JAN 0 2 2020

NO LONGER PROPERTY OF
SEATTLE PUBLIC LIBRARY

BY NASSIM NICHOLAS TALEB

———

INCERTO, an investigation of opacity, luck, uncertainty, probability, human error, risk, and decision making when we don't understand the world, expressed in the form of a personal essay with autobiographical sections, stories, parables, and philosophical, historical, and scientific discussions in nonoverlapping volumes that can be accessed in any order.

FOOLED BY RANDOMNESS (2001, 2004), on how we tend to mistake luck for skills, how randomness does not look random, why there is no point talking about performance when it is easier to buy and sell than fry an egg, and the profound difference between dentists and speculators.

THE BLACK SWAN (2007, 2010), on how high-impact but rare events dominate history, how we retrospectively give ourselves the illusion of understanding them thanks to narratives, how they are impossible to estimate scientifically, how this makes some areas—but not others—totally unpredictable and unforecastable, how confirmatory methods of knowledge don't work, and how thanks to Black Swan–blind "faux experts" we are prone to building systems increasingly fragile to extreme events.

THE BED OF PROCRUSTES (Philosophical Aphorisms) (2010, 2016)

ANTIFRAGILE (2012), on how some things like disorder (hence volatility, time, chaos, variability, and stressors) while others don't, how we can classify things along the lines fragile-robust-antifragile, how we can identify (anti)fragility based on nonlinear response without having to know much about the history of the process (which solves most of the Black Swan problem), and why you are alive if and only if you love (some) volatility.

SKIN IN THE GAME (2018), on symmetry in life and how in its absence systems fail, why our understanding of the world requires some scars, why failed risk takers are more appealing than successful non-risk-takers, why you need engagement rings rather than promises or why belief without sacrifice is a form of theft, and how (motivated) minorities, not majorities, run the world.

INCERTO'S TECHNICAL COMPANION consisting of academic-style papers, miscellaneous notes, and (very) technical remarks and developments.

ANTIFRAGILE

ANTIFRAGILE

THINGS THAT GAIN FROM DISORDER

NASSIM
NICHOLAS TALEB

RANDOM HOUSE
NEW YORK

Copyright © 2012 by Nassim Nicholas Taleb

All rights reserved.

Published in the United States by Random House,
an imprint of The Random House Publishing Group,
a division of Random House, Inc., New York.

RANDOM HOUSE and colophon are registered
trademarks of Random House, Inc.

LIBRARY OF CONGRESS CATALOGING-IN-PUBLICATION DATA

Taleb, Nassim.
Antifragile : things that gain from disorder /
Nassim Nicholas Taleb.
p.   cm.
Includes bibliographical references and index.
ISBN 978-1-4000-6782-4
eBook ISBN 978-0-679-64527-6
1. Uncertainty (Information theory)—Social aspects.   2. Forecasting.
3. Complexity (Philosophy)   I. Title.
Q375.T348 2012
155.2'4—dc23 2012028697

Printed in the United States of America on acid-free paper

www.atrandom.com

12 14 16 18 19 17 15 13 11

To Sarah Josephine Taleb

Contents

———

Chapter Summaries and Map

Boldface terms are in the Glossary at the end of the book.

BOOK I: THE ANTIFRAGILE: AN INTRODUCTION

CHAPTER 1. Explains how we missed the word "antifragility" in classrooms. Fragile-Robust-Antifragile as Damocles-Phoenix-Hydra. Domain dependence.

CHAPTER 2. Where we find overcompensation. Obsessive love is the most antifragile thing outside of economics.

CHAPTER 3. The difference between the organic and the engineered. **Touristification** and attempts to suck volatility out of life.

CHAPTER 4. The antifragility of the whole often depends on the fragility of the parts. Why death is a necessity for life. The benefits of errors for the collective. Why we need risk takers. A few remarks about modernity missing the point. A salute to the entrepreneur and risk taker.

BOOK II: MODERNITY AND THE DENIAL OF ANTIFRAGILITY

THE PROCRUSTEAN BED

CHAPTER 5. Two different randomness categories, seen through the profiles of two brothers. How Switzerland is not controlled from above. The difference between **Mediocristan** and **Extremistan**. The virtues of city-states, bottom-up political systems, and the stabilizing effect of municipal noise.

CHAPTER 6. Systems that like randomness. Annealing inside and outside physics. Explains the effect of overstabilizing organisms and complex systems (political, economic, etc.). The defects of intellectualism. U.S. foreign policy, and pseudostabilization.

went bust. Nonlinearity. The heuristic to detect fragility and antifragility. Convexity biases, **Jensen's inequality,** and their impact on ignorance.

BOOK VI: VIA NEGATIVA

CHAPTER 20. **Neomania.** Looking at the future by *via negativa*. The **Lindy effect:** the old outlives the new in proportion to its age. **Empedocles' Tile.** Why the irrational has an edge over the perceived-to-be-rational.

CHAPTER 21. Medicine and asymmetry. Decision rules in medical problems: why the very ill has a convex payoff and the healthy has concave exposures.

CHAPTER 22. Medicine by subtraction. Introduces the match between individuals and the type of randomness in the environment. Why I don't want to live forever.

BOOK VII: THE ETHICS OF FRAGILITY AND ANTIFRAGILITY

CHAPTER 23. The **agency problem** as transfer of fragility. **Skin in the game.** Doxastic commitment, or **soul in the game.** The **Robert Rubin problem,** the **Joseph Stiglitz problem,** and the **Alan Blinder problem,** all three about agency, and one about **cherry-picking.**

CHAPTER 24. **Ethical inversion.** The collective can be wrong while individuals know it. How people are trapped into an opinion, and how to set them free.

CHAPTER 25. Conclusion.

EPILOGUE. What happens when Nero leaves to go to the Levant to observe the rite of Adonis.

ANTIFRAGILE

Prologue

I. HOW TO LOVE THE WIND

Wind extinguishes a candle and energizes fire.

Likewise with randomness, uncertainty, chaos: you want to use them, not hide from them. You want to be the fire and wish for the wind. This summarizes this author's nonmeek attitude to randomness and uncertainty.

We just don't want to just survive uncertainty, to just about make it. We want to survive uncertainty and, in addition—like a certain class of aggressive Roman Stoics—have the last word. The mission is how to domesticate, even dominate, even conquer, the unseen, the opaque, and the inexplicable.

How?

II. THE ANTIFRAGILE

Some things benefit from shocks; they thrive and grow when exposed to volatility, randomness, disorder, and stressors and love adventure, risk, and uncertainty. Yet, in spite of the ubiquity of the phenomenon, there is no word for the exact opposite of fragile. Let us call it antifragile.

Antifragility is beyond resilience or robustness. The resilient resists shocks and stays the same; the antifragile gets better. This property is behind everything that has changed with time: evolution, culture, ideas, revolutions, political systems, technological innovation, cultural and economic success, corporate survival, good recipes (say, chicken soup or steak tartare with a drop of cognac), the rise of cities, cultures, legal systems, equatorial forests, bacterial resistance . . . even our own existence as a species on this planet. And antifragility determines the boundary between what is living and organic (or complex), say, the human body, and what is inert, say, a physical object like the stapler on your desk.

The antifragile loves randomness and uncertainty, which also means—crucially—a love of errors, a certain class of errors. Antifragility has a singular property of allowing us to deal with the unknown, to do things without understanding them—and do them well. Let me be more aggressive: we are largely better at doing than we are at thinking, thanks to antifragility. I'd rather be dumb and antifragile than extremely smart and fragile, any time.

It is easy to see things around us that like a measure of stressors and volatility: economic systems, your body, your nutrition (diabetes and many similar modern ailments seem to be associated with a lack of randomness in feeding and the absence of the stressor of occasional starvation), your psyche. There are even financial contracts that are antifragile: they are explicitly designed to benefit from market volatility.

Antifragility makes us understand fragility better. Just as we cannot improve health without reducing disease, or increase wealth without first decreasing losses, antifragility and fragility are degrees on a spectrum.

Nonprediction

By grasping the mechanisms of antifragility we can build a systematic and broad guide to *nonpredictive* decision making under uncertainty in business, politics, medicine, and life in general—anywhere the unknown preponderates, any situation in which there is randomness, unpredictability, opacity, or incomplete understanding of things.

It is far easier to figure out if something is fragile than to predict the occurrence of an event that may harm it. Fragility can be measured; risk is not measurable (outside of casinos or the minds of people who call themselves "risk experts"). This provides a solution to what I've called the Black Swan problem—the impossibility of calculating the risks of consequential rare events and predicting their occurrence. Sensitivity to harm from volatility is tractable, more so than forecasting the event that would cause the harm. So we propose to stand our current approaches to prediction, prognostication, and risk management on their heads.

In every domain or area of application, we propose rules for moving from the fragile toward the antifragile, through reduction of fragility or harnessing antifragility. And we can almost always detect antifragility (and fragility) using a simple test of asymmetry: anything that has more upside than downside from random events (or certain shocks) is antifragile; the reverse is fragile.

Deprivation of Antifragility

Crucially, if antifragility is the property of all those natural (and complex) systems that have survived, depriving these systems of volatility, randomness, and stressors will harm them. They will weaken, die, or blow up. We have been fragilizing the economy, our health, political life, education, almost everything . . . by suppressing randomness and volatility. Just as spending a month in bed (preferably with an unabridged version of *War and Peace* and access to *The Sopranos'* entire eighty-six episodes) leads to muscle atrophy, complex systems are weakened, even killed, when deprived of stressors. Much of our modern, structured, world has been harming us with top-down policies and contraptions (dubbed "Soviet-Harvard delusions" in the book) which do precisely this: an insult to the antifragility of systems.

This is the tragedy of modernity: as with neurotically overprotective parents, those trying to help are often hurting us the most.

If about everything top-down fragilizes and blocks antifragility and growth, everything bottom-up thrives under the right amount of stress and disorder. The process of discovery (or innovation, or technological progress) itself depends on antifragile tinkering, aggressive risk bearing rather than formal education.

Upside at the Expense of Others

Which brings us to the largest fragilizer of society, and greatest generator of crises, absence of "skin in the game." Some become antifragile at the expense of others by getting the upside (or gains) from volatility, variations, and disorder and exposing others to the downside risks of losses or harm. And such *antifragility-at-the-cost-of-fragility-of-others* is hidden— given the blindness to antifragility by the Soviet-Harvard intellectual circles, this asymmetry is rarely identified and (so far) never taught. Further, as we discovered during the financial crisis that started in 2008, these blowup risks-to-others are easily concealed owing to the growing complexity of modern institutions and political affairs. While in the past people of rank or status were those and only those who took risks, who had the downside for their actions, and heroes were those who did so for the sake of others, today the exact reverse is taking place. We are witnessing the rise of a new class of inverse heroes, that is, bureaucrats, bankers, Davos-attending members of the I.A.N.D. (International Association of Name Droppers), and academics with too much power and no real downside and/or accountability. They game the system while citizens pay the price.

At no point in history have so many non-risk-takers, that is, those with no personal exposure, exerted so much control.

The chief ethical rule is the following: Thou shalt not have antifragility at the expense of the fragility of others.

III. THE ANTIDOTE TO THE BLACK SWAN

I want to live happily in a world I don't understand.

Black Swans (capitalized) are large-scale unpredictable and irregular events of massive consequence—unpredicted by a certain observer, and such unpredictor is generally called the "turkey" when he is both surprised and harmed by these events. I have made the claim that most of history comes from Black Swan events, while we worry about fine-tuning our understanding of the ordinary, and hence develop models, theories, or representations that cannot possibly track them or measure the possibility of these shocks.

Black Swans hijack our brains, making us feel we "sort of" or "almost" predicted them, because they are retrospectively explainable. We don't realize the role of these Swans in life because of this illusion of predictability. Life is more, a lot more, labyrinthine than shown in our memory—our minds are in the business of turning history into something smooth and linear, which makes us underestimate randomness. But when we see it, we fear it and overreact. Because of this fear and thirst for order, some human systems, by disrupting the invisible or not so visible logic of things, tend to be exposed to harm from Black Swans and almost never get any benefit. You get pseudo-order when you seek order; you only get a measure of order and control when you embrace randomness.

Complex systems are full of interdependencies—hard to detect—and nonlinear responses. "Nonlinear" means that when you double the dose of, say, a medication, or when you double the number of employees in a factory, you don't get twice the initial effect, but rather a lot more or a lot less. Two weekends in Philadelphia are not twice as pleasant as a single one—I've tried. When the response is plotted on a graph, it does not show as a straight line ("linear"), rather as a curve. In such environments, simple causal associations are misplaced; it is hard to see how things work by looking at single parts.

Man-made complex systems tend to develop cascades and runaway chains of reactions that decrease, even eliminate, predictability and cause outsized events. So the modern world may be increasing in technological knowledge, but, paradoxically, it is making things a lot more unpredictable. Now for reasons that have to do with the increase of the artificial, the move away from ancestral and natural models, and the loss in robustness owing to complications in the design of everything, the role of Black Swans is increasing. Further, we are victims to a new disease, called in this book *neomania,* that makes us build Black Swan–vulnerable systems—"progress."

An annoying aspect of the Black Swan problem—in fact the central, and largely missed, point—is that the odds of rare events are simply not computable. We know a lot less about hundred-year floods than five-year floods—model error swells when it comes to small probabilities. *The rarer the event, the less tractable, and the less we know about how frequent its occurrence*—yet the rarer the event, the more confident these "scientists" involved in predicting, modeling, and using PowerPoint in conferences with equations in multicolor background have become.

It is of great help that Mother Nature—thanks to its antifragility—is the best expert at rare events, and the best manager of Black Swans; in its billions of years it succeeded in getting here without much command-and-control instruction from an Ivy League–educated director nominated by a search committee. Antifragility is not just the antidote to the Black Swan; understanding it makes us less intellectually fearful in accepting the role of these events as necessary for history, technology, knowledge, everything.

Robust Is Not Robust Enough

Consider that Mother Nature is not just "safe." It is aggressive in destroying and replacing, in selecting and reshuffling. When it comes to random events, "robust" is certainly not good enough. In the long run everything with the most minute vulnerability breaks, given the ruthlessness of time—yet our planet has been around for perhaps four billion years and, convincingly, robustness can't just be it: you need perfect robustness for a crack not to end up crashing the system. Given the unattainability of perfect robustness, we need a mechanism by which the system regenerates itself continuously by using, rather than suffering from, random events, unpredictable shocks, stressors, and volatility.

The antifragile gains from prediction errors, in the long run. If you follow this idea to its conclusion, then many things that gain from randomness should be dominating the world today—and things that are hurt by it should be gone. Well, this turns out to be the case. We have the illusion that the world functions thanks to programmed design, university research, and bureaucratic funding, but there is compelling—very compelling—evidence to show that this is an illusion, the illusion I call *lecturing birds how to fly*. Technology is the result of antifragility, exploited by risk-takers in the form of tinkering and trial and error, with nerd-driven design confined to the backstage. Engineers and tinkerers develop things while history books are written by academics; we will have to refine historical interpretations of growth, innovation, and many such things.

On the Measurability of (Some) Things

Fragility is quite measurable, risk not so at all, particularly risk associated with rare events.*

I said that we can estimate, even measure, fragility and antifragility, while we cannot calculate risks and probabilities of shocks and rare events, no matter how sophisticated we get. Risk management as practiced is the study of an event taking place in the future, and only some economists and other lunatics can claim—against experience—to "measure" the future incidence of these rare events, with suckers listen-

---

* Outside of casinos and some narrowly defined areas such as man-made situations and constructions.

ing to them—against experience and the track record of such claims. But fragility and antifragility are part of the current property of an object, a coffee table, a company, an industry, a country, a political system. We can detect fragility, see it, even in many cases measure it, or at least measure comparative fragility with a small error while comparisons of risk have been (so far) unreliable. You cannot say with any reliability that a certain remote event or shock is more likely than another (unless you enjoy deceiving yourself), but you can state with a lot more confidence that an object or a structure is more fragile than another should a certain event happen. You can easily tell that your grandmother is more fragile to abrupt changes in temperature than you, that some military dictatorship is more fragile than Switzerland should political change happen, that a bank is more fragile than another should a crisis occur, or that a poorly built modern building is more fragile than the Cathedral of Chartres should an earthquake happen. And—centrally—you can even make the prediction of which one will last longer.

Instead of a discussion of risk (which is both predictive and sissy) I advocate the notion of fragility, which is not predictive—and, unlike risk, has an interesting word that can describe its functional opposite, the nonsissy concept of antifragility.

To measure antifragility, there is a philosopher's-stone-like recipe using a compact and simplified rule that allows us to identify it across domains, from health to the construction of societies.

We have been unconsciously exploiting antifragility in practical life and, consciously, rejecting it—particularly in intellectual life.

The Fragilista

Our idea is to avoid interference with things we don't understand. Well, some people are prone to the opposite. The fragilista belongs to that category of persons who are usually in suit and tie, often on Fridays; he faces your jokes with icy solemnity, and tends to develop back problems early in life from sitting at a desk, riding airplanes, and studying newspapers. He is often involved in a strange ritual, something commonly called "a meeting." Now, in addition to these traits, he defaults to thinking that what he doesn't see is not there, or what he does not understand does not exist. At the core, he tends to mistake the unknown for the nonexistent.

The fragilista falls for the *Soviet-Harvard delusion*, the (unscientific) overestimation of the reach of scientific knowledge. Because of such delusion, he is what is called a *naive rationalist*, a *rationalizer*, or sometimes just a *rationalist*, in the sense that he believes that the *reasons* behind things are automatically accessible to him. And let us not confuse rationalizing with rational—the two are almost always exact opposites. Outside of physics, and generally in complex domains, the reasons behind things have had a tendency to make themselves less obvious to us, and even less to the fragilista. This property of natural things not to advertise themselves in a user's manual is, alas, not much of a hindrance: some fragilistas will get together to write the user's manual themselves, thanks to their definition of "science."

So thanks to the fragilista, modern culture has been increasingly building blindness to the mysterious, the impenetrable, what Nietzsche called the Dionysian, in life.

Or to translate Nietzsche into the less poetic but no less insightful Brooklyn vernacular, this is what our character Fat Tony calls a "sucker game."

In short, the fragilista (medical, economic, social planning) is one who makes you engage in policies and actions, all artificial, in which *the benefits are small and visible, and the side effects potentially severe and invisible*.

There is the medical fragilista who overintervenes in denying the body's natural ability to heal and gives you medications with potentially very severe side effects; the policy fragilista (the interventionist social planner) who mistakes the economy for a washing machine that continuously needs fixing (by him) and blows it up; the psychiatric fragilista who medicates children to "improve" their intellectual and emotional life; the soccer-mom fragilista; the financial fragilista who makes people use "risk" models that destroy the banking system (then uses them again); the military fragilista who disturbs complex systems; the predictor fragilista who encourages you to take more risks; and many more.*

Indeed, the political discourse is lacking a concept. Politicians in their speeches, goals, and promises aim at the timid concepts of "resilience," "solidity," not antifragility, and in the process are stifling the mechanisms of growth and evolution. We didn't get where we are thanks to the sissy

---

* Hayek did not take his idea about organic price formation into risk and fragility. For Hayek, bureaucrats were inefficient, not fragilistas. This discussion starts with fragility and antifragility, and gets us as a side discussion into organic price formation.

notion of resilience. And, what's worse, we didn't get where we are today thanks to policy makers—but thanks to the appetite for risks and errors of a certain class of people we need to encourage, protect, and respect.

Where Simple Is More Sophisticated

A complex system, contrary to what people believe, does not require complicated systems and regulations and intricate policies. The simpler, the better. Complications lead to multiplicative chains of unanticipated effects. Because of opacity, an intervention leads to unforeseen consequences, followed by apologies about the "unforeseen" aspect of the consequences, then to another intervention to correct the secondary effects, leading to an explosive series of branching "unforeseen" responses, each one worse than the preceding one.

Yet simplicity has been difficult to implement in modern life because it is against the spirit of a certain brand of people who seek sophistication so they can justify their profession.

Less is more and usually more effective. Thus I will produce a small number of tricks, directives, and interdicts—how to live in a world we don't understand, or, rather, how to *not be afraid* to work with things we patently don't understand, and, more principally, in what manner we should work with these. Or, even better, how to dare to look our ignorance in the face and not be ashamed of being human—be aggressively and proudly human. But that may require some structural changes.

What I propose is a road map to modify our man-made systems to let the simple—and natural—take their course.

But simplicity is not so simple to attain. Steve Jobs figured out that "you have to work hard to get your thinking clean to make it simple." The Arabs have an expression for trenchant prose: *no skill to understand it, mastery to write it.*

Heuristics are simplified rules of thumb that make things simple and easy to implement. But their main advantage is that the user knows that they are not perfect, just expedient, and is therefore less fooled by their powers. They become dangerous when we forget that.

IV. THIS BOOK

The journey to this idea of antifragility was, if anything, nonlinear.

I suddenly realized one day that fragility—which had been lacking a technical definition—could be expressed as *what does not like volatility,* and that *what does not like volatility* does not like randomness, uncertainty, disorder, errors, stressors, etc. Think of anything fragile, say, objects in your living room such as the glass frame, the television set, or, even better, the china in the cupboards. If you label them "fragile," then you necessarily want them to be left alone in peace, quiet, order, and predictability. A fragile object would not possibly benefit from an earthquake or the visit of your hyperactive nephew. Further, everything that does not like volatility does not like stressors, harm, chaos, events, disorder, "unforeseen" consequences, uncertainty, and, critically, time.

And antifragility flows—sort of—from this explicit definition of fragility. It likes volatility et al. It also likes time. And there is a powerful and helpful link to nonlinearity: everything nonlinear in response is either fragile or antifragile to a certain source of randomness.

The strangest thing is that this obvious property that *anything fragile hates volatility,* and vice versa, has been sitting completely outside the scientific and philosophical discourse. Completely. And the study of the sensitivity of things to volatility is the strange business specialty in which I spent most of my adult life, two decades—I know it is a strange specialty, I promise to explain later. My focus in that profession has been on identifying items that "love volatility" or "hate volatility"; so all I had to do was expand the ideas from the financial domain in which I had been focused to the broader notion of decision making under uncertainty across various fields, from political science to medicine to dinner plans.*

And in that strange profession of people who work with volatility, there were two types. First category, academics, report-writers, and commentators who study future events and write books and papers; and, second category, practitioners who, instead of studying future events, try to understand how things react to volatility (but practitioners are usually too busy practitioning to write books, articles, papers, speeches, equations, theories and get honored by Highly Constipated and Honorable Members of Academies). The difference between the two categories is central: as we saw, it is much easier to understand if

---

* The technical term I used for "hates volatility" was "short vega" or "short gamma," meaning "harmed should volatility increase," and "long vega" or "long gamma" for things that benefit. In the rest of the book we will use "short" and "long" to describe negative and positive exposures, respectively. It is critical that I never believed in our ability to forecast volatility, as I just focused on how things react to it.

something is harmed by volatility—hence fragile—than try to forecast harmful events, such as these oversized Black Swans. But only practitioners (or people who do things) tend to spontaneously get the point.

The (Rather Happy) Disorder Family

One technical comment. We keep saying that fragility and antifragility mean potential gain or harm from exposure to *something* related to volatility. What is that something? Simply, membership in the extended disorder family.

> The Extended Disorder Family (or Cluster): (i) uncertainty, (ii) variability, (iii) imperfect, incomplete knowledge, (iv) chance, (v) chaos, (vi) volatility, (vii) disorder, (viii) entropy, (ix) time, (x) the unknown, (xi) randomness, (xii) turmoil, (xiii) stressor, (xiv) error, (xv) dispersion of outcomes, (xvi) unknowledge.

It happens that uncertainty, disorder, and the unknown are completely equivalent in their effect: antifragile systems benefit (to some degree) from, and the fragile is penalized by, almost all of them—even if you have to find them in separate buildings of the university campuses and some philosophaster who has never taken real risks in his life, or, worse, never had a life, would inform you that "they are *clearly* not the same thing."

Why item (ix), time? Time is functionally similar to volatility: the more time, the more events, the more disorder. Consider that if you can suffer limited harm and are antifragile to small errors, time brings the kind of errors or reverse errors that end up benefiting you. This is simply what your grandmother calls experience. The fragile breaks with time.

Only One Book

This makes this book my central work. I've had only one master idea, each time taken to its next step, the last step—this book—being more like a big jump. I am reconnected to my "practical self," my soul of a practitioner, as this is a merger of my entire history as practitioner and "volatility specialist" combined with my intellectual and philosophical interests in randomness and uncertainty, which had previously taken separate paths.

My writings are not stand-alone essays on specific topics, with beginnings, ends, and expiration dates; rather, they are nonoverlapping chapters from that central idea, a main corpus focused on uncertainty, randomness, probability, disorder, and what to do in a world we don't understand, a world with unseen elements and properties, the random and the complex; that is, decision making under opacity. The corpus is called *Incerto* and is constituted (so far) of a trilogy plus philosophical and technical addenda. The rule is that the distance between a random chapter of one book, say, *Antifragile,* and another random chapter of another, say, *Fooled by Randomness,* should be similar to the one between chapters of a long book. The rule allows the corpus to cross domains (by shifting across science, philosophy, business, psychology, literature, and autobiographical segments) without lapsing into promiscuity.

So the relationship of this book to *The Black Swan* would be as follows: in spite of the chronology (and the fact that this book takes the Black Swan idea to its natural and prescriptive conclusion), *Antifragile* would be the main volume and *The Black Swan* its backup of sorts, and a theoretical one, perhaps even its junior appendix. Why? Because *The Black Swan* (and its predecessor, *Fooled by Randomness*) were written to convince us of a dire situation, and worked hard at it; this one starts from the position that one does not need convincing that (a) Black Swans dominate society and history (and people, because of ex post rationalization, think themselves capable of understanding them); (b) as a consequence, we don't quite know what's going on, particularly under severe nonlinearities; so we can get to practical business right away.

No Guts, No Belief

To accord with the practitioner's ethos, the rule in this book is as follows: I eat my own cooking.

I have only written, in every line I have composed in my professional life, about things I have done, and the risks I have recommended that others take or avoid were risks I have been taking or avoiding myself. I will be the first to be hurt if I am wrong. When I warned about the fragility of the banking system in *The Black Swan,* I was betting on its collapse (particularly when my message went unheeded); otherwise I felt it would not have been ethical to write about it. That personal stricture applies to every domain, including medicine, technical innovation, and simple matters in life. It does not mean that one's personal experiences constitute a sufficient sample to derive a conclusion about an idea; it is just that one's personal experience gives the stamp of authenticity and sincerity of opinion. Experience is devoid of the cherry-picking that we find in studies, particularly those called "observational," ones in which the researcher finds past patterns, and, thanks to the sheer amount of data, can therefore fall into the trap of an invented narrative.

Further, in writing, I feel corrupt and unethical if I have to look up a subject in a library as part of the writing itself. This acts as a filter—it is the only filter. If the subject is not interesting enough for me to look it up *independently*, for my own curiosity or purposes, and I have not done so before, then I should not be writing about it at all, period. It does not mean that libraries (physical and virtual) are not acceptable; it means that they should not be the *source* of any idea. Students pay to write essays on topics for which they have to derive knowledge from a library as a self-enhancement exercise; a professional who is compensated to write and is taken seriously by others should use a more potent filter. Only distilled ideas, ones that sit in us for a long time, are acceptable—and those that come from reality.

It is time to revive the not well-known philosophical notion of *doxastic commitment,* a class of beliefs that go beyond talk, and to which we are committed enough to take personal risks.

If You See Something

Modernity has replaced ethics with legalese, and the law can be gamed with a good lawyer.

So I will expose the transfer of fragility, or rather the theft of antifragility, by people "arbitraging" the system. These people will be named by name. Poets and painters are free, *liberi poetae et pictores,* and there are severe moral imperatives that come with such freedom. First ethical rule:

If you see fraud and do not say fraud, you are a fraud.

Just as being nice to the arrogant is no better than being arrogant toward the nice, being accommodating toward anyone committing a nefarious action condones it.

Further, many writers and scholars speak in private, say, after half a bottle of wine, differently from the way they do in print. Their writing is certifiably fake, fake. And many of the problems of society come from the argument "other people are doing it." So if I call someone a dangerous ethically challenged fragilista in private after the third glass of Lebanese wine (white), I will be obligated to do so here.

Calling people and institutions fraudulent in print when they are not (yet) called so by others carries a cost, but is too small to be a deterrent. After the mathematical scientist Benoît Mandelbrot read the galleys of *The Black Swan,* a book dedicated to him, he called me and quietly said: "In what language should I say 'good luck' to you?" I did not need any luck, it turned out; I was antifragile to all manner of attacks: the more attacks I got from the Central Fragilista Delegation, the more my message spread as it drove people to examine my arguments. I am now ashamed of not having gone further in calling a spade a spade.

Compromising is condoning. The only modern dictum I follow is one by George Santayana: *A man is morally free when . . . he judges the world, and judges other men, with uncompromising sincerity.* This is not just an aim but an obligation.

Defossilizing Things

Second ethical point.

I am obligated to submit myself to the scientific process simply because I require it from others, but no more than that. When I read empirical claims in medicine or other sciences, I like these claims to go through the peer-review mechanism, a fact-checking of sorts, an examination of the rigor of the approach. Logical statements, or those backed by mathematical reasoning, on the other hand, do not require such a mechanism: they can and must stand on their own legs. So I publish technical footnotes for these books in specialized and academic outlets, and nothing more (and limit them to statements that require proofs or more elaborate technical arguments). But for the sake of authenticity and to avoid careerism (the debasing of knowledge by turning it into a competitive sport), I ban myself from publishing anything outside of these footnotes.

After more than twenty years as a transactional trader and businessman in what I called the "strange profession," I tried what one calls an academic career. And I have something to report—actually that was the driver behind this idea of antifragility in life and the dichotomy between the *natural* and the alienation of the *unnatural.* Commerce is fun, thrilling, lively, and natural; academia as currently professionalized is none of these. And for those who think that academia is "quieter" and an emotionally relaxing transition after the volatile and risk-taking business life, a surprise: when in action, new problems and scares emerge every day to displace and eliminate the previous day's headaches, resentments, and conflicts. A nail displaces another nail, with astonishing variety. But academics (particularly in social science) seem to distrust each other; they live in petty obsessions, envy, and icy-cold hatreds, with small snubs developing into grudges, fossilized over time in the loneliness of the transaction with a computer screen and the immutability of their environment. Not to mention a level of envy I have almost never seen in business. . . . My experience is that money and transactions purify relations; ideas and abstract matters like "recognition" and "credit" warp them, creating an atmosphere of perpetual rivalry. I grew to find people greedy for credentials nauseating, repulsive, and untrustworthy.

Commerce, business, Levantine souks (though not large-scale markets and corporations) are activities and places that bring out the best in people, making most of them forgiving, honest, loving, trusting, and open-minded. As a member of the Christian minority in the Near East, I can vouch that commerce, particularly small commerce, is the door to tolerance—the only door, in my opinion, to any form of tolerance. It beats rationalizations and lectures. Like antifragile tinkering, mistakes are small and rapidly forgotten.

I want to be happy to be human and be in an environment in which other people are in love with their fate—and never, until my brush with academia, did I think that that environment was a certain form of commerce (combined with solitary scholarship). The biologist-writer and libertarian economist Matt Ridley made me feel that it was truly the Phoenician trader in me (or, more exactly, the Canaanite) that was the intellectual.*

---

* Once again, please, no, *itisnotresilience*. I am used to facing, at the end of a conference lecture, the question "So what is the difference between robust and antifragile?" or the more unenlightened and even more irritating "Antifragile is resilient, no?" The reaction to my answer is usually "Ah," with the look "Why didn't you say that before?" (of course I had said that before). Even the initial referee of the scientific article I wrote on defining and detecting antifragility entirely missed the point, conflating antifragility and robustness—and that was the scientist who pored over my definitions. It is worth re-explaining the following: the robust or resilient is neither harmed nor helped by volatility and disorder, while the antifragile benefits from them. But it takes some effort for the concept to sink in. A lot of things people call robust or resilient are just robust or resilient, the other half are antifragile.

V. ORGANIZATION

Antifragile is composed of seven books and a notes section.

Why "books"? Most people's first reaction upon reading my ethics and *via negativa* chapters, which I supplied separately, was that each should be a separate book and published as a short or medium-length essay. Someone in the business of "summarizing" books would have to write four or five separate descriptions. But I saw that they were not stand-alone essays at all; each deals with the applications of a central idea, going either deeper or into different territories: evolution, politics, business innovation, scientific discovery, economics, ethics, epistemology, and general philosophy. So I call them books rather than sections or parts. Books to me are not expanded journal articles, but reading experiences; and the academics who tend to read in order to cite in their writing—rather than read for enjoyment, curiosity, or simply because they like to read—tend to be frustrated when they can't rapidly scan the text and summarize it in one sentence that connects it to some existing discourse in which they have been involved. Further, the essay is the polar opposite of the textbook—mixing autobiographical musings and parables with more philosophical and scientific investigations. I write about probability with my entire soul and my entire experiences in the risk-taking business; I write with my scars, hence my thought is inseparable from autobiography. The personal essay form is ideal for the topic of incertitude.

The sequence is as follows.

The Appendix to this prologue presents the Triad as a table, a comprehensive map of the world along the fragility spectrum.

Book I, *The Antifragile: An Introduction,* presents the new property and discusses evolution and the organic as the typical antifragile system. It also looks at the tradeoff between the antifragility of the collective and the fragility of the individual.

Book II, *Modernity and the Denial of Antifragility,* describes what happens when we starve systems—mostly political systems—of volatility. It discusses this invention called the nation-state, as well as the idea of harm done by the healer, someone who tries to help you and ends up harming you very badly.

Book III, *A Nonpredictive View of the World,* introduces Fat Tony and his intuitive detection of fragility and presents the foundational asymmetry of things grounded in the writings of Seneca, the Roman philosopher and doer.

Book IV, *Optionality, Technology, and the Intelligence of Antifragility*, presents the mysterious property of the world, by which a certain asymmetry is behind things, rather than human "intelligence," and how optionality drove us here. It is opposed to what I call the Soviet-Harvard method. And Fat Tony argues with Socrates about how we do things one cannot quite explain.

Book V, *The Nonlinear and the Nonlinear (sic)*, is about the philosopher's stone and its opposite: how to turn lead into gold, and gold into lead. Two chapters constitute the central technical section—the plumbing of the book—mapping fragility (as nonlinearity, more specifically, convexity effects) and showing the edge coming from a certain class of convex strategies.

Book VI, *Via Negativa*, shows the wisdom and effectiveness of subtraction over addition (acts of omission over acts of commission). This section introduces the notion of convexity effects. Of course the first application is to medicine. I look at medicine only from an epistemological, risk-management approach—and it looks different from there.

Book VII, *The Ethics of Fragility and Antifragility*, grounds ethics in transfers of fragility, with one party getting the benefits and the other one the harm, and points out problems arising from absence of skin in the game.

The end of the book consists of graphs, notes, and a technical appendix.

The book is written at three levels.

First, the literary and philosophical, with parables and illustrations but minimal if any technical arguments, except in Book V (the philosopher's stone), which presents the convexity arguments. (The enlightened reader is invited to skip Book V, as the ideas are distilled elsewhere.)

Second, the appendix, with graphs and more technical discussion, but no elaborate derivations.

Third, the backup material with more elaborate arguments, all in the form of technical papers and notes (don't mistake my illustrations and parables for proof; remember, a personal essay is not a scientific document, but a scientific document is a scientific document). All these backup documents are gathered as a freely available electronic technical companion.

APPENDIX: THE TRIAD, OR A MAP OF THE WORLD AND THINGS
ALONG THE THREE PROPERTIES

Now we aim—after some work—to connect in the reader's mind, with a single thread, elements seemingly far apart, such as Cato the Elder, Nietzsche, Thales of Miletus, the potency of the system of city-states, the sustainability of artisans, the process of discovery, the onesidedness of opacity, financial derivatives, antibiotic resistance, bottom-up systems, Socrates' invitation to overrationalize, how to lecture birds, obsessive love, Darwinian evolution, the mathematical concept of Jensen's inequality, optionality and option theory, the idea of ancestral heuristics, the works of Joseph de Maistre and Edmund Burke, Wittgenstein's antirationalism, the fraudulent theories of the economics establishment, tinkering and bricolage, terrorism exacerbated by death of its members, an apologia for artisanal societies, the ethical flaws of the middle class, Paleo-style workouts (and nutrition), the idea of medical iatrogenics, the glorious notion of the magnificent (*megalopsychon*), my obsession with the idea of convexity (and my phobia of concavity), the late-2000s banking and economic crisis, the misunderstanding of redundancy, the difference between tourist and flâneur, etc. All in one single—and, I am certain, simple—thread.

How? We can begin by seeing how things—just about anything that matters—can be mapped or classified into three categories, what I call the Triad.

Things Come in Triples

In the Prologue, we saw that the idea is to focus on fragility rather than predicting and calculating future probabilities, and that fragility and antifragility come on a spectrum of varying degrees. The task here is to build a map of exposures. (This is what is called "real-world solution," though only academics and other non-real-world operators use the expression "real-world solution" instead of simply "solution.")

The Triad classifies items in three columns along the designation

FRAGILE   ROBUST   ANTIFRAGILE

Recall that the fragile wants tranquility, the antifragile grows from disorder, and the robust doesn't care too much. The reader is invited to navigate the Triad to see how the ideas of the book apply across domains. Simply, in a given subject, when you discuss an item or a policy, the task is to find in which category of the Triad one should put it and what to do in order to improve its condition. For example: the centralized nation-state is on the far left of the Triad, squarely in the fragile category, and a decentralized system of city-states on the far right, in the antifragile one. By getting the characteristics of the latter, we can move away from the undesirable fragility of the large state. Or look at errors. On the left, in the fragile category, the mistakes are rare and large when they occur, hence irreversible; to the right the mistakes are small and benign, even reversible and quickly overcome. They are also rich in information. So a certain system of tinkering and trial and error would have the attributes of antifragility. If you want to become antifragile, put yourself in the situation "loves mistakes"— to the right of "hates mistakes"—by making these numerous and small in harm. We will call this process and approach the "barbell" strategy.

Or take the health category. Adding is on the left, removing to the right. *Removing* medication, or some other unnatural stressor—say, gluten, fructose, tranquilizers, nail polish, or some such substance—by trial and error is more robust than *adding* medication, with unknown side effects, unknown in spite of the statements about "evidence" and shmevidence.

As the reader can see, the map uninhibitedly spreads across domains and human pursuits, such as culture, health, biology, political systems, technology, urban organization, socioeconomic life, and other matters of more or less direct interest to the reader. I have even managed to merge decision making and *flâneur* in the same breath. So a simple method would lead us to both a risk-based political philosophy and medical decision-making.

The Triad in Action

Note that fragile and antifragile here are relative terms, not quite absolute properties: one item to the right of the Triad is more antifragile than another to the left. For instance, artisans are more antifragile than small businesses, but a rock star will be more antifragile than any artisan. Debt always puts you on the left, fragilizes economic systems. And things are antifragile up to a certain level of stress. Your body benefits from some amount of mishandling, but up to a point—it would not benefit too much from being thrown down from the top of the Tower of Babel.

The Golden Robust: Further, the *robust* here in the middle column is not equivalent to Aristotle's "golden middle" (commonly mislabeled the "golden mean"), in the way that, say, generosity is the middle between profligacy and stinginess—it can be, but it is not necessarily so. Antifragility is desirable in general, but not always, as there are cases in which antifragility will be costly, extremely so. Further, it is hard to consider robustness as always desirable—to quote Nietzsche, one can die from being immortal.

Finally, by now the reader, grappling with a new word, might ask too much from it. If the designation *antifragile* is rather vague and limited to specific sources of harm or volatility, and up to a certain range of exposure, it is no more and no less so than the designation *fragile*. Antifragility is relative to a given situation. A boxer might be robust, hale when it comes to his physical condition, and might improve from fight to fight, but he can easily be emotionally fragile and break into tears when dumped by his girlfriend. Your grandmother might have opposite qualities, fragile in build but equipped with a strong personality. I remember the following vivid image from the Lebanese civil war: A diminutive old lady, a widow (she was dressed in black), was chastising militiamen from the enemy side for having caused the shattering of the glass in her window during a battle. They were pointing their guns at her; a single bullet would have terminated her but they were visibly having a bad moment, intimidated and scared by her. She was the opposite of the boxer: physically fragile, but not fragile in character.

Now the Triad.

TABLE 1 • THE CENTRAL TRIAD: THREE TYPES OF EXPOSURE

	FRAGILE	ROBUST	ANTIFRAGILE
Mythology— Greek	Sword of Damocles, Rock of Tantalus	Phoenix	Hydra
Mythology— New York and Brooklyn	Dr. John	Nero Tulip	Fat Tony, Yevgenia Krasnova*
Black Swan	Exposed to negative Black Swans		Exposed to positive Black Swans
Businesses	New York: Banking system		Silicon Valley: "Fail fast," "Be foolish"
Biological & economic systems	Efficiency, optimized	Redundancy	Degeneracy (functional redundancy)
Errors	Hates mistakes	Mistakes are just information	Loves mistakes (since they are small)
Errors	Irreversible, large (but rare) errors, blowups		Produces reversible, small errors
Science/ technology	Directed research	Opportunistic research	Stochastic tinkering (antifragile tinkering or bricolage)
Dichotomy event-exposure	Studying events, measuring their risks, statistical properties of events	Studying exposure to events, statistical properties of exposures	Modifying exposure to events
Science	Theory	Phenomenology	Heuristics, practical tricks
Human body	Mollification, atrophy, "aging," sarcopenia	Mithridatization, recovery	Hormesis, hypertrophy

* Dr. John, Nero Tulip, Fat Tony, and Yevgenia Krasnova are characters in *The Black Swan*. Nero Tulip is also a character in *Fooled by Randomness*.

	FRAGILE	*ROBUST*	*ANTIFRAGILE*
Ways of thinking	Modernity	Medieval Europe	Ancient Mediterranean
Human relationships	Friendship	Kinship	Attraction
Ancient culture (Nietzsche)	Apollonian	Dionysian	Balanced mixture of Apollonian and Dionysian
Ethics	The weak	The magnificent	The strong
Ethics	System without skin in the game	System with skin in the game	System with soul in the game
Regulation	Rules	Principles	Virtue
Systems	Concentrated sources of randomness		Distributed sources of randomness
Mathematics (functional)	Nonlinear-concave, or concave-convex	Linear, or convex-concave	Nonlinear-convex
Mathematics (probability)	Left-skewed (or negative skewed)	Low volatility	Right-skewed (or positive skewed)
Option Trading	Short volatility, gamma, vega	Flat volatility	Long volatility, "gamma," "vega"
Knowledge	Explicit	Tacit	Tacit with convexity
Epistemology	True-False		Sucker-Nonsucker
Life and thinking	Tourist, personal and intellectual		Flâneur with a large private library
Financial dependence	Corporate employment, Tantalized class	Dentist, dermatologist, niche worker, minimum-wage earner	Taxi driver, artisan, prostitute, f*** you money
Learning	Classroom	Real life, pathemata mathemata	Real life and library
Political systems	Nation-state; centralized		Collection of city-states; decentralized

	FRAGILE	ROBUST	ANTIFRAGILE
Social system	Ideology		Mythology
	Post-agricultural modern settlements		Nomadic and hunter-gatherer tribes
Knowledge	Academia	Expertise	Erudition
Science	Theory	Phenomenology	Evidence-based phenomenology
Psychological well-being	Post-traumatic stress		Post-traumatic growth
Decision making	Model-based probabilistic decision making	Heuristic-based decision making	Convex heuristics
Thinkers	Plato, Aristotle, Averroes	Early Stoics, Menodotus of Nicomedia, Popper, Burke, Wittgenstein, John Gray	Roman Stoics, Nietzsche, Nietzsche perhaps Hegel (sublation), Jaspers
Economic life	Econophasters cults	Anthropologists	Religion
Economic life (effect on economic life)	Bureaucrats		Entrepreneurs
Reputation (profession)	Academic, corporate executive, pope, bishop, politician	Postal employee, truck driver, train conductor	Artist, writer
Reputation (class)	Middle class	Minimum-wage persons	Bohemian, aristocracy, old money
Medicine	Via positiva Additive treatment (give medication)		Via negativa Subtractive treatment (remove items from consumption, say cigarettes, carbs, etc.)
Philosophy/ science	Rationalism	Empiricism	Skeptical, subtractive empiricism

	FRAGILE	*ROBUST*	*ANTIFRAGILE*
	Separable		Holistic
Economic life		Owner operated	
Finance	Short option		Long option
Knowledge	Positive science	Negative science	Art
Stress	Chronic stressors		Acute stressors, with recovery
Decision making	Acts of commission		Acts of omission ("missed opportunity")
Literature	E-reader	Book	Oral tradition
Business	Industry	Small business	Artisan
Food	Food companies		Restaurants
Finance	Debt	Equity	Venture capital
Finance	Public debt	Private debt with no bailout	Convertible
General	Large	Small but specialized	Small but not specialized
General	Monomodal		Barbell
Risk taking	Markowitz	Kelly criterion	Kelly criterion using finite bets
Legal system	Statutory law, legal code		Common law, equity
Regulation	Code of regulations		Heuristic regulations
Finance	Banks, hedge funds managed by econophasters	Hedge funds (some)	Hedge funds (some)
Business	Agency problem		Principal operated
Noise-signal	Signal only		Stochastic resonance, simulated annealing
Model error	Concave to errors		Convex to errors
Education	Soccer mom	Street life	Barbell: parental library, street fights

	FRAGILE	ROBUST	ANTIFRAGILE
Physical training	Organized sports, gym machines		Street fights
Urbanism	Robert Moses, Le Corbusier		Jane Jacobs

BOOK I

The Antifragile: An Introduction

———

The first two chapters introduce and illustrate antifragility. Chapter 3 introduces a distinction between the organic and the mechanical, say, between your cat and a washing machine. Chapter 4 is about how the antifragility of some comes from the fragility of others, how errors benefit some, not others—the sort of things people tend to call evolution and write a lot, a lot about.

CHAPTER 1

Between Damocles and Hydra

*Please cut my head off—How by some magic, colors become colors—
How to lift weight in Dubai*

―――――

HALF OF LIFE HAS NO NAME

You are in the post office about to send a gift, a package full of champagne glasses, to a cousin in Central Siberia. As the package can be dam-
aged during transportation, you would stamp "fragile," "breakable," or
"handle with care" on it (in red). Now what is the exact opposite of such
situation, the exact opposite of "fragile"?

Almost all people answer that the opposite of "fragile" is "robust,"
"resilient," "solid," or something of the sort. But the resilient, robust
(and company) are items that neither break nor improve, so you would
not need to write anything on them—have you ever seen a package with
"robust" in thick green letters stamped on it? Logically, the exact opposite of a "fragile" parcel would be a package on which one has written
"please mishandle" or "please handle carelessly." Its contents would not
just be unbreakable, but would benefit from shocks and a wide array of
trauma. The fragile is the package that would be *at best* unharmed, the
robust would be *at best* and *at worst* unharmed. And the opposite of
fragile is therefore what is *at worst* unharmed.

We gave the appellation "antifragile" to such a package; a neologism
was necessary as there is no simple, noncompound word in the *Oxford*

English Dictionary that expresses the point of reverse fragility. For the idea of antifragility is not part of our consciousness—but, luckily, it is part of our ancestral behavior, our biological apparatus, and a ubiquitous property of every system that has survived.

FIGURE 1. A package begging for stressors and disorder.
Credit: Giotto Enterprise and George Nasr.

To see how alien the concept is to our minds, repeat the experiment and ask around at the next gathering, picnic, or pre-riot congregation what's the antonym of fragile (and specify insistently that you mean the *exact reverse,* something that has opposite properties and payoff). The likely answers will be, aside from robust: unbreakable, solid, well-built, resilient, strong, something-proof (say, waterproof, windproof, rustproof)—unless they've heard of this book. Wrong—and it is not just individuals but branches of knowledge that are confused by it; this is a mistake made in every dictionary of synonyms and antonyms I've found.

Another way to view it: since the opposite of *positive* is *negative,* not *neutral,* the opposite of positive fragility should be negative fragility (hence my appellation "antifragility"), not neutral, which would just convey robustness, strength, and unbreakability. Indeed, when one writes things down mathematically, antifragility is fragility with a negative sign in front of it.[*]

This blind spot seems universal. There is no word for "antifragility"

---

[*] Just as concavity is convexity with a negative sign in front of it and is sometimes called anticonvexity.

in the main known languages, modern, ancient, colloquial, or slang. Even Russian (Soviet version) and Standard Brooklyn English don't seem to have a designation for antifragility, conflating it with robustness.[*]

Half of life—the interesting half of life—we don't have a name for.

PLEASE BEHEAD ME

If we have no common name for antifragility, we can find a mythological equivalence, the expression of historical intelligence through potent metaphors. In a Roman recycled version of a Greek myth, the Sicilian tyrant Dionysius II has the fawning courtier Damocles enjoy the luxury of a fancy banquet, but with a sword hanging over his head, tied to the ceiling with a single hair from a horse's tail. A horse's hair is the kind of thing that eventually breaks under pressure, followed by a scene of blood, high-pitched screams, and the equivalent of ancient ambulances. Damocles is fragile—it is only a matter of time before the sword strikes him down.

In another ancient legend, this time the Greek recycling of an ancient Semitic and Egyptian legend, we find Phoenix, the bird with splendid colors. Whenever it is destroyed, it is reborn from its own ashes. It always returns to its initial state. Phoenix happens to be the ancient symbol of Beirut, the city where I grew up. According to legend, Berytus (Beirut's historical name) has been destroyed seven times in its close to five-thousand-year history, and has come back seven times. The story seems cogent, as I myself saw the eighth episode; central Beirut (the ancient part of the city) was completely destroyed for the eighth time during my late childhood, thanks to the brutal civil war. I also saw its eighth rebuilding.

But Beirut was, in its latest version, rebuilt in even better shape than the previous incarnation—and with an interesting irony: the earthquake of A.D. 551 had buried the Roman law school, which was discovered, like a bonus from history, during the reconstruction (with archeologists

---

[*] I checked in addition to Brooklyn English most Indo-European languages, both ancient (Latin, Greek) and modern branches: Romance (Italian, French, Spanish, Portuguese), Slavic (Russian, Polish, Serbian, Croatian), Germanic (German, Dutch, Afrikaans), and Indo-Iranian (Hindi, Urdu, Farsi). It is also absent from non-Indo-European families such as Semitic (Arabic, Hebrew, Aramaic) and Turkic (Turkish).

and real estate developers trading public insults). That's not Phoenix, but something else beyond the robust. Which brings us to the third mythological metaphor: Hydra.

Hydra, in Greek mythology, is a serpent-like creature that dwells in the lake of Lerna, near Argos, and has numerous heads. Each time one is cut off, two grow back. So harm is what it likes. Hydra represents antifragility.

The sword of Damocles represents the side effect of power and success: you cannot rise and rule without facing this continuous danger—someone out there will be actively working to topple you. And like the sword, the danger will be silent, inexorable, and discontinuous. It will fall abruptly after long periods of quiet, perhaps at the very moment one has gotten used to it and forgotten about its existence. Black Swans will be out there to get you as you now have much more to lose, a cost of success (and growth), perhaps an unavoidable penalty of excessive success. At the end, what matters is the strength of the string—not the wealth and power of the dining party. But, luckily, this is an identifiable, measurable, and tractable vulnerability, for those who want to listen. The entire point of the Triad is that in many situations we can measure the strength of the string.

Further, consider how toxic such growth-followed-by-a-fall can be to society, as the fall of the dining guest, in response to the fall of the sword of Damocles, will bring what we now call collateral damage, harming others. For instance, the collapse of a large institution will have effects on society.

Sophistication, a certain brand of sophistication, also brings fragility to Black Swans: as societies gain in complexity, with more and more "cutting edge" sophistication in them, and more and more specialization, they become increasingly vulnerable to collapse. This idea has been brilliantly—and convincingly—adumbrated by the archeologist Joseph Tainter. But it does not have to be so: it is so only for those unwilling to go the extra step and understand the matrix of reality. To counter success, you need a high offsetting dose of robustness, even high doses of antifragility. You want to be Phoenix, or possibly Hydra. Otherwise the sword of Damocles will get you.

On the Necessity of Naming

We know more than we think we do, a lot more than we can articulate. If our formal systems of thought denigrate the natural, and in fact we don't have a name for antifragility, and fight the concept whenever we use our brains, it does not mean that our actions neglect it. Our perceptions and intuitions, as expressed in deeds, can be superior to what we know and tabulate, discuss in words, and teach in a classroom. We will have ample discussions of the point particularly with the potent notion of the *apophatic* (what cannot be explicitly said, or directly described, in our current vocabulary); so for now, take this curious phenomenon.

In *Through the Language Glass,* the linguist Guy Deutscher reports that many primitive populations, without being color-blind, have verbal designations for only two or three colors. But when given a simple test, they can successfully match strings to their corresponding colors. They are capable of detecting the differences between the various nuances of the rainbow, but they do not express these in their vocabularies. These populations are culturally, though not biologically, color-blind.

Just as we are intellectually, not organically, antifragility-blind. To see the difference just consider that you need the name "blue" for the construction of a narrative, but not when you engage in action.

It is not well known that many colors we take for granted had no name for a long time, and had no names in the central texts in Western culture. Ancient Mediterranean texts, both Greek and Semitic, also had a reduced vocabulary of a small number of colors polarized around the dark and the light—Homer and his contemporaries were limited to about three or four main colors: black, white, and some indeterminate part of the rainbow, often subsumed as red, or yellow.

I contacted Guy Deutscher. He was extremely generous with his help and pointed out to me that the ancients even lacked words for something as elementary as blue. This absence of the word "blue" in ancient Greek explains the recurring reference by Homer to the "wine-dark sea" (*oinopa ponton*), which has been quite puzzling to readers (including this one).

Interestingly, it was the British Prime Minister William Gladstone who first made this discovery in the 1850s (and was unfairly and thoughtlessly reviled for it by the usual journalists). Gladstone, quite an erudite, wrote, during his interregnum between political positions, an impressive seventeen-hundred-page treatise on Homer. In the last section, Gladstone announced this limitation of color vocabulary, attributing our modern sensitization to many more nuances of color to a cross-generational training of the eye. But regardless of these variations of color in the culture of the time, people were shown to be able to identify the nuances—unless physically color-blind.

Gladstone was impressive in many respects. Aside from his erudition, force of character, respect for the weak, and high level of energy, four very attractive attributes (respect for the weak being, after intellectual courage, the second most attractive quality to this author), he showed remarkable prescience. He figured out what few in his day dared to propose: that the *Iliad* corresponds to a true story (the city of Troy had not been discovered yet). In addition, even more prescient and of great relevance to this book, he was insistent upon a balanced fiscal budget: fiscal deficits have proven to be a prime source of fragility in social and economic systems.

PROTO-ANTIFRAGILITY

There have been names for two starter-antifragility concepts, with two precursor applications that cover some special cases of it. These are mild aspects of antifragility and limited to the medical field. But they are a good way to start.

According to legend, Mithridates IV, king of Pontus in Asia Minor, while hiding after his father's assassination, got himself some protection against poisoning by ingesting sub-lethal doses of toxic material in progressively larger quantities. He later incorporated the process into a complicated religious ritual. But this immunity got him in trouble a bit later as his attempt to take his own life by poisoning failed, "having fortified himself against the drugs of others." So he had to ask for the services of an ally military commander to give him a blow with a sword.

The method named *Antidotum Mithridatium*, celebrated by Celsus, the ancient world's famous doctor, had to be rather fashionable in Rome, since about a century later it brought some complication to the emperor Nero's attempts at matricide. Nero had been obsessed with the idea of killing his mother, Agrippina, who, to make things more colorful, was Caligula's sister (and, even more colorful, was the alleged lover of the philosopher Seneca, more on whom later). But a mother tends to know her son rather well and predict his actions, particularly when he is her only child—and Agrippina knew something about poison, as she might have used the method to kill at least one of her husbands (I said things were quite colorful). So, suspecting that Nero had a contract on her, she got herself Mithridatized against the poisons that would have been available to her son's underlings. Like Mithridates, Agrippina eventually died by more mechanical methods as her son (supposedly) had assassins slay her, thus providing us with the small but meaningful lesson that one cannot be robust against everything. And, two thousand years later, nobody has found a method for us to get "fortified" against swords.

Let us call Mithridatization the result of an exposure to a small dose of a substance that, over time, makes one immune to additional, larger quantities of it. It is the sort of approach used in vaccination and allergy medicine. It is not quite antifragility, still at the more modest level of robustness, but we are on our way. And we already have a hint that perhaps being deprived of poison makes us fragile and that the road to robustification starts with a modicum of harm.

Now consider a case when the poisonous substance, in some dose, makes you better off overall, one step up from robustness. Hormesis, a word coined by pharmacologists, is when a small dose of a harmful substance is actually beneficial for the organism, acting as medicine. A little bit of an otherwise offending substance, not too much, acts to benefit the organism and make it better overall as it triggers some overreaction. This was not interpreted at the time in the sense of "gains from harm" so much as "harm is dose dependent" or "medicine is dose dependent." The interest to scientists has been in the nonlinearity of the dose-response.

Hormesis was well known by the ancients (and like the color blue was known but not expressed). But it was only in 1888 that it was first "scientifically" described (though still not given a name) by a German toxicologist, Hugo Schulz, who observed that small doses of poison stimulate the growth of yeast while larger doses cause harm. Some researchers hold that the benefits of vegetables may not be so much in what we call the "vitamins" or some other rationalizing theories (that is, ideas that seem to make sense in narrative form but have not been subjected to rigorous empirical testing), but in the following: plants protect themselves from harm and fend off predators with poisonous substances that, ingested by us in the right quantities, may stimulate our organisms— or so goes the story. Again, limited, low-dose poisoning triggers healthy benefits.

Many claim that caloric restriction (permanent or episodic) activates healthy reactions and switches that, among other benefits, lengthen life expectancy in laboratory animals. We humans live too long for researchers to test if such restriction increases our life expectancy (if the hypothesis is true, then the subjects of the test would outlive the researchers). But it looks like such restriction makes humans healthier (and may also improve their sense of humor). But since abundance would bring the opposite effect, this episodic caloric restriction can be also interpreted as follows: too much regular food is bad for you, and depriving humans of the stressor of hunger may make them live less than their full potential; so all hormesis seems to be doing is reestablishing the natural dosage for food and hunger in humans. In other words, hormesis is the norm, and its absence is what hurts us.

Hormesis lost some scientific respect, interest, and practice after the 1930s because some people mistakenly associated it with homeopathy. The association was unfair, as the mechanisms are extremely different. Homeopathy is based on other principles, such as the one that minute, highly diluted parts of the agents of a disease (so small they can hardly be perceptible, hence cannot cause hormesis) can help cure us of the disease itself. Homeopathy has shown little empirical backing and because of its testing methodologies belongs today to alternative medicine, while hormesis, as a phenomenon, has ample scientific evidence to back it up.

But the larger point is that we can now see that depriving systems of stressors, vital stressors, is not necessarily a good thing, and can be downright harmful.

DOMAIN INDEPENDENCE IS DOMAIN DEPENDENT

This idea that systems may need some stress and agitation has been missed by those who grasp it in one area and not in another. So we can now also see the *domain dependence* of our minds, a "domain" being an area or category of activity. Some people can understand an idea in one domain, say, medicine, and fail to recognize it in another, say, socioeconomic life. Or they get it in the classroom, but not in the more complicated texture of the street. Humans somehow fail to recognize situations outside the contexts in which they usually learn about them.

I had a vivid illustration of domain dependence in the driveway of a hotel in the pseudocity of Dubai. A fellow who looked like a banker had a uniformed porter carry his luggage (I can instantly tell if someone is a certain type of banker with minimal cues as I have physical allergies to them, even affecting my breathing). About fifteen minutes later I saw the banker lifting free weights at the gym, trying to replicate natural exercises using kettlebells as if he were swinging a suitcase. Domain dependence is pervasive.

Further, the problem is not just that Mithridatization and hormesis can be known in (some) medical circles and missed in other applications such as socioeconomic life. Even within medicine, some get it here and miss it there. The same doctor might recommend exercise so you "get tougher," and a few minutes later write a prescription for antibiotics in response to a trivial infection so you "don't get sick."

Another expression of domain dependence: ask a U.S. citizen if some semi-governmental agency with a great deal of independence (and no interference from Congress) should control the price of cars, morning newspapers, and Malbec wine, as its domain of specialty. He would jump in anger, as it appears to violate every principle the country stands for, and call you a Communist post-Soviet mole for even suggesting it. OK. Then ask him if that same government agency should control foreign exchange, mainly the rate of the dollar against the euro and the Mongolian tugrik. Same reaction: this is not France. Then very gently point out to him that the Federal Reserve Bank of the United States is in the business of controlling and managing the price of another good, another price, called the lending rate, the interest rate in the economy (and has proved to be good at it). The libertarian presidential candidate Ron Paul was called a crank for suggesting the abolition of the Federal Reserve, or even restricting its role. But he would also have been called a crank for suggesting the creation of an agency to control other prices.

Imagine someone gifted in learning languages but unable to transfer concepts from one tongue to another, so he would need to relearn "chair" or "love" or "apple pie" every time he acquires a new language. He would not recognize "house" (English) or "casa" (Spanish) or "byt" (Semitic). We are all, in a way, similarly handicapped, unable to recognize the same idea when it is presented in a different context. It is as if we are doomed to be deceived by the most superficial part of things, the packaging, the gift wrapping. This is why we don't see antifragility in places that are obvious, too obvious. It is not part of the accepted way of thinking about success, economic growth, or innovation that these may result only from overcompensation against stressors. Nor do we see this overcompensation at work elsewhere. (And domain dependence is also why it has been difficult for many researchers to realize that uncertainty, incomplete understanding, disorder, and volatility are members of the same close family.)

This lack of translation is a mental handicap that comes with being a human; and we will only start to attain wisdom or rationality when we make an effort to overcome and break through it.

Let us get deeper into overcompensation.

CHAPTER 2

Overcompensation and Overreaction Everywhere

Is it easy to write on a Heathrow runway?—Try to get the Pope to ban your work—How to beat up an economist (but not too hard, just enough to go to jail)

———

My own domain dependence was revealed to me one day as I was sitting in the office of David Halpern, a U.K. government advisor and policy maker. He informed me—in response to the idea of antifragility—of a phenomenon called post-traumatic growth, the opposite of post-traumatic stress syndrome, by which people harmed by past events surpass themselves. I had never heard about it before, and, to my great shame, had never made the effort to think of its existence: there is a small literature but it is not advertised outside a narrow discipline. We hear about the more lurid post-traumatic disorder, not post-traumatic growth, in the intellectual and so-called learned vocabulary. But popular culture has an awareness of its equivalent, revealed in the expression "it builds character." So do the ancient Mediterranean classics, along with grandmothers.

Intellectuals tend to focus on negative responses from randomness (fragility) rather than the positive ones (antifragility). This is not just in psychology: it prevails across the board.

How do you innovate? First, try to get in trouble. I mean serious, but not terminal, trouble. I hold—it is beyond speculation, rather a conviction—

that innovation and sophistication spark from initial situations of necessity, in ways that go far beyond the satisfaction of such necessity (from the unintended side effects of, say, an initial invention or attempt at invention). Naturally, there are classical thoughts on the subject, with a Latin saying that sophistication is born out of hunger (*artificia docuit fames*). The idea pervades classical literature: in Ovid, difficulty is what wakes up the genius (*ingenium mala saepe movent*), which translates in Brooklyn English into "When life gives you a lemon . . ."

The excess energy released from overreaction to setbacks is what innovates!

This message from the ancients is vastly deeper than it seems. It contradicts modern methods and ideas of innovation and progress on many levels, as we tend to think that innovation comes from bureaucratic funding, through planning, or by putting people through a Harvard Business School class by one Highly Decorated Professor of Innovation and Entrepreneurship (who never innovated anything) or hiring a consultant (who never innovated anything). This is a fallacy—note for now the disproportionate contribution of *uneducated* technicians and entrepreneurs to various technological leaps, from the Industrial Revolution to the emergence of Silicon Valley, and you will see what I mean.

Yet in spite of the visibility of the counterevidence, and the wisdom you can pick up free of charge from the ancients (or grandmothers), moderns try today to create inventions from situations of comfort, safety, and predictability instead of accepting the notion that "necessity really is the mother of invention."

Many, like the great Roman statesman Cato the Censor, looked at comfort, almost any form of comfort, as a road to waste.* He did not like it when we had it too easy, as he worried about the weakening of the will. And the softening he feared was not just at the personal level: an entire society can fall ill. Consider that as I am writing these lines, we are living in a debt crisis. The world as a whole has never been richer, and it has never been more heavily in debt, living off borrowed money. The record shows that, for society, the richer we become, the harder it gets to live within our means. Abundance is harder for us to handle than scarcity.

---

* Cato was the statesman who, three books ago (*Fooled by Randomness*), expelled all philosophers from Rome.

Cato would have smiled hearing about the recently observed effect in aeronautics that the automation of airplanes is underchallenging pilots, making flying too comfortable for them, dangerously comfortable. The dulling of the pilot's attention and skills from too *little* challenge is indeed causing deaths from flying accidents. Part of the problem is a Federal Aviation Administration (FAA) regulation that forced the industry to increase its reliance on automated flying. But, thankfully, the same FAA finally figured out the problem; it has recently found that pilots often "abdicate too much responsibility to automated systems."

HOW TO WIN A HORSE RACE

It is said that the best horses lose when they compete with slower ones, and win against better rivals. Undercompensation from the absence of a stressor, inverse hormesis, absence of challenge, degrades the best of the best. In Baudelaire's poem, "The albatross's giant wings prevent him from walking"—many do better in Calculus 103 than Calculus 101.

This mechanism of overcompensation hides in the most unlikely places. If tired after an intercontinental flight, go to the gym for some exertion instead of resting. Also, it is a well-known trick that if you need something urgently done, give the task to the busiest (or second busiest) person in the office. Most humans manage to squander their free time, as free time makes them dysfunctional, lazy, and unmotivated—the busier they get, the more active they are at other tasks. Overcompensation, here again.

I've discovered a trick when giving lectures. I have been told by conference organizers that one needs to be clear, to speak with the fake articulation of TV announcers, maybe even dance on the stage to get the attention of the crowd. Some try sending authors to "speech school"—the first time it was suggested to me I walked out, resolved to change publishers on the spot. I find it better to whisper, not shout. Better to be slightly inaudible, less clear. When I was a pit trader (one of those crazy people who stand in a crowded arena shouting and screaming in a continuous auction), I learned that the noise produced by the person is inverse to the pecking order: as with mafia dons, the most powerful traders were the least audible. One should have enough self-control to make the audience work hard to listen, which causes them to switch into intellectual overdrive. This paradox of attention has been a little bit investigated: there is empirical evidence of the effect of "disfluency." Mental effort moves us into higher gear, activating more vigorous and more analytical brain machinery.* The management guru Peter Drucker and the psychoanalyst Jacques Lacan, two persons who mesmerized the crowds the most in their respective areas, were the antithesis of the polished-swanky speaker or the consonant-trained television announcer.

The same or a similar mechanism of overcompensation makes us concentrate better in the presence of a modicum of background random noise, as if the act of countering such noise helps us hone our mental focus. Consider this remarkable ability humans have to filter out noise at happy hour and distinguish the signal among so many other loud conversations. So not only are we made to overcompensate, but we sometimes *need* the noise. Like many writers, I like to sit in cafés, working, as they say, against resistance. Consider our bedtime predilection for the rustle of tree leaves or the sound of the ocean: there are even electric contraptions that produce "white noise"† that helps people sleep better. Now these small distractions, like hormetic responses, act up to a point. I haven't tried it yet, but I am certain that it would be hard to write an essay on the runway of Heathrow airport.

Antifragile Responses as Redundancy

Something flashed when I heard "post-traumatic" during that London visit. It hit me right there and then that these antifragile hormetic responses were just a form of redundancy, and all the ideas of Mother Nature converged in my mind. It is all about redundancy. Nature likes to overinsure itself.

Layers of redundancy are the central risk management property of natural systems. We humans have two kidneys (this may even include accountants), extra spare parts, and extra capacity in many, many things (say, lungs, neural system, arterial apparatus), while human design tends to be spare and inversely redundant, so to speak—we have a historical track record of engaging in debt, which is the opposite of redundancy (fifty thousand in extra cash in the bank or, better, under the mattress, is

---

* This little bit of effort seems to activate the switch between two distinct mental systems, one intuitive and the other analytical, what psychologists call "system 1" and "system 2."

† There is nothing particularly "white" in white noise; it is simply random noise that follows a Normal Distribution.

redundancy; owing the bank an equivalent amount, that is, debt, is the opposite of redundancy). Redundancy is ambiguous because it seems like a waste if nothing unusual happens. Except that something unusual happens—usually.

Further, redundancy is not necessarily wussy; it can be extremely aggressive. For instance, if you have extra inventory of, say, fertilizers in the warehouse, just to be safe, and there happens to be a shortage because of disruptions in China, you can sell the excess inventory at a huge premium. Or if you have extra oil reserves, you may sell them at a large profit during a squeeze.

Now, it turns out, the same, very same logic applies to overcompensation: it is just a form of redundancy. An additional head for Hydra is no different from an extra—that is, seemingly redundant—kidney for humans, and no different from the additional capacity to withstand an extra stressor. If you ingest, say, fifteen milligrams of a poisonous substance, your body may prepare for twenty or more, and as a side effect will get stronger overall. These extra five milligrams of poison that you can withstand are no different from additional stockpiles of vital or necessary goods, say extra cash in the bank or more food in the basement. And to return to the drivers of innovation: the additional *quantities* of motivation and willpower, so to speak, stemming from setbacks can be also seen as extra capacity, no different from extra boxes of victuals.

A system that overcompensates is necessarily in overshooting mode, building extra capacity and strength in anticipation of a worse outcome and in response to information about the possibility of a hazard. And of course such extra capacity or strength may become useful by itself, opportunistically. We saw that redundancy is opportunistic, so such extra strength can be used to some benefit even in the absence of the hazard. Tell the next MBA analyst or business school professor you run into that redundancy is not defensive; it is more like investment than insurance. And tell them that what they call "inefficient" is often very efficient.

Indeed, our bodies discover probabilities in a very sophisticated manner and assess risks much better than our intellects do. To take one example, risk management professionals look in the past for information on the so-called *worst-case scenario* and use it to estimate future risks—this method is called "stress testing." They take the worst historical recession, the worst war, the worst historical move in interest rates, or the worst point in unemployment as an exact estimate for the worst future outcome. But they never notice the following inconsistency:

this so-called worst-case event, when it happened, exceeded the worst case at the time.

I have called this mental defect *the Lucretius problem,* after the Latin poetic philosopher who wrote that the fool believes that the tallest mountain in the world will be equal to the tallest one he has observed. We consider the biggest object of any kind that we have seen in our lives or hear about as the largest item that can possibly exist. And we have been doing this for millennia. In Pharaonic Egypt, which happens to be the first complete top-down nation-state managed by bureaucrats, scribes tracked the high-water mark of the Nile and used it as an estimate for a future worst-case scenario.

The same can be seen in the Fukushima nuclear reactor, which experienced a catastrophic failure in 2011 when a tsunami struck. It had been built to withstand the worst past historical earthquake, with the builders not imagining much worse—and not thinking that the worst past event had to be a surprise, as it had no precedent. Likewise, the former chairman of the Federal Reserve, Fragilista Doctor Alan Greenspan, in his apology to Congress offered the classic "It never happened before." Well, nature, unlike Fragilista Greenspan, prepares for what has not happened before, *assuming worse harm is possible.**

If humans fight the last war, nature fights the next one. Your body is more imaginative about the future than you are. Consider how people train in weightlifting: the body overshoots in response to exposures and overprepares (up to the point of biological limit, of course). This is how bodies get stronger.

In the aftermath of the banking crisis, I received all manner of threats, and *The Wall Street Journal* suggested that I "stock up on bodyguards." I tried to tell myself no worries, stay calm, these threats were coming from disgruntled bankers; anyway, people get whacked first, then you read about it in the newspapers, not in the reverse sequence. But the argument did not register in my mind, and, when in New York or London, I could not relax, even after chamomile tea. I started feeling paranoia in public places, scrutinizing people to ascertain that I was not being followed. I started taking the bodyguard suggestion seriously, and I found it more appealing (and considerably more economical) to become one,

---

* The obvious has not been tested empirically: Can the occurrence of extreme events be predicted from past history? Alas, according to a simple test: no, sorry.

or, better, to look like one. I found Lenny "Cake," a trainer, weighing around two hundred and eighty pounds (one hundred and thirty kilograms), who moonlighted as a security person. His nickname and weight both came from his predilection for cakes. Lenny Cake was the most physically intimidating person within five zip codes, and he was sixty. So, rather than taking lessons, I watched him train. He was into the "maximum lifts" type of training and swore by it, as he found it the most effective and least time-consuming. This method consisted of short episodes in the gym in which one focused solely on improving one's past maximum in a single lift, the heaviest weight one could haul, sort of the high-water mark. The workout was limited to trying to exceed that mark once or twice, rather than spending time on un-entertaining time-consuming repetitions. The exercise got me into a naturalistic form of weightlifting, and one that accords with the evidence-based literature: work on the maximum, spend the rest of the time resting and splurging on mafia-sized steaks. I have been trying to push my limit for four years now; it is amazing to see how something in my biology anticipates a higher level than the past maximum—until it reaches its ceiling. When I deadlift (i.e., mimic lifting a stone to waist level) using a bar with three hundred and thirty pounds, then rest, I can safely expect that I will build a certain amount of additional strength as my body *predicts* that next time I may need to lift three hundred and thirty-five pounds. The benefits, beyond the fading of my paranoia and my newfound calm in public places, includes small unexpected conveniences. When I am harassed by limo drivers in the arrival hall at Kennedy airport insistently offering me a ride and I calmly tell them to "f*** off," they go away immediately. But there are severe drawbacks: some of the readers I meet at conferences have a rough time dealing with an intellectual who has the appearance of a bodyguard—intellectuals can be svelte or flabby and out of shape (when they wear a tweed jacket), but they are not supposed to look like butchers.

Something that will give the Darwinists some work, an observation made to me by the risk analyst, my favorite intellectual opponent (and personal friend) Aaron Brown: the term "fitness" itself may be quite imprecise and even ambiguous, which is why the notion of antifragility as something exceeding mere fitness can elucidate the confusion. What does "fitness" mean? Being exactly tuned to a given past history of a specific environment, or extrapolating to an environment with stressors of higher intensity? Many seem to point to the first kind of adaptation, missing the notion of antifragility. But if one were to write down mathematically a standard model of selection, one would get overcompensation rather than mere "fitness."*

Even the psychologists who studied the antifragile response of post-traumatic growth, and show the data for it, don't quite get the full concept, as they lapse, when using words, into the concept of "resilience."

ON THE ANTIFRAGILITY OF RIOTS, LOVE, AND
OTHER UNEXPECTED BENEFICIARIES OF STRESS

Once one makes an effort to overcome domain dependence, the phenomenon of overcompensation appears ubiquitous.

Those who understand bacterial resistance in the biological domain completely fail to grasp the dictum by Seneca in *De clemencia* about the inverse effect of punishments. He wrote: "Repeated punishment, while it crushes the hatred of a few, stirs the hatred of all . . . just as trees that have been trimmed throw out again countless branches." For revolutions feed on repression, growing heads faster and faster as one *literally* cuts a few off by killing demonstrators. There is an Irish revolutionary song that encapsulates the effect:

> *The higher you build your barricades, the stronger we become.*

The crowds, at some point, mutate, blinded by anger and a sense of outrage, fueled by the heroism of a few willing to sacrifice their lives for the cause (although they don't quite see it as sacrifice) and hungry for the privilege to become martyrs. It is that political movements and rebellions can be highly antifragile, and the sucker game is to try to repress them using brute force rather than manipulate them, give in, or find more astute ruses, as Heracles did with Hydra.

If antifragility is what wakes up and overreacts and overcompensates to stressors and damage, then one of the most antifragile things you will find outside economic life is a certain brand of refractory love (or hate),

---

* Set a simple filtering rule: all members of a species need to have a neck forty centimeters long in order to survive. After a few generations, the surviving population would have, on average, a neck *longer* than forty centimeters. (More technically, a stochastic process subjected to an absorbing barrier will have an observed mean higher than the barrier.)

one that seems to overreact and overcompensate for impediments such as distance, family incompatibilities, and every conscious attempt to kill it. Literature is rife with characters trapped in a form of antifragile passion, seemingly against their will. In Proust's long novel *La recherche,* Swann, a socially sophisticated Jewish art dealer, falls for Odette, a demimondaine, a "kept" woman of sorts, a semi- or perhaps just a quarter-prostitute; she treats him badly. Her elusive behavior fuels his obsession, causing him to demean himself for the reward of a bit more time with her. He exhibits overt clinginess, follows her on her trysts with other men, hiding shamelessly in staircases, which of course causes her to treat him even more elusively. Supposedly, the story was a fictionalization of Proust's own entanglement with his (male) driver. Or take Dino Buzzati's semiautobiographical novel *Un amore,* the story of a middle-aged Milanese man who falls—accidentally, of course—for a dancer at the Scala who moonlights as a prostitute. She of course mistreats him, exploits him, takes advantage of him, milks him; and the more she mistreats him, the more he exposes himself to abuse to satisfy the antifragile thirst of a few moments with her. But some form of happy ending there: from his biography, Buzzati himself ended up marrying, at sixty, a twenty-five year old, Almerina, a former dancer, seemingly the character of the story; when he died shortly after that, she became a good caretaker of his literary legacy.

Even when authors such as Lucretius (the same of the high mountains earlier in this chapter) rant against the dependence, imprisonment, and alienation of love, treating it as a (preventable) disease, they end up lying to us or themselves. Legend perhaps: Lucretius the priest of anti-romance might have been himself involved in uncontrollable—antifragile—infatuation.

Like tormenting love, some thoughts are so antifragile that you feed them by trying to get rid of them, turning them into obsessions. Psychologists have shown the irony of the process of thought control: the more energy you put into trying to control your ideas and what you think about, the more your ideas end up controlling you.

Please Ban My Book: The Antifragility of Information

Information is antifragile; it feeds more on attempts to harm it than it does on efforts to promote it. For instance, many wreck their reputations merely by trying to defend them.

The wily Venetians knew how to spread information by disguising it as a secret. Try it out with the following experiment in spreading gossip: tell someone a secret and qualify it by insisting that it is a secret, begging your listener "not to tell anyone"; the more you insist that it remain a secret, the more it will spread.

We all learn early on in life that books and ideas are antifragile and get nourishment from attacks—to borrow from the Roman emperor Marcus Aurelius (one of the doer-Stoic authors), "fire feeds on obstacles." There is the attraction of banned books, their antifragility to interdicts. The first book I read, during my childhood, of Graham Greene's was *The Power and the Glory*, selected for no other reason than its having been put on the *Index* (that is, banned) by the Vatican. Likewise, as a teenager, I gorged on the books of the American expatriate Henry Miller—his major book sold a million copies in one year thanks to having been banned in twenty-three states. The same with *Madame Bovary* or *Lady Chatterley's Lover*.

Criticism, for a book, is a truthful, unfaked badge of attention, signaling that it is not boring; and boring is the only very bad thing for a book. Consider the Ayn Rand phenomenon: her books *Atlas Shrugged* and *The Fountainhead* have been read for more than half a century by millions of people, in spite of, or most likely thanks to, brutally nasty reviews and attempts to discredit her. The first-order information is the intensity: what matters is the effort the critic puts into trying to prevent others from reading the book, or, more generally in life, it is the effort in badmouthing someone that matters, not so much what is said. So if you really want people to read a book, tell them it is "overrated," with a sense of outrage (and use the attribute "underrated" for the opposite effect).

Balzac recounts how actresses paid journalists (often in kind) to write favorable accounts—but the wiliest got them to write unfavorable comments, knowing that it made them more interesting.

I have just bought Tom Holland's book on the rise of Islam for the sole reason that he was attacked by Glen Bowersock, considered to be the most prominent living scholar on the Roman Levant. Until then I had thought that Tom Holland was just a popularizer, and I would not have taken him seriously otherwise. I didn't even attempt to read Bowersock's review. So here is a simple rule of thumb (a heuristic): to estimate the quality of research, take the caliber of the highest detractor, or the caliber of the lowest detractor whom the author answers in print—whichever is lower.

Criticism itself can be antifragile to repression, when the fault finder wants to be attacked in return in order to get some validation. Jean Fréron, said to be a very envious thinker, with the mediocrity of envious thinkers, managed to play a role in intellectual history solely by irritating the otherwise brilliant Voltaire to the point of bringing him to write satirical poems against him. Voltaire, himself a gadfly and expert at ticking off people to benefit from their reactions, forgot how things worked when it came to himself. Perhaps Voltaire's charm was in that he did not know how to save his wit. So the same hidden antifragilities apply to attacks on our ideas and persons: we fear them and dislike negative publicity, but smear campaigns, if you can survive them, help enormously, conditional on the person appearing to be extremely motivated and adequately angry—just as when you hear a woman badmouthing another in front of a man (or vice versa). There is a visible selection bias: why did he attack *you* instead of someone else, one of the millions of persons deserving but not worthy of attack? It is his energy in attacking or badmouthing that will, antifragile style, put you on the map.

My great-grandfather Nicolas Ghosn was a wily politician who managed to stay permanently in power and hold government positions in spite of his numerous enemies (most notably his archenemy, my great-great-grandfather on the Taleb side of the family). As my grandfather, his eldest son, was starting his administrative and hopefully political career, his father summoned him to his deathbed. "My son, I am very disappointed in you," he said. "I never hear anything wrong said about you. You have proven yourself incapable of generating envy."

Get Another Job

As we saw with the Voltaire story, it is not possible to stamp out criticism; if it harms you, get out. It is easier to change jobs than control your reputation or public perception.

Some jobs and professions are fragile to reputational harm, something that in the age of the Internet cannot possibly be controlled—these jobs aren't worth having. You do not want to "control" your reputation; you won't be able to do it by controlling information flow. Instead, focus on altering your exposure, say, by putting yourself in a position impervious to reputational damage. Or even put yourself in a situation to benefit from the antifragility of information. In that sense, a writer is antifragile, but we will see later most modernistic professions are usually not.

I was in Milan trying to explain antifragility to Luca Formenton, my Italian publisher (with great aid from body language and hand gestures). I was there partly for the Moscato dessert wines, partly for a convention in which the other main speaker was a famous fragilista economist. So, suddenly remembering that I was an author, I presented Luca with the following thought experiment: if I beat up the economist publicly, what would happen to me (other than a publicized trial causing great interest in the new notions of *fragilita* and *antifragilita*)? You know, this economist had what is called a *tête à baffe,* a face that invites you to slap it, just like a cannoli invites you to bite into it. Luca thought for a second . . . well, it's not like he would like me to do it, but, you know, it wouldn't hurt book sales. Nothing I can do as an author that makes it to the front page of *Corriere della Sera* would be detrimental for my book. Almost no scandal would hurt an artist or writer.*

Now let's say I were a midlevel executive employee of some corporation listed on the London Stock Exchange, the sort who never take chances by dressing down, always wearing a suit and tie (even on the beach). What would happen to me if I attack the fragilista? My firing and arrest record would plague me forever. I would be the total victim of informational antifragility. But someone earning close to minimum wage, say, a construction worker or a taxi driver, does not overly depend on his reputation and is free to have his own opinions. He would be merely robust compared to the artist, who is antifragile. A midlevel bank employee with a mortgage would be fragile to the extreme. In fact he would be completely a prisoner of the value system that invites him to be corrupt to the core—because of his dependence on the annual vacation in Barbados. The same with a civil servant in Washington. Take this easy-to-use heuristic (which is, to repeat the definition, a simple compressed rule of thumb) to detect the independence and robustness of someone's reputation. With few exceptions, those who dress outrageously are robust or even antifragile in reputation; those clean-shaven types who dress in suits and ties are fragile to information about them.

* The French have a long series of authors who owe part of their status to their criminal record—which includes the poet Ronsard, the writer Jean Genet, and many others.

Large corporations and governments do not seem to understand this rebound power of information and its ability to control those who try to control it. When you hear a corporation or a debt-laden government trying to "reinstill confidence" you know they are fragile, hence doomed. Information is merciless: one press conference "to tranquilize" and the investors will run away, causing a death spiral or a run on the bank. Which explains why I have an obsessive stance against government indebtedness, as a staunch proponent of what is called fiscal conservatism. When you don't have debt you don't care about your reputation in economics circles—and somehow it is only when you don't care about your reputation that you tend to have a good one. Just as in matters of seduction, people lend the most to those who need them the least.

And we are blind to this antifragility of information in even more domains. If I physically beat up a rival in an ancestral environment, I injure him, weaken him, perhaps eliminate him forever—and get some exercise in the process. If I use the mob to put a contract on his head, he is gone. But if I stage a barrage of informational attacks on websites and in journals, I may be just helping him and hurting myself.

So I end this section with a thought. It is quite perplexing that those from whom we have benefited the most aren't those who have tried to help us (say with "advice") but rather those who have actively tried—but eventually failed—to harm us.

Next we turn to a central distinction between the things that like stress and other things that don't.

CHAPTER 3

The Cat and the Washing Machine

Stress is knowledge (and knowledge is stress)—The organic and the mechanical—No translator needed, for now—Waking up the animal in us, after two hundred years of modernity

The bold conjecture made here is that everything that has life in it is to some extent antifragile (but not the reverse). It looks like the secret of life is antifragility.

Typically, the natural—the biological—is both antifragile and fragile, depending on the source (and the range) of variation. A human body can benefit from stressors (to get stronger), but only to a point. For instance, your bones will get denser when episodic stress is applied to them, a mechanism formalized under the name Wolff's Law after an 1892 article by a German surgeon. But a dish, a car, an inanimate object will not—these may be robust but cannot be intrinsically antifragile.

Inanimate—that is, nonliving—material, typically, when subjected to stress, either undergoes material fatigue or breaks. One of the rare exceptions I've seen is in the report of a 2011 experiment by Brent Carey, a graduate student, in which he shows that composite material of carbon nanotubes arranged in a certain manner produces a self-strengthening response previously unseen in synthetic materials, "similar to the localized self-strengthening that occurs in biological structures." This crosses the boundary between the living and the inanimate, as it can lead to the development of adaptable load-bearing material.

We can use the distinction as a marker between living and nonliving. The fact that the artificial needs to be antifragile for us to be able to use it as tissue is quite a telling difference between the biological and the synthetic. Your house, your food processor, and your computer desk eventually wear down and don't self-repair. They may look better with age (when artisanal), just as your jeans will look more fashionable with use, but eventually time will catch up with them and the hardest material will end up looking like Roman ruins. Your jeans may look improved and more fashionable when worn out, but their material did not get stronger, nor do they self-repair. But think of a material that would make them stronger, self-heal, and improve with time.*

True, while humans self-repair, they eventually wear out (hopefully leaving their genes, books, or some other information behind—another discussion). But the phenomenon of aging is misunderstood, largely fraught with mental biases and logical flaws. We observe old people and see them age, so we associate aging with their loss of muscle mass, bone weakness, loss of mental function, taste for Frank Sinatra music, and similar degenerative effects. But these failures to self-repair come largely from maladjustment—either too few stressors or too little time for recovery between them—and maladjustment for this author is the mismatch between one's design and the structure of the randomness of the environment (what I call more technically its "distributional or statistical properties"). What we observe in "aging" is a combination of maladjustment and senescence, and it appears that the two are separable—senescence might not be avoidable, and should not be avoided (it would contradict the logic of life, as we will see in the next chapter); maladjustment is avoidable. Much of aging comes from a misunderstanding of the effect of comfort—a disease of civilization: make life longer and longer, while people are more and more sick. In a natural environment, people die without aging—or after a very short period of aging. For instance, some markers, such as blood pressure, that tend to worsen over time for moderns do not change over the life of hunter-gatherers until the very end.

And this artificial aging comes from stifling internal antifragility.

---

* Another way to see it: machines are harmed by low-level stressors (material fatigue), organisms are harmed by the *absence* of low-level stressors (hormesis).

The Complex

This organic-mechanical dichotomy is a good starter distinction to build intuitions about the difference between two kinds of phenomena, but we can do better. Many things such as society, economic activities and markets, and cultural behavior are apparently man-made but grow on their own to reach some kind of self-organization. They may not be strictly biological, but they resemble the biological in that, in a way, they multiply and replicate—think of rumors, ideas, technologies, and businesses. They are closer to the cat than to the washing machine but tend to be mistaken for washing machines. Accordingly we can generalize our distinction beyond the biological-nonbiological. More effective is the distinction between noncomplex and complex systems.

Artificial, man-made mechanical and engineering contraptions with simple responses are complicated, but not "complex," as they don't have interdependencies. You push a button, say, a light switch, and get an exact response, with no possible ambiguity in the consequences, even in Russia. But with complex systems, interdependencies are severe. You need to think in terms of ecology: if you remove a specific animal you disrupt a food chain: its predators will starve and its prey will grow unchecked, causing complications and series of cascading side effects. Lions are exterminated by the Canaanites, Phoenicians, Romans, and later inhabitants of Mount Lebanon, leading to the proliferation of goats who crave tree roots, contributing to the deforestation of mountain areas, consequences that were hard to see ahead of time. Likewise, if you shut down a bank in New York, it will cause ripple effects from Iceland to Mongolia.

In the complex world, the notion of "cause" itself is suspect; it is either nearly impossible to detect or not really defined—another reason to ignore newspapers, with their constant supply of causes for things.

STRESSORS ARE INFORMATION

Now the crux of complex systems, those with interacting parts, is that they convey information to these component parts through stressors, or thanks to these stressors: your body gets information about the environment not through your logical apparatus, your intelligence and ability to reason, compute, and calculate, but through stress, via hormones or other messengers we haven't discovered yet. As we saw, your bones will get stronger when subjected to gravity, say, after your (short) employment with a piano moving company. They will become weaker after you spend the next Christmas vacation in a space station with zero gravity or (as few people realize) if you spend a lot of time riding a bicycle. The skin on the palms of your hands will get calloused if you spend a summer on a Soviet-style cooperative farm. Your skin lightens in the winter and tans in the summer (especially if you have Mediterranean origins, less so if you are of Irish or African descent or from other places with more uniform weather throughout the year).

Further, errors and their consequences are information; for small children, pain is the only risk management information, as their logical faculties are not very developed. For complex systems are, well, all about information. And there are many more conveyors of information around us than meet the eye. This is what we will call *causal opacity*: it is hard to see the arrow from cause to consequence, making much of conventional methods of analysis, in addition to standard logic, inapplicable. As I said, the predictability of specific events is low, and it is such opacity that makes it low. Not only that, but because of nonlinearities, one needs higher visibility than with regular systems—instead what we have is opacity.

FIGURE 2. This illustrates why I have a thing for bones. You see identical situations of head-loading water or grain in traditional societies in India, Africa, and the Americas. There is even a Levantine love song about an attractive woman with an amphora on her head. The health benefits could beat bone density medication—but such forms of therapy would not benefit pharma's bottom line. Credit: Creative Commons

Let us consider bones again. I have a thing for bones, and the idea I will discuss next made me focus on lifting heavy objects rather than using gym machines. This obsession with the skeleton got started when I found a paper published in the journal *Nature* in 2003 by Gerard Karsenty and colleagues. The tradition has been to think that aging *causes* bone weakness (bones lose density, become more brittle), as if there was a one-way relationship possibly brought about by hormones (females start experiencing osteoporosis after menopause). It turns out, as shown by Karsenty and others who have since embarked on the line of research, that the reverse is also largely true: loss of bone density and degradation of the health of the bones also *causes* aging, diabetes, and, for males, loss of fertility and sexual function. We just cannot isolate any causal relationship in a complex system. Further, the story of the bones and the associated misunderstanding of interconnectedness illustrates how lack of stress (here, bones under a weight-bearing load) can cause aging, and how depriving stress-hungry antifragile systems of stressors brings a great deal of fragility which we will transport to political systems in Book II. Lenny's exercise method, the one I watched and tried to imitate in the last chapter, seemed to be as much about stressing and strengthening the bones as it was about strengthening the muscles—he didn't know much about the mechanism but had discovered, heuristically, that weight bearing did something to his system. The lady in Figure 2, thanks to a lifetime of head-loading water jugs, has outstanding health and excellent posture.

Our antifragilities have conditions. The frequency of stressors matters a bit. Humans tend to do better with acute than with chronic stressors, particularly when the former are followed by ample time for recovery, which allows the stressors to do their jobs as messengers. For instance, having an intense emotional shock from seeing a snake coming out of my keyboard or a vampire entering my room, followed by a period of soothing safety (with chamomile tea and baroque music) long enough for me to regain control of my emotions, would be beneficial for my health, provided of course that I manage to overcome the snake or vampire after an arduous, hopefully heroic fight and have a picture taken next to the dead predator. Such a stressor would be certainly better than the mild but continuous stress of a boss, mortgage, tax problems, guilt over procrastinating with one's tax return, exam pressures, chores, emails to answer, forms to complete, daily commutes—things that make you feel trapped in life. In other words, the pressures brought about by civilization. In fact, neurobiologists show that the former type of stressor is necessary, the second harmful, for one's health. For an idea of how harmful a low-level stressor without recovery can be, consider the so-called Chinese water torture: a drop continuously hitting the same spot on your head, never letting you recover.

Indeed, the way Heracles managed to control Hydra was by cauterizing the wounds on the stumps of the heads that he had just severed. He thus prevented the regrowth of the heads and the exercise of antifragility. In other words, he disrupted the recovery.

Table 2 shows the difference between the two types. Note that there may be intermediate steps between engineered and organic, though things tend to cluster in one bucket or the other.

The reader can get a hint of the central problem we face with top-down tampering with political systems (or similar complex systems), the subject of Book II. The fragilista mistakes the economy for a washing machine that needs monthly maintenance, or misconstrues the properties of your body for those of a compact disc player. Adam Smith himself made the analogy of the economy as a watch or a clock that once set in motion continues on its own. But I am certain that he did not quite think

TABLE 2 • THE MECHANICAL AND THE ORGANIC (BIOLOGICAL OR NONBIOLOGICAL)

THE MECHANICAL, NONCOMPLEX	THE ORGANIC, COMPLEX
Needs continuous repair and maintenance	Self-healing
Hates randomness	Loves randomness (small variations)
No need for recovery	Needs recovery between stressors
No or little interdependence	High degree of interdependence
Stressors cause material fatigue	Absence of stressors cause atrophy
Age with use (wear and tear)	Age with disuse*
Undercompensates from shocks	Overcompensates from shocks
Time brings only senescence	Time brings aging and senescence

* Frano Barović reading this chapter wrote to me: "Machines: use it and lose it; organisms: use it or lose it." Also note that everything alive needs stressors, but not all machines need to be left alone—a point we will visit in our discussion of annealing.

of matters in these terms, that he looked at the economy in terms of organisms but lacked a framework to express it. For Smith understood the opacity of complex systems as well as the interdependencies, since he developed the notion of the "invisible hand."

But alas, unlike Adam Smith, Plato did not quite get it. Promoting the well-known metaphor of the *ship of state*, he likens a state to a naval vessel, which, of course, requires the monitoring of a captain. He ultimately argues that the only men fit to be captain of this ship are philosopher kings, benevolent men with absolute power who have access to the Form of the Good. And once in a while one hears shouts of "who is governing us?" as if the world needs someone to govern it.

Equilibrium, Not Again

Social scientists use the term "equilibrium" to describe balance between opposing forces, say, supply and demand, so small disturbances or deviations in one direction, like those of a pendulum, would be countered with an adjustment in the opposite direction that would bring things back to stability. In short, this is thought to be the goal for an economy.

Looking deeper into what these social scientists want us to get into, such a goal can be death. For the complexity theorist Stuart Kaufman uses the idea of equilibrium to separate the two different worlds of Table 2. *For the nonorganic, noncomplex, say, an object on the table, equilibrium* (as traditionally defined) *happens in a state of inertia. So for something organic, equilibrium* (in that sense) *only happens with death.* Consider an example used by Kaufman: in your bathtub, a vortex starts forming and will keep going after that. Such type of situation is permanently "far from equilibrium"—and it looks like organisms and dynamic systems exist in such a state.* For them, a state of normalcy requires a certain degree of volatility, randomness, the continuous swapping of information, and stress, which explains the harm they may be subjected to when deprived of volatility.

---

* These are the so-called dissipative structures, after the works of the physicist Ilya Prigogine, that have a quite different status from simple equilibrium structures: they are formed and maintained through the effect of exchange of energy and matter in permanent nonequilibrium conditions.

CRIMES AGAINST CHILDREN

Not only are we averse to stressors, and don't understand them, but we are committing crimes against life, the living, science, and wisdom, for the sake of eliminating volatility and variation.

I feel anger and frustration when I think that one in ten Americans beyond the age of high school is on some kind of antidepressant, such as Prozac. Indeed, when you go through mood swings, you now have to justify why you *are not* on some medication. There may be a few good reasons to be on medication, in severely pathological cases, but my mood, my sadness, my bouts of anxiety, are a second source of intelligence—perhaps even the first source. I get mellow and lose physical energy when it rains, become more meditative, and tend to write more and more slowly then, with the raindrops hitting the window, what Verlaine called autumnal "sobs" (*sanglots*). Some days I enter poetic melancholic states, what the Portuguese call *saudade* or the Turks *hüzün* (from the Arabic word for sadness). Other days I am more aggressive, have more energy—and will write less, walk more, do other things, argue with researchers, answer emails, draw graphs on blackboards. Should I be turned into a vegetable or a happy imbecile?

Had Prozac been available last century, Baudelaire's "spleen," Edgar Allan Poe's moods, the poetry of Sylvia Plath, the lamentations of so many other poets, everything with a soul would have been silenced*. . . .

If large pharmaceutical companies were able to eliminate the seasons, they would probably do so—for a profit, of course.

There is another danger: in addition to harming children, we are harming society and our future. Measures that aim at reducing variability and swings in the lives of children are also reducing variability and differences within our said to be Great Culturally Globalized Society.

Punished by Translation

Another forgotten property of stressors is in language acquisition—I don't know anyone who ever learned to speak his mother tongue in a

---

* This does not mean that Sylvia Plath should not have been medicated at all. The point is that pathologies should be medicated when there is a risk of suicide, not mood swings.

textbook, starting with grammar and, checked by biquarterly exams, systematically fitting words to the acquired rules. You pick up a language best thanks to situational difficulty, from error to error, when you need to communicate under more or less straining circumstances, particularly to express urgent needs (say, physical ones, such those arising in the aftermath of dinner in a tropical location).

One learns new words without making a nerd-effort, but rather another type of effort: to communicate, mostly by being forced to read the mind of the other person—suspending one's fear of making mistakes. Success, wealth, and technology, alas, make this mode of acquisition much more difficult. A few years ago, when I was of no interest to anyone, foreign conference organizers did not assign to me the fawning "travel assistant" fluent in Facebook English, so I used to be forced to fend for myself, hence picking up vocabulary by finger pointing and trial and error (just as children do)—no handheld devices, no dictionary, nothing. Now I am punished by privilege and comfort—and I can't resist comfort. The punishment is in the form of a person, fluent in English, greeting me by displaying my misspelled name at the airport, no stress, no ambiguity, and no exposure to Russian, Turkish, Croatian, or Polish outside of ugly (and organized) textbooks. What is worse, the person is unctuous; obsequious verbosity is something rather painful under the condition of jet lag.

Yet the best way to learn a language may be an episode of jail in a foreign country. My friend Chad Gracia improved his Russian thanks to an involuntary stay in the quarantine section of a hospital in Moscow for an imagined disease. It was a cunning brand of medical kidnapping, as during the mess after the end of the Soviet rule, hospitals were able to extort travelers with forced hospital stays unless they paid large sums of money to have their papers cleared. Chad, then barely fluent in the language, was forced to read Tolstoy in the original, and picked up quite a bit of vocabulary.

Touristification

My friend Chad benefited from the kind of disorder that is less and less prevalent thanks to the modern disease of *touristification*. This is my term for an aspect of modern life that treats humans as washing machines, with simplified mechanical responses—and a detailed user's manual. It is the systematic removal of uncertainty and randomness from things, trying to make matters highly predictable in their smallest details. All that for the sake of comfort, convenience, and efficiency.

What a tourist is in relation to an adventurer, or a flâneur, touristification is to life; it consists in converting activities, and not just travel, into the equivalent of a script like those followed by actors. We will see how touristification castrates systems and organisms that like uncertainty by sucking randomness out of them to the last drop—while providing them with the illusion of benefit. The guilty parties are the education system, planning the funding of teleological scientific research, the French baccalaureate, gym machines, etc.

And the electronic calendar.

But the worse touristification is the life we moderns have to lead in captivity, during our leisure hours: Friday night opera, scheduled parties, scheduled laughs. Again, golden jail.

This "goal-driven" attitude hurts deeply inside my existential self.

The Secret Thirst for Chance

Which brings us to the existential aspect of randomness. If you are not a washing machine or a cuckoo clock—in other words, if you are alive—something deep in your soul likes a certain measure of randomness and disorder.

There is a titillating feeling associated with randomness. We like the moderate (and highly domesticated) world of games, from spectator sports to having our breathing suspended between crap shoots during the next visit to Las Vegas. I myself, while writing these lines, try to avoid the tyranny of a precise and explicit plan, drawing from an opaque source inside me that gives me surprises. Writing is only worth it when it provides us with the tingling effect of adventure, which is why I enjoy the composition of books and dislike the straitjacket of the 750-word op-ed, which, even without the philistinism of the editor, bores me to tears. And, remarkably, what the author is bored writing bores the reader.

If I could predict what my day would exactly look like, I would feel a little bit dead.

Further, this randomness is necessary for true life. Consider that all the wealth of the world can't buy a liquid more pleasurable than water after intense thirst. Few objects bring more thrill than a recovered wallet (or laptop) lost on a train. Further, in an ancestral habitat we humans were prompted by natural stimuli—fear, hunger, desire—that made us work out and become fit for our environment. Consider how easy it is to find the energy to lift a car if a crying child is under it, or to run for your life if you see a wild animal crossing the street. Compare this to the heaviness of the obligation to visit the gym at the planned 6 P.M. and be bullied there by some personal trainer—unless of course you are under the imperative to look like a bodyguard. Also consider how easy it is to skip a meal when the randomness in the environment causes us to do so, because of lack of food—as compared to the "discipline" of sticking to some eighteen-day diet plan.

There exist the kind of people for whom life is some kind of project. After talking to them, you stop feeling good for a few hours; life starts tasting like food cooked without salt. I, a thrill-seeking human, have a b***t detector that seems to match my boredom detector, as if we were equipped with a naturalistic filter, dullness-aversion. Ancestral life had no homework, no boss, no civil servants, no academic grades, no conversation with the dean, no consultant with an MBA, no table of procedure, no application form, no trip to New Jersey, no grammatical stickler, no conversation with someone boring you: all life was random stimuli and nothing, good or bad, ever felt like work.* Dangerous, yes, but boring, never.

Finally, an environment with variability (hence randomness) does not expose us to chronic stress injury, unlike human-designed systems. If you walk on uneven, not man-made terrain, no two steps will ever be identical—compare that to the randomness-free gym machine offering the exact opposite: forcing you into endless repetitions of the very same movement.

Much of modern life is preventable chronic stress injury.

Next, let us examine a wrinkle of evolution, that great expert on antifragility.

---

* Neither Rousseau nor Hobbes. True, life then was perhaps "brutal and short," but it is a severe logical mistake to present a tradeoff, to use unsavory aspects of early humanity as a necessary cost of avoiding modern tortures. There is no reason to not want advantages from both eras.

CHAPTER 4

What Kills Me Makes Others Stronger

Antifragility for one is fragility for someone else—Where we introduce the idea that we think too much, do very little—Fail for others to succeed—One day you may get a thank-you note

_____

ANTIFRAGILITY BY LAYERS

This chapter is about error, evolution, and antifragility, with a hitch: it is largely about the errors of others—the antifragility of some comes necessarily at the expense of the fragility of others. In a system, the sacrifices of some units—fragile units, that is, or people—are often necessary for the well-being of other units or the whole. The fragility of every startup is necessary for the economy to be antifragile, and that's what makes, among other things, entrepreneurship work: the fragility of individual entrepreneurs and their necessarily high failure rate.

So antifragility gets a bit more intricate—and more interesting—in the presence of layers and hierarchies. A natural organism is not a single, final unit; it is composed of subunits and itself may be the subunit of some larger collective. These subunits may be contending with each other. Take another business example. Restaurants are fragile; they compete with each other, but the collective of local restaurants is antifragile for that very reason. Had restaurants been individually robust, hence immortal, the overall business would be either stagnant or weak, and would deliver nothing better than cafeteria food—and I mean Soviet-style cafeteria food. Further, it would be marred with systemic shortages, with, once in a while, a complete crisis and government bailout. All that quality, stability, and reliability are owed to the fragility of the restaurant itself.

So some parts *on the inside* of a system may be required to be fragile in order to make the system antifragile as a result. Or the organism itself might be fragile, but the information encoded in the genes reproducing it will be antifragile. The point is not trivial, as it is behind the logic of evolution. This applies equally to entrepreneurs and individual scientific researchers.

Further, we mentioned "sacrifice" a few paragraphs ago. Sadly, the benefits of errors are often conferred on others, the collective—as if individuals were designed to make errors for the greater good, not their own. Alas, we tend to discuss mistakes without taking into consideration this layering and transfer of fragility.

Evolution and Unpredictability

I said that the notions of Mithridatization and hormesis were "proto"-antifragility, introductory concepts: they are even a bit naive, and we will need to refine, even transcend them, in order to look at a complex system as a whole. Hormesis is a metaphor; antifragility is a phenomenon.

Primo, Mithridatization and hormesis are just very weak forms of antifragility, with limited gains from volatility, accident, or harm and a certain reversal of the protective or beneficial effect beyond a certain dosage. Hormesis likes only a little bit of disorder, or, rather, *needs* a little bit of it. They are mostly interesting insofar as their deprivation is harmful, something we don't get intuitively—our minds cannot easily understand the complicated responses (we think linearly, and these dose-dependent responses are nonlinear). Our linear minds do not like nuances and reduce the information to the binary "harmful" or "helpful."

Secundo, and that's the central weakness, they see the organism from the outside and consider it as a whole, a single unit, when things can be a bit more nuanced.

There is a different, stronger variety of antifragility linked to evolution that is beyond hormesis—actually very different from hormesis; it is even its opposite. It can be described as hormesis—getting stronger under harm—if we look from the outside, not from the inside. This other variety of antifragility is evolutionary, and operates at the informational level—genes are information. Unlike with hormesis, the unit does not get stronger in response to stress; it dies. But it accomplishes a transfer of benefits; other units survive—and those that survive have attributes that improve the collective of units, leading to modifications commonly assigned the vague term "evolution" in textbooks and in the *New York Times* Tuesday science section. So the antifragility of concern here is not so much that of the organisms, inherently weak, but rather that of their genetic code, which can survive them. The code doesn't really care about the welfare of the unit itself—quite the contrary, since it destroys many things around it. Robert Trivers figured out the presence of competition between gene and organism in his idea of the "selfish gene."

In fact, the most interesting aspect of evolution is that it only works because of its *antifragility*; it is in love with stressors, randomness, uncertainty, and disorder—while individual organisms are relatively fragile, the gene pool takes advantage of shocks to enhance its fitness.

So from this we can see that there is a tension between nature and individual organisms.

Everything alive or organic in nature has a finite life and dies eventually—even Methuselah lived less than a thousand years. But it usually dies after reproducing offspring with a genetic code in one way or another different from that of the parents, with their information modified. Methuselah's genetic information is still present in Damascus, Jerusalem, and, of course, Brooklyn, New York. Nature does not find its members very helpful after their reproductive abilities are depleted (except perhaps special situations in which animals live in groups, such as the need for grandmothers in the human and elephant domains to assist others in preparing offspring to take charge). Nature prefers to let the game continue at the informational level, the genetic code. So organisms need to die for nature to be antifragile—nature is opportunistic, ruthless, and selfish.

Consider, as a thought experiment, the situation of an immortal organism, one that is built without an expiration date. To survive, it would need to be completely fit for all possible random events that can take place in the environment, all *future* random events. By some nasty property, a random event is, well, random. It does not advertise its arrival ahead of time, allowing the organism to prepare and make adjustments to sustain shocks. For an immortal organism, pre-adaptation for all such events would be a necessity. When a random event happens, it is already too late to react, so the organism should be prepared to withstand the shock, or say goodbye. We saw that our bodies overshoot a bit in response to stressors, but this remains highly insufficient; they still can't see the future. They can prepare for the next war, but not win it. Post-event adaptation, no matter how fast, would always be a bit late.*

To satisfy the conditions for such immortality, the organisms need to predict the future with perfection—near perfection is not enough. But by letting the organisms go one lifespan at a time, with modifications between successive generations, nature does not need to predict future conditions beyond the extremely vague idea of which direction things should be heading. Actually, even a vague direction is not necessary. Every random event will bring its own antidote in the form of ecological variation. It is as if nature changed itself at every step and modified its strategy every instant.

Consider this in terms of economic and institutional life. If nature ran the economy, it would not continuously bail out its living members to make them live forever. Nor would it have permanent administrations and forecasting departments that try to outsmart the future—it would not let the scam artists of the United States Office of Management and Budget make such mistakes of epistemic arrogance.

If one looks at history as a complex system similar to nature, then, like nature, it won't let a single empire dominate the planet forever—even if every superpower from the Babylonians to the Egyptians to the Persians to the Romans to modern America has believed in the permanence of its domination and managed to produce historians to theorize to that effect. Systems subjected to randomness—and unpredictability—build a mechanism beyond the robust to opportunistically reinvent themselves each generation, with a continuous change of population and species.

Black Swan Management 101: nature (and nature-like systems) likes

---

* A technical comment on why the adaptability criterion is innocent of probability (the nontechnical reader should skip the rest of this note). The property in a stochastic process of not seeing at any time period t what would happen in time after t, that is, any period higher than t, hence reacting with a lag, an incompressible lag, is called *nonanticipative strategy*, a requirement of stochastic integration. The incompressibility of the lag is central and unavoidable. Organisms can only have nonanticipative strategies—hence nature can only be nonpredictive. This point is not trivial at all, and has even confused probabilists such as the Russian School represented by Stratonovich and the users of his method of integration, who fell into the common mental distortion of thinking that the future sends some signal detectable by us. We wish.

diversity *between* organisms rather than diversity *within* an immortal organism, unless you consider nature itself the immortal organism, as in the pantheism of Spinoza or that present in Asian religions, or the Stoicism of Chrisippus or Epictetus. If you run into a historian of civilizations, try to explain it to him.

Let us look at how evolution benefits from randomness and volatility (in some dose, of course). The more noise and disturbances in the system, up to a point, barring those extreme shocks that lead to extinction of a species, the more the effect of the reproduction of the fittest and that of random mutations will play a role in defining the properties of the next generation. Say an organism produces ten offspring. If the environment is perfectly stable, all ten will be able to reproduce. But if there is instability, pushing aside five of these descendants (likely to be on average weaker than their surviving siblings), then those that evolution considers (on balance) the better ones will reproduce, making the gene undergo some fitness. Likewise, if there is variability among the offspring, thanks to occasional random spontaneous mutation, a sort of copying mistake in the genetic code, then the best should reproduce, increasing the fitness of the species. So evolution benefits from randomness by two different routes: randomness in the mutations, and randomness in the environment—both act in a similar way to cause changes in the traits of the surviving next generations.

Even when there is extinction of an entire species after some extreme event, no big deal, it is part of the game. This is still evolution at work, as those species that survive are fittest and take over from the lost dinosaurs—evolution is not about a species, but at the service of the whole of nature.

But note that evolution likes randomness only up to some limit.* If a calamity completely kills life on the entire planet, the fittest will not survive. Likewise, if random mutations occur at too high a rate, then the fitness gain might not stick, might perhaps even reverse thanks to a new mutation: as I will keep repeating, nature is antifragile *up to a point* but such point is quite high—it can take a lot, a lot of shocks. Should a nuclear event eradicate most of life on earth, but not all life, some rat or bacteria will emerge out of nowhere, perhaps the bottom of the oceans,

---

* Strong antifragility is when the love of volatility knows no bound—the gains have a remote limit or are truly unlimited—the sky is the limit. These can only exist in artificial, man-made life such as economic contracts and cultural products, not really in natural processes. More in the Appendix.

and the story will start again, without us, and without the members of the Office of Management and Budget, of course.

So, in a way, while hormesis corresponds to situations by which the individual organism benefits from direct harm to itself, evolution occurs when harm makes the individual organism perish and the benefits are transferred to others, the surviving ones, and future generations.

For an illustration of how families of organisms like *harm* in order to evolve (again, up to a point), though not the organisms themselves, consider the phenomenon of antibiotic resistance. The harder you try to harm bacteria, the stronger the survivors will be—unless you can manage to eradicate them completely. The same with cancer therapy: quite often cancer cells that manage to survive the toxicity of chemotherapy and radiation reproduce faster and take over the void made by the weaker cells.

Organisms Are Populations and Populations Are Organisms

The idea of viewing things in terms of populations, not individuals, with benefits to the latter stemming from harm to the former, came to me from the works on antifragility by the physicist turned geneticist Antoine Danchin.* For him, analysis needs to accommodate the fact that an organism is not something isolated and stand-alone: there are layerings and hierarchies. If you view things in terms of populations, you must transcend the terms "hormesis" and "Mithridatization" as a characterization of antifragility. Why? To rephrase the argument made earlier, hormesis is a metaphor for direct antifragility, when an organism directly benefits from harm; with evolution, something hierarchically superior to that organism benefits from the damage. From the outside, it looks like there is hormesis, but from the inside, there are winners and losers.

How does this layering operate? A tree has many branches, and these look like small trees; further, these large branches have many more smaller branches that sort of look like even smaller trees. This is a manifestation of what is called *fractal self-similarity*, a vision by the mathe-

---

* He and his co-authors published in the journal *Genes* a paper on the idea of antifragility in biological systems. Interestingly, the article was in response to a draft of this book; in turn this book was modified in response to Danchin's article.

matician Benoît Mandelbrot. There is a similar hierarchy in things and we just see the top layer from the outside. The cell has a population of intercellular molecules; in turn the organism has a population of cells, and the species has a population of organisms. A strengthening mechanism for the species comes at the expense of some organisms; in turn the organism strengthens at the expense of some cells, all the way down and all the way up as well.

For instance, if you drink a poisonous substance in small amounts, the mechanism by which your organism gets better is, according to Danchin, evolutionary *within* your system, with bad (and weak) proteins in the cells replaced by stronger—and younger—ones and the stronger ones being spared (or some similar operation). When you starve yourself of food, it is the bad proteins that are broken down first and recycled by your own body—a process called *autophagy*. This is a purely evolutionary process, one that selects and *kills* the weakest for fitness. But one does not need to accept the specific biological theory (like aging proteins and autophagy) to buy the general idea that survival pressures within the organism play a role in its overall improvement under external stress.

THANK YOU, ERRORS

Now we get into errors and how the errors of some people carry benefits for others.

We can simplify the relationships between fragility, errors, and antifragility as follows. When you are fragile, you depend on things following the exact planned course, with as little deviation as possible—for deviations are more harmful than helpful. This is why the fragile *needs* to be very predictive in its approach, and, conversely, predictive systems cause fragility. When you want deviations, and you don't care about the possible dispersion of outcomes that the future can bring, since most will be helpful, you are antifragile.

Further, the random element in trial and error is not quite random, if it is carried out rationally, using error as a source of information. If every trial provides you with information about what *does not* work, you start zooming in on a solution—so every attempt becomes more valuable, more like an expense than an error. And of course you make discoveries along the way.

Learning from the Mistakes of Others

But recall that this chapter is about layering, units, hierarchies, fractal structure, and the difference between the interest of a unit and those of its subunits. So it is often the mistakes of others that benefit the rest of us—and, sadly, not them. We saw that stressors are information, in the right context. For the antifragile, harm from errors should be less than the benefits. We are talking about some, not all, errors, of course; those that do not destroy a system help prevent larger calamities. The engineer and historian of engineering Henry Petroski presents a very elegant point. Had the *Titanic* not had that famous accident, as fatal as it was, we would have kept building larger and larger ocean liners and the next disaster would have been even more tragic. So the people who perished were sacrificed for the greater good; they unarguably saved more lives than were lost. The story of the *Titanic* illustrates the difference between gains for the system and harm to some of its individual parts.

The same can be said of the debacle of Fukushima: one can safely say that it made us aware of the problem with nuclear reactors (and small probabilities) and prevented larger catastrophes. (Note that the errors of naive stress testing and reliance on risk models were quite obvious at the time; as with the economic crisis, nobody wanted to listen.)

Every plane crash brings us closer to safety, improves the system, and makes the next flight safer—those who perish contribute to the overall safety of others. Swiss flight 111, TWA flight 800, and Air France flight 447 allowed the improvement of the system. But these systems learn because they are antifragile and set up to exploit small errors; the same cannot be said of economic crashes, since the economic system is not antifragile the way it is presently built. Why? There are hundreds of thousands of plane flights every year, and a crash in one plane does not involve others, so errors remain confined and highly epistemic—whereas globalized economic systems operate as one: errors spread and compound.

Again, crucially, we are talking of partial, not general, mistakes, small, not severe and terminal ones. This creates a separation between good and bad systems. Good systems such as airlines are set up to have small errors, independent from each other—or, in effect, negatively correlated to each other, since mistakes lower the odds of future mistakes. This is one way to see how one environment can be antifragile (aviation)

and the other fragile (modern economic life with "earth is flat" style interconnectedness).

If every plane crash makes the next one less likely, every bank crash
makes the next one more likely. We need to eliminate the second type of
error—the one that produces contagion—in our construction of an ideal
socioeconomic system. Let us examine Mother Nature once again.

The natural was built from nonsystemic mistake to nonsystemic mistake: my errors lifting stones, when I am well calibrated, translate into
small injuries that guide me the next time, as I try to avoid pain—after
all, that's the purpose of pain. Leopards, who move like a true sym-
phony of nature, are not instructed by personal trainers on the "proper
form" to lift a deer up a tree. Human advice might work with artificial
sports, like, say, tennis, bowling, or gun shooting, not with natural
movements.

Some businesses love their *own* mistakes. Reinsurance companies,
who focus on insuring catastrophic risks (and are used by insurance
companies to "re-insure" such non-diversifiable risks), manage to do
well *after* a calamity or tail event that causes them to take a hit. If they
are still in business and "have their powder dry" (few manage to have
plans for such contingency), they make it up by disproportionately raising premia—customers overreact and pay up for insurance. They claim
to have no idea about fair value, that is, proper pricing, for reinsurance,
but they certainly know that it is overpriced at times of stress, which is
sufficient to them to make a long-term shekel. All they need is to keep
their mistakes small enough so they can survive them.

How to Become Mother Teresa

Variability causes mistakes and adaptations; it also allows you to know
who your friends are. Both your failures and your successes will give you
information. But, and this is one of the good things in life, sometimes
you only know about someone's character after you harm them with an
error for which you are solely responsible—I have been astonished at the
generosity of some persons in the way they forgave me for my mistakes.

And of course you learn from the errors of others. You may never
know what type of person someone is unless they are given opportunities to violate moral or ethical codes. I remember a classmate, a girl in
high school who seemed 'nice and honest and part of my childhood

group of anti-materialistic utopists. I learned that against my expectations (and her innocent looks) she didn't turn out to be Mother Teresa or Rosa Luxemburg, as she dumped her first (rich) husband for another, richer person, whom she dumped upon his first financial difficulties for yet another richer and more powerful (and generous) lover. In a non-volatile environment I (and most probably she, too) would have mistaken her for a utopist and a saint. Some members of society—those who did not marry her—got valuable information while others, her victims, paid the price.

Further, my characterization of a loser is someone who, after making a mistake, doesn't introspect, doesn't exploit it, feels embarrassed and defensive rather than enriched with a new piece of information, and tries to explain why he made the mistake rather than moving on. These types often consider themselves the "victims" of some large plot, a bad boss, or bad weather.

Finally, a thought. He who has never sinned is less reliable than he who has only sinned once. And someone who has made plenty of errors—though never the same error more than once—is more reliable than someone who has never made any.

WHY THE AGGREGATE HATES THE INDIVIDUAL

We saw that antifragility in biology works thanks to layers. This rivalry between suborganisms contributes to evolution: cells within our bodies compete; within the cells, proteins compete, all the way through. Let us translate the point into human endeavors. The economy has an equivalent layering: individuals, artisans, small firms, departments within corporations, corporations, industries, the regional economy, and, finally, on top, the general economy—one can even have thinner slicing with a larger number of layers.

For the economy to be antifragile and undergo what is called evolution, every single individual business must *necessarily* be fragile, exposed to breaking—evolution needs organisms (or their genes) to die when supplanted by others, in order to achieve improvement, or to avoid reproduction when they are not as fit as someone else. Accordingly, the antifragility of the higher level may require the fragility—and sacrifice—of the lower one. Every time you use a coffeemaker for your morning cappuccino, you are benefiting from the fragility of the coffeemaking entrepreneur who failed. He failed in order to help put the superior merchandise on your kitchen counter.

Also consider traditional societies. There, too, we have a similar layering: individuals, immediate families, extended families, tribes, people using the same dialects, ethnicities, groups.

While sacrifice as a modus is obvious in the case of ant colonies, I am certain that individual businessmen are not overly interested in hara-kiri for the greater good of the economy; they are therefore necessarily concerned in seeking antifragility or at least some level of robustness for themselves. That's not necessarily compatible with the interest of the collective—that is, the economy. So there is a problem in which the property of the sum (the aggregate) varies from that of each one of the parts—in fact, it wants harm to the parts.

It is painful to think about ruthlessness as an engine of improvement.

Now what is the solution? There is none, alas, that can please everyone—but there are ways to mitigate the harm to the very weak.

The problem is graver than you think. People go to business school to learn how to do well while ensuring their survival—but what the economy, as a collective, wants them to do is to *not* survive, rather to take a lot, a lot of imprudent risks themselves and be blinded by the odds. Their respective industries improve from failure to failure. Natural and naturelike systems want some overconfidence on the part of individual economic agents, i.e., the overestimation of their chances of success and underestimation of the risks of failure in their businesses, provided their failure does not impact others. In other words, they want local, but not global, overconfidence.

We saw that the restaurant business is wonderfully efficient precisely because restaurants, being vulnerable, go bankrupt every minute, and entrepreneurs ignore such a possibility, as they think that they will beat the odds. In other words, some class of rash, even suicidal, risk taking is healthy for the economy—under the condition that not all people take the same risks and that these risks remain small and localized.

Now, by disrupting the model, as we will see, with bailouts, governments typically favor a certain class of firms that are large enough to require being saved in order to avoid contagion to other business. This is the opposite of healthy risk-taking; it is *transferring fragility from the collective to the unfit*. People have difficulty realizing that the solution is building a system in which nobody's fall can drag others down—for continuous failures work to preserve the system. Paradoxically, many government interventions and social policies end up hurting the weak and consolidating the established.

WHAT DOES NOT KILL ME KILLS OTHERS

Time to debunk a myth.

As an advocate of antifragility I need to warn about the illusion of seeing it when it is not really there. We can mistake the antifragility of the system for that of the individual, when in fact it takes place *at the expense* of the individual (the difference between hormesis and selection).

Nietzsche's famous expression "what does not kill me makes me stronger" can be easily misinterpreted as meaning Mithridatization or hormesis. It may be one of these two phenomena, very possible, but it could as well mean "what did not kill me *did not* make me stronger, but spared me *because* I am stronger than others; but it killed others and the average population is now stronger because the weak are gone." In other words, I passed an exit exam. I've discussed the problem in earlier writings of the false illusion of causality, with a newspaper article saying that the new mafia members, former Soviet exiles, had been "hardened by a visit to the Gulag" (the Soviet concentration camps). Since the sojourn in the Gulag killed the weakest, one had the illusion of strengthening. Sometimes we see people having survived trials and imagine, given that the surviving population is sturdier than the original one, that these trials are good for them. In other words, the trial can just be a ruthless exam that kills those who fail. All we may be witnessing is that transfer of fragility (rather, antifragility) from the individual to the system that I discussed earlier. Let me present it in a different way. The surviving cohort, clearly, is stronger than the initial one—but not quite the individuals, since the weaker ones died.

Someone paid a price for the system to improve.

Me and Us

This visible tension between individual and collective interests is new in history: in the past it was dealt with by the near irrelevance of individuals. Sacrifice for the sake of the group is behind the notion of heroism: it is good for the tribe, bad for those who perish under the fever of war. This instinct for heroism and the fading of individual interests in favor of the communal has become aberrant with suicide bombers. These pre-death terrorists get into a mood similar to an ecstatic trance in which their emotions drive them to become indifferent to their own mortality. It is a fallacy that suicide bombers are driven by the promise of a reward of some Islamic paradise with virgins and other entertainment, for, as the anthropologist Scott Atran has pointed out, the first suicide bombers in the Levant were revolutionaries of Greek Orthodox background—my tribe—not Islamists.

There is something like a switch in us that kills the individual in favor of the collective when people engage in communal dances, mass riots, or war. Your mood is now that of the herd. You are part of what Elias Canetti calls the *rhythmic and throbbing crowd*. You can also feel a different variety of crowd experience during your next street riot, when fear of authorities vanishes completely under group fever.

Let us now generalize the point. Looking at the world from a certain distance, I see a total tension between man and nature—a tension in the trade-off of fragilities. We saw how nature wants herself, the aggregate, to survive—not every species—just as, in turn, every single species wants its individuals to be fragile (particularly after reproduction), for evolutionary selection to take place. We saw how such transfer of fragility from individuals to species is necessary for its overall survival: species are potentially antifragile, given that DNA is information, but members of the species are perishable, hence ready to sacrifice and in reality designed to do so for the benefit of the collective.

Antifragility shmantifragility. Some of the ideas about fitness and selection here are not very comfortable to this author, which makes the writing of some sections rather painful—I detest the ruthlessness of selection, the inexorable disloyalty of Mother Nature. I detest the notion of improvement thanks to harm to others. As a humanist, I stand against the antifragility of systems at the expense of individuals, for if you follow the reasoning, this makes us humans individually irrelevant.

The great benefit of the Enlightenment has been to bring the individual to the fore, with his rights, his freedom, his independence, his "pursuit of happiness" (whatever that "happiness" means), and, most of all, his privacy. In spite of its denial of antifragility, the Enlightenment and the political systems that emerged from it freed us (somewhat) from the domination of society, the tribe, and the family that had prevailed throughout history.

The unit in traditional cultures is the collective; and it could be perceived to be harmed by the behavior of an individual—the honor of the family is sullied when, say, a daughter becomes pregnant, or a member of the family engages in large-scale financial swindles and Ponzi schemes, or, worst, may even teach a college course in the charlatanic subject of financial economics. And these mores persist. Even as recently as the late nineteenth century or early twentieth, it was common in, say, rural France for someone to spend all his savings to erase the debts of a remote cousin (a practice called *passer l'éponge*, literally, to use a sponge to erase the liability from the chalkboard), and to do so in order to preserve the dignity and good name of the extended family. It was perceived as a duty. (I confess having done some of that myself in the twenty-first century!)

Clearly the system needs to be there for the individual to survive. So one needs to be careful in glorifying one interest against others in the presence of interdependence and complexity.*

In the Cosa Nostra, the Sicilian mafia, the designation "man of honor" (*uomo d'onore*) implies that the person caught by the police would remain silent and not rat on his friends, regardless of benefits, and that life in prison is preferable to a plea that entails hurting other members. The tribe (Cosa Nostra) comes before the individual. And what broke the back of the mafia was the recent generation of plea bargainers. (Note that "honor" in the mafia is limited to such in-group solidarity— they otherwise lie, and there is nothing honorable about them in other domains. And they kill people from behind, something that on the east side of the Mediterranean is considered the purest form of cowardice.)

Likewise, we humans may have to be self-centered at the expense of other species, at the risk of ecological fragility, if it insures our survival. Our interests—as a human race—prevail over those of nature; and we can tolerate some inefficiency, some fragility, in order to protect individuals, although sacrificing nature too much may eventually hurt ourselves.

We saw the trade-off between the interests of the collective and those of the individual. An economy cannot survive without breaking indi-

---

* Many people think at first that their own death is the worst Black Swan scenario. It is not. Unless they've studied too much modern economics, they would agree explicitly that their death *plus* the death of their loved ones *plus* the termination of humanity would be a vastly worse outcome than their own death. Recall my comment on complex systems. We are a mere part of a large chain, and we are worried about both ourselves and the system, as well as the preservation of parts of that large chain.

vidual eggs; protection is harmful, and constraining the forces of evolution to benefit individuals does not seem required. But we can shield individuals from starvation, provide some social protection. And give them respect. Or more, as we see next.

National Entrepreneur Day

Meanwhile, if as a utopist (indeed), I hate what I am figuring out, I think that there is hope.

Heroism and the respect it commands is a form of compensation by society for those who take risks for others. And entrepreneurship is a risky and heroic activity, necessary for growth or even the mere survival of the economy.

It is also necessarily collective on epistemological grounds—to facilitate the development of expertise. Someone who did *not* find something is providing others with knowledge, the best knowledge, that of *absence* (what does not work)—yet he gets little or no credit for it. He is a central part of the process with incentives going to others and, what is worse, gets no respect.*

I am an ingrate toward the man whose overconfidence caused him to open a restaurant and fail, enjoying my nice meal while he is probably eating canned tuna.

In order to progress, modern society should be treating ruined entrepreneurs in the same way we honor dead soldiers, perhaps not with as much honor, but using exactly the same logic (the entrepreneur is still alive, though perhaps morally broken and socially stigmatized, particularly if he lives in Japan). For there is no such thing as a failed soldier, dead or alive (unless he acted in a cowardly manner)—likewise, there is no such thing as a failed entrepreneur or failed scientific researcher, any more than there is a successful babbler, philosophaster, commentator, consultant, lobbyist, or business school professor who does not take personal risks. (Sorry.)

Psychologists label "overconfidence" a disease, blinding people to the odds of success when engaging in ventures. But there is a difference between the benign, heroic type of risk taking that is beneficial to others,

---

* A correspondent, Jean-Louis Rheault, wrote, "I have noticed that the more people glorify the entrepreneur as an abstraction, the more they will scorn an actual one they meet."

in the antifragile case, and the nastier modern type related to negative Black Swans, such as the overconfidence of "scientists" computing the risks of harm from the Fukushima reactor. In the case of the former, what they call overconfidence is a good thing, not something to medicate.

And compare entrepreneurs to the beancounting managers of companies who climb the ladder of hierarchy with hardly ever any real downside. Their cohort is rarely at risk.

What Erasmus called *ingratitudo vulgi,* the ingratitude of the masses, is increasing in the age of globalization and the Internet.

My dream—the solution—is that we would have a National Entrepreneur Day, with the following message:

> Most of you will fail, disrespected, impoverished, but we are grateful for the risks you are taking and the sacrifices you are making for the sake of the economic growth of the planet and pulling others out of poverty. *You are at the source of our antifragility.* Our nation thanks you.

Modernity and the Denial of Antifragility

As in Baudelaire's sad poem about the albatross, what is made to fly will not do well trapped on the ground, where it is forced to traipse. And it is quite fitting that "volatility" comes from *volare*, "to fly" in Latin. Depriving political (and other) systems of volatility harms them, causing eventually greater volatility of the cascading type.

This section, Book II, deals with the fragility that comes from the denial of hormesis, the natural antifragility of organisms, and how we hurt systems with the very best of intentions by playing conductor. We are fragilizing social and economic systems by denying them stressors and randomness, putting them in the Procrustean bed of cushy and comfortable—but ultimately harmful—modernity.

Procrustes was an inn-keeper in Greek mythology who, in order to make the travelers fit in his bed, cut the limbs of those who were too tall and stretched those who were too short. But he had the bed fitting the visitor with total perfection.

As we saw in Chapter 3, treating an organism like a simple machine is a kind of simplification or approximation or reduction that is exactly like a Procrustean bed. It is often with the most noble intentions that we do so, as we are pressured to "fix" things, so we often blow them up with our fear of randomness and love of smoothness.*

Book II will also discuss the competition between man and natural forces, the craving of volatility by some antifragile systems, and how we make social, political (and other) systems vulnerable to Black Swans when we overstabilize them.

---

* Where simplifications fail, causing the most damage, is when something nonlinear is simplified with the linear as a substitute. That is the most common Procrustean bed.

CHAPTER 5

The Souk and the Office Building

*The Reds and the Whites all go to Zurich—War is not a prison—
The turkey's thwarted projects—Remember we are in Extremistan*

TWO TYPES OF PROFESSIONS

Consider the fate of Ioannis (John) and Georgios (George), two identical twin brothers, born in Cyprus (both of them), currently both living in the Greater London area. John has been employed for twenty-five years as a clerk in the personnel department of a large bank, dealing with the relocation of employees around the globe. George is a taxi driver.

John has a perfectly predictable income (or so he thinks), with benefits, four weeks' annual vacation, and a gold watch every twenty-five years of employment. Every month, £3,082 is deposited in his local Nat West checking account. He spends a portion of it for the mortgage on his house west of London, the utilities, and feta cheese, and has a bit left for his savings. He used to wake up on Saturday morning, the day when people stretch and linger in bed, anxiety free, telling himself "life is good"—until the banking crisis, when he realized that his job could be "made redundant." Unemployment would seriously hit him hard. As a personnel expert, he has seen the implosions of long careers, with persons who, laid off at the age of fifty, never recovered.

George, who lives on the same street as his brother, drives a black taxi—meaning he has a license for which he spent three years expanding his frontal lobes by memorizing streets and itineraries in Greater London, which gives him the right to pick up clients in the streets. His income is extremely variable. Some days are "good," and he earns several hundred pounds; some are worse, when he does not even cover his costs; but, year after year, he averages about the same as his brother. To date, he has only had a single day in his twenty-five-year career without a fare. Because of the variability of his income, he keeps moaning that he does not have the job security of his brother—but in fact this is an illusion, for he has a bit more.

This is the central illusion in life: that randomness is risky, that it is a bad thing—and that eliminating randomness is done by eliminating randomness.

Artisans, say, taxi drivers, prostitutes (a very, very old profession), carpenters, plumbers, tailors, and dentists, have some volatility in their income but they are rather robust to a minor professional Black Swan, one that would bring their income to a complete halt. Their risks are visible. Not so with employees, who have no volatility, but can be surprised to see their income going to zero after a phone call from the personnel department. Employees' risks are hidden.

Thanks to variability, these artisanal careers harbor a bit of antifragility: small variations make them adapt and change continuously by learning from the environment and being, sort of, continuously under pressure to be fit. Remember that stressors are information; these careers face a continuous supply of these stressors that make them adjust opportunistically. In addition, they are open to gifts and positive surprises, free options—the hallmark of antifragility, as we will see in Book IV. George was used to having, once in a while, a crazy request, one he was free to decline: during the Icelandic volcano scare, when U.K. air traffic was shut down, he was asked by a rich old lady to drive her to a wedding in the South of France—a two-thousand-mile round-trip journey. Likewise, a prostitute faces the small probability of seeing a severely infatuated rich client give her a very expensive diamond, or even an offer of matrimony, in what can be expected to be a short transitional period before her widowhood.

And George has the freedom to continue until he drops (many people continue to drive cabs into their eighties, mostly to kill time), since he is his own boss, compared to his brother, who is completely unhireable in his fifties.

The difference between the two volatilities in income applies to political systems—and, as we will see in the next two chapters, to about everything in life. Man-made smoothing of randomness produces the equivalent of John's income: smooth, steady, but fragile. Such income is more vulnerable to large shocks that can make it go to zero (plus some unemployment benefits if he resides in one of the few welfare states). Natural randomness presents itself more like George's income: smaller role for very large shocks, but daily variability. Further, such variability helps improve the system (hence the antifragility). A week with declining earnings for a taxi driver or a prostitute provides information concerning the environment and intimates the need to find a new part of town where clients hang around; a month or so without earnings drives them to revise their skills.

Further, for a self-employed person, a small (nonterminal) mistake is information, valuable information, one that directs him in his adaptive approach; for someone employed like John, a mistake is something that goes into his permanent record, filed in the personnel department. Yogi Berra once said: "We made the wrong mistake"—and for John all mistakes are wrong mistakes. Nature loves small errors (without which genetic variations are impossible), humans don't—hence when you rely on human judgment you are at the mercy of a mental bias that disfavors antifragility.

So, alas, we humans are afraid of the second type of variability and naively fragilize systems—or prevent their antifragility—by protecting them. In other words, a point worth repeating every time it applies, this avoidance of small mistakes makes the large ones more severe.

The centralized state resembles the income of John; the city-state model that of George. John has one large employer, George many small ones—so he can select the ones that fit him the best and hence has, at any point in time, "more options." One has the illusion of stability, but is fragile; the other one the illusion of variability, but is robust and even antifragile.

The more variability you observe in a system, the less Black Swan–prone it is. Let us now examine how this applies to political systems with the story of Switzerland.

Lenin in Zurich

I was recently in a café-turned-expensive-restaurant in Zurich poring over the overpriced menu, with prices at least triple of those in a place of equivalent quality in the United States. The world's recent crisis had made Switzerland even more of a safe haven than it had ever been, causing its currency to rise dramatically—Switzerland is the most antifragile place on the planet; it benefits from shocks that take place in the rest of the world. The friend, a writer, pointed out to me that Lenin, who lived in town, used to play chess in the café with the Dadaist poet Tristan Tzara. Yes, the Russian revolutionary Vladimir Ilyich Ulyanov, later known as Lenin, spent some time in Switzerland concocting his project of the great top-down modernist state and largest human experiment in centralized state control. It hit me that there was something eerie in Lenin's presence there, for, a few days before, I had been at a conference in Montreux, on Lake Geneva, that took place in the same lakefront hotel where Vladimir Nabokov, the émigré Russian aristocrat and victim of Lenin, spent the last couple of decades of his life.

It seemed interesting to me that sheltering the reds and the whites, both the Bolsheviks and the aristocratic White Russians they later displaced, seems to be part of the primary business of the Helvetic Confederation. The main cities such as Zurich, Geneva, or Lausanne bear traces of the political refugees who went there for shelter: émigrés, from the Iranian royals thrown out by the Islamists to the latest African potentate executing "plan B." Even Voltaire spent some time hiding in the place, in Ferney, a French suburb of Geneva near the Swiss border (before it even joined the confederation). Voltaire, the perfectly protected gadfly, would rush to Geneva after insulting the king of France, the Catholic Church, or some other authority—what people don't usually know about him is that he also had an incentive to seek protection there for financial reasons. Voltaire was a self-made man, a wealthy merchant, investor, and speculative dealer. Much of his wealth came from the antifragility of stressors, as he started building his fortune during his early exile.

So, like Voltaire, there are refugees of other types: financial refugees coming from places of turmoil, recognizable by their expensive and boring clothes, bland vocabulary, contrived decorum, and expensive (shiny) watches—in other words, non-Voltaires. Like many rich people, they feel entitled to laugh at their own jokes. These (dull) people are not looking for personal shelter: it is their assets that are seeking refuge. While some political persons might prefer to hide from the risks of their national regime in France or England, more exciting places on Saturday night, it is most certainly in Switzerland that their checking account wants to be. It is economically the most robust place on the planet—and has been so for quite a few centuries.

This great variety of people and their wallets are there, in Switzerland, for its shelter, safety, and stability. But all these refugees don't notice the obvious: the most stable country in the world *does not have* a government. And it is not stable in spite of not having a government; it is stable *because* it does not have one. Ask random Swiss citizens to name their president, and count the proportion of people who can do so—they can usually name the presidents of France or the United States but not their own. Its currency works best (at the time of writing it proved to be the safest), yet its central bank is tiny, even relative to its size.

Do these politicians biding their time before (they hope) returning to power notice such absence of government, accept that they are in Switzerland because of such absence of government, and adapt their ideas on nation-states and political systems accordingly? Not at all.

It is not quite true that the Swiss do not have a government. What they do not have is a large *central* government, or what the common discourse describes as "the" government—what governs them is entirely bottom-up, municipal of sorts, regional entities called cantons, near-sovereign mini-states united in a confederation. There is plenty of volatility, with enmities between residents that stay at the level of fights over water fountains or other such uninspiring debates. This is not necessarily pleasant, since neighbors are transformed into busybodies—this is a dictatorship from the bottom, not from the top, but a dictatorship nevertheless. But this bottom-up form of dictatorship provides protection against the romanticism of utopias, since no big ideas can be generated in such an unintellectual atmosphere—it suffices to spend some time in cafés in the old section of Geneva, particularly on a Sunday afternoon, to understand that the process is highly unintellectual, devoid of any sense of the grandiose, even downright puny (there is a famous quip about how the greatest accomplishment of the Swiss was inventing the cuckoo clock while other nations produced great works—nice story except that the Swiss did not invent the cuckoo clock). But the system produces stability—boring stability—at every possible level.

Also note that the hideously glitzy scenes one encounters in Switzerland, in all of Geneva, in some parts of Zurich (the center), and particularly in the ski resorts such as Gstaadt and San Moritz are not the direct product of the country nor part of its mission, but the result of its success, as Switzerland acts as a magnet for the ugly rich and tax refugees.

Note for now that this is the last major country that is not a nation-state, but rather a collection of small municipalities left to their own devices.

BOTTOM-UP VARIATIONS

What I call bottom-up variations—or noise—is the type of political volatility that takes place within a municipality, the petty fights and frictions in the running of regular affairs. It is not scalable (or what is called *invariant* under scale transformation): in other words, if you increase the size, say, multiply the number of people in a community by a hundred, you will have markedly different dynamics. A large state does not behave at all like a gigantic municipality, much as a baby human does not resemble a smaller adult. The difference is qualitative: the increase in the number of persons in a given community alters the quality of the relationship between parties. Recall the nonlinearity description from the Prologue. If you multiply by ten the number of persons in a given entity, you do not preserve the properties: there is a transformation. Here conversations switch from the mundane—but effective—to abstract numbers, more interesting, more academic perhaps, but, alas, less effective.

A cluster of municipalities with charming provincial enmities, their own internal fights, and people out to get one another aggregates to a quite benign and stable state. Switzerland is similar to the income of the second brother, stable because of the variations and noise at the local level. Just as the income of the cab driver shows instability on a daily basis but annual stability, likewise Switzerland shows stability at the aggregate level, as the ensemble of cantons produces a solid system.

The way people handle local affairs is vastly different from the way they handle large, abstract public expenditures: we have traditionally lived in small units and tribes and managed rather well in small units.*

Further, biology plays a role in a municipal environment, not in a larger system. An administration is shielded from having to feel the sting

---

* I bypass here the economic argument as to whether autonomous city-states were invigorated with economic energy (as Henri Pirenne or Max Weber advocated, in a sort of romantic way); my (mathematical) point is that a collection of small units with semi-independent variations produces vastly different risk characteristics than a single large unit.

of shame (with flushing in his face), a biological reaction to overspending and other failures such as killing people in Vietnam. Eye contact with one's peers changes one's behavior. But for a desk-grounded office leech, a number is just a number. Someone you see in church Sunday morning would feel uncomfortable for his mistakes—and more responsible for them. On the small, local scale, his body and biological response would direct him to avoid causing harm to others. On a large scale, others are abstract items; given the lack of social contact with the people concerned, the civil servant's brain leads rather than his emotions—with numbers, spreadsheets, statistics, more spreadsheets, and theories.

When I expressed this idea to my co-author Mark Blyth, he blurted out the obvious: "Stalin could not have existed in a municipality."

Small is beautiful in so many other ways. Take for now that the small (in the aggregate, that is, a collection of small units) is more antifragile than the large—in fact the large is doomed to breaking, a mathematical property we will explain later, that, sadly, seems universal as it applies to large corporations, very large mammals, and large administrations.*

There is another issue with the abstract state, a psychological one. We humans scorn what is not concrete. We are more easily swayed by a crying baby than by thousands of people dying elsewhere that do not make it to our living room through the TV set. The one case is a tragedy, the other a statistic. Our emotional energy is blind to probability. The media make things worse as they play on our infatuation with anecdotes, our thirst for the sensational, and they cause a great deal of unfairness that way. At the present time, one person is dying of diabetes every seven seconds, but the news can only talk about victims of hurricanes with houses flying in the air.

The problem is that by creating bureaucracies, we put civil servants in a position to make decisions based on abstract and theoretical matters, with the illusion that they will be making them in a rational, accountable way.

Also consider that lobbyists—this annoying race of lobbyists—cannot exist in a municipality or small region. The Europeans, thanks to the centralization of (some) power with the European Commission in Brussels, are quickly discovering the existence of these mutants coming to

---

* It is quite distressing to hear debates about political systems that make comparisons between countries when the size of the entities is not the same—say, comparing Singapore to Malaysia. The size of the unit may matter more than the system.

manipulate democracy for the sake of some large corporation. By influencing one single decision or regulation in Brussels, a single lobbyist gets a large bang. It is a much larger payoff (at low cost) than with municipalities, which would require armies of lobbyists trying to convince people while embedded in their communities.*

Consider, too, the other effect of scale: small corporations are less likely to have lobbyists.

The same bottom-up effect applies to law. The Italian political and legal philosopher Bruno Leoni has argued in favor of the robustness of judge-based law (owing to its diversity) as compared to explicit and rigid codifications. True, the choice of a court could be a lottery—but it helps prevent large-scale mistakes.

I use the example of Switzerland to show the natural antifragility of political systems and how stability is achieved by managing noise, having a mechanism for letting it run its natural course, not by minimizing it.

Note another element of Switzerland: it is perhaps the most successful country in history, yet it has traditionally had a very low level of university education compared to the rest of the rich nations. Its system, even in banking during my days, was based on apprenticeship models, nearly vocational rather than the theoretical ones. In other words, on *techne* (crafts and know how), not *episteme* (book knowledge, know what).

AWAY FROM EXTREMISTAN

Let us now examine the technical aspects of the process, a more statistical view of the effect of human intervention on the volatility of affairs. There is a certain mathematical property to this bottom-up volatility, and to the volatility of natural systems. It generates the kind of randomness I call Mediocristan—plenty of variations that might be scary, but tend to cancel out in the aggregate (over time, or over the collection of municipalities that constitute the larger confederation or entity)—rather than the unruly one called Extremistan, in which you have mostly stability and occasion-

---

* Thankfully, the European Union is legally protected from overcentralization thanks to the principle of subsidiarity: things should be handled by the smallest possible unit that can manage them with efficacy. The idea was inherited from the Catholic Church: philosophically, a unit doesn't need to be very large (the state) nor very small (the individual), but somewhere in between. This is a powerful philosophical statement, particularly in light of both the transfers of fragility we saw in Chapter 4 and the notion that size fragilizes, much on which later.

ally large chaos—errors there have large consequences. One fluctuates, the other jumps. One has a lot of small variations, the other varies in lumps. Just like the income of the driver compared to that of bank employee. The two types of randomness are qualitatively distinct.

Mediocristan has a lot of variations, not a single one of which is extreme; Extremistan has few variations, but those that take place are extreme.

Another way to understand the difference: your caloric intake is from Mediocristan. If you add the calories you consume in a year, even without adjusting for your lies, not a single day will represent much of the total (say, more than 0.5 percent of the total, five thousand calories when you may consume eight hundred thousand in a year). So the exception, the rare event, plays an inconsequential role in the aggregate and the long-term. You cannot double your weight in a single day, not even a month, not possibly in a year—but you can double your net worth or lose half of it in a single moment.

By comparison, if you take the sale of novels, more than half of sales (and perhaps 90 percent of profits) tends to come from the top 0.1 percent, so the exception, the one-in-a-thousand event, is dominant there. So financial matters—and other economic matters—tend to be from Extremistan, just like history, which moves by discontinuities and jumps from one state to another.*

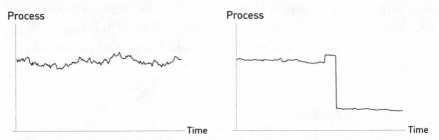

FIGURE 3. Municipal noise, distributed variations in the souks (first) compared to that of centralized or human-managed systems (second)—or, equivalently, the income of a taxi driver (first) and that of an employee (second). The second graph shows moves taking place from cascade to cascade, or Black Swan to Black Swan. Human overintervention to smooth or control processes causes a switch from one kind of system, Mediocristan, into another, Extremistan. This effect applies to all manner of systems with constrained volatility—health, politics, economics, even someone's mood with and without Prozac. Or the difference between the entrepreneur-driven Silicon Valley (first) and the banking system (second).

* When randomness gets distributed across a large number of small units, along with small recurrent political disorder, we get the first type, the benign Mediocristan. When randomness concentrates, we get the second type, the sneaky Extremistan.

Figure 3 illustrates how antifragile systems are hurt when they are deprived of their natural variations (mostly thanks to naive intervention). Beyond municipal noise, the same logic applies to: the child who, after spending time in a sterilized environment, is left out in the open; a system with dictated political stability from the top; the effects of price controls; the advantages of size for a corporation; etc. We switch from a system that produces steady but controllable volatility (Mediocristan), closer to the statistical "bell curve" (from the benign family of the Gaussian or Normal Distribution), into one that is highly unpredictable and moves mostly by jumps, called "fat tails." Fat tails—a synonym for Extremistan—mean that remote events, those in what is called the "tails," play a disproportionate role. One (first graph) is volatile; it fluctuates but does not sink. The other (second graph) sinks without significant fluctuations outside of episodes of turmoil. In the long run the second system will be far more volatile—but volatility comes in lumps. When we constrain the first system we tend to get the second outcome.

Note also that in Extremistan predictability is very low. In the second, pseudo-smooth kind of randomness, mistakes appear to be rare, but they will be large, often devastating when they occur. Actually, an argument we develop in Book IV, anything locked into planning tends to fail precisely because of these attributes—it is quite a myth that planning helps corporations: in fact we saw that the world is too random and unpredictable to base a policy on visibility of the future. What survives comes from the interplay of some fitness and environmental conditions.

The Great Turkey Problem

Let me now move back from the technical jargon and graphs of Fat Tails and Extremistan to colloquial Lebanese. In Extremistan, one is prone to be fooled by the properties of the past and get the story exactly backwards. It is easy, looking at what is happening in the second graph of Figure 3, before the big jump down, to believe that the system is now safe, particularly when the system has made a progressive switch from the "scary" type of visibly volatile randomness at left to the apparently safe right. It looks like a drop in volatility—and it is not.

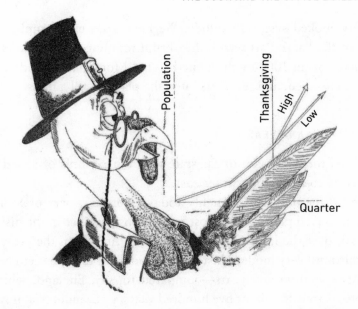

FIGURE 4. A turkey using "evidence"; unaware of Thanksgiving, it is making "rigorous" future projections based on the past. Credit: George Nasr

A turkey is fed for a thousand days by a butcher; every day confirms to its staff of analysts that butchers love turkeys "with increased statistical confidence." The butcher will keep feeding the turkey until a few days before Thanksgiving. Then comes that day when it is really not a very good idea to be a turkey. So with the butcher surprising it, the turkey will have a revision of belief—right when its confidence in the statement that *the butcher loves turkeys* is maximal and "it is very quiet" and soothingly predictable in the life of the turkey. This example builds on an adaptation of a metaphor by Bertrand Russell. The key here is that such a surprise will be a Black Swan event; but just for the turkey, not for the butcher.

We can also see from the turkey story the mother of all harmful mistakes: mistaking absence of evidence (of harm) for evidence of absence, a mistake that we will see tends to prevail in intellectual circles and one that is grounded in the social sciences.

So our mission in life becomes simply "how not to be a turkey," or, if possible, how to be a turkey in reverse—antifragile, that is. "Not being a turkey" starts with figuring out the difference between true and manufactured stability.

The reader can easily imagine what happens when constrained, volatility-choked systems explode. We have a fitting example: the removal of the Baath Party, with the abrupt toppling of Saddam Hussein and his regime in 2003 by the United States. More than a hundred thousand persons died, and ten years later, the place is still a mess.

TWELVE THOUSAND YEARS

We started the discussion of the state with the example of Switzerland. Now let us go a little bit farther east.

The northern Levant, roughly today's northern part of Syria and Lebanon, stayed perhaps the most prosperous province in the history of mankind, over the long, very long stretch of time from the pre-pottery Neolithic until very modern history, the middle of the twentieth century. That's twelve thousand years—compared to, say, England, which has been prosperous for about five hundred years, or Scandinavia, now only prosperous for less than three hundred years. Few areas on the planet have managed to thrive with so much continuity over any protracted stretch of time, what historians call *longue durée*. Other cities came and went; Aleppo, Emesa (today Homs), and Laodicea (Lattakia) stayed relatively affluent.

The northern Levant was since ancient times dominated by traders, largely owing to its position as a central spot on the Silk Road, and by agricultural lords, as the province supplied wheat to much of the Mediterranean world, particularly Rome. The area supplied a few Roman emperors, a few Catholic popes before the schisms, and more than thirty Greek language writers and philosophers (which includes many of the heads of Plato's academy), in addition to the ancestors of the American visionary and computer entrepreneur Steve Jobs, who brought us the Apple computer, on one of which I am recopying these lines (and the iPad tablet, on which you may be reading them). We know of the autonomy of the province from the records during Roman days, as it was then managed by the local elites, a decentralized method of ruling through locals that the Ottoman retained. Cities minted their own coins.

Then two events took place. First, after the Great War, one part of the northern Levant was integrated into the newly created nation of Syria, separated from its other section, now part of Lebanon. The entire area had been until then part of the Ottoman Empire, but functioned as somewhat autonomous regions—Ottomans, like the Romans before them, let local elites run the place so long as sufficient tax was paid, while they focused on their business of war. The Ottoman type of imperial peace, the *pax Ottomana*, like its predecessor the *pax Romana,* was good for commerce. Contracts were enforced, and that is what governments are needed for the most. In the recent nostalgic book *Levant,* Philip Mansel documents how the cities of the Eastern Mediterranean operated as city-states separated from the hinterland.

Then, a few decades into the life of Syria, the modernist Baath Party came to further enforce utopias. As soon as the Baathists centralized the place and enforced their statist laws, Aleppo and Emesa went into instant decline.

What the Baath Party did, in its "modernization" program, was to remove the archaic mess of the souks and replace them with the crisp modernism of the office building.

The effect was immediately visible: overnight the trading families moved to places such as New York and New Jersey (for the Jews), California (for the Armenians), and Beirut (for the Christians). Beirut offered a commerce-friendly atmosphere, and Lebanon was a benign, smaller, disorganized state without any real central government. Lebanon was small enough to be a municipality on its own: it was smaller than a medium-size metropolitan area.

War, Prison, or Both

But while Lebanon had all the right qualities, the state was *too* loose, and by allowing the various Palestinian factions and the Christian militias to own weapons, it caused an arms race between the communities while placidly watching the entire buildup. There was also an imbalance between communities, with the Christians trying to impose their identity on the place. Disorganized is invigorating; but the Lebanese state was one step too disorganized. It would be like allowing each of the New York mafia bosses to have a larger army than the Joint Chiefs of Staff (just imagine John Gotti with missiles). So in 1975 a raging civil war started in Lebanon.

A sentence that still shocks me when I think about it was voiced by one of my grandfather's friends, a wealthy Aleppine merchant who fled the Baath regime. When my grandfather asked his friend during the Lebanese war why he did not go back to Aleppo, his answer was categorical: "We people of Aleppo prefer war to prison." I thought that he meant that they were going to put him in jail, but then I realized that by "prison" he meant the loss of political and economic freedoms.

Economic life, too, seems to prefer war to prison. Lebanon and Northern Syria had very similar wealth per individual (what economists call Gross Domestic Product) about a century ago—and had identical cultures, language, ethnicities, food, and even jokes. Everything was the same except for the rule of the "modernizing" Baath Party in Syria compared to the totally benign state in Lebanon. In spite of a civil war that decimated the population, causing an acute brain drain and setting wealth back by several decades, in addition to every possible form of chaos that rocked the place, today Lebanon has a considerably higher standard of living—between three and six times the wealth of Syria.

Nor did the point escape Machiavelli. Jean-Jacques Rousseau wrote, citing him: "It seemed, wrote Machiavelli, that in the midst of murders and civil wars, our republic became stronger [and] its citizens infused with virtues. . . . A little bit of agitation gives resources to souls and what makes the species prosper isn't peace, but freedom."

Pax Romana

The centralized nation-state is not exactly new in history. In fact, it existed in a nearly identical form in ancient Egypt. But this was an isolated event in history, and it did not survive there for long: the Egyptian high state started collapsing upon contact with the crazy unruly barbaric disorganized harassing invaders coming from Asia Minor with their assault chariots, literally a killer app.

The dynasties of ancient Egypt did not run the place like an empire but like an integrated state, which is markedly different—as we saw, it produces different types of variations. Nation-states rely on centralized bureaucracy, whereas empires, such as the Roman empire and Ottoman dynasties, have relied on local elites, in fact allowing the city-states to prosper and conserve some effective autonomy—and, what was great for peace, such autonomy was commercial, not military. In reality, the Ottomans did these vassals and suzerains a favor by preventing them from involvement in warfare—this took away militaristic temptations and helped them thrive; regardless of how iniquitous the system seemed to be on the surface, it allowed locals to focus on commerce rather than war. It protected them from themselves. This is the argument brought by David Hume in his *History of England* in favor of small states, as large states get tempted by warfare.

Clearly neither the Romans nor the Ottomans were allowing local autonomy out of love of freedom on the part of others; they just did it for convenience. A combination of empire (for some affairs) and semi-independent regions (left alone for their own business) provides more stability than the middle: the centralized nation-state with flags and discrete borders.

But the states, even when centralized, as in Egypt or China, were, in practice, not too different from the Roman and Ottoman ones—except for the centralization of intellect with the scribes and the mandarinate system establishing a monopoly of knowledge. Some of us may remember that there were days with no Internet, no electronic monitoring of wire transfers to supervise tax receipts. And before modernity's communication networks, with the telegraph, the train, and, later, the telephone, states had to rely on messenger services. So a local provincial ruler was king for a large number of matters, even though he was not so nominally. Until recent history, the central state represented about 5 percent of the economy—compared to about ten times that share in modern Europe. And, further, governments were sufficiently distracted by war to leave economic affairs to businessmen.*

War or No War

Let us take a look at Europe before the creations of the nation-states of Germany and Italy (marketed as "re-unification," as if these nations had been crisp units in some romantic past). There was, until the creation of these romantic entities, a fissiparous and amorphous mass of small statelings and city-states in constant tension—but shifting alliances. In most of their history, Genoa and Venice were competing for the Eastern and Southern Mediterranean like two hookers battling for a sidewalk. And here is something comforting about statelings at war: mediocrity cannot handle more than one enemy, so war here turns into an alliance there. Tension was always present somewhere but without large consequences, like precipitation in the British Isles; mild rain and no floods are vastly more manageable than the opposite: long droughts followed by intense rainfall. In other words, Mediocristan.

Then of course the contagious creation of nation-states in the late

---

* Note that people invoke an expression, "Balkanization," about the mess created by fragmented states, as if fragmentation was a bad thing, and as if there was an alternative in the Balkans—but nobody uses "Helvetization" to describe its successes.

nineteenth century led to what we saw with the two world wars and their sequels: more than sixty million (and possibly eighty million) victims. The difference between war and *no war* became huge, with marked discontinuity. This is no different from a switch to "winner take all" effects in industry, the domination of rare events. A collection of statelings is similar to the restaurant business we discussed earlier: volatile, but you never have a generalized restaurant crisis—unlike, say, the banking business. Why? Because it is composed of a lot of independent and competing small units that do not individually threaten the system and make it jump from one state to another. Randomness is distributed rather than concentrated.

Some people have fallen for the naive turkey-style belief that the world is getting safer and safer, and of course they naively attribute it to the holy "state" (though bottom-up Switzerland has about the lowest rate of violence of any place on the planet). It is exactly like saying that nuclear bombs are safer because they explode less often. The world is subjected to fewer and fewer acts of violence, while wars have the potential to be more criminal. We were very close to the mother of all catastrophes in the 1960s when the United States was about to pull the nuclear trigger on the Soviet Union. Very close. When we look at risks in Extremistan, we don't look at evidence (evidence comes too late), we look at potential damage: never has the world been more prone to more damage; never.* It is hard to explain to naive data-driven people that risk is in the future, not in the past.

The messy multi-ethnic empire, the so-called Austro-Hungarian Empire, vanished after the great war, along with its Ottoman neighbor and rival (and, to a large extent, sibling—don't tell them), to be replaced with crisp, clean nation-states. The Ottoman Empire with its messy nationalities—or, rather, what was left of it—became the state of Turkey, modeled after Switzerland, with nobody noticing the inconsistency. Vienna became trapped in Austria, with whom it shared very little outside the formal language. Imagine moving New York City to central Texas

---

* A more rigorous reading of the data—with appropriate adjustment for the unseen—shows that a war that would decimate the planet would be completely consistent with the statistics, and would not even be an "outlier." As we will see, Ben Bernanke was similarly fooled with his *Great Moderation,* a turkey problem; one can be confused by the properties of any process with compressed volatility from the top. Some people, like Steven Pinker, misread the nature of the statistical process and hold such a thesis, similar to the "great moderation" in finance.

and still calling it New York. Stefan Zweig, the Viennese Jewish novelist, then considered the most influential author in the world, expressed his pain in the poignant memoir *The World of Yesterday*. Vienna joined the league of multicultural cities such as Alexandria, Smyrna, Aleppo, Prague, Thessaloniki, Constantinople (now Istanbul), and Trieste, now squeezed into the Procrustean bed of the nation-state, with its citizens left in the grip of intergenerational nostalgia. Unable to handle the loss and integrate elsewhere, Zweig later committed suicide in Brazil. I first read his account as I was put in a similar situation of physical and cultural exile when my Levantine Christian world was shattered by the Lebanese war, and I wondered whether he might have stayed alive had he gone to New York instead.

CHAPTER 6

Tell Them I Love (Some) Randomness

Maxwell in Extremistan—Complicated mechanisms to feed a donkey—
Virgil said to do it, and do it now

———

The point of the previous chapter was that the risk properties of the first brother (the fragile bank employee) are vastly different from those of the second one (the comparatively antifragile artisan taxi driver). Likewise, the risk characteristic of a centralized system is different from that of a messy municipally-led confederation. The second type is stable in the long run *because* of *some* dose of volatility.

A scientific argument showing how tight controls backfire and cause blowups was made by James Clerk Maxwell of electromagnetic theory fame. "Governors" are contraptions meant to control the speed of steam engines by compensating for abrupt variations. They aimed at stabilizing the engines, and they apparently did, but they paradoxically sometimes brought about capricious behavior and crashes. Light control works; close control leads to overreaction, sometimes causing the machinery to break into pieces. In a famous paper "On Governors," published in 1867, Maxwell modeled the behavior and showed mathematically that tightly controlling the speed of engines leads to instability.

It is remarkable how Maxwell's neat mathematical derivations and the dangers of tight control can be generalized across domains and help debunk pseudo-stabilization and hidden long-term fragility.* In the markets, fixing prices, or, equivalently, eliminating speculators, the so-called "noise traders"—and the moderate volatility that they bring—provide an illusion of stability, with periods of calm punctuated with large jumps. Because players are unused to volatility, the slightest price variation will then be attributed to insider information, or to changes in the state of the system, and will cause panics. When a currency never varies, a slight, very slight move makes people believe that the world is ending. Injecting some confusion stabilizes the system.

Indeed, confusing people a little bit is beneficial—it is good for you and good for them. For an application of the point in daily life, imagine someone extremely punctual and predictable who comes home at exactly six o'clock every day for fifteen years. You can use his arrival to set your watch. The fellow will cause his family anxiety if he is barely a few minutes late. Someone with a slightly more volatile—hence unpredictable— schedule, with, say, a half-hour variation, won't do so.

Variations also act as purges. Small forest fires periodically cleanse the system of the most flammable material, so this does not have the opportunity to accumulate. Systematically preventing forest fires from taking place "to be safe" makes the big one much worse. For similar reasons, stability is not good for the economy: firms become very weak during long periods of steady prosperity devoid of setbacks, and hidden vulnerabilities accumulate silently under the surface—so delaying crises is not a very good idea. Likewise, absence of fluctuations in the market causes hidden risks to accumulate with impunity. The longer one goes without a market trauma, the worse the damage when commotion occurs.

This adverse effect of stability is straightforward to model scientifically, but when I became a trader, I was told of a heuristic used by veterans, and only old seasoned veterans: when a market reaches a "new low," that is, drops to a level not seen in a long time, there is "a lot of blood" to come, with people rushing to the exit. Some people unused to losing shekels will be experiencing a large loss and will incur distress. If such a low market level has not been seen in years, say two years, it will be called "a two-year low" and will cause more damage than a one-year

* The financier George Cooper has revived the argument in *The Origin of Financial Crises*—the argument is so crisp that an old trader friend, Peter Nielsen, has distributed it to every person he knows.

low. Tellingly, they call it a "cleanup," getting the "weak hands" out of the way. A "weak hand" is clearly someone who is fragile but doesn't know it and is lulled by a false sense of security. When many such weak hands rush to the door, they collectively cause crashes. A volatile market doesn't let people go such a long time without a "cleanup" of risks, thereby preventing such market collapses.

Fluctuat nec mergitur (fluctuates, or floats, but does not sink) goes the Latin saying.

HUNGRY DONKEYS

So far we have argued that preventing randomness in an antifragile system is not always a good idea. Let us now look at the situation in which *adding* randomness has been a standard operating method, as the needed fuel for an antifragile system permanently hungry for it.

A donkey equally famished and thirsty caught at an equal distance between food and water would unavoidably die of hunger or thirst. But he can be saved thanks to a random nudge one way or the other. This metaphor is named Buridan's Donkey, after the medieval philosopher Jean de Buridan, who—among other, very complicated things—introduced the thought experiment. When some systems are stuck in a dangerous impasse, randomness and only randomness can unlock them and set them free. You can see here that absence of randomness equals guaranteed death.

The idea of injecting random noise into a system to improve its functioning has been applied across fields. By a mechanism called *stochastic resonance,* adding random noise to the background makes you hear the sounds (say, music) with more accuracy. We saw earlier that the psychological effect of overcompensation helps us get signals in the midst of noise; here it is not psychological but a physical property of the system. Weak SOS signals, too weak to get picked up by remote receptors, can become audible in the presence of background noise and random interference. By adding to the signal, random hiss allows it to rise sufficiently above the threshold of detection to become audible—nothing in that situation does better than randomness, which comes for free.

Consider the method of annealing in metallurgy, a technique used to make metal stronger and more homogeneous. It involves the heating and controlled cooling of a material, to increase the size of the crystals and reduce their defects. Just as with Buridan's donkey, the heat causes the atoms to become unstuck from their initial positions and wander randomly through states of higher energy; the cooling gives them more chances of finding new, better configurations.

As a child I was exposed to a version of this annealing effect by watching my father, who was a man of habits, tap a wooden barometer every day upon coming home. He would gently strike the barometer, then get a reading for his homemade weather forecast. The stress on the barometer got the needle unstuck and allowed it to find its true equilibrium position. That's a local brand of antifragility. Inspired by the metallurgical technique, mathematicians use a method of computer simulation called *simulated annealing* to bring more general optimal solutions to problems and situations, solutions that only randomness can deliver.

Randomness works well in search—sometimes better than humans. Nathan Myhrvold brought to my attention a controversial 1975 paper published in *Science* showing that random drilling was superior to whatever search method was being employed at the time.

And, ironically, the so-called chaotic systems, those experiencing a brand of variations called *chaos,* can be stabilized by adding randomness to them. I watched an eerie demonstration of the effects, presented by a doctoral student who first got balls to jump chaotically on a table in response to steady vibrations on the surface. These steady shocks made the balls jump in a jumbled and inelegant manner. Then, as by magic, he moved a switch and the jumps became orderly and smooth. The magic is that such change of regime, from chaos to order, did not take place by removing chaos, but by adding random, completely random but low-intensity shocks. I came out of the beautiful experiment with so much enthusiasm that I wanted to inform strangers on the street, "I love randomness!"

Political Annealing

It has been hard to explain to real people that stressors and uncertainty have their role in life—so you can imagine what it would be like to explain it to politicians. Yet this is where a certain dose of randomness is needed the most.

I was once shown the script of a film based on a parable of a city completely ruled by randomness—very Borgesian. At set intervals, the ruler randomly assigns to the denizens a new role in the city. Say the butcher would now become a baker, and the baker a prisoner, etc. At the end, people end up rebelling against the ruler, asking for stability as their inalienable right.

I immediately thought that perhaps the opposite parable should be written: instead of having the rulers randomize the jobs of citizens, we should have citizens randomize the jobs of rulers, naming them by raffles and removing them at random as well. That is similar to simulated annealing—and it happens to be no less effective. It turned out that the ancients—again, those ancients!—were aware of it: the members of the Athenian assemblies were chosen by lot, a method meant to protect the system from degeneracy. Luckily, this effect has been investigated with modern political systems. In a computer simulation, Alessandro Pluchino and his colleagues showed how adding a certain number of randomly selected politicians to the process can improve the functioning of the parliamentary system.

Or sometimes the system benefits from a different type of stressor. For Voltaire, the best form of government was the one tempered with political assassination. Regicide is sort of the equivalent of tapping on the barometer to make it work better. That, too, creates some often-needed reshuffling, and one that would never have been done voluntarily. The void created at the top allows the annealing effect, causing the new leader to emerge. The secular drop in premature deaths in society has deprived us of a naturalistic managerial turnover. Murder is the standard procedure for succession in the mafia (the last publicized annealing was when John Gotti murdered his predecessor in front of a New York steakhouse to become the capo of the family). Outside the mafia, bosses and board members now stay longer, a fact that impedes many domains: CEOs, tenured academics, politicians, journalists—and we need to offset this condition with random lotteries.

Unfortunately, you cannot randomize a political party out of existence. What is plaguing us in the United States is not the two-party system, but being stuck with the *same* two parties. Parties don't have organic built-in expiration dates.

Finally the ancients perfected the method of random draw in more or less difficult situations—and integrated it into divinations. These draws were really meant to pick a random exit without having to make a decision, so one would not have to live with the burden of the consequences later. You went with what the gods told you to do, so you would not have to second-guess yourself later. One of the methods, called *sortes virgilianae* (fate as decided by the epic poet Virgil), involved opening Virgil's *Aeneid* at random and interpreting the line that presented itself as direction for the course of action. You should use such method for every sticky business decision. I will repeat until I get hoarse: the ancients evolved hidden and sophisticated ways and tricks to exploit randomness. For instance, I actually practice such randomizing heuristic in restaurants. Given the lengthening and complication of menus, subjecting me to what psychologists call the *tyranny of choice,* with the stinging feeling after my decision that I should have ordered something else, I blindly and systematically duplicate the selection by the most overweight male at the table; and when no such person is present, I randomly pick from the menu without reading the name of the item, under the peace of mind that Baal made the choice for me.

THAT TIME BOMB CALLED STABILITY

We saw that absence of fire lets highly flammable material accumulate. People are shocked and outraged when I tell them that absence of political instability, even war, lets explosive material and tendencies accumulate under the surface.

The Second Step: Do (Small) Wars Save Lives?

The anti-Enlightenment political philosopher Joseph de Maistre remarked that conflicts strengthen countries. This is highly debatable—war is not a good thing, and, as the victim of a brutal civil war, I can attest to its horrors. But what I find interesting—and elegant—in his reasoning is his pointing out the mistake of analyzing losses from a given event and ignoring the rest of the story. It is also interesting that people tend to grasp the opposite more easily, that is, spot the error of analyzing immediate gains without taking into account the long-term side effects. For we look at casualties as losses without taking into account the second step, what happens later—unlike gardeners, who understand rather well that pruning trees strengthens them.

Likewise peace—some kind of forced, constrained, non-natural peace—may be costly in lives: just consider the great complacency that led to the Great War after almost a century of relative peace in Europe, coupled with the rise of the heavily armed nation-state.

Again, we all love peace and we all love economic and emotional stability—but do not want to be suckers in the long term. We seek vaccination at every new school year (injecting ourselves with a bit of harm to build immunity) but fail to transfer the mechanism to political and economic domains.

What to Tell the Foreign Policy Makers

To summarize, the problem with artificially suppressed volatility is not just that the system tends to become extremely fragile; it is that, at the same time, it exhibits no *visible* risks. Also remember that volatility is information. In fact, these systems tend to be too calm and exhibit minimal variability as silent risks accumulate beneath the surface. Although the stated intention of political leaders and economic policy makers is to stabilize the system by inhibiting fluctuations, the result tends to be the opposite. These artificially constrained systems become prone to Black Swans. Such environments eventually experience massive blowups, of the type seen in Figure 3, catching everyone off guard and undoing years of stability or, in almost all cases, ending up far worse than they were in their initial volatile state. Indeed, the longer it takes for the blowup to occur, the worse the resulting harm to both economic and political systems.

Seeking stability by achieving stability (and forgetting the second step) has been a great sucker game for economic and foreign policies. The list is depressingly long. Take rotten governments like the one in Egypt before the riots of 2011, supported by the United States for four decades in order "to avoid chaos," with the side effect of a coterie of privileged pillagers using superpowers as a backstop—identical to bankers using their "too big to fail" status to scam taxpayers and pay themselves high bonuses.

Saudi Arabia is the country that at present worries and offends me the most; it is a standard case of top-down stability enforced by a superpower at the expense of every single possible moral and ethical metric—and, of course, at the expense of stability itself.

So a place "allied" to the United States is a total monarchy, devoid of a constitution. But that is not what is morally shocking. A group of between seven and fifteen thousand members of the royal family runs the place, leading a lavish, hedonistic lifestyle in open contradiction with the purist ideas that got them there. Look at the contradiction: the stern desert tribes whose legitimacy is derived from Amish-like austerity can, thanks to a superpower, turn to hedonistic uninhibited pleasure seeking— the king openly travels for pleasure with a retinue that fills four Jumbo jets. Quite a departure from his ancestors. The family members amassed a fortune now largely in Western safes. Without the United States, the country would have had its revolution, a regional breakup, some turmoil, then perhaps—by now—some stability. But preventing noise makes the problem worse in the long run.

Clearly the "alliance" between the Saudi royal family and the United States was meant to provide stability. What stability? How long can one confuse the system? Actually "how long" is irrelevant: this stability is similar to a loan one has to eventually pay back. And there are ethical issues I leave to Chapter 24, particularly casuistry, when someone finds a justification "for the sake of" to violate an otherwise inflexible moral rule.* Few people are aware of the fact that the bitterness of Iranians toward the United States comes from the fact that the United States— a democracy—installed a monarch, the repressive Shah of Iran, who pillaged the place but gave the United States the "stability" of access to the Persian Gulf. The theocratic regime in Iran today is largely the result of such repression. We need to learn to think in second steps, chains of consequences, and side effects.

More worrisome, U.S. policy toward the Middle East has historically, and especially since September 11, 2001, been unduly focused on the repression of any and all political fluctuations in the name of preventing "Islamic fundamentalism"—a trope that almost every regime has used. Aside from the fact that killing Islamists compounds their numbers, the West and its autocratic Arab allies have strengthened Islamic fundamentalists by forcing them underground.

Time for American policy makers to understand that the more they intervene in other countries for the sake of stability, the more they bring instability (except for emergency-room-style cases). Or perhaps time to reduce the role of policy makers in policy affairs.

One of life's packages: no stability without volatility.

---

* Note these double standards on the part of Western governments. As a Christian, parts of Saudi Arabia are off-limits to me, as I would violate the purity of the place. But no public part of the United States or Western Europe is off-limits to Saudi citizens.

WHAT DO WE CALL HERE MODERNITY?

My definition of modernity is humans' large-scale domination of the environment, the systematic smoothing of the world's jaggedness, and the stifling of volatility and stressors.

Modernity corresponds to the systematic extraction of humans from their randomness-laden ecology—physical and social, even epistemological. Modernity is not just the postmedieval, postagrarian, and postfeudal historical period as defined in sociology textbooks. It is rather the spirit of an age marked by rationalization (naive rationalism), the idea that society is understandable, hence must be designed, by humans. With it was born statistical theory, hence the beastly bell curve. So was linear science. So was the notion of "efficiency"—or optimization.

Modernity is a Procrustean bed, good or bad—a reduction of humans to what appears to be efficient and useful. Some aspects of it work: Procrustean beds are not all negative reductions. Some may be beneficial, though these are rare.

Consider the life of the lion in the comfort and predictability of the Bronx Zoo (with Sunday afternoon visitors flocking to look at him in a combination of curiosity, awe, and pity) compared to that of his cousins in freedom. We, at some point, had free-range humans and free-range children before the advent of the golden period of the soccer mom.

We are moving into a phase of modernity marked by the lobbyist, the very, very limited liability corporation, the MBA, sucker problems, secularization (or rather reinvention of new sacred values like flags to replace altars), the tax man, fear of the boss, spending the weekend in interesting places and the workweek in a putatively less interesting one, the separation of "work" and "leisure" (though the two would look identical to someone from a wiser era), the retirement plan, argumentative intellectuals who would disagree with this definition of modernity, literal thinking, inductive inference, philosophy of science, the invention of social science, smooth surfaces, and egocentric architects. Violence is transferred from individuals to states. So is financial indiscipline. At the center of all this is the denial of antifragility.

There is a dependence on narratives, an intellectualization of actions and ventures. Public enterprises and functionaries—even employees of large corporations—can only do things that seem to fit some narrative, unlike businesses that can just follow profits, with or without a good-sounding story. Remember that you need a name for the color blue when you build a narrative, but not in action—the thinker lacking a word for "blue" is handicapped; not the doer. (I've had a hard time conveying to intellectuals the *intellectual* superiority of practice.)

Modernity widened the difference between the sensational and the relevant—in a natural environment the sensational is, well, sensational for a reason; today we depend on the press for such essentially human things as gossip and anecdotes and we care about the private lives of people in very remote places.

Indeed, in the past, when we were not fully aware of antifragility and self-organization and spontaneous healing, we managed to respect these properties by constructing beliefs that served the purpose of managing and surviving uncertainty. We imparted improvements to the agency of god(s). We may have denied that things can take care of themselves without some agency. But it was the gods that were the agents, not Harvard-educated captains of the ship.

So the emergence of the nation-state falls squarely into this progression—the transfer of agency to mere humans. The story of the nation-state is that of the concentration and magnification of human errors. Modernity starts with the state monopoly on violence, and ends with the state's monopoly on fiscal irresponsibility.

We will discuss next two central elements at the core of modernity. Primo, in Chapter 7, naive interventionism, with the costs associated with fixing things that one should leave alone. Secundo, in Chapter 8 and as a transition to Book III, this idea of replacing God and the gods running future events with something even more religiously fundamentalist: the unconditional belief in the idea of scientific prediction regardless of the domain, the aim to squeeze the future into numerical reductions whether reliable or unreliable. For we have managed to transfer religious belief into gullibility for whatever can masquerade as science.

CHAPTER 7

Naive Intervention

A tonsillectomy to kill time—Never do today what can be left to tomorrow—Let's predict revolutions after they happen—Lessons in blackjack

————

Consider this need to "do something" through an illustrative example. In the 1930s, 389 children were presented to New York City doctors; 174 of them were recommended tonsillectomies. The remaining 215 children were again presented to doctors, and 99 were said to need the surgery. When the remaining 116 children were shown to yet a third set of doctors, 52 were recommended the surgery. Note that there is morbidity in 2 to 4 percent of the cases (today, not then, as the risks of surgery were very bad at the time) and that a death occurs in about every 15,000 such operations and you get an idea about the break-even point between medical gains and detriment.

This story allows us to witness probabilistic homicide at work. Every child who undergoes an unnecessary operation has a shortening of her life expectancy. This example not only gives us an idea of harm done by those who intervene, but, worse, it illustrates the lack of awareness of the need to look for a break-even point between benefits and harm.

Let us call this urge to help "naive interventionism." Next we examine its costs.

INTERVENTION AND IATROGENICS

In the case of tonsillectomies, the harm to the children undergoing un-necessary treatment is coupled with the trumpeted gain for *some* others. The name for such net loss, the (usually hidden or delayed) damage from treatment in excess of the benefits, is *iatrogenics,* literally, "caused by the healer," *iatros* being a healer in Greek. We will posit in Chapter 21 that every time you visit a doctor and get a treatment, you incur risks of such medical harm, which should be analyzed the way we analyze other trade-offs: probabilistic benefits minus probabilistic costs.

For a classic example of iatrogenics, consider the death of George Washington in December 1799: we have enough evidence that his doctors greatly helped, or at least hastened, his death, thanks to the then standard treatment that included bloodletting (between five and nine pounds of blood).

Now these risks of harm by the healer can be so overlooked that, depending on how you account for it, until penicillin, medicine had a largely negative balance sheet—going to the doctor increased your chance of death. But it is quite telling that medical iatrogenics seems to have increased over time, along with knowledge, to peak sometime late in the nineteenth century. Thank you, modernity: it was "scientific prog-ress," the birth of the clinic and its substitution for home remedies, that caused death rates to shoot up, mostly from what was then called "hos-pital fever"—Leibniz had called these hospitals *seminaria mortis,* seed-beds of death. The evidence of increase in death rates is about as strong as they come, since all the victims were now gathered in one place: peo-ple were dying in these institutions who would have survived outside them. The famously mistreated Austro-Hungarian doctor Ignaz Sem-melweis had observed that more women died giving birth in hospitals than giving birth on the street. He called the establishment doctors a bunch of criminals—which they were: the doctors who kept killing pa-tients could not accept his facts or act on them since he "had no theory" for his observations. Semmelweis entered a state of depression, helpless to stop what he saw as murders, disgusted at the attitude of the estab-lishment. He ended up in an asylum, where he died, ironically, from the same hospital fever he had been warning against.

Semmelweis's story is sad: a man who was punished, humiliated, and even killed for shouting the truth in order to save others. The worst pun-ishment was his state of helplessness in the face of risks and unfairness.

But the story is also a happy one—the truth came out eventually, and his mission ended up paying off, with some delay. And the final lesson is that one should not expect laurels for bringing the truth.

Medicine is comparatively the good news, perhaps the only good news, in the field of iatrogenics. We see the problem there because things are starting to be brought under control today; it is now just what we call the cost of doing business, although medical error still currently kills between three times (as accepted by doctors) and ten times as many people as car accidents in the United States. It is generally accepted that harm from doctors—not including risks from hospital germs—accounts for more deaths than any single cancer. The methodology used by the medical establishment for decision making is still innocent of proper risk-management principles, but medicine is getting better. We have to worry about the incitation to overtreatment on the part of pharmaceutical companies, lobbies, and special interest groups and the production of harm that is not immediately salient and not accounted for as an "error." Pharma plays the game of concealed and distributed iatrogenics, and it has been growing. It is easy to assess iatrogenics when the surgeon amputates the wrong leg or operates on the wrong kidney, or when the patient dies of a drug reaction. But when you medicate a child for an imagined or invented psychiatric disease, say, ADHD or depression, instead of letting him out of the cage, the long-term harm is largely unaccounted for. Iatrogenics is compounded by the "agency problem" or "principal-agent problem," which emerges when one party (the agent) has personal interests that are divorced from those of the one using his services (the principal). An agency problem, for instance, is present with the stockbroker and medical doctor, whose ultimate interest is their own checking account, not your financial and medical health, respectively, and who give you advice that is geared to benefit themselves. Or with politicians working on their career.

First, Do No Harm

Medicine has known about iatrogenics since at least the fourth century before our era—*primum non nocere* ("first do no harm") is a first principle attributed to Hippocrates and integrated in the so-called Hippocratic Oath taken by every medical doctor on his commencement day. It just took medicine about twenty-four centuries to properly execute the brilliant idea. In spite of the recitations of *non nocere* through the ages, the term "iatrogenics" only appeared in frequent use very, very late, a few decades ago—after so much damage had been done. I for myself did not know the exact word until the writer Bryan Appleyard introduced me to it (I had used "harmful unintended side effects"). So let us leave medicine (to return to it in a dozen chapters or so), and apply this idea born in medicine to other domains of life. Since no intervention implies no iatrogenics, the source of harm lies in the denial of antifragility, and to the impression that we humans are so necessary to making things function.

Enforcing consciousness of generalized iatrogenics is a tall order. The very notion of iatrogenics is quite absent from the discourse outside medicine (which, to repeat, has been a rather slow learner). But just as with the color blue, having a word for something helps spread awareness of it. We will push the idea of iatrogenics into political science, economics, urban planning, education, and more domains. Not one of the consultants and academics in these fields with whom I tried discussing it knew what I was talking about—or thought that they could possibly be the source of any damage. In fact, when you approach the players with such skepticism, they tend to say that you are "against scientific progress."

But the concept can be found in some religious texts. The Koran mentions "those who are wrongful while thinking of themselves that they are righteous."

To sum up, anything in which there is naive interventionism, nay, even just intervention, will have iatrogenics.

The Opposite of Iatrogenics

While we now have a word for causing harm while trying to help, we don't have a designation for the opposite situation, that of someone who ends up helping while trying to cause harm. Just remember that attacking the antifragile will backfire. For instance, hackers make systems stronger. Or as in the case of Ayn Rand, obsessive and intense critics help a book spread.

Incompetence is double-sided. In the Mel Brooks movie *The Producers,* two New York theater fellows get in trouble by finding success instead of the intended failure. They had sold the same shares to multiple investors in a Broadway play, reasoning that should the play fail, they would keep the excess funds—their scheme would not be discovered if the investors got no return on their money. The problem was that they tried so hard to have a bad play—called *Springtime for Hitler*—and they were so bad at it that it turned out to be a huge hit. Uninhibited by their common prejudices, they managed to produce interesting work. I also saw similar irony in trading: a fellow was so upset with his year-end bonus that he started making huge bets with his employer's portfolio— and ended up making them considerable sums of money, more than if he had tried to do so on purpose.

Perhaps the idea behind capitalism is an inverse-iatrogenic effect, the unintended-but-not-so-unintended consequences: the system facilitates the conversion of selfish aims (or, to be correct, not necessarily benevolent ones) at the individual level into beneficial results for the collective.

Iatrogenics in High Places

Two areas have been particularly infected with absence of awareness of iatrogenics: socioeconomic life and (as we just saw in the story of Semmelweis) the human body, matters in which we have historically combined a low degree of competence with a high rate of intervention and a disrespect for spontaneous operation and healing—let alone growth and improvement.

As we saw in Chapter 3, there is a distinction between organisms (biological or nonbiological) and machines. People with an engineering-oriented mind will tend to look at everything around as an engineering problem. This is a very good thing in engineering, but when dealing with cats, it is a much better idea to hire veterinarians than circuits engineers— or even better, let your animal heal by itself.

Table 3 provides a glimpse of these attempts to "improve matters" across domains and their effects. Note the obvious: in all cases they correspond to the denial of antifragility.

TABLE 3 • FRAGILIZING INTERVENTIONISM AND ITS EFFECTS ACROSS DISCIPLINES

FIELD	EXAMPLE OF INTERVENTIONISM	IATROGENICS/ COSTS
Medicine, Health	Overtreatment	Fragility
	Steady feeding, thermal stability, etc.—denying the human body randomness	Medical error
		Sicker (but longer-living) humans, richer pharma, antibiotic-resistant bacteria
	Pharmaceutical addition, not subtraction	
Ecology	Micromanaging forest fires	Worsening total risks— larger "big ones"
Politics	Central planning	Informational opacity
	U.S. supporting rotten regimes "for the sake of stability"	Chaos after a revolution
Economics	"No More Boom and Bust" (Greenspan (US), Labor (UK)), Great Moderation (Bernanke)	Fragility
		Deeper crises when they happen
	State interventionism	
	Optimization	Support for established, state-friendly corporations; stifling of entrepreneurs
	Illusion of pricing rare events, value-at-risk methodologies, illusion of economies of scale, ignorance of second-order effects	Vulnerability, pseudo-efficiency
		Big-time blowups
Business	Positive advice (charlatans), focus on return not risk (what to avoid)	Richer charlatans, bankrupt businesses
Urbanism	City planning	Urban blight, inner cities, depressions, crime
Forecasting	Forecasting in Black Swan Domain (Fourth Quadrant) in spite of the horrible track record	Hidden risks (people take more risks when supplied with a forecast)
Literature	Copy editors trying to change your text	Blander, more *New York Times*–style commoditized writing

FIELD	EXAMPLE OF INTERVENTIONISM	IATROGENICS/ COSTS
Parenting	Soccer mom (or pop): removing every random element from children's lives	Touristification of children's minds
Education	The entire concept is grounded in interventionism	Ludification—transformation of children's brains
Technology	Neomania	Fragility, alienation, nerdification
Media	High-frequency sterile information	Disruption of the noise/ signal filtering mechanism Interventionism

Can a Whale Fly Like an Eagle?

Social scientists and economists have no built-in consciousness of iatrogenics, and of course no name for it—when I decided to teach a class on model error in economics and finance, nobody took me or the idea seriously, and the few who did tried to block me, asking for "a theory" (as in Semmelweis's story) and not realizing that it was precisely the errors of theory that I was addressing and cataloguing, as well as the very idea of using a theory without considering the impact of the possible errors from theory.

For a theory is a very dangerous thing to have.

And of course one can rigorously do science without it. What scientists call phenomenology is the observation of an empirical regularity without a visible theory for it. In the Triad, I put theories in the fragile category, phenomenology in the robust one. Theories are superfragile; they come and go, then come and go, then come and go again; phenomenologies stay, and I can't believe people don't realize that phenomenology is "robust" and usable, and theories, while overhyped, are unreliable for decision making—outside physics.

Physics is privileged; it is the exception, which makes its imitation by other disciplines similar to attempts to make a whale fly like an eagle. Errors in physics get smaller from theory to theory—so saying "Newton was wrong" is attention grabbing, good for lurid science journalism, but ultimately mendacious; it would be far more honest to say "Newton's theory is imprecise in some specific cases." Predictions made by Newtonian mechanics are of astonishing precision except for items traveling close to the speed of light, something you don't expect to do on your next vacation. We also read nonsense-with-headlines to the effect that Einstein was "wrong" about that speed of light—and the tools used to prove him wrong are of such complication and such precision that they've demonstrated how inconsequential such a point will be for you and me in the near and far future.

On the other hand, social science seems to diverge from theory to theory. During the cold war, the University of Chicago was promoting laissez-faire theories, while the University of Moscow taught the exact opposite—but their respective physics departments were in convergence, if not total agreement. This is the reason I put social science theories in the left column of the Triad, as something superfragile for real-world decisions and unusable for risk analyses. The very designation "theory" is even upsetting. In social science we should call these constructs "chimeras" rather than theories.

We will have to construct a methodology to deal with these defects. We cannot afford to wait an additional twenty-four centuries. Unlike with medicine, where iatrogenics is distributed across the population (hence with Mediocristan effects), because of concentration of power, social science and policy iatrogenics can blow us up (hence, Extremistan).

Not Doing Nothing

A main source of the economic crisis that started in 2007 lies in the iatrogenics of the attempt by Überfragilista Alan Greenspan—certainly the top economic iatrogenist of all time—to iron out the "boom-bust cycle" which caused risks to go hide under the carpet and accumulate there until they blew up the economy. The most depressing part of the Greenspan story is that the fellow was a libertarian and seemingly convinced of the idea of leaving systems to their own devices; people can fool themselves endlessly. The same naive interventionism was also applied by the U.K. government of Fragilista Gordon Brown, a student of the Enlightenment whose overt grand mission was to "eliminate" the business cycle. Fragilista Prime Minister Brown, a master iatrogenist though not nearly in the same league as Greenspan, is now trying to lecture the world on "ethics" and "sustainable" finance—but his policy of centralizing information technology (leading to massive cost overruns and delays in implementation) instead of having decentralized small units has proven difficult to reverse. Indeed, the U.K. health service was operating under the principle that a pin falling somewhere in some remote hospital should be heard in Whitehall (the street in London where the government buildings are centralized). The technical argument about the dangers of concentration is provided in Chapter 18.

These attempts to eliminate the business cycle lead to the mother of all fragilities. Just as a little bit of fire here and there gets rid of the flammable material in a forest, a little bit of harm here and there in an economy weeds out the vulnerable firms early enough to allow them to "fail early" (so they can start again) and minimize the long-term damage to the system.

An ethical problem arises when someone is put in charge. Greenspan's actions were harmful, but even if he knew that, it would have taken a bit of heroic courage to justify inaction in a democracy where the incentive is to always promise a better outcome than the other guy, regardless of the actual, delayed cost.

Ingenuous interventionism is very pervasive across professions. Just as with the tonsillectomy, if you supply a typical copy editor with a text, he will propose a certain number of edits, say about five changes per page. Now accept his "corrections" and give this text to another copy editor who tends to have the same average rate of intervention (editors vary in interventionism), and you will see that he will suggest an equivalent number of edits, sometimes reversing changes made by the previous editor. Find a third editor, same.

Incidentally, those who do too much somewhere do too little elsewhere—and editing provides a quite fitting example. Over my writing career I've noticed that those who overedit tend to miss the real typos (and vice versa). I once pulled an op-ed from *The Washington Post* owing to the abundance of completely unnecessary edits, as if every word had been replaced by a synonym from the thesaurus. I gave the article to the *Financial Times* instead. The editor there made one single correction: 1989 became 1990. *The Washington Post* had tried so hard that they missed the only relevant mistake. As we will see, interventionism depletes mental and economic resources; it is rarely available when it is needed the most. (Beware what you wish for: small government might in the end be more effective at whatever it needs to do. Reduction in size and scope may make it even more intrusive than large government.)

Non-Naive Interventionism

Let me warn against misinterpreting the message here. The argument is not against the notion of intervention; in fact I showed above that I am equally worried about underintervention when it is truly necessary. I am just warning against *naive* intervention and lack of awareness and acceptance of harm done by it.

It is certain that the message will be misinterpreted, for a while. When I wrote *Fooled by Randomness,* which argues—a relative of this message—that we have a tendency to underestimate the role of randomness in human affairs, summarized as "it is more random than you think," the message in the media became "it's all random" or "it's all dumb luck," an illustration of the Procrustean bed that changes by reducing. During a radio interview, when I tried explaining to the journalist the nuance and the difference between the two statements I was told that I was "too complicated"; so I simply walked out of the studio, leaving them in the lurch. The depressing part is that those people who were committing such mistakes were educated journalists entrusted to represent the world to us lay persons. Here, all I am saying is that we need to avoid being blind to the natural antifragility of systems, their ability to take care of themselves, and fight our tendency to harm and fragilize them by not giving them a chance to do so.

As we saw with the overzealous editor, over-intervention comes with under-intervention. Indeed, as in medicine, we tend to over-intervene in areas with minimal benefits (and large risks) while under-intervening in areas in which intervention is necessary, like emergencies. So the message here is in favor of staunch intervention in some areas, such as ecology or to limit the economic distortions and moral hazard caused by large corporations.

What should we control? As a rule, intervening to limit size (of companies, airports, or sources of pollution), concentration, and speed are beneficial in reducing Black Swan risks. These actions may be devoid of iatrogenics—but it is hard to get governments to limit the size of government. For instance, it has been argued since the 1970s that limiting speed on the highway (and enforcing it) leads to an extremely effective increase in safety. This can be plausible because risks of accidents increase disproportionally (that is, *nonlinearly*) with speed, and humans are not ancestrally equipped with such intuition. Someone recklessly driving a huge vehicle on the highway is endangering your safety and needs to be stopped before he hits your convertible Mini—or put in a situation in which he is the one exiting the gene pool, not you. Speed is from modernity, and I am always suspicious of hidden fragilities coming from the post-natural—we will further show a technical proof in Chapters 18 and 19.

But I also buy the opposite argument that regulating street signs does not seem to reduce risks; drivers become more placid. Experiments show that alertness is weakened when one relinquishes control to the system (again, lack of overcompensation). Motorists need the stressors and tension coming from the feeling of danger to feed their attention and risk controls, rather than some external regulator—fewer pedestrians die jaywalking than using regulated crossings. Some libertarians use the example of Drachten, a town in the Netherlands, in which a dream experiment was conducted. All street signs were removed. The deregulation led to an increase in safety, confirming the antifragility of attention at work, how it is whetted by a sense of danger and responsibility. As a result, many German and Dutch towns have reduced the number of street signs. We saw a version of the Drachten effect in Chapter 2 in the discussion of the automation of planes, which produces the exact opposite effect than what is intended by making pilots lose alertness. But one needs to be careful not to overgeneralize the Drachten effect, as it does not imply the effectiveness of removing all rules from society. As I said earlier, speed on the highway responds to a different dynamic and its risks are different.

Alas, it has been hard for me to fit these ideas about fragility and antifragility within the current U.S. political discourse—that beastly two-fossil system. Most of the time, the Democratic side of the U.S. spectrum favors hyper-intervention, unconditional regulation, and large government, while the Republican side loves large corporations, unconditional deregulation, and militarism—both are the same to me here. They are even more the same when it comes to debt, as both sides have tended to encourage indebtedness on the part of citizens, corporations, and government (which brings fragility and kills antifragility). I believe that both markets and governments are unintelligent when it comes to Black Swan events—though, again, not Mother Nature, thanks to her construction, or more ancient types of markets (like the souks), unlike the ones we have now.

Let me simplify my take on intervention. To me it is mostly about having a systematic protocol to determine when to intervene and when to leave systems alone. And we may need to intervene to control the iatrogenics of modernity—particularly the large-scale harm to the environment and the concentration of potential (though not yet manifested) damage, the kind of thing we only notice when it is too late. The ideas advanced here are not political, but risk-management based. I do not have a political affiliation or allegiance to a specific party; rather, I am introducing the idea of harm and fragility into the vocabulary so we can formulate appropriate policies to ensure we don't end up blowing up the planet and ourselves.

IN PRAISE OF PROCRASTINATION—THE FABIAN KIND

There is an element of deceit associated with interventionism, accelerating in a professionalized society. It's much easier to sell "Look what I did for you" than "Look what I avoided for you." Of course a bonus system based on "performance" exacerbates the problem. I've looked in history for heroes who became heroes for what they did *not* do, but it is hard to observe *nonaction*; I could not easily find any. The doctor who refrains from operating on a back (a very expensive surgery), instead giving it a chance to heal itself, will not be rewarded and judged as favorably as the doctor who makes the surgery look indispensable, then brings relief to the patient while exposing him to operating risks, while accruing great financial rewards to himself. The latter will be driving the pink Rolls-Royce. The corporate manager who avoids a loss will not often be rewarded. The true hero in the Black Swan world is someone who prevents a calamity and, naturally, because the calamity did not take place, does not get recognition—or a bonus—for it. I will be taking the concept deeper in Book VII, on ethics, about the unfairness of a bonus system and how such unfairness is magnified by complexity.

However, as always, the elders seem to have far more wisdom than we moderns—and much, much simpler wisdom; the Romans revered someone who, at the least, resisted and delayed intervention. One general, Fabius Maximus was nicknamed Cunctator, "the Procrastinator." He drove Hannibal, who had an obvious military superiority, crazy by avoiding and delaying engagement. And it is quite fitting to consider Hannibal's militarism as a form of interventionism (à la George W. Bush, except that Hannibal was actually in battle himself, not in the comfort of an office) and compare it to the Cunctator's wisdom.

A very intelligent group of revolutionary fellows in the United Kingdom created a political movement called the Fabian Society, named after the Cunctator, based on opportunistically delaying the revolution. The society included George Bernard Shaw, H. G. Wells, Leonard and Virginia Woolf, Ramsay MacDonald, and even Bertrand Russell for a moment. In retrospect, it turned out to be a very effective strategy, not so much as a way to achieve their objectives, but rather to accommodate the fact that these objectives are moving targets. Procrastination turned out to be a way to let events take their course and give the activists the chance to change their minds before committing to irreversible policies. And of course members *did* change their minds after seeing the failures and horrors of Stalinism and similar regimes.

There is a Latin expression *festina lente,* "make haste slowly." The Romans were not the only ancients to respect the act of voluntary omission. The Chinese thinker Lao Tzu coined the doctrine of *wu-wei,* "passive achievement."

Few understand that procrastination is our natural defense, letting things take care of themselves and exercise their antifragility; it results from some ecological or naturalistic wisdom, and is not always bad—at an existential level, it is my body rebelling against its entrapment. It is my soul fighting the Procrustean bed of modernity. Granted, in the modern world, my tax return is not going to take care of itself—but by delaying a non-vital visit to a doctor, or deferring the writing of a passage until my body tells me that I am ready for it, I may be using a very potent naturalistic filter. I write only if I feel like it and only on a subject I feel like writing about—and the reader is no fool. So I use procrastination as a message from my inner self and my deep evolutionary past to resist interventionism in my writing. Yet some psychologists and behavioral economists seem to think that procrastination is a *disease* to be remedied and cured.*

---

* Psychologists document the opposite of interventionism, calling it the *status quo bias.* But it seems that the two can coexist, interventionism and procrastination, in one's profession (where one is supposed to do something) and in one's personal life (the opposite). It depends on the domain. So it is a sociological and economic problem, one linked to norms and incentives (though doctors in the tonsillectomy study did not have direct incentives), rather than a mental property.

Given that procrastination has not been sufficiently pathologized yet, some associate it with the condition of *akrasia* discussed in Plato, a form of lack of self-control or weakness of will; others with *aboulia,* lack of will. And pharmaceutical companies might one day come up with a pill for it.

The benefits of procrastination apply similarly to medical procedures: we saw that procrastination protects you from error as it gives nature a chance to do its job, given the inconvenient fact that nature is less error-prone than scientists. Psychologists and economists who study "irrationality" do not realize that humans may have an instinct to procrastinate only when no life is in danger. I do not procrastinate when I see a lion entering my bedroom or fire in my neighbor's library. I do not procrastinate after a severe injury. I do so with unnatural duties and procedures. I once procrastinated and kept delaying a spinal cord operation as a response to a back injury—and was completely cured of the back problem after a hiking vacation in the Alps, followed by weight-lifting sessions. These psychologists and economists want me to kill my naturalistic instinct (the inner b****t detector) that allowed me to delay the elective operation and minimize the risks—an insult to the antifragility of our bodies. Since procrastination is a message from our natural willpower via low motivation, the cure is changing the environment, or one's profession, by selecting one in which one does not have to fight one's impulses. Few can grasp the logical consequence that, instead, one should lead a life in which procrastination is good, as a naturalistic-risk-based form of decision making.

Actually I select the writing of the passages of this book by means of procrastination. If I defer writing a section, it must be eliminated. This is simple ethics: Why should I try to fool people by writing about a subject for which I feel no natural drive?*

Using my ecological reasoning, someone who procrastinates is not irrational; it is his environment that is irrational. And the psychologist or economist calling him irrational is the one who is beyond irrational.

In fact we humans are very bad at filtering information, particularly short-term information, and procrastination can be a way for us to filter

---

* A friend who writes books remarked that painters like painting but authors like "having written." I suggested he stop writing, for his sake and the sake of his readers.

better, to resist the consequences of jumping on information, as we discuss next.

This idea of "naturalistic" has led to confusion. Philosophers refer to an error called the *naturalistic fallacy*, implying that what is natural is not necessarily morally right—something I subscribe to, as we saw in Chapter 4 in the discussion of the problem of applying Darwinian selection to modern society and the need to protect those who fail, something counter to nature. (The problem is that some people misuse the naturalistic fallacy outside the moral domain and misapply it to this idea of reliance on naturalistic instinct when one is in doubt.) However one slices it, it is not a fallacy when it comes to risk considerations. Time is the best test of fragility—it encompasses high doses of disorder—and nature is the only system that has been stamped "robust" by time. But some philosophasters fail to understand the primacy of risk and survival over philosophizing, and those should eventually exit the gene pool—true philosophers would agree with my statement. There is a worse fallacy: people making the opposite mistake and considering that *what is naturalistic is a fallacy*.

NEUROTICISM IN INDUSTRIAL PROPORTIONS

Imagine someone of the type we call neurotic in common parlance. He is wiry, looks contorted, and speaks with an uneven voice. His neck moves around when he tries to express himself. When he has a small pimple, his first reaction is to assume that it is cancerous, that the cancer is of the lethal type, and that it has already spread to his lymph nodes. His hypochondria is not limited to the medical department: he incurs a small setback in business and reacts as if bankruptcy were both near and certain. In the office, he is tuned to every single possible detail, systematically transforming every molehill into a mountain. The last thing you want in life is to be stuck in traffic with him on your way to an important appointment. The verb "overreact" was designed with him in mind: he does not have reactions, just overreactions.

Compare him to someone imperturbable, with the ability to be calm under fire that is considered necessary to become a leader, military commander, or mafia godfather. Usually unruffled and immune to small information, he can impress you with his self-control in difficult circumstances. For a sample of a composed, calm, and pondered voice, listen to interviews with "Sammy the Bull," Salvatore Gravano, who was involved in the murder of nineteen people (all competing mobsters). He speaks with minimal effort, as if what he is discussing is "not a big deal." This second type sometimes reacts when necessary; in the rare situations when he is angry, unlike with the neurotic fellow, everyone knows it and takes it seriously.

The supply of information to which we are exposed thanks to modernity is transforming humans from the equable second fellow into the neurotic first one. For the purpose of our discussion, the second fellow only reacts to real information, the first largely to noise. The difference between the two fellows will show us the difference between *noise* and *signal*. Noise is what you are supposed to ignore, signal what you need to heed.

Indeed, we have loosely mentioned "noise" earlier in the book; time to be precise about it. In science, noise is a generalization beyond the actual sound to describe random information that is totally useless for any purpose, and that you need to clean up to make sense of what you are listening to. Consider, for example, elements in an encrypted message that have absolutely no meaning, just randomized letters to confuse the spies, or the hiss you hear on a telephone line that you try to ignore in order to focus on the voice of your interlocutor.

And this personal or intellectual inability to distinguish noise from signal is behind overintervention.

A Legal Way to Kill People

If you want to accelerate someone's death, give him a personal doctor. I don't mean provide him with a bad doctor: just pay for him to choose his own. Any doctor will do.

This may be the only possible way to murder someone while staying squarely within the law. We can see from the tonsillectomy story that access to data increases intervention, causing us to behave like the neurotic fellow. Rory Sutherland signaled to me that someone with a personal doctor on staff should be particularly vulnerable to naive interventionism, hence iatrogenics; doctors need to justify their salaries and prove to themselves that they have a modicum of work ethic, something that "doing nothing" doesn't satisfy. Indeed, Michael Jackson's personal doctor has been sued for something equivalent to overintervention-to-stifle-antifragility (but it will take the law courts a while to become directly familiar with the concept). Did you ever wonder why heads of state and very rich people with access to all this medical care die just as easily as regular persons? Well, it looks like this is *because* of overmedication and excessive medical care.

Likewise, those in corporations or in policy making (like Fragilista Greenspan) who are endowed with a sophisticated data-gathering department and are therefore getting a lot of "timely" statistics are capable of overreacting and mistaking noise for information—Greenspan kept an eye on such fluctuations as the sales of vacuum cleaners in Cleveland to, as they say, "get a precise idea about where the economy is going," and of course he micromanaged us into chaos.

In business and economic decision making, reliance on data causes severe side effects—data is now plentiful thanks to connectivity, and the proportion of spuriousness in the data increases as one gets more immersed in it. A very rarely discussed property of data: it is toxic in large quantities—even in moderate quantities.

The previous two chapters showed how you can use and take advantage of noise and randomness; but noise and randomness can also use and take advantage of you, particularly when totally unnatural, as with the data you get on the Web or through the media.

The more frequently you look at data, the more noise you are disproportionally likely to get (rather than the valuable part, called the signal); hence the higher the noise-to-signal ratio. And there is a confusion which is not psychological at all, but inherent in the data itself. Say you look at information on a yearly basis, for stock prices, or the fertilizer sales of your father-in-law's factory, or inflation numbers in Vladivostok. Assume further that for what you are observing, at a yearly frequency, the ratio of signal to noise is about one to one (half noise, half signal)—this means that about half the changes are real improvements or degradations, the other half come from randomness. This ratio is what you get from yearly observations. But if you look at the very same data on a daily basis, the composition would change to 95 percent noise, 5 percent signal. And if you observe data on an hourly basis, as people immersed in the news and market price variations do, the split becomes 99.5 percent noise to 0.5 percent signal. That is two hundred times more noise than signal—which is why anyone who listens to news (except when very, very significant events take place) is one step below sucker.

Consider the iatrogenics of newspapers. They need to fill their pages every day with a set of news items—particularly those news items also dealt with by other newspapers. But to do things right, they ought to learn to keep silent in the absence of news of significance. Newspapers should be of two-line length on some days, two hundred pages on others—in proportion with the intensity of the signal. But of course they want to make money and need to sell us junk food. And junk food is iatrogenic.

There is a biological dimension to this story. I have been repeating that in a natural environment, a stressor is information. Too much information would thus be too much stress, exceeding the threshold of antifragility. In medicine, we are discovering the healing powers of fasting, as the avoidance of the hormonal rushes that come with the ingestion of food. Hormones convey information to the different parts of our system, and too much of them confuses our biology. Here again, as with news received at too high a frequency, too much information becomes harmful—daily news and sugar confuse our system in the same manner. And in Chapter 24 (on ethics) I will show how too much data (particularly when it is sterile) causes statistics to be completely meaningless.

Now let's add the psychological to this: we are not made to understand the point, so we overreact emotionally to noise. The best solution is to *only* look at very large changes in data or conditions, never at small ones.

Just as we are not likely to mistake a bear for a stone (but likely to mistake a stone for a bear), it is almost impossible for someone rational, with a clear, uninfected mind, someone who is not drowning in data, to mistake a vital signal, one that matters for his survival, for noise—unless he is overanxious, oversensitive, and neurotic, hence distracted and confused by other messages. Significant signals have a way to reach you. In the tonsillectomies story, the best filter would have been to only consider the children who were very ill, those with periodically recurring throat inflammation.

Media-Driven Neuroticism

There is so much noise coming from the media's glorification of the anecdote. Thanks to this, we are living more and more in virtual reality, separated from the real world, a little bit more every day while realizing it less and less. Consider that every day, 6,200 persons die in the United States, many of preventable causes. But the media only report the most anecdotal and sensational cases (hurricanes, freak accidents, small plane crashes), giving us a more and more distorted map of real risks. In an ancestral environment, the anecdote, the "interesting," is information; today, no longer. Likewise, by presenting us with explanations and theories, the media induce an illusion of understanding the world.

And the understanding of events (and risks) on the part of members of the press is so retrospective that they would put the security checks after the plane ride, or what the ancients call *post bellum auxilium*, sending troops after the battle. Owing to domain dependence, we forget the need to check our map of the world against reality. So we are living in a more and more fragile world, while thinking it is more and more understandable.

To conclude, the best way to mitigate interventionism is to ration the supply of information, as naturalistically as possible. This is hard to accept in the age of the Internet. It has been very hard for me to explain that the more data you get, the less you know what's going on, and the more iatrogenics you will cause. People are still under the illusion that "science" means more data.

THE STATE CAN HELP—WHEN INCOMPETENT

The famine in China that killed 30 million people between 1959 and 1961 can enlighten us about the effect of the state "trying hard." Xin Meng, Nancy Qian, and Pierre Yared examined its variations *between* areas, looking into how the famine was distributed. They discovered that famine was more severe in areas with higher food production in the period before the famine began, meaning that it was government policy of food distribution that was behind much of the problem, owing to the inflexibility in the procurement system. And indeed, a larger than expected share of famine over the past century has occured in economies with central planning.

But often it is the state's incompetence that can help save us from the grip of statism and modernity—inverse iatrogenics. The insightful author Dmitri Orlov showed how calamities were avoided after the breakdown of the Soviet state because food production was inefficient and full of unintentional redundancies, which ended up working in favor of stability. Stalin played with agriculture, causing his share of famine. But he and his successors never managed to get agriculture to become "efficient," that is, centralized and optimized as it is today in America, so every town had the staples growing around it. This was costlier, as they did not get the benefits of specialization, but this local lack of specialization allowed people to have access to all varieties of food in spite of the severe breakdown of the institutions. In the United States, we burn twelve calories in transportation for every calorie of nutrition; in Soviet Russia, it was one to one. One can imagine what could happen to the United States (or Europe) in the event of food disruptions. Further, because of the inefficiency of housing in the Soviet state, people had been living in close quarters for three generations, and had tight bonds that ensured—as in the Lebanese war—that they stayed close to each other and lent to each other. People had real links, unlike in social networks, and fed their hungry friends, expecting that some friend (most likely another one) would help them should they get in dire circumstances.

And the top-down state is not necessarily the one that has the reputation of being so.

France Is Messier than You Think

Next we will debunk the narrative that France works well because it is a Cartesian rationalizing-rationalist top-down state. As with the Russians, the French were lucky that it was for a long time a failed aim.

I spent the past two decades wondering why France, as a country managed in a top-down manner by an oversized state, could fare so well in so many fields. It is the country of Jean-Baptiste Colbert, after all, the grand dreamer of a state that infiltrates everything. Indeed the current culture is ultra-interventionist, sort of "if it ain't broke, fix it." For things work—somewhat—in France, often better than elsewhere; so can France be used as evidence that central bureaucracies that repress municipal mess are favorable for growth, happiness, good science and literature, excellent weather, diversified flora with Mediterranean varieties, tall mountains, excellent transportation, attractive women, and good cuisine? Then I discovered, reading Graham Robb's *The Discovery of France,* a major fact that led me to see the place with completely new eyes and search the literature for a revision of the story of the country.

The story was actually staring us in the face: the nation-state in France was largely nominal, in spite of attempts by Louis XIV, Napoleon, and the national education program of Jules Ferry to own the place. France in 1863 did not speak French (only one in five persons could), but rather a variety of languages and dialects (a surprising fact: the Nobel Prize in Literature in 1904 went to the Frenchman Frédéric

Mistral, who wrote in Provençal, a language of southern France no longer spoken). The lack of linguistic integration—like the variety in cheese (of which there are about four hundred different types)—expresses the difficulties in centralizing the country. There was nothing ethnic or linguistic to bind the place—it was just the property of a king and a weak aristocracy. Roads were horrible and most of the country was inaccessible to travelers. Tax collection was a dangerous profession, requiring tenacity and sagacity. Indeed, the country was progressively "discovered" by Paris, in many cases after its colonies in North Africa and elsewhere. In a thick and captivating book, *La rebellion française*, the historian Jean Nicolas shows how the culture of rioting was extremely sophisticated—historically, it counts as the true French national sport.

Paris itself was barely controlled by France—no more than the Rio slums called *favelas* are currently ruled by the Brazilian central state. Louis XIV, the Sun King, had moved the government to Versailles to escape the Parisian crowd. Paris only became controllable after Haussmann in the 1860s removed the tenements and narrow streets to make large avenues that allowed for police to control the crowds. Effectively France was still Paris and "the desert," as Paris didn't care much about the rest of France. The country was only centralized after long programs and "Five Year Plans" of roads, rail systems, public schools, and the spread of television—a Napoleonic dream of integration that, begun by De Gaulle after the war, was only completed during the reign of Valéry Giscard d'Estaing in the late 1970s, at which point the decentralization started taking place.* France might have benefited from its two decades or so under a large centralized state—but the argument could equally be that it benefited from the happy condition that the large state spurred growth and did not overstay its welcome.

---

* Another discovery—the control of that most organic, most disorderly of things, language. France, through the institution of the French academy, has an official stamp on what can and cannot be considered proper French and written by a pupil in a document or in a letter to the local mayor complaining about the noisy garbage pickup schedules. The result is obvious: a convoluted, difficult, and narrow formal vocabulary compared to English—but an expanded spoken French misdefined as "slang" that is just as rich as English. There are even writers like Céline or Dard who write in parallel literary vocabulary mixed with exquisitely precise and rich slang, a unique brand of colloquial-literary style.

Sweden and the Large State

Aside from France, I was baffled by the puzzle of Sweden and other Nordic states, which are often offered as paragons of the large state "that works"—the government represents a large portion of the total economy. How could we have the happiest nation in the world, Denmark (assuming "happiness" is both measurable and desirable), and a monstrously large state? Is it that these countries are all smaller than the New York metropolitan area? Until my coauthor, the political scientist Mark Blyth, showed me that there, too, was a false narrative: it was almost the same story as in Switzerland (but with a worse climate and no good ski resorts). The state exists as a tax collector, but the money is spent in the communes themselves, directed by the communes—for, say, skills training locally determined as deemed necessary by the community themselves, to respond to private demand for workers. The economic elites have more freedom than in most other democracies—this is far from the statism one can assume from the outside. And, most of all, these nations are the size of city-states.

Further, illustrating a case of gaining from disorder, Sweden and other Nordic countries experienced a severe recession at the end of the cold war, around 1990, to which they responded admirably with a policy of fiscal toughness, thus effectively shielding them from the severe financial crisis that took place about two decades later.

CATALYST-AS-CAUSE CONFUSION

When constrained systems, those hungry for natural disorder, collapse, as they are eventually bound to, since they are fragile, failure is never seen as the result of fragility. Rather, such failure is interpreted as the product of poor forecasting. As with a crumbling sand pile, it would be unintelligent to attribute the collapse of a fragile bridge to the last truck that crossed it, and even more foolish to try to predict in advance which truck might bring it down. Yet it is done all too often.

In 2011, U.S. president Barack Obama blamed an intelligence failure for the government's not foreseeing the revolution in Egypt that took place that spring (just as former U.S. president Jimmy Carter blamed an intelligence failure for his administration's not foreseeing the 1979 Islamic Revolution in Iran), missing the point that it is the suppressed risk in the statistical "tails" that matters—not the failure to see the last grain of sand. One analogy to economics: after the inception of the financial crisis in 2007–2008, many people thought that predicting the subprime meltdown (which seemed in their mind to have triggered it) would have helped. It would not have, for Baal's sake, since it was a symptom of the crisis, not its underlying cause. Likewise, Obama's blaming "bad intelligence" for his administration's failure to predict the uprising that took place in Egypt is symptomatic of both the misunderstanding of complex systems and the bad policies involved. And superpowers are plain turkeys in that story.

Obama's mistake illustrates the illusion of local causal chains—that is, confusing catalysts for causes and assuming that one can know which catalyst will produce which effect. The final episode of the upheaval in Egypt was unpredictable for all observers, especially those involved. As such, blaming the CIA or some other intelligence agency is as injudicious as funding it to forecast such events. Governments are wasting billions of dollars on attempting to predict events that are produced by interdependent systems and are therefore not statistically understandable at the individual level.

Most explanations that are offered for episodes of turmoil follow the catalysts-as-causes confusion. Take the "Arab Spring" of 2011. The riots in Tunisia and Egypt were initially attributed to rising commodity prices, not to stifling and unpopular dictatorships. But Bahrain and Libya were wealthy countries that could afford to import grain and other commodities. Further, we had had considerably higher commodity prices a few years earlier without any uprising at all. Again, the focus is wrong even if the logic is comforting. It is the system and its fragility, not events, that must be studied—what physicists call "percolation theory," in which the properties of the randomness of the terrain are studied, rather than those of a single element of the terrain.

As Mark Abdollahian of Sentia Group, one of the contractors who sell predictive analytics to the U.S. government (those that failed to warn), noted regarding Egypt, policy makers should "think of this like Las Vegas. In blackjack, if you can do four percent better than the average, you're making real money." But the analogy is spurious—pretty much everything I stand against. There is no "four percent better" on Egypt. This was not just money wasted but the construction of a false confidence based on an erroneous focus. It is telling that the intelligence analysts made the same mistake as the risk-management systems that failed to predict the economic crisis—and offered the exact same excuses when they failed. Political and economic "tail events" are unpredictable, and their probabilities are not scientifically measurable. No matter how many dollars are spent on research, predicting revolutions is not the same as counting cards; humans will never be able to turn politics and economics into the tractable randomness of blackjack.

CHAPTER 8

Prediction as a Child of Modernity

Never shout in French—Ms. Bré gains in respect—Black Swan territory

In the fall of 2009, I found myself in Korea with a collection of suit-and-tie-wearing hotshots. On a panel sat one Takatoshi Kato, then the deputy managing director of a powerful international institution. Before the panel discussion, he gave us a rapid PowerPoint presentation showing his and his department's economic projections for 2010, 2011, 2012, 2013, and 2014.

These were the days before I decided to climb up the mountain, speak slowly and in a priestly tone, and try shaming people rather than insulting them. Listening to Kato's presentation, I could not control myself and flew into a rage in front of two thousand Koreans—I was so angry that I almost started shouting in French, forgetting that I was in Korea. I ran to the podium and told the audience that the next time someone in a suit and tie gave them projections for some dates in the future, they should ask him to show what he had projected in the past—in this case, what he had been forecasting for 2008 and 2009 (the crisis years) two to five years earlier, in 2004, 2005, 2006, and 2007. They would then verify that Highly Venerable Kato-san and his colleagues are, to put it mildly, not very good at this predictionizing business. And it is not just Mr. Kato: our track record in figuring out significant rare events in politics and economics is not close to zero; it is *zero*. I improvised, on the spot, my solution. We can't put all false predictors in jail; we can't stop people from asking for predictions; we can't tell people not to hire the next person who makes promises about the future. "All I want is to live in a world in which predictions such as those by Mr. Kato do not harm you. And such a world has unique attributes: robustness."

The idea of proposing the Triad was born there and then as an answer to my frustration: Fragility-Robustness-Antifragility as a replacement for predictive methods.

Ms. Bré Has Competitors

What was getting me in that state of anger was my realization that forecasting was not neutral. It is all in the iatrogenics. Forecasting can be downright injurious to risk-takers—no different from giving people snake oil medicine in place of cancer treatment, or bleeding, as in the story of George Washington. And there was evidence. Danny Kahneman—rightfully—kept admonishing me for my fits of anger and outbursts at respectable members of the establishment (respectable for now), deeming such behavior to be unbecoming of the wise member of the intelligentsia I was supposed to be. Yet he stoked my frustration and sense of outrage the most by showing me the evidence of iatrogenics. There are ample empirical findings to the effect that providing someone with a random numerical forecast increases his risk taking, even if the person *knows* the projections are random.

All I hear is complaints about forecasters, when the next step is obvious yet rarely taken: avoidance of iatrogenics from forecasting. We understand childproofing, but not forecaster-hubris-proofing.

The Predictive

What makes life simple is that the robust and antifragile don't have to have as accurate a comprehension of the world as the fragile—and they do not need forecasting. To see how redundancy is a nonpredictive, or rather a less predictive, mode of action, let us use the argument of Chapter 2: if you have extra cash in the bank (in addition to stockpiles of tradable goods such as cans of Spam and hummus and gold bars in the basement), you don't need to know with precision which event will cause potential difficulties.* It could be a war, a revolution, an earthquake, a recession, an epidemic, a terrorist attack, the secession of the state of New Jersey, anything—you do not need to predict much, unlike those who are in the opposite situation, namely, in debt. Those, because of their fragility, need to predict with more, a lot more, accuracy.

Plus or Minus Bad Teeth

You can control fragility a lot more than you think. So let us refine in three points:

(i) Since detecting (anti)fragility—or, actually, smelling it, as Fat Tony will show us in the next few chapters—is easier, much easier, than prediction and understanding the dynamics of events, the entire mission reduces to the central principle of what to do to minimize harm (and maximize gain) from forecasting errors, that is, to have things that don't fall apart, or even benefit, when we make a mistake.

(ii) We do not want to change the world for now (leave that to the Soviet-Harvard utopists and other fragilistas); we should first make things more robust to defects and forecast errors, or even exploit these errors, making lemonade out of the lemons.

(iii) As for the lemonade, it looks as if history is in the business of making it out of lemons; antifragility is necessarily how things move forward under the mother of all stressors, called time.

Further, after the occurrence of an event, we need to switch the blame from the inability to see an event coming (say a tsunami, an Arabo-Semitic spring or similar riots, an earthquake, a war, or a financial crisis) to the failure to understand (anti)fragility, namely, "why did we build something so fragile to these types of events?" Not seeing a tsunami or an economic event coming is excusable; building something fragile to them is not.

Also, as to the naive type of utopianism, that is, blindness to history, we cannot afford to rely on the rationalistic elimination of greed and other human defects that fragilize society. Humanity has been trying to

---

* From my experiences of the Lebanese war and a couple of storms with power outages in Westchester County, New York, I suggest stocking up on novels, as we tend to underestimate the boredom of these long hours waiting for the trouble to dissipate. And books, being robust, are immune to power outages.

do so for thousands of years and humans remain the same, plus or minus bad teeth, so the last thing we need is even more dangerous moralizers (those who look in a permanent state of gastrointestinal distress). Rather, the more intelligent (and practical) action is to make the world greed-proof, or even hopefully make society benefit from the greed and other perceived defects of the human race.

In spite of their bad press, some people in the nuclear industry seem to be among the rare ones to have gotten the point and taken it to its logical consequence. In the wake of the Fukushima disaster, instead of predicting failure and the probabilities of disaster, these intelligent nuclear firms are now aware that they should instead focus on *exposure to failure*—making the prediction or nonprediction of failure quite irrelevant. This approach leads to building small enough reactors and embedding them deep enough in the ground with enough layers of protection around them that a failure would not affect us much should it happen—costly, but still better than nothing.

Another illustration, this time in economics, is the Swedish government's focus on total fiscal responsibility after their budget troubles in 1991—it makes them much less dependent on economic forecasts. This allowed them to shrug off later crises.*

The Idea of Becoming a Non-Turkey

It is obvious to anyone before drinking time that we can put a man, a family, a village with a mini town hall on the moon, and predict the trajectory of planets or the most minute effect in quantum physics, yet governments with equally sophisticated models cannot forecast revolutions, crises, budget deficits, or climate change. Or even the closing prices of the stock market a few hours from now.

There are two different domains, one in which we can predict (to some extent), the other—the Black Swan domain—in which we should only let turkeys and turkified people operate. And the demarcation is as visible (to non-turkeys) as the one between the cat and the washing machine.

Social, economic, and cultural life lie in the Black Swan domain,

---

* A related idea is expressed in a (perhaps apocryphal) statement by the financier Warren Buffett that he tries to invest in businesses that are "so wonderful that an idiot can run them. Because sooner or later, one will."

physical life much less so. Further, the idea is to separate domains into those in which these Black Swans are both unpredictable and consequential, and those in which rare events are of no serious concern, either because they are predictable or because they are inconsequential.

I mentioned in the Prologue that randomness in the Black Swan domain is intractable. I will repeat it till I get hoarse. The limit is mathematical, period, and there is no way around it on this planet. What is nonmeasurable and nonpredictable will remain nonmeasurable and nonpredictable, no matter how many PhDs with Russian and Indian names you put on the job—and no matter how much hate mail I get. There is, in the Black Swan zone, a limit to knowledge that can never be reached, no matter how sophisticated statistical and risk management science ever gets.

The involvement of this author has not been so much in asserting this impossibility to ever know anything about these matters—the general skeptical problem has been raised throughout history by a long tradition of philosophers, including Sextus Empiricus, Algazel, Hume, and many more skeptics and skeptical empiricists—as in formalizing and modernizing as a background and footnote to my anti-turkey argument. So my work is about *where* one should be skeptical, and where one should not be so. In other words, focus on getting out of the f*** Fourth Quadrant—the Fourth Quadrant is the scientific name I gave to the Black Swan domain, the one in which we have a high exposure to rare, "tail" events *and* these events are incomputable.*

Now, what is worse, because of modernity, the share of Extremistan is increasing. Winner-take-all effects are worsening: success for an author, a company, an idea, a musician, an athlete is planetary, or nothing. These worsen predictability since almost everything in socioeconomic life now is dominated by Black Swans. Our sophistication continuously puts us ahead of ourselves, creating things we are less and less capable of understanding.

---

* A technical footnote (to skip): What are the Quadrants? Combining exposures and types of randomness we get four combinations: Mediocristan randomness, low exposure to extreme events (First Quadrant); Mediocristan randomness, high exposure to extreme events (Second Quadrant); Extremistan randomness, low exposure to extreme events (Third Quadrant); Extremistan randomness, high exposure to extreme events (Fourth Quadrant). The first three quadrants are ones in which knowledge or lack of it bring inconsequential errors. "Robustification" is the modification of exposures to make a switch from the fourth to the third quadrant.

No More Black Swans

Meanwhile, over the past few years, the world has also gone the other way, upon the discovery of the Black Swan idea. Opportunists are now into predicting, predictioning, and predictionizing Black Swans with even more complicated models coming from chaos-complexity-catastrophe-fractal theory. Yet, again, the answer is simple: *less is more;* move the discourse to (anti)fragility.

BOOK III

A Nonpredictive View of the World

———

Welcome, reader, to the nonpredictive view of the world.

Chapter 10 presents Seneca's stoicism as a starting point for understanding antifragility, with applications from philosophy and religion to engineering. Chapter 11 introduces the barbell strategy and explains why the dual strategy of mixing high risks and highly conservative actions is preferable to just a simple medium-risk approach to things.

But first, we open Book III with the story of our two friends who derive some great entertainment from, and make a living by, detecting fragility and playing with the ills of fragilistas.

CHAPTER 9

Fat Tony and the Fragilistas

Olfactory methods with the perception of fragility—The difficulties of lunch—Quickly open the envelope—A certain redivision of the world, as seen from New Jersey—The sea gets deeper and deeper

INDOLENT FELLOW TRAVELERS

Before the economic crisis of 2008, the association between Nero Tulip and Tony DiBenedetto, also known as "Fat Tony" or the more politically acceptable "Tony Horizontal," would have been hard to explain to an outsider.

Nero's principal activity in life is reading books, with a few auxiliary activities in between. As to Fat Tony, he reads so little that, one day when he mentioned he wanted to write his memoirs, Nero joked that "Fat Tony would have written exactly one more book than he had read"—to which Fat Tony, always a few steps ahead of him, quoted Nero back: "You once said that if you felt like reading a novel, you would write one." (Nero had one day cited the British prime minister and novelist Benjamin Disraeli, who wrote novels but didn't like reading them.)

Tony grew up in Brooklyn and moved to New Jersey, and he has exactly the accent you would expect him to have. So, unburdened with time-consuming (and, to him, "useless") reading activities, and highly allergic to structured office work, Fat Tony spent a lot of his time doing nothing, with occasional commercial transactions in between. And, of course, a lot of eating.

The Importance of Lunch

While most people around them were running around fighting the different varieties of unsuccess, Nero and Fat Tony had this in common: they were terrified of boredom, particularly the prospect of waking up early with an empty day ahead. So the proximate reason for their getting together before that crisis was, as Fat Tony would say, "doing lunch." If you live in an active city, say, New York, and have a friendly personality, you will have no trouble finding good dinner partners, people who can hold a conversation of some interest in an almost relaxed way. Lunch, however, is a severe difficulty, particularly during phases of high employment. It is easy to find lunch partners among resident office inmates but trust me, you don't want to get near them. They will have liquefied stress hormones dripping from their pores, they will exhibit anxiety if they discuss anything that may divert them from what they think is in the course of their "work," and when in the process of picking their brain you hit on a less uninteresting mine, they will cut you short with a "I have to run" or "I have a two-fifteen."

Moreover, Fat Tony got respect in exactly the right places. Unlike Nero, whose ruminating philosophical episodes erased his social presence, making him invisible to waiters, Tony elicited warm and enthusiastic responses when he showed up in an Italian restaurant. His arrival triggered a small parade among the waiters and staff; he was theatrically hugged by the restaurant owner, and his departure after the meal was a long procedure with the owner and, sometimes, his mother seeing him outside, with some gift, like perhaps homemade grappa (or some strange liquid in an unmarked bottle), more hugs, and promises to come for the Wednesday special meal.

Accordingly, Nero, when he was in the New York area, could reduce his anxiety about lunchtime, as he could always count on Tony. He would meet Tony at the health club; there our horizontal hero did his triathlon (sauna, Jacuzzi, and steam bath), and from there they would go get some worship from restaurant owners. So Tony once explained to Nero that he had no use for him in the evenings—he could get better, more humorous, more Italian–New Jersey friends, who, unlike Nero, could give him ideas for "something useful."

The Antifragility of Libraries

Nero lived a life of mixed (and transient) asceticism, going to bed as close to nine o'clock as he could, sometimes even earlier in the winter. He tried to leave parties when the effect of alcohol made people start talking to strangers about their personal lives or, worse, turn metaphysical. Nero preferred to conduct his activities by daylight, trying to wake up in the morning with the sun's rays gently penetrating his bedroom, leaving stripes on the walls.

He spent his time ordering books from booksellers on the Web, and very often read them. Having terminated his turbulent, extremely turbulent, adventures, like Sindbad the sailor and Marco Polo the Venetian traveler, he ended up settling for a quiet and sedate life of post-adventure.

Nero was the victim of an aesthetic ailment that brings revulsion, even phobia, toward: people wearing flip-flops, television, bankers, politicians (right-wing, left-wing, centrists), New Jersey, rich persons from New Jersey (like Fat Tony), rich persons who take cruises (and stop in Venice wearing flip-flops), university administrators, grammatical sticklers, name droppers, elevator music, and well-dressed salespersons and businessmen. As for Fat Tony, he had different allergies: the *empty suit*, which we speculate is someone who has a command of all the superfluous and administrative details of things but misses the essential (and isn't even aware of it), so his conversation becomes mere chitchat around the point, never getting to the central idea.

And Fat Tony was a smeller of fragility. Literally. He claimed that he could figure out a person from seeing him just walk into a restaurant, which was almost true. But Nero had noticed that Fat Tony, when talking to people for the first time, got very close to them and sniffed them, just like a dog, a habit of which Fat Tony wasn't even aware.

Nero belonged to a society of sixty volunteer translators collaborating on previously unpublished ancient texts in Greek, Latin, or Aramaic (Syriac) for the French publishing house Les Belles Lettres. The group is organized along libertarian lines, and one of their rules is that university titles and prestige give no seniority in disputes. Another rule is mandatory attendance at two "dignified" commemorations in Paris, every November 7, the death of Plato, and every April 7, the birth of Apollo. His other membership is in a local club of weight lifters that meets on Saturdays in a converted garage. The club is mostly composed of New York doormen, janitors, and mobster-looking fellows who walk around in the summer wearing sleeveless "wife-beater" shirts.

Alas, men of leisure become slaves to inner feelings of dissatisfaction and interests over which they have little control. The freer Nero's time, the more compelled he felt to compensate for lost time in filling gaps in his natural interests, things that he wanted to know a bit deeper. And, as he discovered, the worst thing one can do to feel one knows things a bit deeper is to try to go into them a bit deeper. *The sea gets deeper as you go further into it,* according to a Venetian proverb.

Curiosity is antifragile, like an addiction, and is magnified by attempts to satisfy it—books have a secret mission and ability to multiply, as everyone who has wall-to-wall bookshelves knows well. Nero lived, at the time of writing, among fifteen thousand books, with the stress of how to discard the empty boxes and wrapping material after the arrival of his daily shipment from the bookstore. One subject Nero read for pleasure, rather than the strange duty-to-read-to-become-more-learned, was medical texts, for which he had a natural curiosity. The curiosity came from having had two brushes with death, the first from a cancer and the second from a helicopter crash that alerted him to both the fragility of technology and the self-healing powers of the human body. So he spent a bit of his time reading textbooks (not papers—textbooks) in medicine, or professional texts.

Nero's formal training was in statistics and probability, which he approached as a special branch of philosophy. He had been spending all his adult life writing a philosophical-technical book called *Probability and Metaprobability.* His tendency was to abandon the project every two years and take it up again two years later. He felt that the concept of probability as used was too narrow and incomplete to express the true nature of decisions in the ecology of the real world.

Nero enjoyed taking long walks in old cities, without a map. He used the following method to detouristify his traveling: he tried to inject some randomness into his schedule by never deciding on the next destination until he had spent some time in the first one, driving his travel agent crazy—when he was in Zagreb, his next destination would be determined by his state of mind while in Zagreb. Largely, it was the smell of places that drew him to them; smell cannot be conveyed in a catalogue.

Mostly, when in New York, Nero sat in his study with his writing desk set against the window, occasionally looking dreamily at the New Jersey shore across the Hudson River and reminding himself how happy he was to not live there. So he conveyed to Fat Tony that the "I have no use for you" was reciprocal (in equally nondiplomatic terms), which, as we will see, was not true.

ON SUCKERS AND NONSUCKERS

After the crisis of 2008, it became clear what the two fellows had in common: they were predicting a sucker's fragility crisis. What had gotten them together was that they had both been convinced that a crisis of such magnitude, with a snowballing destruction of the modern economic system in a way and on a scale never seen before, was bound to happen, simply because there were suckers. But our two characters came from two entirely different schools of thought.

Fat Tony believed that nerds, administrators, and, mostly, bankers were the ultimate suckers (that was when everyone still thought they were geniuses). And, what's more, he believed that collectively they were even bigger suckers than they were individually. And he had a natural ability to detect these suckers before they fell apart. Fat Tony derived his income from that activity while leading, as we saw, a life of leisure.

Nero's interests were similar to Tony's, except dressed up in intellectual traditions. To Nero, a system built on illusions of understanding probability is bound to collapse.

By betting against fragility, they were antifragile.

So Tony made a bundle from the crisis, in the high eight to low nine figures—everything other than a bundle for Tony is "tawk." Nero made a bit, though much less than Tony, but he was satisfied that he had won—as we said, he had already been financially independent and he saw money as a waste of time. To put it bluntly, Nero's family's wealth had peaked in 1804, so he did not have the social insecurity of other adventurers, and money to him could not possibly be a social statement—only erudition for now, and perhaps wisdom in old age. Excess wealth, if you don't need it, is a heavy burden. Nothing was more hideous in his eyes than excessive refinement—in clothes, food, lifestyle, manners—and wealth was nonlinear. Beyond some level it forces people into endless complications of their lives, creating worries about whether the housekeeper in one of the country houses is scamming them while doing a poor job and similar headaches that multiply with money.

The ethics of betting against suckers will be discussed in Book VII, but there are two schools of thought. To Nero one should first warn people that they are suckers, while Tony was against the very notion of warning. "You will be ridiculed," he said; "words are for sissies." A system based on verbal warnings will be dominated by non-risk-taking-babblers. These people won't give you and your ideas respect unless you take their money.

Further, Fat Tony insisted that Nero take a ritual look at the physical embodiments of the spoils, such as a bank account statement—as we said, it had nothing to do with the financial value, nor even the purchasing power, of the items, just their symbolic value. He could understand why Julius Caesar needed to incur the cost of having Vercingetorix, the leader of the Gaul rebellion, brought to Rome and paraded in chains, just so he could exhibit victory in the flesh.

There is another dimension to the need to focus on actions and avoid words: the health-eroding dependence on external recognition. People are cruel and unfair in the way they confer recognition, so it is best to stay out of that game. Stay robust to how others treat you. Nero at some stage befriended a scientist of legendary status, a giant for whom he had immense respect. Although the fellow was about as prominent as one could get in his field (in the eyes of others), he spent his time focused on the status he had that week in the scientific community. He would become enraged at authors who did not cite him or at some committee granting a medal he had never received to someone he judged inferior, that impostor!

Nero learned that no matter how satisfied they could be with their work, these hotshots-who-depended-on-words were deprived of Tony's serenity; they remained fragile to the emotional toll from the compliments they did *not* get, the ones others got, and from what someone of lower intellect stole from them. So Nero promised himself to escape all of this with his small ritual—just in case he should fall prone to the hotshot's temptation. Nero's spoils from what he called the "Fat Tony bet," after deducting the cost of a new car (a Mini) and a new $60 Swatch watch, amounted to a dizzyingly large amount sitting in a portfolio, the summary of which was mailed to him monthly from (of all places) a New Jersey address, with three other statements from overseas countries. Again, it is not the amount but the tangibility of his action that counted—the quantities could have been a tenth, even a hundredth as much and the effect would remain the same. So he would cure himself of the game of recognition by opening the envelope containing the statement and then going on with his day, oblivious to the presence of those cruel and unfair users of words.

But to follow ethics to their natural conclusion, Nero should have felt just as proud—and satisfied—had the envelope contained statements of losses. A man is honorable in proportion to the personal risks he takes for his opinion—in other words, the amount of downside he is exposed to. To sum him up, Nero believed in erudition, aesthetics, and risk taking—little else.

As to the funds, to avoid the charity trap, Nero followed Fat Tony's rule of systematically making donations, but not to those who directly asked for gifts. And he never, never gave a penny to any charitable organization, with the possible exception of those in which not a single person earned a salary.

Loneliness

A word on Nero's loneliness. For Nero, in the dark days before the economic crisis of 2008, it sometimes caused him pain to be alone with his ideas—wondering at times, typically Sunday nights, if there was something particularly wrong with him or if there was something wrong with the world. Lunch with Fat Tony was like drinking water after an episode of thirst; it brought immediate relief to realize that he was either not crazy, or at least not *alone* in being crazy. Things out there *did not make sense,* and it was impossible to convey it to others, particularly people deemed intelligent.

Consider that of the close to a million professionals employed in economic activities, whether in government (from Cameroon to Washington, D.C.), academia, media, banking, corporations, or doing their own private homework for economic and investment decisions, fewer than a handful saw it coming—furthermore, an even smaller handful managed to foresee the full extent of the damage.

And of those who saw it coming, not a single one realized that the crisis was a product of modernity.

Nero could stand near the former World Trade Center site in downtown New York, across from the colossal buildings housing mostly banks and brokerage houses, with hundreds of people running around inside them, expending gigawatts of energy just moving and commuting from New Jersey, consuming millions of bagels with cream cheese, with insulin response inflaming their arteries, producing gigabytes of information just by talking and corresponding and writing articles.

But noise it was: wasted effort, cacophony, unaesthetic behavior, increased entropy, production of energy that causes a local warming up of the New York area ecozone, and a large-scale delusion of this thing called "wealth" that was bound to evaporate somehow.

You could stack the books and they would constitute an entire mountain. Alas, to Nero anything in them that deals with probability, statistics, or mathematical models is just *air*, in spite of evidence that and evidence this. And you learn more in a few lunches with Fat Tony than from the social science sections of the Harvard libraries,* with close to two million books and research papers, for a total of 33 million hours of reading, close to nine thousand years' worth of reading as a full-time activity.

Talk about a major sucker problem.

What the Nonpredictor Can Predict

Fat Tony did not believe in predictions. But he made big bucks predicting that some people—the predictors—would go bust.

Isn't that paradoxical? At conferences, Nero used to meet physicists from the Santa Fe Institute who believed in predictions and used fancy prediction models while their business ventures based on predictions did not do that well—while Fat Tony, who did not believe in predictions, got rich from prediction.

You can't predict in general, but you can predict that those who rely on predictions are taking more risks, will have some trouble, perhaps even go bust. Why? Someone who predicts will be fragile to prediction errors. An overconfident pilot will eventually crash the plane. And numerical prediction leads people to take more risks.

Fat Tony is antifragile because he takes a mirror image of his fragile prey.

Fat Tony's model is quite simple. He identifies fragilities, makes a bet on the collapse of the fragile unit, lectures Nero and trades insults with him about sociocultural matters, reacts to Nero's jabs at New Jersey life, collects big after the collapse. Then he has lunch.

---

* The only exception in that social science library is a few small sections in the cognitive science literature—some of it works.

CHAPTER 10

Seneca's Upside and Downside

How to survive advice—To lose nothing or gain nothing—What to do on your next shipwreck

———

A couple of millennia before Fat Tony, another child of the Italian peninsula solved the problem of antifragility. Except that, more intellectual than our horizontal friend, he spoke in a more distinguished prose. In addition, he was no less successful in the real world—actually he was vastly more successful in business than Fat Tony, and no less intellectual than Nero. The fellow was the stoic philosopher Seneca, whom we mentioned earlier was the alleged lover of Nero's mother (he was not).

And he solved the problem of antifragility—what connects the elements of the Triad—using Stoic philosophy.

Is This Really Serious?

Lucius Annaeus Seneca was a philosopher who happened to be the wealthiest person in the Roman Empire, partly owing to his trading acumen, partly for having served as the tutor of the colorful Emperor Nero, the one who tried to whack his mother a few chapters ago. Seneca subscribed to, and was a prominent expositor of, the philosophical school of Stoicism, which advanced a certain indifference to fate. His work has seduced people like me and most of the friends to whom I introduced his books, because he speaks to us; he walked the walk, and he focused on the practical aspect of Stoicism, down to how to take a trip, how to handle oneself while committing suicide (which he was ordered to do), or, mostly, how to handle adversity and poverty and, even more critically, wealth.

Because Seneca was into practical decision making, he has been described—by academics—as not theoretical or philosophical enough. Yet not a single one of his commentators detected in Seneca the ideas about asymmetry that are central to this book, and to life, the key to robustness and antifragility. Not one. My point is that wisdom in decision making is vastly more important—not just practically, but philosophically—than knowledge.

Other philosophers, when they did things, came to practice from theory. Aristotle, when he attempted to provide practical advice, and a few decades earlier Plato, with his ideas of the state and advice to rulers, particularly the ruler of Syracuse, were either ineffectual or caused debacles. To become a successful philosopher king, it is much better to start as a king than as a philosopher, as illustrated in the following contemporary story.

Modern members of the discipline of decision theory, alas, travel a one-way road from theory to practice. They characteristically gravitate to the most complicated but most inapplicable problems, calling the process "doing science." There is an anecdote about one Professor Triffat (I am changing the name because the story might be apocryphal, though from what I have witnessed, it is very characteristic). He is one of the highly cited academics of the field of decision theory, wrote the main textbook and helped develop something grand and useless called "rational decision making," loaded with grand and useless axioms and shmaxioms, grand and even more useless probabilities and shmobabilities. Triffat, then at Columbia University, was agonizing over the decision to accept an appointment at Harvard—many people who talk about risk can spend their lives without encountering more difficult risk taking than this type of decision. A colleague suggested he use some of his Very Highly Respected and Grandly Honored and Decorated academic techniques with something like "maximum expected utility," as, he told him, "you always write about this." Triffat angrily responded, "Come on, this is serious!"

By contrast, Seneca is nothing but "this is serious." He once survived a shipwreck in which other family members perished, and he wrote letters of practical and less practical advice to his friends. In the end, when he took his own life, he followed excellently and in a dignified way the principles he preached in his writings. So while the Harvard economist is only read by people trying to write papers, who in turn are read by people trying to write papers, and will be (hopefully) swallowed by the inexorable b***t detector of history, Lucius Annaeus, known as Seneca the Younger, is still read by real people two millennia after his passing.

Let us get into his message.

Less Downside from Life

We start with the following conflict. We introduced Seneca as the wealthiest person in the Roman Empire. His fortune was three hundred million denarii (for a sense of its equivalence, at about the same period in time, Judas got thirty denarii, the equivalent of a month's salary, to betray Jesus). Admittedly it is certainly not very convincing to read denigrations of material wealth from a fellow writing the lines on one of his several hundred tables (with ivory legs).

The traditional understanding of Stoicism in the literature is of some *indifference* to fate—among other ideas of harmony with the cosmos that I will skip here. It is about continuously degrading the value of earthly possessions. When Zeno of Kition, the founder of the school of Stoicism, suffered a shipwreck (a lot of shipwrecks in ancient texts), he declared himself lucky to be unburdened so he could now do philosophy. And the key phrase reverberating in Seneca's oeuvre is *nihil perditi*, "I lost nothing," after an adverse event. Stoicism makes you desire the challenge of a calamity. And Stoics look down on luxury: about a fellow who led a lavish life, Seneca wrote: "He is in debt, whether he borrowed from another person or from fortune."*

Stoicism, seen this way, becomes pure robustness—for the attainment of a state of immunity from one's external circumstances, good or bad, and an absence of fragility to decisions made by fate, is robustness. Random events won't affect us either way (we are too strong to lose, and not greedy to enjoy the upside), so we stay in the middle column of the Triad.

What we learn from reading Seneca directly, rather than through the

---

* For those readers who wonder about the difference between Buddhism and Stoicism, I have a simple answer. A Stoic is a Buddhist with attitude, one who says "f*** you" to fate.

commentators, is a different story. Seneca's version of that Stoicism is antifragility from fate. No downside from Lady Fortuna, plenty of upside.

True, Seneca's aim on paper was philosophical, trying to stick to the Stoic tradition as described above: Stoicism was not supposed to be about gains and benefits, so on paper it was not at the level of antifragility, just about a sense of control over one's fate and the reduction of psychological fragility. But there is something that commentators have completely missed. If wealth is so much of a burden, while unnecessary, what's the point of having it? Why did Seneca keep it?

As I said concerning the psychologists who in Chapter 2 ignore post-traumatic growth but focus on post-traumatic harm, intellectuals have this thing against antifragility—for them the world tends to stop at robustness. I don't know what it is, but they don't like it. This made them avoid considering that Seneca wanted the upside from fate, and there is nothing wrong with it.

Let us first learn from the great master how he advocated the mitigation of downside, the standard message of the Stoics—robustness, protection against harm from emotions, how to move away from the first column of the Triad, that sort of thing. Second step, we will show how he truly proposed antifragility. And, third step, we will generalize his trick into a general method of detection of antifragility in Chapters 18 and 19.

Stoicism's Emotional Robustification

Success brings an asymmetry: you now have a lot more to lose than to gain. You are hence fragile. Let us return to the story of Damocles' sword. There is no good news in store, just plenty of bad news in the pipeline. When you become rich, the pain of losing your fortune exceeds the emotional gain of getting additional wealth, so you start living under continuous emotional threat. A rich person becomes trapped by belongings that take control of him, degrading his sleep at night, raising the serum concentration of his stress hormones, diminishing his sense of humor, perhaps even causing hair to grow on the tip of his nose and similar ailments. Seneca fathomed that possessions make us worry about downside, thus acting as a punishment as we depend on them. All downside, no upside. Even more: dependence on circumstances—rather, the emotions that arise from circumstances—induces a form of slavery.

This asymmetry between the effects of good and bad, benefit and harm, had to be familiar to the ancients—I found an earlier exposition in Livy: "Men feel the good less intensely than the bad" (*segnius homines bona quam mala sentiunt*), he wrote half a generation before Seneca. Ancients—mostly thanks to Seneca—stay way ahead of modern psychologists and Triffat-style decision theorists who have developed theories around the notion of "risk (or loss) aversion," the ancients remain deeper, more practical, while transcending vulgar therapy.

Let me rephrase it in modern terms. Take the situation in which you have a lot to lose and little to gain. If an additional quantity of wealth, say, a thousand Phoenician shekels, would not benefit you, but you would feel great harm from the loss of an equivalent amount, you have an asymmetry. And it is not a good asymmetry: you are fragile.

Seneca's practical method to counter such fragility was to go through mental exercises to write off possessions, so when losses occurred he would not feel the sting—a way to wrest one's freedom from circumstances. It is similar to buying an insurance contract against losses. For instance, Seneca often started his journeys with almost the same belongings he would have if he were shipwrecked, which included a blanket to sleep on the ground, as inns were sparse at the time (though I need to qualify, to set things in the context of the day, that he had accompanying him "only one or two slaves").

To show how eminently modern this is, I will next reveal how I've applied this brand of Stoicism to wrest back psychological control of the randomness of life. I have always hated employment and the associated dependence on someone else's arbitrary opinion, particularly when much of what's done inside large corporations violates my sense of ethics. So I have, accordingly, except for eight years, been self-employed. But, before that, for my last job, I wrote my resignation letter before starting the new position, locked it up in a drawer, and felt free while I was there. Likewise, when I was a trader, a profession rife with a high dose of randomness, with continuous psychological harm that drills deep into one's soul, I would go through the mental exercise of assuming every morning that the worst possible thing had actually happened—the rest of the day would be a bonus. Actually the method of mentally adjusting "to the worst" had advantages way beyond the therapeutic, as it made me take a certain class of risks for which the worst case is clear and unambiguous, with limited and known downside. It is hard to stick to a good discipline of mental write-off when things are going well, yet that's when one needs the discipline the most. Moreover, once in a while, I travel, Seneca-style, in uncomfortable circumstances (though unlike him I am not accompanied by "one or two" slaves).

An intelligent life is all about such emotional positioning to eliminate the sting of harm, which as we saw is done by mentally writing off belongings so one does not feel any pain from losses. The volatility of the world no longer affects you negatively.

The Domestication of Emotions

Seen this way, Stoicism is about the domestication, not necessarily the elimination, of emotions. It is not about turning humans into vegetables. My idea of the modern Stoic sage is *someone who transforms fear into prudence, pain into information, mistakes into initiation, and desire into undertaking.*

Seneca proposes a complete training program to handle life and use emotions properly—thanks to small but effective tricks. One trick, for instance, that a Roman Stoic would use to separate anger from rightful action and avoid committing harm he would regret later would be to wait at least a day before beating up a servant who committed a violation. We moderns might not see this as particularly righteous, but just compare it to the otherwise thoughtful Emperor Hadrian's act of stabbing a slave in the eye during an episode of uncontrolled anger. When Hadrian's anger abated, and he felt the grip of remorse, the damage was irreversible.

Seneca also provides us a catalogue of social deeds: invest in good actions. Things can be taken away from us—not good deeds and acts of virtue.

How to Become the Master

So far, that story is well known, and we have learned to move from the left of the Triad (fragile) to the center (robust). But Seneca went beyond.

He said that wealth is the slave of the wise man and master of the fool. Thus he broke a bit with the purported Stoic habit: *he kept the upside.* In my opinion, if previous Stoics claimed to prefer poverty to wealth, we need to be suspicious of their attitude, as it may be just all talk. Since most were poor, they might have fit a narrative to the circumstances (we will see with the story of Thales of Miletus the notion of sour grapes—cognitive games to make yourself believe that the grapes that you can't reach taste sour). Seneca was all deeds, and we cannot ignore the fact that he kept the wealth. It is central that he showed his preference of wealth *without harm from wealth* to poverty.

Seneca even outlined his strategy in *De beneficiis,* explicitly calling it a cost-benefit analysis by using the word "bookkeeping": "The bookkeeping of benefits is simple: it is all expenditure; if any one returns it, that is clear *gain* (my emphasis); if he does not return it, it is not lost, I gave it for the sake of giving." Moral bookkeeping, but bookkeeping nevertheless.

So he played a trick on fate: kept the good and ditched the bad; cut the downside and kept the upside. Self-servingly, that is, by eliminating the harm from fate and un-philosophically keeping the upside. This cost-benefit analysis is not quite Stoicism in the way people understand the meaning of Stoicism (people who study Stoicism seem to want Seneca and other Stoics to think like those who study Stoicism). There is an upside-downside asymmetry.

That's antifragility in its purest form.*

The Foundational Asymmetry

Let us put together Seneca's asymmetry in a single rule.

The concept I used earlier is *more to lose* from adversity. If you have more to lose than to benefit from events of fate, there is an asymmetry, and not a good one. And such asymmetry is universal. Let us see how it brings us to fragility.

Consider the package in Chapter 1: it does not like to be shaken, and it hates the members of the disorder family—hence it is fragile (very fragile because it has absolutely nothing to gain, hence it is very asymmetric). The antifragile package has more to gain than to lose from being shaken. Simple test: if I have "nothing to lose" then it is all gain and I am antifragile.

The entire Table 1 with triads across fields and domains can be explained in these terms. Everything.

To see why asymmetric payoffs like volatility, just consider that if

---

* And for those who believe that Zeno, the founder of Stoicism, was completely against material wealth, I have some news: I accidentally found a mention of his activities in maritime financing, where he was an involved investor, not exactly an activity for the anti-wealth utopist.

you have less to lose than to gain, more upside than downside, then you like volatility (it will, on balance, bring benefits), and you are also anti-fragile.

So the job falling upon this author is to make the link between the four elements as follows with the foundational asymmetry.

Fragility implies more to lose than to gain, equals more downside than upside, equals (unfavorable) asymmetry

and

Antifragility implies more to gain than to lose, equals more up-side than downside, equals (favorable) asymmetry

You are antifragile for a source of volatility if potential gains exceed potential losses (and vice versa).

Further, if you have more upside than downside, then you may be harmed by lack of volatility and stressors.

Now, how do we put this idea—reduction of downside, increase in upside—into practice? By the method of the barbell in the next chapter.

CHAPTER 11

Never Marry the Rock Star

A precise protocol on how and with whom to cheat on one's husband—Introduction to barbell strategies—Transforming diplomats into writers, and vice versa

———

The barbell (or bimodal) strategy is a way to achieve antifragility and move to the right side of the Triad. Monogamous birds put it into practice by cheating with the local rock star and writers do better by having as a day job a sinecure devoid of writing activities.

ON THE IRREVERSIBILITY OF BROKEN PACKAGES

The first step toward antifragility consists in first decreasing downside, rather than increasing upside; that is, by lowering exposure to negative Black Swans and letting natural antifragility work by itself.

Mitigating fragility is not an option but a requirement. It may sound obvious but the point seems to be missed. For fragility is very punishing, like a terminal disease. A package doesn't break under adverse conditions, then manage to fix itself when proper conditions are restored. Fragility has a ratchetlike property, the irreversibility of damage. What matters is the route taken, the order of events, not just the destination—what scientists call a *path-dependent* property. Path dependence can be illustrated as follows: your experience in getting a kidney stone operation first and anesthesia later is different from having the procedures done in the opposite sequence. Or your enjoyment of a meal with coffee and dessert first and tomato soup last would not be the same as the inverse order. The consideration of path dependence makes our approach simple: it is easy to identify the fragile and put it in the left column of the Triad, regardless of upside potential—since the broken will tend to stay permanently broken.

This fragility that comes from path dependence is often ignored by businessmen who, trained in static thinking, tend to believe that generating profits is their principal mission, with survival and risk control something to perhaps consider—they miss the strong logical precedence of survival over success. To make profits and buy a BMW, it would be a good idea to, first, survive.

Notions such as speed and growth—anything related to movement—are empty and meaningless when presented without accounting for fragility. Consider that someone driving two hundred and fifty miles per hour in New York City is quite certain to never get anywhere—the effective speed will be exactly zero miles per hour. While it is obvious that one needs to focus on the effective, not the nominal, speed, something in the sociopolitical discourse masks such an elementary point.

Under path dependence, one can no longer separate growth in the economy from risks of recession, financial returns from risks of terminal losses, and "efficiency" from danger of accident. The notion of efficiency becomes quite meaningless on its own. If a gambler has a risk of terminal blowup (losing back everything), the "potential returns" of his strategy are totally inconsequential. A few years ago, a university fellow boasted to me that their endowment fund was earning 20 percent or so, not realizing that these returns were associated with fragilities that would easily turn into catastrophic losses—sure enough, a bad year wiped out all these returns and endangered the university.

In other words, if something is fragile, its risk of breaking makes anything you do to improve it or make it "efficient" inconsequential unless you first reduce that risk of breaking. As Publilius Syrus wrote, nothing can be done both hastily and safely—almost nothing.

As to growth in GDP (gross domestic product), it can be obtained very easily by loading future generations with debt—and the future economy may collapse upon the need to repay such debt. GDP growth, like cholesterol, seems to be a Procrustean bed reduction that has been used to game systems. So just as, for a plane that has a high risk of crashing, the notion of "speed" is irrelevant, since we know it may not get to its destination, economic growth with fragilities is not to be called growth, something that has not yet been understood by governments. Indeed, growth was very modest, less than 1 percent per head, throughout the golden years surrounding the Industrial Revolution, the period that propelled Europe into domination. But as low as it was, it was robust growth—unlike the current fools' race of states shooting for growth like teenage drivers infatuated with speed.

SENECA'S BARBELL

This brings us to the solution in the form of a barbell—about all solutions to uncertainty are in the form of barbells.

What do we mean by barbell? The barbell (a bar with weights on both ends that weight lifters use) is meant to illustrate the idea of a combination of extremes kept separate, with avoidance of the middle. In our context it is not necessarily symmetric: it is just composed of two extremes, with nothing in the center. One can also call it, more technically, a bimodal strategy, as it has two distinct modes rather than a single, central one.

I initially used the image of the barbell to describe a dual attitude of playing it safe in some areas (robust to negative Black Swans) and taking a lot of small risks in others (open to positive Black Swans), hence achieving antifragility. That is extreme risk aversion on one side and extreme risk loving on the other, rather than just the "medium" or the beastly "moderate" risk attitude that in fact is a sucker game (because medium risks can be subjected to huge measurement errors). But the barbell also results, because of its construction, in the reduction of downside risk—the elimination of the risk of ruin.

Let us use an example from vulgar finance, where it is easiest to explain, but misunderstood the most. If you put 90 percent of your funds in boring cash (assuming you are protected from inflation) or something called a "numeraire repository of value," and 10 percent in very risky, maximally risky, securities, you cannot possibly lose more than 10 percent, while you are exposed to massive upside. Someone with 100 percent in so-called "medium" risk securities has a risk of total ruin from the miscomputation of risks. This barbell technique remedies the problem that risks of rare events are incomputable and fragile to estimation error; here the financial barbell has a maximum known loss.

For antifragility is the combination *aggressiveness plus paranoia*—clip your downside, protect yourself from extreme harm, and let the upside, the positive Black Swans, take care of itself. We saw Seneca's asymmetry: more upside than downside can come simply from the reduction of extreme downside (emotional harm) rather than improving things in the middle.

A barbell can be any dual strategy composed of extremes, without the corruption of the middle—somehow they all result in favorable asymmetries.

Again, to see the difference between barbells and nonbarbells, consider that restaurants present the main course, say, grass-fed minute steak cooked rare and salad (with Malbec wine), then, separately, after you are done with the meat, bring you the goat cheese cake (with Muscat wine). Restaurants do not take your order, then cut the cake and the steak in small pieces and mix the whole thing together with those machines that produce a lot of noise. Activities "in the middle" are like such mashing. Recall Nero in Chapter 9 hanging around with janitors and scholars, rarely with middlebrows.

In risky matters, instead of having all members of the staff on an airplane be "cautiously optimistic," or something in the middle, I prefer the flight attendants to be maximally optimistic and the pilot to be maximally pessimistic or, better, paranoid.

The Accountant and the Rock Star

Biological systems are replete with barbell strategies. Take the following mating approach, which we call the 90 percent accountant, 10 percent rock star. (I am just reporting, not condoning.) Females in the animal kingdom, in some monogamous species (which include humans), tend to marry the equivalent of the accountant, or, even more colorless, the economist, someone stable who can provide, and once in a while they cheat with the aggressive alpha, the rock star, as part of a dual strategy. They limit their downside while using extrapair copulation to get the genetic upside, or some great fun, or both. Even the timing of the cheating seems nonrandom, as it corresponds to periods with high likelihood of pregnancy. We see evidence of such a strategy with the so-called monogamous birds: they enjoy cheating, with more than a tenth of the broods coming from males other than the putative father. The phenomenon is real, but the theories around it vary. Evolutionary theorists claim that females want both economic-social stability and good genes for their children. Both cannot be always obtained from someone in the middle with all these virtues (though good gene providers, those alpha males aren't likely to be stable, and vice versa). Why not have the pie and eat it too? Stable life and good genes. But an alternative theory may be that they just want to have pleasure—or stable life and good fun. *

Also recall from Chapter 2 that overcompensation, to work, requires some harm and stressors as tools of discovery. It means letting children play a little bit, not much more than a little bit, with fire and learn from injuries, for the sake of their own future safety.

It also means letting people experience some, not too much, stress, to wake them up a bit. But, at the same time, they need to be protected from high danger—ignore small dangers, invest your energy in protecting them from consequential harm. And only consequential harm. This can visibly be translated into social policy, health care, and many more matters.

One finds similar ideas in ancestral lore: it is explained in a Yiddish proverb that says "Provide for the worst; the best can take care of itself." This may sound like a platitude, but it is not: just observe how people tend to provide for the best and hope that the worst will take care of itself. We have ample evidence that people are averse to small losses, but not so much toward very large Black Swan risks (which they underestimate), since they tend to insure for small probable losses, but not large infrequent ones. Exactly backwards.

Away from the Golden Middle

Now let us continue our exploration of barbells. There are so many fields in which the middle is no "golden middle" and where the bimodal strategy (maximally safe plus maximally speculative) applies.

Take literature, that most uncompromising, most speculative, most demanding, and riskiest of all careers. There is a tradition with French and other European literary writers to look for a sinecure, say, the

---

* There is evidence of such a barbell strategy but no clarity about the theory behind it—evolutionary theorists enjoy narratives but I prefer evidence. We are not sure if the strategy of extrapair copulation in the animal domain actually enhances fitness. So the barbell—accountant plus cheating—while it exists, might not be aiming at the improvement of the species; it can be just be for "fun" at low risk.

anxiety-free profession of civil servant, with few intellectual demands and high job security, the kind of low-risk job that ceases to exist when you leave the office, then spend their spare time writing, free to write whatever they want, under their own standards. There is a shockingly small number of academics among French authors. American writers, on the other hand, tend to become members of the media or academics, which makes them prisoners of a system and corrupts their writing, and, in the case of research academics, makes them live under continuous anxiety, pressures, and indeed, severe bastardization of the soul. Every line you write under someone else's standards, like prostitution, kills a corresponding segment deep inside. On the other hand, sinecure-cum-writing is a quite soothing model, next best to having financial independence, or perhaps even better than financial independence. For instance, the great French poets Paul Claudel and Saint-John Perse and the novelist Stendhal were diplomats; a large segment of English writers were civil servants (Trollope was a post office worker); Kafka was employed by an insurance company. Best of all, Spinoza worked as a lens maker, which left his philosophy completely immune to any form of academic corruption. As a teenager, I thought that the natural way to have a real literary or philosophical career was to enter the lazy, pleasant, and undemanding profession of diplomat, like many members of my family. There was an Ottoman tradition of using Orthodox Christians as emissaries and ambassadors, even ministers of foreign affairs, which was retained by the states of the Levant (my grandfather and great-grandfather had been ministers of foreign affairs). Except that I worried about the wind turning against the Christian minority, and was proved right. But I became a trader and did my writing on my own time, and, as the reader can see, on my own terms. The barbell businessman-scholar situation was ideal; after three or four in the afternoon, when I left the office, my day job ceased to exist until the next day and I was completely free to pursue what I found most valuable and interesting. When I tried to become an academic I felt like a prisoner, forced to follow others' less rigorous, self-promotional programs.

And professions can be serial: something very safe, then something speculative. A friend of mine built himself a very secure profession as a book editor, in which he was known to be very good. Then, after a decade or so, he left completely for something speculative and highly risky. This is a true barbell in every sense of the word: he can fall back on his previous profession should the speculation fail, or fail to bring the expected satisfaction. This is what Seneca elected to do: he initially had a very active, adventurous life, followed by a philosophical withdrawal to write and meditate, rather than a "middle" combination of both. Many of the "doers" turned "thinkers" like Montaigne have done a serial barbell: pure action, then pure reflection.

Or, if I have to work, I find it preferable (and less painful) to work intensely for very short hours, then do nothing for the rest of the time (assuming doing nothing is really doing nothing), until I recover completely and look forward to a repetition, rather than being subjected to the tedium of Japanese style low-intensity interminable office hours with sleep deprivation. Main course and dessert are separate.

Indeed, Georges Simenon, one of the most prolific writers of the twentieth century, only wrote sixty days a year, with three hundred days spent "doing nothing." He published more than two hundred novels.

The Domestication of Uncertainty

We will see many barbells in the rest of this book that share exactly the same asymmetry and somehow, when it comes to risk, produce the same type of protection and help in the harnessing of antifragility. They all look remarkably similar.

Let us take a peek at a few domains. With personal risks, you can easily barbell yourself by removing the chances of ruin in any area. I am personally completely paranoid about certain risks, then very aggressive with others. The rules are: no smoking, no sugar (particularly fructose), no motorcycles, no bicycles in town or more generally outside a traffic-free area such as the Sahara desert, no mixing with the Eastern European mafias, and no getting on a plane not flown by a professional pilot (unless there is a co-pilot). Outside of these I can take all manner of professional and personal risks, particularly those in which there is no risk of terminal injury.

In social policy, it consists in protecting the very weak and letting the strong do their job, rather than helping the middle class to consolidate its privileges, thus blocking evolution and bringing all manner of economic problems that tend to hurt the poor the most.

Before the United Kingdom became a bureaucratic state, it was barbelled into adventurers (both economically and physically) and an aristocracy. The aristocracy didn't really have a major role except to help keep some sense of caution while the adventurers roamed the planet in search of trading opportunities, or stayed home and tinkered with machinery. Now the City of London is composed of bourgeois bohemian bonus earners.

My writing approach is as follows: on one hand a literary essay that can be grasped by anyone and on the other technical papers, nothing in between—such as interviews with journalists or newspaper articles or op-ed pieces, outside of the requirements of publishers.

The reader may remember the exercise regimen of Chapter 2, which consists in going for the maximum weight one can lift, then nothing, compared to other alternatives that entail less intense but very long hours in the gym. This, supplemented with effortless long walks, constitutes an exercise barbell.

More barbells. Do crazy things (break furniture once in a while), like the Greeks during the later stages of a drinking symposium, and stay "rational" in larger decisions. Trashy gossip magazines and classics or sophisticated works; never middlebrow stuff. Talk to either undergraduate students, cab drivers, and gardeners or the highest caliber scholars; never to middling-but-career-conscious academics. If you dislike someone, leave him alone or eliminate him; don't attack him verbally.*

So take for now that a barbell strategy with respect to randomness results in achieving antifragility thanks to the mitigation of fragility, the clipping of downside risks of harm—reduced pain from adverse events, while keeping the benefits of potential gains.

To return to finance, the barbell does not need to be in the form of investment in inflation-protected cash and the rest in speculative securities. Anything that removes the risk of ruin will get us to such a barbell. The legendary investor Ray Dalio has a rule for someone making speculative bets: "Make sure that the probability of the unacceptable (i.e., the risk of ruin) is nil." Such a rule gets one straight to the barbell.†

---

* In finance, I stood in 2008 for banks to be nationalized rather than bailed out, and other forms of speculation not entailing taxpayers left free. Nobody was getting my barbell idea—some hated the libertarian aspect, others hated the nationalization part. Why? Because the halfway—here, the regulation of both—doesn't work, as it can be gamed by a good lawyer. Hedge funds need to be unregulated and banks nationalized, as a barbell, rather than the horror we now have.

† Domain dependence again. People find insuring their house a necessity, not something to be judged against a financial strategy, but when it comes to their portfolios, because of the way things are framed in the press, they don't look at them in the same way. They think that my barbell idea is a strategy that needs to be examined for its *potential return* as an investment. That's not the point. The barbell is simply an idea of insurance of survival; it is a necessity, not an option.

Another idea from Rory Sutherland: the U.K. guidelines for patients with mild problems coming from alcohol are to reduce the daily consumption to under a certain number of grams of alcohol per day. But the optimal policy is to avoid alcohol three times a week (hence give the liver a lengthy vacation) then drink liberally the remaining four. The mathematics behind this and other barbell ideas are outlined with the later discussion of Jensen's inequality.

Most items on the right of the Triad have a barbell component, necessary, but not sufficient.

So just as Stoicism is the domestication, not the elimination, of emotions, so is the barbell a domestication, not the elimination, of uncertainty.

Optionality, Technology, and the Intelligence of Antifragility

———

Now we get into innovation, the concept of options and optionality. How to enter the impenetrable and completely dominate it, conquer it.

DO YOU REALLY KNOW WHERE YOU ARE GOING?

Summa Theologiae by Saint Thomas Aquinas is the kind of book that no longer exists, the book-as-monument, a *summa* being the comprehensive treatment of a given discipline, while freeing it from the structure the authorities had given it before—the antitextbook. In this case its subject matter is theology, meaning everything philosophical, and it comments on every body of knowledge as it relates to his arguments. And it reflects—and largely directs—the thought of the Middle Ages.

Quite a departure from the book with a simple closed-end subject matter.

The erudite mind's denigration of antifragility is best seen in a sentence that dominates the *Summa,* being repeated in many places, one variant of which is as follows: "An agent does not move except out of intention for an end," *agen autem non movet nisi ex intentione finis.* In other words, agents are supposed to know where they are going, a teleological argument (from *telos,* "based on the end") that originates with Aristotle. Everyone, including the Stoics, but excluding the skeptics, fell for such teleological arguments intellectually, but certainly not in action. Incidentally, it is not Aristotle whom Aquinas is quoting—he calls him the Philosopher—but the Arab synthesizer of Aristotle's thinking, Ibn Rushd, also known as Averroes, whom Aquinas calls the Commentator. And the Commentator has caused a great deal of damage. For Western thought is vastly more Arabian than is recognized, while post-Medieval Arabs have managed to escape medieval rationalism.

This entire heritage of thinking, grounded in the sentence "An agent does not move except out of intention for an end," is where the most pervasive human error lies, compounded by two or more centuries of the illusion of unconditional scientific understanding. This error is also the most fragilizing one.

The Teleological Fallacy

So let us call here the teleological fallacy the illusion that you know exactly where you are going, and that you knew exactly where you were going in the past, and that others have succeeded in the past by knowing where they were going.

The rational flâneur is someone who, unlike a tourist, makes a decision at every step to revise his schedule, so he can imbibe things based on new information, what Nero was trying to practice in his travels, often guided by his sense of smell. The flâneur is not a prisoner of a plan. Tourism, actual or figurative, is imbued with the teleological illusion; it assumes completeness of vision and gets one locked into a hard-to-revise program, while the flâneur continuously—and, what is crucial, rationally—modifies his targets as he acquires information.

Now a warning: the opportunism of the flâneur is great in life and business—but not in personal life and matters that involve others. The opposite of opportunism in human relations is loyalty, a noble sentiment—but one that needs to be invested in the right places, that is, in human relations and moral commitments.

The error of thinking you know exactly where you are going and assuming that you know *today* what your preferences will be *tomorrow* has an associated one. It is the illusion of thinking that *others,* too, know where they are going, and that they would tell you what they want if you just asked them.

Never ask people what they want, or where they want to go, or where they think they should go, or, worse, what they think they will desire tomorrow. The strength of the computer entrepreneur Steve Jobs was precisely in distrusting market research and focus groups—those based on asking people what they want—and following his own imagination. His modus was that people don't know what they want until you provide them with it.

This ability to switch from a course of action is an *option* to change. Options—and optionality, the character of the option—are the topic of Book IV. Optionality will take us many places, but at the core, an option is what makes you antifragile and allows you to benefit from the positive side of uncertainty, without a corresponding serious harm from the negative side.

America's Principal Asset

And it is optionality that makes things work and grow—but it takes a certain type of person for that. Many people keep deploring the low level of formal education in the United States (as defined by, say, math grades). Yet these people fail to realize that the *new* comes from here and gets imitated elsewhere. And it is not thanks to universities, which obviously claim a lot more credit than their accomplishments warrant.

Like Britain in the Industrial Revolution, America's asset is, simply, risk taking and the use of optionality, this remarkable ability to engage in rational forms of trial and error, with no comparative shame in failing, starting again, and repeating failure. In modern Japan, by contrast, shame comes with failure, which causes people to hide risks under the rug, financial or nuclear, making small benefits while sitting on dynamite, an attitude that strangely contrasts with their traditional respect for fallen heroes and the so-called nobility of failure.

Book IV will take this idea to its natural conclusion and will show evidence (ranging from medieval architecture to medicine, engineering, and innovation) that, perhaps, our greatest asset is the one we distrust the most: the built-in antifragility of certain risk-taking systems.

CHAPTER 12

Thales' Sweet Grapes

Where we discuss the idea of doing instead of walking the Great Walk—The idea of a free option—Can a philosopher be called nouveau riche?

———

An anecdote appears in Aristotle's *Politics* concerning the pre-Socratic philosopher and mathematician Thales of Miletus. This story, barely covering half a page, expresses both antifragility and its denigration and introduces us to optionality. The remarkable aspect of this story is that Aristotle, arguably the most influential thinker of all time, got the central point of his own anecdote exactly backward. So did his followers, particularly after the Enlightenment and the scientific revolution. I am not saying this to denigrate the great Aristotle, but to show that intelligence makes you discount antifragility and ignore the power of optionality.

Thales was a philosopher, a Greek-speaking Ionian of Phoenician stock from the coastal town of Miletus in Asia Minor, and like *some* philosophers, he enjoyed what he was doing. Miletus was a trading post and had the mercantile spirit usually attributed to Phoenician settlements. But Thales, as a philosopher, was characteristically impecunious. He got tired of his buddies with more transactional lives hinting at him that "those who can, do, and others philosophize." He performed the following prowess: he put a down payment on the seasonal use of every olive press in the vicinity of Miletus and Chios, which he got at low rent.

The harvest turned out to be extremely bountiful and there was demand for olive presses, so he released the owners of olive presses on his own terms, building a substantial fortune in the process. Then he went back to philosophizing.

What he collected was large, perhaps not enough to make him massively wealthy, but enough to make the point—to others but also, I suspect, to himself—that he talked the talk and was truly above, not below, wealth. This kind of sum I've called in my vernacular "f*** you money"—a sum large enough to get most, if not all, of the advantages of wealth (the most important one being independence and the ability to only occupy your mind with matters that interest you) but not its side effects, such as having to attend a black-tie charity event and being forced to listen to a polite exposition of the details of a marble-rich house renovation. The worst side effect of wealth is the social associations it forces on its victims, as people with big houses tend to end up socializing with other people with big houses. Beyond a certain level of opulence and independence, gents tend to be less and less personable and their conversation less and less interesting.

The story of Thales has many morals, all of them linked to asymmetry (and the construction of an antifragile payoff). The central one is related to the following account by Aristotle: *"But from his knowledge of astronomy he had observed while it was still winter that there was going to be a large crop of olives . . ."* So for Aristotle, clearly, the stated reason was Thales' superior knowledge.

Superior knowledge?

Thales put himself in a position to take advantage of his *lack* of knowledge—and the secret property of the asymmetry. The key to our message about this upside-downside asymmetry is that he did not need to understand too much the messages from the stars.

Simply, he had a contract that is the archetype of what an asymmetry is, perhaps the only explicit asymmetry you can find in its purest form. It is an option, "the right but not the obligation" for the buyer and, of course, "the obligation but not the right" for the other party, called the seller. Thales had the right—but not the obligation—to use the olive presses in case there would be a surge in demand; the other party had the obligation, not the right. Thales paid a small price for that privilege, with a limited loss and large possible outcome. That was the very first option on record.

The option is an agent of antifragility.

OPTION AND ASYMMETRY

The olive press episode took place about six hundred years before Seneca's writings on his tables with ivory legs, and three hundred years before Aristotle.

The formula in Chapter 10 was: *antifragility* equals *more to gain than to lose* equals *more upside than downside* equals *asymmetry (favorable)* equals *likes volatility*. And if you make more when you are right than you are hurt when you are wrong, then you will benefit, in the long run, from volatility (and the reverse). You are only harmed if you repeatedly pay too much for the option. But in this case Thales patently got a good deal—and we will see in the rest of Book IV that we don't pay for the options given to us by nature and technological innovation. Financial options may be expensive because people know they are options and *someone* is selling them and charging a price—but most interesting options are free, or at the worst, cheap.

Centrally, we just don't need to *know* what's going on when we buy cheaply—when we have the asymmetry working for us. But this property goes beyond buying cheaply: we do not need to understand things when we have some edge. And the edge from optionality is in the larger payoff when you are right, which makes it unnecessary to be right too often.

The Options of Sweet Grapes

The option I am talking about is no different from what we call options in daily life—the vacation resort with the most options is more likely to provide you with the activity that satisfies your tastes, and the one with the narrowest choices is likely to fail. So you need *less information,* that is, less knowledge, about the resort with broader options.

There are other hidden options in our story of Thales. Financial independence, when used intelligently, can make you robust; it gives you options and allows you to make the right choices. Freedom is the ultimate option.

Further, you will never get to know yourself—your real preferences—unless you face options and choices. Recall that the volatility of life helps provide information to us about others, but also about ourselves. Plenty of people are poor against their initial wish and only become robust by spinning a story that it was their choice to be poor—as if they had the option. Some are genuine; many don't really have the option—they constructed it. Sour grapes—as in Aesop's fable—is when someone convinces himself that the grapes he cannot reach are sour. The essayist Michel de Montaigne sees the Thales episode as a story of immunity to sour grapes: you need to know whether you *do not like* the pursuit of money and wealth because you genuinely do not like it, or because you are rationalizing your inability to be successful at it with the argument that wealth is not a good thing because it is bad for one's digestive system or disturbing for one's sleep or other such arguments. So the episode enlightened Thales about his own choices in life—how genuine his pursuit of philosophy was. He had other *options*. And, it is worth repeating, options, any options, by allowing you more upside than downside, are vectors of antifragility.*

Thales, by funding his own philosophy, became his own Maecenas, perhaps the highest rank one can attain: being both independent and intellectually productive. He now had even more *options*. He did not have to tell others—those funding him—where he was going, because he himself perhaps didn't even know where he was heading. Thanks to the power of options, he didn't have to.

The next few vignettes will help us go deeper into the notion of *optionality*—the property of option-like payoffs and option-like situations.

Saturday Evening in London

It is Saturday afternoon in London. I am coping with a major source of stress: where to go tonight. I am fond of the brand of the unexpected one finds at parties (going to parties has optionality, perhaps the best advice for someone who wants to benefit from uncertainty with low downside). My fear of eating alone in a restaurant while rereading the same passage of Cicero's *Tusculan Discussions* that, thanks to its pocket-fitting size, I have been carrying for a decade (and reading about three and a half pages per year) was alleviated by a telephone call. Someone, not a close friend, upon hearing that I was in town, invited me to a gathering in

---

* I suppose that the main benefit of being rich (over just being independent) is to be able to despise rich people (a good concentration of whom you find in glitzy ski resorts) without any sour grapes. It is even sweeter when these farts don't know that you are richer than they are.

Kensington, but somehow did not ask me to commit, with "drop by if you want." Going to the party is better than eating alone with Cicero's *Tusculan Discussions*, but these are not very interesting people (many are involved in the City, and people employed in financial institutions are rarely interesting and even more rarely likable) and I know I can do better, but I am not certain to be able to do so. So I can call around: if I can do better than the Kensington party, with, say, a dinner with any of my real friends, I would do that. Otherwise I would take a black taxi to Kensington. I have an *option,* not an obligation. It came at no cost since I did not even solicit it. So I have a small, nay, nonexistent, downside, a big upside.

This is a free option because there is no real cost to the privilege.

Your Rent

Second example: assume you are the official tenant of a rent-controlled apartment in New York City, with, of course, wall-to-wall bookshelves. You have the *option* of staying in it as long as you wish, but no obligation to do so. Should you decide to move to Ulan Bator, Mongolia, and start a new life there, you can simply notify the landlord a certain number of days in advance, and thank you goodbye. Otherwise, the landlord is obligated to let you live there somewhat permanently, at a predictable rent. Should rents in town increase enormously, and real estate experience a bubble-like explosion, you are largely protected. On the other hand, should rents collapse, you can easily switch apartments and reduce your monthly payments—or even buy a new apartment and get a mortgage with lower monthly payments.

So consider the asymmetry. You benefit from lower rents, but are not hurt by higher ones. How? Because here again, you have an option, not an obligation. In a way, uncertainty increases the worth of such privilege. Should you face a high degree of uncertainty about future outcomes, with possible huge decreases in real estate value, or huge possible increases in them, your option would become more valuable. The more uncertainty, the more valuable the option.

Again, this is an embedded option, hidden as there is no cost to the privilege.

Asymmetry

Let us examine once again the asymmetry of Thales—along with that of any option. In Figure 5, the horizontal axis represents the rent, the vertical axis the corresponding profits in thekels. Figure 5 shows the asymmetry: in this situation, the payoff is larger one way (if you are right, you "earn big time") than the other (if you are wrong, you "lose small").

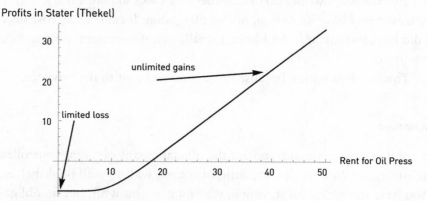

FIGURE 5. Thales' antifragility. He pays little to get a huge potential. We can see the asymmetry between upside and downside.

The vertical axis in Figure 5 represents a function of the rent for oil presses (the payoff from the option). All the reader needs to note from the picture is the nonlinearity (that is, the asymmetry, with more upside than downside; asymmetry is a form of nonlinearity).

Things That Like Dispersion

One property of the option: it does not care about the average outcome, only the favorable ones (since the downside doesn't count beyond a certain point). Authors, artists, and even philosophers are much better off having a very small number of fanatics behind them than a large number of people who appreciate their work. The number of persons who dislike the work don't count—there is no such thing as the *opposite* of buying your book, or the equivalent of losing points in a soccer game, and this absence of negative domain for book sales provides the author with a measure of optionality.

Further, it helps when supporters are both enthusiastic and influential. Wittgenstein, for instance, was largely considered a lunatic, a strange bird, or just a b***t operator by those whose opinion didn't count (he had almost no publications to his name). But he had a small number of cultlike followers, and some, such as Bertrand Russell and J. M. Keynes, were massively influential.

Beyond books, consider this simple heuristic: your work and ideas, whether in politics, the arts, or other domains, are antifragile if, instead of having one hundred percent of the people finding your mission acceptable or mildly commendable, you are better off having a high percentage of people disliking you and your message (even intensely), combined with a low percentage of extremely loyal and enthusiastic supporters. Options like dispersion of outcomes and don't care about the average too much.

Another business that does not care about the average but rather the dispersion around the average is the luxury goods industry—jewelry, watches, art, expensive apartments in fancy locations, expensive collector wines, gourmet farm-raised probiotic dog food, etc. Such businesses only care about the pool of funds available to the very rich. If the population in the Western world had an average income of fifty thousand dollars, with no inequality at all, luxury goods sellers would not survive. But if the average stays the same but with a high degree of inequality, with some incomes higher than two million dollars, and potentially some incomes higher than ten million, then the business has plenty of customers—even if such high incomes are offset by masses of people with lower incomes. The "tails" of the distribution on the higher end of the income brackets, the extreme, are much more determined by changes in inequality than changes in the average. It gains from dispersion, hence is antifragile. This explains the bubble in real estate prices in Central London, determined by inequality in Russia and the Arabian Gulf and totally independent of the real estate dynamics in Britain. Some apartments, those for the very rich, sell for twenty times the average per square foot of a building a few blocks away.

Harvard's former president Larry Summers got in trouble (clumsily) explaining a version of the point and lost his job in the aftermath of the uproar. He was trying to say that males and females have equal intelligence, but the male population has more variations and dispersion (hence volatility), with more highly unintelligent men, and more highly intelligent ones. For Summers, this explained why men were overrepresented in the scientific and intellectual community (and also why men were overrepresented in jails or failures). The number of successful scientists depends on the "tails," the extremes, rather than the average. Just as an option does not care about the adverse outcomes, or an author does not care about the haters.

No one at present dares to state the obvious: growth in society may not come from raising the average the Asian way, but from increasing the number of people in the "tails," that small, very small number of risk takers crazy enough to have ideas of their own, those endowed with that very rare ability called imagination, that rarer quality called courage, and who make things happen.

THE THALESIAN AND THE ARISTOTELIAN

Now some philosophy. As we saw with the exposition of the Black Swan problem earlier in Chapter 8, the decision maker focuses on the payoff, the consequence of the actions (hence includes asymmetries and nonlinear effects). The Aristotelian focuses on being right and wrong—in other words, raw logic. They intersect less often than you think.

Aristotle made the mistake of thinking that knowledge about the event (future crop, or price of the rent for oil presses, what we showed on the horizontal axis) and making profits out of it (vertical) are the same thing. And here, because of asymmetry, the two are not, as is obvious in the graph. As Fat Tony will assert in Chapter 14, "they are not the same thing" (pronounced "ting").

How to Be Stupid

If you "have optionality," you don't have much need for what is commonly called intelligence, knowledge, insight, skills, and these complicated things that take place in our brain cells. For you don't have to be right that often. All you need is the wisdom to *not do* unintelligent things to hurt yourself (some acts of omission) and recognize favorable outcomes when they occur. (The key is that your assessment doesn't need to be made beforehand, only after the outcome.)

This property allowing us to be stupid, or, alternatively, allowing us to get more results than the knowledge may warrant, I will call the "philosopher's stone" for now, or "convexity bias," the result of a mathematical property called Jensen's inequality. The mechanics will be explained later, in Book V when we wax technical, but take for now that evolution can produce astonishingly sophisticated objects without intelligence, simply thanks to a combination of optionality and some type of a selection filter, plus some randomness, as we see next.

Nature and Options

The great French biologist François Jacob introduced into science the notion of options (or option-like characteristics) in natural systems, thanks to trial and error, under a variant called *bricolage* in French. Bricolage is a form of trial and error close to *tweaking*, trying to make do with what you've got by recycling pieces that would be otherwise wasted.

Jacob argued that even within the womb, nature knows how to select: about half of all embryos undergo a spontaneous abortion—easier to do so than design the perfect baby by blueprint. Nature simply keeps what it likes if it meets its standards or does a California-style "fail early"—it has an option and uses it. Nature understands optionality effects vastly better than humans, and certainly better than Aristotle.

Nature is all about the exploitation of optionality; it illustrates how optionality is a substitute for intelligence.*

Let us call trial and error *tinkering* when it presents small errors and large gains. Convexity, a more precise description of such positive asymmetry, will be explained in a bit of depth in Chapter 18.†

The graph in Figure 7 best illustrates the idea present in California, and voiced by Steve Jobs at a famous speech: "Stay hungry, stay foolish." He probably meant "Be crazy but retain the rationality of choosing the upper bound when you see it." Any trial and error can be seen as the expression of an option, so long as one is capable of identifying a favorable result and exploiting it, as we see next.

---

* We will use nature as a model to show how its operational outperformance arises from optionality rather than intelligence—but let us not fall for the naturalistic fallacy: ethical rules do not have to spring from optionality.
† Everyone talks about luck and about trial and error, but it has led to so little difference. Why? Because it is not about luck, but about optionality. By definition luck cannot be exploited; trial and error can lead to errors. Optionality is about getting the upper half of luck.

Changes in Value

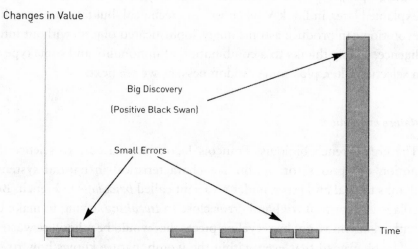

FIGURE 6. The mechanism of optionlike trial and error (the fail-fast model), a.k.a. convex tinkering. Low-cost mistakes, with known maximum losses, and large potential payoff (unbounded). A central feature of positive Black Swans: the gains are unbounded (unlike a lottery ticket), or, rather, with an unknown limit; but the losses from errors are limited and known.

Changes in Value

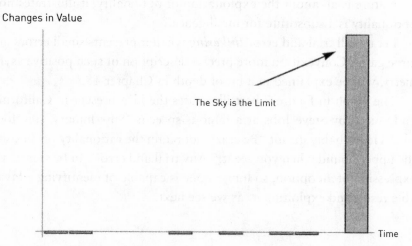

FIGURE 7. Same situation as in Figure 6, but in Extremistan the payoff can be monstrous.

The Rationality

To crystallize, take this description of an option:

$$Option = asymmetry + rationality$$

The rationality part lies in keeping what is good and ditching the bad, knowing to take the profits. As we saw, nature has a filter to keep the good baby and get rid of the bad. The difference between the antifragile and the fragile lies there. The fragile has no option. But the antifragile needs to select what's best—the best option.

It is worth insisting that the most wonderful attribute of nature is the rationality with which it selects its options and picks the best for itself—thanks to the testing process involved in evolution. Unlike the researcher afraid of doing something different, it sees an option—the asymmetry—when there is one. So it ratchets up—biological systems get locked in a state that is better than the previous one, the path-dependent property I mentioned earlier. In trial and error, the rationality consists in not rejecting something that is markedly better than what you had before.

As I said, in business, people pay for the option when it is identified and mapped in a contract, so explicit options tend to be expensive to purchase, much like insurance contracts. They are often overhyped. But because of the domain dependence of our minds, we don't recognize it in other places, where these options tend to remain underpriced or not priced at all.

I learned about the asymmetry of the option in class at the Wharton School, in the lecture on financial options that determined my career, and immediately realized that the professor did not himself see the implications. Simply, he did not understand nonlinearities and the fact that the optionality came from some asymmetry! Domain dependence: he missed it in places where the textbook did not point to the asymmetry—he understood optionality mathematically, but not really outside the equation. He did not think of trial and error as options. He did not think of model error as negative options. And, thirty years later, little has changed in the understanding of the asymmetries by many who, ironically, teach the subject of options.[*]

---

[*] I usually hesitate to discuss my career in options, as I worry that the reader will associate the idea with finance rather than the more scientific applications. I go ballistic when I use technical insights derived from derivatives and people mistake it for a financial discussion—these are only techniques, portable techniques, very portable techniques, for Baal's sake!

An option hides where we don't want it to hide. I will repeat that options benefit from variability, but also from situations in which errors carry small costs. So these errors are like options—in the long run, happy errors bring gains, unhappy errors bring losses. That is exactly what Fat Tony was taking advantage of: certain models can have only unhappy errors, particularly derivatives models and other fragilizing situations.

What also struck me was the option blindness of us humans and intellectuals. These options were, as we will see in the next chapter, out there in plain sight.

Life Is Long Gamma

Indeed, in plain sight.

One day, my friend Anthony Glickman, a rabbi and Talmudic scholar turned option trader, then turned again rabbi and Talmudic scholar (so far), after one of these conversations about how this optionality applies to everything around us, perhaps after one of my tirades on Stoicism, calmly announced: "Life is long gamma." (To repeat, in the jargon, "long" means "benefits from" and "short" "hurt by," and "gamma" is a name for the nonlinearity of options, so "long gamma" means "benefits from volatility and variability." Anthony even had as his mail address "@longgamma.com.")

There is an ample academic literature trying to convince us that options are not rational to own because *some* options are overpriced, and they are deemed overpriced according to business school methods of computing risks that do not take into account the possibility of rare events. Further, researchers invoke something called the "long shot bias" or lottery effects by which people stretch themselves and overpay for these long shots in casinos and in gambling situations. These results, of course, are charlatanism dressed in the garb of science, with non–risk takers who, Triffat-style, when they want to think about risk, only think of casinos. As in other treatments of uncertainty by economists, these are marred with mistaking the randomness of life for the well-tractable one of the casinos, what I call the "ludic fallacy" (after *ludes,* which means "games" in Latin)—the mistake we saw made by the blackjack fellow of Chapter 7. In fact, criticizing all bets on rare events based on the fact that lottery tickets are overpriced is as foolish as criticizing all risk taking on grounds that casinos make money in the long run from gamblers, forgetting that we are here because of risk taking *outside* the casinos. Further, casino bets and lottery tickets also have a known maximum upside—in real life, the sky is often the limit, and the difference between the two cases can be significant.

Risk taking *ain't* gambling, and optionality *ain't* lottery tickets.

In addition, these arguments about "long shots" are ludicrously cherry-picked. If you list the businesses that have generated the most wealth in history, you would see that they all have optionality. There is unfortunately the optionality of people stealing options from others and from the taxpayer (as we will see in the ethical section in Book VII), such as CEOs of companies with upside and no downside to themselves. But the largest generators of wealth in America historically have been, first, real estate (investors have the option at the expense of the banks), and, second, technology (which relies almost completely on trial and error). Further, businesses with negative optionality (that is, the opposite of having optionality) such as banking have had a horrible performance through history: banks lose periodically every penny made in their history thanks to blowups.

But these are all dwarfed by the role of optionality in the two evolutions: natural and scientific-technological, the latter of which we will examine in Book IV.

Roman Politics Likes Optionality

Even political systems follow a form of rational tinkering, when people are rational hence take the better option: the Romans got their political system by tinkering, not by "reason." Polybius in his *Histories* compares the Greek legislator Lycurgus, who constructed his political system while "untaught by adversity," to the more experiential Romans, who, a few centuries later, "have not reached it by *any process of reasoning* [emphasis mine], but by the discipline of many struggles and troubles, and always choosing the best by the light of the experience gained in disaster."

Next

Let me summarize. In Chapter 10 we saw the foundational asymmetry as embedded in Seneca's ideas: more upside than downside and vice versa. This chapter refined the point and presented a manifestation of such asymmetry in the form of an option, by which one can take the upside if one likes, but without the downside. An option is the weapon of antifragility.

The other point of the chapter and Book IV is that the option is a substitute for knowledge—actually I don't quite understand what sterile knowledge is, since it is necessarily vague and sterile. So I make the bold speculation that many things we think are derived by skill come largely from options, but well-used options, much like Thales' situation—and much like nature—rather than from what we claim to be understanding.

The implication is nontrivial. For if you think that education causes wealth, rather than being a result of wealth, or that intelligent actions and discoveries are the result of intelligent ideas, you will be in for a surprise. Let us see what kind of surprise.

CHAPTER 13

Lecturing Birds on How to Fly

Finally, the wheel—Proto-Fat Tony thinking—The central problem is that birds rarely write more than ornithologists—Combining stupidity with wisdom rather than the opposite

Consider the story of the wheeled suitcase.

I carry a large wheeled suitcase mostly filled with books on almost all my travels. It is heavy (books that interest me when I travel always happen to be in hardcover).

In June 2012, I was rolling that generic, heavy, book-filled suitcase outside the JFK international terminal and, looking at the small wheels at the bottom of the case and the metal handle that helps pull it, I suddenly remembered the days when I had to haul my book-stuffed luggage through the very same terminal, with regular stops to rest and let the lactic acid flow out of my sore arms. I could not afford a porter, and even if I could, I would not have felt comfortable doing it. I have been going through the same terminal for three decades, with and without wheels, and the contrast was eerie. It struck me how lacking in imagination we are: we had been putting our suitcases on top of a cart with wheels, but nobody thought of putting tiny wheels directly under the suitcase.

Can you imagine that it took close to six thousand years between the invention of the wheel (by, we assume, the Mesopotamians) and this brilliant implementation (by some luggage maker in a drab industrial suburb)? And billions of hours spent by travelers like myself schlepping luggage through corridors full of rude customs officers.

Worse, this took place three decades or so after we put a man on the moon. And consider all this sophistication used in sending someone into space, and its totally negligible impact on my life, and compare it to this lactic acid in my arms, pain in my lower back, soreness in the palms of my hands, and sense of helplessness in front of a long corridor. Indeed, though extremely consequential, we are talking about something trivial: a very simple technology.

But the technology is only trivial retrospectively—not prospectively. All those brilliant minds, usually disheveled and rumpled, who go to faraway conferences to discuss Gödel, Shmodel, Riemann's Conjecture, quarks, shmarks, had to carry their suitcases through airport terminals, without thinking about applying their brain to such an insignificant transportation problem. (We said that the intellectual society rewards "difficult" derivations, compared to practice in which there is no penalty for simplicity.) And even if these brilliant minds had applied their supposedly overdeveloped brains to such an obvious and trivial problem, they probably would not have gotten anywhere.

This tells us something about the way we map the future. We humans lack imagination, to the point of not even knowing what tomorrow's important things look like. We use randomness to spoon-feed us with discoveries—which is why antifragility is necessary.

The story of the wheel itself is even more humbling than that of the suitcase: we keep being reminded that the Mesoamericans did not invent the wheel. They did. They had wheels. But the wheels were on small toys for children. It was just like the story of the suitcase: the Mayans and Zapotecs did not make the leap to the application. They used vast quantities of human labor, corn maize, and lactic acid to move gigantic slabs of stone in the flat spaces ideal for pushcarts and chariots where they built their pyramids. They even rolled them on logs of wood. Meanwhile, their small children were rolling their toys on the stucco floors (or perhaps not even doing that, as the toys might have been solely used for mortuary purposes).

The same story holds for the steam engine: the Greeks had an operating version of it, for amusement, of course: the aeolipyle, a turbine that spins when heated, as described by Hero of Alexandria. But it took the Industrial Revolution for us to discover this earlier discovery.

Just as great geniuses invent their predecessors, practical innovations create their theoretical ancestry.

There is something sneaky in the process of discovery and implementation—something people usually call evolution. We are managed by small (or large) accidental changes, more accidental than we admit. We talk big but hardly have any imagination, except for a few visionaries who seem to recognize the optionality of things. We need some randomness to help us out—with a double dose of antifragility. For randomness plays a role at two levels: the invention and the implementation. The first point is not overly surprising, though we play down the role of chance, especially when it comes to our own discoveries.

But it took me a lifetime to figure out the second point: implementation does not necessarily proceed from invention. It, too, requires luck and circumstances. The history of medicine is littered with the strange sequence of discovery of a cure followed, much later, by the implementation—as if the two were completely separate ventures, the second harder, much harder, than the first. Just taking something to market requires struggling against a collection of naysayers, administrators, empty suits, formalists, mountains of details that invite you to drown, and one's own discouraged mood on occasion. In other words, to identify the option (again, there is this option blindness). This is where all you need is the wisdom to realize what you have on your hands.

The Half-Invented. For there is a category of things that we can call half-invented, and taking the half-invented into the invented is often the real breakthrough. Sometimes you need a visionary to figure out what to do with a discovery, a vision that he and only he can have. For instance, take the computer mouse, or what is called the graphical interface: it took Steve Jobs to put it on your desk, then laptop—only he had a vision of the dialectic between images and humans—later adding sounds to a trilectic. The things, as they say, that are "staring at us."

Further, the simplest "technologies," or perhaps not even technologies but tools, such as the wheel, are the ones that seem to run the world. In spite of the hype, what we call technologies have a very high mortality rate, as I will show in Chapter 20. Just consider that of all the means of transportation that have been designed in the past three thousand years or more since the attack weapons of the Hyksos and the drawings of Hero of Alexandria, individual transportation today is limited to bicycles and cars (and a few variants in between the two). Even then, technologies seem to go backward and forward, with the more natural and less fragile superseding the technological. The wheel, born in the Middle East, seems to have disappeared after the Arab invasion introduced to the Levant a more generalized use of the camel and the inhabitants figured out that the camel was more robust—hence more efficient in the long run—than the fragile technology of the wheel. In addition, since one person could control six camels but only one carriage, the regression away from technology proved more economically sound.

Once More, Less Is More

This story of the suitcase came to tease me when I realized, looking at a porcelain coffee cup, that there existed a simple definition of fragility, hence a straightforward and practical testing heuristic: the simpler and more obvious the discovery, the less equipped we are to figure it out by complicated methods. The key is that the significant can only be revealed through practice. How many of these simple, trivially simple heuristics are currently looking and laughing at us?

The story of the wheel also illustrates the point of this chapter: both governments and universities have done very, very little for innovation and discovery, precisely because, in addition to their blinding rationalism, they look for the complicated, the lurid, the newsworthy, the narrated, the scientist, and the grandiose, rarely for the wheel on the suitcase. Simplicity, I realized, does not lead to laurels.

Mind the Gaps

As we saw with the stories of Thales and the wheel, antifragility (thanks to the asymmetry effects of trial and error) supersedes intelligence. But *some* intelligence is needed. From our discussion on rationality, we see that all we need is the ability to accept that what we have on our hands is better than what we had before—in other words, to recognize the existence of the option (or "exercise the option" as people say in the business, that is, take advantage of a valuable alternative that is superior to what precedes it, with a certain gain from switching from one into the other, the only part of the process where rationality is required). And from the history of technology, this ability to use the option given to us by antifragility is not guaranteed: things can be looking at us for a long time. We saw the gap between the wheel and its use. Medical researchers call such lag the "translational gap," the time difference between formal discovery and first implementation, which, if anything, owing to excessive noise and academic interests, has been shown by Contopoulos-Ioannidis and her peers to be lengthening in modern times.

The historian David Wooton relates a gap of two centuries between the discovery of germs and the acceptance of germs as a cause of disease, a delay of thirty years between the germ theory of putrefaction and the development of antisepsis, and a delay of sixty years between antisepsis and drug therapy.

But things can get bad. In the dark ages of medicine, doctors used to rely on the naive rationalistic idea of a balance of humors in the body, and disease was assumed to originate with some imbalance, leading to a series of treatments that were perceived as needed to restore such balance. In her book on humors, Noga Arikha shows that after William Harvey demonstrated the mechanism of blood circulation in the 1620s, one would have expected that such theories and related practices should have disappeared. Yet people continued to refer to spirit and humors, and doctors continued to prescribe, for centuries more, phlebotomies (bloodletting), enemas (I prefer to not explain), and cataplasms (application of a moist piece of bread or cereal on inflamed tissue). This continued even after Pasteur's evidence that germs were the cause of these infectious diseases.

Now, as a skeptical empiricist, I do not consider that resisting new technology is *necessarily* irrational: waiting for time to operate its testing might be a valid approach if one holds that we have an incomplete picture of things. This is what naturalistic risk management is about. However, it is downright irrational if one holds on to an old technology that is not naturalistic at all yet visibly harmful, or when the switch to a new technology (like the wheel on the suitcase) is obviously free of possible side effects that did not exist with the previous one. And resisting removal is downright incompetent and criminal (as I keep saying, removal of something non-natural does not carry long-term side effects; it is typically iatrogenics-free).

In other words, I do not give the resistance to the implementation of such discoveries any intellectual credit, or explain it by some hidden wisdom and risk management attitude: this is plainly mistaken. It partakes of the chronic lack of heroism and cowardice on the part of professionals: few want to jeopardize their jobs and reputation for the sake of change.

Search and How Errors Can Be Investments

Trial and error has one overriding value people fail to understand: it is not really random, rather, thanks to optionality, it requires some rationality. One needs to be intelligent in recognizing the favorable outcome and knowing what to discard.

And one needs to be rational in not making trial and error completely random. If you are looking for your misplaced wallet in your living room, in a trial and error mode, you exercise rationality by not looking in the same place twice. In many pursuits, every trial, every failure provides additional information, each more valuable than the previous one—if you know what does not work, or where the wallet is not located. With every trial one gets closer to something, assuming an environment in which one knows exactly what one is looking for. We can, from the trial that fails to deliver, figure out progressively *where* to go.

I can illustrate it best with the modus operandi of Greg Stemm, who specializes in pulling long-lost shipwrecks from the bottom of the sea. In 2007, he called his (then) biggest find "the Black Swan" after the idea of looking for positive extreme payoffs. The find was quite sizable, a treasure with precious metals now worth a billion dollars. His Black Swan is a Spanish frigate called *Nuestra Señora de las Mercedes,* which was sunk by the British off the southern coast of Portugal in 1804. Stemm proved to be a representative hunter of positive Black Swans, and someone who can illustrate that such a search is a highly controlled form of randomness.

I met him and shared ideas with him: his investors (like mine at the time, as I was still involved in that business) were for the most part not programmed to understand that for a treasure hunter, a "bad" quarter (meaning expenses of searching but no finds) was not indicative of distress, as it would be with a steady cash flow business like that of a dentist or prostitute. By some mental domain dependence, people can spend money on, say, office furniture and not call it a "loss," rather an investment, but would treat cost of search as "loss."

Stemm's method is as follows. He does an extensive analysis of the general area where the ship could be. That data is synthesized into a map drawn with squares of probability. A search area is then designed, taking into account that they must have certainty that the shipwreck is not in a specific area before moving on to a lower probability area. It looks random but it is not. It is the equivalent of looking for a treasure in your house: every search has incrementally a higher probability of yielding a result, but only if you can be certain that the area you have searched does not hold the treasure.

Some readers might not be too excited about the morality of shipwreck-hunting, and could consider that these treasures are national, not private, property. So let us change domain. The method used by Stemm applies to oil and gas exploration, particularly at the bottom of the unexplored oceans, with a difference: in a shipwreck, the upside is limited to the value of the treasure, whereas oil fields and other natural resources are nearly unlimited (or have a very high limit).

Finally, recall my discussion of random drilling in Chapter 6 and how it seemed superior to more directed techniques. This optionality-driven method of search is not foolishly random. Thanks to optionality, it becomes tamed and harvested randomness.

Creative and Uncreative Destructions

Someone who got a (minor) version of the point that generalized trial and error has, well, *errors,* but without much grasp of asymmetry (or what, since Chapter 12, we have been calling optionality), is the economist Joseph Schumpeter. He realized that some things need to break for the system to improve—what is labeled *creative destruction*—a notion developed, among so many other ones, by the philosopher Karl Marx and a concept discovered, we will show in Chapter 17, by Nietzsche. But a reading of Schumpeter shows that he did not think in terms of uncertainty and opacity; he was completely smoked by interventionism, under the illusion that governments could innovate by fiat, something that we will contradict in a few pages. Nor did he grasp the notion of layering of evolutionary tensions. More crucially, both he and his detractors (Harvard economists who thought that he did not know mathematics) missed the notion of antifragility as asymmetry (optionality) effects, hence the philosopher's stone—on which, later—as the agent of growth. That is, they missed half of life.

THE SOVIET-HARVARD DEPARTMENT OF ORNITHOLOGY

Now, since a very large share of technological know-how comes from the antifragility, the optionality, of trial and error, some people and some institutions want to hide the fact from us (and themselves), or downplay its role.

Consider two types of knowledge. The first type is not exactly "knowledge"; its ambiguous character prevents us from associating it with the strict definitions of knowledge. It is a way of doing things that we cannot really express in clear and direct language—it is sometimes called *apophatic*—but that we do nevertheless, and do well. The second type is more like what we call "knowledge"; it is what you acquire in school, can get grades for, can codify, what is explainable, academizable, rationalizable, formalizable, theoretizable, codifiable, Sovietizable, bureaucratizable, Harvardifiable, provable, etc.

The error of naive rationalism leads to overestimating the role and necessity of the second type, academic knowledge, in human affairs—and degrading the uncodifiable, more complex, intuitive, or experience-based type.

There is no proof against the statement that the role such explainable knowledge plays in life is so minor that it is not even funny.

We are very likely to believe that skills and ideas that we actually acquired by antifragile *doing,* or that came naturally to us (from our innate biological instinct), came from books, ideas, and reasoning. We get blinded by it; there may even be something in our brains that makes us suckers for the point. Let us see how.

I recently looked for definitions of technology. Most texts define it as *the application of scientific knowledge to practical projects*—leading us to believe in a flow of knowledge going chiefly, even exclusively, from lofty "science" (organized around a priestly group of persons with titles before their names) to lowly practice (exercised by uninitiated people without the intellectual attainments to gain membership into the priestly group).

So, in the corpus, knowledge is presented as derived in the following manner: basic research yields scientific knowledge, which in turn generates technologies, which in turn lead to practical applications, which in turn lead to economic growth and other seemingly interesting matters. The payoff from the "investment" in basic research will be partly directed to more investments in basic research, and the citizens will prosper and enjoy the benefits of such knowledge-derived wealth with Volvo cars, ski vacations, Mediterranean diets, and long summer hikes in beautifully maintained public parks.

This is called the Baconian linear model, after the philosopher of science Francis Bacon; I am adapting its representation by the scientist Terence Kealey (who, crucially, as a biochemist, is a practicing scientist, not a historian of science) as follows:

Academia → *Applied Science and Technology* → *Practice*

While this model may be valid in some very narrow (but highly advertised instances), such as building the atomic bomb, the exact reverse seems to be true in most of the domains I've examined. Or, at least, this model is not guaranteed to be true and, what is shocking, we have no rigorous evidence that it is true. It may be that academia helps science and technology, which in turn help practice, but in unintended, non-teleological ways, as we will see later (in other words, it is *directed research* that may well be an illusion).

Let us return to the metaphor of the birds. Think of the following event: A collection of hieratic persons (from Harvard or some such place) lecture birds on how to fly. Imagine bald males in their sixties, dressed in black robes, officiating in a form of English that is full of jargon, with equations here and there for good measure. The bird flies. Wonderful confirmation! They rush to the department of ornithology to write books, articles, and reports stating that the bird has obeyed them, an impeccable causal inference. The Harvard Department of Ornithology is now indispensable for bird flying. It will get government research funds for its contribution.

Mathematics → *Ornithological navigation and wing-flapping technologies* → *(ungrateful) birds fly*

It also happens that birds write no such papers and books, conceivably because they are just birds, so we never get their side of the story. Meanwhile, the priests keep broadcasting theirs to the new generation of humans who are completely unaware of the conditions of the pre-Harvard lecturing days. Nobody discusses the possibility of the birds' not needing lectures—and nobody has any incentive to look at the number of birds that fly without such help from the great scientific establishment.

The problem is that what I wrote above looks ridiculous, but a change of domain makes it look reasonable. Clearly, we never think that it is thanks to ornithologists that birds learn to fly—and if some people do hold such a belief, it would be hard for them to convince the birds. But why is it that when we anthropomorphize and replace "birds" with "men," the idea that people learn to do things thanks to lectures becomes plausible? When it comes to human agency, matters suddenly become confusing to us.

So the illusion grows and grows, with government funding, tax dollars, swelling (and self-feeding) bureaucracies in Washington all devoted to helping birds fly better. Problems occur when people start cutting such funding—with a spate of accusations of killing birds by not helping them fly.

As per the Yiddish saying: "If the student is smart, the teacher takes the credit." These illusions of contribution result largely from confirmation fallacies: in addition to the sad fact that history belongs to those who can write about it (whether winners or losers), a second bias appears, as those who write the accounts can deliver confirmatory facts (what has worked) but not a complete picture of what has worked and what has failed. For instance, directed research would tell you what has worked from funding (like AIDS drugs or some modern designer drugs), not what has failed—so you may have the impression that it fares better than random.

And of course iatrogenics is never part of the discourse. They never tell you if education hurt you in some places.

So we are blind to the possibility of the alternative process, or the role of such a process, a loop:

> *Random Tinkering (antifragile)* → *Heuristics (technology)* →
> *Practice and Apprenticeship* → *Random Tinkering (antifragile)*
> → *Heuristics (technology)* → *Practice and Apprenticeship . . .*

In parallel to the above loop,

> *Practice* → *Academic Theories* → *Academic Theories* →
> *Academic Theories* → *Academic Theories . . . (with of course*
> *some exceptions, some accidental leaks, though these are indeed*
> *rare and overhyped and grossly generalized).*

Now, crucially, one can detect the scam in the so-called Baconian model by looking at events in the days that preceded the Harvard lectures on flying and examining the birds. This is what I accidentally found (indeed, accidentally) in my own career as practitioner turned researcher in volatility, thanks to some lucky turn of events. But before that, let me explain epiphenomena and the arrow of education.

EPIPHENOMENA

The Soviet-Harvard illusion (lecturing birds on flying and believing that the lecture is the cause of these wonderful skills) belongs to a class of causal illusions called *epiphenomena*. What are these illusions? When you spend time on the bridge of a ship or in the coxswain's station with a large compass in front, you can easily develop the impression that the compass is directing the ship rather than merely reflecting its direction.

The lecturing-birds-how-to-fly effect is an example of epiphenomenal belief: we see a high degree of academic research in countries that are wealthy and developed, leading us to think uncritically that research is the generator of wealth. In an epiphenomenon, you don't usually observe A without observing B with it, so you are likely to think that A causes B, or that B causes A, depending on the cultural framework or what seems plausible to the local journalist.

One rarely has the illusion that, given that so many boys have short hair, short hair determines gender, or that wearing a tie causes one to become a businessman. But it is easy to fall into other epiphenomena, particularly when one is immersed in a news-driven culture.

And one can easily see the trap of having these epiphenomena fuel action, then justify it retrospectively. A dictator—just like a government—will feel indispensable because the alternative is not easily visible, or is hidden by special interest groups. The Federal Reserve Bank of the United States, for instance, can wreak havoc on the economy yet feel convinced of its effectiveness. People are scared of the alternative.

Greed as a Cause

Whenever an economic crisis occurs, greed is pointed to as the cause, which leaves us with the impression that if we could go to the root of greed and extract it from life, crises would be eliminated. Further, we tend to believe that greed is new, since these wild economic crises are new. This is an epiphenomenon: greed is much older than systemic fragility. It existed as far back as the eye can go into history. From Virgil's mention of *greed of gold* and the expression *radix malorum est cupiditas* (from the Latin version of the New Testament), both expressed more than twenty centuries ago, we know that the same problems of greed have been propounded through the centuries, with no cure, of course, in spite of the variety of political systems we have developed since then. Trollope's novel *The Way We Live Now,* published close to a century and a half ago, shows the exact same complaint of a resurgence of greed and con operators that I heard in 1988 with cries over of the "greed decade," or in 2008 with denunciations of the "greed of capitalism." With astonishing regularity, greed is seen as something (a) new and (b) curable. A Procrustean bed approach; we cannot change humans as easily as we can build greed-proof systems, and nobody thinks of simple solutions.*

Likewise "lack of vigilance" is often proposed as the cause of an error (as we will see with the Société Générale story in Book V, the cause was size and fragility). But lack of vigilance is not the cause of the death of a mafia don; the cause of death is making enemies, and the cure is making friends.

Debunking Epiphenomena

We can dig out epiphenomena in the cultural discourse and consciousness by looking at the sequence of events and checking whether one always precedes the other. This is a method refined by the late Clive Granger (himself a refined gentleman), a well-deserved "Nobel" in Economics, that Bank of Sweden (Sveriges Riksbank) prize in honor of Alfred Nobel that has been given to a large number of fragilistas. It is the only rigorously scientific technique that philosophers of science can use to establish causation, as they can now extract, if not measure, the

---

* Is democracy epiphenomenal? Supposedly, democracy works because of this hallowed rational decision making on the part of voters. But consider that democracy may be something completely accidental to something else, the side effect of people liking to cast ballots for completely obscure reasons, just as people enjoy expressing themselves just to express themselves. (I once put this question at a political science conference and got absolutely nothing beyond blank nerdy faces, not even a smile.)

so-called "Granger cause" by looking at sequences. In epiphenomenal situations, you end up seeing A and B together. But if you refine your analysis by considering the sequence, thus introducing a time dimension —which takes place first, A or B?—and analyze evidence, then you will see if truly A causes B.

Further, Granger had the great idea of studying differences, that is, *changes* in A and B, not just levels of A and B. While I do not believe that Granger's method can lead me to believe that "A causes B" with certainty, it can most certainly help me debunk fake causation, and allow me to make the claim that "the statement that B causes A is wrong" or has insufficient evidence from the sequence.

The important difference between theory and practice lies precisely in the detection of the sequence of events and retaining the sequence in memory. If life is lived forward but remembered backward, as Kierkegaard observed, then books exacerbate this effect—our own memories, learning, and instinct have sequences in them. Someone standing today looking at events *without having lived them* would be inclined to develop illusions of causality, mostly from being mixed-up by the sequence of events. In real life, in spite of all the biases, we do not have the same number of asynchronies that appear to the student of history. Nasty history, full of lies, full of biases!

For one example of a trick for debunking causality: I am not even dead yet, but am already seeing distortions about my work. Authors theorize about some ancestry of my ideas, as if people read books then developed ideas, not wondering whether perhaps it is the other way around; people look for books that support their mental program. So one journalist (Anatole Kaletsky) saw the influence of Benoît Mandelbrot on my book *Fooled by Randomness,* published in 2001 when I did not know who Mandelbrot was. It is simple: the journalist noticed similarities of thought in one type of domain, and seniority of age, and immediately drew the false inference. He did not consider that like-minded people are inclined to hang together and that such intellectual similarity caused the relationship rather than the reverse. This makes me suspicious of the master-pupil relationships we read about in cultural history: about all the people that have been called my pupils have been my pupils because we were like-minded.

Cherry-picking (or the Fallacy of Confirmation)

Consider the tourist brochures used by countries to advertise their wares: you can expect that the pictures presented to you will look much, much better than anything you will encounter in the place. And the bias, the difference (for which humans correct, thanks to common sense), can be measured as *the country shown in the tourist brochure* minus *the country seen with your naked eyes*. That difference can be small, or large. We also make such corrections with commercial products, not overly trusting advertising.

But we don't correct for the difference in science, medicine, and mathematics, for the same reasons we didn't pay attention to iatrogenics. We are suckers for the sophisticated.

In institutional research, one can selectively report facts that confirm one's story, without revealing facts that disprove it or don't apply to it—so the public perception of science is biased into believing in the necessity of the highly conceptualized, crisp, and purified Harvardized methods. And statistical research tends to be marred with this one-sidedness. Another reason one should trust the disconfirmatory more than the confirmatory.

Academia is well equipped to tell us what it did for us, not what it did not—hence how indispensable its methods are. This ranges across many things in life. Traders talk about their successes, so one is led to believe that they are intelligent—not looking at the hidden failures. As to academic science: a few years ago, the great Anglo-Lebanese mathematician Michael Atiyah of string theory fame came to New York to raise funds for a research center in mathematics based in Lebanon. In his speech, he enumerated applications in which mathematics turned out to be useful for society and modern life, such as traffic signaling. Fine. But what about areas where mathematics led us to disaster (as in, say, economics or finance, where it blew up the system)? And how about areas out of the reach of mathematics? I thought right there of a different project: a catalog of where mathematics fails to produce results, hence causes harm.

Cherry-picking has optionality: the one telling the story (and publishing it) has the advantage of being able to show the confirmatory examples and completely ignore the rest—and the more volatility and dispersion, the rosier the best story will be (and the darker the worst story). Someone with optionality—the right to pick and choose his story—is only reporting on what suits his purpose. You take the upside of your story and hide the downside, so only the sensational seems to count.

The real world relies on the intelligence of antifragility, but no university would swallow that—just as interventionists don't accept that things can improve without their intervention. Let us return to the idea that universities generate wealth and the growth of useful knowledge in society. There is a causal illusion here; time to bust it.

CHAPTER 14

When Two Things Are Not the "Same Thing"

Green lumber another "blue"—Where we look for the arrow of discovery—
Putting Iraq in the middle of Pakistan—Prometheus never looked back

———

I am writing these lines in an appropriate place to think about the arrow of knowledge: Abu Dhabi, a city that sprang out of the desert, as if watered by oil.

It makes me queasy to see the building of these huge universities, funded by the oil revenues of governments, under the postulation that oil reserves can be turned into knowledge by hiring professors from prestigious universities and putting their kids through school (or, as is the case, waiting for their kids to feel the desire to go to school, as many students in Abu Dhabi are from Bulgaria, Serbia, or Macedonia getting a free education). Even better, they can, with a single check, import an entire school from overseas, such as the Sorbonne and New York University (among many more). So, in a few years, members of this society will be reaping the benefits of a great technological improvement.

It would seem a reasonable investment if one accepts the notion that *university knowledge generates economic wealth*. But this is a belief that comes more from superstition than empiricism. Remember the story of Switzerland in Chapter 5—a place with a very low level of formal education.* I wonder if my nausea comes from the feeling that these desert tribes are being separated from their money by the establishment that has been sucking dry their resources and diverting them to administrators from Western universities. Their wealth came from oil, not from some vocational know-how, so I am certain that their spending on education is completely sterile and a great transfer of resources (rather than milking antifragility by forcing their citizens to make money naturally, through circumstances).

Where Are the Stressors?

There is something that escapes the Abu Dhabi model. Where are the stressors?

Recall the quote by Seneca and Ovid to the effect that sophistication is born of need, and success of difficulties—in fact many such variations, sourced in medieval days (such as *necessitas magistra* in Erasmus), found their way into our daily vernaculars, as in "necessity is the mother of invention." The best is, as usual, from the master aphorist Publilius Syrus: "poverty makes experiences" (*hominem experiri multa paupertas iubet*). But the expression and idea appear in one form or another in so many classical writers, including Euripides, Pseudo-Theoctitus, Plautus, Apuleus, Zenobius, Juvenal, and of course it is now labeled "post-traumatic growth."

I saw ancient wisdom at work in the exact opposite of the situation in Abu Dhabi. My Levantine village of origin, Amioun, was pillaged and evacuated during the war, sending its inhabitants into exile across the planet. Twenty-five years later, it became opulent, having bounced back with a vengeance: my own house, dynamited, is now *bigger* than the previous version. My father, showing me the multiplication of villas in the countryside while bemoaning these nouveaux riches, calmly told me, "You, too, had you stayed here, would have become a beach bum. People from Amioun only do well when shaken." That's antifragility.

---

* Switzerland's education system has traditionally been apprenticeship-based. But it is now more and more oriented toward formal education, and might lose its edge. Success and wealth bring transformations that end up bringing fragilities.

L'Art pour l'Art, *to Learn for Learning's Sake*

Now let's look at evidence of the direction of the causal arrow, that is, whether it is true that lecture-driven knowledge leads to prosperity. Serious empirical investigation (largely thanks to one Lant Pritchet, then a World Bank economist) shows no evidence that raising the general level of education raises income at the level of a country. But we know the opposite is true, that wealth leads to the rise of education—not an optical illusion. We don't need to resort to the World Bank figures, we could derive this from an armchair. Let us figure out the direction of the arrow:

$$Education \rightarrow Wealth \ and \ Economic \ Growth$$

or

$$Wealth \ and \ Economic \ Growth \rightarrow Education$$

And the evidence is so easy to check, just lying out there in front of us. It can be obtained by looking at countries that are both wealthy and have some level of education and considering which condition preceded the other. Take the following potent and *less-is-more*-style argument by the rogue economist Ha-Joon Chang. In 1960 Taiwan had a much lower literacy rate than the Philippines and half the income per person; today Taiwan has ten times the income. At the same time, Korea had a much lower literacy rate than Argentina (which had one of the highest in the world) and about one-fifth the income per person; today it has three times as much. Further, over the same period, sub-Saharan Africa saw markedly increasing literacy rates, accompanied with a decrease in their standard of living. We can multiply the examples (Pritchet's study is quite thorough), but I wonder why people don't realize the simple truism, that is, the *fooled by randomness* effect: mistaking the merely associative for the causal, that is, if rich countries are educated, immediately inferring that education makes a country rich, without even checking. Epiphenomenon here again. (The error in reasoning is a bit from wishful thinking, because education is considered "good"; I wonder why people don't make the epiphenomenal association between the wealth of a country and something "bad," say, decadence, and infer that decadence, or some other disease of wealth like a high suicide rate, also generates wealth.)

I am not saying that for an individual, education is useless: it builds helpful credentials for one's own career—but such effect washes out at the country level. Education stabilizes the income of families across generations. A merchant makes money, then his children go to the Sorbonne, they become doctors and magistrates. The family retains wealth because the diplomas allow members to remain in the middle class long after the ancestral wealth is depleted. But these effects don't count for countries.

Further, Alison Wolf debunks the flaw in logic in going from the point that it is hard to imagine Microsoft or British Aerospace without advanced knowledge to the idea that more education means more wealth. "The simple one-way relationship which so entrances our politicians and commentators—education spending in, economic growth out—simply doesn't exist. Moreover, the larger and more complex the education sector, the less obvious any links to productivity become." And, similar to Pritchet, she looks at countries such as, say, Egypt, and shows how the giant leap in education it underwent did not translate into the Highly Cherished Golden GDP Growth That Makes Countries Important or Unimportant on the Ranking Tables.

This argument is not against adopting governmental educational policies for noble aims such as reducing inequality in the population, allowing the poor to access good literature and read Dickens, Victor Hugo, or Julien Gracq, or increasing the freedom of women in poor countries, which happens to decrease the birth rate. But then one should not use the excuses of "growth" or "wealth" in such matters.

I once ran into Alison Wolf at a party (parties are great for optionality). As I got her to explain to other people her evidence about the lack of effectiveness of funding formal education, one person got frustrated with our skepticism. Wolf's answer to him was "real education is this," pointing at the room full of people chatting. Accordingly, I am not saying that knowledge is not important; the skepticism in this discussion applies to the brand of commoditized, prepackaged, and pink-coated knowledge, stuff one can buy in the open market and use for self-promotion. Further, let me remind the reader that scholarship and organized education are not the same.

Another party story. Once, at a formal fancy dinner, a fellow in a quick speech deplored the education level in the United States—falling for low-math-grades alarmism. Although I agreed with all his other views, I felt compelled to intervene. I interrupted him to state the point that America's values were "convex" risk taking and that I am glad that we are not like these helicopter-mom cultures—the kind of thing I am writing here. Everyone was shocked, either confused or in heavy but passive disagreement, except for one person who came to lend her support to me. It turned out that she was the head of the New York City school system.

Also, note that I am not saying that universities do not generate knowledge at all and do not help growth (outside, of course, of most standard economics and other superstitions that set us back); all I am saying is that their role is overly hyped-up and that their members seem to exploit some of our gullibility in establishing wrong causal links, mostly on superficial impressions.

Polished Dinner Partners

Education has benefits aside from stabilizing family incomes. Education makes individuals more polished dinner partners, for instance, something non-negligible. But the idea of educating people to improve the economy is rather novel. The British government documents, as early as fifty years ago, an aim for education other than the one we have today: raising values, making good citizens, and "learning," not economic growth (they were not suckers at the time)—a point also made by Alison Wolf.

Likewise, in ancient times, learning was for learning's sake, to make someone a good person, worth talking to, not to increase the stock of gold in the city's heavily guarded coffers. Entrepreneurs, particularly those in technical jobs, are not necessarily the best people to have dinner with. I recall a heuristic I used in my previous profession when hiring people (called "separate those who, when they go to a museum, look at the Cézanne on the wall from those who focus on the contents of the trash can"): the more interesting their conversation, the more cultured they are, the more they will be trapped into thinking that they are effective at what they are doing in real business (something psychologists call the *halo effect*, the mistake of thinking that skills in, say, skiing translate unfailingly into skills in managing a pottery workshop or a bank department, or that a good chess player would be a good strategist in real life).*

Clearly, it is unrigorous to equate *skills at doing* with *skills at talking*.

---

* The halo effect is largely the opposite of domain dependence.

My experience of good practitioners is that they can be totally incomprehensible—they do not have to put much energy into turning their insights and internal coherence into elegant style and narratives. Entrepreneurs are selected to be just doers, not thinkers, and doers do, they don't talk, and it would be unfair, wrong, and downright insulting to measure them in the talk department. The same with artisans: the quality lies in their product, not their conversation—in fact they can easily have false beliefs that, as a side effect (inverse iatrogenics), lead them to make better products, so what? Bureaucrats, on the other hand, because of the lack of an objective metric of success and the absence of market forces, are selected on the "halo effects" of shallow looks and elegance. The side effect is to make them better at conversation. I am quite certain a dinner with a United Nations employee would cover more interesting subjects than one with some of Fat Tony's cousins or a computer entrepreneur obsessed with circuits.

Let us look deeper at this flaw in thinking.

THE GREEN LUMBER FALLACY

In one of the rare noncharlatanic books in finance, descriptively called *What I Learned Losing a Million Dollars,* the protagonist makes a big discovery. He remarks that a fellow named Joe Siegel, one of the most successful traders in a commodity called "green lumber," actually thought that it was lumber painted green (rather than freshly cut lumber, called green because it had not been dried). And he made it his profession to trade the stuff! Meanwhile the narrator was into grand intellectual theories and narratives of what caused the price of commodities to move, and went bust.

It is not just that the successful expert on lumber was ignorant of central matters like the designation "green." He also knew things about lumber that nonexperts think are unimportant. People we call ignorant might not be ignorant.

The fact is that predicting the order flow in lumber and the usual narrative had little to do with the details one would assume from the outside are important. People who do things in the field are not subjected to a set exam; they are selected in the most non-narrative manner—nice arguments don't make much difference. Evolution does not rely on narratives, humans do. Evolution does not need a word for the color blue.

So let us call the *green lumber fallacy* the situation in which one mistakes a source of necessary knowledge—the greenness of lumber—for another, less visible from the outside, less tractable, less narratable.

My intellectual world was shattered as if everything I had studied was not just useless but a well-organized scam—as follows. When I first became a derivatives or "volatility" professional (I specialized in nonlinearities), I focused on exchange rates, a field in which I was embedded for several years. I had to cohabit with foreign exchange traders—people who were not involved in technical instruments as I was; their job simply consisted of buying and selling currencies. Money changing is a very old profession with a long tradition and craft; recall the story of Jesus Christ and the money changers. Coming to this from a highly polished Ivy League environment, I was in for a bit of a shock. You would think that the people who specialized in foreign exchange understood economics, geopolitics, mathematics, the future price of currencies, differentials between prices in countries. Or that they read assiduously the economics reports published in glossy papers by various institutes. You might also imagine cosmopolitan fellows who wear ascots at the opera on Saturday night, make wine sommeliers nervous, and take tango lessons on Wednesday afternoons. Or spoke intelligible English. None of that.

My first day on the job was an astounding discovery of the real world. The population in foreign exchange was at the time mostly composed of New Jersey/Brooklyn Italian fellows. Those were street, very street people who had started in the back office of banks doing wire transfers, and when the market expanded, even exploded, with the growth of commerce and the free-floating of currencies, they developed into traders and became prominent in the business. And prosperous.

My first conversation with an expert was with a fellow called B. Something-that-ends-with-a-vowel dressed in a handmade Brioni suit. I was told that he was the biggest Swiss franc trader in the world, a legend in his day—he had predicted the big dollar collapse in the 1980s and controlled huge positions. But a short conversation with him revealed that he could not place Switzerland on the map—foolish as I was, I thought he was Swiss Italian, yet he did not know there were Italian-speaking people in Switzerland. He had never been there. When I saw that he was not the exception, I started freaking out watching all these years of education evaporating in front of my eyes. That very same day I stopped reading economic reports. I felt nauseous for a while during this enterprise of "deintellectualization"—in fact I may not have re-covered yet.

If New York was blue collar in origin, London was sub–blue collar, and even more successful. The players were entirely cockney, even more separated from sentence-forming society. They were East Londoners, street people (extremely street) with a distinctive accent, using their own numbering system. Five is "Lady Godiva" or "ching," fifteen is a "com-modore," twenty-five is a "pony," etc. I had to learn cockney just to communicate, and mostly to go drinking, with my colleagues during my visits there; at the time, London traders got drunk almost every day at lunch, especially on Friday before New York opened. "Beer turns you into a lion," one fellow told me as he hurried to finish his drink before the New York open.

The most hilarious scenes were hearing on loudspeakers transatlantic conversations between New York Bensonhurst folks and cockney bro-kers, particularly when the Brooklyn fellow tried to put on a little bit of a cockney pronunciation to be understood (these cockneys sometimes spoke *no* standard English).

So that is how I learned the lesson that price and reality as seen by economists *are not the same thing*. One may be a function of the other but the function is too complex to map mathematically. The relation may have optionality in places, something that these non-sentence-savvy people knew deep inside.*

How Fat Tony Got Rich (and Fat)

Fat Tony got to become (literally) Fat Tony, rich and heavier, in the af-termath of the Kuwait war (the sequence was conventional, that is, first

---

* At first I thought that economic theories were not necessary to understand short-term movements in exchange rates, but it turned out that the same limitation applied to long-term movements as well. Many economists toying with foreign exchange have used the notion of "purchasing power parity" to try to predict exchange rates on the basis that in the long run "equilibrium" prices cannot diverge too much and currency rates need to adjust so a pound of ham will eventually need to carry a similar price in London and Newark, New Jersey. Put under scrutiny, there seems to be no operational validity to this theory—currencies that get expensive tend to get even more expensive, and most Fat Tonys in fact made fortunes following the inverse rule. But theoreticians would tell you that "in the long run" it should work. Which long run? It is impossible to make a decision based on such a theory, yet they still teach it to students, because being academics, lacking heuristics, and needing something complicated, they never found anything better to teach.

rich, then fat). It was in January 1991, on the day the United States attacked Baghdad to restitute Kuwait, which Iraq had invaded.

Every intelligent person in socioeconomics had his theory, probabilities, scenarios, and all that. Except Fat Tony. He didn't even know where Iraq was, whether it was a province in Morocco or some emirate with spicy food east of Pakistan—he didn't know the food, so the place did not exist for him.

All he knew is that suckers exist.

If you asked any intelligent "analyst" or journalist at the time, he would have predicted a rise in the price of oil *in the event* of war. But that causal link was precisely what Tony could not take for granted. So he bet against it: they are all prepared for a rise in oil from war, so the price must have adjusted to it. War could cause a rise in oil prices, but not *scheduled* war—since prices adjust to expectations. It has to be "in the price," as he said.

Indeed, on the news of war, oil collapsed from around $39 a barrel to almost half that value, and Tony turned his investment of three hundred thousand into eighteen million dollars. "There are so few occasions in one's life, you can't miss them," he later told Nero during one of their lunches as he was convincing his non–New Jersey friend to bet on a collapse of the financial system. "Good speculative bets come to you, you don't get them by just staying focused on the news."

And note the main Fat Tony statement: "Kuwait and oil are not the same ting [thing]." This will be a platform for our notion of conflation. Tony had greater upside than downside, and for him, that was it.

Indeed many people lost their shirt from the drop of oil—while *correctly predicting* war. They just thought it was the same *ting*. But there had been too much hoarding, too much inventory. I remember going around that time into the office of a large fund manager who had a map of Iraq on the wall in a war-room-like setting. Members of the team knew every possible thing about Kuwait, Iraq, Washington, the United Nations. Except for the very simple fact that it had nothing to do with oil—*not the same "ting."* All these analyses were nice, but not too connected to anything. Of course the fellow got subsequently shellacked by the drop in oil price, and, from what I heard, went to law school.

Aside from the non-narrative view of things, another lesson. People with too much smoke and complicated tricks and methods in their brains start missing elementary, very elementary things. Persons in the real world can't afford to miss these things; otherwise they crash the plane. Unlike researchers, they were selected for survival, not complications. So I saw the less is more in action: the more studies, the less obvious elementary but fundamental things become; activity, on the other hand, strips things to their simplest possible model.

CONFLATION

Of course, so many things are *not the same "ting"* in life. Let us generalize the conflation.

This lesson "not the same thing" is quite general. When you have optionality, or some antifragility, and can identify betting opportunities with big upside and small downside, what you do is only remotely connected to what Aristotle thinks you do.

There is *something* (here, perception, ideas, theories) and a *function of something* (here, a price or reality, or something real). The conflation problem is to mistake one for the other, forgetting that there is a "function" and that such function has different properties.

Now, the more asymmetries there are between the *something* and the *function of something,* then the more difference there is between the two. They may end up having nothing to do with each other.

This seems trivial, but there are big-time implications. As usual science—not "social" science, but smart science—gets it. Someone who escaped the conflation problem is Jim Simons, the great mathematician who made a fortune building a huge machine to transact across markets. It replicates the buying and selling methods of these sub–blue collar people and has more statistical significance than anyone on planet Earth. He claims to never hire economists and finance people, just physicists and mathematicians, those involved in pattern recognition accessing the internal logic of things, without theorizing. Nor does he ever listen to economists or read their reports.

The great economist Ariel Rubinstein gets the green lumber fallacy—it requires a great deal of intellect and honesty to see things that way. Rubinstein is one of the leaders in the field of game theory, which consists in thought experiments; he is also the greatest expert in cafés for thinking and writing across the planet. Rubinstein refuses to claim that his knowledge of theoretical matters can be translated—by him—into anything directly practical. To him, economics is like a fable—a fable writer is there to stimulate ideas, indirectly inspire practice perhaps, but certainly not to direct or determine practice. Theory should stay independent from practice and vice versa—and we should not extract academic economists from their campuses and put them in positions of decision making. Economics is not a science and should not be there to advise policy.

In his intellectual memoirs, Rubinstein recounts how he tried to get a Levantine vendor in the souk to apply ideas from game theory to his bargaining in place of ancestral mechanisms. The suggested method failed to produce a price acceptable to both parties. Then the fellow told him: "For generations, we have bargained in our way and you come and try to change it?" Rubinstein concluded: "I parted from him shamefaced." All we need is another two people like Rubinstein in that profession and things will be better on planet Earth.

Sometimes, even when an economic theory makes sense, its application cannot be imposed from a model, in a top-down manner, so one needs the organic self-driven trial and error to get us to it. For instance, the concept of specialization that has obsessed economists since Ricardo (and before) blows up countries when imposed by policy makers, as it makes the economies error-prone; but it works well when reached progressively by evolutionary means, with the right buffers and layers of redundancies. Another case where economists may inspire us but should never tell us what to do—more on that in the discussion of Ricardian comparative advantage and model fragility in the Appendix.

The difference between a narrative and practice—the important things that cannot be easily narrated—lies mainly in optionality, the missed optionality of things. The "right thing" here is typically an antifragile payoff. And my argument is that you don't go to school to learn optionality, but the reverse: to become blind to it.

PROMETHEUS AND EPIMETHEUS

In Greek legend, there were two Titan brothers, Prometheus and Epimetheus. Prometheus means "fore-thinker" while Epimetheus means "after-thinker," equivalent to someone who falls for the retrospective distortion of fitting theories to past events in an ex post narrative manner. Prometheus gave us fire and represents the progress of civilization, while Epimetheus represents backward thinking, staleness, and lack of intelligence. It was Epimetheus who accepted Pandora's gift, the large jar, with irreversible consequences.

Optionality is Promethean, narratives are Epimethean—one has reversible and benign mistakes, the other symbolizes the gravity and irreversibility of the consequences of opening Pandora's box.

You make forays into the future by opportunism and optionality. So far in Book IV we have seen the power of optionality as an alternative way of doing things, opportunistically, with some large edge coming from asymmetry with large benefits and benign harm. It is a way—the only way—to domesticate uncertainty, to work rationally without understanding the future, while reliance on narratives is the exact opposite: one is domesticated by uncertainty, and ironically set back. You cannot look at the future by naive projection of the past.

This brings us to the difference between doing and thinking. The point is hard to understand from the vantage point of intellectuals. As Yogi Berra said, "In theory there is no difference between theory and practice; in practice there is." So far we have seen arguments that intellect is associated with fragility and instills methods that conflict with tinkering. So far we saw the option as the expression of antifragility. We separated knowledge into two categories, the formal and the Fat Tony-ish, heavily grounded in the antifragility of trial and error and risk taking with less downside, barbell-style—a de-intellectualized form of risk taking (or, rather, intellectual in its own way). In an opaque world, that is the only way to go.

Table 4 summarizes the different aspects of the opposition between narrating and tinkering, the subject of the next three chapters.

TABLE 4 • THE DIFFERENCE BETWEEN THE TELEOLOGICAL AND OPTIONALITY

NARRATIVE KNOWLEDGE	*ANTIFRAGILE: OPTIONALITY-DRIVEN TINKERING, TRIAL AND ERROR*
Hates uncertainty (fragile to change, or turkey-style misunderstanding of the past)	Domesticates uncertainty (antifragile to the unknown)
Looks at the past, subject to overfitting to past	Looks at the future
Epimetheus	Prometheus
Teleological action	Opportunistic action
Tourist-style	Flâneur-style
Fragile, naive rationality	Robust rationality
Psychologically comfortable	Psychologically uncomfortable, but sense of thrill and adventure
Concave (visible known gains, unknown errors)	Convex (small known errors, large possible gains)
Subject to turkey problems (mistaking evidence of absence for absence of evidence)	Can benefit from suckers and turkey problems
Subject to epiphenomena and the green lumber fallacy	Escapes the green lumber fallacy
Academia's sole mechanism outside laboratory and physical science	Practice's main mechanism
Narrative is epistemological	Narrative is instrumental
Trapped into a story	No meaningful dependence on a story—the narrative can be just for motivation
Narrow domain, closed space of action	Broad domain, open space of action
Needs to understand logic of things	Little understanding is necessary, just rationality in comparing two outcomes (exercising the better option)
Doesn't benefit from the philosopher's stone (a.k.a. convexity bias; see Chapter 19)	Relies on the philosopher's stone

All this does not mean that tinkering and trial and error are devoid of narrative: they are just not overly dependent on the narrative being true—the narrative is not epistemological but instrumental. For instance, religious stories might have no value as narratives, but they may get you to do something convex and antifragile you otherwise would not do, like mitigate risks. English parents controlled children with the false narrative that if they didn't behave or eat their dinner, Boney (Napoleon Bonaparte) or some wild animal might come and take them away. Religions often use the equivalent method to help adults get out of trouble, or avoid debt. But intellectuals tend to believe their own b***t and take their ideas too literally, and that is vastly dangerous.

Consider the role of heuristic (rule-of-thumb) knowledge embedded in traditions. Simply, just as evolution operates on individuals, so does it act on these tacit, unexplainable rules of thumb transmitted through generations—what Karl Popper has called evolutionary epistemology. But let me change Popper's idea ever so slightly (actually quite a bit): my take is that this evolution is not a competition between ideas, but between humans and systems based on such ideas. An idea does not survive because it is better than the competition, but rather because the person who holds it has survived! Accordingly, wisdom you learn from your grandmother should be vastly superior (empirically, hence scientifically) to what you get from a class in business school (and, of course, considerably cheaper). My sadness is that we have been moving farther and farther away from grandmothers.

Expert problems (in which the expert knows a lot but less than he thinks he does) often bring fragilities, and acceptance of ignorance the reverse.[*] Expert problems put you on the wrong side of asymmetry. Let us examine the point with respect to risk. When you are fragile you need to know a lot more than when you are antifragile. Conversely, when you think you know more than you do, you are fragile (to error).

We showed earlier the evidence that classroom education does not

---

[*] Overconfidence leads to reliance on forecasts, which causes borrowing, then to the fragility of leverage. Further, there is convincing evidence that a PhD in economics or finance causes people to build vastly more fragile portfolios. George Martin and I listed all the major financial economists who were involved with funds, calculated the blowups by funds, and observed a far higher proportional incidence of such blowups on the part of finance professors—the most famous one being Long Term Capital Management, which employed Fragilistas Robert Merton, Myron Scholes, Chi-Fu Huang, and others.

lead to wealth as much as it comes from wealth (an epiphenomenon). Next let us see how, similarly, antifragile risk taking—not education and formal, organized research—is largely responsible for innovation and growth, while the story is dressed up by textbook writers. It does not mean that theories and research play no role; it is that just as we are fooled by randomness, so we are fooled into overestimating the role of good-sounding ideas. We will look at the confabulations committed by historians of economic thought, medicine, technology, and other fields that tend to systematically downgrade practitioners and fall into the green lumber fallacy.

CHAPTER 15

History Written by the Losers

The birds may perhaps listen—Combining stupidity with wisdom rather than the opposite—Where we look for the arrow of discovery—A vindication of trial and error

———

Because of a spate of biases, historians are prone to epiphenomena and other illusions of cause and effect. To understand the history of technology, you need accounts by nonhistorians, or historians with the right frame of mind who developed their ideas by watching the formation of technologies, instead of just reading accounts concerning it. I mentioned earlier Terence Kealey's debunking of the so-called linear model and that he was a practicing scientist.* A practicing laboratory scientist, or an engineer, can witness the real-life production of, say, pharmacological innovations or the jet engine and can thus avoid falling for epiphenomena, unless he was brainwashed prior to starting practice.

I have seen evidence—as an eyewitness—of results that owe *nothing* to academizing science, rather evolutionary tinkering that was dressed up and claimed to have come from academia.

---

* According to David Edgerton, the so-called linear model was not believed in much in the early twentieth century; it is just that we believe *now* that we believed *then* in the supremacy of teleological science.

TABLE 5 • THE LECTURING-BIRDS-HOW-TO-FLY EFFECT ACROSS DOMAINS: EXAMPLE OF MISATTRIBUTION OF RESULTS IN TEXTBOOKS

FIELD	ORIGINATION AND DEVELOPMENT AS MARKETED BY BIRDS LECTURERS	REAL ORIGINATION AND DEVELOPMENT
Jet Engine	Physicists (busted by Scranton)	Tinkering engineers with no understanding of "why it works"
Architecture	Euclidian geometry, mathematics (busted by Beaujouan)	Heuristics and secret recipes (guilds)
Cybernetics	Norbert Wiener (busted by Mindell)	Programmers "wiki-style"
Derivatives formulas	Black, Scholes, and Fragilista Merton (busted by Haug and Taleb)	Traders and practitioners, Regnauld, Bachelier, Thorp
Medicine	Biological understanding (busted by a long series of doctors)	Luck, trial and error, side effects of other medicines, or sometimes poisoning (mustard gas)
Industrial Revolution	Growth in knowledge, Scientific Revolution (busted by Kealey)	Adventurers, hobbyists
Technology	Formal science	Technology, businesses

Long before I knew of the results in Table 5, of other scholars debunking the lecturing-birds-how-to-fly effect, the problem started screaming at me, as follows, around 1998. I was sitting in a Chicago restaurant with the late Fred A., an economist, though a true, thoughtful gentleman. He was the chief economist of one of the local exchanges and had to advise them on new, complicated financial products and wanted my opinion on these, as I specialized in and had published a textbook of sorts on the so-called very complicated "exotic options." He recognized that the demand for these products was going to be very large, but he wondered "how traders could handle these complicated exotics if they do not understand the Girsanov theorem." The Girsanov theorem is something mathematically complicated that at the time was only known by a very small number of persons. And we were talking about pit traders who—as we saw in the last chapter—would most certainly mistake

Girsanov for a vodka brand. Traders, usually uneducated, were considered overeducated if they could spell their street address correctly, while the professor was truly under the epiphenomenal impression that traders studied mathematics to produce an option price. I for myself had figured out by trial and error and picking the brains of experienced people how to play with these complicated payoffs before I heard of these theorems.

Something hit me then. Nobody worries that a child ignorant of the various theorems of aerodynamics and incapable of solving an equation of motion would be unable to ride a bicycle. So why didn't he transfer the point from one domain to another? Didn't he realize that these Chicago pit traders respond to supply and demand, little more, in competing to make a buck, with no need for the Girsanov theorem, any more than a trader of pistachios in the Souk of Damascus needs to solve general equilibrium equations to set the price of his product?

For a minute I wondered if I was living on another planet or if the gentleman's PhD and research career had led to this blindness and his strange loss of common sense—or if people without practical sense usually manage to get the energy and interest to acquire a PhD in the fictional world of equation economics. Is there a selection bias?

I smelled a rat and got extremely excited but realized that for someone to be able to help me, he had to be both a practitioner and a researcher, with practice coming before research. I knew of only one other person, a trader turned researcher, Espen Haug, who had to have observed the same mechanism. Like me, he got his doctorate *after* spending time in trading rooms. So we immediately embarked on an investigation about the source of the option pricing formula that we were using: what did people use before? Is it thanks to the academically derived formula that we are able to operate, or did the formula come through some antifragile evolutionary discovery process based on trial and error, now expropriated by academics? I already had a hint, as I had worked as a pit trader in Chicago and had observed veteran traders who refused to touch mathematical formulas, using simple heuristics and saying "real men don't use sheets," the "sheets" being the printouts of output from the complex formulas that came out of computers. Yet these people had survived. Their prices were sophisticated and more efficient than those produced by the formula, and it was obvious what came first. For instance, the prices accounted for Extremistan and "fat tails," which the standard formulas ignored.

Haug has some interests that diverge from mine: he was into the subject of finance and eager to collect historical papers by practitioners. He called himself "the collector," even used it as a signature, as he went to assemble and collect books and articles on option theory written before the Great War, and from there we built a very precise image of what had taken place. To our great excitement, we had proof after proof that traders had vastly, vastly more sophistication than the formula. And their sophistication preceded the formula by at least a century. It was of course picked up through natural selection, survivorship, apprenticeship to experienced practitioners, and one's own experience.

> *Traders trade* → *traders figure out techniques and products* → *academic economists find formulas and claim traders are using them* → *new traders believe academics* → *blowups (from theory-induced fragility)*

Our paper sat for close to seven years before publication by an academic economics journal—until then, a strange phenomenon: it became one the most downloaded papers in the history of economics, but was not cited at all during its first few years. Nobody wanted to stir the pot.*

Practitioners don't write; they do. Birds fly and those who lecture them are the ones who write their story. So it is easy to see that history is truly written by losers with time on their hands and a protected academic position.

The greatest irony is that we watched firsthand how narratives of thought are made, as we were lucky enough to face another episode of blatant intellectual expropriation. We received an invitation to publish our side of the story—being option practitioners—in the honorable *Wiley Encyclopedia of Quantitative Finance*. So we wrote a version of the previous paper mixed with our own experiences. Shock: we caught the editor of the historical section, one Barnard College professor, red-handed trying to modify our account. A historian of economic thought, he proceeded to rewrite our story to play down, if not reverse, its message and change the arrow of the formation of knowledge. This was scientific history in the making. The fellow sitting in his office in

---

* We also figured out that two fragilistas, Myron Scholes and Robert Merton, got the Memorial Prize in Economics called "Nobel" for the packaging of a formula that other people discovered in much more sophisticated form before them. Furthermore, they used fictional mathematics. It is quite unsettling.

Barnard College was now dictating to us what we saw as traders—we were supposed to override what we saw with our own eyes with his logic.

I came to notice a few similar inversions of the formation of knowledge. For instance, in his book written in the late 1990s, the Berkeley professor Highly Certified Fragilista Mark Rubinstein attributed to publications by finance professors techniques and heuristics that we practitioners had been extremely familiar with (often in more sophisticated forms) since the 1980s, when I got involved in the business.

No, we don't put theories into practice. We create theories out of practice. That was our story, and it is easy to infer from it—and from similar stories—that the confusion is generalized. The theory is the child of the cure, not the opposite—*ex cura theoria nascitur*.

The Evidence Staring at Us

It turned out that engineers, too, get sandbagged by historians.

Right after the previous nauseating episode I presented the joint paper I had written with Haug on the idea of lecturing birds on how to fly in finance at the London School of Economics, in their sociology of science seminar. I was, of course, heckled (but was by then very well trained at being heckled by economists). Then, surprise. At the conclusion of the session, the organizers informed me that, exactly a week earlier, Phil Scranton, a professor from Rutgers, had delivered the exact same story. But it was not about the option formula; it was about the jet engine.

Scranton showed that we have been building and using jet engines in a completely trial-and-error experiential manner, without anyone truly understanding the theory. Builders needed the original engineers who knew how to twist things to make the engine work. *Theory came later,* in a lame way, to satisfy the intellectual bean counter. But that's not what you tend to read in standard histories of technology: my son, who studies aerospace engineering, was not aware of this. Scranton was polite and focused on situations in which innovation is messy, "distinguished from more familiar analytic and synthetic innovation approaches," as if the latter were the norm, which it is obviously not.

I looked for more stories, and the historian of technology David Edgerton presented me with a quite shocking one. We think of cybernetics—

which led to the "cyber" in cyberspace—as invented by Norbert Wiener in 1948. The historian of engineering David Mindell debunked the story; he showed that Wiener was articulating ideas about feedback control and digital computing that had long been in practice in the engineering world. Yet people—even today's engineers—have the illusion that we owe the field to Wiener's mathematical thinking.

Then I was hit with the following idea. We all learn geometry from textbooks based on axioms, like, say, Euclid's *Book of Elements,* and tend to think that it is thanks to such learning that we today have these beautiful geometric shapes in buildings, from houses to cathedrals; to think the opposite would be anathema. So I speculated immediately that the ancients developed an interest in Euclid's geometry and other mathematics because they were already using these methods, derived by tinkering and experiential knowledge, otherwise they would not have bothered at all. This is similar to the story of the wheel: recall that the steam engine had been discovered and developed by the Greeks some two millennia before the Industrial Revolution. It is just that things that are implemented tend to want to be born from practice, not theory.

Now take a look at architectural objects around us: they appear so geometrically sophisticated, from the pyramids to the beautiful cathedrals of Europe. So a sucker problem would make us tend to believe that mathematics led to these beautiful objects, with exceptions here and there such as the pyramids, as these preceded the more formal mathematics we had after Euclid and other Greek theorists. Some facts: architects (or what were then called Masters of Works) relied on heuristics, empirical methods, and tools, and almost nobody knew any mathematics—according to the medieval science historian Guy Beaujouan, before the thirteenth century no more than five persons in the whole of Europe knew how to perform a division. No theorem, shmeorem. But builders could figure out the resistance of materials without the equations we have today—buildings that are, for the most part, still standing. The thirteenth-century French architect Villard de Honnecourt documents with his series of drawings and notebooks in Picard (the language of the Picardie region in France) how cathedrals were built: experimental heuristics, small tricks and rules, later tabulated by Philibert de l'Orme in his architectural treatises. For instance, a triangle was visualized as the head of a horse. Experimentation can make people much more careful than theories.

Further, we are quite certain that the Romans, admirable engineers, built aqueducts without mathematics (Roman numerals did not make quantitative analysis very easy). Otherwise, I believe, these would not be here, as a patent side effect of mathematics is making people over-optimize and cut corners, causing fragility. Just look how the new is increasingly more perishable than the old.

And take a look at Vitruvius' manual, *De architectura,* the bible of architects, written about three hundred years after Euclid's *Elements.* There is little formal geometry in it, and, of course, no mention of Euclid, mostly heuristics, the kind of knowledge that comes out of a master guiding his apprentices. (Tellingly, the main mathematical result he mentions is Pythagoras's theorem, amazed that the right angle could be formed "without the contrivances of the artisan.") Mathematics had to have been limited to mental puzzles until the Renaissance.

Now I am not saying that theories or academic science are not behind some practical technologies at all, directly derived from science for their final use (not for some tangential use)—what the researcher Joel Mokyr calls an "epistemic base," or propositional knowledge, a sort of repository of formal "knowledge" that embeds the theoretical and empirical discoveries and becomes a rulebook of sorts, used to generate more knowledge and (he thinks) more applications. In other words, a body of theories from which further theories can be directly derived.

But let's not be suckers: following Mr. Mokyr would make one want to study economic geography to predict foreign exchange prices (I would have loved to introduce him to the expert in green lumber). While I accept the notion of epistemic base, what I question is the role it has really played in the history of technology. The evidence of a strong effect is not there, and I am waiting for someone to show it to me. Mokyr and the advocates of such view provide no evidence that it is not epiphenomenal—nor do they appear to understand the implications of asymmetric effects. Where is the role of optionality in this?

There is a body of know-how that was transmitted from master to apprentice, and transmitted *only* in such a manner—with degrees necessary as a selection process or to make the profession more respectable, or to help here and there, but not systematically. And the role of such formal knowledge will be overappreciated precisely because it is highly visible.

Is It Like Cooking?

Cooking seems to be the perfect business that depends on optionality. You add an ingredient and have the option of keeping the result if it is in agreement with Fat Tony's taste buds, or fuhgetaboudit if it's not. We also have wiki-style collaborative experimentation leading to a certain body of recipes. These recipes are derived entirely without conjectures about the chemistry of taste buds, with no role for any "epistemic base" to generate theories out of theories. Nobody is fooled so far by the process. As Dan Ariely once observed, we cannot reverse engineer the taste of food from looking at the nutritional label. And we can observe ancestral heuristics at work: generations of collective tinkering resulting in the evolution of recipes. These food recipes are embedded in cultures. Cooking schools are entirely apprenticeship based.

On the other side, we have pure physics, with theories used to generate theories with some empirical validation. There the "epistemic base" can play a role. The discovery of the Higgs Boson is a modern case of a particle entirely expected from theoretical derivations. So was Einstein's relativity. (Prior to the Higgs Boson, one spectacular case of a discovery with a small number of existing external data is that of the French astronomer Le Verrier's derivation of the existence of the planet Neptune. He did that on the basis of solitary computation, from the behavior of the surrounding planets. When the planet was actually sighted he refused to look at it, so comfortable was he with his result. These are exceptions, and tend to take place in physics and other places I call "linear," where errors are from Mediocristan, not from Extremistan.)

Now use this idea of cooking as a platform to grasp other pursuits: do other activities resemble it? If we put technologies through scrutiny, we would see that most do in fact resemble cooking a lot more than physics, particularly those in the complex domain.

Even medicine today remains an apprenticeship model with some theoretical science in the background, but made to look entirely like science. And if it leaves the apprenticeship model, it would be for the "evidence-based" method that relies less on biological theories and more on the cataloging of empirical regularities, the phenomenology I explained in Chapter 7. Why is it that science comes and goes and technologies remain stable?

Now, one can see a possible role for basic science, but not in the way it is intended to be.* For an example of a chain of unintended uses, let us start with Phase One, the computer. The mathematical discipline of combinatorics, here basic science, derived from propositional knowledge, led to the building of computers, or so the story goes. (And, of course, to remind the reader of cherry-picking, we need to take into account the body of theoretical knowledge that went nowhere.) But at first, nobody had an idea what to do with these enormous boxes full of circuits as they were cumbersome, expensive, and their applications were not too widespread, outside of database management, only good to process quantities of data. It is as if one needed to invent an application for the thrill of technology. Baby boomers will remember those mysterious punch cards. Then someone introduced the console to input with the aid of a screen monitor, using a keyboard. This led, of course, to word processing, and the computer took off because of its fitness to word processing, particularly with the microcomputer in the early 1980s. It was convenient, but not much more than that until some other unintended consequence came to be mixed into it. Now Phase Two, the Internet. It had been set up as a resilient military communication network device, developed by a research unit of the Department of Defense called DARPA and got a boost in the days when Ronald Reagan was obsessed with the Soviets. It was meant to allow the United States to survive a generalized military attack. Great idea, but add the personal computer *plus* Internet and we get social networks, broken marriages, a rise in nerdiness, the ability for a post-Soviet person with social difficulties to find a matching spouse. All that thanks to initial U.S. tax dollars (or rather budget deficit) during Reagan's anti-Soviet crusade.

So for now we are looking at the forward arrow and at no point, although science was of *some* use along the way since computer technology relies on science in most of its aspects; at no point did academic science serve in setting its direction, rather it served as a slave to chance discoveries in an opaque environment, with almost no one but college dropouts and overgrown high school students benefiting along the way. The process remained self-directed and unpredictable at every step. And the great fallacy is to make it sound irrational—the irrational resides in not seeing a free option when it is handed to us.

---

* I remind the reader that the bone in Book IV is teleology and sense of direction, and while this is largely skeptical of formal academia (i.e. anti-universities), this is staunchingly anti-pseudoscience (or cosmetic science) and ultra-pro-science. It is just that what many call science is highly unscientific. Science is an anti-sucker problem.

China might be a quite convincing story, through the works of a genius observer, Joseph Needham, who debunked quite a few Western beliefs and figured out the powers of Chinese science. As China became a top-down mandarinate (that is, a state managed by Soviet-Harvard centralized scribes, as Egypt had been before), the players somehow lost the zest for bricolage, the hunger for trial and error. Needham's biographer Simon Winchester cites the sinologist Mark Elvin's description of the problem, as the Chinese did not have, or, rather, no longer had, what he called the "European mania for tinkering and improving." They had all the means to develop a spinning machine, but "nobody tried"—another example of knowledge hampering optionality. They probably needed someone like Steve Jobs—blessed with an absence of college education and the right aggressiveness of temperament—to take the elements to their natural conclusion. As we will see in the next section, it is precisely this type of uninhibited doer who made the Industrial Revolution happen.

We will next examine two cases, first, the Industrial Revolution, and second, medicine. So let us start by debunking a causal myth about the Industrial Revolution, the overstatement of the role of science in it.

The Industrial Revolution

Knowledge formation, even when theoretical, takes time, some boredom, and the freedom that comes from having another occupation, therefore allowing one to escape the journalistic-style pressure of modern publish-and-perish academia to produce cosmetic knowledge, much like the counterfeit watches one buys in Chinatown in New York City, the type that you know is counterfeit although it looks like the real thing. There were two main sources of technical knowledge and innovation in the nineteenth and early twentieth centuries: the hobbyist and the English rector, both of whom were generally in barbell situations.

An extraordinary proportion of work came out of the rector, the English parish priest with no worries, erudition, a large or at least comfortable house, domestic help, a reliable supply of tea and scones with clotted cream, and an abundance of free time. And, of course, optionality. The enlightened amateur, that is. The Reverends Thomas Bayes (as in Bayesian probability) and Thomas Malthus (Malthusian overpopulation) are the most famous. But there are many more surprises, cataloged in Bill Bryson's *Home,* in which the author found ten times more vicars and clergymen leaving recorded traces for posterity than scientists, physicists, economists, and even inventors. In addition to the previous two giants, I randomly list contributions by country clergymen: Rev. Edmund Cartwright invented the power loom, contributing to the Industrial Revolution; Rev. Jack Russell bred the terrier; Rev. William Buckland was the first authority on dinosaurs; Rev. William Greenwell invented modern archaeology; Rev. Octavius Pickard-Cambridge was the foremost authority on spiders; Rev. George Garrett invented the submarine; Rev. Gilbert White was the most esteemed naturalist of his day; Rev. M. J. Berkeley was the top expert on fungi; Rev. John Michell helped discover Uranus; and many more. Note that, just as with our episode documented with Haug, that organized science tends to skip the "not made here," so the list of visible contribution by hobbyists and doers is most certainly shorter than the real one, as some academic might have appropriated the innovation by his predecessor.*

Let me get poetic for a moment. Self-directed scholarship has an aesthetic dimension. For a long time I had on the wall of my study the following quote by Jacques Le Goff, the great French medievalist, who believes that the Renaissance came out of independent humanists, not professional scholars. He examined the striking contrast in period paintings, drawings, and renditions that compare medieval university members and humanists:

> One is a professor surrounded and besieged by huddled students. The other is a solitary scholar, sitting in the tranquility and privacy of his chambers, at ease in the spacious and comfy room where his thoughts can move freely. Here we encounter the tumult of schools, the dust of classrooms, the indifference to beauty in collective workplaces,
>> There, it is all order and beauty,
>> *Luxe, calme et volupté*

As to the hobbyist in general, evidence shows him (along with the hungry adventurer and the private investor) to be at the source of the Industrial Revolution. Kealey, who we mentioned was not a historian and, thankfully, not an economist, in *The Economic Laws of Scientific*

* Remarkably, Johan Jensen, of Jensen's inequality, which provides the major technical support behind the ideas of this book, was an amateur mathematician who never held any academic position.

Research questions the conventional "linear model" (that is, the belief that academic science leads to technology)—for him, universities prospered as a consequence of national wealth, not the other way around. He even went further and claimed that like naive interventions, these had iatrogenics that provided a negative contribution. He showed that in countries in which the government intervened by funding research with tax money, private investment decreased and moved away. For instance, in Japan, the almighty MITI (Ministry for Technology and Investment) has a horrible record of investment. I am not using his ideas to prop up a political program against science funding, only to debunk causal arrows in the discovery of important things.

The Industrial Revolution, for a refresher, came from "technologists building technology," or what he calls "hobby science." Take again the steam engine, the one artifact that more than anything else embodies the Industrial Revolution. As we saw, we had a blueprint of how to build it from Hero of Alexandria. Yet the theory didn't interest anyone for about two millennia. So practice and rediscovery had to be the cause of the interest in Hero's blueprint, not the other way around.

Kealey presents a convincing—very convincing—argument that the steam engine emerged from preexisting technology and was created by uneducated, often isolated men who applied practical common sense and intuition to address the mechanical problems that beset them, and whose solutions would yield obvious economic reward.

Now, second, consider textile technologies. Again, the main technologies that led to the jump into the modern world owe, according to Kealey, nothing to science. "In 1733," he writes, "John Kay invented the flying shuttle, which mechanized weaving, and in 1770 James Hargreaves invented the spinning jenny, which as its name implies, mechanized spinning. These major developments in textile technology, as well as those of Wyatt and Paul (spinning frame, 1758), Arkwright (water frame, 1769), presaged the Industrial Revolution, yet they owed nothing to science; they were empirical developments based on the trial, error, and experimentation of skilled craftsmen who were trying to improve the productivity, and so the profits, of their factories."

David Edgerton did some work questioning the link between academic science and economic prosperity, along with the idea that people believed in the "linear model" (that is, that academic science was at the source of technology) in the past. People were *no suckers* in the nineteenth and twentieth centuries; we believe today that they believed in the said linear model then but they did not. In fact academics were mostly just teachers, not researchers, until well into the twentieth century.

Now, instead of looking into a scholar's writings to see whether he is credible or not, it is always best to consider what his detractors say—they will uncover what's worst in his argument. So I looked for the detractors of Kealey, or people opposing his ideas, to see if they address anything of merit—and to see where they come from. Aside from some comments by Joel Mokyr, who, as I said, has not yet discovered optionality, and an attack by an economist of the type that doesn't count, given the devaluation of the currency of the economics profession, the main critique against Kealey, published in the influential journal *Nature* by a science bureaucrat, was that he uses data from government-sponsored agencies such as the OECD in his argument against tax-funded research. So far, no substantive evidence that Kealey was wrong. But, let us flip the burden of evidence: there is *zero* evidence that the opposite of his thesis is remotely right. Much of all of this is a religious belief in the *unconditional* power of organized science, one that has replaced unconditional religious belief in organized religion.

Governments Should Spend on Nonteleological Tinkering, Not Research

Note that I do not believe that the argument set forth above should logically lead us to say that *no* money should be spent by government. This reasoning is more against teleology than research in general. There has to be a form of spending that works. By some vicious turn of events, governments have gotten huge payoffs from research, but not as intended—just consider the Internet. And look at the recapture we've had of military expenditures with innovations, and, as we will see, medical cures. It is just that functionaries are too teleological in the way they look for things (particularly the Japanese), and so are large corporations. Most large corporations, such as Big Pharma, are their own enemies.

Consider *blue sky* research, whereby research grants and funding are given to people, not projects, and spread in small amounts across many researchers. The sociologist of science Steve Shapin, who spent time in California observing venture capitalists, reports that investors tend to back entrepreneurs, not ideas. Decisions are largely a matter of opinion strengthened with "who you know" and "who said what," as, to use the venture capitalist's lingo, you bet on the jockey, not the horse. Why?

Because innovations drift, and one needs flâneur-like abilities to keep capturing the opportunities that arise, not stay locked up in a bureaucratic mold. The significant venture capital decisions, Shapin showed, were made without real business plans. So if there was any "analysis," it had to be of a backup, confirmatory nature. I myself spent some time with venture capitalists in California, with an eye on investing myself, and sure enough, that was the mold.

Visibly the money should go to the tinkerers, the aggressive tinkerers who you trust will milk the option.

Let us use statistical arguments and get technical for a paragraph. Payoffs from research are from Extremistan; they follow a power-law type of statistical distribution, with big, near-unlimited upside but, because of optionality, limited downside. Consequently, payoff from research should necessarily be linear to number of trials, not total funds involved in the trials. Since, as in Figure 7, the winner will have an explosive payoff, uncapped, the right approach requires a certain style of blind funding. It means the right policy would be what is called "one divided by n" or "1/N" style, spreading attempts in as large a number of trials as possible: if you face n options, invest in all of them in equal amounts.* Small amounts per trial, lots of trials, broader than you want. Why? Because in Extremistan, it is more important to be in something in a small amount than to miss it. As one venture capitalist told me: "The payoff can be so large that you can't afford not to be in everything."

THE CASE IN MEDICINE

Unlike technology, medicine has a long history of domestication of luck; it now has accepted randomness in its practice. But not quite.

Medical data allow us to assess the performance of teleological research compared to randomly generated discoveries. The U.S. government provides us with the ideal dataset for that: the activities of the National Cancer Institute that came out of the Nixon "war on cancer" in the early 1970s. Morton Meyers, a practicing doctor and researcher, writes in his wonderful *Happy Accidents: Serendipity in Modern Medical Breakthroughs:* "Over a twenty-year period of screening more than

* This is a technical comment. "1/N" is the argument Mandelbrot and I used in 2005 to debunk optimized portfolios and modern finance theory on simple mathematical grounds; under Extremistan effects, we favor broad, very broad diversification with small equal allocations rather than what modern financial theory stipulates.

144,000 plant extracts, representing about 15,000 species, not a single plant-based anticancer drug reached approved status. This failure stands in stark contrast to the discovery in the late 1950s of a major group of plant-derived cancer drugs, the Vinca Alcaloids—a discovery that came about by chance, not through directed research."

John LaMatina, an insider who described what he saw after leaving the pharmaceutical business, shows statistics illustrating the gap between public perception of academic contributions and truth: private industry develops nine drugs out of ten. Even the tax-funded National Institutes of Health found that out of forty-six drugs on the market with significant sales, about three had anything to do with federal funding.

We have not digested the fact that cures for cancer had been coming from other branches of research. You search for noncancer drugs (or noncancer nondrugs) and find something you were not looking for (and vice versa). But the interesting constant is that when a result is initially discovered by an academic researcher, he is likely to disregard the consequences because it is not what he wanted to find—an academic has a script to follow. So, to put it in option terms, he does not exercise his option in spite of its value, a strict violation of rationality (no matter how you define rationality), like someone who both is greedy and does not pick up a large sum of money found in his garden. Meyers also shows the lecturing-birds-how-to-fly effect as discoveries are ex post narrated back to some academic research, contributing to our illusion.

In some cases, because the source of the discovery is military, we don't know exactly what's going on. Take for instance chemotherapy for cancer, as discussed in Meyers's book. An American ship carrying mustard gas off Bari in Italy was bombed by the Germans in 1942. It helped develop chemotherapy owing to the effect of the gas on the condition of the soldiers who had liquid cancers (eradication of white blood cells). But mustard gas was banned by the Geneva Conventions, so the story was kept secret—Churchill purged all mention from U.K. records, and in the United States, the information was stifled, though not the research on the effect of nitrogen mustard.

James Le Fanu, the doctor and writer about medicine, wrote that the therapeutic revolution, or the period in the postwar years that saw a large number of effective therapies, was not ignited by a major scientific insight. It came from the exact opposite, "the realization by doctors and scientists that it was not necessary to understand in any detail what was wrong, but that synthetic chemistry blindly and randomly would deliver the remedies that had eluded doctors for centuries." (He uses as a central example the sulfonamides identified by Gerhard Domagk.)

Further, the increase in our theoretical understanding—the "epistemic base," to use Mokyr's term—came with a *decrease* in the number of new drugs. This is something Fat Tony or the green lumber fellow could have told us. Now, one can argue that we depleted the low-hanging fruits, but I go further, with more cues from other parts (such as the payoff from the Human Genome Project or the stalling of medical cures of the past two decades in the face of the growing research expenditures)—knowledge, or what is called "knowledge," in complex domains inhibits research.

Or, another way to see it, studying the chemical composition of ingredients will make you neither a better cook nor a more expert taster—it might even make you worse at both. (Cooking is particularly humbling for teleology-driven fellows.)

One can make a list of medications that came Black Swan–style from serendipity and compare it to the list of medications that came from design. I was about to embark on such a list until I realized that the notable exceptions, that is, drugs that were discovered in a teleological manner, are too few—mostly AZT, AIDS drugs. Designer drugs have a main property—they are designed (and are therefore teleological). But it does not look as if we are capable of designing a drug while taking into account the potential side effects. Hence a problem for the future of designer drugs. The more drugs there are on the market, the more interactions with one another—so we end up with a swelling number of possible interactions with every new drug introduced. If there are twenty unrelated drugs, the twenty-first would need to consider twenty interactions, no big deal. But if there are a thousand, we would need to predict a little less than a thousand. And there are tens of thousands of drugs available today. Further, there is research showing that we may be underestimating the interactions of *current* drugs, those already on the market, by a factor of four so, if anything, the pool of available drugs should be shrinking rather than growing.

There is an obvious drift in that business, as a drug can be invented for something and find new applications, what the economist John Kay calls *obliquity*—aspirin, for instance, changed many times in uses; or the ideas of Judah Folkman about restricting the blood supply of tumors (angiogenesis inhibitors) have led to the treatment of macular degeneration (bevacizumab, known as Avastin), an effect that is more effective than the original intent.

Now, instead of giving my laundry list of drugs here (too inelegant), I refer the reader to, in addition to Meyers's book, Claude Bohuon and Claude Monneret, *Fabuleux hasards, histoire de la découverte des médicaments,* and Jie Jack Li's *Laughing Gas, Viagra and Lipitor.*

Matt Ridley's Anti-Teleological Argument

The great medieval Arabic-language skeptic philosopher Algazel, aka Al-Ghazali, who tried to destroy the teleology of Averroes and his rationalism, came up with the famous metaphor of the pin—now falsely attributed to Adam Smith. The pin doesn't have a single maker, but twenty-five persons involved; these are all collaborating in the absence of a central planner—a collaboration guided by an invisible hand. For not a single one knows how to produce it on his own.

In the eyes of Algazel, a skeptic fideist (i.e., a skeptic with religious faith), knowledge was not in the hands of humans, but in those of God, while Adam Smith calls it the law of the market and some modern theorist presents it as self-organization. If the reader wonders why fideism is epistemologically equivalent to pure skepticism about human knowledge and embracing the hidden logics of things, just replace God with nature, fate, the Invisible, Opaque, and Inaccessible, and you mostly get the same result. The logic of things stands outside of us (in the hands of God or natural or spontaneous forces); and given that nobody these days is in direct communication with God, even in Texas, there is little difference between God and opacity. Not a single individual has a clue about the general process, and that is central.

The author Matt Ridley produces a more potent argument thanks to his background in biology. The difference between humans and animals lies in the ability to collaborate, engage in business, let ideas, pardon the expression, copulate. Collaboration has explosive upside, what is mathematically called a superadditive function, i.e., one plus one equals more than two, and one plus one plus one equals much, much more than three. That is pure nonlinearity with explosive benefits—we will get into details on how it benefits from the philosopher's stone. Crucially, this is an argument for unpredictability and Black Swan effects: since you cannot forecast collaborations and cannot direct them, you cannot see where the world is going. All you can do is create an environment that facilitates these collaborations, and lay the foundation for prosperity. And, no, you cannot centralize innovations, we tried that in Russia.

Remarkably, to get a bit more philosophical with the ideas of Algazel, one can see religion's effect here in reducing dependence on the fallibility of human theories and agency—so Adam Smith meets Algazel in that sense. For one the invisible hand is the market, for the other it is God. It has been difficult for people to understand that, historically, skepticism has been mostly skepticism of expert knowledge rather than skepticism about abstract entities like God, and that all the great skeptics have been largely either religious or, at least, pro-religion (that is, in favor of *others* being religious).

Corporate Teleology

When I was in business school I rarely attended lectures in something called strategic planning, a required course, and when I showed my face in class, I did not listen for a nanosecond to what was said there; did not even buy the books. There is something about the common sense of student culture; we knew that it was all babble. I passed the required classes in management by confusing the professors, playing with complicated logics, and I felt it intellectually dishonest to enroll in more classes than the strictly necessary.

Corporations are in love with the idea of the strategic plan. They need to pay to figure out where they are going. Yet there is no evidence that strategic planning works—we even seem to have evidence against it. A management scholar, William Starbuck, has published a few papers debunking the effectiveness of planning—it makes the corporation option-blind, as it gets locked into a non-opportunistic course of action.

Almost everything theoretical in management, from Taylorism to all productivity stories, upon empirical testing, has been exposed as pseudoscience—and like most economic theories, lives in a world parallel to the evidence. Matthew Stewart, who, trained as a philosopher, found himself in a management consultant job, gives a pretty revolting, if funny, inside story in *The Management Myth*. It is similar to the self-serving approach of bankers. Abrahamson and Friedman, in their beautiful book *A Perfect Mess*, also debunk many of these neat, crisp, teleological approaches. It turns out, strategic planning is just superstitious babble.

For an illustration of business drift, rational and opportunistic business drift, take the following. Coca-Cola began as a pharmaceutical product. Tiffany & Co., the fancy jewelry store company, started life as a stationery store. The last two examples are close, perhaps, but consider next: Raytheon, which made the first missile guidance system, was a refrigerator maker (one of the founders was no other than Vannevar Bush, who conceived the teleological linear model of science we saw earlier; go figure). Now, worse: Nokia, who used to be the top mobile phone maker, began as a paper mill (at some stage they were into rubber shoes). DuPont, now famous for Teflon nonstick cooking pans, Corian countertops, and the durable fabric Kevlar, actually started out as an explosives company. Avon, the cosmetics company, started out in door-to-door book sales. And, the strangest of all, Oneida Silversmiths was a community religious cult but for regulatory reasons they needed to use as cover a joint stock company.

THE INVERSE TURKEY PROBLEM

Now some plumbing behind what I am saying—epistemology of statistical statements. The following discussion will show how the unknown, what you don't see, can contain good news in one case and bad news in another. And in Extremistan territory, things get even more accentuated.

To repeat (it is necessary to repeat because intellectuals tend to forget it), absence of evidence is not evidence of absence, a simple point that has the following implications: for the antifragile, good news tends to be absent from past data, and for the fragile it is the bad news that doesn't show easily.

Imagine going to Mexico with a notebook and trying to figure out the average wealth of the population from talking to people you randomly encounter. Odds are that, without Carlos Slim in your sample, you have little information. For out of the hundred or so million Mexicans, Slim would (I estimate) be richer than the bottom seventy to ninety million all taken together. So you may sample fifty million persons and unless you include that "rare event," you may have nothing in your sample and underestimate the total wealth.

Remember the graphs in Figures 6 or 7 illustrating the payoff from trial and error. When engaging in tinkering, you incur a lot of small losses, then once in a while you find something rather significant. Such methodology will show nasty attributes when seen from the outside—it hides its qualities, not its defects.

> *In the antifragile case (of positive asymmetries, positive Black Swan businesses), such as trial and error, the sample track record will tend to underestimate the long-term average; it will hide the qualities, not the defects.*

(A chart is included in the appendix for those who like to look at the point graphically.)

Recall our mission to "not be a turkey." The take-home is that, when facing a long sample subjected to turkey problems, one tends to estimate a *lower* number of adverse events—simply, rare events are rare, and tend not to show up in past samples, and given that *the rare is almost always negative*, we get a rosier picture than reality. But here we face the mirror image, the reverse situation. Under positive asymmetries, that is, the antifragile case, the "unseen" is positive. So "empirical evidence" tends to miss positive events and underestimate the total benefits.

As to the classic turkey problem, the rule is as follows.

> *In the fragile case of negative asymmetries (turkey problems), the sample track record will tend to overestimate the long-term average; it will hide the defects and display the qualities.*

The consequences make life simple. But since standard methodologies do not take asymmetries into account, about anyone who studied conventional statistics without getting very deep into the subject (just to theorize in social science or teach students) will get the turkey problem wrong. I have a simple rule, that those who teach at Harvard should be expected to have much less understanding of things than cab drivers or people innocent of canned methods of inference (it is a heuristic, it can be wrong, but it works; it came to my attention as the Harvard Business School used to include Fragilista Robert C. Merton on its staff).

So let us pick on Harvard Business School professors who deserve it quite a bit. When it comes to the first case (the error of ignoring positive asymmetries), one Harvard Business School professor, Gary Pisano, writing about the potential of biotech, made the elementary inverse-turkey mistake, not realizing that in a business with limited losses and unlimited potential (the exact opposite of banking), what you don't see can be both significant and hidden from the past. He writes: "Despite the commercial success of several companies and the stunning growth in revenues for the industry as a whole, most biotechnology firms earn no profit." This may be correct, but the inference from it is wrong, possibly backward, on two counts, and it helps to repeat the logic owing to the gravity of the consequences. First, "most companies" in Extremistan make no profit—the rare event dominates, and a small number of companies generate all the shekels. And whatever point he may have, in the presence of the kind of asymmetry and optionality we see in Figure 7, it is inconclusive, so it is better to write about another subject, something less harmful that may interest Harvard students, like how to make a convincing PowerPoint presentation or the difference in managerial cultures between the Japanese and the French. Again, he may be right about the pitiful potential of biotech investments, but not on the basis of the data he showed.

Now why is such thinking by the likes of Professor Pisano dangerous? It is not a matter of whether or not he would inhibit research in biotech. The problem is that such a mistake inhibits everything in economic life that has antifragile properties (more technically, "right-skewed"). And it would fragilize by favoring matters that are "sure bets."

Remarkably, another Harvard professor, Kenneth Froot, made the exact same mistake, but in the opposite direction, with the negative asymmetries. Looking at reinsurance companies (those that insure catastrophic events), he thought that he found an aberration. They made too much profit given the risks they took, as catastrophes seemed to occur *less often* than what was reflected in the premia. He missed the point that catastrophic events hit them only negatively, and tend to be absent from past data (again, they are rare). Remember the turkey problem. One single episode, the asbestos liabilities, bankrupted families of Lloyd underwriters, losing income made over generations. One single episode.

We will return to these two distinct payoffs, with "bounded left" (limited losses, like Thales' bet) and "bounded right" (limited gains, like insurance or banking). The distinction is crucial, as most payoffs in life fall in either one or the other category.

To Fail Seven Times, Plus or Minus Two

Let me stop to issue rules based on the chapter so far. (i) Look for optionality; in fact, rank things according to optionality, (ii) preferably with open-ended, not closed-ended, payoffs; (iii) Do not invest in business plans but in people, so look for someone capable of changing six or seven times over his career, or more (an idea that is part of the modus operandi of the venture capitalist Marc Andreessen); one gets immunity from the backfit narratives of the business plan by investing in people. It is simply more robust to do so; (iv) Make sure you are barbelled, whatever that means in your business.

THE CHARLATAN, THE ACADEMIC, AND THE SHOWMAN

I end the chapter on a sad note: our ingratitude toward many who have helped us get here—letting our ancestors survive.

Our misunderstanding of convex tinkering, antifragility, and how to tame randomness is woven into our institutions—though not consciously and explicitly. There is a category of people in medicine called the empirics, or empirical skeptics, the doers, and that is about it—we do not have many names for them as they have not written a lot of books. Many of their works were destroyed or hidden from cultural consciousness, or have naturally dropped out of the archives, and their memory has been treated very badly by history. Formal thinkers and theorizing theorizers tend to write books; seat-of-the-pants people tend to be practitioners who are often content to get the excitement, make or lose the money, and discourse at the pub. Their experiences are often formalized by academics; indeed, history has been written by those who want you to believe that reasoning has a monopoly or near monopoly on the production of knowledge.

So the final point here is about those called charlatans. Some were, others were less so; some were not; and many were borderline. For a long time official medicine had to compete with crowds of flashy showmen, mountebanks, quacks, sorcerers and sorceresses, and all manner of unlicensed practitioners. Some were itinerant, going from town to town carrying out their curative acts in front of large gatherings. They would perform surgery on occasion while repeating incantations.

This category included doctors who did not subscribe to the dominant Graeco-Arabic school of rational medicine, developed in the Hellenistic world of Asia Minor and later grown by the Arabic language school. The Romans were an anti-theoretical pragmatic bunch; the Arabs loved everything philosophical and "scientific" and put Aristotle, about whom nobody seemed to have cared much until then, on a pedestal. For instance we know very, very little of the skeptical empirical school of Menodotus of Nicomedia—we know a lot more about Galen, the rationalist. Medicine, for the Arabs, was a scholarly pursuit and founded on the logic of Aristotle and the methods of Galen; they abhorred experience.* Medical practitioners were the Other.

The regulation of the medical establishment corresponds to worries about the empirics for economic reasons as competition made their incomes drop. So no wonder these were bundled with the thieves, to wit this long title for an Elizabethan treatise: *A short discourse, or, discouery of certaine stratagems, whereby our London-empericks, haue bene obserued strongly to oppugne, and oft times to expugne their poore patients purses.*

"Charlatan" was held to be a synonym for *empirick*. The word "empiric" designated someone who relied on experiment and experience to ascertain what was correct. In other words, trial and error and tinkering. That was held to be inferior—professionally, socially, and intellectually. It is still not considered to be very "intelligent."

But luckily for us, the empirics enjoyed immense popular support and could not be uprooted. You do not see their works, but they left a huge imprint on medicine.

Note the initial peaking of iatrogenics after the academization—and institutionalization—of medicine with the onset of modernity. It has only recently started to reverse. Also, formal academics, seen in the light of history, were not better than those they called charlatans—they just hid their fraud under the weight of more convincing rationalizations. They were just *organized* quacks. My hope is for that to change.

Now, I agree that most nonacademically vetted medical practitioners were scoundrels, mountebanks, quacks, and often even worse than these. But let's hold off jumping to the wrong conclusions. Formalists, to protect their turf, have always played on the logical fallacy that if quacks are found among nonacademics, nonacademics are all quacks. They keep doing it: the statement *all that is nonrigorous is nonacademic* (as-

---

* It is not very well noticed that Arabic thought favors abstract thinking and science in the most theoretical sense of the word — violently rationalistic, away from empiricism.

suming one is a sucker and believes it) does not imply that *all that is nonacademic is nonrigorous.* The fight between the "legitimate" doctors and the Others is quite enlightening, particularly when you note that doctors were silently (and reluctantly) copying some of the remedies and cures developed and promoted by the Others. They had to do so for economic reasons. They benefited from the collective trial and error of the Others. And the process led to cures, now integrated into medicine.

Now, reader, let us take a minute and pay some respect. Consider our ingratitude to those who got us here, got our disrespect, and do not even know that they were heroes.

CHAPTER 16

A Lesson In Disorder

Where is the next street fight?—How to decommoditize, detouristify—
The intelligent student (also in reverse)—Flâneur as options

Let us continue with teleology and disorder—in private life and individual education. Then an autobiographical vignette.

THE ECOLOGICAL AND THE LUDIC

As we saw with the fellow making the common but false analogy to blackjack in Chapter 7, there are two domains, the ludic, which is set up like a game, with its rules supplied in advance in an explicit way, and the ecological, where we don't know the rules and cannot isolate variables, as in real life. Seeing the nontransferability of skills from one domain to the other led me to skepticism in general about whatever skills are acquired in a classroom, anything in a non-ecological way, as compared to street fights and real-life situations.

It is not well advertised that there is no evidence that abilities in chess lead to better reasoning off the chessboard—even those who play blind chess games with an entire cohort can't remember things outside the board better than a regular person. We accept the domain-specificity of games, the fact that they do not really train you for life, that there are severe losses in translation. But we find it hard to apply this lesson to technical skills acquired in schools, that is, to accept the crucial fact that what is picked up in the classroom *stays* largely in the classroom. Worse even, the classroom can bring some detectable harm, a measure of iatrogenics hardly ever discussed: Laura Martignon showed me results from her doctoral student Birgit Ulmer demonstrating that children's ability to *count* degrades right after they are taught arithmetic. When you ask children how many intervals there are between fifteen poles, those who don't know arithmetic figure out that there are fourteen of them. Those who studied arithmetic get confused and often make the mistake that there are fifteen.

The Touristification of the Soccer Mom

The biologist and intellectual E. O. Wilson was once asked what represented the most hindrance to the development of children; his answer was the soccer mom. He did not use the notion of the Procrustean bed, but he outlined it perfectly. His argument is that they repress children's natural biophilia, their love of living things. But the problem is more general; soccer moms try to eliminate the trial and error, the antifragility, from children's lives, move them away from the ecological and transform them into nerds working on preexisting (soccer-mom-compatible) maps of reality. Good students, but nerds—that is, they are like computers except slower. Further, they are now totally untrained to handle ambiguity. As a child of civil war, I disbelieve in structured learning— actually I believe that one can be an intellectual without being a nerd, provided one has a private library instead of a classroom, and spends time as an aimless (but rational) flâneur benefiting from what randomness can give us inside and outside the library. Provided we have the right type of rigor, we need randomness, mess, adventures, uncertainty, self-discovery, near-traumatic episodes, all these things that make life worth living, compared to the structured, fake, and ineffective life of an empty-suit CEO with a preset schedule and an alarm clock. Even their leisure is subjected to a clock, squash between four and five, as their life is sandwiched between appointments. It is as if the mission of modernity was to squeeze every drop of variability and randomness out of life—with (as we saw in Chapter 5) the ironic result of making the world a lot more unpredictable, as if the goddesses of chance wanted to have the last word.

Only the autodidacts are free. And not just in school matters—those who decommoditize, detouristify their lives. Sports try to put randomness in a box like the ones sold in aisle six next to canned tuna—a form of alienation.

If you want to understand how vapid are the current modernistic arguments (and understand your existential priorities), consider the difference between lions in the wild and those in captivity. Lions in captivity live longer; they are technically richer, and they are guaranteed job security for life, if these are the criteria you are focusing on . . .

As usual, an ancient, here Seneca, detected the problem (and the difference) with his saying "We do not study for life, but only for the lecture room," *non vitae, sed scolae discimus,* which to my great horror has been corrupted and self-servingly changed to fit the motto of many colleges in the United States, with *non scolae, sed vitae discimus* as their motto, meaning that "We study [here] for life, not for the lecture hall."

Most of the tension in life will take place when the one who reduces and fragilizes (say the policy maker) invokes rationality.

AN ANTIFRAGILE (BARBELL) EDUCATION

Something cured me of the effect of education, and made me very skeptical of the very notion of standardized learning.

For I am a pure autodidact, in spite of acquiring degrees.

My father was known in Lebanon as the "Intelligent Student Student Intelligent," a play on words, as the Arabic phrase for "intelligent student" (or scholar) is *taleb nagib* and his name was Nagib Taleb. That was the way the newspaper published his name for having the highest grade on the Lebanese high school exit exam. He was a national valedictorian of sorts, and the main newspaper announced his passing in 2002 with a front-page headline with a pun on his predestined name, THE INTELLIGENT STUDENT STUDENT INTELLIGENT IS NO LONGER. His school education was harrowing, though, as he attended the elite Jesuit school. The Jesuits' mission was to produce the mandarins who ran the place, by filtering and filtering students after every year. They were successful beyond their aim, as in addition to having one of the highest success rates in the world in the French baccalaureate (in spite of the war), their school had a world-class roster of former students. The Jesuits also deprived pupils of free time, so many gave up voluntarily. So one can surmise that having a father as national valedictorian would definitely have provided me with a cure against school, and it did. My father himself did not seem to overvalue school education, since he did not put me in the

Jesuit school—to spare me what he went through. But this clearly left me to seek ego fulfillment elsewhere.

Observing my father close up made me realize what being a valedictorian meant, what being an *Intelligent Student* meant, mostly in the negative: they were things that intelligent students were unable to understand. Some blindness came with the package. This idea followed me for a long time, as when I worked in trading rooms, where you sit most of the time waiting for things to happen, a situation similar to that of people sitting in bars or mafia men "hanging around." I figured out how to select people on their ability to integrate socially with others while sitting around doing nothing and enjoying fuzziness. You select people on their ability to hang around, as a filter, and studious people were not good at hanging around: they needed to have a clear task.

When I was about ten I realized that good grades weren't as good outside school as they were in it, as they carried some side effects. They had to correspond to a sacrifice, an intellectual sacrifice of sorts. Actually my father kept hinting to me the problem of getting good grades himself: the person who was at the exact bottom of his class (and ironically, the father of a classmate at Wharton) turned out to be a self-made merchant, by far the most successful person in his class (he had a huge yacht with his initials prominently displayed on it); another one made a killing buying wood in Africa, retired before forty, then became an amateur historian (mostly in ancient Mediterranean history) and entered politics. In a way my father did not seem to value education, rather culture or money—and he prompted me to go for these two (I initially went for culture). He had a total fascination with erudites and businessmen, people whose position did not depend on credentials.

My idea was to be rigorous in the open market. This made me focus on what an intelligent antistudent needed to be: an autodidact—or a person of knowledge compared to the students called "swallowers" in Lebanese dialect, those who "swallow school material" and whose knowledge is only derived from the curriculum. The edge, I realized, isn't in the package of what was on the official program of the baccalaureate, which everyone knew with small variations multiplying into large discrepancies in grades, but exactly what lay outside it.

Some can be more intelligent than others in a structured environment—in fact school has a selection bias as it favors those quicker in such an environment, and like anything competitive, at the expense of performance outside it. Although I was not yet familiar with gyms, my idea of knowledge was as follows. People who build their strength using these modern expensive gym machines can lift extremely large weights, show great numbers and develop impressive-looking muscles, but fail to lift a stone; they get completely hammered in a street fight by someone trained in more disorderly settings. Their strength is extremely domain-specific and their domain doesn't exist outside of ludic—extremely organized—constructs. In fact their strength, as with overspecialized athletes, is the result of a deformity. I thought it was the same with people who were selected for trying to get high grades in a small number of subjects rather than follow their curiosity: try taking them slightly away from what they studied and watch their decomposition, loss of confidence, and denial. (Just like corporate executives are selected for their ability to put up with the boredom of meetings, many of these people were selected for their ability to concentrate on boring material.) I've debated many economists who claim to specialize in risk and probability: when one takes them slightly outside their narrow focus, but within the discipline of probability, they fall apart, with the disconsolate face of a gym rat in front of a gangster hit man.

Again, I wasn't exactly an autodidact, since I did get degrees; I was rather a barbell autodidact as I studied the exact minimum necessary to pass any exam, overshooting accidentally once in a while, and only getting in trouble a few times by undershooting. But I read voraciously, wholesale, initially in the humanities, later in mathematics and science, and now in history—outside a curriculum, away from the gym machine so to speak. I figured out that whatever I selected myself I could read with more depth and more breadth—there was a match to my curiosity. And I could take advantage of what people later pathologized as Attention Deficit Hyperactive Disorder (ADHD) by using natural stimulation as a main driver to scholarship. The enterprise needed to be totally effortless in order to be worthwhile. The minute I was bored with a book or a subject I moved to another one, instead of giving up on reading altogether—when you are limited to the school material and you get bored, you have a tendency to give up and do nothing or play hooky out of discouragement. The trick is to be bored with a specific book, rather than with the act of reading. So the number of pages absorbed could grow faster than otherwise. And you find gold, so to speak, effortlessly, just as in rational but undirected trial-and-error-based research. It is exactly like options, trial and error, not getting stuck, bifurcating when necessary but keeping a sense of broad freedom and opportunism. Trial and error is freedom.

(I confess I still use that method at the time of this writing. Avoidance of boredom is the only worthy mode of action. Life otherwise is not worth living.)

My parents had an account with the largest bookstore in Beirut and I would pick up books in what seemed to me unlimited quantities. There was such a difference between the shelves of the library and the narrow school material; so I realized that school was a plot designed to deprive people of erudition by squeezing their knowledge into a narrow set of authors. I started, around the age of thirteen, to keep a log of my reading hours, shooting for between thirty and sixty a week, a practice I've kept up for a long time. I read the likes of Dostoyevsky, Turgenev, Chekhov, Bishop Bossuet, Stendhal, Dante, Proust, Borges, Calvino, Céline, Schultz, Zweig (didn't like), Henry Miller, Max Brod, Kafka, Ionesco, the surrealists, Faulkner, Malraux (along with other wild adventurers such as Conrad and Melville; the first book I read in English was *Moby-Dick*) and similar authors in literature, many of them obscure, and Hegel, Schopenhauer, Nietzsche, Marx, Jaspers, Husserl, Lévi-Strauss, Levinas, Scholem, Benjamin, and similar ones in philosophy because they had the golden status of not being on the school program, and I managed to read *nothing* that was prescribed by school so to this day I haven't read Racine, Corneille, and other bores. One summer I decided to read the twenty novels by Émile Zola in twenty days, one a day, and managed to do so at great expense. Perhaps joining an underground anti-government group motivated me to look into Marxist studies, and I picked up the most about Hegel indirectly, mostly through Alexandre Kojève.

When I decided to come to the United States, I repeated, around the age of eighteen, the marathon exercise by buying a few hundred books in English (by authors ranging from Trollope to Burke, Macaulay, and Gibbon, with Anaïs Nin and other then fashionable authors *de scandale*), not showing up to class, and keeping the thirty- to sixty-hour discipline.

In school, I had figured out that when one could write essays with a rich, literary, but precise vocabulary (though not inadequate to the topic at hand), and maintain some coherence throughout, what one writes about becomes secondary and the examiners get a hint about one's style and rigor from that. And my father gave me a complete break after I got published as a teenager in the local paper—"just don't flunk" was his condition. It was a barbell—play it safe at school and read on your own, have *zero* expectation from school. Later, after I was jailed for assaulting a policeman in a student riot, he acted scared of me and let me do whatever I wanted. When I reached the "f*** you money" stage in my twenties, at the time when it was much, much rarer than today, in spite of a war raging in the home country, my father took credit for it by attributing it to the breadth of the education he allowed me to have and how it differentiated me from others like him with narrow background.

When, at Wharton, I discovered that I wanted to specialize in a profession linked to probability and rare events, a probability and randomness obsession took control of my mind. I also smelled some flaws with statistical stuff that the professor could not explain, brushing them away—it was what the professor was brushing away that had to be the meat. I realized that there was a fraud somewhere, that "six sigma" events (measures of very rare events) were grossly miscomputed and we had no basis for their computation, but I could not articulate my realization clearly, and was getting humiliated by people who started smoking me with complicated math. I saw the limits of probability in front of me, clear as crystal, but could not find the words to express the point. So I went to the bookstore and ordered (there was no Web at the time) almost every book with "probability" or "stochastic" in its title. I read nothing else for a couple of years, no course material, no newspaper, no literature, nothing. I read them in bed, jumping from one book to the next when stuck with something I did not get immediately or felt ever so slightly bored. And I kept ordering those books. I was hungry to go deeper into the problem of small probabilities. It was effortless. That was my best investment—risk turned out to be the topic I know the best. Five years later I was set for life and now I am making a research career out of various aspects of small probability events. Had I studied the subject by prepackaged means, I would be now brainwashed into thinking that uncertainty was something to be found in a casino, that kind of thing. There is such a thing as nonnerdy applied mathematics: find a problem first, and figure out the math that works for it (just as one acquires language), rather than study in a vacuum through theorems and artificial examples, then change reality to make it look like these examples.

One day in the 1980s I had dinner with a famous speculator, a hugely successful man. He muttered the hyperbole that hit home: "much of what other people know isn't worth knowing."

To this day I still have the instinct that the treasure, what one needs to know for a profession, is necessarily what lies outside the corpus, as far away from the center as possible. But there is something central in following one's own direction in the selection of readings: what I was given to study in school I have forgotten; what I decided to read on my own, I still remember.

CHAPTER 17

Fat Tony Debates Socrates

Piety for the impious—Fat Tony does not drink milk—Always ask poets to explain their poetry—Mystagogue philosophaster

———

Fat Tony believes that they were totally justified in putting Socrates to death.

This chapter will allow us to complete the discussion of the difference between narrated, intelligible knowledge, and the more opaque kind that is entirely probed by tinkering—the two columns of Table 4 separating narrative and non-narrative action. There is this error of thinking that things always have a *reason* that is accessible to us—that we can comprehend easily.

Indeed, the most severe mistake made in life is to mistake the unintelligible for the unintelligent—something Nietzsche figured out. In a way, it resembles the turkey problem, mistaking what we don't see for the nonexistent, a sibling to mistaking absence of evidence for evidence of absence.

We've been falling for the green lumber problem since the beginning of the golden age of philosophy—we saw Aristotle mistaking the source of Thales' success; now we turn to Socrates, the greatest of the great masters.

EUTHYPHRO

Plato expressed himself chiefly through his use of the person who no doubt became the most influential philosopher in history, Socrates the Athenian, the first philosopher in the modern sense. Socrates left no writing of his own, so we get direct representation of him mainly through Plato and Xenophon. And just as Fat Tony has, as his self-appointed biographer, yours truly trying to satisfy his own agenda, leading to distortions in his character and self-serving representation of some of the said author's ideas, so I am certain that the Socrates of Plato is a more Platonic character than the true Socrates.*

In one of Plato's dialogues, *Euthyphro,* Socrates was outside the courthouse, awaiting the trial in which he was eventually put to death, when the eponymous Euthyphro, a religious expert and prophet of sorts, struck up a conversation with him. Socrates started explaining that for the "activities" with which he was charged by the court (corrupting the youth and introducing new gods at the expense of the older ones), not only he did not charge a fee, but he was in perfect readiness to pay for people to listen to him.

It turned out that Euthyphro was on his way to charge his father with manslaughter, not a bad conversation starter. So Socrates started out by wondering how charging his own father with manslaughter was compatible with Euthyphro's religious duties.

Socrates' technique was to make his interlocutor, who started with a thesis, agree to a series of statements, then proceed to show him how the statements he agreed to are inconsistent with the original thesis, thus establishing that he has no clue as to what he was talking about. Socrates used it mostly to show people how lacking in clarity they were in their thoughts, how little they knew about the concepts they used routinely—and the need for philosophy to elucidate these concepts.

In the beginning of the *Euthypro* dialogue, he catches his interlocutor using the word "piety," characterizing the prosecution of his father as a

---

* The other biographer of Socrates, Xenophon, presents a different picture. The Socrates of the *Memorabilia* is no-nonsense and down to earth; he despises sterile knowledge, and the experts who study matters without practical consequence when so many useful and important things are neglected (instead of looking at stars to understand causes, figure out how you can use them to navigate; use geometry to measure land, but no more).

pious act and so giving the impression that he was conducting the prosecution on grounds of piety. But he could not come up with a definition that suited Socrates. Socrates kept pestering the poor fellow as he could not produce a definition of piety. The dialogue continued with more definitions (what is "moral rectitude"?), until Euthyphro found some polite excuse to run away. The dialogue ended abruptly, but the reader is left with the impression that it could have gone on until today, twenty-five centuries later, without it bringing us any closer to anything.

Let us reopen it.

FAT TONY VERSUS SOCRATES

How would Fat Tony have handled the cross-examination by the relentless Athenian? Now that the reader is acquainted with our hefty character, let us examine, as a thought experiment, an equivalent dialogue between Fat Tony and Socrates, properly translated of course.

Clearly, there are similarities between the two characters. Both had time on their hands and enjoyed unlimited leisure, though, in Tony's case, free time was the result of productive insights. Both like to argue, and both look at active conversation (instead of TV screen or concert hall passivity) as a main source of entertainment. Both dislike writing: Socrates because he did not like the definitive and immutable character that is associated with the written word when for him answers are never final and should not be fixed. Nothing should be written in stone, even literally: Socrates in the *Euthyphro* boasts for ancestry the sculptor Daedalus, whose statues came alive as soon as the work was completed. When you talk to one of Daedalus' statues, it talks back to you, unlike the ones you see in the Metropolitan Museum of Art in New York City. Tony, for his part, did not like writing for other, no less respectable reasons: he almost flunked out of high school in Bay Ridge, Brooklyn.

But the similarities stop somewhere, which would be good enough for a dialogue. Of course we can expect a bit of surprise on the part of Fat Tony standing in front of the man described to him by Nero as the greatest philosopher of all time: Socrates, we are told, had looks beyond unprepossessing. Socrates was repeatedly described as having a protruding belly, thin limbs, bulging eyes, a snub nose. He looked haggard. He might even have had body odor, as he was said to bathe much less than his peers. You can imagine Fat Tony sneering while pointing his finger at the fellow: "Look, Neeero, you want me to talk to . . . *dis?*" Or perhaps not: Socrates was said to have a presence, a certain personal confidence and a serenity of mind that made some young men find him "beautiful."

What Nero was certain of was that Fat Tony would initially get close to Socrates and form his opinion on the fellow after some olfactory investigation—and as we said, Fat Tony doesn't even realize that this is part of his modus operandi.

Now assume Fat Tony was asked by Socrates how he defined piety. Fat Tony's answer would have been most certainly to *get lost*—Fat Tony, aware of Socrates' statement that not only would he debate for free, but he would be ready to pay for conversation, would have claimed one doesn't argue with someone who is ready to pay you to argue with him.

But Fat Tony's power in life is that he never lets the other person frame the question. He taught Nero that an answer is planted in every question; never respond with a straight answer to a question that makes no sense to you.

> FAT TONY: "You are asking me to define what characteristic makes a difference between pious and nonpious. Do I really *need* to be able to tell you what it is to be able to conduct a pious action?"
>
> SOCRATES: "How can you use a word like 'piety' without knowing what it means, while pretending to know what it means?"
>
> FAT TONY: "Do I actually have to be able to tell you in plain barbarian non-Greek English, or in pure Greek, what it means to prove that I know and understand what it means? I don't know it in words but I know what it is."

No doubt Fat Tony would have taken Socrates of Athens further down his own road and be the one doing the framing of the question:

> FAT TONY: "Tell me, old man. Does a child need to define mother's milk to understand the need to drink it?"
>
> SOCRATES: "No, he does not need to."
>
> FAT TONY (using the same repetitive pattern of Socrates in the Plato dialogues): "And my dear Socrates, does a dog need to define what an owner is to be loyal to him?"
>
> SOCRATES (puzzled to have someone ask him questions): "A dog has . . . instinct. It does not reflect on its life. He doesn't examine his life. We are not dogs."

FAT TONY: "I agree, my dear Socrates, that a dog has instinct and that we are not dogs. But are we humans so fundamentally different as to be completely stripped of instinct leading us to do things we have no clue about? Do we have to limit life to what we can answer in proto-Brooklyn English?"

Without waiting for Socrates' answer (only suckers wait for answers; questions are not made for answers):

FAT TONY: "Then, my good Socrates, why do you think that we need to fix the meaning of things?"

SOCRATES: "My dear Mega-Tony, we need to know what we are talking about when we talk about things. The entire idea of philosophy is to be able to reflect and understand what we are doing, examine our lives. An unexamined life is not worth living."

FAT TONY: "The problem, my poor old Greek, is that you are killing the things we can know but not express. And if I asked someone riding a bicycle just fine to give me the theory behind his bicycle riding, he would fall from it. By bullying and questioning people you confuse them and hurt them."

Then, looking at him patronizingly, with a smirk, very calmly:

FAT TONY: "My dear Socrates . . . you know why they are putting you to death? It is because you make people feel stupid for blindly following habits, instincts, and traditions. You may be occasionally right. But you may confuse them about things they've been doing just fine without getting in trouble. You are destroying people's illusions about themselves. You are taking the joy of ignorance out of the things we don't understand. And you have *no* answer; you have *no* answer to offer them."

PRIMACY OF DEFINITIONAL KNOWLEDGE

You can see that what Fat Tony is hitting here is the very core of philosophy: it is indeed with Socrates that the main questions that became philosophy today were first raised, questions such as "what is existence?," "what are morals?," "what is a proof?," "what is science?," "what is this?" and "what is that?"

The question we saw in *Euthyphro* pervades the various dialogues written by Plato. What Socrates is seeking relentlessly are definitions of the essential nature of the thing concerned rather than descriptions of the properties by means of which we can recognize them.

Socrates went even as far as questioning the poets and reported that they had no more clue than the public about their own works. In Plato's account of his trial in the *Apology*, Socrates recounted how he cross-examined the poets in vain: "I took them some of the most elaborate passages in their own writings, and asked what was the meaning of them. I am almost ashamed to speak of this, but still I must say that there is hardly a person present who wouldn't have talked better about their poetry than they did themselves."

And this priority of definitional knowledge led to Plato's thesis that you cannot know anything unless you know the Forms, which are what definitions specify. If we cannot define piety from working with particulars, then let us start with the universals from which these particulars should flow. In other words, if you cannot get a map from a territory, build a territory out of the map.

In defense of Socrates, his questions lead to a major result: if they could not allow him to define what something was, at least they allowed him to be certain about what a thing was not.

Mistaking the Unintelligible for the Unintelligent

Fat Tony, of course, had many precursors. Many we will not hear about, because of the primacy of philosophy and the way it got integrated into daily practices by Christianity and Islam. By "philosophy," I mean theoretical and conceptual knowledge, all knowledge, things we can write down. For, until recently, the term largely referred to what we call today science—natural philosophy, this attempt to rationalize Nature, penetrate her logic.

A vivid modern attack on the point came from the young Friedrich Nietzsche, though dressed up in literary flights on optimism and pessimism mixed with a hallucination on what "West," a "typical Hellene," and "the German soul" mean. The young Nietzsche wrote his first book, *The Birth of Tragedy*, while in his early twenties. He went after Socrates, whom he called the "mystagogue of science," for "making existence appear comprehensible." This brilliant passage exposes what I call the sucker-rationalistic fallacy:

Perhaps—thus he [Socrates] should have asked himself—what is not intelligible to me is not necessarily unintelligent? Perhaps there is a realm of wisdom from which the logician is exiled?

"What is not intelligible to me is not necessarily unintelligent" is perhaps the most potent sentence in all of Nietzsche's century—and we used a version of it in the prologue, in the very definition of the fragilista who mistakes what he does not understand for nonsense.

Nietzsche is also allergic to Socrates' version of truth, largely motivated by the agenda of the promotion of understanding, since according to Socrates, one does not knowingly do evil—an argument that seems to have pervaded the Enlightenment as such thinkers as Condorcet made truth the only and sufficient source for the good.

This argument is precisely what Nietzsche vituperated against: knowledge is the panacea; error is evil; hence science is an optimistic enterprise. The mandate of scientific optimism irritated Nietzsche: this use of reasoning and knowledge at the service of utopia. Forget the optimism/pessimism business that is addressed when people discuss Nietzsche, as the so-called Nietzschean pessimism distracts from the point: it is the very *goodness* of knowledge that he questioned.

It took me a long time to figure out the central problem that Nietzsche addressed in *The Birth of Tragedy*. He sees two forces, the Apollonian and the Dionysian. One is measured, balanced, rational, imbued with reason and self-restraint; the other is dark, visceral, wild, untamed, hard to understand, emerging from the inner layers of our selves. Ancient Greek culture represented a balance of the two, until the influence of Socrates on Euripides gave a larger share to the Apollonian and disrupted the Dionysian, causing this excessive rise of rationalism. It is equivalent to disrupting the natural chemistry of your body by the injection of hormones. The Apollonian without the Dionysian is, as the Chinese would say, yang without yin.

Nietzsche's potency as a thinker continues to surprise me: he figured out antifragility. While many attribute (mistakenly) the notion of "creative destruction" to the economist Joseph Schumpeter (not wondering how something insightful and deep can come out of an economist),*

---

* Adam Smith was first and last a moral philosopher. Marx was a philosopher. Kahneman and Simon are psychologist and cognitive scientist, respectively. The exception is, of course, Hayek.

while, as we saw, the more erudite source it to Karl Marx, it is indeed Nietzsche who was first to coin the term with reference to Dionysus, whom he called "creatively destructive" and "destructively creative." Nietzsche indeed figured out—in his own way—antifragility.

I read Nietzsche's *The Birth of Tragedy* twice, first as a child when I was very green. The second time, after a life thinking of randomness, it hit me that Nietzsche understood something that I did not find explicitly stated in his work: that growth in knowledge—or in anything—cannot proceed without the Dionysian. It reveals matters that we can select at some point, given that we have optionality. In other words, it can be the source of stochastic tinkering, and the Apollonian can be part of the rationality in the selection process.

Let me bring the big boss, Seneca, into the picture. He, too, referred to Dionysian and Apollonian attributes. He appeared to present, in one of his writings a richer version of our human tendencies. Talking about a God (whom he also calls "destiny," equating him with the interaction of causes), he gives him three manifestations. First, the "Liber Pater," the Bacchic force (that is, the Dionysos to whom Nietzsche referred) that gives seminal power to the continuation of life; second, Hercules, who embodies strength; and third, Mercury, who represented (for Seneca's contemporaries) craft, science, and reason (what for Nietzsche appeared to be the Apollonian). Richer than Nietzsche, he included strength as an additional dimension.

As I said, earlier attacks on "philosophy" in the sense of rationalistic knowledge from the Plato and Aristotle traditions came from a variety of people, not necessarily visible in the corpus, mostly in forgotten or rarely mentioned texts. Why forgotten? Because structured learning likes the impoverishment and simplification of naive rationalism, easy to teach, not the rich texture of empiricism, and, as I said, those who attacked academic thinking had little representation (something that we will see is starkly apparent in the history of medicine).

An even more accomplished, and far more open-minded, classical scholar than Nietzsche, the nineteenth-century French thinker Ernest Renan, knew, in addition to the usual Greek and Latin, Hebrew, Aramaic (Syriac), and Arabic. In his attack on Averroes, he expressed the famous idea that logic excludes—by definition—nuances, and since truth resides exclusively in the nuances, it is "a useless instrument for finding Truth in the moral and political sciences."

Tradition

As Fat Tony said, Socrates was put to death because he disrupted something that, in the eyes of the Athenian establishment, was working just fine. Things are too complicated to be expressed in words; by doing so, you kill humans. Or people—as with the green lumber—may be focusing on the right things but we are not good enough to figure it out intellectually.

Death and martyrdom make good marketing, particularly when one faces destiny while unwavering in his opinions. A hero is someone imbued with intellectual confidence and ego, and death is something too small for him. While most of the accounts we hear of Socrates make him heroic, thanks to his death and his resignation to die in a philosophical way, he had some classical critics who believed that Socrates was destroying the foundations of society—the heuristics that are transmitted by the elders and that we may not be mature enough to question.

Cato the Elder, whom we met in Chapter 2, was highly allergic to Socrates. Cato had the bottom-line mind of Fat Tony, but with a much higher civic sense, sense of mission, respect for tradition, and commitment to moral rectitude. He was also allergic to things Greek, as exhibited in his allergy to philosophers and doctors—an allergy which, as we will see in later chapters, had remarkably modern justifications. Cato's commitment to democracy led him to believe in both freedom and the rules of custom, in combination with fear of tyranny. Plutarch quotes him as saying: "Socrates was a mighty babbler who tried to make himself tyrant of his country in order to destroy its customs and entice its citizens into holding views contrary to law and order."

So the reader can see how the ancients saw naive rationalism: by impoverishing—rather than enhancing—thought, it introduces fragility. They knew that incompleteness—half-knowledge—is always dangerous.

Many other people than the ancients have been involved in defending—and inviting us to respect—this different type of knowledge. First, Edmund Burke, the Irish statesman and political philosopher, who also countered the French Revolution for disrupting the "collected reasons of the ages." He believed that large social variations can expose us to unseen effects and thus advocated the notion of small trial-and-error experiments (in effect, convex tinkering) in social systems, coupled with respect for the complex heuristics of tradition. Also Michael Oakeshot, the twentieth-century conservative political philosopher and philosopher of history who believed that traditions provide an aggregation of filtered collective knowledge. Another one in that league would be Joseph de Maistre, who as we saw thought in "second steps." He was a French-language royalist and counter-Enlightenment thinker who was vocal against the ills of the Revolution and believed in the fundamental depravity of men unless checked by some dictatorship.

Clearly, Wittgenstein would be at the top of the list of modern antifragile thinkers, with his remarkable insight into the inexpressible with words. And of all thinkers he best understands the green lumber issue—he may be the first ever to express a version of it when he doubted the ability of language to express the literal. In addition, the fellow was a saint—he sacrificed his life, his friendships, his fortune, his reputation, everything, for the sake of philosophy.

We may be drawn to think that Friedrich Hayek would be in that antifragile, antirationalist category. He is the twentieth-century philosopher and economist who opposed social planning on the grounds that the pricing system reveals through transactions the knowledge embedded in society, knowledge not accessible to a social planner. But Hayek missed the notion of optionality as a substitute for the social planner. In a way, he believed in intelligence, but as a distributed or collective intelligence—not in optionality as a replacement for intelligence.*

The anthropologist Claude Lévi-Strauss showed that nonliterate peoples had their own "science of the concrete," a holistic way of thinking about their environment in terms of objects and their "secondary," sensuous qualities which was not necessarily less coherent than many of our scientific approaches and, in many respects, can be as rich as and even richer than ours. Again, green lumber.

Finally, John Gray, the contemporary political philosopher and essayist who stands against human hubris and has been fighting the prevailing ideas that the Enlightenment is a panacea—treating a certain category of thinkers as Enlightenment fundamentalists. Gray showed repeatedly how what we call scientific progress can be just a mirage. When he, myself, and the essayist Bryan Appleyard got together for lunch I was mentally prepared to discuss ideas, and advocate my own. I was pleasantly surprised by what turned out to be the best lunch I ever

---

* The philosopher Rupert Read convinced me that Hayek harbored in fact a strain of naive rationalism, as did Popper, and presents convincing arguments that the two should not be included in the category of antifragile thinkers.

had in my entire life. There was this smoothness of knowing that the three of us tacitly understood the same point and, instead, went to the second step of discussing applications—something as mundane as replacing our currency holdings with precious metals, as these are not owned by governments. Gray worked in an office next to Hayek and told me that Hayek was quite a dull fellow, lacking playfulness—hence optionality.

THE SUCKER-NONSUCKER DISTINCTION

Let us introduce the philosopher's stone back into this conversation. Socrates is about knowledge. Not Fat Tony, who has no idea what it is.

For Tony, the distinction in life isn't True or False, but rather sucker or nonsucker. Things are always simpler with him. In real life, as we saw with the ideas of Seneca and the bets of Thales, exposure is more important than knowledge; decision effects supersede logic. Textbook "knowledge" misses a dimension, the hidden asymmetry of benefits—just like the notion of average. The need to focus on the payoff from your actions instead of studying the structure of the world (or understanding the "True" and the "False") has been largely missed in intellectual history. Horribly missed. *The payoff, what happens to you (the benefits or harm from it), is always the most important thing, not the event itself.*

> *Philosophers talk about truth and falsehood. People in life talk*
> *about payoff, exposure, and consequences (risks and rewards),*
> *hence fragility and antifragility. And sometimes philosophers*
> *and thinkers and those who study conflate Truth with risks*
> *and rewards.*

My point taken further is that True and False (hence what we call "belief") play a poor, secondary role in human decisions; it is the payoff from the True and the False that dominates—and it is almost always asymmetric, with one consequence much bigger than the other, i.e., harboring positive and negative asymmetries (fragile or antifragile). Let me explain.

Fragility, Not Probability

We check people for weapons before they board the plane. Do we believe that they are terrorists: True or False? False, as they are not likely to be terrorists (a tiny probability). But we check them nevertheless because we are fragile to terrorism. There is an asymmetry. We are interested in the payoff, and the consequence, or payoff, of the True (that they turn out to be terrorists) is too large and the costs of checking are too low. Do you think the nuclear reactor is likely to explode in the next year? False. Yet you want to behave as if it were True and spend millions on additional safety, because we are fragile to nuclear events. A third example: Do you think that this random medicine will harm you? False. Do you ingest these pills? No, no, no.

If you sat with a pencil and jotted down all the decisions you've taken in the past week, or, if you could, over your lifetime, you would realize that almost all of them have had asymmetric payoff, with one side carrying a larger consequence than the other. *You decide principally based on fragility, not probability.* Or to rephrase, *You decide principally based on fragility, not so much on True/False.*

Let us discuss the idea of the insufficiency of True/False in decision making in the real world, particularly when probabilities are involved. True or False are interpretations corresponding to high or low probabilities. Scientists have something called "confidence level"; a result obtained with a 95 percent confidence level means that there is no more than a 5 percent probability of the result being wrong. The idea of course is inapplicable as it ignores the size of the effects, which of course, makes things worse with extreme events. If I tell you that some result is true with 95 percent confidence level, you would be quite satisfied. But what if I told you that the plane was safe with 95 percent confidence level? Even 99 percent confidence level would not do, as a 1 percent probability of a crash would be quite a bit alarming (today commercial planes operate with less than one in several hundred thousand probabilities of crashing, and the ratio is improving, as we saw that every error leads to the improvement of overall safety). So, to repeat, the probability (hence True/False) does not work in the real world; it is the payoff that matters.

You have taken probably a billion decisions in your life. How many times have you computed probabilities? Of course, you may do so in casinos, but not elsewhere.

Conflation of Events and Exposure

This brings us again to the green lumber fallacy. A Black Swan event and how it affects you—its impact on your finances, emotions, the destruction it will cause—are *not the same "ting."* And the problem is deeply ingrained in standard reactions; the predictors' reply when we point out their failures has typically been "we need better computation" in order to predict the event better and figure out the probabilities, instead of the vastly more effective "modify your exposure" and learn to get out of trouble, something religions and traditional heuristics have been better at enforcing than naive and cosmetic science.

CONCLUSION TO BOOK IV

In addition to the medical empirics, this section has attempted to vindicate the unreasonable mavericks, engineers, freelance entrepreneurs, innovative artists, and anti-academic thinkers who have been reviled by history. Some of them had great courage—not just the courage to put forth their ideas, but the courage to accept to live in a world they knew they did not understand. And they enjoyed it.

To conclude this section, note that doing is wiser than you are prone to believe—and more rational. What I did here is just debunk the *Lecturing-Birds-How-to-Fly* epiphenomenon and the "linear model," using among other things the simple mathematical properties of optionality, which does not require knowledge or intelligence, merely rationality in choice.

Remember that there is no empirical evidence to support the statement that organized research in the sense it is currently marketed leads to the great things promised by universities. And the promoters of the Soviet-Harvard idea do not use optionality, or second-order effects—this absence of optionality in their accounts invalidates their views about the role of teleological science. They need to rewrite the history of technology.

What Will Happen Next?

When I last met Alison Wolf we discussed this dire problem with education and illusions of academic contribution, with Ivy League universities becoming in the eyes of the new Asian and U.S. upper class a status luxury good. Harvard is like a Vuitton bag or a Cartier watch. It is a huge drag on the middle-class parents who have been plowing an increased share of their savings into these institutions, transferring their money to administrators, real estate developers, professors, and other agents. In the United States, we have a buildup of student loans that automatically transfer to these rent extractors. In a way it is no different from racketeering: one needs a decent university "name" to get ahead in life; but we know that collectively society doesn't appear to advance with organized education.

She requested that I write to her my thoughts about the future of education—as I told her that I was optimistic on the subject. My answer: b**t is fragile. Which scam in history has lasted forever? I have an enormous faith in Time and History as eventual debunkers of fragility. Education is an institution that has been growing without external stressors; eventually the thing will collapse.

The next two books, V and VI, will deal with the notion that fragile things break—predictably. Book V will show how to detect fragility (in a more technical manner) and will present the mechanics behind the philosopher's stone. Book VI is based on the idea that Time is an eraser rather than a builder, and a good one at breaking the fragile—whether buildings or ideas.*

---

* The reader might wonder about the connection between education and disorder. Education is teleological and hates disorder. It tends to cater to fragilistas.

BOOK V

The Nonlinear and the Nonlinear*

———

Time for another autobiographical vignette. As Charles Darwin wrote in a historical section of his *On the Origin of Species,* presenting a sketch of the progress of opinion: "I hope I may be excused for entering on these personal details, as I give them to show that I have not been hasty in coming to a decision." For it is not quite true that there is no exact word, concept, and application for antifragility. My colleagues and I had one without knowing it. And I had it for a long, very long time. So I have been thinking about the exact same problem most of my life, partly consciously, partly without being aware of it. Book V explores the journey and the idea that came with it.

ON THE IMPORTANCE OF ATTICS

In the mid-1990s, I quietly deposited my necktie in the trash can at the corner of Forty-fifth Street and Park Avenue in New York. I decided to take a few years off and locked myself in the attic, trying to express what was coming out of my guts, trying to frame what I called "hidden nonlinearities" and their effects.

What I had wasn't quite an idea, rather, just a method, for the deeper central idea eluded me. But using this method, I produced close to a

---

* The nontechnical reader can skip Book V without any loss: the definition of antifragility from Seneca's asymmetry is amply sufficient for a literary read of the rest of the book. This is a more technical rephrasing of it.

six-hundred-page-long discussion of managing nonlinear effects, with graphs and tables. Recall from the prologue that "nonlinearity" means that the response is not a straight line. But I was going further and looking at the link with volatility, something that should be clear soon. And I went deep into the volatility of volatility, and such higher-order effects.

The book that came out of this solitary investigation in the attic, finally called *Dynamic Hedging,* was about the "techniques to manage and handle complicated nonlinear derivative exposures." It was a technical document that was completely *ab ovo* (from the egg), and as I was going, I knew in my guts that the point had vastly more import than the limited cases I was using in my profession; I knew that my profession was the perfect platform to start thinking about these issues, but I was too lazy and too conventional to venture beyond. That book remained by far my favorite work (before this one), and I fondly remember the two harsh New York winters in the near-complete silence of the attic, with the luminous effect of the sun shining on the snow warming up both the room and the project. I thought of nothing else for years.

I also learned something quite amusing from the episode. My book was mistakenly submitted to four referees, all four of them academic financial economists instead of "quants" (quantitative analysts who work in finance using mathematical models). The person who made the submissions wasn't quite aware of the difference. The four academics rejected my book, interestingly, for four sets of completely different reasons, with absolutely no intersection in their arguments. We practitioners and quants aren't too fazed by remarks on the part of academics—it would be like prostitutes listening to technical commentary by nuns. What struck me was that if I had been wrong, all of them would have provided the exact same reason for rejection. That's antifragility. Then, of course, as the publisher saw the mistake, the book was submitted to quantitative reviewers, and it saw the light of day.*

The Procrustean bed in life consists precisely in simplifying the nonlinear and making it linear—the simplification that distorts.

Then my interest in the nonlinearity of exposures went away as I began to deal with other matters related to uncertainty, which seemed more intellectual and philosophical to me, like the nature of

---

* A similar test: when a collection of people write "There is nothing new here" and each one cites a different originator of the idea, one can safely say there is something effectively new.

randomness—rather than how things react to random events. This may also have been due to the fact that I moved and no longer had that attic.

But some events brought me back to a second phase of intense seclusion.

After the crisis of the late 2000s, I went through an episode of hell owing to contact with the press. I was suddenly deintellectualized, corrupted, extracted from my habitat, propelled into being a public commodity. I had not realized that it is hard for members of the media and the public to accept that the job of a scholar is to ignore insignificant current affairs, to write books, not emails, and not to give lectures dancing on a stage; that he has other things to do, like read in bed in the morning, write at a desk in front of a window, take long walks (slowly), drink espressos (mornings), chamomile tea (afternoons), Lebanese wine (evenings), and Muscat wines (after dinner), take more long walks (slowly), argue with friends and family members (but never in the morning), and read (again) in bed before sleeping, not keep rewriting one's book and ideas for the benefit of strangers and members of the local chapter of Networking International who haven't read it.

Then I opted out of public life. When I managed to retake control of my schedule and my brain, recovered from the injuries deep into my soul, learned to use email filters and autodelete functions, and restarted my life, Lady Fortuna brought two ideas to me, making me feel stupid—for I realized I had had them inside me all along.

Clearly, the tools of analysis of nonlinear effects are quite universal. The sad part is that until that day in my new-new life of solitary walker cum chamomile drinker, when I looked at a porcelain cup I had not realized that everything nonlinear around me could be subjected to the same techniques of detection as the ones that hit me in my previous episode of seclusion.

What I found is described in the next two chapters.

CHAPTER 18

On the Difference Between a
Large Stone and a Thousand Pebbles

How to punish with a stone—I landed early (once)—Why attics are always useful—On the great benefits of avoiding Heathrow unless you have a guitar

———

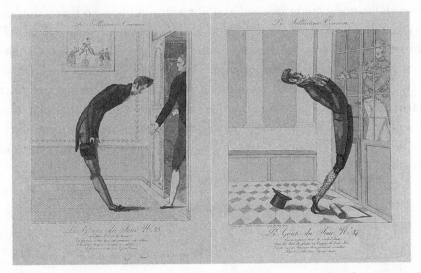

FIGURE 8. The solicitor knocking on doors in concave (left) and convex (right) position. He illustrates the two forms of nonlinearity; if he were "linear" he would be upright, standing straight. This chapter will show—a refinement of Seneca's asymmetry—how one position (the convex) represents antifragility in all its forms, the other, fragility (the concave), and how we can easily detect and even measure fragility by evaluating how humped (convex) or how slumped (concave) the courtier is standing.

I noticed looking at the porcelain cup that it did not like volatility or variability or action. It just wanted calm and to be left alone in the tranquility of the home study-library. The realization that fragility was simply *vulnerability to the volatility of the things that affect it* was a huge personal embarrassment for me, since my specialty was the link between volatility and nonlinearity; I know, I know, a very strange specialty. So let us start with the result.

A SIMPLE RULE TO DETECT THE FRAGILE

A story present in the rabbinical literature (*Midrash Tehillim*), probably originating from earlier Near Eastern lore, says the following. A king, angry at his son, swore that he would crush him with a large stone. After he calmed down, he realized he was in trouble, as a king who breaks his oath is unfit to rule. His sage advisor came up with a solution. Have the stone cut into very small pebbles, and have the mischievous son pelted with them.

The difference between a thousand pebbles and a large stone of equivalent weight is a potent illustration of how fragility stems from nonlinear effects. Nonlinear? Once again, "nonlinear" means that the response is not straightforward and not a straight line, so if you double, say, the dose, you get a lot more or a lot less than double the effect—if I throw at someone's head a ten-pound stone, it will cause more than twice the harm of a five-pound stone, more than five times the harm of a two-pound stone, etc. It is simple: if you draw a line on a graph, with harm on the vertical axis and the size of the stone on the horizontal axis, it will be curved, not a straight line. That is a refinement of asymmetry.

Now the very simple point, in fact, that allows for a detection of fragility:

For the fragile, shocks bring higher harm as their intensity increases (up to a certain level).

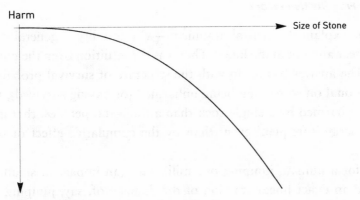

FIGURE 9. The King and His Son. The harm from the size of the stone as a function of the size of the stone (up to a point). Every additional weight of the stone harms more than the previous one. You see nonlinearity (the harm curves inward, with a steeper and steeper vertical slope).

The example is shown in Figure 9. Let us generalize. Your car is fragile. If you drive it into the wall at 50 miles per hour, it would cause more damage than if you drove it into the same wall ten times at 5 mph. The harm at 50 mph is more than ten times the harm at 5 mph.

Other examples. Drinking seven bottles of wine (Bordeaux) in one sitting, then purified water with lemon twist for the remaining six days is more harmful than drinking one bottle of wine a day for seven days (spread out in two glasses per meal). Every additional glass of wine harms you more than the preceding one, hence your system is fragile to alcoholic consumption. Letting a porcelain cup drop on the floor from a height of one foot (about thirty centimeters) is worse than twelve times the damage from a drop from a height of one inch (two and a half centimeters).

Jumping from a height of thirty feet (ten meters) brings more than ten times the harm of jumping from a height of three feet (one meter)—actually, thirty feet seems to be the cutoff point for death from free fall.

Note that this is a simple expansion of the foundational asymmetry we saw two chapters ago, as we used Seneca's thinking as a pretext to talk about nonlinearity. Asymmetry is necessarily nonlinearity. More harm than benefits: simply, an increase in intensity brings more harm than a corresponding decrease offers benefits.

Why Is Fragility Nonlinear?

Let me explain the central argument—why fragility is generally in the nonlinear and not in the linear. That was the intuition from the porcelain cup. The answer has to do with the structure of survival probabilities: conditional on something being unharmed (or having survived), then it is more harmed by a single rock than a thousand pebbles, that is, by a single large infrequent event than by the cumulative effect of smaller shocks.

If for a human, jumping one millimeter (an impact of small force) caused an exact linear fraction of the damage of, say, jumping to the ground from thirty feet, then the person would already be dead from cumulative harm. Actually a simple computation shows that he would have expired within hours from touching objects or pacing in his living room, given the multitude of such stressors and their total effect. The fragility that comes from linearity is immediately visible, so we rule it out because the object would be already broken. This leaves us with the following: what is fragile is something that is both unbroken and subjected to nonlinear effects—and extreme, rare events, since impacts of large size (or high speed) are rarer than ones of small size (and slow speed).

Let me rephrase this idea in connection with Black Swans and extreme events. There are a lot more ordinary events than extreme events. In the financial markets, there are at least ten thousand times more events of 0.1 percent magnitude than events of 10 percent magnitude. There are close to eight thousand microearthquakes daily on planet Earth, that is, those below 2 on the Richter scale—about three million a year. These are totally harmless, and, with three million per year, you would need them to be so. But shocks of intensity 6 and higher on the scale make the newspapers. Take objects such as porcelain cups. They get a lot of hits, a million more hits of, say, one hundredth of a pound per square inch (to take an arbitrary measure) than hits of a hundred pounds per square inch. Accordingly, we are necessarily immune to the *cumulative* effect of small deviations, or shocks of very small magnitude, which implies that these affect us disproportionally less (that is, nonlinearly less) than larger ones.

Let me reexpress my previous rule:

For the fragile, the cumulative effect of small shocks is smaller than the single effect of an equivalent single large shock.

This leaves me with the principle that the fragile is what is hurt a lot more by extreme events than by a succession of intermediate ones. Finito—and there is *no other* way to be fragile.

Now let us flip the argument and consider the antifragile. Antifragility, too, is grounded in nonlinearities, nonlinear responses.

For the antifragile, shocks bring more benefits (equivalently, less harm) as their intensity increases (up to a point).

A simple case—known heuristically by weight lifters. In the bodyguard-emulating story in Chapter 2, I focused only on the maximum I could do. Lifting one hundred pounds once brings more benefits than lifting fifty pounds twice, and certainly a lot more than lifting one pound a hundred times. Benefits here are in weight-lifter terms: strengthening the body, muscle mass, and bar-fight looks rather than resistance and the ability to run a marathon. The second fifty pounds play a larger role, hence the nonlinear (that is, we will see, *convexity*) effect. Every additional pound brings more benefits, until one gets close to the limit, what weight lifters call "failure."*

For now, note the reach of this simple curve: it affects about just anything in sight, even medical error, government size, innovation—anything that touches uncertainty. And it helps put the "plumbing" behind the statements on size and concentration in Book II.

When to Smile and When to Frown

Nonlinearity comes in two kinds: concave (curves inward), as in the case of the king and the stone, or its opposite, convex (curves outward). And of course, mixed, with concave and convex sections.

Figures 10 and 11 show the following simplifications of nonlinearity: the convex and the concave resemble a smile and a frown, respectively.

---

* Actually there are different muscle fibers, each one responding to different sets of conditions with varied asymmetries of responses. The so-called "fast-twitch" fibers, the ones used to lift very heavy objects, are very antifragile, as they are convex to weight. And they die in the absence of intensity.

FIGURE 10. The two types of nonlinearities, the convex (left) and the concave (right). The convex curves outward, the concave inward.

FIGURE 11. Smile! A better way to understand convexity and concavity. What curves outward looks like a smile—what curves inward makes a sad face. The convex (left) is antifragile, the concave (right) is fragile (has negative convexity effects).

I use the term "convexity effect" for both, in order to simplify the vocabulary, saying "positive convexity effects" and "negative convexity effects."

Why does asymmetry map to convexity or concavity? Simply, if for a given variation you have more upside than downside and you draw the curve, it will be convex; the opposite for the concave. Figure 12 shows the asymmetry reexpressed in terms of nonlinearities. It also shows the magical effect of mathematics that allowed us to treat steak tartare, entrepreneurship, and financial risk in the same breath: the convex graph turns into concave when one simply puts a minus sign in front of it. For instance, Fat Tony had the exact opposite payoff than, say, a bank or financial institution in a certain transaction: he made a buck whenever they lost one, and vice versa. The profits and losses are mirror images of each other at the end of the day, except that one is the minus sign times the other.

Figure 12 also shows why the convex *likes volatility*. If you earn more than you lose from fluctuations, you want a lot of fluctuations.

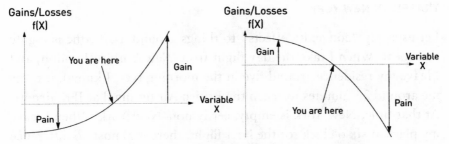

FIGURE 12. Pain More than Gain, or Gain More than Pain. Assume you start from the "You Are Here" spot. In the first case, should the variable x increase, i.e., move to the right on the horizontal axis, the gains (vertical axis) are larger than the losses encountered by moving left, i.e., an equivalent decrease in the variable x. The graph illustrates how positive asymmetry (first graph) turns into convex (inward) curving and negative asymmetry (second graph) turns into concave (outward) curving. To repeat, for a set deviation in a variable, in equivalent amounts in both directions, the convex gains more than it loses, and the reverse for the concave.

Why Is the Concave Hurt by Black Swan Events?

Now the idea that has inhabited me all my life—I never realized it could show so clearly when put in graphical form. Figure 13 illustrates the effect of harm and the unexpected. The more concave an exposure, the more harm from the unexpected, and disproportionately so. So very large deviations have a disproportionately larger and larger effect.

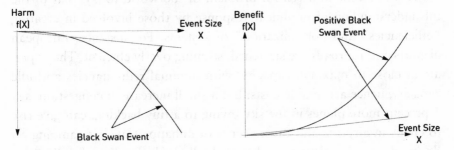

FIGURE 13. Two exposures, one linear, one nonlinear, with negative convexity—that is, concavity—in the first graph, positive convexity in the second. An unexpected event affects the nonlinear disproportionately more. The larger the event, the larger the difference.

Next, let us apply this very simple technique to the detection of fragility and position in the Triad.

TRAFFIC IN NEW YORK

Let us apply "convexity effects" to things around us. Traffic is highly nonlinear. When I take the day flight from New York to London, and I leave my residence around five in the morning (yes, I know), it takes me around 26 minutes to reach the British Air terminal at JFK airport. At that time, New York is empty, eerily non–New York. When I leave my place at six o'clock for the later flight, there is almost no difference in travel time, although traffic is a bit denser. One can add more and more cars on the highway, with no or minimal impact on time spent in traffic.

Then, a mystery—increase the number of cars by 10 percent and watch the travel time jump by 50 percent (I am using approximate numbers). Look at the convexity effect at work: the average number of cars on the road does not matter at all for traffic speed. If you have 90,000 cars for one hour, then 110,000 cars for another hour, traffic would be much slower than if you had 100,000 cars for two hours. Note that travel time is a negative, so I count it as a cost, like an expense, and a rise is a bad thing.

So travel cost is fragile to the *volatility* of the number of cars on the highway; it does not depend so much on their average number. Every additional car increases travel time more than the previous one.

This is a hint to a central problem of the world today, that of the misunderstanding of nonlinear response by those involved in creating "efficiencies" and "optimization" of systems. For instance, European airports and railroads are stretched, seeming overly efficient. They operate at close to maximal capacity, with minimal redundancies and idle capacity, hence acceptable costs; but a small increase in congestion, say 5 percent more planes in the sky owing to a tiny backlog, can give rise to chaos in airports and cause scenes of unhappy travelers camping on floors, their only solace some bearded fellow playing French folk songs on his guitar.

We can see applications of the point across economic domains: central banks can print money; they print and print with no effect (and claim the "safety" of such a measure), then, "unexpectedly," the printing causes a jump in inflation. Many economic results are completely canceled by convexity effects—and the happy news is that we know why. Alas, the tools (and culture) of policy makers are based on the overly linear, ignoring these hidden effects. They call it "approximation." When you hear of a "second-order" effect, it means convexity is causing the failure of approximation to represent the real story.

I have put a (very hypothetical) graph of the response of traffic to cars on the road in Figure 14. Note for now the curved shape of the graph. It curves inward.

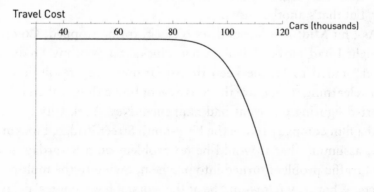

FIGURE 14. The graph shows how the author's travel time (and travel costs) to JFK depend, beyond a certain point, nonlinearly on the number of cars on the road. We show travel costs as curving inward—concave, not a good thing.

Someone Call New York City Officials

An apt illustration of how convexity effects affect an overoptimized system, along with misforecasting large deviations, is this simple story of an underestimation made by New York City officials of the effect of a line closure on traffic congestion. This error is remarkably general: a small modification with compounded results in a system that is extremely stretched, hence fragile.

One Saturday evening in November 2011, I drove to New York City to meet the philosopher Paul Boghossian for dinner in the Village— typically a forty-minute trip. Ironically, I was meeting him to talk about my book, this book, and more particularly, my ideas on redundancy in systems. I have been advocating the injection of redundancy into people's lives and had been boasting to him and others that, since my New Year's resolution of 2007, I have never been late to anything, not even by a minute (well, almost). Recall in Chapter 2 my advocacy of redundancies as an aggressive stance. Such personal discipline forces me to build buffers, and, as I carry a notebook, it allowed me to write an entire book of aphorisms. Not counting long visits to bookstores. Or I can sit in a café and read hate mail. With, of course, no stress, as I have no fear of being late. But the greatest benefit of such discipline is that it prevents me from cramming my day with appointments (typically, appointments are neither useful nor pleasant). Actually, by another rule of personal discipline I do not make appointments (other than lectures) except the very same morning, as a date on the calendar makes me feel like a prisoner, but that's another story.

As I hit Midtown, around six o'clock, traffic stopped. Completely. By eight I had moved hardly a few blocks. So even my "redundancy buffer" failed to let me keep the so-far-unbroken resolution. Then, after relearning to operate the noisy cacophonic thing called the radio, I started figuring out what had happened: New York City had authorized a film company to use the Fifty-ninth Street Bridge, blocking part of it, assuming that it would be no problem on a Saturday. And the small traffic problem turned into mayhem, owing to the multiplicative effects. What they felt would be at the worst a few minutes' delays was multiplied by two orders of magnitude; minutes became hours. Simply, the authorities running New York City did not understand nonlinearities.

This is the central problem of efficiency: these types of errors compound, multiply, swell, with an effect that only goes in one direction—the wrong direction.

WHERE MORE IS DIFFERENT

Another intuitive way to look at convexity effects: consider the scaling property. If you double the exposure to something, do you more than double the harm it will cause? If so, then this is a situation of fragility. Otherwise, you are robust.

The point has been aptly expressed by P. W. Anderson in the title of his paper "More Is Different." And what scientists involved in complexity call "emerging properties" is the nonlinear result of adding units, as the sum becomes increasingly different from the parts. Just look at how different the large stone is from the pebbles: the latter have the same weight and the same general shape, but that's about it. Likewise, we saw in Chapter 5 that a city is not a large village; a corporation is not a larger small business. We also saw how randomness changes in nature from Mediocristan to Extremistan, how a state is not a large village, and many alterations that come from size—and speed. All these show non-linearity in action.

A "Balanced Meal"

Another example of missing the hidden dimension, that is, variability: we are currently told by the Soviet-Harvard U.S. health authorities to eat set quantities of nutrients (total calories, protein, vitamins, etc.) every day, in some recommended amounts of each. Every food item has a "percentage daily allowance." Aside from the total lack of empirical rigor in the way these recommendations are currently derived (more on that in the medical chapters), there is another sloppiness in the edict: an insistence in the discourse on the *regularity*. Those recommending the nutritional policies fail to understand that "steadily" getting your calories and nutrients throughout the day, with "balanced" composition and metronomic regularity, does not necessarily have the same effect as consuming them unevenly or randomly, say by having a lot of proteins one day, fasting completely another, feasting the third, etc.

This is a denial of hormesis, the slight stressor of episodic deprivation. For a long time, nobody even bothered to try to figure out whether variability in distribution—the second-order effect—mattered as much as long-term composition. Now research is starting to catch up to such a very, very simple point. It turns out that the effect of variability in food sources and the nonlinearity in the physiological response is central to biological systems. Consuming no protein at all on Monday and catching up on Wednesday seemingly causes a different—better—physiological response, possibly because the deprivation, as a stressor, activates some pathways that facilitate the subsequent absorption of the nutrients (or something similar). And, until a few recent (and disconnected) empirical studies, this convexity effect has been totally missed by science—though not by religions, ancestral heuristics, and traditions. And if scientists get some convexity effects (as we said about domain dependence, doctors, just like weight lifters, understand here and there nonlinearities in dose response), the notion of convexity effects itself appears to be completely missing from their language and methods.

Run, Don't Walk

Another illustration, this time a situation that benefits from variation—positive convexity effects. Take two brothers, Castor and Polydeuces, who need to travel a mile. Castor walks the mile at a leisurely pace and arrives at the destination in twenty minutes. Polydeuces spends fourteen minutes playing with his handheld device getting updates on the gossip, then runs the same mile in six minutes, arriving at the same time as Castor.

So both persons have covered the exact same distance, in exactly the same time—same average. Castor, who walked all the way, presumably will not get the same health benefits and gains in strength as Polydeuces, who sprinted. Health benefits are *convex* to speed (up to a point, of course).

The very idea of exercise is to gain from antifragility to workout stressors—as we saw, all kinds of exercise are just exploitations of convexity effects.

SMALL MAY BE UGLY, IT IS CERTAINLY LESS FRAGILE

We often hear the expression "small is beautiful." It is potent and appealing; many ideas have been offered in its support—almost all of them anecdotal, romantic, or existential. Let us present it within our approach of *fragility* equals *concavity* equals *dislike of randomness* and see how we can measure such an effect.

How to Be Squeezed

A squeeze occurs when people have no choice but to do something, and do it right away, regardless of the costs.

Your other half is to defend a doctoral thesis in the history of German dance and you need to fly to Marburg to be present at such an important moment, meet the parents, and get formally engaged. You live in New York and manage to buy an economy ticket to Frankfurt for $400 and you are excited about how cheap it is. But you need to go through London. Upon getting to New York's Kennedy airport, you are apprised by the airline agent that the flights to London are canceled, sorry, delays due to backlog due to weather problems, that type of thing. Something about Heathrow's fragility. You can get a last-minute flight to Frankfurt, but now you need to pay $4,000, close to ten times the price, and hurry, as there are very few seats left. You fume, shout, curse, blame yourself, your upbringing and parents who taught you to save, then shell out the $4,000. That's a squeeze.

Squeezes are exacerbated by size. When one is large, one becomes vulnerable to some errors, particularly horrendous squeezes. The squeezes become nonlinearly costlier as size increases.

To see how size becomes a handicap, consider the reasons one should not own an elephant as a pet, regardless of what emotional attachment you may have to the animal. Say you can afford an elephant as part of your postpromotion household budget and have one delivered to your backyard. Should there be a water shortage—hence a squeeze, since you have no choice but to shell out the money for water—you would have to pay a higher and higher price for each additional gallon of water. That's fragility, right there, a negative convexity effect coming from getting too big. The unexpected cost, as a percentage of the total, would be monstrous. Owning, say, a cat or a dog would not bring about such high unexpected additional costs at times of squeeze—the overruns taken as a percentage of the total costs would be very low.

In spite of what is studied in business schools concerning "economies of scale," size hurts you at times of stress; it is not a good idea to be large during difficult times. Some economists have been wondering why mergers of corporations do not appear to play out. The combined unit is now much larger, hence more powerful, and according to the theories of economies of scale, it should be more "efficient." But the numbers show, at best, no gain from such increase in size—that was already true in 1978, when Richard Roll voiced the "hubris hypothesis," finding it irrational for companies to engage in mergers given their poor historical record. Recent data, more than three decades later, still confirm both the poor record of mergers and the same hubris as managers seem to ignore the bad economic aspect of the transaction. There appears to be something about size that is harmful to corporations.

As with the idea of having elephants as pets, squeezes are much, much more expensive (relative to size) for large corporations. The gains from size are visible but the risks are hidden, and some concealed risks seem to bring frailties into the companies.

Large animals, such as elephants, boa constrictors, mammoths, and other animals of size tend to become rapidly extinct. Aside from the squeeze when resources are tight, there are mechanical considerations. Large animals are more fragile to shocks than small ones—again, stone and pebbles. Jared Diamond, always ahead of others, figured out such vulnerability in a paper called "Why Cats Have Nine Lives." If you throw a cat or a mouse from an elevation of several times their height, they will typically manage to survive. Elephants, by comparison, break limbs very easily.

Kerviel and Micro-Kerviel

Let us look at a case study from vulgar finance, a field in which participants are very good at making mistakes. On January 21, 2008, the Parisian bank Societé Générale rushed to sell in the market close to seventy billion dollars' worth of stocks, a very large amount for any single "fire sale." Markets were not very active (called "thin"), as it was Martin Luther King Day in the United States, and markets worldwide dropped precipitously, close to 10 percent, costing the company close to six billion dollars in losses just from their fire sale. The entire point of the squeeze is that they couldn't wait, and they had no option but to turn a sale into a fire sale. For they had, over the weekend, uncovered a fraud. Jerome Kerviel, a rogue back office employee, was playing with humongous sums in the market and hiding these exposures from the main computer system. They had no choice but to sell, immediately, these stocks they didn't know they owned.

Now, to see the effect of fragility from size, look at Figure 15 showing losses as a function of quantity sold. A fire sale of $70 billion worth of stocks leads to a loss of $6 billion. But a fire sale a tenth of the size, $7 billion would result in no loss at all, as markets would absorb the quantities without panic, maybe without even noticing. So this tells us that if, instead of having one very large bank, with Monsieur Kerviel as a rogue trader, we had ten smaller banks, each with a proportional Monsieur Micro-Kerviel, and each conducted his rogue trading independently and at random times, the total losses for the ten banks would be close to nothing.

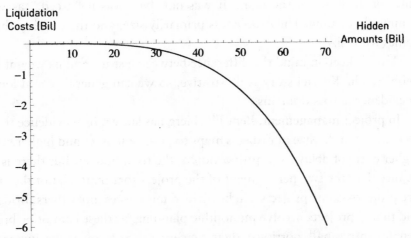

FIGURE 15. Small may be beautiful; it is certainly less fragile. The graph shows transaction costs as a function of the size of the error: they increase nonlinearly, and we can see the megafragility.

About a few weeks before the Kerviel episode, a French business school hired me to present to the board of executives of the Societé Générale meeting in Prague my ideas of Black Swan risks. In the eyes of the bankers, I was like a Jesuit preacher visiting Mecca in the middle of the annual Hajj—their "quants" and risk people hated me with passion, and I regretted not having insisted on speaking in Arabic given that they had simultaneous translation. My talk was about pseudo risk techniques à la Triffat—methods commonly used, as I said, to measure and predict events, methods that have never worked before—and how we needed to focus on fragility and barbells. During the talk I was heckled relentlessly by Kerviel's boss and his colleague, the head of risk management. After my talk, everyone ignored me, as if I were a Martian, with a "who brought this guy here" awkward situation (I had been selected by the school, not the bank). The only person who was nice to me was the chairman, as he mistook me for someone else and had no clue about what I was discussing.

So the reader can imagine my state of mind when, shortly after my return to New York, the Kerviel trading scandal broke. It was also tantalizing that I had to keep my mouth shut (which I did, except for a few slips) for legal reasons.

Clearly, the postmortem analyses were mistaken, attributing the problem to *bad* controls by the *bad* capitalistic system, and lack of vigilance on the part of the bank. It was not. Nor was it "greed," as we commonly assume. The problem is primarily size, and the fragility that comes from size.

Always keep in mind the difference between a stone and its weight in pebbles. The Kerviel story is illustrative, so we can generalize and look at evidence across domains.

In project management, Bent Flyvbjerg has shown firm evidence that an increase in the size of projects maps to poor outcomes and higher and higher costs of delays as a proportion of the total budget. But there is a nuance: it is the size per segment of the project that matters, not the entire project—some projects can be divided into pieces, not others. Bridge and tunnel projects involve monolithic planning, as these cannot be broken up into small portions; their percentage costs overruns increase markedly with size. Same with dams. For roads, built by small segments, there is no serious size effect, as the project managers incur only small errors and can adapt to them. Small segments go one small error at the time, with no serious role for squeezes.

Another aspect of size: large corporations also end up endangering neighborhoods. I've used the following argument against large superstore chains in spite of the advertised benefits. A large super-megastore wanted to acquire an entire neighborhood near where I live, causing uproar owing to the change it would bring to the character of the neighborhood. The argument in favor was the revitalization of the area, that type of story. I fought the proposal on the following grounds: should the company go bust (and the statistical elephant in the room is that it eventually will), we would end up with a massive war zone. This is the type of argument the British advisors Rohan Silva and Steve Hilton have used in favor of small merchants, along the poetic "small is beautiful." It is completely wrong to use the calculus of benefits without including the probability of failure.*

---

* A nuance: the notions of "large" and "small" are relative to a given ecology or business structure. Small for an airplane maker is different from "small" when it comes to a bakery. As with the European Union's subsidiarity principle, "small" here means the smallest possible unit for a given function or task that can operate with a certain level of efficiency.

How to Exit a Movie Theater

Another example of the costs of a squeeze: Imagine how people exit a movie theater. Someone shouts "fire," and you have a dozen persons squashed to death. So we have a fragility of the theater to size, stemming from the fact that every additional person exiting brings more and more trauma (such disproportional harm is a negative convexity effect). A thousand people exiting (or trying to exit) in one minute is not the same as the same number exiting in half an hour. Someone unfamiliar with the business who naively *optimizes* the size of the place (Heathrow airport, for example) might miss the idea that smooth functioning at regular times is different from the rough functioning at times of stress.

It so happens that contemporary economic optimized life causes us to build larger and larger theaters, but with the exact same door. They no longer make this mistake too often while building cinemas, theaters, and stadiums, but we tend to make the mistake in other domains, such as, for instance, natural resources and food supplies. Just consider that the price of wheat more than tripled in the years 2004–2007 in response to a small increase in net demand, around 1 percent.*

Bottlenecks are the mothers of all squeezes.

PROJECTS AND PREDICTION

Why Planes Don't Arrive Early

Let us start as usual with a transportation problem, and generalize to other areas. Travelers (typically) do not like uncertainty—especially when they are on a set schedule. Why? There is a one-way effect.

I've taken the very same London–New York flight most of my life. The flight takes about seven hours, the equivalent of a short book plus a

---

* The other problem is that of misunderstanding the nonlinearity of natural resources, or anything particularly scarce and vital. Economists have the so-called law of scarcity, by which things increase in value according to the demand for them—but they ignore the consequences of nonlinearities on risk. My former thesis director, Hélyette Geman, and I are currently studying a "law of convexity" that makes commodities, particularly vital ones, even dearer than previously thought.

brief polite chat with a neighbor and a meal with port wine, stilton cheese, and crackers. I recall a few instances in which I arrived early, about twenty minutes, no more. But there have been instances in which I got there more than two or three hours late, and in at least one instance it has taken me more than two days to reach my destination.

Because travel time cannot be really negative, uncertainty tends to cause delays, making arrival time increase, almost never decrease. Or it makes arrival time decrease by just minutes, but increase by hours, an obvious asymmetry. Anything unexpected, any shock, any volatility, is much more likely to extend the total flying time.

This also explains the irreversibility of time, in a way, if you consider the passage of time as an increase in disorder.

Let us now apply this concept to projects. Just as when you add uncertainty to a flight, the planes tend to land later, not earlier (and these laws of physics are so universal that they even work in Russia), when you add uncertainty to projects, they tend to cost more and take longer to complete. This applies to many, in fact almost all, projects.

The interpretation I had in the past was that a psychological bias, the underestimation of the random structure of the world, was the cause behind such underestimation—projects take longer than planned because the estimates are too optimistic. We have evidence of such bias, called overconfidence. Decision scientists and business psychologists have theorized something called the "planning fallacy," in which they try to explain the fact that projects take longer, rarely less time, using psychological factors.

But the puzzle was that such underestimation did not seem to exist in the past century or so, though we were dealing with the very same humans, endowed with the same biases. Many large-scale projects a century and a half ago were completed on time; many of the tall buildings and monuments we see today are not just more elegant than modernistic structures but were completed within, and often ahead of, schedule. These include not just the Empire State Building (still standing in New York), but the London Crystal Palace, erected for the Great Exhibition of 1851, the hallmark of the Victorian reign, based on the inventive ideas of a gardener. The Palace, which housed the exhibition, went from concept to grand opening in just nine months. The building took the form of a massive glass house, 1,848 feet long by 454 feet wide; it was constructed from cast iron frame components and glass made almost exclusively in Birmingham and Smethwick.

The obvious is usually missed here: the Crystal Palace project did not use computers, and the parts were built not far from the source, with a small number of businesses involved in the supply chain. Further, there were no business schools at the time to teach something called "project management" and increase overconfidence. There were no consulting firms. The agency problem (which we defined as the divergence between the interest of the agent and that of his client) was not significant. In other words, it was a much more linear economy—less complex—than today. And we have more nonlinearities—asymmetries, convexities—in today's world.

Black Swan effects are necessarily increasing, as a result of complexity, interdependence between parts, globalization, and the beastly thing called "efficiency" that makes people now sail too close to the wind. Add to that consultants and business schools. One problem somewhere can halt the entire project—so the projects tend to get as weak as the weakest link in their chain (an acute negative convexity effect). The world is getting less and less predictable, and we rely more and more on technologies that have errors and interactions that are harder to estimate, let alone predict.

And the information economy is the culprit. Bent Flyvbjerg, the one of bridge and road projects mentioned earlier in this chapter, showed another result. The problem of cost overruns and delays is much more acute in the presence of information technologies (IT), as computer projects cause a large share of these cost overruns, and it is better to focus on these principally. But even outside of these IT-heavy projects, we tend to have very severe delays.

But the logic is simple: again, negative convexity effects are the main culprit, a direct and visible cause. There is an asymmetry in the way errors hit you—the same as with travel.

No psychologist who has discussed the "planning fallacy" has realized that, at the core, it is not essentially a psychological problem, not an issue with human errors; it is inherent to the nonlinear structure of the projects. Just as time cannot be negative, a three-month project cannot be completed in zero or negative time. So, on a timeline going left to right, errors add to the right end, not the left end of it. If uncertainty were linear we would observe some projects completed extremely early (just as we would arrive sometimes very early, sometimes very late). But this is not the case.

Wars, Deficits, and Deficits

The Great War was estimated to last only a few months; by the time it was over, it had gotten France and Britain heavily in debt; they incurred at least ten times what they thought their financial costs would be, aside from all the horrors, suffering, and destruction. The same of course for the second war, which added to the U.K. debt, causing it to become heavily indebted, mostly to the United States.

In the United States the prime example remains the Iraq war, expected by George W. Bush and his friends to cost thirty to sixty billion, which so far, taking into account all the indirect costs, may have swelled to more than two trillion—indirect costs multiply, causing chains, explosive chains of interactions, all going in the same direction of more costs, not less. Complexity plus asymmetry (plus such types as George W. Bush), once again, lead to explosive errors.

The larger the military, the disproportionally larger the cost overruns.

But wars—with more than twentyfold errors—are only illustrative of the way governments underestimate explosive nonlinearities (convexity effects) and why they should not be trusted with finances or any large-scale decisions. Indeed, governments do not need wars at all to get us in trouble with deficits: the underestimation of the costs of their projects is chronic for the very same reason 98 percent of contemporary projects have overruns. They just end up spending more than they tell us. This has led me to install a governmental golden rule: no borrowing allowed, forced fiscal balance.

WHERE THE "EFFICIENT" IS NOT EFFICIENT

We can easily see the costs of fragility swelling in front of us, visible to the naked eye. Global disaster costs are today more than three times what they were in the 1980s, adjusting for inflation. The effect, noted a while ago by the visionary researcher on extreme events Daniel Zajdenweber, seems to be accelerating. The economy can get more and more "efficient," but fragility is causing the costs of errors to be higher.

The stock exchanges have converted from "open outcry" where wild traders face each other, yelling and screaming as in a souk, then go drink together. Traders were replaced by computers, for very small visible benefits and massively large risks. While errors made by traders are confined and distributed, those made by computerized systems go wild—in August 2010, a computer error made the entire market crash (the "flash crash"); in August 2012, as this manuscript was heading to the printer, the Knight Capital Group had its computer system go wild and cause $10 million dollars of losses a minute, losing $480 million.

And naive cost-benefit analyses can be a bit harmful, an effect that of course swells with size. For instance, the French have in the past focused on nuclear energy as it seemed "clean" and cheap. And "optimal" on a computer screen. Then, after the wake-up call of the Fukushima disaster of 2011, they realized that they needed additional safety features and scrambled to add them, at any cost. In a way this is similar to the squeeze I mentioned earlier: they are forced to invest, regardless of price. Such additional expense was not part of the cost-benefit analysis that went into the initial decision and looked good on a computer screen. So when deciding on one source of fuel against another, or similar comparisons, we do not realize that model error may hit one side more than the other.

Pollution and Harm to the Planet

From this we can generate a simple ecological policy. We know that fossil fuels are harmful in a nonlinear way. The harm is necessarily concave (if a little bit of it is devoid of harm, a lot can cause climatic disturbances). While on epistemological grounds, because of opacity, we do not need to believe in anthropogenic climate change (caused by humans) in order to be ecologically conservative, we can put these convexity effects to use in producing a risk management rule for pollution. Simply, just as with size, split your sources of pollution among many natural sources. The harm from polluting with ten different sources is smaller than the equivalent pollution from a single source.*

Let's look at naturelike ancestral mechanisms for regulating the concentration effects. We contemporary humans go to the stores to purchase the same items, say tuna, coffee or tea, rice, mozzarella, Cabernet

---

* Volatility and uncertainty are equivalent, as we saw with the table of the Disorder family. Accordingly, note that the fragile is harmed by an increase in uncertainty.

wine, olive oil, and other items that appear to us as not easily substitut-able. Because of sticky contemporary habits, cultural contagion, and the rigidity of factories, we are led to the excessive use of specific products. This concentration is harmful. Extreme consumption of, say, tuna, can hurt other animals, mess with the ecosystem, and lead species to extinc-tion. And not only does the harm scale nonlinearly, but the shortages lead to disproportional rises in prices.

Ancestral humans did it differently. Jennifer Dunne, a complexity researcher who studies hunter-gatherers, examined evidence about the behavior of the Aleuts, a North American native tribe, for which we have ample data, covering five millennia. They exhibit a remarkable lack of concentration in their predatorial behavior, with a strategy of prey switching. They were not as sticky and rigid as us in their habits. When-ever they got low on a resource, they switched to another one, as if to preserve the ecosystem. So they understood convexity effects—or, rather, their habits did.

Note that globalization has had the effect of making contagions planetary—as if the entire world became a huge room with narrow exits and people rushing to the same doors, with accelerated harm. Just as about every child reads Harry Potter and joins (for now) Facebook, people when they get rich are starting to engage in the same activities and buy the same items. They drink Cabernet wine, hope to visit Venice and Florence, dream of buying a second home in the South of France, etc. Tourist locations are becoming unbearable: just go to Venice next July.

The Nonlinearity of Wealth

We can certainly attribute the fragilizing effect of contemporary global-ization to complexity, and how connectivity and cultural contagions make gyrations in economic variables much more severe—the classic switch to Extremistan. But there is another effect: wealth. Wealth means more, and because of nonlinear scaling, more is different. We are prone to make more severe errors because we are simply wealthier. Just as projects of one hundred million dollars are more unpredictable and more likely to incur overruns than five-million-dollar ones, simply by being richer, the world is troubled with additional unpredictability and fragility. This comes with growth—at a country level, this Highly Dreamed-of GDP Growth. Even at an individual level, wealth means more headaches; we may need to work harder at mitigating the complications arising from wealth than we do at acquiring it.

Conclusion

To conclude this chapter, fragility in any domain, from a porcelain cup to an organism, to a political system, to the size of a firm, or to delays in airports, resides in the nonlinear. Further, discovery can be seen as an antideficit. Think of the exact opposite of airplane delays or project overruns—something that benefits from uncertainty. And discovery presents the mirror image of what we saw as fragile, randomness-hating situations.

CHAPTER 19

The Philosopher's Stone and Its Inverse

They tell you when they are going bust—Gold is sometimes a special variety of lead

———

And now, reader, after the Herculean effort I put into making the ideas of the last few chapters clearer to you, my turn to take it easy and express things technically, sort of. Accordingly, this chapter—a deepening of the ideas of the previous one—will be denser and should be skipped by the enlightened reader.

HOW TO DETECT WHO WILL GO BUST

Let us examine a method to detect fragility—the inverse philosopher's stone. We can illustrate it with the story of the giant government-sponsored lending firm called Fannie Mae, a corporation that collapsed leaving the United States taxpayer with hundreds of billions of dollars of losses (and, alas, still counting).

One day in 2003, Alex Berenson, a *New York Times* journalist, came into my office with the secret risk reports of Fannie Mae, given to him by a defector. It was the kind of report getting into the guts of the methodology for risk calculation that only an insider can see—Fannie Mae made its own risk calculations and disclosed what it wanted to whomever it wanted, the public or someone else. But only a defector could show us the guts to see how the risk was calculated.

We looked at the report: simply, a move upward in an economic variable led to massive losses, a move downward (in the opposite direction), to small profits. Further moves upward led to even larger additional losses and further moves downward to even smaller profits. It looked exactly like the story of the stone in Figure 9. Acceleration of harm was obvious—in fact it was monstrous. So we immediately saw that their blowup was inevitable: their exposures were severely "concave," similar to the graph of traffic in Figure 14: losses that accelerate as one deviates economic variables (I did not even need to understand which one, as fragility to one variable of this magnitude implies fragility to all other parameters). I worked with my emotions, not my brain, and I had a pang before even understanding what numbers I had been looking at. It was the mother of all fragilities and, thanks to Berenson, *The New York Times* presented my concern. A smear campaign ensued, but nothing too notable. For I had in the meantime called a few key people charlatans and they were not too excited about it.

The key is that the nonlinear is vastly more affected by extreme events—and nobody was interested in extreme events since they had a mental block against them.

I kept telling anyone who would listen to me, including random taxi drivers (well, almost), that the company Fannie Mae was "sitting on a barrel of dynamite." Of course, blowups don't happen every day (just as poorly built bridges don't collapse immediately), and people kept saying that my opinion was wrong and unfounded (using some argument that the stock was going up or something even more circular). I also inferred that other institutions, almost all banks, were in the same situation. After checking similar institutions, and seeing that the problem was general, I realized that a total collapse of the banking system was a certainty. I was so certain I could not see straight and went back to the markets to get my revenge against the turkeys. As in the scene from *The Godfather* (III), "Just when I thought I was out, they pull me back in."

Things happened as if they were planned by destiny. Fannie Mae went bust, along with other banks. It just took a bit longer than expected, no big deal.

The stupid part of the story is that I had not seen the link between financial and general fragility—nor did I use the term "fragility." Maybe I didn't look at too many porcelain cups. However, thanks to the episode of the attic I had a measure for fragility, hence antifragility.

It all boils down to the following: figuring out if our miscalculations or misforecasts are on balance more harmful than they are beneficial, and how accelerating the damage is. Exactly as in the story of the king, in which the damage from a ten-kilogram stone is more than twice the damage from a five-kilogram one. Such accelerating damage means that a large stone would eventually kill the person. Likewise a large market deviation would eventually kill the company.

Once I figured out that fragility was directly from nonlinearity and convexity effects, and that convexity was measurable, I got all excited. The technique—detecting *acceleration* of harm—applies to anything that entails decision making under uncertainty, and risk management. While it was the most interesting in medicine and technology, the immediate demand was in economics. So I suggested to the International Monetary Fund a measure of fragility to substitute for their measures of risk that they knew didn't work. Most people in the risk business had been frustrated by the poor (rather, the random) performance of their models, but they didn't like my earlier stance: "don't use any model." They wanted something. And a risk measure was there.*

So here is something to use. The technique, a simple heuristic called the *fragility (and antifragility) detection heuristic,* works as follows. Let's say you want to check whether a town is overoptimized. Say you measure that when traffic increases by ten thousand cars, travel time grows by ten minutes. But if traffic increases by ten thousand more cars, travel time now extends by an extra thirty minutes. Such acceleration of traffic time shows that traffic is fragile and you have too many cars and need to reduce traffic until the acceleration becomes mild (acceleration, I repeat, is acute concavity, or negative convexity effect).

Likewise, government deficits are particularly concave to changes in economic conditions. Every additional deviation in, say, the unemployment rate—particularly when the government has debt—makes deficits incrementally worse. And financial leverage for a company has the same

---

* The method does not require a good model for risk measurement. Take a ruler. You know it is wrong. It will not be able to measure the height of the child. But it can certainly tell you if he is growing. In fact the error you get about the rate of growth of the child is much, much smaller than the error you would get measuring his height. The same with a scale: no matter how defective, it will almost always be able to tell you if you are gaining weight, so stop blaming it.

Convexity is about acceleration. The remarkable thing about measuring convexity effects to detect model errors is that even if the model used for the computation is wrong, it can tell you if an entity is fragile and by how much it is fragile. As with the defective scale, we are only looking for second-order effects.

effect: you need to borrow more and more to get the same effect. Just as in a Ponzi scheme.

The same with operational leverage on the part of a fragile company. Should sales increase 10 percent, then profits would increase less than they would decrease should sales drop 10 percent.

That was in a way the technique I used intuitively to declare that the Highly Respected Firm Fannie Mae was on its way to the cemetery—and it was easy to produce a rule of thumb out of it. Now with the IMF we had a simple measure with a stamp. It looks simple, too simple, so the initial reaction from "experts" was that it was "trivial" (said by people who visibly never detected these risks before—academics and quantitative analysts scorn what they can understand too easily and get ticked off by what they did not think of themselves).

According to the wonderful principle that one should use people's stupidity to have fun, I invited my friend Raphael Douady to collaborate in expressing this simple idea using the most opaque mathematical derivations, with incomprehensible theorems that would take half a day (for a professional) to understand. Raphael, Bruno Dupire, and I had been involved in an almost two-decades-long continuous conversation on how everything entailing risk—everything—can be seen with a lot more rigor and clarity from the vantage point of an option professional. Raphael and I managed to prove the link between nonlinearity, dislike of volatility, and fragility. Remarkably—as has been shown—if you can say something straightforward in a complicated manner with complex theorems, even if there is no large gain in rigor from these complicated equations, people take the idea very seriously. We got nothing but positive reactions, and we were now told that this simple detection heuristic was "intelligent" (by the same people who had found it trivial). The only problem is that mathematics is addictive.

The Idea of Positive and Negative Model Error

Now what I believe is my true specialty: error in models.

When I was in the transaction business, I used to make plenty of errors of execution. You buy one thousand units and in fact you discover the next day that you bought two thousand. If the price went up in the meantime you had a handsome profit. Otherwise you had a large loss. So these errors are in the long run neutral in effect, since they can affect you both ways. They increase the variance, but they don't affect your business too much. There is no one-sidedness to them. And these errors can be kept under control thanks to size limits—you make a lot of small transactions, so errors remain small. And at year end, typically, the errors "wash out," as they say.

But that is not the case with most things we build, and with errors related to things that are fragile, in the presence of negative convexity effects. This class of errors has a one-way outcome, that is, negative, and tends to make planes land later, not earlier. Wars tend to get worse, not better. As we saw with traffic, variations (now called disturbances) tend to increase travel time from South Kensington to Piccadilly Circus, never shorten it. Some things, like traffic, do rarely experience the equivalent of positive disturbances.

This one-sidedness brings both underestimation of randomness and underestimation of harm, since one is more exposed to harm than benefit from error. If in the long run we get as much variation in the source of randomness one way as the other, the harm would severely outweigh the benefits.

So—and this is the key to the Triad—we can classify things by three simple distinctions: things that, in the long run, like disturbances (or errors), things that are neutral to them, and those that dislike them. By now we have seen that evolution likes disturbances. We saw that discovery likes disturbances. Some forecasts are hurt by uncertainty—and, like travel time, one needs a buffer. Airlines figured out how to do it, but not governments, when they estimate deficits.

This method is very general. I even used it with Fukushima-style computations and realized how fragile their computation of small probabilities was—in fact all small probabilities tend to be very fragile to errors, as a small change in the assumptions can make the probability rise dramatically, from one per million to one per hundred. Indeed, a ten-thousand-fold underestimation.

Finally, this method can show us where the math in economic models is bogus—which models are fragile and which ones are not. Simply do a small change in the assumptions, and look at how large the effect, and if there is acceleration of such effect. Acceleration implies—as with Fannie Mae—that someone relying on the model blows up from Black Swan effects. *Molto facile*. A detailed methodology to detect which results are bogus in economics—along with a discussion of small probabilities—is provided in the Appendix. What I can say for now is that much of what is taught in economics that has an equation, as well as econometrics, should be immediately ditched—which explains why economics is largely a charlatanic profession. Fragilistas, *semper fragilisti*!

HOW TO LOSE A GRANDMOTHER

Next I will explain the following effect of nonlinearity: conditions under which the average—the first order effect—does not matter. As a first step before getting into the workings of the philosopher's stone.

As the saying goes:

> *Do not cross a river if it is on average four feet deep.*

You have just been informed that your grandmother will spend the next two hours at the very desirable average temperature of seventy degrees Fahrenheit (about twenty-one degrees Celsius). Excellent, you think, since seventy degrees is the optimal temperature for grandmothers. Since you went to business school, you are a "big picture" type of person and are satisfied with the summary information.

But there is a second piece of data. Your grandmother, it turns out, will spend the first hour at zero degrees Fahrenheit (around minus eighteen Celsius), and the second hour at one hundred and forty degrees (around 60° C), for an average of the very desirable Mediterranean-style seventy degrees (21° C). So it looks as though you will most certainly end up with no grandmother, a funeral, and, possibly, an inheritance.

Clearly, temperature changes become more and more harmful as they deviate from seventy degrees. As you see, the second piece of information, the variability, turned out to be more important than the first. The notion of average is of no significance when one is fragile to variations—the dispersion in possible thermal outcomes here matters much more. Your grandmother is fragile to variations of temperature, to the volatility of the weather. Let us call that second piece of information the *second-order effect*, or, more precisely, the *convexity effect*.

Here, consider that, as much as a good simplification the notion of average can be, it can also be a Procrustean bed. The information that the average temperature is seventy degrees Fahrenheit does not simplify the situation for your grandmother. It is information squeezed into a Procrustean bed—and these are necessarily committed by scientific modelers, since a model is *by its very nature* a simplification. You just don't want the simplification to distort the situation to the point of being harmful.

Figure 16 shows the fragility of the health of the grandmother to variations. If I plot health on the vertical axis, and temperature on the horizontal one, I see a shape that curves inward—a "concave" shape, or *negative* convexity effect.

If the grandmother's response was "linear" (no curve, a straight line), then the harm of temperature below seventy degrees would be offset by the benefits of temperature above it. And the fact is that the health of the grandmother has to be capped at a maximum, otherwise she would keep improving.

Health of Grandmother

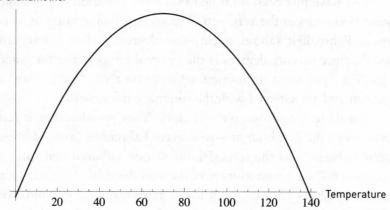

Temperature

FIGURE 16. Megafragility. Health as a function of temperature curves inward. A combination of 0 and 140 degrees (F) is worse for your grandmother's health than just 70 degrees. In fact almost *any* combination averaging 70 degrees is worse than just 70 degrees.[*] The graph shows concavity or negative convexity effects—curves inward.

Take this for now as we rapidly move to the more general attributes; in the case of the grandmother's health response to temperature: (a) there is nonlinearity (the response is not a straight line, not "linear"),

---

[*] I am simplifying a bit. There may be a few degrees' variation around 70 at which the grandmother might be better off than just at 70, but I skip this nuance here. In fact younger humans are antifragile to thermal variations, up to a point, benefiting from some variability, then losing such antifragility with age (or disuse, as I suspect that thermal comfort ages people and makes them fragile).

(b) it curves inward, too much so, and, finally, (c) the more nonlinear the response, the less relevant the average, and the more relevant the stability around such average.

NOW THE PHILOSOPHER'S STONE *

Much of medieval thinking went into finding the philosopher's stone. It is always good to be reminded that chemistry is the child of alchemy, much of which consisted of looking into the chemical powers of substances. The main efforts went into creating value by transforming metals into gold by the method of *transmutation*. The necessary substance was called the philosopher's stone—*lapis philosophorum*. Many people fell for it, a list that includes such scholars as Albertus Magnus, Isaac Newton, and Roger Bacon and great thinkers who were not quite scholars, such as Paracelsus.

It is a matter of no small import that the operation of transmutation was called the *Magnus Opus*—the great(est) work. I truly believe that the operation I will discuss—based on some properties of optionality—is about as close as we can get to the philosopher's stone.

The following note would allow us to understand:

(a) The severity of the problem of conflation (mistaking the price of oil for geopolitics, or mistaking a profitable bet for good forecasting—not convexity of payoff and optionality).

(b) Why anything with optionality has a long-term advantage— and how to measure it.

(c) An additional subtle property called Jensen's inequality.

Recall from our traffic example in Chapter 18 that 90,000 cars for an hour, then 110,000 cars for the next one, for an average of 100,000, and traffic will be horrendous. On the other hand, assume we have 100,000 cars for two hours, and traffic will be smooth and time in traffic short.

The number of cars is the *something,* a variable; traffic time is the *function of something*. The behavior of the *function* is such that it is, as

---

* I remind the reader that this section is technical and can be skipped.

we said, "not the same thing." We can see here that the *function of something* becomes different from the *something* under nonlinearities.

(a) The more nonlinear, the more the *function of something* divorces itself from the *something*. If traffic were linear, then there would be no difference in traffic time between the two following situations: 90,000, then 110,000 cars on the one hand, or 100,000 cars on the other.

(b) The more volatile the *something*—the more uncertainty—the more the *function* divorces itself from the *something*. Let us consider the average number of cars again. The function (travel time) depends more on the volatility around the average. Things degrade if there is unevenness of distribution. For the same average you prefer to have 100,000 cars for both time periods; 80,000 then 120,000, would be even worse than 90,000 and 110,000.

(c) If the function is convex (antifragile), then the average of the function *of something* is going to be higher than the function of the average *of something*. And the reverse when the function is concave (fragile).

As an example for (c), which is a more complicated version of the bias, assume that the function under question is the squaring function (multiply a number by itself). This is a convex function. Take a conventional die (six sides) and consider a payoff equal to the number it lands on, that is, you get paid a number equivalent to what the die shows— 1 if it lands on 1, 2 if it lands on 2, up to 6 if it lands on 6. The square of the expected (average) payoff is then $(1+2+3+4+5+6$ divided by $6)^2$, equals 3.5^2, here 12.25. So the *function of the average* equals 12.25.

But the average of the function is as follows. Take the square of every payoff, $1^2+2^2+3^2+4^2+5^2+6^2$ divided by 6, that is, the average square payoff, and you can see that *the average of the function* equals 15.17.

So, since squaring is a convex function, the average of the square payoff is higher than the square of the average payoff. The difference here between 15.17 and 12.25 is what I call the hidden benefit of antifragility—here, a 24 percent "edge."

There are two biases: one elementary convexity effect, leading to mistaking the properties of the average of something (here 3.5) and those of a (convex) function of something (here 15.17), and the second, more involved, in mistaking an average of a function for the function of an average, here 15.17 for 12.25. The latter represents optionality.

Someone with a linear payoff needs to be right more than 50 percent of the time. Someone with a convex payoff, much less. The hidden benefit of antifragility is that you can guess worse than random and still end up outperforming. Here lies the power of optionality—your *function of something* is very convex, so you can be wrong and still do fine—the more uncertainty, the better.

This explains my statement that you can be dumb and antifragile and still do very well.

This hidden "convexity bias" comes from a mathematical property called Jensen's inequality. This is what the common discourse on innovation is missing. If you ignore the convexity bias, you are missing a chunk of what makes the nonlinear world go round. And it is a fact that such an idea is missing from the discourse. Sorry.*

How to Transform Gold into Mud: The Inverse Philosopher's Stone

Let us take the same example as before, using as the function the square root (the exact inverse of squaring, which is concave, but much less concave than the square function is convex).

The square root of the expected (average) payoff is then $\sqrt{(1+2+3+4+5+6}$ divided by 6), equals $\sqrt{3.5}$, here 1.87. The *function of the average* equals 1.87.

But the average of the function is as follows. Take the square root of every payoff, $(\sqrt{1}+\sqrt{2}+\sqrt{3}+\sqrt{4}+\sqrt{5}+\sqrt{6})$, divided by 6, that is, the average square root payoff, and you can see that *the average of the function* equals 1.80.

The difference is called the "negative convexity bias" (or, if you are a stickler, "concavity bias"). The hidden harm of fragility is that you need to be much, much better than random in your prediction and knowing where you are going, just to offset the negative effect.

---

* The grandmother does better at 70 degrees Fahrenheit than at an average of 70 degrees with one hour at 0, another at 140 degrees. The more dispersion around the average, the more harm for her. Let us see the counterintuitive effect in terms of x and function of x, $f(x)$. Let us write the health of the grandmother as $f(x)$, with x the temperature. We have a function of the average temperature, $f\{(0 + 140)/2\}$, showing the grandmother in excellent shape. But $\{f(o) + f(140)\}/2$ leaves us with a dead grandmother at $f(0)$ and a dead grandmother at $f(140)$, for an "average" of a dead grandmother. We can see an explanation of the statement that the properties of $f(x)$ and those of x become divorced from each other when $f(x)$ is nonlinear. The average of $f(x)$ is different from f(average of x).

Let me summarize the argument: if you have favorable asymmetries, or positive convexity, options being a special case, then in the long run you will do reasonably well, outperforming the average in the presence of uncertainty. The more uncertainty, the more role for optionality to kick in, and the more you will outperform. This property is very central to life.

BOOK VI

Via Negativa

———

Recall that we had no name for the color blue but managed rather well without it—we stayed for a long part of our history culturally, not biologically, color blind. And before the composition of Chapter 1, we did not have a name for antifragility, yet systems have relied on it effectively in the absence of human intervention. There are many things without words, matters that we know and can act on but cannot describe directly, cannot capture in human language or within the narrow human concepts that are available to us. Almost anything around us of significance is hard to grasp linguistically—and in fact the more powerful, the more incomplete our linguistic grasp.

But if we cannot express what something is exactly, we can say something about what it is not—the indirect rather than the direct expression. The "apophatic" focuses on what cannot be said directly in words, from the Greek *apophasis* (saying no, or mentioning without mentioning). The method began as an avoidance of direct description, leading to a focus on negative description, what is called in Latin *via negativa*, the negative way, after theological traditions, particularly in the Eastern Orthodox Church. *Via negativa* does not try to express what God is—leave that to the primitive brand of contemporary thinkers and philosophasters with scientistic tendencies. It just lists what God is *not* and proceeds by the process of elimination. The idea is mostly associated with the mystical theologian Pseudo-Dionysos the Areopagite. He was some obscure Near Easterner by the name of Dionysos who wrote powerful mystical treatises and was for a long time confused with Dionysos the

Areopagite, a judge in Athens who was converted by the preaching of Paul the Apostle. Hence the qualifier of "Pseudo" added to his name.

Neoplatonists were followers of Plato's ideas; they focused mainly on Plato's forms, those abstract objects that had a distinct existence on their own. Pseudo-Dionysos was the disciple of Proclus the Neoplatonist (himself the student of Syrianus, another Syrian Neoplatonist). Proclus was known to repeat the metaphor that statues are carved by subtraction. I have often read a more recent version of the idea, with the following apocryphal pun. Michelangelo was asked by the pope about the secret of his genius, particularly how he carved the statue of David, largely considered the masterpiece of all masterpieces. His answer was: "It's simple. I just remove everything that is not David."

The reader might thus recognize the logic behind the barbell. Remember from the logic of the barbell that it is necessary to first remove fragilities.

Where Is the Charlatan?

Recall that the interventionista focuses on positive action—*doing*. Just like positive definitions, we saw that acts of commission are respected and glorified by our primitive minds and lead to, say, naive government interventions that end in disaster, followed by generalized complaints about naive government interventions, as these, it is now accepted, end in disaster, followed by more naive government interventions. Acts of omission, *not* doing something, are not considered acts and do not appear to be part of one's mission. Table 3 showed how generalized this effect can be across domains, from medicine to business.

I have used all my life a wonderfully simple heuristic: charlatans are recognizable in that they will give you positive advice, and only positive advice, exploiting our gullibility and sucker-proneness for recipes that hit you in a flash as just obvious, then evaporate later as you forget them. Just look at the "how to" books with, in their title, "Ten Steps for—" (fill in: enrichment, weight loss, making friends, innovation, getting elected, building muscles, finding a husband, running an orphanage, etc.). Yet in practice it is the negative that's used by the pros, those selected by evolution: chess grandmasters usually win by not losing; people become rich by not going bust (particularly when others do); religions are mostly about interdicts; the learning of life is about what to avoid. You reduce most of your personal risks of accident thanks to a small number of measures.

Further, being fooled by randomness is that in most circumstances fraught with a high degree of randomness, one cannot really tell if a successful person has skills, or if a person with skills will succeed—but we can pretty much predict the negative, that a person totally devoid of skills will eventually fail.

Subtractive Knowledge

Now when it comes to knowledge, the same applies. The greatest—and most robust—contribution to knowledge consists in removing what we think is wrong—subtractive epistemology.

In life, antifragility is reached by *not* being a sucker. In *Peri mystikes theologias,* Pseudo-Dionysos did not use these exact words, nor did he discuss disconfirmation, nor did he get the idea with clarity, but in my view he figured out this subtractive epistemology and asymmetries in knowledge. I have called "Platonicity" the love of some crisp abstract forms, the theoretical forms and universals that make us blind to the mess of reality and cause Black Swan effects. Then I realized that there was an asymmetry. I truly believe in Platonic ideas when they come in reverse, like negative universals.

So the central tenet of the epistemology I advocate is as follows: we know a lot more what is wrong than what is right, or, phrased according to the fragile/robust classification, negative knowledge (what is wrong, what does not work) is more robust to error than positive knowledge (what is right, what works). So knowledge grows by subtraction much more than by addition—given that what we know today might turn out to be wrong but what we know to be wrong cannot turn out to be right, at least not easily. If I spot a black swan (not capitalized), I can be quite certain that the statement "all swans are white" is wrong. But even if I have never seen a black swan, I can never hold such a statement to be true. Rephrasing it again: since one small observation can disprove a statement, while millions can hardly confirm it, disconfirmation is more rigorous than confirmation.

This idea has been associated in our times with the philosopher Karl Popper, and I quite mistakenly thought that he was its originator (though he is at the origin of an even more potent idea on the fundamental inability to predict the course of history). The notion, in fact, is vastly more ancient, and was one of the central tenets of the skeptical-empirical school of medicine of the postclassical era in the Eastern Mediterranean. It was well known to a group of nineteenth-century French scholars who rediscovered these works. And this idea of the power of disconfirmation permeates the way we do hard science.

As you can see, we can link this to the general tableaus of positive (additive) and negative (subtractive): negative knowledge is more robust. But it is not perfect. Popper has been criticized by philosophers for his treatment of disconfirmation as hard, unequivocal, black-and-white. It is not clear-cut: it is impossible to figure out whether an experiment failed to produce the intended results—hence "falsifying" the theory—because of the failure of the tools, because of bad luck, or because of fraud by the scientist. Say you saw a black swan. That would certainly invalidate the idea that all swans are white. But what if you had been drinking Lebanese wine, or hallucinating from spending too much time on the Web? What if it was a dark night, in which all swans look gray? Let us say that, in general, failure (and disconfirmation) are more informative than success and confirmation, which is why I claim that negative knowledge is just "more robust."

Now, before starting to write this section, I spent some time scouring Popper's complete works wondering how the great thinker, with his obsessive approach to falsification, completely missed the idea of fragility. His masterpiece, *The Poverty of Historicism,* in which he presents the limits of forecasting, shows the impossibility of an acceptable representation of the future. But he missed the point that if an incompetent surgeon is operating on a brain, one can safely predict serious damage, even the death of the patient. Yet such subtractive representation of the future is perfectly in line with his idea of disconfirmation, its logical second step. What he calls falsification of a theory should lead, in practice, to the breaking of the object of its application.

In political systems, a good mechanism is one that helps remove the bad guy; it's not about what to do or who to put in. For the bad guy can cause more harm than the collective actions of good ones. Jon Elster goes further. And presents another kind of *via negativa*: A good system is one that protects the ordinary guy from bad influences. He recently wrote a book with the telling title *Preventing Mischief* in which he bases negative action on Bentham's idea that "the art of the legislator is limited to the prevention of everything that might prevent the development of their [members of the assembly] liberty and their intelligence."

And, as expected, *via negativa* is part of classical wisdom. For the Arab scholar and religious leader Ali Bin Abi-Taleb (no relation), keeping one's distance from an ignorant person is equivalent to keeping company with a wise man.

Finally, consider this modernized version in a saying from Steve Jobs: "People think focus means saying yes to the thing you've got to focus on. But that's not what it means at all. It means saying no to the hundred other good ideas that there are. You have to pick carefully. I'm actually as proud of the things we haven't done as the things I have done. Innovation is saying no to 1,000 things."

BARBELLS, AGAIN

Subtractive knowledge is a form of barbell. Critically, it is convex. What is wrong is quite robust, what you don't know is fragile and speculative, but you do not take it seriously so you make sure it does not harm you in case it turns out to be false.

Now another application of *via negativa* lies in the less-is-more idea.

Less Is More

The less-is-more idea in decision making can be traced to Spyros Makridakis, Robyn Dawes, Dan Goldstein, and Gerd Gigerenzer, who have all found in various contexts that simpler methods for forecasting and inference can work much, much better than complicated ones. Their simple rules of thumb are not perfect, but are designed to not be perfect; adopting some intellectual humility and abandoning the aim at sophistication can yield powerful effects. The pair of Goldstein and Gigerenzer coined the notion of "fast and frugal" heuristics that make good decisions despite limited time, knowledge, and computing power.

I realized that the less-is-more heuristic fell squarely into my work in two places. First, extreme effects: there are domains in which the rare event (I repeat, good or bad) plays a disproportionate share and we tend to be blind to it, so focusing on the exploitation of such a rare event, or protection against it, changes a lot, a lot of the risky exposure. Just worry about Black Swan exposures, and life is easy.

Less is more has proved to be shockingly easy to find and apply—and "robust" to mistakes and change of minds. There may not be an easily identifiable cause for a large share of the problems, but often there is an easy solution (not to all problems, but good enough; I mean really good enough), and such a solution is immediately identifiable, sometimes with the naked eye rather than the use of complicated analyses and highly fragile, error-prone, cause-ferreting nerdiness.

Some people are aware of the *eighty/twenty* idea, based on the discovery by Vilfredo Pareto more than a century ago that 20 percent of the people in Italy owned 80 percent of the land, and vice versa. Of these 20 percent, 20 percent (that is, 4 percent) would have owned around 80 percent of the 80 percent (that is, 64 percent). We end up with less than 1 percent representing about 50 percent of the total. These describe winner-take-all Extremistan effects. These effects are very general, from the distribution of wealth to book sales per author.

Few realize that we are moving into the far more uneven distribution of 99/1 across many things that used to be 80/20: 99 percent of Internet traffic is attributable to less than 1 percent of sites, 99 percent of book sales come from less than 1 percent of authors . . . and I need to stop because numbers are emotionally stirring. Almost everything contemporary has winner-take-all effects, which includes sources of harm and benefits. Accordingly, as I will show, 1 percent modification of systems can lower fragility (or increase antifragility) by about 99 percent—and all it takes is a few steps, very few steps, often at low cost, to make things better and safer.

For instance, a small number of homeless people cost the states a disproportionate share of the bills, which makes it obvious where to look for the savings. A small number of employees in a corporation cause the most problems, corrupt the general attitude—and vice versa—so getting rid of these is a great solution. A small number of customers generate a large share of the revenues. I get 95 percent of my smear postings from the same three obsessive persons, all representing the same prototypes of failure (one of whom has written, I estimate, close to one hundred thousand words in posts—he needs to write more and more and find more and more stuff to critique in my work and personality to get the same effect). When it comes to health care, Ezekiel Emanuel showed that half the population accounts for less than 3 percent of the costs, with the sickest 10 percent consuming 64 percent of the total pie. Bent Flyvbjerg (of Chapter 18) showed in his *Black Swan management* idea that the bulk of cost overruns by corporations are simply attributable to large technology projects—implying that that's what we need to focus on instead of talking and talking and writing complicated papers.

As they say in the mafia, just work on removing the pebble in your shoe.

There are some domains, like, say, real estate, in which problems and solutions are crisply summarized by a heuristic, a rule of thumb to look for the three most important properties: "location, location, and location"—much of the rest is supposed to be chickensh***t. Not quite and not always true, but it shows the central thing to worry about, as the rest takes care of itself.

Yet people want more data to "solve problems." I once testified in Congress against a project to fund a crisis forecasting project. The people involved were blind to the paradox that we have never had more data than we have now, yet have less predictability than ever. More data—such as paying attention to the eye colors of the people around when crossing the street—can make you miss the big truck. When you cross the street, you remove data, anything but the essential threat.* As Paul Valéry once wrote: *que de choses il faut ignorer pour agir*—how many things one should disregard in order to act.

Convincing—and confident—disciplines, say, physics, tend to use little statistical backup, while political science and economics, which have never produced anything of note, are full of elaborate statistics and statistical "evidence" (and you know that once you remove the smoke, the evidence is not evidence). The situation in science is similar to detective novels in which the person with the largest number of alibis turns out to be to be the guilty one. And you do not need reams of paper full of data to destroy the megatons of papers using statistics in economics: the simple argument that Black Swans and tail events run the socioeconomic world—and these events cannot be predicted—is sufficient to invalidate their statistics.

We have further evidence of the potency of less-is-more from the following experiment. Christopher Chabris and Daniel Simons, in their book *The Invisible Gorilla*, show how people watching a video of a

---

* Recall that the overediting interventionist missed the main mistake in Chapter 7. The 663-page document *Financial Crisis Inquiry Report* by the Financial Crisis Inquiry Commission missed what I believe are the main reasons: fragility and absence of skin in the game. But of course they listed every possible epiphenomenon you can think of as cause.

basketball game, when diverted with attention-absorbing details such as counting passes, can completely miss a gorilla stepping into the middle of the court.

I discovered that I had been intuitively using the less-is-more idea as an aid in decision making (contrary to the method of putting a series of pros and cons side by side on a computer screen). For instance, if you have more than one reason to do something (choose a doctor or veterinarian, hire a gardener or an employee, marry a person, go on a trip), just don't do it. It does not mean that one reason is better than two, just that by invoking more than one reason you are trying to convince yourself to do something. Obvious decisions (robust to error) *require* no more than a single reason. Likewise the French army had a heuristic to reject excuses for absenteeism for more than one reason, like death of grandmother, cold virus, and being bitten by a boar. If someone attacks a book or idea using more than one argument, you know it is not real: nobody says "he is a criminal, he killed many people, and he also has bad table manners and bad breath and is a very poor driver."

I have often followed what I call Bergson's razor: "A philosopher should be known for one single idea, not more" (I can't source it to Bergson, but the rule is good enough). The French essayist and poet Paul Valéry once asked Einstein if he carried a notebook to write down ideas. "I never have ideas" was the reply (in fact he just did not have chickens***t ideas). So, a heuristic: if someone has a long bio, I skip him—at a conference a friend invited me to have lunch with an overachieving hotshot whose résumé "can cover more than two or three lives"; I skipped to sit at a table with the trainees and stage engineers.* Likewise when I am told that someone has three hundred academic papers and twenty-two honorary doctorates, but no other single compelling contribution or main idea behind it, I avoid him like the bubonic plague.

---

* Even the Nobel, with all its ills of inducing competition in something as holy as science, is not granted for a collection of papers but rarely for more than a single, but major, contribution.

CHAPTER 20

Time and Fragility

Prophecy, like knowledge, is subtractive, not additive—The Lindy effect, or how the old prevails over the new, especially in technology, no matter what they say in California—Prophecy not a recommended and voluntary career

---

Antifragility implies—contrary to initial instinct—that the old is superior to the new, and much more than you think. No matter how something looks to your intellectual machinery, or how well or poorly it narrates, time will know more about its fragilities and break it when necessary. Here, I expose a contemporary disease—linked to interventionism—called *neomania,* which brings fragility but I believe may be treatable if one is patient enough.

What survives must be good at serving some (mostly hidden) purpose that time can see but our eyes and logical faculties can't capture. In this chapter we use the notion of fragility as a central driver of prediction.

Recall the foundational asymmetry: the antifragile benefits from volatility and disorder, the fragile is harmed. Well, time is the same as disorder.

FROM SIMONIDES TO JENSEN

As an exercise in the use of the distinction between fragility and antifragility, let us play prophet, with the understanding that it is not a good career choice unless you have a thick skin, a good circle of friends, little access to the Internet, a library with a good set of ancient proverbs, and, if possible, the ability to derive personal benefits from your prophecy. As shown from the track record of the prophets: before you are proven right, you will be reviled; after you are proven right, you will be hated for a while, or, what's worse, your ideas will appear to be "trivial" thanks to retrospective distortion. This makes it far more convincing to follow the Fat Tony method of focusing on shekels more than recognition. And such treatment has continued in modern times: twentieth-century intellectuals who have embraced the wrong ideas, such as Communism or even Stalinism, have remained fashionable—and their books remain on the bookstore shelves—while those who, like the political philosopher Raymond Aron, saw the problems got short shrift both before and after being acknowledged as having seen things right.

Now close your eyes and try to imagine your future surroundings in, say, five, ten, or twenty-five years. Odds are your imagination will produce *new* things in it, things we call *innovation, improvements, killer technologies,* and other inelegant and hackneyed words from the business jargon. These common concepts concerning innovation, we will see, are not just offensive aesthetically, but they are nonsense both empirically and philosophically.

Why? Odds are that your imagination will be adding things to the present world. I am sorry, but I will show in this chapter that this approach is exactly backward: the way to do it rigorously, according to the notions of fragility and antifragility, is to *take away* from the future, reduce from it, simply, things that do not belong to the coming times. *Via negativa.* What is fragile will eventually break; and, luckily, we can easily tell what is fragile. Positive Black Swans are more unpredictable than negative ones.

"Time has sharp teeth that destroy everything," declaimed the sixth-century (B.C.) poet Simonides of Ceos, perhaps starting a tradition in Western literature about the inexorable effect of time. I can trace a plethora of elegant classical expressions, from Ovid (*tempus edax rerum*—time devours everything) to the no less poetic twentieth-century Franco-Russian poetess Elsa Triolet ("time burns but leaves no ashes"). Naturally, this exercise triggered some poetic waxing, so I am now humming a French poem put to music titled *"Avec le temps"* about how time erases things, even bad memories (though it doesn't say that it erases us as well in the process). Now, thanks to convexity effects, we can put a little bit of science in these, and produce our own taxonomy of what should be devoured the fastest by that inexorable time. The fragile will eventually break—and, luckily, we are capable of figuring out what is fragile. Even what we believe is antifragile will eventually break, but it should take much, much longer to do so (wine does well with time, but up to a point; and not if you put it in the crater of a volcano).

The verse by Simonides that started the previous paragraph continues with the stipulation "even the most solid." So Simonides had the adumbration of the idea, quite useful, that the most solid will be swallowed with more difficulty, hence last. Naturally, he did not think that something could be antifragile, hence never swallowed.

Now, I insist on the *via negativa* method of prophecy as being the only valid one: there is no other way to produce a forecast without being a turkey somewhere, particularly in the complex environment in which we live today. Now, I am not saying that new technologies will not emerge—something new will rule its day, for a while. What is currently fragile will be replaced by something else, of course. But this "something else" is unpredictable. In all likelihood, the technologies you have in your mind are not the ones that will make it, no matter your perception of their fitness and applicability—with all due respect to your imagination.

Recall that the most fragile is the predictive, what is built on the basis of predictability—in other words, those who underestimate Black Swans will eventually exit the population.

An interesting apparent paradox is that, according to these principles, longer-term predictions are more reliable than short-term ones, given that one can be quite certain that what is Black Swan–prone will be eventually swallowed by history since time augments the probability of such an event. On the other hand, typical predictions (not involving the currently fragile) degrade with time; in the presence of nonlinearities, the longer the forecast the worse its accuracy. Your error rate for a ten-year forecast of, say, the sales of a computer plant or the profits of a commodity vendor can be a thousand times that of a one-year projection.

LEARNING TO SUBTRACT

Consider the futuristic projections made throughout the past century and a half, as expressed in literary novels such as those by Jules Verne,

H. G. Wells, or George Orwell, or in now forgotten narratives of the future produced by scientists or futurists. It is remarkable that the tools that seem to currently dominate the world, such as the Internet, or more mundane matters such as the wheel on the suitcase of Book IV, were completely missing from these forecasts. But it is not here that the major error lies. The problem is that almost everything that was imagined never took place, except for a few overexploited anecdotes (such as the steam engine by Hero the Alexandrian or the assault vehicle by Leonardo da Vinci). Our world looks too close to theirs, much closer to theirs than they ever imagined or wanted to imagine. And we tend to be blind to that fact—there seems to be no correcting mechanism that can make us aware of the point as we go along forecasting a highly technocratic future.

There may be a selection bias: those people who engage in producing these accounts of the future will tend to have (incurable and untreatable) *neomania,* the love of the modern for its own sake.

Tonight I will be meeting friends in a restaurant (tavernas have existed for at least twenty-five centuries). I will be walking there wearing shoes hardly different from those worn fifty-three hundred years ago by the mummified man discovered in a glacier in the Austrian Alps. At the restaurant, I will be using silverware, a Mesopotamian technology, which qualifies as a "killer application" given what it allows me to do to the leg of lamb, such as tear it apart while sparing my fingers from burns. I will be drinking wine, a liquid that has been in use for at least six millennia. The wine will be poured into glasses, an innovation claimed by my Lebanese compatriots to come from their Phoenician ancestors, and if you disagree about the source, we can say that glass objects have been sold by them as trinkets for at least twenty-nine hundred years. After the main course, I will have a somewhat younger technology, artisanal cheese, paying higher prices for those that have not changed in their preparation for several centuries.

Had someone in 1950 predicted such a minor gathering, he would have imagined something quite different. So, thank God, I will not be dressed in a shiny synthetic space-style suit, consuming nutritionally optimized pills while communicating with my dinner peers by means of screens. The dinner partners, in turn, will be expelling airborne germs on my face, as they will not be located in remote human colonies across the galaxy. The food will be prepared using a very archaic technology (fire), with the aid of kitchen tools and implements that have not changed since the Romans (except in the quality of some of the metals used). I will be sitting on an (at least) three-thousand-year-old device commonly known as the chair (which will be, if anything, less ornate than its majestic Egyptian ancestor). And I will be not be repairing to the restaurant with the aid of a flying motorcycle. I will be walking or, if late, using a cab from a century-old technology, driven by an immigrant—immigrants were driving cabs in Paris a century ago (Russian aristocrats), same as in Berlin and Stockholm (Iraqis and Kurdish refugees), Washington, D.C. (Ethiopian postdoc students), Los Angeles (musically oriented Armenians), and New York (multinationals) today.

David Edgerton showed that in the early 2000s we produce two and a half times as many bicycles as we do cars and invest most of our technological resources in maintaining existing equipment or refining old technologies (note that this is not just a Chinese phenomenon: Western cities are aggressively trying to become bicycle-friendly). Also consider that one of the most consequential technologies seems to be the one people talk about the least: the condom. Ironically, it wants to look like less of a technology; it has been undergoing meaningful improvements, with the precise aim of being less and less noticeable.

FIGURE 17. Cooking utensils from Pompeii, hardly different from those found in today's (good) kitchens

So, the prime error is as follows. When asked to imagine the future, we have the tendency to take the present as a baseline, then produce a speculative destiny by adding new technologies and products to it and what sort of *makes sense,* given an interpolation of past developments. We also represent society according to our utopia of the moment, largely driven by our wishes—except for a few people called doomsayers, the future will be largely inhabited by our desires. So we will tend to over-technologize it and underestimate the might of the equivalent of these small wheels on suitcases that will be staring at us for the next millennia.

A word on the blindness to this over-technologizing. After I left finance, I started attending some of the fashionable conferences attended by pre-rich and post-rich technology people and the new category of technology intellectuals. I was initially exhilarated to see them wearing no ties, as, living among tie-wearing abhorrent bankers, I had developed the illusion that anyone who doesn't wear a tie was not an empty suit. But these conferences, while colorful and slick with computerized images and fancy animations, felt depressing. I knew I did not belong. It was not just their additive approach to the future (failure to subtract the fragile rather than add to destiny). It was not entirely their blindness by uncompromising neomania. It took a while for me to realize the reason: a profound lack of elegance. Technothinkers tend to have an "engineering mind"—to put it less politely, they have autistic tendencies. While they don't usually wear ties, these types tend, of course, to exhibit all the textbook characteristics of nerdiness—mostly lack of charm, interest in objects instead of persons, causing them to neglect their looks. They love precision at the expense of applicability. And they typically share an absence of literary culture.

This absence of literary culture is actually a marker of future blindness because it is usually accompanied by a denigration of history, a byproduct of unconditional neomania. Outside of the niche and isolated genre of science fiction, literature is about the past. We do not learn physics or biology from medieval textbooks, but we still read Homer, Plato, or the very modern Shakespeare. We cannot talk about sculpture without knowledge of the works of Phidias, Michelangelo, or the great Canova. These are in the past, not in the future. Just by setting foot into a museum, the aesthetically minded person is connecting with the elders. Whether overtly or not, he will tend to acquire and respect historical knowledge, even if it is to reject it. And the past—properly handled, as we will see in the next section—is a much better teacher about the properties of the future than the present. To understand the future, you do not need technoautistic jargon, obsession with "killer apps," these sort of things. You just need the following: some respect for the past, some curiosity about the historical record, a hunger for the wisdom of the elders, and a grasp of the notion of "heuristics," these often unwritten rules of thumb that are so determining of survival. In other words, you will be forced to give weight to things that have been around, things that have survived.

Technology at Its Best

But technology can cancel the effect of bad technologies, by self-subtraction.

Technology is at its best when it is invisible. I am convinced that technology is of greatest benefit when it displaces the deleterious, unnatural, alienating, and, most of all, inherently fragile preceding technology. Many of the modern applications that have managed to survive today came to disrupt the deleterious effect of the philistinism of modernity, particularly the twentieth century: the large multinational bureaucratic corporation with "empty suits" at the top; the isolated family (nuclear) in a one-way relationship with the television set, even more isolated thanks to car-designed suburban society; the dominance of the state, particularly the militaristic nation-state, with border controls; the destructive dictatorship on thought and culture by the established media; the tight control on publication and dissemination of economic ideas by the charlatanic economics establishment; large corporations that tend to control their markets now threatened by the Internet; pseudorigor that has been busted by the Web; and many others. You no longer have to "press 1 for English" or wait in line for a rude operator to make bookings for your honeymoon in Cyprus. In many respects, as unnatural as it is, the Internet removed some of the even more unnatural elements around us. For instance, the absence of paperwork makes bureaucracy—something modernistic—more palatable than it was in the days of paper files. With a little bit of luck a computer virus will wipe out all records and free people from their past mistakes.

Even now, we are using technology to reverse technology. Recall my walk to the restaurant wearing shoes not too dissimilar to those worn by the ancient, preclassical person found in the Alps. The shoe industry, after spending decades "engineering" the perfect walking and running shoe, with all manner of "support" mechanisms and material for cushioning, is now selling us shoes that replicate being barefoot—they want to be so unobtrusive that their only claimed function is to protect our feet from the elements, not to dictate how we walk as the more modernistic mission was. In a way they are selling us the calloused feet of a hunter-gatherer that we can put on, use, and then remove upon returning to civilization. It is quite exhilarating to wear these shoes when walking in nature as one wakes up to a new dimension while feeling the three dimensions of the terrain. Regular shoes feel like casts that separate us from the environment. And they don't have to be inelegant: the technology is in the sole, not the shoe, as the new soles can be both robust and very thin, thus allowing the foot to hug the ground as if one were barefoot—my best discovery is an Italian-looking moccasin made in Brazil that allows me to both run on stones and go to dinner in restaurants.

Then again, perhaps they should just sell us reinforced waterproof socks (in effect, what the Alpine fellow had), but it would not be very profitable for these firms.*

And the great use of the tablet computer (notably the iPad) is that it allows us to return to Babylonian and Phoenician roots of writing and take notes on a tablet (which is how it started). One can now jot down handwritten, or rather fingerwritten, notes—it is much more soothing to write longhand, instead of having to go through the agency of a keyboard. My dream would be to someday write everything longhand, as almost every writer did before modernity.

So it may be a natural property of technology to only want to be displaced by itself.

Next let me show how the future is mostly in the past.

TO AGE IN REVERSE: THE LINDY EFFECT

Time to get more technical, so a distinction is helpful at this stage. Let us separate the perishable (humans, single items) from the nonperishable, the potentially perennial. The nonperishable is anything that does not have an organic unavoidable expiration date. The perishable is typically an object, the nonperishable has an informational nature to it. A

---

* There is anecdotal evidence from barefoot runners and users of "five finger" style athletic shoes—which includes myself—that one's feet store some memory of the terrain, remembering where they have been in the past.

single car is perishable, but the automobile as a technology has survived about a century (and we will speculate should survive another one). Humans die, but their genes—a code—do not necessarily. The physical book is perishable—say, a specific copy of the Old Testament—but its contents are not, as they can be expressed into another physical book.

Let me express my idea in Lebanese dialect first. When you see a young and an old human, you can be confident that the younger will survive the elder. With something nonperishable, say a technology, that is not the case. We have two possibilities: either both are expected to have the same additional life expectancy (the case in which the probability distribution is called *exponential*), or the old is expected to have a longer expectancy than the young, in proportion to their relative age. In that situation, if the old is eighty and the young is ten, the elder is expected to live eight times as long as the younger one.

TABLE 6 • DOMAINS AND COMPARISON OF LIFE EXPECTANCY WHEN WE COMPARE THE "OLD" TO THE "YOUNG"

COMPARATIVE LIFE EXPECTANCY	DOMAIN	PROBABILITY DISTRIBUTION
The young is expected to live longer than the old.	Perishable: life of humans and other animals	Gaussian (or close, from same type of family)
Both the young and the old have equivalent life expectancy.	Non-perishable informational: lifetime of species	Exponential
LINDY EFFECT. The old is expected to stay longer than the young in proportion to their age.	Non-perishable informational: life of intellectual production, lifetime of genera	Power law

Now conditional on something belonging to either category, I propose the following (building on the so-called Lindy effect in the version later developed by the great Benoît Mandelbrot):*

For the perishable, every additional day in its life translates into a

---

* If something does not have a natural upper bound then the distribution of any specified event time is constrained only by fragility.

<u>shorter</u> *additional life expectancy. For the nonperishable, every additional day may imply a* <u>longer</u> *life expectancy.*

So the longer a technology lives, the longer it can be expected to live. Let me illustrate the point (people have difficulty understanding it at the first go). Say I have for sole information about a gentleman that he is 40 years old and I want to predict how long he will live. I can look at actuarial tables and find his age-adjusted life expectancy as used by insur-· ance companies. The table will predict that he has an extra 44 to go. Next year, when he turns 41 (or, equivalently, if applying the reasoning today to another person currently 41), he will have a little more than 43 years to go. So every year that elapses reduces his life expectancy by about a year (actually, a little less than a year, so if his life expectancy at birth is 80, his life expectancy at 80 will not be zero, but another decade or so).*

The opposite applies to nonperishable items. I am simplifying numbers here for clarity. If a book has been in print for forty years, I can expect it to be in print for another forty years. But, and that is the main difference, if it survives another decade, then it will be expected to be in print another fifty years. This, simply, as a rule, tells you why things that have been around for a long time are not "aging" like persons, but "aging" in reverse. Every year that passes without extinction doubles the additional life expectancy.† This is an indicator of some robustness. The robustness of an item is proportional to its life!

The physicist Richard Gott applied what seems to be completely different reasoning to state that whatever we observe in a randomly selected way is likely to be neither in the beginning nor in the end of its life, most likely in its middle. His argument was criticized for being rather incomplete. But by testing his argument he tested the one I just outlined above, that the expected life of an item is proportional to its past life. Gott made a list of Broadway shows on a given day, May 17, 1993, and

---

* The phrase originates, it seems, with a June 13, 1964, article in *The New Republic,* though the article made the mistake of applying it to perishable items. The author wrote that "the future career expectations of a television comedian is proportional to the total amount of his past exposure on the medium." This would work for a young comedian, not an older one (comedians are, alas, perishable items). But technologies and books do not have such constraint.

† This is where my simplification lies: I am assuming that every year doubles the additional life expectancy. It can actually get better, increase by 2½ or more. So the Lindy effect, says, mathematically, that the nonperishable has a life expectancy that *increases* with every day it survives.

predicted that *the longest-running ones would last longest, and vice versa*. He was proven right with 95 percent accuracy. He had, as a child, visited both the Great Pyramid (fifty-seven hundred years old), and the Berlin Wall (twelve years old), and correctly guessed that the former would outlive the latter.

The proportionality of life expectancy does not need to be tested explicitly—it is the direct result of "winner-take-all" effects in longevity.

Two mistakes are commonly made when I present this idea—people have difficulties grasping probabilistic notions, particularly when they have spent too much time on the Internet (not that they need the Internet to be confused; we are naturally probability-challenged). The first mistake is usually in the form of the presentation of the counterexample of a technology that we currently see as inefficient and dying, like, say, telephone land lines, print newspapers, and cabinets containing paper receipts for tax purposes. These arguments come with anger as many neomaniacs get offended by my point. But my argument is not about *every* technology, but about life expectancy, which is simply a probabilistically derived average. If I know that a forty-year-old has terminal pancreatic cancer, I will no longer estimate his life expectancy using unconditional insurance tables; it would be a mistake to think that he has forty-four more years to live, like others in his age group who are cancer-free. Likewise someone (a technology guru) interpreted my idea as suggesting that the World Wide Web, being currently less than about twenty years old, will *only* have another twenty to go—this is a noisy estimator that should work on average, not in every case. But in general, the older the technology, not only the longer it is expected to last, but the more certainty I can attach to such a statement.*

Remember the following principle: I am not saying that *all* technologies do not age, only that those technologies that were prone to aging are already dead.

The second mistake is to believe that one would be acting "young" by adopting a "young" technology, revealing both a logical error and mental bias. It leads to the inversion of the power of generational contributions, producing the illusion of the contribution of the new generations over the old—statistically, the "young" do almost nothing. This

---

* Note also that the Lindy effect is invariant to the definition of the technology. You can define a technology as a "convertible car," a more general "car," a "bound book," or a broadly defined "book" (which would include electronic texts); the life expectancy will concern the item as defined.

mistake has been made by many people, but most recently I saw an angry "futuristic" consultant who accuses people who don't jump into technology of "thinking old" (he is actually older than I am and, like most technomaniacs I know, looks sickly and pear-shaped and has an undefined transition between his jaw and his neck). I didn't understand why one would be acting particularly "old" by loving things historical. So by loving the classics ("older") I would be acting "older" than if I were interested in the "younger" medieval themes. This is a mistake similar to believing that one would turn into a cow by eating cow meat. It is actually a worse fallacy than the inference from eating: a technology, being informational rather than physical, does not age organically, like humans, at least not necessarily so. The wheel is not "old" in the sense of experiencing degeneracy.

This idea of "young" and "old" attached to certain crowd behavior is even more dangerous. Supposedly, if those who don't watch prepackaged 18-minute hyped-up lectures on the Web paid attention to people in their teens and twenties, who do, and in whom supposedly the key to the future lies, they would be thinking differently. Much progress comes from the young because of their relative freedom from the system and courage to take action that older people lose as they become trapped in life. But it is precisely the young who propose ideas that are fragile, not because they are young, but because most unseasoned ideas are fragile. And, of course, someone who sells "futuristic" ideas will not make a lot of money selling the value of the past! New technology is easier to hype up.

I received an interesting letter from Paul Doolan from Zurich, who was wondering how we could teach children skills for the twenty-first century since we do not know which skills will be needed in the twenty-first century—he figured out an elegant application of the large problem that Karl Popper called the error of historicism. Effectively my answer would be to make them read the classics. The future is in the past. Actually there is an Arabic proverb to that effect: *he who does not have a past has no future.**

---

* By the same Lindy effect, diseases and conditions that were not known to be diseases a hundred or so years ago are likely to be either (1) diseases of civilization, curable by *via negativa,* or (2) not diseases, just invented conditions. This applies most to psychological "conditions" and buzzwords putting people in silly buckets: "Type A," "passive aggressive," etc.

A FEW MENTAL BIASES

Next I present an application of the *fooled by randomness* effect. Information has a nasty property: it hides failures. Many people have been drawn to, say, financial markets after hearing success stories of someone getting rich in the stock market and building a large mansion across the street—but since failures are buried and we don't hear about them, investors are led to overestimate their chances of success. The same applies to the writing of novels: we do not see the wonderful novels that are now completely out of print, we just think that because the novels that have done well are well written (whatever that means), that what is well written will do well. So we confuse the necessary and the causal: because all surviving technologies have some obvious benefits, we are led to believe that all technologies offering obvious benefits will survive. I will leave the discussion of what impenetrable property may help survival to the section on Empedocles' dog. But note here the mental bias that causes people to believe in the "power of" some technology and its ability to run the world.

Another mental bias causing the overhyping of technology comes from the fact that we notice change, not statics. The classic example, discovered by the psychologists Daniel Kahneman and Amos Tversky, applies to wealth. (The pair developed the idea that our brains like minimal effort and get trapped that way, and they pioneered a tradition of cataloging and mapping human biases with respect to perception of random outcomes and decision making under uncertainty). If you announce to someone "you lost $10,000," he will be much more upset than if you tell him "your portfolio value, which was $785,000, is now $775,000." Our brains have a predilection for shortcuts, and the variation is easier to notice (and store) than the entire record. It requires less memory storage. This psychological heuristic (often operating without our awareness), the error of variation in place of total, is quite pervasive, even with matters that are visual.

We notice what varies and changes more than what plays a large role but doesn't change. We rely more on water than on cell phones but because water does not change and cell phones do, we are prone to thinking that cell phones play a larger role than they do. Second, because the new generations are more aggressive with technology, we notice that they try more things, but we ignore that these implementations don't usually stick. Most "innovations" are failures, just as most books are flops, which should not discourage anyone from trying.

Neomania and Treadmill Effects

You are driving on the highway in your two-year-old Japanese car when you are overtaken by a vehicle of the same make, the latest version, that looks markedly different. And markedly better. Markedly better? The bumper is slightly larger and the taillights are wider. Other than these cosmetic details (and perhaps some hidden technical improvements) representing less than a few percentage points in variation, the car looks the same, but you can't tell by just looking at it. You just see the lights and feel that you are due an upgrade. And the upgrade will cost you, after you sell your car, about the third of the price of a new vehicle—all that motivated by small, mostly cosmetic variations. But switching cars is a small cost compared to switching computers—the recovery value of an old computer is so negligible.

You use an Apple Mac computer. You just bought a new version a week before. The person on the plane next to you just pulled out of his bag an older version. It has a family resemblance to yours, but looks so inferior. It is thicker and has a much less elegant screen. But you forget the days when you used to have the same model and were thrilled with it.

The same with a cell phone: you look down at those carrying older, larger models. But a few years ago you would have considered these small and slick.

So with so many technologically driven and modernistic items—skis, cars, computers, computer programs—it seems that we notice differences between versions rather than commonalities. We even rapidly tire of what we have, continuously searching for versions 2.0 and similar iterations. And after that, another "improved" reincarnation. These impulses to buy new things that will eventually lose their novelty, particularly when compared to newer things, are called *treadmill effects*. As the reader can see, they arise from the same generator of biases as the one about the salience of variations mentioned in the section before: we notice differences and become dissatisfied with some items and some classes of goods. This treadmill effect has been investigated by Danny Kahneman and his peers when they studied the psychology of what they call hedonic states. People acquire a new item, feel *more satisfied* after an initial boost, then rapidly revert to their baseline of well-being. So, when you "upgrade," you feel a boost of satisfaction with *changes* in technology. But then you get used to it and start hunting for the *new* new thing.

But it looks as though we don't incur the same treadmilling techno-dissatisfaction with classical art, older furniture—whatever we do not put in the category of the technological. You may have an oil painting and a flat-screen television set inhabiting the same room of your house. The oil painting is an imitation of a classic Flemish scene made close to a century ago, with the dark ominous skies of Flanders, majestic trees, and an uninspiring but calmative rural scene. I am quite certain that you are not eager to upgrade the oil painting but that soon your flat-screen TV set will be donated to the local chapter of some kidney foundation.

The same with dishes—recall that we try to replicate nineteenth-century dinner customs. So there is at least one other domain in which we do not try to optimize matters.

I am initially writing these lines longhand, using a seasoned fountain pen. I do not fuss over the state of my pens. Many of them are old enough to cross decades; one of them (the best) I have had for at least thirty years. Nor do I obsess over small variations in the paper. I prefer to use Clairefontaine paper and notebooks that have hardly changed since my early childhood—if anything, they have degraded in quality.

But when it comes to transcribing my writing into electronic form, then I get worried that my Mac computer may not be the best tool for the job. I heard somewhere that the new version had a longer-lasting battery and I plan to upgrade soon, during my next impulse buying episode.

Note here is a strange inconsistency in the way we perceive items across the technological and real domains. Whenever I sit on an airplane next to some businessman reading the usual trash businessmen read on an e-reader, said businessperson will not resist disparaging my use of the book by comparing the two items. Supposedly, an e-reader is more "efficient." It delivers the essence of the book, which said businessman assumes is information, but in a more convenient way, as he can carry a library on his device and "optimize" his time between golf outings. I have never heard anyone address the large differences between e-readers and physical books, like smell, texture, dimension (books are in three dimensions), color, ability to change pages, physicality of an object compared to a computer screen, and hidden properties causing unexplained differences in enjoyment. The focus of the discussion will be commonalities (how close to a book this wonderful device is). Yet when he compares his version of an e-reader to another e-reader, he will invariably focus on minute differences. Just as when Lebanese run into Syrians, they focus on the tiny variations in their respective Levantine dialects, but when Lebanese run into Italians, they focus on similarities.

There may be a heuristic that helps put such items in categories. First, the electronic on-off switch. Whatever has an "off" or "on" switch that I need to turn off before I get yelled at by the flight attendant will necessarily be in one category (but not the opposite as many items without an on-off switch will be prone to neomania). For these items, I focus on variations, with attendant neomania. But consider the difference between the artisanal—the other category—and the industrial. What is artisanal has the love of the maker infused in it, and tends to satisfy—we don't have this nagging impression of incompleteness we encounter with electronics.

It also so happens that whatever is technological happens to be fragile. Articles made by an artisan cause fewer treadmill effects. And they tend to have some antifragility—recall how my artisanal shoes take months before becoming comfortable. Items with an on-off switch tend to have no such redeeming antifragility.

But alas, some things we wish were a bit more fragile—which brings us to architecture.

ARCHITECTURE AND THE IRREVERSIBLE NEOMANIA

There is some evolutionary warfare between architects producing a compounded form of neomania. The problem with modernistic—and functional—architecture is that it is not fragile enough to break physically, so these buildings stick out just to torture our consciousness—you cannot exercise your prophetic powers by leaning on their fragility.

Urban planning, incidentally, demonstrates the central property of the so-called top-down effect: top-down is usually irreversible, so mistakes tend to stick, whereas bottom-up is gradual and incremental, with creation and destruction along the way, though presumably with a positive slope.

Further, things that grow in a natural way, whether cities or individual houses, have a fractal quality to them. Like everything alive, all organisms, like lungs, or trees, grow in some form of self-guided but tame randomness. What is fractal? Recall Mandelbrot's insight in Chapter 3: "fractal" entails both jaggedness and a form of self-similarity in things (Mandelbrot preferred "self-affinity"), such as trees spreading into branches that look like small trees, and smaller and smaller branches that look like a slightly modified, but recognizable, version of the whole. These fractals induce a certain wealth of detail based on a small number of rules of repetition of nested patterns. The fractal require some jaggedness, but one that has some method to its madness. Everything in nature is fractal, jagged, and rich in detail, though with a certain pattern. The smooth, by comparison, belongs to the class of Euclidian geometry we study in school, simplified shapes that lose this layer of wealth.

Alas, contemporary architecture is smooth, even when it tries to look whimsical. What is top-down is generally unwrinkled (that is, unfractal) and feels dead.

Sometimes modernism can take a naturalistic turn, then stop in its tracks. Gaudi's buildings in Barcelona, from around the turn of the twentieth century, are inspired by nature and rich architecture (Baroque and Moorish). I managed to visit a rent-controlled apartment there: it felt like an improved cavern with rich, jagged details. I was convinced that I had been there in a previous life. Wealth of details, ironically, leads to inner peace. Yet Gaudi's idea went nowhere, except in promoting modernism in its unnatural and naive versions: later modernistic structures are smooth and completely stripped of fractal jaggedness.

I also enjoy writing facing trees, and, if possible, wild untamed gardens with ferns. But white walls with sharp corners and Euclidian angles and crisp shapes strain me. And once they are built, there is no way to get rid of them. Almost everything built since World War II has an unnatural smoothness to it.

For some, these buildings cause even more than aesthetic harm—many Romanians are bitter about the dictator Nicolae Ceausescu's destruction of traditional villages replaced by modern high-rises. Neomania and dictatorship are an explosive combination. In France, some blame the modernistic architecture of housing projects for the immigrant riots. As the journalist Christopher Caldwell wrote about the unnatural living conditions: "Le Corbusier called houses 'machines for living.' France's housing projects, as we now know, became machines for alienation."

Jane Jacobs, the New York urban activist, took a heroic stance as a political-style resistant against neomania in architecture and urban planning, as the modernistic dream was carried by Robert Moses, who wanted to improve New York by razing tenements and installing large roads and highways, committing a greater crime against natural order than Haussmann, who, as we saw in Chapter 7, removed during the nineteenth century entire neighborhoods of Paris to make room for the "Grand Boulevards." Jacobs stood against tall buildings as they deform the experience of urban living, which is conducted at street level. Further, her bone with Robert Moses concerns the highway, as these engines for travel suck life out of the city—to her a city should be devoted to pedestrians. Again, we have the machine-organism dichotomy: to her the city is an organism, for Moses it is a machine to be improved upon. Indeed, Moses had plans to raze the West Village; it is thanks to her petitions and unremitting resistance that the neighborhood—the prettiest in Manhattan—has survived nearly intact. One might want to give Moses some credit, for not all his projects turned out to be nefarious—some might have been beneficial, such as the parks and beaches now accessible to the middle class thanks to the highways.

Recall the discussion of municipal properties—they don't translate into something larger because problems become more abstract as they scale up, and the abstract is not something human nature can manage properly. The same principle needs to apply to urban life: neighborhoods are villages, and need to remain villages.

I was recently stuck in a traffic jam in London where, one hears, the speed of traveling is equal to what it was a century and a half ago, if not slower. It took me almost two hours to cross London from one end to the other. As I was depleting the topics of conversation with the (Polish) driver, I wondered whether Haussmann was not right, and whether London would be better off if it had its Haussmann razing neighborhoods and plowing wide arteries to facilitate circulation. Until it hit me that, in fact, if there was so much traffic in London, as compared to other cities, it was because people wanted to be there, and being there for them exceeded the costs. More than a third of the residents in London are foreign-born, and, in addition to immigrants, most high net worth individuals on the planet get their starter pied-à-terre in Central London. It could be that the absence of these large avenues and absence of a dominating state is part of its appeal. Nobody would buy a pied-à-terre in Brasilia, the perfectly top-down city built from scratch on a map.

I also checked and saw that the most expensive neighborhoods in

Paris today (such as the Sixth Arrondissement or Île Saint-Louis) were the ones that had been left alone by the nineteenth-century renovators.

Finally, the best argument against teleological design is as follows. Even after they are built, buildings keep incurring mutations as if they needed to slowly evolve and be taken over by the dynamical environment: they change colors, shapes, windows—and character. In his book *How Buildings Learn,* Stewart Brand shows in pictures how buildings change through time, as if they needed to metamorphose into unrecognizable shapes—strangely buildings, when erected, do not account for the optionality of future alterations.

Wall to Wall Windows

The skepticism about architectural modernism that I am proposing is not unconditional. While most of it brings unnatural stress, some elements are a certain improvement. For instance, floor-to-ceiling windows in a rural environment expose us to nature—here again technology making itself (literally) invisible. In the past, the size of windows was dictated by thermal considerations, as insulation was not possible—heat escaped rather quickly from windows. Today's materials allow us to avoid such constraint. Further, much French architecture was a response to the tax on windows and doors installed after the Revolution, so many buildings have a very small number of windows.

Just as with the unintrusive shoes that allow us to feel the terrain, modern technology allows some of us to reverse that trend, as expressed by Oswald Spengler, which makes civilization go from plants to stone, that is, from the fractal to the Euclidian. We are now moving back from the smooth stone to the rich fractal and natural. Benoît Mandelbrot wrote in front of a window overlooking trees: he craved fractal aesthetics so much that the alternative would have been inconceivable. Now modern technology allows us to merge with nature, and instead of a small window, an entire wall can be transparent and face lush and densely forested areas.

Metrification

One example of the neomania of states: the campaign for metrification, that is, the use of the metric system to replace "archaic" ones on grounds of efficiency—it "makes sense." The logic might be impeccable (until of course one supersedes it with a better, less naive logic, an attempt I will make here). Let us look at the wedge between rationalism and empiricism in this effort.

Warwick Cairns, a fellow similar to Jane Jacobs, has been fighting in courts to let market farmers in Britain keep selling bananas by the pound, and similar matters as they have resisted the use of the more "rational" kilogram. The idea of metrification was born out of the French Revolution, as part of the utopian mood, which includes changing the names of the winter months to *Nivôse, Pluviôse, Ventôse,* descriptive of weather, having decimal time, ten-day weeks, and similar naively rational matters. Luckily the project of changing time has failed. However, after repeated failures, the metric system was implemented there—but the old system has remained refractory in the United States and England. The French writer Edmond About, who visited Greece in 1832, a dozen years after its independence, reports how peasants struggled with the metric system as it was completely unnatural to them and stuck to Ottoman standards instead. (Likewise, the "modernization" of the Arabic alphabet from the easy-to-memorize old Semitic sequence made to sound like words, ABJAD, HAWWAZ, to the logical sequence A-B-T-TH has created a generation of Arabic speakers without the ability to recite their alphabet.)

But few realize that naturally born weights have a logic to them: we use feet, miles, pounds, inches, furlongs, stones (in Britain) because these are remarkably intuitive and we can use them with a minimal expenditure of cognitive effort—and all cultures seem to have similar measurements with some physical correspondence to the everyday. A meter does not match anything; a foot does. I can imagine the meaning of "thirty feet" with minimal effort. A mile, from the Latin *milia passum,* is a thousand paces. Likewise a stone (14 pounds) corresponds to . . . well, a stone. An inch (or *pouce*) corresponds to a thumb. A furlong is the distance one can sprint before running out of breath. A pound, from *libra,* is what you can imagine holding in your hands. Recall from the story of Thales in Chapter 12 that we used *thekel* or *shekel:* these mean "weight" in Canaanite-Semitic languages, something with a physical connotation, similar to the pound. There is a certain nonrandomness to how these units came to be in an ancestral environment—and the digital system itself comes from the correspondence to the ten fingers.

As I am writing these lines, no doubt, some European Union official of the type who eats 200 grams of well-cooked meat with 200 centiliters' worth of red wine every day for dinner (the optimal quantity for his health benefits) is concocting plans to promote the "efficiency" of the metric system deep into the countryside of the member countries.

TURNING SCIENCE INTO JOURNALISM

So, we can apply criteria of fragility and robustness to the handling of information—the fragile in that context is, like technology, what does not stand the test of time. The best filtering heuristic, therefore, consists in taking into account the age of books and scientific papers. Books that are one year old are usually not worth reading (a very low probability of having the qualities for "surviving"), no matter the hype and how "earth-shattering" they may seem to be. So I follow the Lindy effect as a guide in selecting what to read: books that have been around for ten years will be around for ten more; books that have been around for two millennia should be around for quite a bit of time, and so forth. Many understand this point but do not apply it to academic work, which is, in much of its modern practice, hardly different from journalism (except for the occasional original production). Academic work, because of its attention-seeking orientation, can be easily subjected to Lindy effects: think of the hundreds of thousands of papers that are just noise, in spite of how hyped they were at the time of publication.

The problem in deciding whether a scientific result or a new "innovation" is a breakthrough, that is, the opposite of noise, is that one needs to see all aspects of the idea—and there is always some opacity that time, and only time, can dissipate. Like many people watching cancer research like a hawk, I fell for the following. There was at some point a great deal of excitement about the work of Judah Folkman, who, as we saw in Chapter 15, believed that one could cure cancer by choking the blood supply (tumors require nutrition and tend to create new blood vessels, what is called *neovascularization*). The idea looked impeccable on paper, but, about a decade and a half later, it appears that the only significant result we got was completely outside cancer, in the mitigation of macular degeneration.

Likewise, seemingly uninteresting results that go unnoticed, can, years later turn out to be breakthroughs.

So time can act as a cleanser of noise by confining to its dustbins all these overhyped works. Some organizations even turn such scientific production into a cheap spectator sport, with ranking of the "ten hottest papers" in, say, rectal oncology or some such sub-sub-specialty.

If we replace scientific results with scientists, we often get the same neomaniac hype. There is a disease to grant a prize for a promising scientist "under forty," a disease that is infecting economics, mathematics, finance, etc. Mathematics is a bit special because the value of its results can be immediately seen—so I skip the criticism. Of the fields I am familiar with, such as literature, finance, and economics, I can pretty much ascertain that the prizes given to those under forty are the best reverse indicator of value (much like the belief—well tested—by traders that companies that get hyped up for their potential and called "best" on the cover of magazines or in books such as *Good to Great* are about to underperform and one can derive an abnormal profit by shorting their stock). The worst effect of these prizes is penalizing those who don't get them and debasing the field by turning it into an athletic competition.

Should we have a prize, it should be for "over a hundred": it took close to one hundred and forty years to validate the contribution of one Jules Regnault, who discovered optionality and mapped it mathematically—along with what we dubbed the philosopher's stone. His work stayed obscure all this time.

Now if you want to be convinced of my point of how noisy science can be, take any elementary textbook you read in high school or college with interest then—in any discipline. Open it to a random chapter, and see if the idea is still relevant. Odds are that it may be boring, but still relevant—or nonboring, and still relevant. It could be the famous 1215 Magna Carta (British history), Caesar's Gallic wars (Roman history), a historical presentation of the school of Stoics (philosophy), an introduction to quantum mechanics (physics), or the genetic trees of cats and dogs (biology).

Now try to get the proceedings of a random conference about the subject matter concerned that took place five years ago. Odds are it will feel no different from a five-year-old newspaper, perhaps even less interesting. So attending breakthrough conferences might be, statistically speaking, as much a waste of time as buying a mediocre lottery ticket, one with a small payoff. The odds of the paper's being relevant—and interesting—in five years is no better than one in ten thousand. The fragility of science!

Even the conversation of a high school teacher or that of an unsuccessful college professor is likely to be more worthwhile than the latest academic paper, less corrupted with neomania. My best conversations in philosophy have been with French lycée teachers who love the topic but are not interested in pursuing a career writing papers in it (in France they teach philosophy in the last year of high school). Amateurs in any discipline are the best, if you can connect with them. Unlike dilettantes, career professionals are to knowledge what prostitutes are to love.

Of course you may be lucky enough to hit on a jewel here and there, but in general, at best, conversation with an academic would be like the conversation of plumbers, at the worst that of a concierge bandying the worst brand of gossip: gossip about uninteresting people (other academics), small talk. True, the conversation of top scientists can sometimes be captivating, those people who aggregate knowledge and for whom cruising the subject is effortless as the entire small parts of the field come glued together. But these people are just currently too rare on this planet.

I complete this section with the following anecdote. One of my students (who was majoring in, of all subjects, economics) asked me for a rule on what to read. "As little as feasible from the last twenty years, except history books that are not about the last fifty years," I blurted out, with irritation as I hate such questions as "what's the best book you've ever read," or "what are the ten best books,"—my "ten best books ever" change at the end of every summer. Also, I have been hyping Daniel Kahneman's recent book, because it is largely an exposition of his research of thirty-five and forty years ago, with filtering and modernization. My recommendation seemed impractical, but, after a while, the student developed a culture in original texts such as Adam Smith, Karl Marx, and Hayek, texts he believes he will cite at the age of eighty. He told me that after his detoxification, he realized that all his peers do is read *timely* material that becomes instantly obsolete.

WHAT SHOULD BREAK

In 2010, *The Economist* magazine asked me to partake in an exercise imagining the world in 2036. As they were aware of my reticence concerning forecasters, their intention was to bring a critical "balance" and use me as a counter to the numerous imaginative forecasts, hoping for my usual angry, dismissive, and irascible philippic.

Quite surprised they were when, after a two-hour (slow) walk, I wrote a series of forecasts at one go and sent them the text. They probably thought at first that I was pulling a prank on them, or that someone got the wrong email and was impersonating me. Outlining the reasoning on fragility and asymmetry (concavity to errors), I explained that I would expect the future to be populated with wall-to-wall bookshelves, the device called the telephone, artisans, and such, using the notion that most technologies that are now twenty-five years old should be around in another twenty-five years—once again, most, not all.* But the fragile should disappear, or be weakened. Now, what is fragile? The large, optimized, overreliant on technology, overreliant on the so-called scientific method instead of age-tested heuristics. Corporations that are large today should be gone, as they have always been weakened by what they think is their strength: size, which is the enemy of corporations as it causes disproportionate fragility to Black Swans. City-states and small corporations are more likely to be around, even thrive. The nation-state, the currency-printing central bank, these things called economics departments, may stay nominally, but they will have their powers severely eroded. In other words, what we saw in the left column of the Triad should be gone—alas to be replaced by other fragile items.

PROPHETS AND THE PRESENT

By issuing warnings based on vulnerability—that is, subtractive prophecy—we are closer to the original role of the prophet: to warn, not necessarily to predict, and to predict calamities *if people don't listen.*

The classical role of the prophet, at least in the Levantine sense, is not to look into the future but to talk about the present. He tells people what to do, or, rather, in my opinion, the more robust what *not* to do. In the Near Eastern monotheistic traditions, Judaism, Christianity, and Islam, the major role of the prophets is the protection of monotheism from its idolatrous and pagan enemies that may bring calamities on the straying population. The prophet is someone who is in communication with the unique God, or at least can read his mind—and, what is key, issues warnings to His subjects. The Semitic *nby,* expressed as *Nevi* or *nebi* (in the original Hebrew), the same with minor differences in pronunciation in Aramaic (*nabi'y*) and Arabic (*nabi*), is principally someone connecting with God, expressing what is on God's mind—the meaning of *nab'*

---

* I have had the privilege of reading a five-hundred-year-old book, an experience hardly different from that of reading a modern book. Compare such robustness to the lifespan of electronic documents: some of the computer files of my manuscripts that are less than a decade old are now irretrievable.

in Arabic is "news" (the original Semitic root in Acadian, *nabu,* meant "to call"). The initial Greek translation, *pro-phetes,* meant "spokesman," which is retained in Islam, as a dual role for Mohammed the Prophet is that of the Messenger (*rasoul*)—there were some small ranking differences between the roles of spokesman (*nabi*) and messenger (*rasoul*). The job of mere forecasting is rather limited to seers, or the variety of people involved in divination such as the "astrologers" so dismissed by the Koran and the Old Testament. Again, the Canaanites had been too promiscuous in their theologies and various approaches to handling the future, and the prophet is precisely someone who deals only with the One God, not with the future like a mere Baalite.

Nor has the vocation of Levantine prophet been a particularly desirable professional occupation. As I said at the beginning of the chapter, acceptance was far from guaranteed: Jesus, mentioning the fate of Elijah (who warned against Baal, then ironically had to go find solace in Sidon, where Baal was worshipped), announced that *no one becomes a prophet in his own land.* And the prophetic mission was not necessarily voluntary. Consider Jeremiah's life, laden with *jeremiads* (lamentations), as his unpleasant warnings about destruction and captivity (and their causes) did not make him particularly popular and he was the personification of the notion of "shoot the messenger" and the expression *veritas odium parit*—truth brings hatred. Jeremiah was beaten, punished, persecuted, and the victim of numerous plots, which involved his own brothers. Apocryphal and imaginative accounts even have him stoned to death in Egypt.

Further north of the Semites, in the Greek tradition, we find the same focus on messages, warnings about the present, and the same punishment inflicted on those able to understand things others don't. For example, Cassandra gets the gift of prophecy, along with the curse of not being believed, when the temple snakes cleaned her ears so she could hear some special messages. Tiresias was made blind and transformed into a woman for revealing the secrets of the gods—but, as a consolation, Athena licked his ears so he could understand secrets in the songs of birds.

Recall the inability we saw in Chapter 2 to learn from past behavior. The problem with lack of recursion in learning—lack of second-order thinking—is as follows. If those delivering some messages deemed valuable for the long term have been persecuted in past history, one would expect that there would be a correcting mechanism, that intelligent people would end up learning from such historical experience so those delivering new messages would be greeted with the new understanding in mind. But nothing of the sort takes place.

This lack of recursive thinking applies not just to prophecy, but to other human activities as well: if you believe that what will work and do well is going to be a *new* idea that others did not think of, what we commonly call "innovation," then you would expect people to pick up on it and have a clearer eye for new ideas without too much reference to the perception of others. But they don't: something deemed "original" tends to be modeled on something that was new at the time but is no longer new, so being an Einstein for many scientists means solving a similar problem to the one Einstein solved when at the time Einstein was not solving a standard problem at all. The very idea of being an Einstein in physics is no longer original. I've detected in the area of risk management the similar error, made by scientists trying to be new in a standard way. People in risk management only consider risky things that have hurt them in the past (given their focus on "evidence"), not realizing that, in the past, before these events took place, these occurrences that hurt them severely were completely without precedent, escaping standards. And my personal efforts to make them step outside their shoes to consider these second-order considerations have failed—as have my efforts to make them aware of the notion of fragility.

EMPEDOCLES' DOG

In Aristotle's *Magna Moralia,* there is a possibly apocryphal story about Empedocles, the pre-Socratic philosopher, who was asked why a dog prefers to always sleep on the same tile. His answer was that there had to be some *likeness* between the dog and that tile. (Actually the story might be even twice as apocryphal since we don't know if *Magna Moralia* was actually written by Aristotle himself.)

Consider the match between the dog and the tile. A natural, biological, explainable or nonexplainable match, confirmed by long series of recurrent frequentation—in place of rationalism, just consider the history of it.

Which brings me to the conclusion of our exercise in prophecy.

I surmise that those human technologies such as writing and reading that have survived are like the tile to the dog, a match between natural friends, because they correspond to something deep in our nature.

Every time I hear someone trying to make a comparison between a book and an e-reader, or something ancient and a new technology, "opinions" pop up, as if reality cared about opinions and narratives. There are secrets to our world that only practice can reveal, and no opinion or analysis will ever capture in full.

This secret property is, of course, revealed through time, and, thankfully, only through time.

What Does Not Make Sense

Let's take this idea of Empedocles' dog a bit further: If something that makes no sense to you (say, religion—if you are an atheist—or some age-old habit or practice called irrational); if that something has been around for a very, very long time, then, irrational or not, you can expect it to stick around much longer, and outlive those who call for its demise.

CHAPTER 21

Medicine, Convexity, and Opacity

What they call nonevidence—Where medicine fragilizes humans, then tries to save them—Newton's law or evidence?

The history of medicine is the story—largely documented—of the dialectic between doing and thinking—and how to make decisions under opacity. In the medieval Mediterranean, Maimonides, Avicenna, Al-Ruhawi, and the Syriac doctors such as Hunain Ibn Ishaq were at once philosophers and doctors. A doctor in the medieval Semitic world was called Al-Hakim, "the wise," or "practitioner of wisdom," a synonym for philosopher or rabbi (*hkm* is the Semitic root for "wisdom"). Even in the earlier period there was a crop of Hellenized fellows who stood in the exact middle between medicine and the practice of philosophy—the great skeptic philosopher Sextus Empiricus was himself a doctor member of the skeptical empirical school. So were Menodotus of Nicomedia and the experience-based predecessor of evidence-based medicine—on whom a bit more in a few pages. The works of these thinkers, or whatever remains extant are quite refreshing for those of us who distrust those who talk without doing.

Simple, quite simple decision rules and heuristics emerge from this chapter. *Via negativa,* of course (by removal of the unnatural): only resort to medical techniques when the health payoff is very large (say, saving a life) and visibly exceeds its potential harm, such as incontrovertibly needed surgery or lifesaving medicine (penicillin). It is the same as with government intervention. This is squarely Thalesian, not Aristotelian (that is, decision making based on payoffs, not knowledge). For in these cases medicine has positive asymmetries—convexity effects—and the outcome will be less likely to produce fragility. Otherwise, in situations in which the benefits of a particular medicine, procedure, or nutritional or lifestyle modification appear small—say, those aiming for comfort—we have a large potential sucker problem (hence putting us on the wrong side of convexity effects). Actually, one of the unintended side benefits of the theorems that Raphael Douady and I developed in our paper mapping risk detection techniques (in Chapter 19) is an exact link between (a) nonlinearity in exposure or dose-response and (b) potential fragility or antifragility.

I also extend the problem to epistemological grounds and make rules for *what should be considered evidence*: as with whether a cup should be considered half-empty or half-full, there are situations in which we focus on *absence* of evidence, others in which we focus on evidence. In some cases one can be confirmatory, not others—it depends on the risks. Take smoking, which was, at some stage, viewed as bringing small gains in pleasure and even health (truly, people thought it was a good thing). It took decades for its harm to become visible. Yet had someone questioned it, he would have faced the canned-naive-academized and faux-expert response "do you have *evidence* that this is harmful?" (the same type of response as "is there evidence that polluting is harmful?"). As usual, the solution is simple, an extension of *via negativa* and Fat Tony's *don't-be-a-sucker* rule: the non-natural needs to prove its benefits, not the natural—according to the statistical principle outlined earlier that nature is to be considered much less of a sucker than humans. In a complex domain, only time—a long time— is evidence.

For any decision, the unknown will preponderate on one side more than the other.

The "do you have evidence" fallacy, mistaking evidence of no harm for no evidence of harm, is similar to the one of misinterpreting NED (no evidence of disease) for evidence of no disease. This is the same error as mistaking absence of evidence for evidence of absence, the one that tends to affect smart and educated people, as if education made people more confirmatory in their responses and more liable to fall into simple logical errors.

And recall that under nonlinearities, the simple statements "harmful" or "beneficial" break down: it is all in the dosage.

HOW TO ARGUE IN AN EMERGENCY ROOM

I once broke my nose . . . walking. For the sake of antifragility, of course. I was trying to walk on uneven surfaces, as part of my antifragility program, under the influence of Erwan Le Corre, who believes in naturalistic exercise. It was exhilarating; I felt the world was richer, more fractal, and when I contrasted this terrain with the smooth surfaces of sidewalks and corporate offices, those felt like prisons. Unfortunately, I was carrying something much less ancestral, a cellular phone, which had the insolence to ring in the middle of my walk.

In the emergency room, the doctor and staff insisted that I should "ice" my nose, meaning apply an ice-cold patch to it. In the middle of the pain, it hit me that the swelling that Mother Nature gave me was most certainly not directly caused by the trauma. It was my own body's response to the injury. It seemed to me that it was an insult to Mother Nature to override her programmed reactions unless we had a good reason to do so, backed by proper empirical testing to show that we humans can do better; the burden of evidence falls on us humans. So I mumbled to the emergency room doctor whether he had any statistical evidence of benefits from applying ice to my nose or if it resulted from a naive version of an *interventionism*.

His response was: "You have a nose the size of Cleveland and you are now interested in . . . numbers?" I recall developing from his blurry remarks the thought that he had no answer.

Effectively, he had no answer, because as soon as I got to a computer, I was able to confirm that there is no compelling empirical evidence in favor of the reduction of swelling. At least, not outside of the very rare cases in which the swelling would threaten the patient, which was clearly not the case. It was pure sucker-rationalism in the mind of doctors, following what made sense to boundedly intelligent humans, coupled with interventionism, this need to *do something*, this defect of thinking that we knew better, and denigration of the unobserved. This defect is not limited to our control of swelling: this confabulation plagues the entire history of medicine, along with, of course, many other fields of practice. The researchers Paul Meehl and Robin Dawes pioneered a tradition to catalog the tension between "clinical" and actuarial (that is, statistical) knowledge, and examine how many things believed to be true by professionals and clinicians aren't so and don't match empirical evidence. The problem is of course that these researchers did not have a clear idea of where the burden of empirical evidence lies (the difference between naive or pseudo empiricism and rigorous empiricism)—the onus is on the doctors to show us why reducing fever is good, why eating breakfast before engaging in activity is healthy (there is no evidence), or why bleeding patients is the best alternative (they've stopped doing so). Sometimes I get the answer that they have no clue when they have to utter defensively "I am a doctor" or "are you a doctor?" But worst, I sometimes get some letters of support and sympathy from the alternative medicine fellows, which makes me go postal: the approach in this book is ultra-orthodox, ultra-rigorous, and ultra-scientific, certainly not in favor of alternative medicine.

The hidden costs of health care are largely in the denial of antifragility. But it may not be just medicine—what we call diseases of civilization result from the attempt by humans to make life comfortable for ourselves against our own interest, since the comfortable is what fragilizes. The rest of this chapter focuses on specific medical cases with hidden negative convexity effects (small gains, large losses)—and reframes the ideas of iatrogenics in connection with my notion of fragility and nonlinearities.

FIRST PRINCIPLE OF IATROGENICS (EMPIRICISM)

The first principle of iatrogenics is as follows: we do not need *evidence of harm* to claim that a drug or an unnatural *via positiva* procedure is dangerous. Recall my comment earlier with the turkey problem that harm is in the future, not in the narrowly defined past. In other words, empiricism is not naive empiricism.

We saw the smoking argument. Now consider the adventure of a human-invented fat, trans fat. Somehow, humans discovered how to make fat products and, as it was the great era of scientism, they were convinced they could make it *better* than nature. Not just equal; better. Chemists assumed that they could produce a fat replacement that was superior to lard or butter from so many standpoints. First, it was more convenient: synthetic products such as margarine stay soft in the refrigerator, so you can immediately spread them on a piece of bread without the usual wait while listening to the radio. Second, it was economical, as the synthetic fats were derived from vegetables. Finally, what is worst, trans fat was assumed to be healthier. Its use propagated very widely and after a few hundred million years of consumption of animal fat, people suddenly started getting scared of it (particularly something called "saturated" fat), mainly from shoddy statistical interpretations. Today trans fat is widely banned as it turned out that it kills people, as it is behind heart disease and cardiovascular problems.

For another murderous example of such sucker (and fragilizing) rationalism, consider the story of Thalidomide. It was a drug meant to reduce the nausea episodes of pregnant women. It led to birth defects. Another drug, Diethylstilbestrol, silently harmed the fetus and led to delayed gynecological cancer among daughters.

These two mistakes are quite telling because, in both cases, the benefits appeared to be obvious and immediate, though small, and the harm remained delayed for years, at least three-quarters of a generation. The next discussion will be about the burden of evidence, as you can easily imagine that someone defending these treatments would have immediately raised the objection, "Monsieur Taleb, do you have *evidence* for your statement?"

Now we can see the pattern: iatrogenics, being a cost-benefit situation, usually results from the treacherous condition in which the benefits are small, and visible—and the costs very large, delayed, and hidden. And of course, the potential costs are much worse than the cumulative gains.

For those into graphs, the appendix shows the potential risks from different angles and expresses iatrogenics as a probability distribution.

SECOND PRINCIPLE OF IATROGENICS (NONLINEARITY IN RESPONSE)

Second principle of iatrogenics: it is not linear. We should not take risks with near-healthy people; but we should take a lot, a lot more risks with those deemed in danger.*

Why do we need to focus treatment on more serious cases, not mar-

* A technical comment. This is a straightforward result of convexity effects on the probability distribution of outcomes. By the "inverse barbell effect," when the gains are small to iatrogenics, uncertainty harms the situation. But by the "barbell effect," when the gains are large in relation to potential side effects, uncertainty tends to be helpful. An explanation with ample graphs is provided in the Appendix.

ginal ones? Take this example showing nonlinearity (convexity). When hypertension is mild, say marginally higher than the zone accepted as "normotensive," the chance of benefiting from a certain drug is close to 5.6 percent (only one person in eighteen benefit from the treatment). But when blood pressure is considered to be in the "high" or "severe" range, the chances of benefiting are now 26 and 72 percent, respectively (that is, one person in four and two persons out of three will benefit from the treatment). So the treatment benefits are convex to condition (the benefits rise disproportionally, in an accelerated manner). But consider that the iatrogenics should be constant for all categories! In the very ill condition, the benefits are large relative to iatrogenics; in the borderline one, they are small. This means that we need to focus on high-symptom conditions and ignore, I mean really ignore, other situations in which the patient is not very ill.

The argument here is based on the structure of conditional survival probabilities, similar to the one that we used to prove that harm needs to be nonlinear for porcelain cups. Consider that Mother Nature had to have tinkered through selection in inverse proportion to the rarity of the condition. Of the hundred and twenty thousand drugs available today, I can hardly find a *via positiva* one that makes a healthy person unconditionally "better" (and if someone shows me one, I will be skeptical of yet-unseen side effects). Once in a while we come up with drugs that enhance performance, such as, say, steroids, only to discover what people in finance have known for a while: in a "mature" market there is no free lunch anymore, and what appears as a free lunch has a hidden risk. When you think you have found a free lunch, say, steroids or trans fat, something that helps the healthy without visible downside, it is most likely that there is a concealed trap somewhere. Actually, my days in trading, it was called a "sucker's trade."

And there is a simple statistical reason that explains why we have not been able to find drugs that make us feel unconditionally better when we are well (or unconditionally stronger, etc.): nature would have been likely to find this magic pill by itself. But consider that illness is rare, and the more ill the person the less likely nature would have found the solution by itself, in an accelerating way. A condition that is, say, three units of deviation away from the norm is more than three hundred times rarer than normal; an illness that is five units of deviation from the norm is more than a million times rarer!

The medical community has not modeled such nonlinearity of benefits to iatrogenics, and if they do so in words, I have not seen it formalized in papers, hence into a decision-making methodology that takes probability into account (as we will see in the next section, there is little explicit use of convexity biases). Even risks seem to be linearly extrapolated, causing both underestimation and overestimation, most certainly miscalculation of degrees of harm—for instance, a paper on the effect of radiation states the following: "The standard model currently in use applies a linear scale, extrapolating cancer risk from high doses to low doses of ionizing radiation." Further, pharmaceutical companies are under financial pressures to find diseases and satisfy the security analysts. They have been scraping the bottom of the barrel, looking for disease among healthier and healthier people, lobbying for reclassifications of conditions, and fine-tuning sales tricks to get doctors to overprescribe. Now, if your blood pressure is in the upper part of the range that used to be called "normal," you are no longer "normotensive" but "pre-hypertensive," even if there are no symptoms in view. There is nothing wrong with the classification if it leads to healthier lifestyle and robust *via negativa* measures—but what is behind such classification, often, is a drive for more medication.

I am not against the function and mission of pharma, rather, its business practice: they should focus *for their own benefit* on extreme diseases, not on reclassifications or pressuring doctors to prescribe medicines. Indeed, pharma plays on the interventionism of doctors.

Another way to view it: the iatrogenics is in the patient, not in the treatment. If the patient is close to death, all speculative treatments should be encouraged—no holds barred. Conversely, if the patient is near healthy, then Mother Nature should be the doctor.

Jensen's Inequality in Medicine

The philosopher's stone explained that the volatility of an exposure can matter more than its average—the difference is the "convexity bias." If you are antifragile (i.e., convex) to a given substance, then you are better off having it randomly distributed, rather than provided steadily.

I've found very few medical papers making use of nonlinearity by applying convexity effects to medical problems, in spite of the ubiquity of nonlinear responses in biology. (I am being generous; I actually found only one explicit use of Jensen's inequality in one single application—

thanks to my friend Eric Briys—and only one that used it properly, so the response "we know that" by medical researchers when the consequence nonlinearity is explained to them is rather lame.)

Remarkably, convexity effects work in an identical way with options, innovations, anything convex. Now let us apply it . . . to lungs.

The next paragraph is a bit technical and can be skipped.

People with a variety of lung diseases, including acute respiratory distress syndrome, used to be put on mechanical ventilators. The belief was that constant pressure and volume were desirable—steadiness seemed a good idea. But the reaction of the patient is nonlinear to the pressure (convex over an initial range, then concave above it), and he suffers from such regularity. Further, people with very sick lungs cannot take high pressure for a long time—while they need a lot of volume. J. F. Brewster and his associates figured out that dispensing higher pressure on occasion, and low pressure at other times, allowed them to provide a lot more volume to the lungs for a given mean pressure and thus decrease patient mortality. An additional benefit is that an occasional spike in pressure helps to open up collapsed alveoli. Actually, that's how our lungs function when healthy: with variations and "noise" rather than steady airflow. Humans are antifragile to lung pressure. And this arises directly from the nonlinearity of the response since as we saw everything convex is antifragile, up to a certain dosage. Brewster's paper went through empirical validation, but this is not even necessary: you don't need empirical data to prove that one plus one equals two, or that probabilities need to add up to 100 percent.*

It does not look as though people who deal with nutrition have examined the difference between random calories and steady nutrition, something to which we will return in the next chapter.

Not using models of nonlinear effects such as convexity biases while "doing empirical work" is like having to catalog every apple falling from a tree and call the operation "empiricism" instead of just using Newton's equation.

---

* In other words, the response for, say, 50 percent of a certain dose during one period, followed by 150 percent of the dose in a subsequent period in convex cases, is superior to 100 percent of the dose in both periods. We do not need much empiricism to estimate the convexity bias: by theorem, such bias is a necessary result of convexity.

BURYING THE EVIDENCE

Now some historical background. What made medicine mislead people for so long is that its successes were prominently displayed, and its mistakes literally buried—just like so many other interesting stories in the cemetery of history.

I cannot resist the following illustration of intervention bias (with negative convexity effects). In the 1940s and 1950s many children and teenagers received radiation for acne, thymus gland enlargement, tonsillitis, to remove birthmarks and treat ringworm of the scalp. In addition to the goiters and other late complications, approximately 7 percent of patients who received this radiation developed thyroid cancer two to four decades later. But let's not write off radiation, when it comes from Mother Nature. We are necessarily antifragile to some dose of radiation—at naturally found levels. It may be that small doses prevent injuries and cancers coming from larger ones, as the body develops some kind of immunity. And, talking about radiation, few wonder why, after hundreds of million of years of having our skins exposed to sun rays, we suddenly need so much protection from them—is it that our exposure is more harmful than before because of changes in the atmosphere, or populations living in an environment mismatching the pigmentation of their skin—or rather, that makers of sun protection products need to make some profits?

The Never-ending History of Turkey Situations

The list of such attempts to outsmart nature driven by naive rationalism is long—always meant to "improve" things—with continuous first-order learning, that is, banning the offending drug or medical procedure but not figuring out that we could be making the mistake again, elsewhere.

Statins. Statin drugs are meant to lower cholesterol in your blood. But there is an asymmetry, and a severe one. One needs to treat fifty high risk persons for five years to avoid a single cardiovascular event. Statins can potentially harm people who are not very sick, for whom the benefits are either minimal or totally nonexistent. We will not be able to get an evidence-based picture of the hidden harm in the short term (we need years for that—remember smoking) and, further, the arguments currently made in favor of the routine administration of these drugs often lie in a few statistical illusions or even manipulation (the experiments used by drug companies seem to play on nonlinearities and bundle the very ill and the less ill, in addition to assuming that the metric "cholesterol" equates 100 percent with health). Statins fail in their application the first principle of iatrogenics (unseen harm); further, they certainly *do* lower cholesterol, but as a human your objective function is not to lower a certain metric to get a grade to pass a school-like test, but get in better health. Further, it is not certain whether these indicators people try to lower are causes or manifestations that correlate to a condition—just as muzzling a baby would certainly prevent him from crying but would not remove the cause of his emotions. Metric-lowering drugs are particularly vicious because of a legal complexity. The doctor has the incentive to prescribe it because should the patient have a heart attack, he would be sued for negligence; but the error in the opposite direction is not penalized at all, as side effects do not appear at all as being caused by the medicine.

The same problem of naive interpretation mixed with intervention bias applies to cancer detection: there is a marked bias in favor of treatment, even when it brings more harm, because the legal system favors intervention.

Surgery. Historians show that surgery had, for a long time, a much better track record than medicine; it was checked by the necessary rigor of visible results. Consider that, when operating on victims of very severe trauma, say, to extract a bullet or to push bowels back in their place, the iatrogenics is reduced; the downside of the operation is small compared to the benefits—hence positive convexity effects. Unlike with the usual pharmaceutical interventions, it is hard to say that Mother Nature would have done a better job. The surgeons used to be blue-collar workers, or closer to artisans than high science, so they did not feel too obligated to theorize.

The two professions of medical doctor and surgeon were kept professionally and socially separate, one was an *ars*, the other *scientia*, hence one was a craft built around experience-driven heuristics and the other reposed on theories, nay, a general theory of humans. Surgeons were there for emergencies. In England, France, and some Italian cities, surgeons' guilds were merged with those of barbers. So the Soviet-Harvardification of surgery was for a long time constrained by the visibility of the results—you can't fool the eye. Given that for a long time people operated without anesthetics, one did not have to overly justify *doing nothing* and waiting for Nature to play her role.

But today's surgery, thanks to anesthesia, is done with a much smaller hurdle—and surgeons now need to attend medical school, albeit a less theoretical one than the Sorbonne or Bologna of the Middle Ages. By contrast, in the past, letting blood (phlebotomy) was one of the few operations performed by surgeons without any disincentive. For instance, back surgery done in modern times to correct sciatica is often useless, minus the possible harm from the operation. Evidence shows that six years later, such an operation is, on average, equivalent to doing nothing, so we have a certain potential deficit from the back operation as every operation brings risks such as brain damage from anesthesia, medical error (the doctor harming the spinal cord), or exposure to hospital germs. Yet spinal cord surgery such as lumbar disc fusion is still practiced liberally, particularly as it is very lucrative for the doctor.*

Antibiotics. Every time you take an antibiotic, you help, to some degree, the mutation of germs into antibiotic-resistant strains. Add to that the toying with your immune system. You transfer the antifragility from your body to the germ. The solution, of course, is to do it only when the benefits are large. Hygiene, or excessive hygiene, has the same effect, particularly when people clean their hands with chemicals after every social exposure.

Here are some verified and potential examples of iatrogenics (in terms of larger downside outside of very ill patients, whether such downside has been verified or not)†: Vioxx, the anti-inflammatory medicine with delayed heart problems as side effects. Antidepressants (used beyond the necessary cases). Bariatric surgery (in place of starvation of overweight diabetic patients). Cortisone. Disinfectants, cleaning products potentially giving rise to autoimmune diseases. Hormone replacement therapy. Hysterectomies. Cesarean births beyond the strictly necessary. Ear tubes in babies as an immediate response to ear infection. Lobotomies. Iron supplementation. Whitening of rice and wheat—it was considered progress. The sunscreen creams suspected to cause harm.

---

* Stuart McGill, an evidence-based scientist who specializes in back conditions, describes the self-healing process as follows: the sciatic nerve, when trapped in too narrow a cavity, causing the common back problem that is thought (by doctors) to be curable only by (lucrative) surgery, produces acid substances that cut through the bone and, over time, carves itself a larger passage. The body does a better job than surgeons.
† The core point in this chapter and the next is nonlinearity as it links to fragility, and how to make use of it in medical decision making, not specific medical treatments and errors. These examples are just illustrative of things we look at without considering concave responses.

Hygiene (beyond a certain point, hygiene may make you fragile by deny-ing hormesis—our own antifragility). We ingest probiotics because we don't eat enough "dirt" anymore. Lysol and other disinfectants killing so many "germs" that kids' developing immune systems are robbed of necessary workout (or robbed of the "good" friendly germs and para-sites). Dental hygiene: I wonder if brushing our teeth with toothpaste full of chemical substances is not mostly to generate profits for the tooth-paste industry—the brush is natural, the toothpaste might just be to counter the abnormal products we consume, such as starches, sugars and high fructose corn syrup. Speaking of which, high fructose corn syrup was the result of neomania, financed by a Nixon administration in love with technology and victim of some urge to subsidize corn farmers. Insulin injections for Type II diabetics, based on the assumption that the harm from diabetes comes from blood sugar, not insulin resistance (or something else associated with it). Soy milk. Cow milk for people of Mediterranean and Asian descent. Heroin, the most dangerously addic-tive substance one can imagine, was developed as a morphine substitute for cough suppressants that did not have morphine's addictive side ef-fects. Psychiatry, particularly child psychiatry—but I guess I don't need to convince anyone about its dangers. I stop here.

Again, my statements here are risk-management-based: if the person is very ill, there are no iatrogenics to worry about. So it is the marginal case that brings dangers.

The cases I have been discussing so far are easy to understand, but some applications are far more subtle. For instance, counter to "what makes sense" at a primitive level, there is no clear evidence that sugar-free sweetened drinks make you lose weight in accordance with the calories saved. But it took thirty years of confusing the biology of millions of people for us to start asking such questions. Somehow those recom-mending these drinks are under the impression, driven by the laws of physics (naive translation from thermodynamics), that the concept that we gain weight from calories is sufficient for further analysis. This would be certainly true in thermodynamics, as in a simple machine responding to energy without feedback, say, a car that burns fuel. But the reasoning does not hold in an informational dimension in which food is not just a source of energy; it conveys information about the environment (like stressors). The ingestion of food combined with one's activity brings about hormonal cascades (or something similar that conveys informa-tion), causing cravings (hence consumption of other foods) or changes in the way your body burns the energy, whether it needs to conserve fat and burn muscle, or vice versa. Complex systems have feedback loops, so what you "burn" depends on what you consume, and how you consume it.

NATURE'S OPAQUE LOGIC

At the time of this writing, the biologist Craig Venter is engaging in the creation of artificial life. He conducted experiments and stated them in a famous paper titled "Creation of a Bacterial Cell Controlled by a Chemically Synthesized Genome." I have an immense respect for Craig Venter, whom I consider one of the smartest men who ever breathed, and a "doer" in the full sense of the word, but giving fallible humans such powers is similar to giving a small child a bunch of explosives.

If I understand this well, to the creationists, this should be an insult to God; but, further, to the evolutionist, this is certainly an insult to evolution. And to the probabilist, like myself and my peers, this is an insult to human prudence, the beginning of the mother of all exposures to Black Swans.

Let me repeat the argument here in one block to make it clearer. Evolution proceeds by undirected, convex bricolage or tinkering, inherently robust, i.e., with the achievement of potential stochastic gains thanks to continuous, repetitive, small, localized mistakes. What men have done with top-down, command-and-control science has been exactly the reverse: interventions with negative convexity effects, i.e., the achievement of small certain gains through exposure to massive potential mistakes. Our record of understanding risks in complex systems (biology, economics, climate) has been pitiful, marred with retrospective distortions (we only understand the risks after the damage takes place, yet we keep making the mistake), and there is nothing to convince me that we have gotten better at risk management. In this particular case, because of the scalability of the errors, you are exposed to the wildest possible form of randomness.

Simply, humans should not be given explosive toys (like atomic bombs, financial derivatives, or tools to create life).

Guilty or Innocent

Let me phrase the last point a bit differently. If there is something in nature you don't understand, odds are it makes sense in a deeper way that is beyond your understanding. So there is a logic to natural things that is much superior to our own. Just as there is a dichotomy in law: *innocent until proven guilty* as opposed to *guilty until proven innocent,* let me express my rule as follows: what Mother Nature does is rigorous until proven otherwise; what humans and science do is flawed until proven otherwise.

Let us close on this business of b***t "evidence." If you want to talk about the "statistically significant," nothing on the planet can be as close to "statistically significant" as nature. This is in deference to her track record and the sheer statistical significance of her massively large experience—the way she has managed to survive Black Swan events. So overriding her requires some very convincing justification on our part, rather than the reverse, as is commonly done, and it is very hard to beat her on statistical grounds—as I wrote in Chapter 7 in the discussion on procrastination, we can invoke the naturalistic fallacy when it comes to ethics, not when it comes to risk management.*

Let me repeat violations of logic in the name of "evidence" owing to their gravity. I am not joking: just as I face the shocking request "Do you have evidence?" when I question a given unnatural treatment, such as icing one's swollen nose, in the past, many faced the question "Do you have evidence that trans fat is harmful?" and needed to produce proofs—which they were obviously unable to do because it took decades before the harm became apparent. These questions are offered more often than not by smart people, even doctors. So when the (present) inhabitants of Mother Earth want to do something counter to nature, they are the ones that need to produce the evidence, if they can.

Everything nonstable or breakable has had ample chance to break over time. Further, the interactions between components of Mother Nature had to modulate in such a way as to keep the overall system alive. What emerges over millions of years is a wonderful combination of so-

---

* A common mistake is to argue that the human body is not perfectly adapted, as if the point had consequences for decision making. This is not the point here; the idea is that nature is computationally more able than humans (and has proven to be so), not that it is perfect. Just look at it as the master of high-dimensional trial and error.

lidity, antifragility, and local fragility, sacrifices in one area made in order for nature to function better. We sacrifice ourselves in favor of our genes, trading our fragility for their survival. We age, but they stay young and get fitter and fitter outside us. Things break on a small scale all the time, in order to avoid large-scale generalized catastrophes.

Plead Ignorance of Biology: Phenomenology

I have explained that phenomenology is more potent than theories—and should lead to more rigorous policy making. Let me illustrate here.

I was in a gym in Barcelona next to the senior partner of a consulting firm, a profession grounded in building narratives and naive rationalization. Like many people who have lost weight, the fellow was eager to talk about it—it is easier to talk about weight loss theories than to stick to them. The fellow told me that he did not believe in such diets as the low-carbohydrate Atkins or Dukan diet, until he was told of the mechanism of "insulin," which convinced him to embark on the regimen. He then lost thirty pounds—he had to wait for a theory before taking any action. That was in spite of the empirical evidence showing people losing one hundred pounds by avoiding carbohydrates, without changing their total food intake—just the composition! Now, being the exact opposite of the consultant, I believe that "insulin" as a cause is a fragile theory but that the phenomenology, the empirical effect, is real. Let me introduce the ideas of the postclassical school of the skeptical empiricists.

We are built to be dupes for theories. But theories come and go; experience stays. Explanations change all the time, and have changed all the time in history (because of causal opacity, the invisibility of causes) with people involved in the incremental development of ideas thinking they always had a definitive theory; experience remains constant.

As we saw in Chapter 7, what physicists call the phenomenology of the process is the empirical manifestation, without looking at how it glues to existing general theories. Take for instance the following statement, entirely evidence-based: *if you build muscle, you can eat more without getting more fat deposits in your belly* and can gorge on lamb chops without having to buy a new belt. Now in the past the theory to rationalize it was "Your metabolism is higher because muscles burn calories." Currently I tend to hear "You become more insulin-sensitive and store less fat." Insulin, shminsulin; metabolism, shmetabolism: another theory will emerge in the future and some other substance will come about, but the exact same effect will continue to prevail.

The same holds for the statement *Lifting weights increases your muscle mass.* In the past they used to say that weight lifting caused the "micro-tearing of muscles," with subsequent healing and increase in size. Today some people discuss hormonal signaling or genetic mechanisms, tomorrow they will discuss something else. But the effect has held forever and will continue to do so.

When it comes to narratives, the brain seems to be the last province of the theoretician-charlatan. Add *neurosomething* to a field, and suddenly it rises in respectability and becomes more convincing as people now have the illusion of a strong causal link—yet the brain is too complex for that; it is both the most complex part of the human anatomy and the one that seems most susceptible to sucker-causation. Christopher Chabris and Daniel Simons brought to my attention the evidence I had been looking for: whatever theory has a reference in it to brain circuitry seems more "scientific" and more convincing, even when it is just randomized psychoneurobabble.

But this causation is highly rooted in orthodox medicine as it was traditionally built. Avicenna in his *Canon* (which in Arabic means law): "We must know the causes of health and illness if we wish to make [medicine] a *scientia.*"

I am writing about health, but I do not want to rely on biology beyond the minimum required (not in the theoretical sense)—and I believe that my strength will lie there. I just want to understand as little as possible to be able to look at regularities of experience.

So the *modus operandi* in every venture is to remain as robust as possible to changes in theories (let me repeat that my deference to Mother Nature is entirely statistical and risk-management-based, i.e., again, grounded in the notion of fragility). The doctor and medical essayist James Le Fanu showed how our understanding of the biological processes was coupled with a decline of pharmaceutical discoveries, as if rationalistic theories were blinding and somehow a handicap.

In other words, we have in biology a green lumber problem!

Now, a bit of history of ancient and medieval medicine. Traditionally, medicine used to be split into three traditions: rationalists (based on preset theories, the need of global understanding of what things were made *for*), skeptical empiricists (who refused theories and were skeptical of ideas making claims about the unseen), and methodists (who taught each other some simple medical heuristics stripped of theories and found an even more practical way to be empiricists). While differences can be overplayed by the categorization, one can look at the three traditions not as entirely dogmatic approaches, but rather ones varying in their starting point, the weight of the prior beliefs: some start with theories, others with evidence.

Tensions among the three tendencies have always existed over time—and I put myself squarely in the camp attempting to vindicate the empiricists, who, as a philosophical school, were swallowed by late antiquity. I have been trying to bring alive these ideas of Aenesidemus of Knossos, Antiochus of Laodicea, Menodotus of Nicomedia, Herodotus of Tarsus, and of course Sextus Empiricus. The empiricists insisted on the "I did not know" while facing situations *not exactly seen* in the past, that is, in nearly identical conditions. The methodists did not have the same strictures against analogy, but were still careful.

The Ancients Were More Caustic

This problem of iatrogenics is not new—and doctors have been traditionally the butt of jokes.

Martial in his epigrams gives us an idea of the perceived expert problem in medicine in his time: "I thought that Diaulus was a doctor, not a caretaker—but for him it appears to be the same job" (*Nuper erat medicus, nunc est uispillo Diaulus: quod uispillo facit, fecerat et medicus*) or "I did not feel ill, Symmache; now I do (after your ministrations)." (*Non habui febrem, Symmache, nunc habeo*).

The Greek term *pharmakon* is ambiguous, as it can mean both "poison" and "cure" and has been used as a pun to warn against iatrogenics by the Arab doctor Ruhawi.

An *attribution problem* arises when the person imputes his positive results to his own skills and his failures to luck. Nicocles, as early as the fourth century B.C., asserts that doctors claimed responsibility for success and blamed failure on nature, or on some external cause. The very same idea was rediscovered by psychologists some twenty-four centuries later, and applied to stockbrokers, doctors, and managers of companies.

According to an ancient anecdote, the Emperor Hadrian continually exclaimed, as he was dying, that it was his doctors who had killed him.

Montaigne, mostly a synthesizer of classical writers, has his *Essays* replete with anecdotes: A Lacedaemonian was asked what had made him live so long; he answered, "Ignoring medicine." Montaigne also detected the agency problem, or why the last thing a doctor needs is for you to be healthy: "No doctor derives pleasure from the health of his friends, wrote the ancient Greek satirist, no soldier from the peace of his city, etc." *(Nul médecin ne prent plaisir à la santé de ses amis mesmes, dit l'ancien Comique Grec, ny soldat à la paix de sa ville: ainsi du reste.)*

How to Medicate Half the Population

Recall how a personal doctor can kill you.

We saw in the story of the grandmother our inability to distinguish in our logical reasoning (though not in intuitive actions) between average and other, richer properties of what we observe.

I was once attending a lunch party at the country house of a friend when someone produced a handheld blood pressure measuring tool. Tempted, I measured my arterial pressure, and it turned out to be slightly higher than average. A doctor, who was part of the party and had a very friendly disposition, immediately pulled out a piece of paper prescribing some medication to lower it—which I later threw in the garbage can. I subsequently bought the same measuring tool and discovered that my blood pressure was much lower (hence better) than average, except once in a while, when it peaked episodically. In short, it exhibits some variability. Like everything in life.

This random variability is often mistaken for information, hence leading to intervention. Let us play a thought experiment, without making any assumption on the link between blood pressure and health. Further, assume that "normal" pressure is a certain, known number. Take a cohort of healthy persons. Suppose that because of randomness, half the time a given person's pressure will be above that number, and half the time, for the same person, the measurement will be below. So on about half the doctor's visits they will show the alarming "above normal." If the doctor automatically prescribes medication on the days the patients are above normal, then half the *normal* population will be on medication. And note that we are quite certain that their life expectancy will be reduced by unnecessary treatments. Clearly I am simplifying here; sophisticated doctors are aware of the variable nature of the measurements and do not prescribe medication when the numbers are not compelling (though it is easy to fall into the trap, and not all doctors are sophisticated). But the thought experiment can show how frequent visits to the doctor, particularly outside the cases of a life-threatening ailment or an uncomfortable condition—just like frequent access to information—can be harmful. This example also shows us the process outlined in Chapter 7 by which a personal doctor ends up killing the patient—simply by overreacting to noise.

This is more serious than you think: it seems that medicine has a hard time grasping normal variability in samples—it is hard sometimes to translate the difference between "statistically significant" and "significant" in effect. A certain disease might marginally lower your life expectancy, but it can be deemed to do so with "high statistical significance," prompting panics when in fact all these studies might be saying is they established *with a significant statistical margin* that in some cases, say, 1 percent of the cases, patients are likely to be harmed by it. Let me rephrase: the magnitude of the result, the importance of the effect, is not captured by what is called "statistical significance," something that tends to deceive specialists. We need to look in two dimensions: how much a condition, say, blood pressure a certain number of points higher than normal, is likely to affect your life expectancy; and how significant the result is.

Why is this serious? If you think that the statistician really understands "statistical significance" in the complicated texture of real life (the "large world," as opposed to the "small world" of textbooks), some surprises. Kahneman and Tversky showed that statisticians themselves made practical mistakes in real life in violation of their teachings, forgetting that they were statisticians (thinking, I remind the reader, requires effort). My colleague Daniel Goldstein and I did some research on "quants," professionals of quantitative finance, and realized that the overwhelming majority did not understand the practical effect of elementary notions such as "variance" or "standard deviation," concepts they used in about every one of their equations. A recent powerful study by Emre Soyer and Robin Hogarth showed that many professionals and experts in the field of econometrics supplying pompous numbers such as "regression" and "correlation" made egregious mistakes translating into practice the numbers they were producing themselves—they get the equation right but make severe translation mistakes when expressing it into reality. In all cases they underestimate randomness and underestimate the uncertainty in the results. And we are talking about errors of interpretation *made by the statisticians,* not by the users of statistics such as social scientists and doctors.

Alas, all these biases lead to action, almost never inaction.

In addition, we now know that the craze against fats and the "fat free" slogans result from an elementary mistake in interpreting the results of a regression: when two variables are jointly responsible for an effect (here, carbohydrates and fat), sometimes one of them shows sole responsibility. Many fell into the error of attributing problems under joint consumption of fat and carbohydrates to fat rather than carbohydrates. Further, the great statistician and debunker of statistical misinterpretation David Freedman showed (very convincingly) with a coauthor that the link everyone is obsessing about between salt and blood pressure has no statistical basis. It may exist for some hypertensive people, but it is more likely the exception than the rule.

The "Rigor of Mathematics" in Medicine

For those of us who laugh at the charlatanism hidden behind fictional mathematics in social science, one may wonder why this did not happen to medicine.

And indeed the cemetery of bad ideas (and hidden ideas) shows that mathematics fooled us there. There have been many forgotten attempts to mathematize medicine. There was a period during which medicine derived its explanatory models from the physical sciences. Giovanni Borelli, in *De motu animalium,* compared the body to a machine consisting of animal levers—hence we could apply the rules of linear physics.

Let me repeat: I am not against rationalized learned discourse, provided it is not fragile to error; I am first and last a decision maker hybrid and will never separate the philosopher-probabilist from the decision maker, so I am that joint person all the time, in the morning when I drink the ancient liquid called coffee, at noon when I eat with my friends, and at night when I go to bed clutching a book. What I am against is *naive* rationalized, pseudolearned discourse, with green lumber problems—one that focuses solely on the known and *ignores the unknown.* Nor am I against the use of mathematics when it comes to gauging the importance of the unknown—this is the robust application of mathematics. Actually

the arguments in this chapter and the next are all based on the mathematics of probability—but it is not a rationalistic use of mathematics
and much of it allows the detection of blatant inconsistencies between
statements about severity of disease and intensity of treatment. On the
other hand, the use of mathematics in social science is like interventionism. Those who practice it professionally tend to use it everywhere except where it can be useful.

The only condition for such brand of more sophisticated rationalism:
to believe and act as if one does not have the full story—to be sophisticated you need to accept that you are not so.

Next

This chapter has introduced the idea of convexity effects and burden of
evidence into medicine and into the assessment of risk of iatrogenics.
Next, let us look at more applications of convexity effects and discuss
via negativa as a rigorous approach to life.

CHAPTER 22

To Live Long, but Not Too Long

*Wednesdays and Fridays, plus Lent—How to live forever, according to
Nietzsche or others—Or why, when you think about it, not to live longer*

LIFE EXPECTANCY AND CONVEXITY

Whenever you question some aspects of medicine—or unconditional
technological "progress"—you are invariably and promptly provided
the sophistry that "we tend to live longer" than past generations. Note
that some make the even sillier argument that a propensity to natural
things implies favoring a return to a day of "brutish and short" lives, not
realizing it is the exact same argument as saying that eating fresh, non-
canned foods implies rejecting civilization, the rule of law, and human-
ism. So there are a lot of nuances in this life expectancy argument.

Life expectancy has increased (conditional on no nuclear war) because of the combination of many factors: sanitation, penicillin, a drop
in crime, life-saving surgery, and of course, *some* medical practitioners
operating in severe life-threatening situations. If we live longer, it is
thanks to medicine's benefits in cases that are lethal, in which the condition is severe—hence low iatrogenics, as we saw, the convex cases. So it
is a serious error to infer that if we live longer because of medicine, that
all medical treatments make us live longer.

Further, to account for the effect of "progress," we need to deduct of
course, from the gains in medical treatment, the costs of the diseases of

civilization (primitive societies are largely free of cardiovascular disease, cancer, dental cavities, economic theories, lounge music, and other modern ailments); advances in lung cancer treatment need to be offset by the effect of smoking. From the research papers, one can estimate that medical practice may have contributed a small number of years to the increase, but again, this depends greatly on the gravity of the disease (cancer doctors certainly provide a positive contribution in advanced—and curable—cases, while interventionistic personal doctors, patently, provide a negative one). We need to take into account the unfortunate fact that iatrogenics, hence medicine, reduces life expectancy in a set—and easy to map—number of cases, the concave ones. We have a few pieces of data from the small number of hospital strikes during which only a small number of operations are conducted (for the most urgent cases), and elective surgery is postponed. Depending on whose side in the debate you join, life expectancy either increases in these cases or, at the least, does not seem to drop. Further, which is significant, many of the elective surgeries are subsequently canceled upon the return to normalcy—evidence of the denigration of Mother Nature's work by *some* doctors.

Another fooled-by-randomness-style mistake is to think that because life expectancy at birth used to be thirty until the last century, that people lived *just* thirty years. The distribution was massively skewed, with the bulk of the deaths coming from birth and childhood mortality. Conditional life expectancy was high—just consider that ancestral men tended to die of trauma.* Perhaps legal enforcement contributed more than doctors to the increase in length of life—so the gains in life expectancy are more societal than from the result of scientific advance.

As a case study, consider mammograms. It has been shown that administering them to women over forty on an annual basis does not lead to an increase in life expectancy (at best; it could even lead to a decrease). While female mortality from breast cancer decreases for the cohort subjected to mammograms, the death *from other causes*

---

* While there are some controversies concerning conditional life expectancy, the numbers are quite revealing. For instance, on one extreme, Richard Lewontin estimates, "in the last 50 years, only four months have been added to the expected life span of a person who is already 60 years old." Data from the Centers for Disease Control and Prevention (CDC) show a few more years (but we are still unsure how much of it came from medicine as compared to improvements in life conditions and social mores). Still, the CDC shows that life expectancy at age 20 only increased from 42.79 (additional years) in 1900–1902 to 51.2 in 1949–1951 and to 58.2 in 2002.

increases markedly. We can spot here simple measurable iatrogenics. The doctor, seeing the tumor, cannot avoid doing something harmful, like surgery followed by radiation, chemotherapy, or both—that is, more harmful than the tumor. There is a break-even point that is easily crossed by panicked doctors and patients: treating *the tumor that will not kill you* shortens your life—chemotherapy is toxic. We have built up so much paranoia against cancer, looking at the chain backward, an error of logic called *affirming the consequent*. If all of those dying prematurely from cancer had a malignant tumor, that does not mean that all malignant tumors lead to death from cancer. Most equally intelligent persons do not infer from the fact that all Cretans are liars that all liars are Cretan, or from the condition that all bankers are corrupt that all corrupt people are bankers. Only in extreme cases does nature allow us to make such violations of logic (called *modus ponens*) in order to help us survive. Overreaction is beneficial in an ancestral environment. *

Misunderstanding of the problems with mammograms has led to overreactions on the part of politicians (another reason to have a society immune from the stupidity of lawmakers by decentralization of important decisions). One politician of the primitive kind, Hillary Clinton, went so far as to claim that critics of the usefulness of mammograms were killing women.

We can generalize the mammogram problem to unconditional laboratory tests, finding deviations from the norm, and acting to "cure" them.

Subtraction Adds to Your Life

Now I speculate the following, having looked closely at data with my friend Spyros Makridakis, a statistician and decision scientist who we introduced a few chapters ago as the first to find flaws in statistical forecasting methods. We estimated that cutting medical expenditures by a certain amount (while limiting the cuts to elective surgeries and treatments) would extend people's lives in most rich countries, especially the United States. Why? Simple basic convexity analysis; a simple examina-

---

* A technical comment: in the so-called Bayesian (or conditional probability) analysis, it would be equivalent to looking at A conditional on B rather than B conditional on A.

tion of conditional iatrogenics: the error of treating the mildly ill puts them in a concave position. And it looks as if we know very well how to do this. Just raise the hurdle of medical intervention in favor of cases that are most severe, for which the iatrogenics effect is very small. It may even be better to increase expenditures on these and reduce the one on elective ones.

In other words, reason backward, starting from the iatrogenics to the cure, rather than the other way around. Whenever possible, replace the doctor with human antifragility. But otherwise don't be shy with aggressive treatments.

Another application of *via negativa:* spend less, live longer is a subtractive strategy. We saw that iatrogenics comes from the intervention bias, *via positiva,* the propensity to want to *do something,* causing all the problems we've discussed. But let's do some *via negativa* here: removing things can be quite a potent (and, empirically, a more rigorous) action.

Why? Subtraction of a substance not seasoned by our evolutionary history reduces the possibility of Black Swans while leaving one open to improvements. Should the improvements occur, we can be pretty comfortable that they are as free of unseen side effects as one can get.

So there are many hidden jewels in *via negativa* applied to medicine. For instance, telling people *not* to smoke seems to be the greatest medical contribution of the last sixty years. Druin Burch, in *Taking the Medicine,* writes: "The harmful effects of smoking are roughly equivalent to the combined good ones of *every* medical intervention developed since the war. . . . Getting rid of smoking provides more benefit than being able to cure people of every possible type of cancer."

As usual, the ancients. As Ennius wrote, "The good is mostly in the absence of bad"; *Nimium boni est, cui nihil est mali.*

Likewise, happiness is best dealt with as a negative concept; the same nonlinearity applies. Modern happiness researchers (who usually look quite unhappy), often psychologists turned economists (or vice versa), do not use nonlinearities and convexity effects when they lecture us about happiness as if we knew what it was and whether that's what we should be after. Instead, they should be lecturing us about unhappiness (I speculate that just as those who lecture on happiness look unhappy, those who lecture on unhappiness would look happy); the "pursuit of happiness" is not equivalent to the "avoidance of unhappiness." Each of us certainly knows not only what makes us unhappy (for instance, copy editors, commuting, bad odors, pain, the sight of a certain magazine in a waiting room, etc.), but what to do about it.

Let us probe the wisdom of the ages. "Sometimes scantiness of nourishment restores the system," wrote Plotinus—and the ancients believed in purges (one manifestation of which was the oft-harmful, though often beneficial, routine of bloodletting). The regimen of the Salerno School of Medicine: joyful mood, rest, and scant nourishment. *Si tibi deficiant medici, medici tibi fiant haec tria: mens laeta, requies, moderata diaeta.*

There is a seemingly apocryphal (but nevertheless interesting) story about Pomponius Atticus, famous for being Cicero's relative and epistolary recipient. Being ill, incurably ill, he tried to put an end to both his life and his suffering by abstinence, and only succeeded in ending the latter, as, according to Montaigne, his health was restored. But I am citing the story in spite of its apocryphal nature simply because, from a scientific perspective, it seems that the only way we may manage to extend people's lives is through caloric restriction—which seems to cure many ailments in humans and extend lives in laboratory animals. But, as we will see in the next section, such restriction does not need to be permanent—just an occasional (but painful) fast might do.

We know we can cure many cases of diabetes by putting people on a very strict starvation-style diet, shocking their system—in fact the mechanism had to have been known heuristically for a long time since there are institutes and sanatoria for curative starvation in Siberia.

It has been shown that many people benefit from the removal of products that did not exist in their ancestral habitat: sugars and other carbohydrates in unnatural format, wheat products (those with celiac disease, but almost all of us are somewhat ill-adapted to this new addition to the human diet), milk and other cow products (for those of non–Northern European origin who did not develop lactose tolerance), sodas (both diet and regular), wine (for those of Asian origin who do not have the history of exposure), vitamin pills, food supplements, the family doctor, headache medicine and other painkillers. Reliance on painkillers encourages people to avoid addressing the cause of the headache with trial and error, which can be sleep deprivation, tension in the neck, or bad stressors—it allows them to keep destroying themselves in a

Procrustean-bed-style life. But one does not have to go far, just start re-moving the medications that your doctor gave you, or, preferably, re-move your doctor—as Oliver Wendell Holmes Sr. put it, "if all the medications were dumped in the sea, it would be better for mankind but worse for the fishes." My father, an oncologist (who also did research in anthropology) raised me under that maxim (alas, while not completely following it in practice; he cited it enough, though).

I, for my part, resist eating fruits not found in the ancient Eastern Mediterranean (I use "I" here in order to show that I am not narrowly generalizing to the rest of humanity). I avoid any fruit that does not have an ancient Greek or Hebrew name, such as mangoes, papayas, even or-anges. Oranges seem to be the postmedieval equivalent of candy; they did not exist in the ancient Mediterranean. Apparently, the Portuguese found a sweet citrus tree in Goa or elsewhere and started breeding it for sweeter and sweeter fruits, like a modern confectionary company. Even the apples we see in the stores are to be regarded with some suspicion: original apples were devoid of sweet taste and fruit corporations bred them for maximal sweetness—the mountain apples of my childhood were acid, bitter, crunchy, and much smaller than the shiny variety in U.S. stores said to keep the doctor away.

As to liquid, my rule is drink no liquid that is not at least a thousand years old—so its fitness has been tested. I drink just wine, water, and coffee. No soft drinks. Perhaps the most possibly deceitfully noxious drink is the orange juice we make poor innocent people imbibe at the breakfast table while, thanks to marketing, we convince them it is "healthy." (Aside from the point that the citrus our ancestors ingested was not sweet, they never ingested carbohydrates without large, very large quantities of fiber. Eating an orange or an apple is not biologically equivalent to drinking orange or apple juice.) From such examples, I derived the rule that what is called "healthy" is generally unhealthy, just as "social" networks are antisocial, and the "knowledge"-based econ-omy is typically ignorant.

I would add that, in my own experience, a considerable jump in my personal health has been achieved by removing offensive irritants: the morning newspapers (the mere mention of the names of the fragilista journalists Thomas Friedman or Paul Krugman can lead to explosive bouts of unrequited anger on my part), the boss, the daily commute, air-conditioning (though not heating), television, emails from documentary filmmakers, economic forecasts, news about the stock market, gym "strength training" machines, and many more.*

The Iatrogenics of Money

To understand the outright denial of antifragility in the way we seek wealth, consider that construction laborers seem happier with a ham and cheese baguette than businessmen with a Michelin three-star meal. Food tastes so much better after exertion. The Romans had a strange relation to wealth: anything that "softens" or "mollifies" was seen negatively. Their reputation for decadence is a bit overdone—history likes the lurid; they disliked comfort and understood its side effects. The same with the Semites, split between desert tribes and city dwellers, with city dwellers harboring a certain cross-generational nostalgia for their roots and their original culture; so there is the culture of the desert, full of poetry, chivalry, contemplation, rough episodes, and frugality, plotted against the cities' comfort, which is associated with physical and moral decay, gossip, and decadence. The city dweller repairs to the desert for purification, as Christ did for forty days in the Judean desert, or Saint Mark in the Egyptian desert, starting a tradition of such asceticism. There was at some point an epidemic of monasticism in the Levant, perhaps the most impressive being Saint Simeon, who spent forty years on top of a column in Northern Syria. The Arabs kept the tradition, shedding possessions to go to silent, barren, empty spaces. And of course, with mandatory fasting, on which a bit later.

Note that medical iatrogenics is the result of wealth and sophistication rather than poverty and artlessness, and of course the product of partial knowledge rather than ignorance. So this idea of shedding possessions to go to the desert can be quite potent as a *via negativa*-style subtractive strategy. Few have considered that money has its own iatrogenics, and that separating some people from their fortune would simplify their lives and bring great benefits in the form of healthy stressors. So being poorer might not be completely devoid of benefits if one does it right. We need modern civilization for many things, such as the legal

---

* One example of lack of empirical wisdom in the use of "evidence": in a *New York Times Magazine* article, a doctor who claimed that he stopped eating sugar because of its potential harm was apologetic for doing so "without full evidence." The best test of empirical wisdom in someone is in where he puts the burden of evidence.

system and emergency room surgery. But just imagine how by the subtractive perspective, *via negativa*, we can be better off by getting tougher: no sunscreen, no sunglasses if you have brown eyes, no air-conditioning, no orange juice (just water), no smooth surfaces, no soft drinks, no complicated pills, no loud music, no elevator, no juicer, no . . . I stop.

When I see pictures of my friend the godfather of the Paleo ancestral lifestyle, Art De Vany, who is extremely fit in his seventies (much more than most people thirty years younger than him), and those of the pear-shaped billionaires Rupert Murdoch or Warren Buffett or others in the same age group, I am invariably hit with the following idea. If true wealth consists in worriless sleeping, clear conscience, reciprocal gratitude, absence of envy, good appetite, muscle strength, physical energy, frequent laughs, no meals alone, no gym class, some physical labor (or hobby), good bowel movements, no meeting rooms, and periodic surprises, then it is largely subtractive (elimination of iatrogenics).

Religion and Naive Interventionism

Religion has invisible purposes beyond what the literal-minded scientistic-scientifiers identify—one of which is to protect us from scientism, that is, them. We can see in the corpus of inscriptions (on graves) accounts of people erecting fountains or even temples to their favorite gods after these succeeded where doctors failed. Indeed we rarely look at religion's benefits in limiting the intervention bias and its iatrogenics: *in a large set of circumstances (marginal disease), anything that takes you away from the doctor and allows you to do nothing (hence gives nature a chance to do its work) will be beneficial.* So going to church (or the temple of Apollo) for mild cases—say, those devoid of trauma, like a mild discomfort, not injuries from a car accident, those situations in which the risk of iatrogenics exceeds the benefit of cure, to repeat it again, the cases with negative convexity—will certainly help. We have so many inscriptions on temples of the type *Apollo saved me, my doctors tried to kill me*—typically the patient has bequeathed his fortune to the temple.

And it seems to me that human nature does, deep down, know when to resort to the solace of religion, and when to switch to science.*

---

* I am trying to avoid discussing the placebo effect; I am in the business of nonlinearities and it does not relate to the nonlinearities argument.

IF IT'S WEDNESDAY, I MUST BE VEGAN

Sometimes, for a conference dinner, the organizers send me a form asking me if I have dietary requirements. Some do so close to six months in advance. In the past, my usual answer had been that I avoid eating cats, dogs, rats, and humans (especially economists). Today, after my personal evolution, I truly need to figure out the day of the week to know if I will be vegan then or capable of eating those thick monstrous steaks. How? Just by looking at the Greek Orthodox calendar and its required fasts. This confuses the usual categorizing business-reader-TED-conference modern version of the naive fellow who cannot place me in the "Paleo camp" or the "vegan camp." (The "Paleo" people are carnivores who try to replicate the supposed ancestral high-meat, high-animal-fat diet of hunter-gatherers; vegans are people who eat no animal product, not even butter). We will see further down why it is a naive rationalistic mistake to be in either category (except for religious or spiritual reasons) except episodically.

I believe in the heuristics of religion and blindly accommodate its rules (as an Orthodox Christian, I can cheat once in a while, as it is part of the game). Among other things the role of religion is to tame the iatrogenics of abundance—fasting makes you lose your sense of entitlement. But there are more subtle aspects.

Convexity Effects and Random Nutrition

Recall from the lung ventilator discussion this practical consequence of Jensen's inequality: irregularity has its benefits in some areas; regularity has its detriments. Where Jensen's inequality applies, irregularity might be medicine.

Perhaps what we mostly need to remove is a few meals at random, or at least avoid steadiness in food consumption. The error of missing non-linearities is found in two places, in the mixture and in the frequency of food intake.

The problem with the mixture is as follows. We humans are said to be omnivorous, compared to more specialized mammals, such as cows and elephants (who eat salads) and lions (who eat prey, generally salad-eating prey). But such ability to be omnivorous had to come in response to more variegated environments with unplanned, haphazard, and, what is key, serial availability of sources—specialization is the response to a very stable habitat free of abrupt changes, redundancy of pathways the response to a more variegated one. Diversification of function had to come in response to variety. And a variety of a certain structure.

Note a subtlety in the way we are built: the cow and other herbivores are subjected to much less randomness than the lion in their food intake; they eat steadily but need to work extremely hard in order to metabolize all these nutrients, spending several hours a day just eating. Not to count the boredom of standing there eating salads. The lion, on the other hand, needs to rely on more luck; it succeeds in a small percentage of the kills, less than 20 percent, but when it eats, it gets in a quick and easy way all these nutrients produced thanks to very hard and boring work by the prey. So take the following principles derived from the random structure of the environment: when we are herbivores, we eat steadily; but when we are predators we eat more randomly. Hence our proteins need to be consumed randomly for statistical reasons.

So if you agree that we need "balanced" nutrition of a certain combination, it is wrong to immediately assume that we need such balance *at every meal* rather than serially so. Assuming that we need on average certain quantities of the various nutrients that have been identified, say a certain quantity of carbohydrates, proteins, and fats.* There is a big difference between getting them together, at every meal, with the classical steak, salad, followed by fresh fruits, or having them separately, serially.

Why? Because deprivation is a stressor—and we know what stressors do when allowed adequate recovery. Convexity effects at work here again: getting three times the daily dose of protein in one day and nothing the next two is certainly not biologically equivalent to "steady" moderate consumption if our metabolic reactions are nonlinear. It should have some benefits—at least this is how we are designed to be.

I speculate; in fact I more than speculate: I am convinced (an inevitable result of nonlinearity) that we are antifragile to randomness in food delivery and composition—at least over a certain range, or number of days.

---

* Some people claim that we need more fat than carbohydrates; others offer the opposite (they all tend to agree on protein, though few realize we need to randomize protein intake). Both sides still advocate nonrandomness in the mixing and ignore the nonlinearities from sequence and composition.

And one blatant denial of convexity bias is the theory about the benefits of the so-called Cretan (or Mediterranean) diet that triggered a change in the eating habits of the U.S. enlightened class, away from steak and potatoes in favor of grilled fish with salad and feta cheese. It happened as follows. Someone looked at the longevity of Cretans, cataloged what they ate, then inferred—naively—that they lived longer because of the types of food they consumed. It could be true, but the second-order effect (the variations in intake) could be dominant, something that went unnoticed by mechanistic researchers. Indeed, it took a while to notice the following: the Greek Orthodox church has, depending on the severity of the local culture, almost two hundred days of fasting per year; and these are harrowing fasts.

Yes, harrowing fasts, as I am feeling it right now. For I am writing these lines during Orthodox Lent, a forty-day period in which almost no animal product can be consumed, no sweets, and, for some sticklers, no olive oil. As there are several gradations, I try to stick to a semistrict level, and life is not very easy, as is meant to be. I just spent a long weekend in Amioun, my ancestral village in Northern Lebanon, in the Greek Orthodox area called the Koura valley. There traditional "ruse" foods are perfected, with great imagination: Levantine kibbeh made with herbs and beans in place of meat, meatballs made of matzoh-style small brown balls in a lentil soup. Remarkably, while fish is banned, most days, shellfish is allowed, probably as it was not considered a luxury item. The compensation for the absence of some nutrients from my daily diet will take place in lumps. I will make up my deprivation of what researchers (for now) call protein with fish on days when it is allowed, and of course I will ravenously eat lamb on Easter Day, then consume disproportionally high quantities of fatty red meat for a while thereafter. I dream of the red steak served in Fat Tony–patronized restaurants in unapologetically monstrous portions.

And there is this antifragility to the stressor of the fast, as it makes the wanted food taste better and can produce euphoria in one's system. Breaking a fast feels like the exact opposite of a hangover.*

---

* The principal disease of abundance can be seen in habituation and jadedness (what biologists currently call dulling of receptors); Seneca: "To a sick person, honey tastes better."

How to Eat Yourself

I wonder how people can accept that the stressors of exercise are good for you, but do not transfer to the point that food deprivation can have the same effect. But scientists are in the process of discovering the effects of episodic deprivation of some, or all, foods. Somehow, evidence shows, we get sharper and fitter in response to the stress of the constraint.

We can look at biological studies not to generalize or use in the rationalistic sense, but to verify the existence of a human response to hunger: that biological mechanisms are activated by food deprivation. And we have experiments on cohorts showing the positive effect of hunger—or deprivation of a food group—on the human body. Researchers rationalize now with the mechanism of *autophagy* (eating oneself): when deprived of external sources, the theories are that your cells start eating themselves, or breaking down proteins and recombining amino acids to provide material for building other cells. It is assumed by some researchers (for now) that the "vacuum cleaner" effect of autophagy is the key to longevity—though my ideas of the natural are impervious to their theories: as I will show further down, occasional starvation produces some health benefits and that's that.

The response to hunger, our antifragility, has been underestimated. We've been telling people to eat a good meal for breakfast so they can face the travails of the day. And it is not a new theory by empirically blind modern-day nutritionists—for instance I was struck by a dialogue in Stendhal's monumental novel *Le rouge et le noir* in which the protagonist, Julien Sorel, is told "the work for the day will be long and rough, so let us *fortify* ourselves with a breakfast" (which in the French of the period was called "the first lunch"). Indeed, the idea of breakfast as a main meal with cereals and other such materials has been progressively shown to be harming humans—I wonder why it took so long before anyone realized that such an unnatural idea needs to be tested; further, the tests show that harm, or, at least, no benefits are derived from breakfast unless one has worked for it beforehand.

Let us remember that we are not designed to be receiving foods from the delivery person. In nature, we had to expend some energy to eat. Lions hunt to eat, they don't eat their meal then hunt for pleasure. Giving people food before they expend energy would certainly confuse their signaling process. And we have ample evidence that intermittently (and only intermittently) depriving organisms of food has been shown to engender beneficial effects on many functions—Valter Longo, for instance, noted that prisoners in concentration camps got less sick in the first phase of food restriction, then broke down later. He tried the result experimentally and found out that mice, in the initial phases of starvation, can withstand high doses of chemotherapy without visible side effects. Scientists use the narrative that starvation causes the expression of a gene coding a protein called SIRT, SIRT1, or sirtuin, which brings longevity and other effects. The antifragility of humans manifests itself in the response with up-regulation of some genes in response to hunger.

So once again, religions with ritual fasts have more answers than assumed by those who look at them too literally. In fact what these ritual fasts do is try to bring nonlinearities in consumption to match biological properties. The Appendix shows graphically the standard dose responses in biology: a little bit of anything seems to harbor positive convexity effects (whether beneficial or harmful); add to it and the effect weakens. Clearly at the upper end, the dose has no additional effect since one reaches saturation.

Walk-Deprived

Another source of harm from naive rationalism. Just as for a long time people tried to shorten their sleep, as it seemed useless to our earthling logic, many people think that walking is useless, so they use mechanical transportation (car, bicycle, etc.) and get their exercise working out at the gym. And when they walk, they do this ignominious "power walk," sometimes with weights on their arms. They do not realize that for reasons still opaque to them, walking effortlessly, at a pace below the stress level, can have some benefits—or, as I speculate, is necessary for humans, perhaps as necessary as sleep, which at some point modernity could not rationalize and tried to reduce. Now it may or may not be true that walking effortlessly is as necessary as sleep, but since all my ancestors until the advent of the automobile spent much of their time walking around (and sleeping), I try to just follow the logic, even before some medical journal catches up to the idea and produces what referees of medical journals call "evidence."

I Want to Live Forever

All I hear is how to live longer, richer, and, of course, more laden with electronic gadgets. We are not the first generation to believe that the worst possible thing to befall us is death. But for the ancients, the worst possible outcome was not death, but a dishonorable death, or even just a regular one. For a classical hero, dying in a retirement home with a rude nurse and a network of tubes coming into and out of your nose would not be the attractive *telos* for a life.

And, of course, we have this modern illusion that we should live as long as we can. As if we were each the end product. This idea of the "me" as a unit can be traced to the Enlightenment. And, with it, fragility.

Before that, we were part of the present collective and future progeny. Both present and the future tribes exploited the fragility of individuals to strengthen themselves. People engaged in sacrifices, sought martyrdom, died for the group, and derived pride from doing so; they worked hard for future generations.

Sadly, as I am writing these lines, the economic system is loading future generations with public governmental debt, causing depletion of resources, and environmental blight to satisfy the requirements of the security analysts and the banking establishment (once again, we cannot separate fragility from ethics).

As I wrote in Chapter 4, while the gene is antifragile, since it is information, the carrier of the gene is fragile, and needs to be so for the gene to get stronger. We live to produce information, or improve on it. Nietzsche had the Latin pun *aut liberi, aut libri*—either children or books, both information that carries through the centuries.

I was just reading in John Gray's wonderful *The Immortalization Commission* about attempts to use science, in a postreligious world, to achieve immortality. I felt some deep disgust—as would any ancient—at the efforts of the "singularity" thinkers (such as Ray Kurzweil) who believe in humans' potential to live forever. Note that if I had to find the anti-me, the person with diametrically opposite ideas and lifestyle on the planet, it would be that Ray Kurzweil fellow. It is not just neomania. While I propose removing offensive elements from people's diets (and lives), he works by adding, popping close to two hundred pills daily. Beyond that, these attempts at immortality leave me with deep moral revulsion.

It is the same kind of deep internal disgust that takes hold of me when I see a rich eighty-two-year-old man surrounded with "babes," twentysomething mistresses (often Russian or Ukrainian). I am not here to live forever, as a sick animal. Recall that the antifragility of a system comes from the mortality of its components—and I am part of that larger population called humans. I am here to die a heroic death for the sake of the collective, to produce offspring (and prepare them for life and provide for them), or eventually, books—my information, that is, my genes, the antifragile in me, should be the ones seeking immortality, not me.

Then say goodbye, have a nice funeral in St. Sergius (Mar Sarkis) in Amioun, and, as the French say, *place aux autres*—make room for others.

BOOK VII

The Ethics of Fragility and Antifragility

———

Now, ethics. Under opacity and in the newfound complexity of the world, people can hide risks and hurt others, with the law incapable of catching them. Iatrogenics has both delayed and invisible consequences. It is hard to see causal links, to fully understand what's going on.

Under such epistemic limitations, skin in the game is the only true mitigator of fragility. Hammurabi's code provided a simple solution—close to thirty-seven hundred years ago. This solution has been increasingly abandoned in modern times, as we have developed a fondness for neomanic complication over archaic simplicity. We need to understand the everlasting solidity of such a solution.

CHAPTER 23

Skin in the Game: Antifragility and Optionality at the Expense of Others

Making talk less cheap—Looking at the spoils—Corporations with random acts of pity?—Predict and inverse predict

This chapter will look at what we are getting ourselves into when someone gets the upside, and a different person gets the downside.

The worst problem of modernity lies in the malignant transfer of fragility and antifragility from one party to the other, with one getting the benefits, the other one (unwittingly) getting the harm, with such transfer facilitated by the growing wedge between the ethical and the legal. This state of affairs has existed before, but is acute today—modernity hides it especially well.

It is, of course, an agency problem.

And the agency problem, is of course, an asymmetry.

We are witnessing a fundamental change. Consider older societies—those societies that have survived. The main difference between us and them is the disappearance of a sense of heroism; a shift away from a certain respect—and power—to those who take downside risks for others. For heroism is the exact inverse of the agency problem: someone elects to bear the disadvantage (risks his own life, or harm to himself, or, in milder forms, accepts to deprive himself of some benefits) for the sake of others. What we have currently is the opposite: power seems to go to those, like bankers, corporate executives (nonentrepreneurs), and politicians, who steal a free option from society.

And heroism is not just about riots and wars. An example of an inverse agency problem: as a child I was most impressed with the story of a nanny who died in order to save a child from being hit by a car. I find nothing more honorable than accepting death in someone else's place.

In other words, what is called sacrifice. And the word "sacrifice" is related to *sacred*, the domain of the holy that is separate from that of the profane.

In traditional societies, a person is only as respectable and as worthy as the downside he (or, more, a lot more, than expected, *she*) is willing to face for the sake of others. The most courageous, or valorous, occupy the highest rank in their society: knights, generals, commanders. Even mafia dons accept that such rank in the hierarchy makes them the most exposed to be whacked by competitors and the most penalized by the authorities. The same applies to saints, those who abdicate, devote their lives to serve others—to help the weak, the deprived, and the dispossessed.

So Table 7 presents another Triad: there are those with no skin in the game but who benefit from others, those who neither benefit from nor harm others, and, finally, the grand category of those sacrificial ones who take the harm for the sake of others.

TABLE 7 • ETHICS AND THE FOUNDATIONAL ASYMMETRY

NO SKIN IN THE GAME	SKIN IN THE GAME	SKIN IN THE GAME FOR THE SAKE OF OTHERS, OR SOUL IN THE GAME
(Keeps upside, transfers downside to others, owns a hidden option at someone else's expense)	(Keeps his own downside, takes his own risk)	(Takes the downside on behalf of others, or universal values)
Bureaucrats	Citizens	Saints, knights, warriors, soldiers
Cheap talk ("tawk" in Fat Tony's lingo)	Actions, no tawk	Expensive talk
Consultants, sophists	Merchants, businessmen	Prophets, philosophers (in the pre-modern sense)
Businesses	Artisans	Artists, some artisans
Corporate executives (with suit)	Entrepreneurs	Entrepreneurs/Innovators
Theoreticians, data miners, observational studies	Laboratory and field experimenters	Maverick scientists
Centralized government	Government of city-states	Municipal government
Editors	Writers	Great writers
Journalists who "analyze" and predict	Speculators	Journalists who take risks and *expose* frauds (powerful regimes, corporations)
Politicians	Activists	Rebels, dissidents, revolutionaries
Bankers	Traders	(They would not engage in vulgar commerce)
Fragilista Prof. Dr. Joseph Stiglitz	Fat Tony	Nero Tulip
Risk vendors		Taxpayers (not quite voluntarily soul in the game, but they are victims)

Let me follow my emotions and start with the third column, on the far right, the one about heroes and people of courage. The robustness—even antifragility—of society depends on them; if we are here today, it is because someone, at some stage, took some risks for us. But courage and heroism do not mean blind risk taking—it is not necessarily recklessness. There is a pseudocourage that comes from risk blindness, in which people underestimate the odds of failure. We have ample evidence that the very same people become chicken and overreact in the face of real risks; the exact opposite. For the Stoics, prudence is connatural to courage—the courage to fight your own impulses (in an aphorism by—who else—Publilius Syrus, prudence was deemed the courage of the general).

Heroism has evolved through civilization from the martial arena to that of ideas. Initially, in preclassical times, the Homeric hero was someone principally endowed with physical courage—since everything was physical. In later classical times, for such people as the great Lacedaemonian king Agiselaus, a truly happy life was one crowned by the privilege of death in battle, little else, perhaps even nothing else. But for Agiselaus, courage had already evolved from purely martial prowess into something greater. Courage was often seen in acts of renunciation, as when one is ready to sacrifice himself for the benefit of others, of the collective, something altruistic.

Finally, a new form of courage was born, that of the Socratic Plato, which is the very definition of the modern man: the courage to stand up for an idea, and enjoy death in a state of thrill, simply because the privilege of dying for truth, or standing up for one's values, had become the highest form of honor. And no one has had more prestige in history than two thinkers who overtly and defiantly sacrificed their lives for their ideas—two Eastern Mediterraneans; one Greek and one Semite.

We should pause a little when we hear *happiness* defined as an economic or otherwise puny materialistic condition. You can imagine how distraught I feel when I hear about the glorified heroism-free "middle class values," which, thanks to globalization and the Internet, have spread to any place easily reached by British Air, enshrining the usual opiates of the deified classes: "hard work" for a bank or a tobacco company, diligent newspaper reading, obedience to most, but not all, traffic laws, captivity in some corporate structure, dependence on the opinion of a boss (with one's job records filed in the personnel department), good legal compliance, reliance on stock market investments, tropical vacations, and a suburban life (under some mortgage) with a nice-looking dog and Saturday night wine tasting. Those who meet with some success enter the gallery of the annual billionaire list, where they will hope to spend some time before their fertilizer sales are challenged by competitors from China. They will be called heroes—rather than lucky. Further, if success is random, a conscious act of heroism is nonrandom. And the "ethical" middle class may work for a tobacco company—and thanks to casuistry call themselves ethical.

I am even more distraught for the future of the human race when I see a nerd behind a computer in a D.C. suburb, walking distance from a Starbucks coffeehouse, or a shopping mall, capable of blowing up an entire battalion in a remote place, say Pakistan, and afterward going to the gym for a "workout" (compare his culture to that of knights or samurai). Cowardice enhanced by technology is all connected: society is fragilized by spineless politicians, draft dodgers afraid of polls, and journalists building narratives, who create explosive deficits and compound agency problems because they want to look good in the short term.

A disclaimer. Table 7 does not imply that those with soul in the game are necessarily right or that dying for one's ideas makes one necessarily good for the rest of us: many messianic utopians have caused quite a bit of harm. Nor is a grandiose death a necessity: many people fight evil in the patient grind of their daily lives without looking like heroes; they suffer society's ingratitude even more—while media-friendly pseudo-heroes rise in status. These people will not get a statue from future generations.

A half-man (or, rather, half-person) is not someone who does not have an opinion, just someone who does not take risks for it.

The great historian Paul Veyne has recently shown that it is a big myth that gladiators were forced labor. Most were volunteers who wanted the chance to become heroes by risking their lives and winning, or, when failing, to show in front of the largest crowd in the world how they were able to die honorably, without cowering—when a gladiator loses the fight the crowd decides whether he should be spared or put to death by the opponent. And spectators did not care for nonvolunteers, as these did not have their soul in the fight.

My greatest lesson in courage came from my father—as a child, I had admired him before for his erudition, but was not overly fazed since erudition on its own does not make a man. He had a large ego and immense dignity, and he demanded respect. He was once insulted by a militiaman at a road check during the Lebanese war. He refused to comply, and got angry at the militiaman for being disrespectful. As he drove away, the gunman shot him in the back. The bullet stayed in his chest for the rest of his life so he had to carry an X-ray image through airport terminals. This set the bar very high for me: dignity is worth nothing unless you earn it, unless you are willing to pay a price for it.

A lesson I learned from this ancient culture is the notion of *megalopsychon* (a term expressed in Aristotle's ethics), a sense of grandeur that was superseded by the Christian value of "humility." There is no word for it in Romance languages; in Arabic it is called *Shhm*—best translated as *nonsmall*. If you take risks and face your fate with dignity, there is nothing you can do that makes you small; if you don't take risks, there is nothing you can do that makes you grand, nothing. And when you take risks, insults by half-men (small men, those who don't risk anything) are similar to barks by nonhuman animals: you can't feel insulted by a dog.

HAMMURABI

Let us now work with the elements of Table 7 and bring the unifying foundational asymmetry (between upside and downside) into our central theme, ethics. Just as only business school professors and similar fragilistas separate robustness and growth, we cannot separate fragility and ethics.

Some people have options, or have optionality, at the expense of others. And the others don't know it.

The effects of transfers of fragility are becoming more acute, as modernity is building up more and more people on the left column—inverse heroes, so to say. So many professions, most arising from modernity, are affected, becoming more antifragile at the expense of our fragility—tenured government employees, academic researchers, journalists (of the non-myth-busting variety), the medical establishment, Big Pharma, and many more. Now how do we solve the problem? As usual, with some great help from the ancients.

Hammurabi's code—now about 3,800 years old—identifies the need to reestablish a symmetry of fragility, spelled out as follows:

> If a builder builds a house and the house collapses and causes the death of the owner of the house—the builder shall be put to

death. If it causes the death of the son of the owner of the house, a son of that builder shall be put to death. If it causes the death of a slave of the owner of the house—he shall give to the owner of the house a slave of equal value.

It looks like they were much more advanced 3,800 years ago than we are today. The entire idea is that the builder knows more, a lot more, than any safety inspector, particularly about what lies hidden in the foundations—making it the best risk management rule ever, as the foundation, with delayed collapse, is the best place to hide risk. Hammurabi and his advisors understood small probabilities.

Now, clearly the object here is not to punish retrospectively, but to save lives by providing up-front disincentive in case of harm to others during the fulfillment of one's profession.

These asymmetries are particularly severe when it comes to small-probability extreme events, that is, Black Swans—as these are the most misunderstood and their exposure is easiest to hide.

Fat Tony has two heuristics.

First, *never get on a plane if the pilot is not on board.*

Second, *make sure there is also a copilot.*

The first heuristic addresses the asymmetry in rewards and punishment, or transfer of fragility between individuals. Ralph Nader has a simple rule: people voting for war need to have at least one descendant (child or grandchild) exposed to combat. For the Romans, engineers needed to spend some time under the bridge they built—something that should be required of financial engineers today. The English went further and had the families of the engineers spend time with them under the bridge after it was built.

To me, every opinion maker needs to have "skin in the game" in the event of harm caused by reliance on his information or opinion (not having such persons as, say, the people who helped cause the criminal Iraq invasion come out of it completely unscathed). Further, anyone producing a forecast or making an economic analysis needs to have something to lose from it, given that others rely on those forecasts (to repeat, forecasts induce risk taking; they are more toxic to us than any other form of human pollution).

We can derive plenty of sub-heuristics from Fat Tony's rules, particularly to mitigate the weaknesses of predictive systems. Predicting—any prediction—without skin in the game can be as dangerous for others as unmanned nuclear plants without the engineer sleeping on the premises. Pilots should be on the plane.

The second heuristic is that we need to build redundancy, a margin of safety, avoiding optimization, mitigating (even removing) asymmetries in our sensitivity to risk.

The rest of this chapter will present a few syndromes, with, of course, some ancient remedies.

THE TALKER'S FREE OPTION

We closed Book I by arguing that we need to put entrepreneurs and risk takers, "failed" or not, on top of the pyramid, and, unless they take personal risks when they expose others, academizing academics, talkers, and political politicians at the bottom. The problem is that society is currently doing the exact opposite, granting mere talkers a free option.

The idea that Fat Tony milked suckers when they ran to the exit door seemed at first quite inelegant to Nero. Benefiting from the misfortune of others—no matter how hideous these are and can be—is not the most graceful approach to life. But Tony had something at risk, and would have been personally harmed by an adverse outcome. Fat Tony had no agency problem. This makes it permissible. For there is an even worse problem associated with the opposite situation: people who just *talk,* prognosticate, theorize.

In fact, speculative risk taking is not just permissible; it is mandatory. No opinion without risk; and, of course, no risk without hope for return. If Fat Tony had an opinion, he felt he needed, for ethical reasons, to have a corresponding exposure. As they say in Bensonhurst, you got to do so if you have an opinion. Otherwise, you do not really have an opinion at all. You need to be earmarked as someone who has no downside for his opinion, with a special status in society, perhaps something below that of ordinary citizen. Commentators need to have a status *below* ordinary citizens. Regular citizens, at least, face the downside of their statements.

So counter to the entire idea of the intellectual and commentator as a detached and protected member of society, I am stating here that I find it profoundly unethical to talk without doing, without exposure to harm, without having one's skin in the game, without having something at risk. You express your opinion; it can hurt others (who rely on it), yet you incur no liability. Is this fair?

But this is the information age. This effect of transferring fragility might have been present throughout history, but it is much more acute now, under modernity's connectivity, and the newfound invisibility of causal chains. The intellectual today is vastly more powerful and dangerous than before. The "knowledge world" causes separation of knowing and doing (within the same person) and leads to the fragility of society. How?

In the old days, privilege came with obligations—except for the small class of intellectuals who served a patron or, in some cases, the state. You want to be a feudal lord—you will be first to die. You want war? First in battle. Let us not forget something embedded in the U.S. Constitution: the president is commander in chief. Caesar, Alexander, and Hannibal were on the battlefield—the last, according to Livy, was first-in, last-out of combat zones. George Washington, too, went to battle, unlike Ronald Reagan and George W. Bush, who played video games while threatening the lives of others. Even Napoleon was personally exposed to risks; his showing up during a battle was the equivalent of adding twenty-five thousand troops. Churchill showed an impressive amount of physical courage. They were in it; they believed in it. Status implied you took physical risks.

Note that in traditional societies even those who fail—but have taken risks—have a higher status than those who are not exposed.

Now, again, the idiocy of predictive systems, making me emotional. We may have more social justice today than before the Enlightenment, but we also have more, a lot more transfers of optionality, more than ever—a patent setback. Let me explain. This knowledge shknowledge business necessarily means shifting to talk. Talk by academics, consultants, and journalists, when it comes to predictions, can be just *talk*, devoid of embodiment and stripped of true evidence. As in anything with words, it is not the victory of the most correct, but that of the most charming—or the one who can produce the most academic-sounding material.

We mentioned earlier how the political philosopher Raymond Aron sounded uninteresting in spite of his predictive abilities, while those who were wrong about Stalinism survived beautifully. Aron was about as colorless as they come: in spite of his prophetic insights he looked, wrote, and lived like a tax accountant while his enemy, say, Jean-Paul Sartre, who led a flamboyant lifestyle, got just about everything wrong and even put up with the occupying Germans in an extremely cowardly manner. Sartre the coward looked radiant, impressive, and, alas, his books survived (please stop calling him a Voltaire; he was no Voltaire).

I got nauseous in Davos making eye contact with the fragilista journalist Thomas Friedman who, thanks to his influential newspaper op-eds, helped cause the Iraq war. He paid no price for the mistake. The real reason for my malaise was perhaps not just that I saw someone I consider vile and harmful. I just get disturbed when I see wrong and do nothing about it; it is biological. It is guilt, for Baal's sake, and guilt is what I do not have to put up with. There is another central element of ancient Mediterranean ethics: *Factum tacendo, crimen facias acrius:* For Publilius Syrus, he who does not stop a crime is an accomplice. (I've stated my own version of this in the prologue, which needs to be reiterated: if you see fraud and don't say fraud, you are a fraud.)

Thomas Friedman was a bit responsible for the Iraq invasion of 2003, and not only paid no penalty for it but continues to write for the op-ed page of *The New York Times,* confusing innocent people. He got—and kept—the upside, others get the downside. A writer with arguments can harm more people than any serial criminal. I am singling him out here because, at the core, the problem is his promotion of the misunderstanding of iatrogenics in complex systems. He promoted the "earth is flat" idea of globalization without realizing that globalization brings fragilities, causes more extreme events as a side effect, and requires a great deal of redundancies to operate properly. And the very same error holds with the Iraq invasion: in such a complex system, the predictability of the consequences is very low, so invading was epistemologically irresponsible.

Natural and ancestral systems work by penalties: no perpetual free option given to anyone. So does society in many things with visible effects. If someone drives a school bus blindfolded, and has an accident, he either exits the gene pool the old-fashioned way, or, if for some reason he is not harmed by the accident, he will incur enough penalties to be prevented from driving other people ever again. The problem is that the journalist Thomas Friedman is still driving the bus. There is no penalty for opinion makers who harm society. And this is a very bad practice.

The Obama administration was after the crisis of 2008 populated with people who drove the bus blindfolded. The iatrogenists got promoted.

Postdicting

Words are dangerous: postdictors, who explain things after the fact—because they are in the business of talking—always look smarter than predictors.

Because of the retrospective distortion, people who of course did not see an event coming will remember some thought to the effect that they did, and will manage to convince themselves that they predicted it, before proceeding to convince others. There will be after every event many more postdictors than true predictors, people who had an idea in the shower without taking it to its logical conclusion, and, given that many people take a lot of showers, say, nearly twice a day (if you include the gym or the episode with the mistress), they will have a large repertoire to draw from. They will not remember the numerous bath-generated ideas they had in the past that were either noise, or that contradicted the observed present—but as humans crave self-consistency, they will retain those elements of what they thought in the past that cohere with their perception of the present.

So opinion makers who were so proudly and professionally providing idle babble will eventually appear to win an argument, since they are the ones writing, and suckers who got in trouble from reading them will again look to them for future guidance, and will again get in trouble.

The past is fluid, marred with selection biases and constantly revised memories. It is a central property of suckers that they will never know they were the suckers because that's how our minds work. (Even so, one is struck with the following fact: the fragilista crisis that started in 2007–2008 had many, many fewer *near-predictors* than random.)

> *The asymmetry (antifragility of postdictors): postdictors can cherry-pick and produce instances in which their opinions played out and discard mispredictions into the bowels of history. It is like a free option—to them; we pay for it.*

Since they have the option, the fragilistas are personally antifragile: volatility tends to benefit them: the more volatility, the higher the illusion of intelligence.

But evidence of whether one has been a sucker or a nonsucker is easy to ferret out by looking at actual records, actions. Actions are symmetric, do not allow cherry-picking, remove the free option. When you look at the actual history of someone's activities, instead of what thoughts he will deliver after the facts, things become crystal clear. The option is gone. Reality removes the uncertainty, the imprecision, the vagueness, the self-serving mental biases that make us appear more intelligent. Mistakes are costly, no longer free, but being right brings actual rewards. Of course, there are other checks one can do to assess the b***t component of life: investigate people's decisions as expressed through their own investments. You would discover that many people who claim to have foreseen the collapse of the financial system had financial companies in their portfolios. Indeed, there was no need to "profit" from events like Tony and Nero to show nonsuckerness: just avoiding being hurt by them would have been sufficient.

> *I want predictors to have visible scars on their body from prediction errors, not distribute these errors to society.*

You cannot sit and moan about the world. You need to come out on top. So Tony was right to insist that Nero take a ritual look at the physical embodiment of the spoils, like a bank account statement—as we said, it had nothing to do with financial value, nor purchasing power, just symbolic value. We saw in Chapter 9 how Julius Caesar needed to incur the cost of having Vercingetorix brought to Rome and paraded. An intangible victory has no value.

Verba volent, words fly. Never have people who talk and don't do been more visible, and played a larger role, than in modern times. This is the product of modernism and division of tasks.

Recall that I said that America's strength was risk taking and harboring risk takers (the right kind, the Thalesian king of high-failure, long-optionality type). Sorry, but we have been moving away from this model.

The Stiglitz Syndrome

There is something more severe than the problem with Thomas Friedman, which can be generalized to represent someone causing action while being completely unaccountable for his words.

The phenomenon I will call the Stiglitz syndrome, after an academic economist of the so-called "intelligent" variety called Joseph Stiglitz, is as follows.

Remember the fragility detection in Chapter 19 and my obsession with Fannie Mae. Luckily, I had some skin in the game for my opinions, be it through exposure to a smear campaign. And, in 2008, no surprise, Fannie Mae went bust, I repeat, costing the U.S. taxpayer hundreds of billions (and counting)—generally, the financial system, with similar risks, exploded. The entire banking system had similar exposures.

But around the same period, Joseph Stiglitz, with two colleagues, the Orszag brothers (Peter and Jonathan), looked at the very same Fannie Mae. They assessed, in a report, that "on the basis of historical experience, the risk to the government from a potential default on GSE debt is effectively zero."* Supposedly, they ran simulations—but didn't see the obvious. They also said that the probability of a default was found to be "so small that it is difficult to detect." It is statements like these and, to me, only statements like these (intellectual hubris and the illusion of understanding of rare events) that caused the buildup of these exposures to rare events in the economy. This is the Black Swan problem that I was fighting. This is Fukushima.

Now the culmination is that Stiglitz writes in 2010 in his *I-told-you-so* book that he claims to have "predicted" the crisis that started in 2007–2008.

Look at this aberrant case of antifragility provided to Stiglitz and his colleagues by society. It turns out that Stiglitz was not just a nonpredictor (by my standards) but was also part of the problem that caused the events, these accumulations of exposures to small probabilities. But he did not notice it! An academic is not designed to remember his opinions because he doesn't have anything at risk from them.

At the core, people are dangerous when they have that strange skill that allows their papers to be published in journals but decreases their understanding of risk. So the very same economist who caused the problem then postdicted the crisis, and then became a theorist on what happened. No wonder we will have larger crises.

The central point: had Stiglitz been a businessman with his own money on the line, he would have blown up, terminated. Or had he been in nature, his genes would have been made extinct—so people with such

* GSE is Fannie Mae and Freddie Mac—they both blew up.

misunderstanding of probability would eventually disappear from our DNA. What I found nauseating was the government hiring one of his coauthors.*

I am reluctantly calling the syndrome by Stiglitz's name because I find him the smartest of economists, one with the most developed intellect for things *on paper*—except that he has no clue about the fragility of systems. And Stiglitz symbolizes harmful misunderstanding of small probabilities by the economics establishment. It is a severe disease, one that explains why economists will blow us up again.

The Stiglitz syndrome corresponds to a form of cherry-picking, the nastiest variety because the perpetrator is not aware of what he is doing. It is a situation in which someone doesn't just fail to detect a hazard but contributes to its cause while ending up convincing himself—and sometimes others—of the opposite, namely, that he predicted it and warned against it. It corresponds to a combination of remarkable analytical skills, blindness to fragility, selective memory, and absence of skin in the game.

Stiglitz Syndrome = fragilista (with good intentions) + ex post cherry-picking

There are other lessons here, related to the absence of penalty. This is an illustration of the academics-who-write-papers-and-talk syndrome in its greatest severity (unless, as we will see, they have their soul in it). So many academics propose something in one paper, then the opposite in another paper, without penalty to themselves from having been wrong in the first paper since there is a need only for consistency *within* a single paper, not *across* one's career. This would be fine, as someone may evolve and contradict earlier beliefs, but then the earlier "result" should be withdrawn from circulation and superseded with a new one—with books, the new edition supersedes the preceding one. This absence of penalty makes them antifragile at the expense of the society that accepts the "rigor" of their results. Further, I am not doubting Stiglitz's sincerity, or some weak form of sincerity: I believe he genuinely thinks he predicted the financial crisis, so let me rephrase the problem: the problem

---

* I find it truly disgusting that one of the Orszag brothers, Peter, after the crisis got a job with the Obama administration—another rehiring of blindfolded bus drivers. Then he became vice chairman of Citibank, which explains why Citibank will blow up again (and we taxpayers will end up subsidizing his high salary).

with people who do not incur harm is that they can cherry-pick from statements they've made in the past, many of them contradictory, and end up convincing themselves of their intellectual lucidity on the way to the World Economic Forum at Davos.

There is the iatrogenics of the medical charlatan and snake oil salesperson causing harm, but he sort of knows it and lies low after he is caught. And there is a far more vicious form of iatrogenics by experts who use their more acceptable status to claim later that they warned of harm. As these did not know they were causing iatrogenics, they cure iatrogenics with iatrogenics. Then things explode.

Finally, the cure to many ethical problems maps to the exact cure for the Stiglitz effect, which I state now.

> *Never ask anyone for their opinion, forecast, or recommendation. Just ask them what they have—or don't have—in their portfolio.*

We now know that many innocent retirees have been harmed by the incompetence of the rating agencies—it was a bit more than incompetence. Many subprime loans were toxic waste dressed as "AAA," meaning near-government grade in safety. People were innocently led into putting their savings into them—and, further, regulators were forcing portfolio managers to use the assessment of the rating agencies. But rating agencies are protected: they present themselves as press—without the noble mission of the press to expose frauds. And they benefit from the protection of free speech—the "First Amendment" so ingrained in American habits. My humble proposal: one should say whatever he wants, but one's portfolio needs to line up with it. And, of course, regulators should not be fragilistas by giving their stamp to predictive approaches—hence junk science.

The psychologist Gerd Gigerenzer has a simple heuristic. Never ask the doctor what *you* should do. Ask him what *he* would do if he were in your place. You would be surprised at the difference.

The Problem of Frequency, or How to Lose Arguments

Recall that Fat Tony was in favor of just "making a buck" as opposed to being "proven right." The point has a statistical dimension. Let us return to the distinction between Thalesian and Aristotelian for a minute and look at evolution from the following point of view. The frequency, i.e., how *often* someone is right is largely irrelevant in the real world, but alas, one needs to be a practitioner, not a talker, to figure it out. On paper, the frequency of being right matters, but only on paper—typically, fragile payoffs have little (sometimes no) upside, and antifragile payoffs have little downside. This means that one makes pennies to lose dollars in the fragile case; makes dollars to lose pennies in the antifragile one. So the antifragile can lose for a long time with impunity, so long as he happens to be right once; for the fragile, a single loss can be terminal.

Accordingly if you were betting on the downfall of, say, a portfolio of financial institutions because of their fragilities, it would have cost you pennies over the years preceding their eventual demise in 2008, as Nero and Tony did. (Note again that taking the other side of fragility makes you antifragile.) You were wrong for years, right for a moment, losing small, winning big, so vastly more successful than the other way (actually the other way would be bust). So you would have made the Thekels like Thales because betting against the fragile is antifragile. But someone who had merely "predicted" the event with just words would have been called by the journalists "wrong for years," "wrong most of the time," etc.

Should we keep tally of opinion makers' "right" and "wrong," the proportion does not matter, as we need to include consequences. And given that this is impossible, we are now in a quandary.

Look at it again, the way we looked at entrepreneurs. They are usually wrong and make "mistakes"—plenty of mistakes. They are convex. So what counts is the payoff from success.

Let me rephrase again. Decision making in the real world, that is, deeds, are Thalesian, while forecasting *in words* is Aristotelian. As we saw in the discussion in Chapter 12, one side of a decision has larger consequences than the other—we don't have evidence that people are terrorists but we check them for weapons; we don't believe the water is poisonous but we avoid drinking it; something that would be absurd for someone narrowly applying Aristotelian logic. To put in Fat Tony terms: suckers try to be right, nonsuckers try to make the buck, or:

Suckers try to win arguments, nonsuckers try to win.

To put it again in other words: it is rather a good thing to lose arguments.

The Right Decision for the Wrong Reason

More generally, for Mother Nature, opinions and predictions don't count; surviving is what matters.

There is an evolutionary argument here. It appears to be the most underestimated argument in favor of free enterprise and a society driven by individual doers, what Adam Smith called "adventurers," not central planners and bureaucratic apparatuses. We saw that bureaucrats (whether in government or large corporations) live in a system of rewards based on narratives, "tawk," and the opinion of others, with job evaluation and peer reviews—in other words, what we call marketing. Aristotelian, that is. Yet the biological world evolves by survival, not opinions and "I predicted" and "I told you so." Evolution dislikes the confirmation fallacy, endemic in society.

The economic world should, too, but institutions mess things up, as suckers may get bigger—institutions block evolution with bailouts and statism. Note that, in the long term, social and economic evolution nastily takes place by surprises, discontinuities, and jumps.*

We mentioned earlier Karl Popper's ideas on evolutionary epistemology; not being a decision maker, he was under the illusion that ideas compete with each other, with the least wrong surviving at any point in time. He missed the point that it is not ideas that survive, but people who have the right ones, or societies that have the correct heuristics, or the ones, right or wrong, that lead them to do the good thing. He missed the Thalesian effect, the fact that a wrong idea that is harmless can survive. Those who have wrong heuristics—but with a small harm in the event of error—will survive. Behavior called "irrational" can be good if it is harmless.

Let me give an example of a type of false belief that is helpful for survival. In your opinion, which is more dangerous, to mistake a bear for a stone, or mistake a stone for a bear? It is hard for humans to make the first mistake; our intuitions make us overreact at the smallest probability of harm and fall for a certain class of false patterns—those who

---

* My suggestion to deter "too big to fail" and prevent employers from taking advantage of the public is as follows. A company that is classified as potentially *bailable out* should it fail should not be able to pay anyone more than a corresponding civil servant. Otherwise people should be free to pay each other what they want since it does not affect the taxpayer. Such limitation would force companies to stay small enough that they would not be considered for a bailout in the event of their failure.

overreact upon seeing what may look like a bear have had a survival advantage, those who made the opposite mistake left the gene pool.

Our mission is to make talk less cheap.

THE ANCIENTS AND THE STIGLITZ SYNDROME

We saw how the ancients understood the Stiglitz syndrome—and associated ones—rather well. In fact they had quite sophisticated mechanisms to counter most aspects of agency problems, whether individual or collective (the circular effect of hiding behind the collective). Earlier, I mentioned the Romans forcing engineers to spend time under the bridge they built. They would have had Stiglitz and Orszag sleep under the bridge of Fannie Mae and exit the gene pool (so they wouldn't harm us again).

The Romans had even more powerful heuristics for situations few today have thought about, solving potent game-theoretic problems. Roman soldiers were forced to sign a *sacramentum* accepting punishment in the event of failure—a kind of pact between the soldier and the army spelling out commitment for upside and downside.

Assume that you and I are facing a small leopard or a wild animal in the jungle. The two of us can possibly overcome it by joining forces—but each one of us is individually weak. Now, if you run away, all you need to be is just faster than me, not faster than the animal. So it would be optimal for the one who can run away the fastest, that is, the most cowardly, to just be a coward and let the other one perish.

The Romans removed the soldiers' incentive to be a coward and hurt others thanks to a process called *decimation*. If a legion loses a battle and there is suspicion of cowardice, 10 percent of the soldiers and commanders are put to death, usually by random lottery. Decimation—meaning eliminating one in ten—has been corrupted by modern language. The magic number is one in ten (or something equivalent): putting more than 10 per cent to death would lead to weakening of the army; too little, and cowardice would be a dominant strategy.

And the mechanism must have worked well as a deterrent against cowardice, since it was not commonly applied.

The English applied a version of it. Admiral John Byng was court-martialed and sentenced to death as he was found guilty of failing to "do his utmost" to prevent Minorca from falling to the French following the Battle of Minorca in 1757.

To Burn One's Vessels

Playing on one's inner agency problem can go beyond symmetry: give soldiers no options and see how antifragile they can get.

On April 29, 711, the armies of the Arab commander Tarek crossed the Strait of Gibraltar from Morocco into Spain with a small army (the name Gibraltar is derived from the Arabic *Jabal Tarek*, meaning "mount of Tarek"). Upon landing, Tarek had his ships put to the fire. He then made a famous speech every schoolchild memorized during my school days that I translate loosely: "Behind you is the sea, before you, the enemy. You are vastly outnumbered. All you have is sword and courage."

And Tarek and his small army took control of Spain. The same heuristic seems to have played out throughout history, from Cortés in Mexico, eight hundred years later, to Agathocles of Syracuse, eight hundred years earlier—ironically, Agathocles was heading southward, in the opposite direction as Tarek, as he was fighting the Carthaginians and landed in Africa.

Never put your enemy's back to the wall.

How Poetry Can Kill You

Ask a polyglot who knows Arabic who he considers the best poet—in any language—and odds are that he would answer Almutanabbi, who lived about a thousand years ago; his poetry in the original has a hypnotic effect on the reader (listener), rivaled only by the grip of Pushkin on Russian speakers. The problem is that Almutanabbi knew it; his name was literally "He who thinks of himself as a prophet," on account of his perceived oversized ego. For a taste of his bombast, one of his poems informs us that his poetry is so potent "that blind people can read it" and "deaf people can listen to it." Well, Almutanabbi was that rare case of a poet with skin in the game, dying for his poetry.

For in the same egotistical poem, Almutanabbi boasts, in a breathtaking display of linguistic magic, that he walks the walk, in addition to being the most imaginably potent poet—which I insist he was—he knew "the horse, the night, the desert, the pen, the book"—and thanks to his courage he got respect from the lion.

Well, the poem cost him his life. For Almutanabbi had—characteristically—vilified a desert tribe in one of his poems and they were out to get him. They reached him as he was traveling. As he was outnumbered, he started to do the rational thing and run away, nothing shameful, except that one of his companions started reciting "the horse, the night . . ." back at him. He turned around and confronted the tribe to his certain death. Thus Almutanabbi remains, a thousand years later, the poet who died simply to avoid the dishonor of running away, and when we recite his verses we know they are genuine.

My childhood role model was the French adventurer and writer André Malraux. He imbued his writings with his own risk taking: Malraux was a school dropout—while extremely well read—who became an adventurer in Asia in his twenties. He was an active pilot during the Spanish Civil War and later an active member of the French underground resistance during the Second World War. He turned out to be a bit of a mythomaniac, unnecessarily glorifying his meetings with great men and statesmen. He just could not bear the idea of a writer being an intellectual. But unlike Hemingway, who was mostly into image building, he was the real thing. And he never engaged in small talk—his biographer reports that while other writers were discussing copyrights and royalties, he would steer the conversation to theology (he supposedly said *the twenty-first century will be religious or will not be*). One of my saddest days was when he died.

The Problem of Insulation

The system does not give researchers the incentive to be a Malraux. The great skeptic Hume was said to leave his skeptical angst in the philosophical cabinet, then go party with his friends in Edinburgh (though his idea of partying was rather too . . . Edinburgh). The philosopher Myles Burnyeat called this the "problem of insulation," particularly with skeptics who are skeptics in one domain but not another. He provides the example of a philosopher who puzzles about the reality of time, but who nonetheless applies for a research grant to work on the philosophical problem of time during next year's sabbatical—without doubting the reality of next year's arrival. For Burnyeat, the philosopher "insulates his ordinary first order judgments from the effects of his philosophizing." Sorry, Professor Doctor Burnyeat; I agree that philosophy is the only field (and its sibling, pure mathematics) that does not need to connect to reality. But then make it a parlor game and give it another name . . .

Likewise, Gerd Gigerenzer reports a more serious violation on the part of Harry Markowitz, who started a method called "portfolio selection" and received the same iatrogenic Swedish Riskbank prize (called "Nobel" in economics) for it, like other fragilistas such as Fragilista Merton and Fragilista Stiglitz. I spent part of my adult life calling it charlatanism, as it has no validity outside of academic endorsements and causes blowups (as explained in the Appendix). Well, Doctor Professor Fragilista Markowitz does not use his method for his own portfolio; he has recourse to more sophisticated (and simpler to implement) cabdrivers' methodologies, closer to the one Mandelbrot and I have proposed.

I believe that forcing researchers to eat their own cooking whenever possible solves a serious problem in science. Take this simple heuristic—does the scientific researcher whose ideas are applicable to the real world apply his ideas to his daily life? If so, take him seriously. Otherwise, ignore him. (If the fellow is doing pure mathematics or theology, or teaching poetry, then there is no problem. But if he is doing something applicable, then: red flag.)

This brings us to Triffat-type fakeness compared to Seneca, the talker versus the doer. I applied this method of ignoring what an academic writes and focusing on what he does when I met a researcher on happiness who held that *anything one makes beyond $50,000 does not bring any additional happiness*—he was then earning more than twice that at a university, so according to his metric he was safe. The argument seen through his "experiments" published in "highly cited papers" (that is, by other academics) seemed convincing on paper—although I am not particularly crazy about the notion of "happiness" or the vulgarity of the modern interpretation of "seeking happiness." So, like an idiot, I believed him. But a year or so later, I heard that he was particularly avid for dollars and spent his time on the road speaking for fees. That, to me, was more sufficient evidence than thousands of citations.

Champagne Socialism

Another blatant case of insulation. Sometimes the divorce between one's "tawk" and one's life can be overtly and convincingly visible: take people who want others to live a certain way but don't really like it for themselves.

Never listen to a leftist who does not give away his fortune or does not live the exact lifestyle he wants others to follow. What the French call "the caviar left," *la gauche caviar,* or what Anglo-Saxons call champagne socialists, are people who advocate socialism, sometimes even communism, or some political system with sumptuary limitations, while overtly leading a lavish lifestyle, often financed by inheritance—not realizing the contradiction that they want others to avoid just such a lifestyle. It is not too different from the womanizing popes, such as John XII, or the Borgias. The contradiction can exceed the ludicrous as with French president François Mitterrand of France who, coming in on a socialist platform, emulated the pomp of French monarchs. Even more ironic, his traditional archenemy, the conservative General de Gaulle, led a life of old-style austerity and had his wife sew his socks.

I have witnessed even worse. A former client of mine, a rich fellow with what appeared to be a social mission, tried to pressure me to write a check to a candidate in an election on a platform of higher taxes. I resisted, on ethical grounds. But I thought that the fellow was heroic, for, should the candidate win, his own taxes would increase by a considerable amount. A year later I discovered that the client was being investigated for his involvement in a very large scheme to be shielded from taxes. He wanted to be sure that *others* paid more taxes.

I developed a friendship over the past few years with the activist Ralph Nader and saw contrasting attributes. Aside from an astonishing amount of personal courage and total indifference toward smear campaigns, he exhibits absolutely no divorce between what he preaches and his lifestyle, none. Just like saints who have soul in their game. The man is a secular saint.

Soul in the Game

There is a class of people who escape bureaucrato-journalistic "tawk": those who have more than their skin in the game. *They have their soul in the game.*

Consider prophets. Prophecy is a pledge of belief, little else. A prophet is not someone who first had an idea; he is the one to first believe in it—and take it to its conclusion.

Chapter 20 discussed prophecy, when done right, as subtraction, and detection of fragility. But if having skin in the game (and accepting downside) is what distinguishes the genuine thinker from ex post "tawk," there is one step beyond needed to reach the rank of prophet. It is a matter of commitment, or what philosophers call *doxastic commitment,* a type of belief-pledge that to Fat Tony and Nero needed to be translated into deeds (the reverse-Stiglitz). *Doxa* in Greek used to mean "belief," but distinguished from "knowledge" (episteme); to see how it involves a commitment of sorts beyond just words, consider that in church Greek it took the meaning of *glorification.*

Incidentally, this notion also applies to all manner of ideas and theories: the main person behind a theory, the person to be called the originator, is someone who believed in it, in a doxastic way, with a costly commitment to take it to its natural conclusion; and not necessarily the first person to mention it over dessert wine or in a footnote.

Only he who has true beliefs will avoid eventually contradicting himself and falling into the errors of postdicting.

OPTIONS, ANTIFRAGILITY, AND SOCIAL FAIRNESS

The stock market: the greatest, industrial-sized, transfer of antifragility in history—due to a vicious form of asymmetric skin in the game. I am not talking about investment here—but the current system of packaging investments into shares of "public" corporations, with managers allowed to game the system, and of course, getting more prestige than the real risk takers, the entrepreneurs.

A blatant manifestation of the agency problem is the following. There is a difference between a manager running a company that is not his own and an owner-operated business in which the manager does not need to report numbers to anyone but himself, and for which he has a downside. Corporate managers have incentives without disincentives— something the general public doesn't quite get, as they have the illusion that managers are properly "incentivized." Somehow these managers have been given free options by innocent savers and investors. I am concerned here with managers of businesses that are *not* owner-operated.

As I am writing these lines the United States stock market has cost retirees more than three trillion dollars in losses over the past dozen years compared to leaving money in government money market funds (I am being generous, the difference is even higher), while managers of the companies composing the stock market, thanks to the asymmetry of the stock option, are richer by close to four hundred billion dollars. They pulled a Thales on these poor savers. Even more outrageous is the fate of the banking industry: banks have lost more than they ever made in their history, with their managers being paid billions in compensation—taxpayers take the downside, bankers get the upside. And the policies aiming at correcting the problem are hurting innocent people while bankers are sipping the Rosé de Provence brand of summer wine on their yachts in St. Tropez.

The asymmetry is visibly present: volatility benefits managers since they only get one side of the payoffs. The main point (alas, missed by almost everyone) is that they stand to gain from volatility—the more variations, the more value to this asymmetry. Hence they are antifragile.

To see how transfer of antifragility works, consider two scenarios, in which the market does the same thing on average but following different paths.

Path 1: market goes up 50 percent, then goes back down to erase all gains.

Path 2: market does not move at all.

Visibly Path 1, the more volatile, is more profitable to the managers, who can cash in their stock options. So the more jagged the route, the better it is for them.

And of course society—here the retirees—has the exact opposite payoff since they finance bankers and chief executives. Retirees get less upside than downside. Society pays for the losses of the bankers, but gets no bonuses from them. If you don't see this transfer of antifragility as theft, you certainly have a problem.

What is worse, this system is called "incentive-based" and supposed to correspond to capitalism. Supposedly managers' interests are aligned with those of the shareholders. What incentive? There is upside and no downside, no disincentive at all.

The Robert Rubin Free Option

Robert Rubin, former treasury secretary, earned $120 million from Citibank in bonuses over about a decade. The risks taken by the institution were hidden but the numbers looked good . . . until they didn't look good (upon the turkey's surprise). Citibank collapsed, but he kept his money—we taxpayers had to compensate him retrospectively since the government took over the banks' losses and helped them stand on their feet. This type of payoff is very common, thousands of other executives had it.

This is the same story as the one of the architect hiding risks in the basement for delayed collapse and cashing big checks while protected by the complexities of the legal system.

Some people suggest enforcing a "clawback provision" as a remedy, which consists of making people repay past bonuses in cases of subsequent failure. It would be done as follows: managers cannot cash their bonuses immediately, they can only do so three or five years later if there are no losses. But this does not solve the problem: the managers still have a net upside, and no net downside. At no point is their own net worth endangered. So the system still contains a high degree of optionality and transfer of fragility.

The same applies to the fund manager involved in managing a pension fund—he, too, has no downside.

But bankers used to be subjected to Hammurabi's rule. The tradition in Catalonia was to behead bankers in front of their own banks (bankers tended to skip town before failure was apparent, but that was the fate of at least one banker, Francesco Castello, in 1360). In modern times, only the mafia executes these types of strategies to remove the free option. In 1980, the "Vatican banker" Roberto Calvi, the chief executive of Banco Ambrosiano that went bust, ran to take refuge in London. There, he supposedly committed suicide—as if Italy was no longer a good place for acts of drama such as taking one's own life. It was recently discovered that it was not quite suicide; the mafia killed him for losing their money. The same fate befell the Las Vegas pioneer Bugsy Siegel, who ran an unprofitable casino in which the mafia had investments.

And in some countries such as Brazil, even today, top bankers are made unconditionally liable to the extent of their own assets.

Which Adam Smith?

Many right-wingers-in-love-with-large-corporations keep citing Adam Smith, famous patron saint of "capitalism," a word he never uttered, without reading him, using his ideas in a self-serving selective manner— ideas that he most certainly did not endorse in the form they are presented.*

---

* I have had the same experience with journalists citing each other about my books without the smallest effort to go to my writings—my experience is that most journalists, professional academics, and other in similar phony professions don't read original sources, but each other, largely because they need to figure out the consensus before making a pronouncement.

In Book IV of *The Wealth of Nations,* Smith was extremely chary of the idea of giving someone upside without downside and had doubts about the limited liability of joint-stock companies (the ancestor of the modern limited liability corporation). He did not get the idea of transfer of antifragility, but he came close enough. And he detected—sort of—the problem that comes with managing other people's business, the lack of a pilot on the plane:

> The directors of such companies, however, being the managers rather of other people's money than of their own, it cannot well be expected, that they should watch over it with the same anxious vigilance with which the partners in a private copartnery frequently watch over their own.

Further, Smith is even suspicious of their economic performance as he writes: "Joint-stock companies for foreign trade have seldom been able to maintain the competition against private adventurers."

Let me make the point clearer: the version of "capitalism" or whatever economic system you need to have is with the minimum number of people in the left column of the Triad. Nobody realizes that the central problem of the Soviet system was that it put everyone in charge of economic life in that nasty fragilizing left column.

THE ANTIFRAGILITY AND ETHICS OF (LARGE) CORPORATIONS

Have you noticed that while corporations sell you junk drinks, artisans sell you cheese and wine? And there is a transfer of antifragility from the small in favor of the large—until the large goes bust.

The problem of the commercial world is that it only works by addition (*via positiva*), not subtraction (*via negativa*): pharmaceutical companies don't gain if you avoid sugar; the manufacturer of health club machines doesn't benefit from your deciding to lift stones and walk on rocks (without a cell phone); your stockbroker doesn't gain from your decision to limit your investments to what you see with your own eyes, say your cousin's restaurant or an apartment building in your neighborhood; all these firms have to produce "growth in revenues" to satisfy the metric of some slow thinking or, at best, semi-slow thinking MBA analyst sitting in New York. Of course they will eventually self-destruct, but that's another conversation.

Now consider companies like Coke or Pepsi, which I assume are, as the reader is poring over these lines, still in existence—which is unfortunate. What business are they in? Selling you sugary water or substitutes for sugar, putting into your body stuff that messes up your biological signaling system, *causing* diabetes and making diabetes vendors rich thanks to their compensatory drugs. Large corporations certainly can't make money selling you tap water and cannot produce wine (wine seems to be the best argument in favor of the artisanal economy). But they dress their products up with a huge marketing apparatus, with images that fool the drinker and slogans such as "125 years of providing happiness" or some such. I fail to see why the arguments we've used against tobacco firms don't apply—to some extent—to all other large companies that try to sell us things that may make us ill.

The historian Niall Ferguson and I once debated the chairperson of Pepsi-Cola as part of an event at the New York Public Library. It was a great lesson in antifragility, as neither Niall nor I cared about who she was (I did not even bother to know her name). Authors are antifragile. Both of us came totally unprepared (not even a single piece of paper) and she showed up with a staff of aides who, judging from their thick files, had probably studied us down to our shoe sizes (I saw in the speakers' lounge an aide perusing a document with an ugly picture of yours truly in my pre-bone-obsession, pre-weight-lifting days). We could say anything we wanted with total impunity and she had to hew to her party line, lest the security analysts issue a bad report that would cause a drop of two dollars and thirty cents in the stock price before the year-end bonus. In addition, my experience of company executives, as evidenced by their appetite for spending thousands of hours in dull meetings or reading bad memos, is that they cannot possibly be remarkably bright. They are no entrepreneurs—just actors, slick actors (business schools are more like acting schools). Someone intelligent—or free—would likely implode under such a regimen. So Niall immediately detected her weak point and went straight for the jugular: her slogan was that she contributed to employment by having six hundred thousand persons on her staff. He immediately exposed her propaganda with the counterargument—actually developed by Marx and Engels—that large bureaucratic corporations seized control of the state just by being "big employers," and can then extract benefits at the expense of small businesses. So a company that employs six hundred thousand persons is allowed to wreck the health of citizens with impunity, and to benefit from the implied protection of bailouts (just like American car companies), whereas artisans like hairdressers and cobblers do not get such immunity.

A rule then hit me: with the exception of, say, drug dealers, small companies and artisans tend to sell us healthy products, ones that seem naturally and spontaneously needed; larger ones—including pharmaceutical giants—are likely to be in the business of producing wholesale iatrogenics, taking our money, and then, to add insult to injury, hijacking the state thanks to their army of lobbyists. Further, anything that requires marketing appears to carry such side effects. You certainly need an advertising apparatus to convince people that Coke brings them "happiness"—and it works.

There are, of course, exceptions: corporations with the soul of artisans, some with even the soul of artists. Rohan Silva once remarked that Steve Jobs wanted the inside of the Apple products to look aesthetically appealing, although they are designed to remain unseen by the customer. This is something only a true artisan would do—carpenters with personal pride feel fake when treating the inside of cabinets differently from the outside. Again, this is a form of redundancy, one with an aesthetic and ethical payoff. But Steve Jobs was one of the rare exceptions in the Highly Talked About Completely Misunderstood Said to Be Efficient Corporate Global Economy.

Artisans, Marketing, and the Cheapest to Deliver

Another attribute of the artisanal. There is no product that I particularly like that I have discovered through advertising and marketing: cheeses, wine, meats, eggs, tomatoes, basil leaves, apples, restaurants, barbers, art, books, hotels, shoes, shirts, eyeglasses, pants (my father and I have used three generations of Armenian tailors in Beirut), olives, olive oil, etc. The same applies to cities, museums, art, novels, music, painting, sculpture (I had at some point an obsession with ancient artifacts and Roman heads). These may have been "marketed" in some sense, by making people aware of their existence, but this isn't how I came to use them—word of mouth is a potent naturalistic filter. Actually, the only filter.

The mechanism of *cheapest-to-deliver-for-a-given-specification* pervades whatever you see on the shelves. Corporations, when they sell you what they call cheese, have an incentive to provide you with the cheapest-to-produce piece of rubber containing the appropriate ingredients that can still be called cheese—and do their homework by studying how to fool your taste buds. Actually, it is more than just an incentive: they are structurally designed and extremely expert at delivering the cheapest possible product that meets their specifications. The same with, say, business books: publishers and authors want to grab your attention and put in your hands the most perishable journalistic item available that still can be called a book. This is optimization at work, in maximizing (image and packaging) or minimizing (costs and efforts).

I said about marketing by soft drink companies that it is meant to maximally confuse the drinker. Anything one needs to market heavily is necessarily either an inferior product or an evil one. And it is highly unethical to portray something in a more favorable light than it actually is. One may make others aware of the existence of a product, say a new belly dancing belt, but I wonder why people don't realize that, by definition, what is being marketed is necessarily inferior, otherwise it would not be advertised.

Marketing is bad manners—and I rely on my naturalistic and ecological instincts. Say you run into a person during a boat cruise. What would you do if he started boasting of his accomplishments, telling you how great, rich, tall, impressive, skilled, famous, muscular, well educated, efficient, and good in bed he is, plus other attributes? You would certainly run away (or put him in contact with another talkative bore to get rid of both of them). It is clearly much better if others (preferably someone other than his mother) are the ones saying good things about him, and it would be nice if he acted with some personal humility.

Actually this is not at all far-fetched. As I was writing this book, I overheard on a British Air flight a gentleman explain to the flight attendant less than two seconds into the conversation (meant to be about whether he liked cream and sugar in his coffee) that he won the Nobel Prize in Medicine "and Physiology" in addition to being the president of a famous monarchal academy. The flight attendant did not know what the Nobel was, but was polite, so he kept repeating "the Nobel Prize" hoping that she would wake up from her ignorance. I turned around and recognized him, and the character suddenly deflated. As the saying goes, it is hardest to be a great man to one's chambermaid. And marketing beyond conveying information is insecurity.

We accept that people who boast are boastful and turn people off. How about companies? Why aren't we turned off by companies that advertise how great they are? We have three layers of violations:

First layer, the mild violation: companies are shamelessly self-promotional, like the man on the British Air flight, and it only harms them. Second layer, the more serious violation: companies trying to represent themselves in the most favorable light possible, hiding the defects of their products—still harmless, as we tend to expect it and rely on the opinion of users. Third layer, the even more serious violation: companies trying to misrepresent the product they sell by playing with our cognitive biases, our unconscious associations, and that's sneaky. The latter is done by, say, showing a poetic picture of a sunset with a cowboy smoking and forcing an association between great romantic moments and some given product that, logically, has no possible connection to it. You seek a romantic moment and what you get is cancer.

It seems that the corporate system pushes companies progressively into the third layer. At the core of the problem with capitalism—again, please do not invoke Adam Smith—lies the problem of units that are different from individuals. A corporation does not have natural ethics; it just obeys the balance sheet. The problem is that its sole mission is the satisfaction of some metric imposed by security analysts, themselves (very) prone to charlatanism.

A (publicly listed) corporation does not feel shame. We humans are restrained by some physical, natural inhibition.

A corporation does not feel pity.

A corporation does not have a sense of honor—while, alas, marketing documents mention "pride."

A corporation does not have generosity. Only self-serving actions are acceptable. Just imagine what would happen to a corporation that decided to unilaterally cancel its receivables—just to be nice. Yet societies function thanks to random acts of generosity between people, even sometimes strangers.

All of these defects are the result of the absence of skin in the game, cultural or biological—an asymmetry that harms others for their benefit.

Now, such systems should tend to implode. And they do. As they say, you can't fool too many people for too long a period of time. But the problem of implosion is that it does not matter to the managers—because of the agency problem, their allegiance is to their own personal cash flow. They will not be harmed by subsequent failures; they will keep their bonuses, as there is currently no such thing as negative manager compensation.

In sum, corporations are so fragile, long-term, that they eventually collapse under the weight of the agency problem, while managers milk them for bonuses and ditch the bones to taxpayers. They would collapse sooner if not for the lobby machines: they start hijacking the state to help them inject sugary drinks into your esophagus. In the United States large corporations control some members of Congress. All this does is delay the corporation's funeral at our expense.*

Lawrence of Arabia or Meyer Lansky

Finally, if you ever have to choose between a mobster's promise and a civil servant's, go with the mobster. Any time. Institutions do not have a sense of honor, individuals do.

During the Great War, T. E. Lawrence, nicknamed Lawrence of Arabia, struck a deal with the Arab desert tribes to help the British against the Ottoman Empire. His promise: to deliver to them in return an Arab state. As the tribes did not know better, they made good on their side of the bargain. But, it turned out, the French and British governments had made a secret agreement, the Sykes-Picot Agreement, to divide the area in question between themselves. After the war, Lawrence went back to live in the U.K., supposedly in a state of frustration, but, of course, not much more. But he left us with a good lesson: never trust the words of a man who is not free.

Now on the other hand, a mobster's greatest asset is that "his word is gold." It was said that "a handshake from the famous mobster Meyer Lansky was worth more than the strongest contracts that a battery of lawyers could put together." In fact he held in his mind the assets and liabilities of the Sicilian mafia, and was their bank account, without a single record. Just his honor.

As a trader I never trusted transactions with "representatives" of institutions; pit traders are bound by their bonds, and I've never known a single self-employed trader over a two-decade-long career who did not live up to his handshake.

Only a sense of honor can lead to commerce. Any commerce.

---

* There seems to be a survival advantage to small or medium-sized owner-operated or family-owned companies.

Next

We saw how, thanks to the misunderstanding of antifragility (and asymmetry or convexity), some classes of people use hidden options and harm the collective without anyone realizing. We also saw the solution in forcing skin in the game. Next, we will look at another form of optionality: how people can cherry-pick ethical rules to fit their actions. Or how they use public office as a means to satisfy personal greed.

CHAPTER 24

Fitting Ethics to a Profession

How the slaves can snatch control—Squeezing the sissies—The tantalized class, permanently tantalized

———

At no time in the history of mankind has the following situation been seen in such an acute form. Say Mr. John Smith Jr., JD, is employed as lobbyist for the tobacco industry in Washington, D.C., which, as we all know, is engaged in the business of killing people for profit (we saw with the powers of subtraction that if we stopped such industries from existing by, say, banning cigarettes, then everything else done by medicine becomes a footnote). Ask any of his relatives (or friends) why they can tolerate it and don't just ostracize him or harass him to tears, avoid him at the next family funeral. The answer is likely to be "everyone needs to make a living"—as they are hedging the possibility of their falling into the same situation some day.

We need to test the direction of the arrow (using the same logic as in our discussion of lecturing birds on flying):

Ethics (and Beliefs) → *Profession*

or

Profession → *Ethics (and Beliefs)*

Prior to Fat Tony's debate with Socrates, Nero was curious about the first minute of encounter, since there is a gap of about twenty-five centuries. It is not a simple matter to identify the elements of our physical environment that would surprise Socrates the most. Questioned on the point by Fat Tony, who had some grudging respect for Nero's knowledge of history, Nero's speculative reply was "It would most certainly be the absence of slaves."

"These people never did small domestic things themselves. So imagine Socrates' sorry figure of a bulging belly, spindly legs, wondering *Opou oi douloi?*"

"But, Neeroh Toolip, there are still slaves around," Fat Tony blurted out. "They often distinguish themselves by wearing this intricate device called a necktie."

Nero: "Signore Ingeniere Tony, some of these tie-wearers are very rich, even richer than you."

Tony: "Nero, you sucker. Don't be fooled by money. These are just numbers. Being self-owned is a state of mind."

Wealth Without Independence

There is a phenomenon called the *treadmill effect,* similar to what we saw with neomania: you need to make more and more to stay in the same place. Greed is antifragile—though not its victims.

Back to the sucker problem in believing that wealth makes people more independent. We need no more evidence for it than what is taking place now: recall that we have never been richer in the history of mankind. And we have never been more in debt (for the ancients, someone in debt was not free, he was in bondage). So much for "economic growth."

At the local level, it looks like we get socialized in a certain milieu, hence exposed to a treadmill. You do better, move to Greenwich, Connecticut, then become a pauper next to a twenty-million-dollar mansion and million-dollar birthday parties. And you become more and more dependent on your job, particularly as your neighbors get big tax-sponsored Wall Street bonuses.

This class of persons is like Tantalus, who was subjected to an eternal punishment: he stood in a pool of water underneath a fruit tree and whenever he tried to grab the fruit it moved away and whenever he tried to drink, the water receded.

And such a permanently tantalized class is a modern condition. The Romans circumvented these social treadmill effects: much of social life took place between a patron and his less fortunate clients who benefited from his largesse and ate at his table—and relied on his assistance in times of trouble. There was no welfare at the time, and no church to distribute or recommend charity: everything was private (Seneca's book *De beneficiis* I mentioned earlier was exactly about which obligations one had in such situations). There was little exposure to the other wealthy biggies, just as mafia dons don't socialize with other mafia dons but with their constituents. To a large extent, that's how my grandfather and great-grandfather lived, as they were local landowners and politicians; power was accompanied by a coterie of dependents. Provincial landowners were required to maintain an occasional "open house," with an open table for people to come help themselves to the fruits of the wealth. Court life, on the other hand, leads to corruption—the nobleman comes from the provinces, where he is now brought down to size; he faces more flamboyant, wittier persons and feels pressure to prop up his self-esteem. People who would have lost their status in the cities conserve it in the provinces.

You cannot possibly trust someone on a treadmill.

THE PROFESSIONALS AND THE COLLECTIVE

It is a fact that one can rapidly, after a phase of indoctrination, become enslaved to a profession, to the point of having one's opinions on any subject become self-serving, hence unreliable for the collective. This is the bone the Greeks had to pick with professionals.

One of my first jobs was for a Wall Street firm. After I'd been employed for a few months, the managing director called us up and told us that we needed to contribute to a few politicians' campaigns, with a "recommended" payment of a certain proportion of our income. These politicians were said to be "good." By "good" was meant good for their business of investment banking, as these politicians would help with legislation that would protect their business. Had I done that, I would no longer have been eligible ethically to voice a political opinion "for the sake of the public."

In a story well argued throughout the centuries, Demades the Athenian condemned a man who traded in funeral goods on the grounds that he could only derive profits by the death of the great many people. Mon-

410 THE ETHICS OF FRAGILITY AND ANTIFRAGILITY

taigne, rephrasing the argument made by Seneca in his *De beneficiis,* argued that we would then be obligated to condemn every single professional. According to him, the merchant only thrives by the debauchery of youth, the farmer by the dearness of grain, the architect by the ruin of buildings, lawyers and officers of justice by the suits and contentions of men. A physician takes no pleasure in the health of even his friends, a soldier does not wish for the peace of his country, etc. And, even worse, should we go into people's inner and private thoughts and motivations, we would see that their wishes and hopes are almost invariably at someone else's expense.

But Montaigne and Seneca were a bit too indulgent toward self-interest and missed something quite central. They clearly got the point that economic life does not necessarily depend on altruistic motives, and that the aggregate works differently from the individual. Remarkably, Seneca was born about eighteen centuries before Adam Smith, and Montaigne about three, so we should be quite impressed with their thinking while retaining a certain abhorrence of the fundamental dishonesty of men. We have known since Adam Smith that the collective does not require the benevolence of individuals, as self-interest can be the driver of growth. But all this does not make people less unreliable *in their personal opinions* about the collective. For they are involving the skin of others, so to speak.

What Montaigne and Seneca missed, in addition to the notion of skin in the game, was that one can draw the line with public affairs. They missed the agency problem—although the problem was known heuristically (Hammurabi, golden rules), it was not part of their consciousness.

The point isn't that making a living in a profession is inherently bad; rather, it's that such a person becomes automatically suspect when dealing with public affairs, matters that involve others. The definition of the *free man,* according to Aristotle, is one who is free with his opinions—as a side effect of being free with his time.

Freedom in this sense is only a matter of sincerity in political opinions.

The Greeks saw the world in three professions. The *banausikai technai,* the artisans; the craft of war, *polemike techne;* and that of farming, *georgia.* The last two professions, war and farming, were worthy of a gentleman—mainly because they were not self-serving and were free of conflicts of interest with the collective. But the Athenians despised the *banausoi,* the artisans who worked for a living in dark rooms making objects—generally sitting down. For Xenophon, such crafts degraded the craftsmen's bodily strength, softened his spirit, and left him no time for his friends and city. The illiberal arts confine one to the workshop and narrow one's interests *to his own welfare;* the crafts of war and farming give one a wider scope so that he can attend to his friends and city. To Xenophon, farming is the mother and nurse of the other *technai.* (The ancients did not have corporations; if Xenophon were alive today he would transfer his distrust from artisans to corporate employees.)

There are Arabic and Hebrew sayings, *Yad el hurr mizan / Yad ben horin moznayim*—"the hand of the free is a scale." It is just that the definition of the free is not well understood: he is free who owns his own opinion.

For Metternich, humanity started at the rank of baron; for Aristotle, as well as, though in a separate form, the English up until the twentieth century, it started at the rank of idle freeman, unpreoccupied with work. It never meant *not* working; it just meant not deriving your personal and emotional identity from your work, and viewing work as something optional, more like a hobby. In a way your profession does not identify you so much as other attributes, here your birth (but it could be something else). This is the *f*** you money* that allowed Thales of Miletus to gauge his own sincerity. For the Spartans, it was all about courage. For Fat Tony, humanity started at the level of "self-ownership."

Now self-ownership for our horizontal friend was vastly more democratic than for his thinking predecessors. It simply meant being the owner of your opinion. And it has nothing to do with wealth, birth, intelligence, looks, shoe size, rather with personal courage.

In other words, for Fat Tony, it was a very, very specific definition of a free person: someone who cannot be squeezed into doing something he would otherwise never do.

Consider this leap in sophistication from Athens to Brooklyn: if for the Greeks, only he who is free with his time is free with his opinion, for our horizontal friend and advisor, only he who has courage is free with his opinion. *Sissies are born, not made. They stay sissies no matter how much independence you give them, no matter how rich they get.*

Another facet of the difference between abstract modernistic nation-states and local government. In an antique city-state, or a modern municipality, shame is the penalty for the violation of ethics—making things more symmetric. Banishment and exile, or, worse, ostracism were severe penalties—people did not move around voluntarily and considered up-rooting a horrible calamity. In larger organisms like the mega holy nation-state, with a smaller role for face-to-face encounters, and social roots, shame ceases to fulfill its duty of disciplinarian. We need to rees-tablish it.

And aside from shame, there is friendship, socialization in a certain milieu, being part of a group of people that have diverging interests from the collective. Cleon, the hero of the Peloponnesian War, advocated the public renouncement of friends upon taking up public affairs—he paid for it with some revilement by historians.

A simple solution, but quite drastic: anyone who goes into public service should not be allowed to *subsequently* earn more from any com-mercial activity than the income of the highest paid civil servant. It is like a voluntary cap (it would prevent people from using public office as a credential-building temporary accommodation, then going to Wall Street to earn several million dollars). This would get priestly people into of-fice.

Just as Cleon was reviled, in the modern world, there seems to be an inverse agency problem for those who do the right thing: you pay for your service to the public with smear campaigns and harassment. The activist and advocate Ralph Nader suffered numerous smear campaigns as the auto industry went after him.

THE ETHICAL AND THE LEGAL

I felt ashamed not having exposed the following scam for a long time. (As I said, *if you see fraud* . . .) Let us call it the Alan Blinder problem.

The story is as follows. At Davos, during a private coffee conversa-tion that I thought aimed at saving the world from, among other things, moral hazard and agency problems, I was interrupted by Alan Blinder, a former vice chairman of the Federal Reserve Bank of the United States, who tried to sell me a peculiar investment product that aims at legally hoodwinking taxpayers. It allowed the high net worth investor to get around the regulations limiting deposit insurance (at the time, $100,000) and benefit from coverage for near-unlimited amounts. The investor would deposit funds in any amount and Prof. Blinder's company would break it up into smaller accounts and invest in banks, thus escaping the limit; it would look like a single account but would be insured in full. In other words, it would allow the super-rich to scam taxpayers by getting free government-sponsored insurance. Yes, *scam* taxpayers. Legally. With the help of former civil servants who have an insider edge.

I blurted out: "Isn't this unethical?" I was then told in response "It is perfectly legal," adding the even more incriminating "we have plenty of former regulators on the staff," (a) implying that what was legal was ethical and (b) asserting that former regulators have an edge over citizens.

It took a long time, a couple of years, before I reacted to the event and did my public *J'accuse*. Alan Blinder is certainly not the worst violator of my sense of ethics; he probably irritated me because of the prominence of his previous public position, while the Davos conversation was meant to save the world from evil (I was presenting to him my idea of how bankers take risks at the expense of taxpayers). But what we have here is a model of how people use public office to, at some point, legally profit from the public.

Tell me if you understand the problem in its full simplicity: former regulators and public officials who were employed by the citizens to represent their best interests can use the expertise and contacts acquired on the job to benefit from glitches in the system upon joining private employment—law firms, etc.

Think about it a bit further: the more complex the regulation, the more bureaucratic the network, the more a regulator who knows the loops and glitches would benefit from it later, as his regulator edge would be a convex function of his differential knowledge. This is a franchise, an asymmetry one has at the expense of others. (Note that this franchise is spread across the economy; the car company Toyota hired former U.S. regulators and used their "expertise" to handle investigations of its car defects.)

Now stage two—things get worse. Blinder and the dean of Columbia University Business School wrote an op-ed opposing the government's raising the insurance limit on individuals. The article argued that the public should not have the unlimited insurance that Blinder's clients benefit from.

A few remarks.

First, the more complicated the regulation, the more prone to arbitrages by insiders. This is another argument in favor of heuristics. Twenty-three hundred pages of regulation—something I can replace with Hammurabi's rule—will be a gold mine for former regulators. The incentive of a regulator is to have complex regulation. Again, the insiders are the enemies of the *less-is-more* rule.

Second, the difference between the letter and the spirit of regulation is harder to detect in a complex system. The point is technical, but complex environments with nonlinearities are easier to game than linear ones with a small number of variables. The same applies to the gap between the legal and the ethical.

Third, in African countries, government officials get explicit bribes. In the United States they have the implicit, never mentioned, promise to go work for a bank at a later date with a sinecure offering, say $5 million a year, if they are seen favorably by the industry. And the "regulations" of such activities are easily skirted.

What upset me the most about the Alan Blinder problem is the reactions by those with whom I discussed it: people found it natural that a former official would try to "make money" thanks to his former position—at our expense. *Don't people like to make money?* goes the argument.

Casuistry as Optionality

You can always find an argument or an ethical reason to defend an opinion ex post. This is a dicey point, but, as with cherry-picking, one should propose an ethical rule before an action, not after. You want to prevent fitting a narrative to what you are doing—and for a long time "casuistry," the art of arguing the nuances of decisions, was just that, fitting narratives.

Let me first define a fraudulent opinion. It is simply one with vested interests generalized to the public good—in which, say a hairdresser recommends haircuts "for the health of people," or a gun lobbyist claims gun ownership is "good for America," simply making statements that benefit him personally, while the statements are dressed up to look as if they were made for the benefit of the collective. In other words, is he in the left column of Table 7? Likewise, Alan Blinder wrote that he opposed generalized deposit insurance, not because his company would lose business, but *because of the public good.*

But the heuristic is easy to implement, with a simple question. I was in Cyprus at a conference dinner in which another speaker, a Cypriot professor of petrochemical engineering in an American university, was ranting against the climate activist Lord Nicholas Stern. Stern was part of the conference but absent from the dinner. The Cypriot was extremely animated. I had no idea what the issues were, but saw the notion of "absence of evidence" mixed with "evidence of absence" and pounced on him in defense of Stern, whom I had never met. The petrochemical engineer was saying that we had *no evidence* that fossil fuels caused harm to the planet, turning his point semantically into something equivalent in decision making to the statement that that we had *evidence that fossil fuels did not harm.* He made the mistake of saying that Stern was recommending useless insurance, causing me to jump to ask him if he had car, health, and other insurance for events that did not take place, that sort of argument. I started bringing up the idea that we are doing something new to the planet, that the burden of evidence is on those who disturb natural systems, that Mother Nature knows more than he will ever know, not the other way around. But it was like talking to a defense lawyer—sophistry, and absence of convergence to truth.

Then a heuristic came to mind. I surreptitiously asked a host sitting next to me if the fellow had anything to gain from his argument: it turned out that he was deep into oil companies, as an advisor, an investor, and a consultant. I immediately lost interest in what he had to say and the energy to debate him in front of others—his words were nugatory, just babble.

Note how this fits into the idea of skin in the game. If someone has an opinion, like, say, the banking system is fragile and should collapse, I want him invested in it so he is harmed if the audience for his opinion are harmed—as a token that he is not an empty suit. But when general statements about the collective welfare are made, instead, *absence* of investment is what is required. *Via negativa.*

I have just presented the mechanism of ethical optionality by which *people fit their beliefs to actions rather than fit their actions to their beliefs.* Table 8 compares professions with respect to such ethical backfitting.

TABLE 8 • COMPARING PROFESSIONS AND ACTIVITIES

INVITED TO BE OPPORTUNIST (FITS ETHICS TO PROFESSION)	PROTECTED FROM PLAYING THE PSEUDOETHICS GAME
Gold-digger	Prostitute
Networker	Social person
Compromises	Doesn't compromise
Someone "here to help"	Erudite, dilettante, amateur
Merchant, professional (Classical period)	Landowner (Classical period)
Employee	Artisan
Academic at a research university, researcher depending on "grants"	Lens maker, philosophy teacher in a college or Lycée high school, independent scholar

There exists an inverse Alan Blinder problem, called "evidence against one's interest." One should give more weight to witnesses and opinions when they present the opposite of a conflict of interest. A pharmacist or an executive of Big Pharma who advocates starvation and *via negativa* methods to cure diabetes would be more credible than another one who favors the ingestion of drugs.

BIG DATA AND THE RESEARCHER'S OPTION

This is a bit technical, so the reader can skip this section with no loss. But optionality is everywhere, and here is a place to discuss a version of cherry-picking that destroys the entire spirit of research and makes the abundance of data extremely harmful to knowledge. More data means more information, perhaps, but it also means more false information. We are discovering that fewer and fewer papers replicate—textbooks in, say, psychology need to be revised. As to economics, fuhgetaboudit. You can hardly trust many statistically oriented sciences—especially when the researcher is under pressure to publish for his career. Yet the claim will be "to advance knowledge."

Recall the notion of epiphenomenon as a distinction between real life and libraries. Someone looking at history from the vantage point of a library will necessarily find many more spurious relationships than one who sees matters in the making, in the usual sequences one observes in real life. He will be duped by more epiphenomena, one of which is the direct result of the excess of data as compared to real signals.

We discussed the rise of noise in Chapter 7. Here it becomes a worse problem, because there is an optionality on the part of the researcher, no different from that of a banker. The researcher gets the upside, truth gets the downside. The researcher's free option is in his ability to pick whatever statistics can confirm his belief—or show a good result—and ditch the rest. He has the *option* to stop once he has the right result. But beyond that, he can find statistical relationships—the spurious rises to the surface. There is a certain property of data: in large data sets, large deviations are vastly more attributable to noise (or variance) than to information (or signal).*

Spurious Correlations

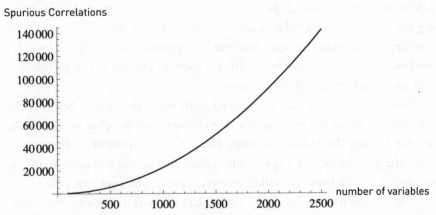

FIGURE 18. The Tragedy of Big Data. The more variables, the more correlations that can show significance in the hands of a "skilled" researcher. Falsity grows faster than information; it is nonlinear (convex) with respect to data.

There is a difference in medical research between (a) observational studies, in which the researcher looks at statistical relationships on his computer, and (b) the double-blind cohort experiments that extract information in a realistic way that mimics real life.

The former, that is, observation from a computer, produces all man-

---

* It is a property of sampling. In real life, if you are observing things in real time, then large deviations matter a lot. But when a researcher looks for them, then they are likely to be bogus—in real life there is no cherry-picking, but on the researcher's computer, there is.

ner of results that tend to be, as last computed by John Ioannides, now more than eight times out of ten, spurious—yet these observational studies get reported in the papers and in *some* scientific journals. Thankfully, these observational studies are not accepted by the Food and Drug Administration, as the agency's scientists know better. The great Stan Young, an activist against spurious statistics, and I found a genetics-based study in *The New England Journal of Medicine* claiming significance from statistical data—while the results to us were no better than random. We wrote to the journal, to no avail.

Figure 18 shows the swelling number of potential spurious relationships. The idea is as follows. If I have a set of 200 random variables, completely unrelated to each other, then it would be near impossible not to find in it a high correlation of sorts, say 30 percent, but that is entirely spurious. There are techniques to control the cherry-picking (one of which is known as the Bonferoni adjustment), but even then they don't catch the culprits—much as regulation doesn't stop insiders from gaming the system. This explains why in the twelve years or so since we've decoded the human genome, not much of significance has been found. I am not saying that there is no information in the data: the problem is that the needle comes in a haystack.

Even experiments can be marred with bias: the researcher has the incentive to select the experiment that corresponds to what he was looking for, hiding the failed attempts. He can also formulate a hypothesis after the results of the experiment—thus fitting the hypothesis to the experiment. The bias is smaller, though, than in the previous case.

The fooled-by-data effect is accelerating. There is a nasty phenomenon called "Big Data" in which researchers have brought cherry-picking to an industrial level. Modernity provides too many variables (but too little data per variable), and the spurious relationships grow much, much faster than real information, as noise is convex and information is concave.

Increasingly, data can only truly deliver *via negativa*-style knowledge—it can be effectively used to debunk, not confirm.

The tragedy is that it is very hard to get funding to replicate—and reject—existing studies. And even if there were money for it, it would be hard to find takers: trying to replicate studies will not make anyone a hero. So we are crippled with a distrust of empirical results, except for those that are negative. To return to my romantic idea of the amateur and tea-drinking English clergyman: the professional researcher competes to "find" relationships. Science must not be a competition; it must not have rankings—we can see how such a system will end up blowing up. Knowledge must not have an agency problem.

THE TYRANNY OF THE COLLECTIVE

Mistakes made collectively, not individually, are the hallmark of organized knowledge—and the best argument against it. The argument "because everyone is doing it" or "that's how others do it" abounds. It is not trivial: people who on their own would not do something because they find it silly now engage in the same thing but in groups. And this is where academia in its institutional structure tends to violate science.

One doctoral student at the University of Massachusetts, Chris S., once came to tell me that he believed in my ideas of "fat tails" and my skepticism of current methods of risk management, but that it would not help him get an academic job. "It's what everybody teaches and uses in papers," he said. Another student explained that he wanted a job at a good university so he could make money testifying as an expert witness—they would not buy my ideas on robust risk management because "everyone uses these textbooks." Likewise, I was asked by the administration of a university to teach standard risk methods that I believe are pure charlatanism (I refused). Is my duty as a professor to get students a job at the expense of society, or to fulfill my civic obligations? Well, if the former is the case, then economics and business schools have a severe ethical problem. For the point is generalized and that's why economics hasn't collapsed yet in spite of the obvious nonsense in it—and *scientifically proven* nonsense in it. (In my "fourth quadrant" paper—see discussion in the Appendix—I show how these methods are empirically invalid, in addition to being severely mathematically inconsistent, in other words, a scientific swindle). Recall that professors are not penalized when they teach you something that blows up the financial system, which perpetuates the fraud. Departments need to teach *something* so students get jobs, even if they are teaching snake oil—this got us trapped in a circular system in which everyone knows that the material is wrong but nobody is free enough or has enough courage to do anything about it.

The problem is that the last place on the planet where the "other people think so" argument can be used is science: science is precisely about arguments standing on their own legs, and something proven to be wrong empirically or mathematically is plain wrong, whether a hundred "experts" or three trillion disagree with the statement. And the very use of "other people" to back up one's claims is indicative that the person—or the entire collective that composes the "other"—is a wimp. The appendix shows what has been busted in economics, and what people keep using because they are not harmed by error, and that's the optimal strategy for keeping a job or getting a promotion.

But the good news is that I am convinced that a single person with courage can bring down a collective composed of wimps.

And here, once again, we need to go back into history for the cure. The scriptures were quite aware of the problem of the diffusion of responsibility and made it a sin to follow the crowd in doing evil—as well as to give false testimony in order to conform to the multitude.

I close Book VII with a thought. Whenever I hear the phrase "I am ethical" uttered, I get tense. When I hear about classes in ethics, I get even more tense. All I want is to remove the optionality, reduce the antifragility of some at the expense of others. It is simple *via negativa*. The rest will take care of itself.

CHAPTER 25

Conclusion

As usual at the end of the journey, while I was looking at the entire manuscript on a restaurant table, someone from a Semitic culture asked me to explain my book standing on one leg. This time it was Shaiy Pilpel, a probabilist with whom I've had a two-decades-long calm conversation without a single episode of small talk. It is hard to find people knowledgeable and confident enough to like to extract the essence of things, instead of nitpicking.

With the previous book, one of his compatriots asked me the same question, but I had to think about it. This time I did not even have to make an effort.

It was so obvious that Shaiy summed it up it himself in the same breath. He actually believes that all real ideas can be distilled down to a central issue that the great majority of people in a given field, by dint of specialization and empty-suitedness, completely miss. Everything in religious law comes down to the refinements, applications, and interpretations of the Golden Rule, "Don't do unto others what you don't want them to do to you." This we saw was the logic behind Hammurabi's rule. And the Golden Rule was a true distillation, not a Procrustean bed. A central argument is never a summary—it is more like a generator.

Shaiy's extraction was: *Everything gains or loses from volatility. Fragility is what loses from volatility and uncertainty*. The glass on the table is short volatility.

In the novel *The Plague* by Albert Camus, a character spends part of his life searching for the perfect opening sentence for a novel. Once he had that sentence, he had the full book as a derivation of the opening. But the reader, to understand and appreciate the first sentence, will have to read the entire book.

I glanced at the manuscript with a feeling of calm elation. Every sentence in the book was a derivation, an application, or an interpretation of the short maxim. Some details and extensions can be counterintuitive and elaborate, particularly when it comes to decision making under opacity, but at the end everything flows from it.

The reader is invited to do the same. Look around you, at your life, at objects, at relationships, at entities. You may replace *volatility* with other members of the disorder cluster here and there for clarity, but it is not even necessary—when formally expressed, it is all the same symbol. Time is volatility. Education, in the sense of the formation of character, personality, and acquisition of true knowledge, likes disorder; label-driven education and educators abhor disorder. Some things break because of error, others don't. Some theories fall apart, not others. Innovation is precisely something that gains from uncertainty: and some people sit around waiting for uncertainty and using it as raw material, just like our ancestral hunters.

Prometheus is long disorder; Epimetheus is short disorder. We can separate people and the quality of their experiences based on exposure to disorder and appetite for it: Spartan hoplites contra bloggers, adventurers contra copy editors, Phoenician traders contra Latin grammarians, and pirates contra tango instructors.

It so happens that everything nonlinear is convex or concave, or both, depending on the intensity of the stressor. We saw the link between convexity and liking volatility. So everything likes or hates volatility up to a point. Everything.

We can detect what likes volatility thanks to convexity or acceleration and higher orders, since convexity is the response by a thing that likes disorder. We can build Black Swan–protected systems thanks to detection of concavity. We can take medical decisions by understanding the convexity of harm and the logic of Mother Nature's tinkering, on which side we face opacity, which error we should risk. Ethics is largely about stolen convexities and optionality.

More technically, we may never get to know x, but we can play with the exposure to x, barbell things to defang them; we can control a function of x, $f(x)$, even if x remains vastly beyond our understanding. We can keep changing $f(x)$ until we are comfortable with it by a mechanism called *convex transformation*, the fancier name for the barbell.

This short maxim also tells you where fragility supersedes truth, why we lie to children, and why we humans got a bit ahead of ourselves in this large enterprise called modernity.

Distributed randomness (as opposed to the concentrated type) is a necessity, not an option: everything big is short volatility. So is everything fast. Big and fast are abominations. Modern times don't like volatility.

And the Triad gives us some indication of what should be done to live in a world that does not want us to understand it, a world whose charm comes from our inability to truly understand it.

The glass is dead; living things are long volatility. The best way to verify that you are alive is by checking if you like variations. Remember that food would not have a taste if it weren't for hunger; results are meaningless without effort, joy without sadness, convictions without uncertainty, and an ethical life isn't so when stripped of personal risks.

And once again, reader, thank you for reading my book.

From Resurrection
to Resurrection

It was an aortic aneurism.

Nero was in the Levant for his annual celebration of the death and rebirth of Adonis. It was a period of mourning with wailing women, followed by a celebration of resurrection. He watched nature waking up from the mild Mediterranean winter, when the rivers are full of reddish water, the blood of the Phoenician god wounded by the boar, as the melted snow from the mountains swelled the rivers and rivulets.

Things in nature move ahead from resurrection to resurrection.

That was when Tony's driver called. His name was also Tony, and while identified as Tony-the-driver he pretended he was a bodyguard (when in fact it looked like, given the comparative size, he was the one bodyguarded by Tony). Nero never liked him, always had that strange feeling of distrust, so the moment of sharing the news was odd. During his silence on the line, he felt sympathy for Tony-the-driver.

Nero was designated as the executor of Tony's will, which made him initially nervous. He had somehow a fear that Tony's wisdom would have a gigantic Achilles' heel somewhere. But, it turned out, there was nothing serious, a flawless estate, of course debt-free, conservative, fairly distributed. There were some funds to discreetly provide to a woman likely to be a prostitute, for whom Tony had some antifragile obsessive love, of course helped by the fact that she was both older and much less attractive than Tony's wife, that sort of thing. So nothing serious.

Except for the posthumous prank. Tony bequeathed to Nero a sum of twenty million dollars to spend at his discretion on . . . It was to be a secret mission; noble of course, but secret. And, of course, vague. And dangerous. It was the best compliment Nero ever got from Tony: trusting that Nero would be able to read his mind.

Which he did.

Glossary

Triad: The triplet Antifragility, Robustness, Fragility.

Fundamental Asymmetry (also **Seneca's Asymmetry**): When someone has *more upside than downside* in a certain situation, he is antifragile and tends to gain from (a) volatility, (b) randomness, (c) errors, (d) uncertainty, (e) stressors, (f) time. And the reverse.

Procrustean bed: Procrustes got people to fit perfectly into his bed by cutting or stretching their limbs. Corresponds to situations in which simplifications are not simplifications.

Fragilista: Someone who causes fragility because he thinks he understands what's going on. Also usually lacks sense of humor. See **Iatrogenics**. Often Fragilistas fragilize by depriving variability-loving systems of variability and error-loving systems of errors. They tend to mistake organisms for machines and engineering projects.

Lecturing-Birds-How-to-Fly Effect: Inverting the arrow of knowledge to read academia → practice, or education → wealth, to make it look as though technology owes more to institutional science than it actually does.

Touristification: The attempt to suck randomness out of life. Applies to soccer moms, Washington civil servants, strategic planners, social engineers, "nudge" manipulators, etc. Opposite: **rational flâneur**.

Rational flâneur (or just **flâneur**): Someone who, unlike a tourist, makes a decision opportunistically at every step to revise his schedule (or his destination) so he can imbibe things based on new information obtained. In research and entrepreneurship, being a flâneur is called "looking for optionality." A non-narrative approach to life.

Barbell Strategy: A dual strategy, a combination of two extremes, one safe and one speculative, deemed more robust than a "monomodal" strategy; often a necessary condition for antifragility. For instance, in biological systems, the equivalent of marrying an accountant and having an occasional fling with a rock star; for a writer, getting a stable sinecure and writing without the pressures of the market during spare time. Even trial and error are a form of barbell.

Iatrogenics: Harm done by the healer, as when the doctor's interventions do more harm than good.

Generalized Iatrogenics: By extension, applies to the harmful side effects of actions by policy makers and activities of academics.

Tantalized Class: An economic condition of making more than minimum wage *and* wishing for more wealth. Workers, monks, hippies, some artists, and English aristocrats escape it. The middle class tends to fall into it; so do Russian billionaires, lobbyists, most bankers, and bureaucrats. Members are bribable provided they are given an adequate narrative, mostly with the use of casuistry.

Black Swan Errors

> **Nonpredictive Approach:** Building stuff in a manner immune to perturbations—hence robust to changes in future outcomes.

> **Thalesian versus Aristotelian:** The Thalesian focuses on exposure, payoff from decision; the Aristotelian focuses on logic, the True-False distinction. For Fat Tony, the problem is all about sucker-nonsucker, or risks and rewards. (Also see **nonlinearities, convexity effects**.)

> **Conflation of Event and Exposure:** Mistaking a function of a variable for the variable itself.

Naturalistic Risk Management: The belief that, when it comes to risk management, Mother Nature has a much, much more significant track record than rationalistic humans. It is imperfect, but much better.

Burden of evidence: The burden of evidence falls on those who disrupt the natural, or those who propose *via positiva* policies.

Ludic Fallacy: Mistaking the well-posed problems of mathematics and laboratory experiments for the ecologically complex real world. Includes mistaking the randomness in casinos for that in real life.

Antifragile Tinkering, Bricolage: A certain class of trial and error, with small errors being "the right" kind of mistakes. All equivalent to **rational flâneur.**

Hormesis: A bit of a harmful substance, or stressor, in the right dose or with the right intensity, stimulates the organism and makes it better, stronger, healthier, and prepared for a stronger dose the next exposure. (Think of bones and karate.)

Naive Interventionism: Intervention with disregard to **iatrogenics.** The preference, even obligation, to "do something" over doing nothing. While this instinct can be beneficial in emergency rooms or ancestral environments, it hurts in others in which there is an "expert problem."

Naive Rationalism: Thinking that the reasons for things are, by default, accessible to university buildings. Also called the **Soviet-Harvard illusion.**

Turkey and Inverse Turkey: The turkey is fed by the butcher for a thousand days, and every day the turkey pronounces with increased statistical confidence that the butcher "will never hurt it"—until Thanksgiving, which brings a Black Swan revision of belief for the turkey. The **inverse turkey** error is the mirror confusion, not seeing opportunities—pronouncing that one has evidence that someone digging for gold or searching for cures will "never find" anything.

Doxastic Commitment, or "Soul in the Game": You must only believe predictions and opinions by those who committed themselves to a certain belief, and had something to lose, in a way to pay a cost in being wrong.

Heuristics: Simple, practical, easy-to-apply rules of thumb that make life easy. These are necessary (we do not have the mental power to absorb all information and tend to be confused by details) but they can get us in trouble as we do not know we are using them when forming judgments.

Opaque Heuristic: Routine performed by societies that does not seem to make sense yet has been done for a long time and sticks for unknown reasons.

Dionysian: Opaque heuristic seemingly irrational, named after Dionysos (or Bacchus for Romans), the god of wine and revelling. Is contrasted to the Apollonian, which represents order.

Agency Problem: Situation in which the manager of a business is not the true owner, so he follows a strategy that cosmetically seems to be sound, but in a hidden way benefits him and makes him antifragile at the expense (fragility) of the true owners or society. When he is right, he collects large benefits; when he is wrong, others pay the price. Typically this problem leads to fragility, as it is easy to hide risks. It also affects politicians and academics. A major source of fragility.

Hammurabi Risk Management: The idea that a builder has more knowledge than the inspector and can hide risks in the foundations where they can be most invisible; the remedy is to remove the incentive in favor of delayed risk.

Green Lumber Fallacy: Mistaking the source of important or even necessary knowledge—the greenness of lumber—for another, less visible from the outside, less tractable one. How theoreticians impute wrong weights to what one should know in a certain business or, more generally, how many things we call "relevant knowledge" aren't so much so.

Skin in the Game / Captain and Ship Rule: Every captain goes down with every ship. This removes the **agency problem** and the lack of **doxastic commitment.**

Empedocles' Tile: A dog sleeps on the same tile because of a natural, biological, explainable or nonexplainable match, confirmed by long series of recurrent frequentation. We may never know the reason, but the match is there. Example: why we read books.

Cherry-picking: Selecting from the data what serves to prove one's point and ignoring disconfirming elements.

Ethical Problems as Transfers of Asymmetry (fragility): Someone steals antifragility and optionality from others, getting the upside and sticking others with the downside. "Others' skin in the game."

> **The Robert Rubin violation:** Stolen optionality. Getting upside from a strategy without downside for oneself, leaving the harm to society. Rubin got $120 million in compensation from Citibank; taxpayers are retrospectively paying for his errors.

> **The Alan Blinder problem:** (1) Using privileges of office retrospectively at the expense of citizens. (2) Violating moral rules while complying perfectly with the law; confusion of ethical and legal. (3) The regulator's incentive to make complicated regulations in order to subsequently sell his "expertise" to the private sector.

> **The Joseph Stiglitz problem:** Lack of penalty from bad recommendation causing harm to others. Mental **cherry-picking,** leading to contributing to the cause of a crisis while being convinced of the opposite—and thinking he predicted it. Applies to people with opinions without skin in the game.

Rational Optionality: Not being locked into a given program, so one can change his mind as he goes along based on discovery or new information. Also applies to **rational flâneur.**

Ethical Inversion: Fitting one's ethics to actions (or profession) rather than the reverse.

Narrative Fallacy: Our need to fit a story, or pattern, to a series of connected or disconnected facts. The statistical application is data mining.

Narrative Discipline: Discipline that consists of fitting a convincing and good-sounding story to the past. Opposed to experimental discipline. A great way to fool people is to use statistics as part of the narrative, by ferreting out "good stories" from the data thanks to cherry picking; in medicine, epidemiological studies tend to be marred with the narrative fallacy, less so controlled experiments. Controlled experiments are more rigorous, less subjected to **cherry-picking.**

Non-narrative action: Does not depend on a narrative for the action to be right—the narrative is just there to motivate, entertain, or prompt action. See **flâneur.**

Robust Narrative: When the narrative does not produce opposite conclusions or recommendations for action under change of assumption or environment. The narrative is otherwise fragile. Similarly, a robust model or mathematical tool does not lead to different policies when you change some parts of the model.

Subtractive Knowledge: You know what is wrong with more certainty than you know anything else. An application of *via negativa.*

Via negativa: In theology and philosophy, the focus on what something is not, an indirect definition. In action, it is a recipe for what to avoid, what not to do—subtraction, not addition, say, in medicine.

Subtractive Prophecy: Predicting the future by removing what is fragile from it rather than naively adding to it. An application of *via negativa.*

Lindy Effect: A technology, or anything nonperishable, increases in life expectancy with every day of its life—unlike perishable items (such as humans, cats, dogs, and tomatoes). So a book that has been a hundred years in print is likely to stay in print another hundred years.

Neomania: A love of change for its own sake, a form of philistinism that does not comply with the **Lindy effect** and understands fragility. Forecasts the future by adding, not subtracting.

Opacity: You do not see the barrel when someone is playing Russian roulette. More generally, some things remain opaque to us, leading to illusions of understanding.

Mediocristan: A process dominated by the mediocre, with few extreme successes or failures (say, income for a dentist). No single observation can meaningfully affect the aggregate. Also called "thin-tailed," or member of the Gaussian family of distributions.

Extremistan: A process where the total can be conceivably impacted by a single observation (say, income for a writer). Also called "fat-tailed." Includes the fractal, or power-law, family of distributions.

Nonlinearities, Convexity Effects (smiles and frowns): Nonlinearities can be concave or convex, or a mix of both. The term **convexity effects** is an extension and generalization of the fundamental asymmetry. The technical name for fragility is negative convexity effects and for antifragility is positive convexity effects. Convex is good (a smiley), concave is bad (a frowny).

Philosopher's Stone, also called **Convexity Bias** (very technical): The exact measure of benefits derived from nonlinearity or optionality (or, even more technically, the difference between x and a convex function of x). For instance, such bias can quantify the health benefits of variable intensity of pulmonary ventilation over steady pressure, or compute the gains from infrequent feeding. The **Procrustean bed** from the neglect of nonlinearity (to "simplify") lies in assuming such convexity bias does not exist.

Appendix I:
A GRAPHICAL TOUR OF THE BOOK

For those nonliterary folks who like to see things in graphs, rather than words, and those only.

NONLINEARITY AND LESS IS MORE (& PROCRUSTEAN BED)

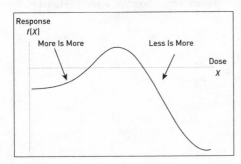

FIGURE 19. *This graph explains both the nonlinear response and the "less is more" idea. As the dose increases beyond a certain point, benefits reverse. We saw that everything nonlinear is either convex, concave, or, as in this graph, mixed. Also shows how under nonlinearities, reductions fail: the Procrustean bed of words "good for you" or "bad" is severely distorting.*

    Also shows why tinkering-derived heuristics matter because they don't take you into the danger zone—words and narratives do. Note how the "more is more" zone is convex, meaning accelerated initial benefits. (In Levantine Arabic, the zone beyond the saturation has a name: كترتا متل قلتا *"more of it is like less of it.")*

    Finally, it shows why competitive "sophistication" (rather, complication masked as sophistication) is harmful, as compared to the practitioner's craving for optimal simplicity.

Fragility Transfer Theorem:
Note that by the Fragility Transfer Theorem,

CONVEX EXPOSURE [OVER SOME RANGE] ↔ LIKES VOLATILITY [UP TO SOME POINT]

(volatility and other members of the disorder cluster), and

CONCAVE EXPOSURE ↔ DISLIKES VOLATILITY

MAPPING OF FRAGILITIES

In Time Series Space

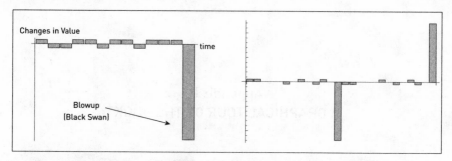

FIGURE 20. *Fragile variations through time, two types of fragilities. A representative series. The horizontal axis shows time, the vertical one shows variations. This can apply to anything: a health indicator, changes in wealth, your happiness, etc. We can see small (or no) benefits and variations most of the time and occasional large adverse outcomes. Uncertainty can hit in a rather hard way. Notice that the loss can occur at any time and exceed the previous cumulative gains. Type 2 (left) and Type 1 (right) differ in that Type 2 does not experience large positive effects from uncertainty while Type 1 does.*

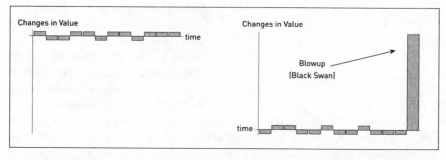

FIGURE 21. *The Just Robust (but not antifragile) (on the left): It experiences small or no variations through time. Never large ones. The Antifragile system (right): Uncertainty benefits a lot more than it hurts—the exact opposite of the first graph in Figure 20.*

Seen in Probabilities

FIGURE 22. *The horizontal axis represents outcomes, the vertical their probability (i.e., their frequency). The Robust: Small positive and negative outcomes. The Fragile (Type 1, very rare): Can deliver both large negative and large positive outcomes. Why is it rare? Symmetry is very, very rare empirically yet all statistical distributions tend to simplify by using it. The Fragile (Type 2): We see large improbable downside (often hidden and ignored), small upside. There is a possibility of a se-*

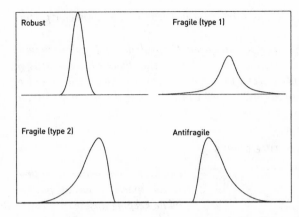

*vere unfavorable outcome (left), much more than a hugely favorable one, as the left side is thicker than the right one. **The Antifragile:** Large upside, small downside. Large favorable outcomes are possible, large unfavorable ones less so (if not impossible). The right "tail," for favorable outcomes, is larger than the left one.*

TABLE 9 • THE FOUR DIFFERENT CLASSES OF PAYOFFS

Left Tail of the Distribution	Right Tail of the Distribution	Condition
Thin	Thick	Antifragile
Thick	Thick	Fragile (Type 1) [Very Rare]
Thick	Thin	Fragile (Type 2)
Thin	Thin	Robust

Fragility has a left tail and, what is crucial, is therefore sensitive to perturbations of the left side of the probability distribution.

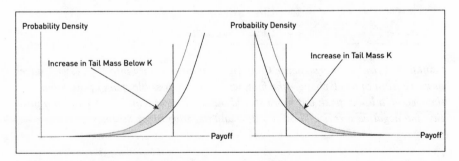

FIGURE 23. *Definition of Fragility (left graph): Fragility is the shaded area, the increase in the mass in left tail below a certain level K of the target variable in response to any change in parameter of the source variable—mostly the "volatility" or something a bit more tuned. We subsume all these changes in s⁻, about which later in the notes section (where I managed to hide equations).*

*For a **definition of antifragility** (right graph), which is not exactly symmetric, the* *same mirror image for right tail plus robustness in left tail. The parameter pertur-bated is s⁺.*

It is key that while we may not be able to specify the probability distribution with any precision, we can probe the response through heuristics thanks to the "transfer theorem" in Taleb and Douady (2012). In other words, we do not need to understand the future probability of events, but we can figure out the fragility to these events.

BARBELL TRANSFORMATION IN TIME SERIES

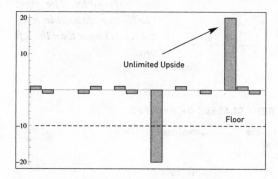

FIGURE 24. *Barbell seen in time series space. Flooring payoffs while keeping upside.*

BARBELLS (CONVEX TRANSFORMATIONS) AND THEIR PROPERTIES IN PROBABILITY SPACE

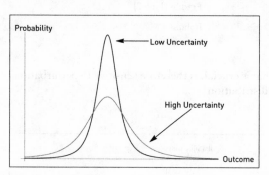

A graphical expression of the bar-bell idea.

FIGURE 25. *Case 1, the Symmetric Case. Injecting uncertainty into the system makes us move from one bell shape—the first, with narrow possible spate of outcomes—to the second, a lower peak but more spread out. So it causes an increase of both posi-tive and negative surprises, both positive and negative Black Swans.*

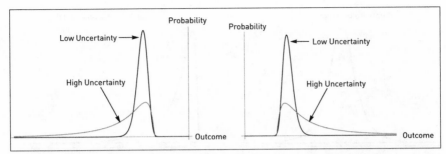

FIGURE 26. *Case 2 (left): Fragile. Limited gains, larger losses. Increasing uncertainty in the system causes an augmentation of mostly (sometimes only) negative outcomes, just negative Black Swans. Case 3 (right): Antifragile. Increasing randomness and uncertainty in the system raises the probability of very favorable outcomes, and accordingly expand the expected payoff. It shows how discovery is, mathematically, exactly like an anti–airplane delay.*

TECHNICAL VERSION OF FAT TONY'S "NOT THE SAME 'TING,' " OR THE CONFLATION OF EVENTS AND EXPOSURE TO EVENTS

This note will also explain a "convex transformation."

$f(x)$ is *exposure* to the variable x. $f(x)$ can equivalently be called "payoff from x," "exposure to x," even "utility of payoff from x" where we introduce in f a utility function. x can be anything.

> **Example:** x is the intensity of an earthquake on some scale in some specific area, $f(x)$ is the number of persons dying from it. We can easily see that $f(x)$ can be made more predictable than x (if we force people to stay away from a specific area or build to some standards, etc.).

> **Example:** x is the number of meters of my fall to the ground when someone pushes me from height x, $f(x)$ is a measure of my physical condition from the effect of the fall. Clearly I cannot predict x (who will push me, rather $f(x)$).

> **Example:** x is the number of cars in NYC at noon tomorrow, $f(x)$ is travel time from point A to point B for a certain agent. $f(x)$ can be made more predictable than x (take the subway, or, even better, walk).

Some people talk about $f(x)$ thinking they are talking about x. This is the problem of the **conflation of event and exposure.** This error present in Aristotle is virtually ubiquitous in the philosophy of probability (say, Hacking).

One can become antifragile to x without understanding x, through convexity of $f(x)$.

The answer to the question "what do you do in a world you don't understand?" is, simply, work on the undesirable states of $f(x)$.

It is often easier to modify $f(x)$ than to get better knowledge of x. (In other words, robustification rather than forecasting Black Swans.)

> **Example:** If I buy an insurance on the market, here x, dropping more than 20 percent, $f(x)$ will be independent of the part of the probability distribution of x that is below 20 percent and impervious to changes in its scale parameter. (This is an example of a barbell.)

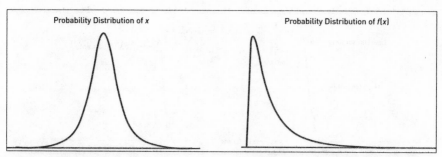

Probability Distribution of *x*   Probability Distribution of *f*(*x*)

FIGURE 27. *Convex Transformation (f(x) is a convex function of x). The difference between x and exposure to x. There is no downside risk in the second graph. The key is to modify f(x) in order to make knowledge of the properties of x on the left side of the distribution as irrelevant as possible. This operation is called convex transformation, nicknamed "barbell" here.*

Green lumber fallacy: When one confuses $f(x)$ for another function $g(x)$, one that has different nonlinearities.

More technically: If one is antifragile to x, then the variance (or volatility, or other measures of variation) of x benefit $f(x)$, since distributions that are skewed have their mean depend on the variance and when skewed right, their expectation increases with variance (the lognormal, for instance, has for mean a term that includes $+\frac{1}{2}\sigma^2$).

Further, the probability distribution of $f(x)$ is markedly different from that of x, particularly in the presence of nonlinearities.

> When $f(x)$ is convex (concave) monotonically, $f(x)$ is right (left) skewed.

> When $f(x)$ is increasing and convex on the left then concave to the right, the probability distribution of $f(x)$ is thinner-tailed than that of x. For instance, in Kahneman-Tversky's prospect theory, the so-called utility of changes in wealth is more "robust" than that of wealth.

Why payoff matters more than probability (technical): Where $p(x)$ is the density, the expectation, that is $\int f(x)p(x)dx$, will depend increasingly on f rather than p, and the more nonlinear f, the more it will depend on f rather than p.

THE FOURTH QUADRANT (TALEB, 2009)

The idea is that tail events are not computable (in fat-tailed domains), but we can assess our exposure to the problem. Assume $f(x)$ is an increasing function, Table 10 connects the idea to the notion of the Fourth Quadrant.

TABLE 10

	THIN-TAILED DISTRIBUTION FOR X	FAT-TAILED DISTRIBUTION FOR X
$f(x)$ "mitigating" by clipping extreme outcomes, i.e., convex-concave	Very robust outcome	Quite robust outcome
$f(x)$ concave-convex, exacerbates remote outcomes	Robust outcome (sort of)	FOURTH QUADRANT Fragile (if $f(x)$ is concave) or antifragile

LOCAL AND GLOBAL CONVEXITIES (TECHNICAL)

Nothing is open-ended in nature—death is a maximum outcome for a unit. So things end up convex on one end, concave on the other.

In fact, there is maximum harm at some point in things biological. Let us revisit the concave figure of the stone and pebbles in Chapter 18: by widening the range we see that boundedness of harm brings convexities somewhere. Concavity was dominant, but local. Figure 28 looks at the continuation of the story of the stone and pebbles.

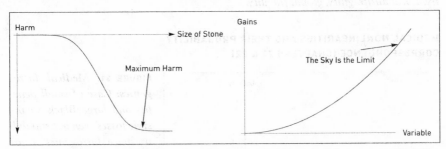

FIGURE 28. *The left graph shows a broader range in the story of the stone and pebbles in Chapter 18. At some point, the concave turns convex as we hit maximum harm. The right graph shows strong antifragility, with no known upper limit (leading to Extremistan). These payoffs are only available in economic variables, say, sales of books, or matters unbounded or near-unbounded. I am unable to find such an effect in nature.*

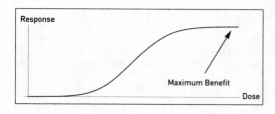

FIGURE 29. *Weak Antifragility (Mediocristan), with bounded maximum. Typical in nature.*

FREAK NONLINEARITIES (VERY TECHNICAL)

The next two types of nonlinearities are almost never seen outside of economic variables; they are particularly limited to those caused by derivatives.

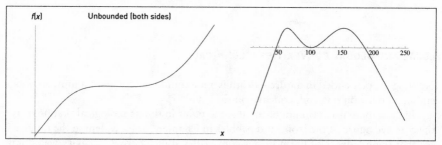

FIGURE 30. *The left graph shows a convex-concave increasing function, the opposite of the bounded dose-response functions we see in nature. It leads to Type 2, Fragile (very, very fat tails). The right graph shows the most dangerous of all: pseudoconvexity. Local antifragility, global fragility.*

MEDICAL NONLINEARITIES AND THEIR PROBABILITY CORRESPONDENCE (CHAPTERS 21 & 22)

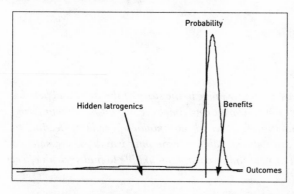

FIGURE 31. *Medical Iatrogenics: Case of small benefits and large Black Swan–style losses seen in probability space. Iatrogenics occurs when we have small identifiable gains (say, avoidance of small discomfort or a minor infection) and exposure to Black Swans with delayed invisible large side effects (say, death). These concave benefits from medicine are just like selling a financial option (plenty of risk) against small tiny immediate gains while claiming "evidence of no harm."*

In short, for a healthy person, there is a small probability of disastrous outcomes (discounted because unseen and not taken into account), and a high probability of mild benefits.

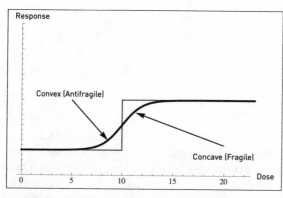

FIGURE 32. *Nonlinearities in biology. The shape convex-concave necessarily flows from anything increasing (monotone, i.e., never decreasing) and bounded, with maximum and minimum values, i.e., does not reach infinity from either side. At low levels, the dose response is convex (gradually more and more effective).*

Additional doses tend to become gradually ineffective or start hurting. The same can apply to anything consumed in too much regularity. This type of graph necessarily applies to any situation bounded on both sides, with a known minimum and maximum (saturation), which includes happiness.

For instance, if one considers that there exists a maximum level of happiness and unhappiness, then the general shape of this curve with convexity on the left and concavity on the right has to hold for happiness (replace "dose" with "wealth" and "response" with "happiness"). Kahneman-Tversky prospect theory models a similar shape for "utility" of changes in wealth, which they discovered empirically.

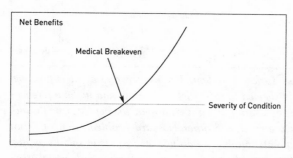

FIGURE 33. *Recall the hypertension example. On the vertical axis, we have the benefits of a treatment, on the horizontal, the severity of the condition. The arrow points at the level where probabilistic gains match probabilistic harm. Iatrogenics disappears nonlin-*early *as a function of the severity of the condition. This implies that when the patient is very ill, the distribution shifts to antifragile (thicker right tail), with large benefits from the treatment over possible iatrogenics, little to lose.*

Note that if you increase the treatment you hit concavity from maximum benefits, a zone not covered in the graph—seen more broadly, it would look like the preceding graph.

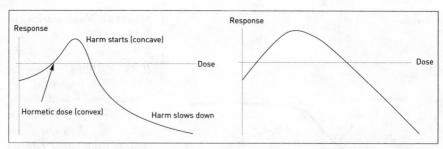

FIGURE 34. *The left graph shows hormesis for an organism (similar to Figure 19): we can see a stage of benefits as the dose increases (initially convex) slowing down into a phase of harm as we increase the dose a bit further (initially concave); then we see things flattening out at the level of maximum harm (beyond a certain point, the organism is dead so there is such a thing as a bounded and known worst case scenario in biology). To the right, a wrong graph of hormesis in medical textbooks showing initial concavity, with a beginning that looks linear or slightly concave.*

THE INVERSE TURKEY PROBLEM

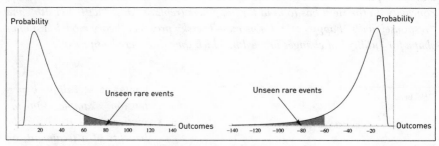

FIGURE 35. *Antifragile, Inverse Turkey Problem: The unseen rare event is positive. When you look at a positively skewed (antifragile) time series and make inferences about the unseen, you miss the good stuff and underestimate the benefits (the Pisano, 2006a, 2006b, mistake). On the right, the other Harvard problem, that of Froot (2001). The filled area corresponds to what we do not tend to see in small samples, from insufficiency of points. Interestingly the shaded area increases with model error. The more technical sections call this zone ω_B (turkey) and ω_C (inverse turkey).*

DIFFERENCE BETWEEN POINT ESTIMATES AND DISTRIBUTIONS

Let us apply this analysis to how planners make the mistakes they make, and why deficits tend to be worse than planned:

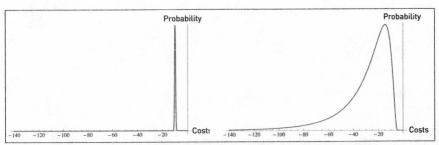

FIGURE 36. *The gap between predictions and reality: probability distribution of outcomes from costs of projects in the minds of planners (left) and in reality (right). In the first graph they assume that the costs will be both low and quite certain. The graph on the right shows outcomes to be both worse and more spread out, particularly with higher possibility of unfavorable outcomes. Note the fragility increase owing to the swelling left tail.*

This misunderstanding of the effect of uncertainty applies to government deficits, plans that have IT components, travel time (to a lesser degree), and many more. We will use the same graph to show model error from underestimating fragility by assuming that a parameter is constant when it is random. This is what plagues bureaucrat-driven economics (next discussion).

Appendix II (Very Technical):
WHERE MOST ECONOMIC MODELS
FRAGILIZE AND BLOW PEOPLE UP

When I said "technical" in the main text, I may have been fibbing. Here I am not.

The Markowitz incoherence: Assume that someone tells you that the probability of an event is exactly zero. You ask him where he got this from. "Baal told me" is the answer. In such case, the person is coherent, but would be deemed unrealistic by non-Baalists. But if on the other hand, the person tells you "I *estimated* it to be zero," we have a problem. The person is both unrealistic and inconsistent. Something estimated needs to have an estimation error. So probability cannot be zero if it is estimated, its lower bound is linked to the estimation error; the higher the estimation error, the higher the probability, up to a point. As with Laplace's argument of total ignorance, an infinite estimation error pushes the probability toward ½.

We will return to the implication of the mistake; take for now that anything estimating a parameter and then putting it into an equation is different from estimating the equation across parameters (same story as the health of the grandmother, the average temperature, here "estimated" is irrelevant, what we need is average health across temperatures). And Markowitz showed his incoherence by starting his "seminal" paper with "Assume you know E and V" (that is, the expectation and the variance). At the end of the paper he accepts that they need to be estimated, and what is worse, with a combination of statistical techniques and the "judgment of practical men." Well, if these parameters need to be estimated, with an error, then the derivations need to be written differently and, of course, we would have no paper—and no Markowitz paper, no blowups, no modern finance, no fragilistas teaching junk to students. . . . Economic models are extremely fragile to assumptions, in the sense that a slight alteration in these assumptions can, as we will see, lead to extremely consequential differences in the results. And, to make matters worse, many of these models are "back-fit" to assumptions, in the sense that the hypotheses are selected to make the math work, which makes them ultrafragile and ultrafragilizing.

Simple example: Government deficits.

We use the following deficit example owing to the way calculations by governments and government agencies currently miss convexity terms (and have a hard time accepting it). Really, they don't take them into account. The example illustrates:

(a) missing the stochastic character of a variable known to affect the model but deemed deterministic (and fixed), and

(b) *F*, the function of such variable, is convex or concave with respect to the variable.

Say a government estimates unemployment for the next three years as averaging 9 percent; it uses its econometric models to issue a forecast balance *B* of a two-hundred-billion deficit in the local currency. But it misses (like almost everything in economics) that unemployment is a stochastic variable. Employment over a three-year period has fluctuated by 1 percent on average. We can calculate the effect of the error with the following:

Unemployment at 8%, Balance B(8%) = –75 bn (improvement of 125 bn)

Unemployment at 9%, Balance B(9%)= –200 bn

Unemployment at 10%, Balance B(10%)= –550 bn (worsening of 350 bn)

The concavity bias, or negative convexity bias, from underestimation of the deficit is –112.5 bn, since ½ {B(8%) + B(10%)} = –312 bn, not –200 bn. This is the exact case of the **inverse philosopher's stone**.

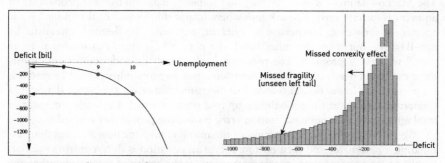

FIGURE 37. *Nonlinear transformations allow the detection of both model convexity bias and fragility. Illustration of the example: histogram from Monte Carlo simulation of government deficit as a left-tailed random variable simply as a result of randomizing unemployment, of which it is a concave function. The method of point estimate would assume a Dirac stick at –200, thus underestimating both the expected deficit (–312) and the tail fragility of it. (From Taleb and Douady, 2012).*

Application: Ricardian Model and Left Tail—The Price of Wine Happens to Vary

For almost two hundred years, we've been talking about an idea by the economist David Ricardo called "comparative advantage." In short, it says that a country should have a certain policy based on its comparative advantage in wine or clothes. Say a country is good at both wine and clothes, better than its neighbors with whom it can trade freely. Then the visible *optimal* strategy would be to specialize in either wine or clothes, whichever fits the best and minimizes opportunity costs. Everyone would then be happy. The analogy by the economist Paul Samuelson is that if some-one happens to be the best doctor in town and, at the same time, the best secretary, then it would be preferable to be the higher-earning doctor—as it would minimize opportunity losses—and let someone else be the secretary and buy secretarial services from him.

I agree that there are benefits in *some* form of specialization, but not from the models used to prove it. The flaw with such reasoning is as follows. True, it would be inconceivable for a doctor to become a part-time secretary just because he is good at it. But, at the same time, we can safely assume that being a doctor insures some professional stability: People will not cease to get sick and there is a higher social status associated with the profession than that of secretary, making the profession more desirable. But assume now that in a two-country world, a country specialized in wine, hoping to sell its specialty in the market to the other country, and that *suddenly the price of wine drops precipitously*. Some change in taste caused the price to change. Ricardo's analysis assumes that both the market price of wine and the costs of production remain constant, and there is no "second order" part of the story.

TABLE 11 • RICARDO'S ORIGINAL EXAMPLE (COSTS OF PRODUCTION PER UNIT)

	CLOTH	WINE
Britain	100	110
Portugal	90	80

The logic: The table above shows the cost of production, normalized to a selling price of one unit each, that is, assuming that these trade at equal price (1 unit of cloth for 1 unit of wine). What looks like the paradox is as follows: that Portugal produces cloth cheaper than Britain, but should buy cloth from there instead, using the gains from the sales of wine. In the absence of transaction and transportation costs, it is efficient for Britain to produce just cloth, and Portugal to only produce wine.

The idea has always attracted economists because of its paradoxical and counterintuitive aspect. For instance, in an article "Why Intellectuals Don't Understand Comparative Advantage" (Krugman, 1998), Paul Krugman, who fails to understand the concept himself, as this essay and his technical work show him to be completely innocent of tail events and risk management, makes fun of other intellectuals such as S. J. Gould who understand tail events albeit intuitively rather than analytically. (Clearly one cannot talk about returns and gains without discounting these benefits by the offsetting risks.) The article shows Krugman falling into the critical and dangerous mistake of confusing function of average and average of function. (Traditional Ricardian analysis assumes the variables are endogenous, but does not add a layer of stochasticity.)

Now consider the price of wine and clothes *variable*—which Ricardo did not assume—with the numbers above the unbiased average long-term value. Further assume that they follow a fat-tailed distribution. Or consider that their costs of production vary according to a fat-tailed distribution.

If the price of wine in the international markets rises by, say, 40 percent, then there are clear benefits. But should the price drop by an equal percentage, –40 percent, then massive harm would ensue, in magnitude larger than the benefits should there be an equal rise. There are concavities to the exposure—severe concavities.

And clearly, should the price drop by 90 percent, the effect would be disastrous. Just imagine what would happen to your household should you get an instant and unpredicted 40 percent pay cut. Indeed, we have had problems in history with countries specializing in some goods, commodities, and crops that happen to be not just volatile, but extremely volatile. And disaster does not necessarily come from variation in price, but problems in production: suddenly, you can't produce the crop because of a germ, bad weather, or some other hindrance.

A bad crop, such as the one that caused the Irish potato famine in the decade around 1850, caused the death of a million and the emigration of a million more (Ireland's entire population at the time of this writing is only about six million, if one includes the northern part). It is very hard to reconvert resources—unlike the case in the doctor-typist story, countries don't have the ability to change. Indeed, monoculture (focus on a single crop) has turned out to be lethal in history—one bad crop leads to devastating famines.

The other part missed in the doctor-secretary analogy is that countries don't have family and friends. A doctor has a support community, a circle of friends, a collective that takes care of him, a father-in-law to borrow from in the event that he needs to reconvert into some other profession, a state above him to help. Countries don't. Further, a doctor has savings; countries tend to be borrowers.

So here again we have fragility to second-order effects.

Probability Matching: The idea of comparative advantage has an analog in probability: if you sample from an urn (with replacement) and get a black ball 60 percent of the time, and a white one the remaining 40 percent, the optimal strategy, according to textbooks, is to bet 100 percent of the time on black. The strategy of betting 60 percent of the time on black and 40 percent on white is called "probability matching" and considered to be an error in the decision-science literature (which I remind the reader is what was used by Triffat in Chapter 10). People's instinct to engage in probability matching appears to be sound, not a mistake. In nature, probabilities are unstable (or unknown), and probability matching is similar to redundancy, as a buffer. So if the probabilities change, in other words if there is another layer of randomness, then the optimal strategy is probability matching.

How specialization works: The reader should not interpret what I am saying to mean that specialization is not a good thing—only that one should establish such specialization after addressing fragility and second-order effects. Now I do believe that Ricardo is ultimately right, but not from the models shown. Organically, systems without top-down controls would specialize progressively, slowly, and over a long time, through trial and error, get the right amount of specialization—not through some bureaucrat using a model. To repeat, systems make small errors, design makes large ones.

So the imposition of Ricardo's insight-turned-model by some social planner would lead to a blowup; letting tinkering work slowly would lead to efficiency—true efficiency. The role of policy makers should be to, *via negativa* style, allow the emergence of specialization by preventing what hinders the process.

A More General Methodology to Spot Model Error

Model second-order effects and fragility: Assume we have the right model (which is a very generous assumption) but are uncertain about the parameters. As a generalization of the deficit/employment example used in the previous section, say we are using f, a simple function: $f(x|\bar{\alpha})$, where $\bar{\alpha}$ is supposed to be the average expected input variable, where we take φ as the distribution of α over its domain $\wp_\alpha$, $\bar\alpha = \int_{\wp_\alpha} \alpha\, \varphi(\alpha)\, d\alpha$.

The philosopher's stone: The mere fact that α is uncertain (since it is estimated) might lead to a bias if we perturbate from the *inside* (of the integral), i.e., stochasticize the parameter deemed fixed. Accordingly, the convexity bias is easily measured as the difference between (a) the function f integrated across values of potential α, and (b) f estimated for a single value of α deemed to be its average. The convexity bias (philosopher's stone) ω_A becomes:[*]

$$\omega_A = \int_{\wp_x}\int_{\wp_\alpha} f\big(x\,\big|\,\alpha\big)\varphi\big(\alpha\big)\, d\alpha\, dx - \int_{\wp_x} f\Big(x\,\Big|\Big(\int_{\wp_\alpha} \alpha\,\varphi\big(\alpha\big)\, d\alpha\Big)\Big)dx$$

The central equation: Fragility is a partial philosopher's stone below K, hence ω_B the missed fragility is assessed by comparing the two integrals below K in order to capture the effect on the left tail:

$$\omega_B(K) \equiv \int_{-\infty}^{K}\int_{\wp_\alpha} f\big(x\,\big|\,\alpha\big)\varphi(\alpha)\, d\alpha\, dx - \int_{-\infty}^{K} f\Big(x\,\Big|\Big(\int_{\wp_\alpha} \alpha\,\varphi\big(\alpha\big)\, d\alpha\Big)\Big)dx$$

which can be approximated by an interpolated estimate obtained with two values of α separated from a midpoint by $\Delta\alpha$ its mean deviation of α and estimating

$$\omega_B(K) \equiv \int_{-\infty}^{K} \frac{1}{2}\big(f(x\,|\,\bar\alpha + \Delta\alpha) + f(x\,|\,\bar\alpha - \Delta\alpha)\big)dx - \int_{-\infty}^{K} f(x\,|\,\bar\alpha)\, dx$$

Note that antifragility ω_C is integrating from K to infinity. We can probe ω_B by point estimates of f at a level of $X \leq K$

$$\omega_B'(X) = \frac{1}{2}\big(f(X\,|\,\bar\alpha + \Delta\alpha) + f(X\,|\,\bar\alpha - \Delta\alpha)\big) - f(X\,|\,\bar\alpha)$$

so that

$$\omega_B(K) = \int_{-\infty}^{K} \omega_B'(x)\, dx$$

which leads us to the fragility detection heuristic (Taleb, Canetti, et al., 2012). In particular, if we assume that $\omega_B'(X)$ has a constant sign for $X \leq K$, then $\omega_B(K)$ has the same sign. The detection heuristic is a perturbation in the tails to probe fragility, by checking the function $\omega_B'(X)$ at any level X.

---

[*] The difference between the two sides of Jensen's inequality corresponds to a notion in information theory, the Bregman divergence. Briys, Magdalou, and Nock, 2012.

TABLE 12

MODEL	SOURCE OF FRAGILITY	REMEDY
Portfolio theory, mean-variance, etc.	Assuming knowledge of the parameters, not integrating models across parameters, relying on (very unstable) correlations. Assumes ω_A (bias) and ω_B (fragility) = 0	1/n (spread as large a number of exposures as manageable), barbells, progressive and organic construction, etc.
Ricardian comparative advantage	Missing layer of randomness in the price of wine may imply total reversal of allocation. Assumes ω_A (bias) and ω_B (fragility) = 0	Natural systems find their own allocation through tinkering
Samuelson optimization	Concentration of sources of randomness under concavity of loss function. Assumes ω_A (bias) and ω_B (fragility) = 0	Distributed randomness
Arrow-Debreu lattice state-space	Ludic fallacy: assumes exhaustive knowledge of outcomes and knowledge of probabilities. Assumes ω_A (bias), ω_B (fragility), and ω_C (antifragility) = 0	Use of metaprobabilities changes entire model implications
Dividend cash flow models	Missing stochasticity causing convexity effects. Mostly considers ω_C (antifragility) =0	Heuristics

Portfolio fallacies: Note one fallacy promoted by Markowitz users: *portfolio theory entices people to diversify, hence it is better than nothing.* Wrong, you finance fools: it pushes them to optimize, hence overallocate. It does not drive people to take less risk based on diversification, but causes them to take more open positions owing to perception of offsetting statistical properties—making them vulnerable to model error, and especially vulnerable to the underestimation of tail events. To see how, consider two investors facing a choice of allocation across three items: cash, and securities A and B. The investor who does not know the statistical properties of A and B and knows he doesn't know will allocate, say, the portion he does not want to lose to cash, the rest into A and B—according to whatever heuristic has been in traditional use. The investor who thinks he knows the statistical properties, with parameters σ_A, σ_B, $\rho_{A,B}$, will allocate ω_A, ω_B in a way to put the total risk at some target level (let us ignore the expected return for this). The lower his perception of the correlation $\rho_{A,B}$, the worse his exposure to model error. Assuming he thinks that the correlation $\rho_{A,B}$ is 0, he will be overallocated by $\frac{1}{3}$ for extreme events. But if the poor investor has the illusion that the correlation is –1, he will be maximally overallocated to his A and B investments. If the investor uses leverage, we end up with the story of Long-Term Capital Management, which turned out to be fooled by the parameters. (In real life, unlike in economic papers, things tend to change; for Baal's sake, they change!) We can repeat the idea for each parameter σ and see how lower perception of this σ leads to overallocation.

I noticed as a trader—and obsessed over the idea—that correlations were never the same in different measurements. Unstable would be a mild word for them: 0.8 over a long period becomes –0.2 over another long period. A pure sucker game. At times of stress, correlations experience even more abrupt changes—without any reliable regularity, in spite of attempts to model "stress correlations." Taleb (1997) deals with the effects of stochastic correlations: One is only safe shorting a correlation at 1, and buying it at –1—which seems to correspond to what the 1/n heuristic does.

Kelly Criterion vs. Markowitz: In order to implement a full Markowitz-style optimization, one needs to know the entire joint probability distribution of all assets for the entire future, plus the exact utility function for wealth at all future times. And without errors! (We saw that estimation errors make the system explode.) Kelly's method, developed around the same period, requires no joint distribution or utility function. In practice one needs the ratio of expected profit to worst-case return—dynamically adjusted to avoid ruin. In the case of barbell transformations, the worst case is guaranteed. And model error is much, much milder under Kelly criterion. Thorp (1971, 1998), Haigh (2000).

The formidable Aaron Brown holds that Kelly's ideas were rejected by economists—in spite of the practical appeal—because of their love of general theories for all asset prices.

Note that bounded trial and error is compatible with the Kelly criterion when one has an idea of the potential return—even when one is ignorant of the returns, if losses are bounded, the payoff will be robust and the method should outperform that of Fragilista Markowitz.

Corporate Finance: In short, corporate finance seems to be based on point projections, not distributional projections; thus if one perturbates cash flow projections, say, in the Gordon valuation model, replacing the fixed—and known—growth (and other parameters) by continuously varying jumps (particularly under fat-tailed distributions), companies deemed "expensive," or those with high growth, but low earnings, could markedly increase in expected value, something the market prices heuristically but without explicit reason.

Conclusion and summary: Something the economics establishment has been missing is that having the right model (which is a very generous assumption), but being uncertain about the parameters will invariably lead to an increase in fragility in the presence of convexity and nonlinearities.

FUHGETABOUD SMALL PROBABILITIES

Now the meat, beyond economics, the more general problem with probability and its mismeasurement.

How Fat Tails (Extremistan) Come from
Nonlinear Responses to Model Parameters

Rare events have a certain property—missed so far at the time of this writing. We deal with them using a model, a mathematical contraption that takes input parameters and outputs the probability. The more parameter uncertainty there is in a model designed to compute probabilities, the more small probabilities tend to be underestimated. Simply, small probabilities are convex to errors of computation, as an airplane ride is concave to errors and disturbances (remember, it gets longer, not shorter). The more sources of disturbance one forgets to take into account, the longer the airplane ride compared to the naive estimation.

We all know that to compute probability using a standard Normal statistical distribution, one needs a parameter called *standard deviation*—or something similar that characterizes the scale or dispersion of outcomes. But uncertainty about such standard deviation has the effect of making the small probabilities rise. For instance, for a deviation that is called "three sigma," events that should take place no more than one in 740 observations, the probability rises by 60% if one moves the standard deviation up by 5%, and drops by 40% if we move the standard deviation down by 5%. So if your error is on average a tiny 5%, the underestimation from a naive model is about 20%. Great asymmetry, but nothing yet. It gets worse as one looks for more deviations, the "six sigma" ones (alas, chronically frequent in economics): a rise of five times more. The rarer the event (i.e., the higher the "sigma"), the worse the effect from small uncertainty about what to put in the equation. With events such as ten sigma, the difference is more than a billion times. We can use the argument to show how smaller and smaller probabilities require more precision in computation. The smaller the probability, the more a small, very small rounding in the computation makes the asymmetry massively insignificant. For tiny, very small probabilities, you need near-infinite precision in the parameters; the slightest uncertainty there causes mayhem. They are very convex to perturbations. This in a way is the argument I've used to show that small probabilities are incomputable, even if one has the right model—which we of course don't.

The same argument relates to deriving probabilities nonparametrically, from past frequencies. If the probability gets close to 1/ sample size, the error explodes.

This of course explains the error of Fukushima. Similar to Fannie Mae. To summarize, small probabilities increase in an accelerated manner as one changes the parameter that enters their computation.

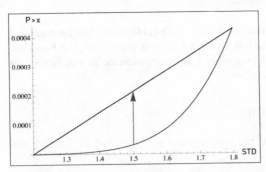

FIGURE 38. *The probability is convex to standard deviation in a Gaussian model. The plot shows the STD effect on P>x, and compares P>6 with an STD of 1.5 compared to P>6 assuming a linear combination of 1.2 and 1.8 (here a(1)=1/5).*

The worrisome fact is that a perturbation in σ extends well into the tail of the distribution in a convex way; the risks of a portfolio that is sensitive to the tails would explode. That is, we are still here in the Gaussian world! Such explosive uncertainty isn't the result of natural fat tails in the distribution, merely small imprecision about a future parameter. It is just epistemic! So those who use these models while admitting parameters uncertainty are necessarily committing a severe inconsistency.[*]

Of course, uncertainty explodes even more when we replicate conditions of the non-Gaussian real world upon perturbating tail exponents. Even with a powerlaw distribution, the results are severe, particularly under variations of the tail exponent as these have massive consequences. Really, fat tails mean incomputability of tail events, little else.

Compounding Uncertainty (Fukushima)

Using the earlier statement that *estimation implies error*, let us extend the logic: errors have errors; these in turn have errors. Taking into account the effect makes all small probabilities rise regardless of model—even in the Gaussian—to the point of reaching fat tails and powerlaw effects (even the so-called infinite variance) when higher orders of uncertainty are large. Even taking a Gaussian with σ the standard deviation having a proportional error $a(1)$; $a(1)$ has an error rate $a(2)$, etc. Now it depends on the higher order error rate $a(n)$ related to $a(n-1)$; if these are in constant proportion, then we converge to a very thick-tailed distribution. If proportional errors decline, we still have fat tails. In all cases mere error is not a good thing for small probability.

The sad part is that getting people to accept that every measure has an error has been nearly impossible—the event in Fukushima held to happen once per million years would turn into one per 30 if one percolates the different layers of uncertainty in the adequate manner.

[*] This further shows the defects of the notion of "Knightian uncertainty," since *all tails* are uncertain under the slightest perturbation and their effect is severe in fat-tailed domains, that is, economic life.

ADDITIONAL NOTES, AFTERTHOUGHTS,
AND FURTHER READING

These are both additional readings and ideas that came to me after the composition of the book, like whether God is considered robust or antifragile by theologians or the history of measurement as a sucker problem in the probability domain. As to further reading, I am avoiding the duplication of those mentioned in earlier books, particularly those concerning the philosophical problem of induction, Black Swan problems, and the psychology of uncertainty. I managed to bury some mathematical material in the text without Alexis K., the math-phobic London editor, catching me (particularly my definition of fragility in the notes for Book V and my summary derivation of "small is beautiful"). Note that there are more involved technical discussions on the Web.

Seclusion: Since *The Black Swan,* I've spent 1,150 days in physical seclusion, a soothing state of more than three hundred days a year with minimal contact with the outside world—plus twenty years of thinking about the problem of nonlinearities and nonlinear exposures. So I've sort of lost patience with institutional and cosmetic knowledge. Science and knowledge are convincing and deepened rigorous argument taken to its conclusion, not naive (*via positiva*) empiricism or fluff, which is why I refuse the commoditized (and highly gamed) journalistic idea of "reference"—rather, "further reading." My results should not depend, and do not depend on a single paper or result, except for *via negativa* debunking—these are illustrative.

Charlatans: In the "fourth quadrant" paper published in *International Journal of Forecasting* (one of the backup documents for *The Black Swan* that had been sitting on the Web) I showed *empirically* using all economic data available that fat tails are both severe and intractable—hence all methods with "squares" don't work with socioeconomic variables: regression, standard deviation, correlation, etc. (technically 80% of the Kurtosis in 10,000 pieces of data can come from *one single* observation, meaning all measures of fat tails are just sampling errors). This is a very strong *via negativa* statement: it means we can't use covariance matrices—they are unreliable and uninformative. Actually just accepting fat tails would have led us to such result—no need for empiricism; I processed the data nevertheless. Now any honest scientific profession would say: "what do we do with such evidence?"—the economics and finance establishment just ignored it. A bunch of charlatans, by any scientific norm and ethical metric. Many "Nobels" (Engle, Merton, Scholes, Markowitz, Miller, Samuelson, Sharpe, and a few more) have their results grounded in such central assumptions, and all their works would evaporate otherwise. Charlatans (and fragilistas) do well in institutions. It is a matter of ethics; see notes on Book VII.

For our purpose here, I ignore any economic paper that uses regression in fat-tailed domains—as just hot air—except in some cases, such as Pritchet (2001), where the result is not impacted by fat tails.

PROLOGUE & BOOK I: The Antifragile: An Introduction

Wind energizes fire: Resembles La Rochefoucauld's comment on love.

Antifragility and complexity: Bar-Yam and Epstein (2004) define sensitivity, the possibility of large response to small stimuli, and robustness, the possibility of small response to large stimuli. In fact this sensitivity, when the response is positive, resembles antifragility.

Private Correspondence with Bar-Yam: Yaneer Bar-Yam, generously in his comments: "If we take a step back and more generally consider the issue of partitioned versus connected systems, partitioned systems are more stable, and connected systems are both more vulnerable and have more opportunities for collective action. Vulnerability (fragility) is connectivity without responsiveness. Responsiveness enables connectivity to lead to opportunity. If collective action can be employed to address threats, or to take advantage of opportunities, then the vulnerability can be mitigated and outweighed by the benefits. This is the basic relationship between the idea of sensitivity as we described it and your concept of antifragility." (With permission.)

Damocles and complexification: Tainter (1988) argues that sophistication leads to fragility—but following a very different line of reasoning.

Post-Traumatic Growth: Bonanno (2004), Tedeschi and Calhoun (1996), Calhoun and Tedeschi (2006), Alter et al. (2007), Shah et al. (2007), Pat-Horenczyk and Brom (2007).

Pilots abdicate responsibility to the system: FAA report: John Lowy, AP, Aug. 29, 2011.

Lucretius Effect: Fourth Quadrant discussion in the Postscript of *The Black Swan* and empirical evidence in associated papers.

High-water mark: Kahneman (2011), using as backup the works of the very insightful Howard Kunreuther, that "protective actions, whether by individuals or by governments, are usually designed to be adequate to the worst disaster actually experienced. . . . Images of even worse disaster do not come easily to mind."

Psychologists and "resilience": Seery 2011, courtesy Peter Bevelin. "However, some theory and empirical evidence suggest that the experience of facing difficulties can also promote benefits in the form of greater propensity for resilience when dealing with subsequent stressful situations." They use resilience! Once again *itsnotresilience.*

Danchin's paper: Danchin et al. (2011).

Engineering errors and sequential effect on safety: Petroski (2006).

Noise and effort: Mehta et al. (2012).

Effort and fluency: Shan and Oppenheimer (2007), Alter et al. (2007).

Barricades: Idea communicated by Saifedean Ammous.

Buzzati: Una felice sintesi di quell'ultimo capitolo della vita di Buzzati è contenuto nel libro di Lucia Bellaspiga «Dio che non esisti, ti prego. Dino Buzzati, la fatica di credere»

Self-knowledge: Daniel Wegner's illusion of conscious will, in *Fooled by Randomness.*

Book sales and bad reviews: For Ayn Rand: Michael Shermer, "The Unlikeliest Cult in History," *Skeptic* vol. 2, no. 2, 1993, pp. 74–81. This is an example; please do not mistake this author for a fan of Ayn Rand.

Smear campaigns: Note that the German philosopher Brentano waged an anonymous attack on Marx. Initially it was the accusation of covering up some sub-minor fact completely irrelevant to the ideas of *Das Kapital;* Brentano got the discussion completely diverted away from the central theme, even posthumously, with Engels vigorously continuing the debate defending Marx in the preface of the third volume of the treatise.

How to run a smear campaign from Louis XIV to Napoleon: Darnton (2010).

Wolff's law and bones, exercise, bone mineral density in swimmers: Wolff (1892), Carbuhn (2010), Guadaluppe-Grau (2009), Hallström et al. (2010), Mudd (2007), Velez (2008).

Aesthetics of disorder: Arnheim (1971).

Nanocomposites: Carey et al. (2011).

Karsenty and Bones: I thank Jacques Merab for discussion and introduction to Karsenty; Karsenty (2003, 2012a), Fukumoto and Martin (2009); for male fertility and bones, Karsenty (2011, 2012b).

Mistaking the Economy for a Clock: A typical, infuriating error in Grant (2001): "Society is conceived as a huge and intricate clockwork that functions automatically and predictably once it has been set in motion. The whole system is governed by mechanical laws that organize the relations of each part. Just as Newton discovered the laws of gravity that govern motion in the natural world, Adam Smith discovered the laws of supply and demand that govern the motion of the economy. Smith used the metaphor of the watch and the machine in describing social systems."

Selfish gene: The "selfish gene" is (convincingly) an idea of Robert Trivers often attributed to Richard Dawkins—private communication with Robert Trivers. A sad story.

Danchin's systemic antifragility and redefinition of hormesis: Danchin and I wrote our papers in feedback mode. Danchin et al. (2011): "The idea behind is that in the fate of a collection of entities, exposed to serious challenges, it may be possible to obtain a positive overall outcome. Within the collection, one of the entities would fare extremely well, compensating for the collapse of all the others and even doing much better than the bulk if unchallenged. With this view, hormesis is just a holistic description of underlying scenarios acting at the level of a population of processes, structures or molecules, just noting the positive outcome for the whole. For living organisms this could act at the level of the population of organisms, the population of cells, or the population of intracellular molecules. We explore here how antifragility could operate at the latter level, noting that its implementation has features highly reminiscent of what we name natural selection. In particular, if antifragility is a built-in process that permits some individual entities to stand out from the bulk in a challenging situation, thereby improving the fate of the whole, it would illustrate the implementation of a process that gathers and utilises information."

Steve Jobs: "Death is the most wonderful invention of life. It purges the system of these old models that are obsolete." Beahm (2011).

Swiss cuckoo clock: Orson Welles, *The Third Man.*

Bruno Leoni: I thank Alberto Mingardi for making me aware of the idea of legal robustness—and for the privilege of being invited to give the Leoni lecture in Milan in 2009. Leoni (1957, 1991).

Great Moderation: A turkey problem. Before the turmoil that started in 2008, a gentleman called Benjamin Bernanke, then a Princeton professor, later to be chairman of the Federal Reserve Bank of the United States and the most powerful person in the world of economics and finance, dubbed the period we witnessed the "great moderation"—putting me in a very difficult position to argue for increase of fragility. This is like pronouncing that someone who has just spent a decade in a sterilized room is in "great health"—when he is the most vulnerable.

Note that the turkey problem is an evolution of Russell's chicken (*The Black Swan*).

Rousseau: In *Contrat Social.* See also Joseph de Maistre, *Oeuvres,* Éditions Robert Laffont.

BOOK II: Modernity and the Denial of Antifragility

City-states: Great arguments in support of the movement toward semiautonomous cities. Benjamin Barber, Long Now Foundation Lecture (2012), Khanna (2010), Glaeser (2011). Mayors are better than presidents at dealing with trash collection— and less likely to drag us into war. Also Mansel (2012) for the Levant.

Austro-Hungarian Empire: Fejtö (1989). Counterfactual history: Fejtö holds that the first war would have been avoided.

Random search and oil exploration: Menard and Sharman (1976), controversy White et al. (1976), Singer et al. (1981).

Randomizing politicians: Pluchino et al. (2011).

Switzerland: Exposition in Fossedal and Berkeley (2005).

Modern State: Scott (1998) provides a critique of the high modernistic state.

Levantine economies: Mansel (2012) on city-states. Economic history, Pamuk (2006), Issawi (1966, 1988), von Heyd (1886). Insights in Edmond About (About, 1855).

City-States in history: Stasavage (2012) is critical of the oligarchic city-state as an engine of long-term growth (though initially high growth rate). However, the paper is totally unconvincing econometrically owing to missing fat tails. The issue is fragility and risk management, not cosmetic growth. Aside from Weber and Pirenne, advocates of the model, Delong and Schleifer (1993). See Ogilvie (2011).

Tonsillectomies: Bakwin (1945), cited by Bornstein and Emler (2001), discussion in Freidson (1970). Redone by Avanian and Berwick (1991).

Orlov: Orlov (2011).

Naive interventionism in development: Easterly (2006) reports a green lumber problem: "The fallacy is to assume that because I have studied and lived in a society that somehow wound up with prosperity and peace, I know enough to plan for other societies to have prosperity and peace. As my friend April once said, this is like thinking the racehorses can be put in charge of building the racetracks."

Also luck in development, Easterly et al. (1993), Easterly and Levine (2003), Easterly (2001).

China famine: Meng et al. (2010).

Washington's death: Morens (1999); Wallenborn (1997).

Koran and Iatrogenics:

وإذا قيل لهم لا تفسدوا في الأرض قالوا انما نحن مصلحون. الا انهم هم المفسدون ولكن لا يشعرون

وإذا قيل لهم آمنوا كما آمن الناس قالوا أنؤمن كما آمن السفهاء ألا إنهم هم السفهاء ولكن لا يعلمون

Semmelweiss: Of the most unlikely references, see Louis-Ferdinand Céline's doctoral thesis, reprinted in Gallimard (1999), courtesy Gloria Origgi.

Fake stabilization: Some of the arguments in Chapter 7 were co-developed with Mark Blyth in *Foreign Affairs,* Taleb and Blyth (2011).

Sweden: "Economic elites had more autonomy than in any successful democracy," Steinmo (2011).

Traffic and removal of signs: Vanderbilt (2008).

History of China: Eberhard (reprint, 2006).

Nudge: They call it the *status quo bias* and some people want to get the government to manipulate people into breaking out of it. Good idea, except when the "expert" nudging us is not an expert.

Procrastination and the priority heuristic: Brandstetter and Gigerenzer (2006).

France's variety: Robb (2007). French riots as a national sport, Nicolas (2008). Nation-state in France, between 1680 and 1800, Bell (2001).

Complexity: We are more interested here in the effect on fat tails than other attributes. See Kaufman (1995), Hilland (1995), Bar-Yam (2001), Miller and Page (2007), Sornette (2004).

Complexity and fat tails: There is no need to load the math here (left to the technical companion); simple rigorous arguments can prove with minimal words how fat tails emerge from some attributes of complex systems. The important mathematical effect comes from lack of independence of random variables which prevents convergence to the Gaussian basin.

Let us examine the effect from dynamic hedging and portfolio revisions.

A—Why fat tails emerge from leverage and feedback loops, single agent simplified case.

A1 [leverage]—If an agent with some leverage L buys securities in response to increase in his wealth (from the increase of the value of these securities held), and sells them in response to decrease in their value, in an attempt to maintain a certain level of leverage L (he is concave in exposure), and

A2 [feedback effects]—If securities rise nonlinearly in value in response to purchasers and decline in value in response to sales, then, by the violation of the independence between the variations of securities, CLT (the central limit theorem) no longer holds (no convergence to the Gaussian basin). So fat tails are an immediate result of feedback and leverage, exacerbated by the concavity from the level of leverage L.

A3—If feedback effects are concave to size (it costs more per unit to sell 10 than to sell 1), then negative skewness of the security and the wealth process will emerge. (Simply, like the "negative gamma" of portfolio insurance, the agent has an option in buying, but no option in selling, hence negative skewness. The forced selling is exactly like the hedging of a short option.)

Note on path dependence exacerbating skewness: More specifically, if wealth increases first, this causes more risk and skew. Squeezes and forced selling on the way down: the market drops more (but less frequently) than it rises on the way up.

B—Multiagents: if, furthermore, more than one agent is involved, then the effect is compounded by the dynamic adjustment (hedging) of one agent causing the adjustment of another, something commonly called "contagion."

C—One can generalize to anything, such as home prices rising in response to home purchases from excess liquidity, etc.

The same general idea of forced execution plus concavity of costs leads to the superiority of systems with distributed randomness.

Increase of risk upon being provided numbers: See the literature on anchoring (reviewed in *The Black Swan*). Also Mary Kate Stimmler's doctoral thesis at Berkeley (2012), courtesy Phil Tetlock.

Stimmler's experiment is as follows. In the simple condition, subjects were told:

For your reference, you have been provided with the following formula for calculating the total amount of money (T) the investment will make three months after the initial investment (I) given the rate of return (R):

$$T = I*R$$

In the complex condition, subjects were told:

For your reference, you have been provided with the following formula for calculating the total amount of money A_n the investment will make three months after the initial investment A_{n-1} given the rate of return r.

$$A_n = A_{n-1} + (n+1) \sum_{j=1}^{n-1} [A_j r_j \frac{j}{n^2 - n + j} - j A_{j-1} r_{j-1} \frac{1}{j + (n-1)^2 + n - 2} + A_j r_{j-1} \frac{1}{j + (n-1)^2 + n - 2}]$$

Needless to mention that the simple condition and the complex one produced the same output. But those who had the complex condition took more risks.

The delusion of probabilistic measurement: Something that is obvious to cabdrivers and grandmothers disappears inside university hallways. In his book *The Measure of Reality* (Crosby, 1997), the historian Alfred Crosby presented the following thesis: what distinguished Western Europe from the rest of the world is obsession with measurement, the transformation of the qualitative into the quantitative. (This is not strictly true, the ancients were also obsessed with measurements, but they did not have the Arabic numerals to do proper calculations.) His idea was that we learned to be precise about things—and that was the precursor of the scientific revolution. He cites the first mechanical clock (which quantized time), marine charts and perspective painting (which quantized space), and double-entry bookkeeping (which quantized financial accounts). The obsession with measurement started with the right places, and progressively invaded the wrong ones.

Now our problem is that such measurement started to be applied to elements that have a high measurement error—in some case infinitely high. (Recall Fukushima in the previous section.) Errors from Mediocristan are inconsequential, those from Extremistan are acute. When measurement errors are prohibitively large, we should not be using the word "measure." Clearly I can "measure" the table on which I am writing these lines. I can "measure" the temperature. But I cannot "measure" future risks. Nor can I "measure" probability—unlike this table it cannot lend itself to our investigation. This is at best a speculative estimation of something that *can* happen.

Note that Hacking (2006) does not for a single second consider fat tails! Same with Hald (1998, 2003), von Plato (1994), Salsburg (2001), and from one who should know better, Stigler (1990). A book that promoted bad risk models, Bernstein (1996). Daston (1988) links probabilistic measurement to the Enlightenment.

The idea of probability as a quantitative not a qualitative construct has indeed been plaguing us. And the notion that science *equals* measurement free of error—it is, largely but not in everything—can lead us to all manner of fictions, delusions, and dreams.

An excellent understanding of probability linked to skepticism: Franklin (2001). Few other philosophers go back to the real problem of probability.

Fourth Quadrant: See the discussion in *The Black Swan* or paper Taleb (1999).

Nuclear, new risk management: Private communication, Atlanta, INPO, Nov. 2011.

Anecdotal knowledge and power of evidence: A reader, Karl Schluze, wrote: "An old teacher and colleague told me (between his sips of bourbon) 'If you cut off the head of a dog and it barks, you don't have to repeat the experiment.'" Easy to get examples: no lawyer would invoke an "N=1" argument in defense of a person, saying "he only killed once"; nobody considers a plane crash as "anecdotal."

I would go further and map disconfirmation as exactly where N=1 is sufficient.

Sometimes researchers call a result "anecdotal" as a knee-jerk reaction when the result is exactly the reverse. Steven Pinker called John Gray's pointing out the two world wars as counterevidence to his story of great moderation "anecdotal." My experience is that social science people rarely know what they are talking about when they talk about "evidence."

BOOK III: A Nonpredictive View of the World

Decision theorists teaching practitioners: To add more insults to us, decision scientists use the notion of "practical," an inverse designation. See Hammond, Keeney, and Raiffa (1999) trying to teach us how to make decisions. For a book describing exactly how practitioners don't act, but how academics think practitioners act: Schon (1983).

The asymmetry between good and bad: Segnius homines bona quam mala sentiunt in Livy's *Annals* (XXX, 21).

Stoics and emotions: Contradicts common beliefs that Stoicism is about being a vegetable, Graver (2007).

Economic growth was not so fast: Crafts (1985), Crafts and Harley (1992).

Cheating with the rock star: Arnavist and Kirkpatrick (2005), Griffith et al. (2002), Townsend et al. (2010).

Simenon: "Georges Simenon, profession: rentier," Nicole de Jassy *Le Soir illustré* 9 janvier 1958, N° 1333, pp. 8–9, 12.

Dalio: Bridgewater-Associates-Ray-Dalio-Principles.

BOOK IV: Optionality, Technology, and the Intelligence of Antifragility

The Teleological

Aristotle and his influence: Rashed (2007), both an Arabist and a Hellenist.
The nobility of failure: Morris (1975).

Optionality

Bricolage: Jacob (1977a, 1977b), Esnault (2001).
Rich getting richer: On the total wealth for HNWI (High Net Worth Individuals) increasing, see Merrill Lynch data in "World's wealthiest people now richer than

before the credit crunch," Jill Treanor, *The Guardian*, June 2012. The next graph shows why it has nothing to do with growth and total wealth formation.

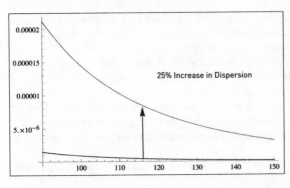

FIGURE 39. *Luxury goods and optionality. On the vertical the probability, on the horizontal the integral of wealth. Antifragility city: the effect of change in inequality on the pool of very rich increases nonlinearly in the tails: the money of the superrich reacts to inequality rather than total wealth in the world. Their share of wealth multiplies by close to 50 times in response to a change of 25% in dispersion of wealth. A small change of 0.01 in the GINI coefficient (0 when perfect inequality, 1.00 when one person has all) equivalent to 8% rise in real Gross Domestic Product—the effect is stark regardless of the probability distribution.*

Camel in Arabia: Lindsay (2005).

Obliquity: Kay (2010).

Real options literature: Trigeorgis (1993), review in Dixit and Pindyck (1994), Trigeorgis (1996), Luehrman (1998), McGrath (1999)—the focus is on reversible and irreversible investments.

Translational gap: Wooton (2007); Arikha (2008b); modern Contopoulos-Ioannidis et al. (2003, 2008), commentary Bosco and Watts (2007).

Criticism of Wootton: Brosco and Watts (2007).

Epiphenomena and Granger-causality: See Granger (1999) for a review.

Lecturing birds how to fly: There are antecedents in Erasmus, "teaching fish how to swim." *Adages*, 2519, III, VI, 19. *"Piscem nature doces* Ἰχθὺν νήχεσθαι διδάσκεις, *id est piscem nature doces. Perinde est ac si dicas : Doctum doces. Confine illi, quod alibi retulimus :* Δελφῖνα νήχεσθαι διδάσκεις, *id est Delphinum natare doces."* The expression was first coined in Haug and Taleb (2010), posted in 2006, leading to a book, Triana (2009). We weren't aware of the Erasmus imagery, which we would have selected instead.

Education and its effect on growth and wealth: Pritchett (2001), Wolf (2002), Chang (2011).

Schumpeter's ideas on destruction for advancement: Schumpeter (1942). Criticism by Harvard economists about lack of technical approach in McCraw (2007).

Amateurs: Bryson (2010), Kealey (1996).

Scientific misattribution of the works of Bachelier, Thorpe, and others: Haug and Taleb (2010). Discussion in Triana (2009, 2011).

Ex cura theoria nascitur: In Coulter (2000), attributed to Paracelsus.

Jet engine: Scranton (2006, 2007, 2009), Gibbert and Scranton (2009).

Busting the episteme theory of cybernetics: Mindell, 2002. I thank David Edgerton for introducing me to his works.

Cathedrals and theoretical and axiomatic geometry: Beaujoan (1973, 1991), Portet (2002). Ball (2008) for the history of the construction of Chartres cathedral.

Epistemic base and conflation: The epistemic base is sort of the *x*, not *f*(*x*). A great way to see the difference between x and $f(x)$ in technology, offered by Michael Polanyi: one can patent $f(x)$, a technique, but not x, scientific knowledge. In Mokyr (2005).

Epistemic Base: Mokyr (1999, 2002, 2005, 2009). The biggest problem with Mokyr: not getting ω_C. Further, this notion of the East missing trial and error (also see argument about China): see Tetlock in Tetlock et al. (2009). Mokyr and Meisenzahl have a different spin, with microinventions feeding macroinventions. Still intellectually weak.

Techne-Episteme in economics: Marglin (1996), but the tradition did not go very far.

Needham's works on China: Winchester (2008).

Tenure: Kealey (1996): "Adam Smith attributed the English professors' decay to their guaranteed salaries and tenured jobs. (As compared to Scottish Universities.)"

Fideism: Popkin (2003).

Linear Model: Edgerton (1996a, 1996b, 2004). Edgerton showed that it was a backward-fit idea, that is, fit to the past. Edgerton also writes: "This profoundly academic-research-oriented model of twentieth-century science is all the more surprising in view of the long tradition of *stressing the non-academic origins of modern science* [emphasis mine], particularly the craft traditions, and the insistence of much history of science, strengthened in the last 20 years, on the significance of industrial contexts for science, from dyeing to brewing to engine making."

Convexity bias: It was discovered early in commodity and financial futures; Burghardt and Hoskins (1994), Taleb (1997), Burghardt and Liu (2002), Burghardt and Panos (2001), Kirikos and Novak (1997), Pieterbarg and Renedo (2004). Many people blew up on misunderstanding the effect.

Example of detection and mapping of convexity bias (ω_A), from author's doctoral thesis: The method is to find what needs dynamic hedging and dynamic revisions. Among the members of the class of instruments considered that are not options *strictosensu* but require dynamic hedging can be rapidly mentioned a broad class of convex instruments: (1) Low coupon long dated bonds. Assume a discrete time framework. Take $B(r,T,C)$ the bond maturing period T, paying a coupon C where $rt = \int rs \, ds$. We have the convexity $\partial^2 B/\partial r^2$ increasing with T and decreasing with C. (2) Contracts where the financing is extremely correlated with the price of the Future. (3) Baskets with a geometric feature in its computation. (4) A largely neglected class of assets is the "quanto-defined" contracts (in which the payoff is not in the native currency of the contract), such as the Japanese NIKEI Future where the payoff is in U.S. currency. In short, while a Japanese yen denominated NIKEI contract is linear, a U.S. dollars denominated one is nonlinear and requires dynamic hedging.

Take at initial time t_0, the final condition $V(S,T) = S_T$ where T is the expiration date. More simply, the security just described is a plain forward, assumed to be linear. There appears to be no Ito term there yet. However should there be an intermediate payoff such that, having an accounting period i/T, the variation margin is paid in cash disbursement, some complexity would arise. Assume $\Delta(t_i)$ the changes in the value of the portfolio during period (t_i, t_{i-1}), $\Delta(t_i) = (V(S,t_i) - V(S, t_{i-1}))$. If the variation is to be paid at period t_i, then the operator would have to borrow at the forward rate between periods t_i and T, here $r(t_i,T)$. This financing is necessary to make $V(S,T)$ and S_T comparable in present value. In expectation, we will have to discount the variation using forward cash flow method for the accounting period between t_{i-1} and t_i. Seen from period T, the value of the variation becomes $E_t[exp[-r(t_i,T)(T-t_i)] \Delta(t_i)]$, where E_t is the expectation operator at time t (under, say, the risk-neutral probability measure). Therefore we are delivering at period T, in expectation, as seen from period t_0, the expected value of a stream of future variation $E_{t0}[\Sigma \ exp[-r(t_i,T)(T-t_i)] \ \Delta(t_i)]$. However we need to discount to the present using the term rate $r(T)$. The previous equation becomes $V(S,T)|_{t=t0}= V[S,t_0]+ exp[r(T)] \ E_{t0} \ [\Sigma \ exp[-r(t_i,T)(T-t_i)] \ \Delta(t_i)]$, which will be different from S_T when any of the interest rate forwards is stochastic. **Result** (a polite way to say "theorem"): *When the variances of the forward discount rate $r(t_i,T)$ and the underlying security S_T are strictly positive and the correlation between the two is lower than 1, $V(S,T)|_{t=t0} \neq S_T$.* Proof: by examining the properties of the expectation operator. Therefore: $F(S, \ t_0) = F(S,t_0+\Delta t)$, while a nonlinear instrument will merely satisfy: $E[V(S,t_0)]=E[V(S,t_0+\Delta t)]$.

Critique of Kealey: Posner (1996).

General History of Technology: Missing convexity biases, Basalla (1988), Stokes (1997), Geison (1995).

Ideas of innovation: Berkun (2007), Latour and Woolfar (1996), Khosla (2009), Johnson (2010).

Medical discoveries and absence of causative knowledge: Morton (2007), Li (2006), Le Fanu (2002), Bohuon and Monneret (2009). Le Fanu (2002): "It is perhaps predictable that doctors and scientists should assume the credit for the ascendency of modern medicine without acknowledging, or indeed recognizing, the mysteries of nature that have played so important a part. Not surprisingly, they came to believe their intellectual contribution to be greater than it really was, and that they understood more than they really did. They failed to acknowledge the overwhelmingly empirical nature of technological and drug innovation, which made possible spectacular breakthroughs in the treatment of disease without the requirement of any profound understanding of its causation or natural history."

Commerce as convex: Ridley (2010) has comments on Phoenicians; Aubet (2001).

Pharma's insider: La Matina (2009).

Multiplicative side effects: Underestimation of interactions in Tatonetti et al. (2012): they simply uncovered the side effects of people taking joint drugs together, which effectively swells the side effects (they show something as large as a multiplication of the effect by 4).

Strategic planning: Starbuck et al. (1992, 2008), Abrahamson and Freedman (2007). The latter is a beautiful ode to disorder and "mess."

Entrepreneurship: Elkington and Hartigan (2008).

Harvard Business School professors' pathological misunderstanding of small probabilities: This is not an empirical statement, but just to have fun: for an illustrative example of a sucker who misses ω_B and ω_C, always start looking in Harvard. Froot (2001), Pisano (2006a, 2006b). Froot: "Because managers of insurance companies purchase reinsurance at far above the fair price, they must believe that risk management adds considerable value." He thinks *he* knows the fair price.

Le Goff: Le Goff (1985): "*L'un est un professeur, saisi dans son enseignement, entouré d'élèves, assiégé par les bans, où se presse l'auditoire. L'autre est un savant solitaire, dans son cabinet tranquille, à l'aise au milieu de la pièce où se meuvent librement ses pensées. Ici c'est le tumulte des écoles, la poussière des salles, l'indifférence au décor du labeur collectif," "Là tout n'est qu'ordre et beauté / Luxe, calme, et volupté.*"

Martignon: Geschlechtsspezifische Unterschiede im Gehirn und mögliche Auswirkungen auf den Mathematikunterricht. Wissenschaftliche Hausarbeit zur Ersten Staatsprüfung für das Lehramt an Realschulen nach der RPO I v. 16.12.1999. Vorgelegt von: Ulmer, Birgit. Erste Staatsprüfung im Anschluss an das Wintersemester 2004/05, Pädagogische Hochschule Ludwigsburg. Studienfach: Mathematik. Dozenten: Prof. Dr. Laura Martignon, Prof. Dr. Otto Ungerer.

Renan: Averroès et l'averroïsme, p. 323 (1852).

Socrates: Conversation with Mark Vernon (Vernon, 2009), who believes that Socrates was more like Fat Tony. Wakefield (2009) a great context. Calder et al. (2002) presents portraits more or less hagiographic.

Socratic Fallacy: Geach (1966).

Episteme-Techne: Alexander of Aphrodisias, *On Aristotle's Metaphysics, On Aristotle's Prior Analytics* 1.1–7, *On Aristotle's Topics* 1, *Quaestiones* 2.16–3.15.

Tacit-Explicit knowledge: Colins (2010), Polanyi (1958), Mitchell (2006).

TABLE 13 • KNOW HOW VS KNOW WHAT AND THEIR SIBLINGS

TYPE 1	TYPE 2
Know *what*	Know *how*
Explicit	Implicit, Tacit
Demonstrative knowledge	Nondemonstrative knowledge
Episteme	Techne
Epistemic base	Experiential knowledge
Propositional knowledge	**Heuristic**
Literal	Figurative
Targeted activity	Bricolage
Rationalism	**Empiricism**
Scholarship	Practice
Mathematics	Engineering
Inductive knowledge, using Aristotle's teleological principles	Epilogism (Menodotus of Nicomedia and the school of empirical medicine)
Causative historiography	*Historia a sensate cognitio*
Diagnostic	*Autopsia*
Letter of the law	Spirit of the law
Ideas	Customs
Ludic probability, statistics textbooks	Ecological uncertainty, not tractable in textbook
Logos	Mythos
Kerygma (the explainable and teachable part of religion)	Dogma (in the religious sense, the unexplainable)
Exoteric theology (Averroes and Spinoza)	Esoteric theology (Averroes and Spinoza)

All the terms on the left seem to be connected. We can easily explain how *rationalism, explicit,* and *literal* fit together. But the terms on the right do not appear to be logically connected. What connects *customs, bricolage, myths, knowhow,* and *figurative*? What is the connection between religious dogma and tinkering? There is *something,* but I can't explain it in a compressed form, but there is the Wittgenstein family resemblance.

Lévi-Strauss: Lévi-Strauss (1962) on different forms of intelligence. However, in Charbonnier (2010), in interviews in the 1980s, he seems to believe that some day in the future, science will allow us to predict with acceptable precision very soon, "once we get the theory of things." Wilken (2010) for bio. See also Bourdieu (1972) for a similar problem seen from a sociologist.

Evolutionary heuristics: This is central but I hide it here. To summarize the view— a merger of what it is in the literature and the ideas of this book: an evolutionary heuristic in a given activity has the following attributes: (a) you don't know you are using it, (b) it has been done for a long time in the very same, or rather similar environment, by generations of practitioners, and reflects some evolutionary collective wisdom, (c) it is free of the agency problem and those who use it survived (this excludes medical heuristics used by doctors since the patient might not have survived, and is in favor of collective heuristics used by society), (d) it replaces complex problems that require a mathematical solution, (e) you can only learn it by practicing and watching others, (f) you can always do "better" on a computer, as these do better on a computer than in real life. For some reason, these heuristics that are second best do better than those that seem to be best, (g) the field in which it was developed allows for rapid feedback, in the sense that those who make mistakes are penalized and don't stick around for too long. Finally, as the psychologists Kahneman and Tversky have shown, outside the domains in which they were formed, these can go awfully wrong.

Argumentation and the green lumber problem: In Mercier and Sperber (2011). The post-Socratic idea of reasoning as an instrument for seeking the truth has been recently devalued further—though it appears that the Socratic method of discussion might be beneficial, but only in a dialogue form. Mercier and Sperber have debunked the notion that we use reasoning in order to search for the truth. They showed in a remarkable study that the purpose of arguments is not to make decisions but to convince others—since decisions we arrive at by reasoning are fraught with massive distortions. They showed it experimentally, producing evidence that individuals are better at forging arguments in a social setting (when there are others to convince) than when they are alone.

Anti-Enlightenment: For a review, Sternhell (2010), McMahon (2001), Delon (1997). Horkheimer and Adorno provide a powerful critique of the cosmeticism and sucker-traps in the ideas of modernity. And of course the works of John Gray, particularly Gray (1998) and *Straw Dogs,* Gray (2002).

Wittgenstein and tacit knowledge: Pears (2006).

On Joseph de Maistre: Companion (2005).

Ecological, non-soccer-mom economics: Smith (2008), also Nobel lecture given along with Kahneman's. Gigerenzer further down.

Wisdom of the ages: Oakeshott (1962, 1975, 1991). Note that Oakeshott conservatism means accepting the necessity of a certain rate of change. It seems to me that what he wanted was organic, not rationalistic change.

BOOK V: The Nonlinear and the Nonlinear

More formally, to complement the graphical exposition, from Taleb and Douady (2012), the **local fragility** of a random variable X_λ depending on parameter λ, at stress level K and semi-deviation level $s^-(\lambda)$ with pdf f_λ is its **K-left-tailed semi-vega sensitivity** ("vega" being sensitivity to some measure of volatility), $V(X, f\lambda, K, s^-)$ to s^-, the mean absolute semi-deviation below Ω, here $s^-(\lambda) = \int_{-\infty}^{\Omega} (\Omega - x) f_\lambda(x) dx$, $\xi(K, s^-) = \int_{-\infty}^{K} (\Omega - x) f_{\lambda(s^-)}(x) dx$, $V(X, f_\lambda, K, s^-) = \frac{\partial \xi}{\partial s}(K, s^-)$. The **inherited fragility** of Y with respect to X at stress level $L = \varphi(K)$ and left-semi-deviation level $s^-(\lambda)$ of X is the partial derivative $V_s(Y, g_\lambda, L, s^-(\lambda)) = \frac{\partial \zeta}{\partial s}(L, u^-(\lambda))$. Note that the stress level and the pdf are defined for the variable Y, but the parameter used for differentiation is the left-semi-absolute deviation of X. For antifragility, the flip above Ω, in addition to robustness below the same stress level K. The **transfer theorems** relate the fragility of Y to the second derivative $\varphi(K)$ and show the effect of convex (concave or mixed nonlinear) transformations on the tails via the **transfer function** H^K. For the antifragile, use s^+, the integral above K.

Fragility is not psychological: We start from the definition of fragility as tail vega sensitivity and end up with nonlinearity as a necessary attribute of the source of such fragility in the inherited case—a cause of the disease rather than the disease itself. However, there is a long literature by economists and decision scientists embedding risk into psychological preferences—historically, risk has been described as derived from risk aversion as a result of the structure of choices under uncertainty with a concavity of the muddled concept of "utility" of payoff; see Pratt (1964), Arrow (1965), Rothschild and Stiglitz (1970, 1971). But this "utility" business never led anywhere except the circularity, expressed by Machina and Rothschild (2008), "risk is what risk-averters hate." Indeed limiting risk to aversion to concavity of choices is a quite unhappy result.

The porcelain cup and its concavity: Clearly, a coffee cup, a house, or a bridge doesn't have psychological preferences, subjective utility, etc. Yet each is concave in its reaction to harm: simply, taking z as a stress level and $\Pi(z)$ the harm function, it suffices to see that, with $n>1$, $\Pi(n\,z) < n\,\Pi(z)$ for all $0< n\,z<Z^*$, where Z^* is the level (not necessarily specified) at which the item is broken. Such inequality leads to $\Pi(z)$ having a negative second derivative at the initial value z. So if a coffee cup is less harmed by n times a stressor of intensity Z than once a stressor of $n\,Z$, then harm (as a negative function) needs to be concave to stressors up to the point of breaking; such stricture is imposed by the structure of survival probabilities and the distribution of harmful events, nothing to do with subjective utility or some other figments.

Scaling in a positive way, convexity of cities: Bettencourt and West (2010, 2011), West (2011). Cities are 3-D items like animals, and these beneficial nonlinearities correspond to efficiencies. But consider traffic!

"More Is Different": Anderson (1972).

Comparative fragility of animals: Diamond (1988).

Flyvbjerg and colleagues on delays: Flyvbjerg (2009), Flyvbjerg and Buzier (2011).

Small Is Beautiful, the romantic views: Dahl and Tufte (1973), Schumacher (1973) for the soundbite. Kohr (1957) for the first manifesto against the size of the governing unit.

Size of government: I can't find people thinking in terms of convexity effects, not even libertarians—take Kahn (2011).

Small states do better: A long research tradition on governance of city-states. It looks like what we interpret as political systems might come from size. Evidence in Easterly and Kraay (2000).

The age of increasing fragility: Zajdenwebber, see the discussion in *The Black Swan.* Numbers redone recently in *The Economist,* "Counting the Cost of Calamities," Jan. 14, 2012.

Convexity effect on mean: Jensen (1906), Van Zwet (1966). While Jensen deals with monotone functions, Van Zwet deals with concave-convex and other mixtures— but these remain simple nonlinearities. Taleb and Douady (2012) applies it to all forms of local nonlinearities.

Empirical record of bigger: Mergers and hubris hypothesis: in Roll (1986); since then Cartwright and Schoenberg (2006).

Debt in ancient history: Babylonian jubilees, Hudson et al. (2002). Athens, Harrison (1998), Finley (1953). History of debt, Barty-King (1997), Muldrew (1993), Glaeser (2001). The latter has an anarchist view. He actually believes that debt precedes barter exchange.

Food networks: Dunne et al. (2002), Perchey and Dunne (2012), Valdovinos and Ramos-Jiliberto (2010). Fragility and resources, Nasr (2008, 2009).

Fannie Mae: They were concave across all meaningful variables. Some probability-and-nonlinearity-challenged fellow in the Obama commission investigating the cause of the crisis spread the rumor that I only detected interest rate risk of Fannie Mae: not true.

Costs of execution: "Price impact," that is, execution costs, increase with size; they tend to follow the square root—meaning the total price is convex and grows at exponent 3/2 (meaning costs are concave). But the problem is that for large deviations, such as the Société Générale case, it is a lot worse; transaction costs accelerate, in a less and less precise manner—all these papers on price impact by the new research tradition are meaningless when you need them. Remarkably, Bent Flyvbjerg found a similar effect, but slightly less concave in total, for bridges and tunnels with proportional costs growing at 10 Log[x] of size.

Small Is Beautiful, a technical approach: To explain how city-states, small firms, etc. are more robust to harmful events, take X, a random variable for the "unintended exposure," the source of uncertainty (for Soc Gen it was the position that it did not see, for a corporation it might be an emergency need to some inventory, etc.). Assume the size of this unintended harm is proportional to the size of the unit— for smaller entities engage in smaller transactions than larger ones. We use for probability distribution the variable of all unintended exposures $\sum X_i$ where X_i are independent random variables, simply scaled as $X_i = X/N$. With k the tail amplitude and α the tail exponent, $\pi(k, \alpha, X) = \alpha\, k^\alpha\, x^{-1-\alpha}$. The N-convoluted Pareto distribution for the unintended total position $N \sum X_i$: $\pi(k/N, \alpha, X)_N$ where N is the number of convolutions for the distribution. The mean of the distribution, invariant with respect to N, is $\alpha\, k/\alpha-1$).

Losses from squeezes and overruns: for the loss function, take $C[X]= -b\, X^\beta$, where costs of harm is a concave function of X. Note that for small deviations, $\beta = 3/2$ in the microstructure and execution literature.

Resulting probability distribution of harm: As we are interested in the distribution of y, we make a transformation of stochastic variable. The harm $y=C[X]$ has for distribution: $\pi[C^{-1}[x]]/C'[C^{-1}[x]]$. Consider that it follows a Pareto distribution with tail amplitude k^β and tail exponent α/β, $L_1(Y) = \frac{\alpha}{\beta} K^\alpha Y^{-1-\alpha/\beta}$ which has for mean $\frac{k^\beta \alpha}{\alpha-\beta}$. Now the sum: for the convoluted sum of N entities, the asymptotic distribution becomes: $L_N(Y) = N\frac{\alpha}{\beta}\left(\frac{K}{N}\right)^\alpha Y^{-1-\alpha/\beta}$ with mean (owing to additivity) as a function of the variables which include N:

$$M(\alpha,\beta,k,N) = \frac{N\left(\frac{k}{N}\right)^\beta \alpha}{\alpha-\beta}.$$

If we check the ratio of expected

losses in the tails for $N=1$ to $N=10$ at different values of the ratio of β over α, the ratio of the expectation for 1 unit over 10 units $\frac{M(\alpha=3,\beta/\alpha,k,N=1)}{M(\alpha=3,\beta/\alpha,k,N=10)}$ reveals the "small is beautiful" effect across different levels of concavity.

BOOK VI: Via Negativa

Subtractive Knowledge

Maps: A reader, Jean-Louis, a mapmaker, writes to me: "As a mapmaker, I learned a long time ago that the key to good mapmaking is precisely the info you choose to leave out. I have made numerous clients notice that if a map is too literal and precise, it confuses people."

Imam Ali: Nahj-el-Balagha, Letter. 31.

The mosaic god is not antifragile: For God—the Abrahamic-Mosaic God (of Jews, Christians, and Moslems)—is the representation of total robustness and infallibility. Note that counter to initial impressions, the essence of perfection is robustness, not antifragility. I've received many messages suggesting that the (Levantine) God should be put in the antifragile category. This would be a severe mistake according to Eastern Mediterranean religions. Antifragility for a deity may apply to Babylonian, Greek, Syrian, and Egyptian mythologies. But Levantine monotheistic theology, from the ancient Semitic El (or Al) to the modern Allah or, to a lesser extent, what people call "the Lord" in the Bible Belt, from Genesis to the Koran, progressed into a definition of an increasingly abstract God—hence closest to the definition of pure robustness. The monotheistic God is certainly not fragile; but he is not antifragile. By definition, thanks to his maximally abstract quality, he is what cannot be improved, which is the very property of perfection—only imperfect mortals can improve, therefore need antifragility to try to improve. In the Koran, one of the properties of God is *Smd,* a word that has no synonym even in Arabic, hence cannot be translated; its meaning can only be conveyed through the iteration of partial descriptions. *Smd* is that which has reached such degree of completeness that it does not depend on external circumstances, anything or anyone; a bulwark against all manner of attacks; He transcends the notion of time. The idea is also present in other Levantine systems. Orthodox theology, through *theosis,* seeks merger with God, the aspiration to a level of completeness, hence independence from anything else.

Interdicts in religion: Fourest and Venner (2010) presents a list across all persuasions.

Steve Jobs: Beahm (2011).

Gladwell: "If you totted up all his hospital bills for the ten years that he had been on the streets—as well as substance-abuse-treatment costs, doctors' fees, and other expenses—Murray Barr probably ran up a medical bill as large as anyone in the state of Nevada. 'It cost us one million dollars not to do something about Murray,' O'Bryan said." Gladwell (2009).

Falsification and problems of induction: See references in *The Black Swan.*

Smoking and overall medical effect: Burch (2009).

Fractality: Mandelbrot (1983).

Edgerton's shock of the old: Edgerton (2007).

Less Is More in Decision Theory

Simplicity and Steve Jobs: "That's been one of my mantras—focus and simplicity. Simple can be harder than complex: You have to work hard to get your thinking clean to make it simple. But it's worth it in the end because once you get there, you can move mountains." *BusinessWeek*, May 25, 1998.

Heuristics as powerful—and necessary—shortcuts: Gigerenzer and Brighton (2009) bust the following myth, as presented in *The Selfish Gene* by Richard Dawkins, in which we find the following about how a baseball outfielder catches a ball: "[H]e behaves as if he had solved a set of differential equations in predicting the trajectory of the ball. . . . At some subconscious level, something functionally equivalent to the mathematical calculations is going on."

Not quite, Professor Dawkins. Gerd Gigerenzer et al. counter by saying that none of that is done. They write the following:

Instead, experiments have shown that players rely on several heuristics. The gaze heuristic is the simplest one and works if the ball is already high up in the air: Fix your gaze on the ball, start running, and adjust your running speed so that the angle of gaze remains constant. A player who relies on the gaze heuristic can ignore all causal variables necessary to compute the trajectory of the ball—the initial distance, velocity, angle, air resistance, speed and direction of wind, and spin, among others. By paying attention to only one variable, the player will end up where the ball comes down without computing the exact spot.

The same heuristic is also used by animal species for catching prey and for intercepting potential mates. In pursuit and predation, bats, birds, and dragon-flies maintain a constant optical angle between themselves and their prey, as do dogs when catching a Frisbee.

Additional examples:

To choose a mate, a peahen uses a heuristic: Rather than investigating all peacocks posing and displaying in a lek eager to get her attention or weighting and adding all male features to calculate the one with the highest expected utility, she investigates only three or four, and chooses the one with the largest number of eyespots.

Just like humans. Another example:

To measure the area of a nest cavity, a narrow crack in a rock, an ant has no yardstick but a rule of thumb: Run around on an irregular path for a fixed period while laying down a pheromone trail, and then leave. Return, move around on a different irregular path, and estimate the size of the cavity by the frequency of encountering the old trail. This heuristic is remarkably precise.

Other: Czerlinski and Gigerenzer et al. (1999), Goldstein and Gigerenzer (1999), Gigerenzer (2008).

Makridakis, forecasting, and less is more: Makridakis et al. (1982, 1993), Makridakis and Hibon (2000), Makridakis and Taleb (2009).

Heuristic to measure risks: Taleb, Canetti et al. (2012)—with IMF staff.

Lindy Effects and Associated Topics

The Lindy effect was demonstrated in Mandelbrot (1997). Initially he used it for the artistic production, bounded by the life of the producer. In our conversations toward the end of his life, I suggested the boundary perishable/nonperishable and he agreed that the nonperishable would be powerlaw distributed while the perishable (the initial Lindy story) worked as a mere metaphor. Depending on whether we condition for knowledge of the initial time, the remaining lifetime for the exponential remains constant regardless of future condition, for power-law increases with time since inception, by a factor of $(\alpha/1-\alpha)$, where α is the tail exponent; for Gaussian or semi-Gaussian it decreases.

Gott: Gott (1993, 1994) presented the Copernican idea but did not properly condition the probability; corrected in Caves (2000). See discussion in Rees (2003), a treatment of the paradox in Bostrom (2002).

Survival papers and distributional properties: Often powerlaws are mistaken for exponential distributions, owing to lack of data in the tails. So I assume a priori that an exponential is likely to be powerlaw, but not the reverse, as the error in the opposite direction is vastly less likely. Pigolotti et al. (2005). For empires, Arbesman (2011), Khmaladze et al. (2007, 2010), Taagepera (1978, 1979). For firms: Fujiwara. Also Turchin (2003, 2009).

Conditional expected time of survival across distributions: Sornette and Knopoff (1997). They show how, paradoxically, the longer one waits for an earthquake, the longer he would be expected to wait.

Other Neomania

Le Corbusier: Christopher Caldwell, "Revolting High Rises," *New York Times,* November 27, 2005.

Cairns and ancient measures: Cairns (2007). His work was brought to my attention by Yoav Brand, who graciously offered me his book after a lecture.

Nonteleological design: How buildings mutate and change, Brand (1995).

The Dog: Moral, ii. 11; 1208 b 11. "And he says that when a dog was accustomed always to sleep on the same tile, Empedokles was asked why the dog always sleeps on the same tile, and he answered that the dog had some likeness to the tile, so that the likeness is the reason for its frequenting it."

General and Philosophical Discussions of Medicine

Medicina soror philosophiae: For reflective histories of medicine, Mudry (2006), Pigeaud (2006); Camguillem (1995) discussion of iatrogenics. For the spirit, Pager (1996), Bates (1995).

Islamic medicine: Porman and Savage-Smith (2007), Djebbar (2001).

De motu animali *and attempts to mathematize medicine:* In Wear (1995). Let me reiterate: math is good, the wrong math is not good.

Ancient medicine: Edelstein (1987), Lonrig (1998). Vivian Nutton's *Ancient Medicine* (Nutton [2004]) is informative, but near-silent about the empiricists, and not too detailed about ancient practices outside of a few standard treatises. More on medicine (skeptics and methodists) in the monumental Zeller (1905) or even better the superb *Les Sceptiques Grecs* by Brochard.

Oranges: As they are named in Modern Greek, *portokali,* a corruption of "Portuguese"—further corrupted in Levantine Arabic into *burduqan,* and present under that name in the Sicilian dialect.

Medical heuristics: Palmieri (2003).

Medieval and Renaissance: French (2003).

General history: Conrad et al. (1995), Porter (2002, 2003), Meslin et al. (2006), Kennedy (2004).

Iatrogenics: Sharpe and Faden (1998), most complete; Illich (1995) the first movement; Hadler (2009) for the back, Duffin (1999), Welsh et al. (2011) on overdiagnosis (though no argument about noise/signal and filtering), Lebrun (1995).

Agency and iatrogenics: Just a random example: "Surgeons do more operations if they're on the board of surgery centers," June 22, 2012, "The Daily Stat," *Harvard Business Review.*

More amusing historical perspective of iatrogenics: Gustave Jules A. Witkowski, 1889, *Le mal qu'on a dit des médecins.*

Rationalism/Galenism: Garicia-Ballester (1995).

Montaigne: "*Mais ils ont cet heur, selon Nicocles, que le soleil esclaire leur succez, et la terre cache leur faute; et, outre-cela, ils ont une façon bien avantageuse de se servir de toutes sortes d'evenemens, car ce que la fortune, ce que la nature, ou quelque autre cause estrangere (desquelles le nombre est infini) produit en nous de bon et de salutaire, c'est le privilege de la medecine de se l'attribuer. Tous les heureux succez qui arrivent au patient qui est soubs son regime, c'est d'elle qu'il les tient. Les occasions qui m'ont guery, moy, et qui guerissent mille autres qui n'appellent point les medecins à leurs secours, ils les usurpent en leurs subjects; et, quant aux mauvais accidents, ou ils les desavouent tout à fait, en attribuant la coulpe au patient par des raisons si vaines qu'ils n'ont garde de faillir d'en trouver tousjours assez bon nombre de telles. . . .*" [Note the detection of the attribution problem.]

    On demandoit à un Lacedemonien qui l'avoit fait vivre sain si long temps: L'ignorance de la medecine, respondit il.

    Et Adrian l'Empereur crioit sans cesse, en mourant, que la presse des medecins l'avoit tué.

Modern alternative medicine: Singh and Edzard (2008)—they had their skin in the game, as they were sued for it.

Homeopathy and empirical evidence: Goldacre (2007). See also the highly readable *Bad Science,* Goldacre (2009).

Modern evidence-based medicine: Manual in Sacket et al. (1998). Flaws of rationalistic methods, Silverman (1999), Gauch (2009), Sestini and Irving (2009).

Icing: Collins (2008): "There is insufficient evidence to suggest that cryotherapy improves clinical outcome in the management of soft tissue injuries." I could not find papers saying the opposite. What benefits are proffered seem so marginal it is not even funny.

Convexity of blood pressure: Numbers from Welch et al. (2011).

Jensen's inequality and pulmonary ventilators: Brewster et al. (2005), Graham et al. (2005), Mutch et al. (2007).

Paracelsus: Interesting character as a rebel; alas, seems to have been hijacked by homeopathy advocates such as Coulter (2000). Biographies in Ball (2006), Bechtel (1970), Alendy (1937).

Immortalization: Gray (2011).

Stendhal: Le Rouge et le noir: "*La besogne de cette journée sera longue et rude, fortifions-nous par un premier déjeuner; le second viendra à dix heures pendant la grand'messe.*" Chapitre XXVIII.

Specific Medical Topics

Note that the concern of this author is not evidence, but rather absence of it and how researchers manage such a problem. The focus is in detecting missed convexities.

Effectiveness of low-calorie sweeteners: One gets plenty of information by looking at studies by defenders with vested interests. De la Hunty et al. (2006) shows "advantages" to aspartame, with a meta-analysis, but focusing on the calorie-in calorie-out method, not overall weight gains. But reading it closely uncovers that the core is missing: "Some compensation for the substituted energy occurs but this is only about one-third of the energy replaced and is *probably* [emphasis mine] less than when using soft drinks sweetened with aspartame. Nevertheless these compensation values are derived from short-term studies." Obviously, the paper was financed by a maker of aspartame. A better study, Anderson et al. (2012), though marred with conflict of interest (authors' support from food companies), concludes: "there is no evidence that LCS (low calorie sweeteners) can be claimed to be a cause of higher body weight in adults. Similarly evidence supporting a role in weight management is lacking." The last sentence is the only one that I can pay attention to as it is evidence "against interest." Had there been benefits, we would have known about them. In other words, we are incurring iatrogenics of these sweets-without-calories without evidence, as of 2012, that they even work!

Mithridatization and hormesis: In Pliny, Kaiser (2003), Rattan (2008), Calabrese and Baldwin (2002, 2003a, 2003b). Note that they miss the convexity argument or the insight about the departure from the norm—hormesis might just be reinstatement of normalcy.

Fasting and hormesis: Martin, Mattson et al. (2006). Cancer treatment and fasting, Longo et al. (2008), Safdie et al. (2009), Raffaghelo et al. (2010)); on yeast and longevity under restriction, Fabrizio et al. (2001); SIRT1, Longo et al. (2006), Michan et al. (2010); review work in Blagosklonny et al. (2010).

Definition of hormesis: Mattson (2008) for local definition, Danchin et al. (2011) for more complex-systems approach.

Aging, longevity, and hormesis: An extremely rich research; Radak et al. (2005), Rattan (2008), Cypster and Johnson (2002) for the C-elegans; Gems and Partridge (2008), Haylick (2001), Masoro (1998), Parsons (2000); for inflammation and Alzheimer's, Finch et al. (2001).

Bone density and load: Dook (1997) for females, Andreoli et al. (2001) for more general athletes; Scott, Khan, et al. (2008) for general exercise. Aging for females: Solomon (1997), Rautava et al. (2007); Conroy et al. (1993) for young females.

Bone density and bicycle riding: Nichols et al. (2003), Barry et al. (2008).

Bone density and Olympic-style weightlifting: Some "weightlifting" studies mistake the resistance exercise on machines for real naturalistic weightlifting that stresses the skeleton. Conroy et al. (1993) is a more ecologically robust study because it focuses on weight.

Thyroid: Earle (1975).

Cholesterol: Non-naive look, Scanu and Edelstein (2008).

Lewontin and life expectancy: Lewontin (1993). Got idea for the potential unreliability of the Lewontin estimation and was directed to the CDC data from some article on the Web I can't remember.

Outdoors not sports: Rose et al. (2008). Higher levels of total time spent outdoors, rather than at sports per se, were associated with less myopia and a more hyperopic mean refraction, after adjusting for near work, parental myopia, and ethnicity.

"Neurobabble," "brain porn" studies: Weisberg (2008), McCabe (2008), also "neuroscience and the law," report by the U.K. Royal Society. Note that the writer Jonah Lehrer used brain porn quite effectively, building a narrative using some loose brain story, playing the narrative fallacy to the hilt—until he was caught creating both narrative and data to back it up.

The pressure on dentists to generate revenues: "Dental Abuse Seen Driven by Private Equity Investments," Sydney P. Freedberg, Bloomberg News, May 17, 2012.

Significance: Simply, people in social science should not be using statistics any more than an accountant should be given a surgeon's knife. The problem of misunderstanding significance affects professionals. See McCloskey and Ziliak (1996),

Ziliak and McCloskey (2008), Soyer and Hogarth (2011), Kahneman and Tversky (1971), Taleb and Goldstein (2012).

Practitioners and theoreticians in mathematical finance failing to understand an elementary notion in statistics in spite of all the hype: Evidence in Taleb and Goldstein (2007).

Missing nonlinearities of dose response: The case of radiation is rather stark, Neumaier et al. (2012). "The standard model currently in use applies a linear scale, extrapolating cancer risk from high doses to low doses of ionizing radiation. However, our discovery of DSB clustering over such large distances casts considerable doubts on the general assumption that risk to ionizing radiation is proportional to dose, and instead provides a mechanism that could more accurately address risk dose dependency of ionizing radiation." Radiation hormesis is the idea that low-level radiation causes hormetic overreaction with protective effects. Also see Aurengo (2005).

Statins and convexity: For instance, with statin drugs routinely prescribed to lower blood lipids, although the result is statistically significant for a certain class of people, the effect is minor. "High-risk men aged 30–69 years should be advised that about 50 patients need to be treated for 5 years to prevent one [cardiovascular] event" (Abramson and Wright, 2007).

Statins side effects and (more or less) hidden risks: Side effects in musculoskeletal harm or just pain, Women, Speed et al. (2012). General assessment, Hilton-Jones (2009), Hu Chung et al. (2012). Roberts (2012) shows another aspect of convexity of benefits, hence harm in marginal cases. Fernandez et al. (2011) shows where clinical trials do not reflect myopathy risks. Blaha et al. (2012) shows "increased risks for healthy patients." Also, Reedberg and Katz (2012); Hamazaki et al.: "The absolute effect of statins on all-cause mortality is rather small, if any."

Harlan Krumholz, *Forbes*, April 29, 2011:

Problem is that drugs that improve blood test results may not lower risk. For example, many drugs that reduce LDL or raise HDL or lower blood sugar or blood pressure, do not, against all expectations, lower risk—and in some cases they increase risk.

This is particularly true when considering treatment options to prevent a future event such as a heart attack. Unfortunately, for many drugs that affect risk factors, studies that investigate whether patients benefit are either not done or delayed. This is the case with ezetimibe, a Merck agent that reduces LDL. Because the study that will include information about patient outcomes will only be completed when ezetimibe comes off patent, we will not know how it actually affects risk for a few more years. This billion dollar drug's approval and sales have been solely based on its effect on a blood test.

For the fibrates, though, we are more fortunate. There are studies of patient outcomes, and fenofibrate, the Abbott drug, has been tested twice in large studies. In both, the drug failed to reduce the risk of the patients taking it even as it very effectively lowered their triglyceride levels. Most recently, in a $300 million trial by the National Institutes of Health, no benefit was shown for the Abbott drug when it was combined with a statin—compounded by a suggested harm for women. The former concern is sufficiently high to have prompted the FDA to convene an advisory committee to review the findings.

Back: McGill (2007); iatrogenics surgery or epidural, Hadler (2009), Sayre (2010).

Doctor's strikes: There have been a few episodes of hospital strikes, leading to the cancellation of elective surgeries but not emergency-related services. The data are not ample, but can give us insights if interpreted in *via negativa* mode. Extracting the effect of elective surgery, Argeseanu et al. (2008). See also Allebeck (1985), Gruber and Kleiner (2010), Siegel-Iztkovich (2000).

Diabetes and pharmacological treatments (ACCORD study): The ACCORD study (Action to Control Cardiovascular Risk in Diabetes) found no gain from lowering blood glucose, or other metrics—it may be more opaque than a simple glucose problem remedied by pharmacological means. Synthesis, Skyler et al. (2009), old methods, Westman and Vernon (2008).

Discussions of diabetes and diet: Taylor (2008), reversal in Lim et al. (2011), Boucher et al. (2004), Shimakuru et al. (2010); diabetes management by diet alone, early insights in Wilson et al. (1980). Couzin, "Deaths in Diabetes Trial Challenge a Long-Held Theory," *Science* 15 (February 2008): 884–885. Diabetes reversal and bariatric (or other) surgery: Pories (1995), Guidone et al. (2006), Rubino et al. 2006.

Autophagy for cancer: Kondo et al. (2005).

Autophagy (general): Danchin et al. (2011), Congcong et al. (2012).

Jensen's inequality in medicine and workout: Many such as Schnohr and Marott (2011) got close to dealing with the fact that extreme sprinting and nothing (as a barbell) outperforms steady exercise, but missed the convexity bias part.

Art De Vany and Jensen's inequality: Art De Vany, private correspondence: "Tissue gains are increasing but convex with nutrient intake (the curve is rising, but at a diminishing rate). This has to be the case for the point of origin to be a steady state solution. This implies that weight gain, including fat, is higher at the average intake than it is on a varying intake of the same calories and nutrients. Muscle and fat compete for substrate, so a fatter person will shift nutrient partitioning toward muscle because body fat induces insulin resistance in muscle. Insulin operates in a pulsate release and is far more effective with that pattern than with the chronic elevation induced by six meals a day. On the downside, where fat and muscle are lost, the curve is negatively sloped but declines at a diminishing rate (concave). This means you lose more fat feeding intermittently than continuously. The loss at the average intake (six per day keeps the variation of the average small) is less than the loss at the same intake but one that varies between a small intake and a large one. A more subtle point: you lose more weight when you eat at the average than intermittently, but that is because you lose more muscle in chronic deprivation than intermittent deprivation. Intermittent eating yields a superior body composition."

Starvation, intermittent fasting, and aging: For the neuronal resistance and brain aging, Anson, Guo, et al. (2003), Mattson et al. (2005), Martin, Mattson et al. (2006), Halagappa, Guo, et al. (2007), Stranahan and Mattson (2012).

Caloric restriction: Harrison (1984), Wiendruch (1996), Pischon (2008).

Intense exercise: Synthesis of the literature on the effect of episodic energy imbalance, in De Vany (2011), who also, as a bonus, examines powerlaw effects.

Missing the point that pills are more speculative: Stip (2010) spends time on *via positiva* methods to extend life with complicated pharma stories.

Glucose and willpower: Note the effect of glucose making people sharper and helping willpower from experiments by Baumeister, see Kahneman (2011), might only apply to metabolically unfit persons. See Kurzban (2011) for a look at the statistical tools.

Cluster of ailments from lack of randomness, as presented in prologue: Yaffe and Blackwell (2004), Razay and Wilcock (1994); Alzheimer and hyperinsulenemia, Luchsinger, Tang, et al. (2004), Janson, Laedtke, et al. (2004).

Starvation and the brain: Stranahan and Mattson (2012). Long-held belief that the brain needed glucose, not ketones, and that the brain does not go through autophagy, progressively corrected.

Ramadan and effect of fasting: Ramadan is not interesting because people fast for only about 12 hours, depending on the season (someone who fasts from dinner to lunch can get 17 hours without food, which is practiced by this author). Further, they gorge themselves at dawn, and load on carbohydrates with, in my experience, the sweets of Tripoli (Lebanon). Nevertheless, some significance. Trabelsi et al. (2012), Akanji et al. (2012).

Benefits of stress: For the different effects of the two types of stressors, short and chronic, Dhabar (2009); for the benefits of stress on boosting immunity and cancer resistance, Dhabhar et al. (2010), Dhabhar et al. (2012).

Iatrogenics of hygiene and systematic elimination of germs: Rook (2011), Garner et al. (2006), Mégraud and Lamouliatte (1992) for Helyobacter.

The Paleo crowd, De Vany, Gary Taubes, and friends: Taubes (2008, 2011), De Vany (2011); evolutionary anthropology, Carrera-Bastos et al. (2011), Kaplan et al. (2000).

BOOK VII: The Ethics of Fragility and Antifragility

Modern philosophical discussions on capitalism: No interest in such a simple heuristic as skin in the game, even in insightful discourses such as Cuillerai (2009).

Courage in history: Berns et al. (2010).

Gladiators: Veyne (1999).

Treadmill: Lucretius, *Nimirum quia non bene norat quæ esset habendi / Finis, et omnino quoad crescat vera voluptas.*

Group and collective: Haidt (2012).

Adam Smith on capitalism: "A word he never uttered": Simon Schama, private communication.

Stiglitz et al. dangerous report: Joseph E. Stiglitz, Jonathan M. Orszag, and Peter R. Orszag, "Implications of the New Fannie Mae and Freddie Mac Risk-based Capital Standard," *Fannie Mae Papers,* Volume I, Issue 2, March 2002.

Meyer Lansky: Attributed to Ralph Salerno, retired NYPD mob investigator, in Ferrante (2011).

Unsavory activities by pharma finding patients rather than treatments: Stories of direct and indirect corruption, particularly in the psychiatric domain. A professor of psychiatry at Harvard Medical School received $1.6 million from pharma. "Thanks to him, children as young as two years old are now being diagnosed with bipolar disorder . . ." Marcia Angell, *The New York Review of Books.* Angell used to be the editor of *The New England Journal of Medicine* and distrusts a large number of clinical studies. Further, how money is not spent on speculative research, but on "safe" bets with regular drugs, Light and Lexchin (2012).

Contradicting studies: Kahneman brought to my attention studies such as Malmendier and Tate (2008, 2009) showing managers investing more than needed in their companies, hence excess skin in the game as a result of overconfidence. Myron Scholes and Robert Merton had investments in LTCM. Indeed—but overall the free option dominates (just measure the aggregate payment of managers relative to gains by shareholders). There are "fools of randomness" and "crooks of randomness"; we often observe a combination. (Credit: Nicolas Tabardel.)

Asymmetries and extractive: Acemoglu and Robinson (2012) discusses an asymmetry with their notion of extractive economic institutions and environment, in which someone gets rich at the expense of someone else, the opposite of the convex collaborative framework in which one's wealth leads to a compounding pie. Role of institutions, North (1990).

Caviar socialism and Burnyeat's problem: Riffard (2004), Burnyeat (1984), Wai-Hung (2002).

Collective blindness and diffusion of responsibility: In the animal domain (ants), Deneubourg, Goss et al. (1983), Deneubourg, Pasteels et al. (1983).

Life and socialization in Rome: Veyne (2001).

Elephant in the room: Things that everyone knows but remain undiscussed. Zerubavel (2006).

Mortality of large firms: Higher than expected, Greenwood and Suddaby (2006), comment Stubbart and Knight (2006). The best test is to take the S&P 100 or S&P 500 and look at its composition through time. The other one of course is in the literature on mergers.

Information cascades: The mechanism by which the crowd exacerbates fallacies, illusions, and rumors, Sunstein (2009) for a synthesis.

Alan Blinder problem: *Wall Street Journal* article with undisclosed conflict of interest: "Blanket Deposit Insurance Is a Bad Idea," Oct. 15, 2008, coauthored with R. Glenn Hubbard, dean of Columbia University Business School.

Comparative performance of family businesses: McConaughy and Fialco (2001), Le Breton–Miller and Miller (2006), Mackie (2001).

Skin in the game: Taleb and Martin (2012a).

Data Mining, Big Data, and the Researcher's Option, etc.

Misunderstanding in social science literature: Typical mistake, consider the ignorance of the problem by hyperactive promoters of the idea such as Ayres (2007): "Want to hedge a large purchase of Euros? Turns out you should sell a carefully balanced portfolio of twenty-six other stocks and commodities that might include Wal-Mart stock," p. 11.

Stan Young's crusade: Young and Carr (2011). Also Ioannides (2005, 2007).

Doxastic commitment: Levi (1980).

Salt: Very convincing Freedman and Petitti (2001), relies on visualization of data rather than metrics. Note "neither author consults for the salt industry," the kind of thing I read *first*.

Graph on Big Data: By Monte Carlo simulation; used >0.1, or beyond what correlations are loved in social science (it is hard to analytically do the analysis because of the need for large matrices to remain positive-definite). The convexity is invariant to the correlation threshold.

Solution to the researcher's bias in clinical trials: Goldacre (2009) suggests the establishment of a database of trials, forcing researchers to record their failures. Anything is better than what we got.

The collective and fragility: The power of the collective rests on benefits from efficiency, hence fragility: people start substituting collective judgment for individual judgment. This works fine—it is faster and cheaper (hence more *efficient*) than having to reinvent the wheel individually. But like everything that is a shortcut, it ends blowing up in our faces. In the world in which we live the effect is compounded—the scale is larger and larger; the collective is planetary.

Jobs and artisan ethics: This makes me worry: "Playboy: 'Are you saying that the people who made PCjr don't have that kind of pride in the product?' Jobs: 'If they did, they wouldn't have made the PCjr.'" *Playboy* [*sic*], Feb. 1, 1985.

Busting the hypothesis of hyperbolic discounting: Read and Airoldi (2012).

Other discussions of Big Data and researchers gaming the system: Baumeister et al. (2007) about self-reporting in psychology. Kerr (1998) about hypothesis following the results, and post hoc in Yauan and Maxwell; Yarkoni for the large M (dimension) low N (data) problem.

Bibliography

About, Edmond, 1855, *La Grèce contemporaine*.

Abrahamson, Eric, and David H. Freedman, 2007, *A Perfect Mess: The Hidden Benefits of Disorder: How Crammed Closets, Cluttered Offices, and On-the-Fly Planning Make the World a Better Place*. Little, Brown.

Abramson, J., and J. Wright, 2007, "Are Lipid-Lowering Guidelines Evidence-Based?" *Lancet* 369(9557): 168–169.

Acemoglu, Daron, and James A. Robinson, 2012, *Why Nations Fail: The Origins of Power, Prosperity and Poverty*. New York: Crown Books.

ACCORD Study Group, 2007, "Action to Control Cardiovascular Risk in Diabetes (ACCORD) Trial: Design and Methods." *American Journal of Cardiology* 99 (suppl): 21i–33i.

Akanji, A. O., O. A. Mojiminiyi, and N. Abdella, 2000, "Beneficial Changes in Serum Apo A-1 and Its Ratio to Apo B and HDL in Stable Hyperlipidaemic Subjects After Ramadan Fasting in Kuwait." *European Journal of Clinical Nutrition* 54(6): 508–13.

Allebeck, P., 1985, "The General Labour Conflict in Sweden 1980: Effects on the Mortality in Stockholm County." *Public Health* 99(1): 10–17.

Allendy, René, 1937, *Paracelse; le médecin maudit*. Gallimard.

Alter, A. L., D. M. Oppenheimer, et al., 2007, "Overcoming Intuition: Metacognitive Difficulty Activates Analytic Reasoning." *Journal of Experimental Psychology: General* 136(4): 569.

Anderson, G., J. Foreyt, M. Sigman-Grant, and D. Allison, 2012, "The Use of Low-Calorie Sweeteners by Adults: Impact on Weight Management." *Journal of Nutrition* 142(6): 1163s–1169s.

Anderson, P. W., 1972, *Science*, New Series, Vol. 177, No. 4047 (Aug. 4), pp. 393–396.

Anderson, R. C., and D. M. Reeb, 2004, "Board Composition: Balancing Family Influence in S&P 500 Firms." *Administrative Science Quarterly* 209–237.

Andreoli, A., M. Monteleone, M. Van Loan, L. Promenzio, U. Tarantino, and A. De Lorenzo, 2001, "Effects of Different Sports on Bone Density and Muscle Mass in Highly Trained Athletes." *Medicine & Science in Sports & Exercise* 33(4): 507–511.

Anson, R. M., Z. Guo, et al., 2003, "Intermittent Fasting Dissociates Beneficial Effects of Dietary Restriction on Glucose Metabolism and Neuronal Resistance to

Injury from Calorie Intake." *Proceedings of the National Academy of Sciences of the United States of America* 100(10): 6216.

Arbesman, S., 2011, "The Life-Spans of Empires." *Historical Methods: A Journal of Quantitative and Interdisciplinary History* 44(3): 127–129.

Arikha, Noga, 2008a, *Passions and Tempers: A History of the Humours.* Harper Perennial.

Arikha, Noga, 2008b, "Just Life in a Nutshell: Humours as Common Sense," *Philosophical Forum Quarterly* XXXIX: 3.

Arnheim, Rudolf, 1971, *Entropy and Art: An Essay on Disorder and Order.* Berkeley: University of California Press.

Arnqvist, G., and M. Kirkpatrick, 2005, "The Evolution of Infidelity in Socially Monogamous Passerines: The Strength of Direct and Indirect Selection on Extrapair Copulation Behavior in Females." *American Naturalist* 165 (s5).

Aron, Raymond, 1964, *Dimensions de la conscience historique.* Agora/Librairie Plon.

Arrow, Kenneth, 1971, "Aspects of the Theory of Risk-Bearing," Yrjö Jahnsson Lectures (1965), reprinted in *Essays in the Theory of Risk Bearing,* edited by Kenneth Arrow. Chicago: Markum.

Atamas, S. P., and J. Bell, 2009, "Degeneracy-Driven Self-Structuring Dynamics in Selective Repertoires." *Bulletin of Mathematical Biology* 71(6): 1349–1365.

Athavale, Y., P. Hosseinizadeh, et al., 2009, "Identifying the Potential for Failure of Businesses in the Technology, Pharmaceutical, and Banking Sectors Using Kernel-Based Machine Learning Methods." IEEE.

Aubet, Maria Eugenia, 2001, *The Phoenicians and the West: Politics, Colonies and Trade,* Cambridge: Cambridge University Press.

Audard, Catherine, ed., 1993, *Le respect: De l'estime à la déférence: une question de limite.* Paris: Éditions Autrement.

Aurengo, André, 2005, "Dose-Effect Relationships and Estimation of the Carcinogenic Effects of Low Doses of Ionizing Radiation." Académie des Sciences et Académie Nationale de Médecine.

Ayanian, J. Z., and D. M. Berwick 1991, "Do Physicans Have a Bias Toward Action?" *Medical Decision Making* 11(3): 154–158.

Ayres, Ian, 2007, *Super Crunchers: Why Thinking-by-Numbers Is the New Way to Be Smart.* New York: Bantam.

Bakwin, H., 1945, "Pseudodoxia Pediatrica." *New England Journal of Medicine* 232(24): 692.

Ball, Philip, 2006, *The Devil's Doctor: Paracelsus and the World of Renaissance Magic and Science.* New York: Farrar, Straus and Giroux.

Ball, Philip, 2008, *Universe of Stone: A Biography of Chartres Cathedral.* New York: Harper.

Bar-Yam, Yaneer, and I. Epstein, 2004. "Response of Complex Networks to Stimuli." *Proceedings of the National Academy of Sciences of the United States of America* 101(13): 4341.

Bar-Yam, Yaneer, 2001, *Introducing Complex Systems.* Cambridge, Mass.: New England Complex Systems Institute, 57.

Barkan, I., 1936, "Imprisonment as a Penalty in Ancient Athens." *Classical Philology* 31(4): 338–341.

Barry, D. W., and W. M. Kohrt, 2008, "BMD Decreases over the Course of a Year in Competitive Male Cyclists." *Journal of Bone and Mineral Research* 23(4): 484–491.

Barty-King, H., 1997, *The Worst Poverty: A History of Debt and Debtors.* Budding Books.

Basalla, George, 1988, *The Evolution of Technology*. Cambridge: Cambridge University Press.

Bates, Don, ed., 1995, *Knowledge and the Scholarly Medical Traditions*. Cambridge: Cambridge University Press.

Baumeister, R. F., K. D. Vohs, and D. C. Funder, 2007, "Psychology as the Science of Self-Reports and Finger Movements: Whatever Happened to Actual Behavior?" *Perspectives on Psychological Science* 2: 396–403.

Beahm, George, 2011, *I, Steve: Steve Jobs in His Own Words*. Perseus Books Group.

Beaujouan, G., 1991, *Par raison de nombres: L'art du calcul et les savoirs scientifiques médiévaux*. Variorum Publishing.

Beaujouan, G., 1973, *Réflexions sur les rapports entre théorie et pratique au moyen age*. D. Reidel Publ. Co.

Bechtel, Guy, 1970, *Paracelse et la naissance de la médecine alchimique*. Culture, Art, Loisirs.

Bell, David A., 2001, *The Cult of the Nation in France: Inventing Nationalism 1680–1800*. Cambridge, Mass.: Harvard University Press.

Bennett, G., N. Gilman, et al., 2009, "From Synthetic Biology to Biohacking: Are We Prepared?" *Nature Biotechnology* 27(12): 1109–1111.

Berkun, Scott, 2007, *The Myths of Innovation*. Sebastol, Calif.: O'Reilly.

Berlin, Isaiah, 1990, *The Crooked Timber of Humanity*. Princeton, N.J.: Princeton University Press.

Berns, Thomas, Laurence Blésin, and Gaelle Jeanmart, 2010, *Du courage: une histoire philosophique*. Encre Marine.

Bernstein, Peter L., 1996, *Against the Gods: The Remarkable Story of Risk*. New York: Wiley.

Bettencourt, L., and G. West, 2010, "A unified theory of urban living," *Nature* 467(7318): 912–913.

Bettencourt, L., and G. West, 2011, "Bigger Cities Do More with Less." *Scientific American* 305(3): 52–53.

Beunza, D., and D. Stark, 2010, "Models, Reflexivity, and Systemic Risk: A Critique of Behavioral Finance." Preprint.

Biezunski, Michel, ed., 1983, *La recherche en histoire des sciences*. Paris: Éditions du Seuil.

Blagosklonny, M., J. Campisi, D. Sinclair, A. Bartke, M. Blasco, W. Bonner, V. Bohr, R. Brosh Jr., A. Brunet, and R. DePinho, 2010, "Impact Papers on Aging in 2009." *Aging* (Albany, N.Y.), 2(3): 111.

Blaha, M. J., K. Nasir, R. S. Blumenthal, 2012, "Statin Therapy for Healthy Men Identified as 'Increased Risk.'" JAMA 307(14): 1489–90.

Bliss, Michael, 2007, *The Discovery of Insulin*. Chicago: University of Chicago Press.

Blundell-Wignall, A., G. Wehinger, et al., 2009, "The Elephant in the Room: The Need to Deal with What Banks Do." *OECD Journal: Financial Market Trends* (2).

Boehlje, M., 1999, "Structural Changes in the Agricultural Industries: How Do We Measure, Analyze and Understand Them?" *American Journal of Agricultural Economics* 81(5): 1028–1041.

Bohuon, Claude, and Claude Monneret, 2009, *Fabuleux hasards: histoire de la découverte des médicaments*. EDP Sciences.

Bonanno, G. A., 2004, "Loss, Trauma, and Human Resilience: Have We Underestimated the Human Capacity to Thrive After Extremely Aversive Events?" *American Psychologist* 59: 20–28.

Borkowski, M., B. Podaima, et al., 2009, "Epidemic Modeling with Discrete-Space

Scheduled Walkers: Extensions and Research Opportunities." *BMC Public Health* 9 (Suppl 1): S14.

Bostrom, Nick, 2002, *Anthropic Bias: Observation Selection Effects in Science and Philosophy*. London: Routledge.

Boucher, A., et al., 2004, "Biochemical Mechanism of Lipid-Induced Impairment of Glucose-Stimulated Insulin Secretion and Reversal with a Malate Analogue." *Journal of Biological Chemistry* 279: 27263–27271.

Bourdieu, Pierre, 1972, *Esquisse d'une théorie de la pratique*. Paris: Éditions du Seuil.

Brand, Stewart, 1995, *How Buildings Learn: What Happens After They're Built*. Penguin.

Brandstätter, E., G. Gigerenzer, et al., 2006, "The Priority Heuristic: Making Choices Without Trade-offs." *Psychological Review* 113(2): 409.

Brewster, J. F., M. R. Graham, et al., 2005, "Convexity, Jensen's Inequality and Benefits of Noisy Mechanical Ventilation." *Journal of the Royal Society* 2(4): 393–396.

Brosco, J., and S. Watts, 2007, "Two Views: 'Bad Medicine: Doctors Doing Harm Since Hippocrates.' By David Wootton." *Journal of Social History* 41(2): 481.

Bryson, Bill, 2010, *At Home: A Short History of Private Life*. New York: Doubleday.

Burch, Druin, 2009, *Taking the Medicine: A Short History of Medicine's Beautiful Idea, and Our Difficulty Swallowing It*. Chatto and Windus.

Burghardt, G., and W. Hoskins, 1994, "The Convexity Bias in Eurodollar Futures." *Carr Futures Research Note*, September.

Burghardt, G., and G. Panos, 2001, "Hedging Convexity Bias." *Carr Futures Research Note*, August.

Burnyeat, F., 1984, "The Sceptic in His Place and Time." In R. Rorty, J. B. Schneewind, and Q. Skinner, eds., *Philosophy in History*. Cambridge: Cambridge University Press, p. 225.

Cairns, Warwick, 2007, *About the Size of It: The Common Sense Approach to Measuring Things*. London: Pan Books.

Calabrese, E. J., 2005, "Paradigm Lost, Paradigm Found: The Re-emergence of Hormesis as a Fundamental Dose Response Model in the Toxicological Sciences." *Environmental Pollution* 138(3): 378–411.

Calabrese, E. J., and L. Baldwin, 2002, "Defining Hormesis." *Human & Experimental Toxicology* 21(2): 91.

Calabrese, E. J., and L. A. Baldwin, 2003a, "Toxicology Rethinks Its Central Belief." *Nature* 421(6924): 691–692.

Calabrese, E. J., and L. A. Baldwin, 2003b, "Hormesis: The Dose-Response Revolution." *Annual Review of Pharmacology and Toxicology* 43(1): 175–197.

Calder, William M. III, Bernhard Huss, Marc Mastrangelo, R. Scott Smith, and Stephen M. Trzaskoma, 2002, *The Unknown Socrates*. Wauconda, Ill: Bolchazy-Carducci Publishers.

Calhoun, L. G., and R. G. Tedeschi, 2006, *Expert Companions: Post-Traumatic Growth in Clinical Practice*. Lawrence Erlbaum Associates Publishers.

Canguilhem, Georges, 1966, *Le normal et le pathologique*. Presses Universitaires de France.

Canguilhem, Georges, 1995, *Études d'histoire et de philosophie des sciences*. Librairie Philosophique J. Vrin.

Carbuhn, A., T. Fernandez, A. Bragg, J. Green, and S. Crouse, 2010, "Sport and Training Influence Bone and Body Composition in Women Collegiate Athletes." *Journal of Strength and Conditioning Research* 24(7): 1710–1717.

Carey, B., P. K. Patra, et al., 2011, "Observation of Dynamic Strain Hardening in Polymer Nanocomposites." *ACS Nano.* 5(4): 2715–2722.

Carrera-Bastos, P., M. Fontes Villalba, et al., 2011, "The Western Diet and Lifestyle and Diseases of Civilization." *Research Reports in Clinical Cardiology* 2: 215–235.

Cartwright, S., and R. Schoenberg, 2006, "Thirty Years of Mergers and Acquisitions Research: Recent Advances and Future Opportunities." *British Journal of Management* 17(S1): S1–S5.

Caves, Carlton M., 2000, "Predicting Future Duration from Present Age: A Critical Assessment," *Contemporary Physics* 41: 143–153.

Chang, H. J., 2011, *23 Things They Don't Tell You About Capitalism*. London: Bloomsbury Press.

Charbonnier, Georges, 2010, *Entretiens avec Claude Lévi-Strass*. Les Belles Lettres.

Collins, Harry, 2010, *Tacit and Explicit Knowledge*. Chicago: University of Chicago Press.

Collins, N. C., 2008, "Is Ice Right? Does Cryotherapy Improve Outcome for Acute Soft Tissue Injury?" *Emergency Medicine Journal* 25: 65–68.

Compagnon, Antoine, 2005, *Les antimodernes de Joseph de Maistre à Roland Barthes*. Paris: Gallimard.

Congcong, He, et al., 2012, "Exercise-Induced BCL2-Regulated Autophagy Is Required for Muscle Glucose Homeostasis." *Nature*, 2012.

Conrad, Lawrence I., Michael Neve, Vivian Nutton, Roy Porter, and Andrew Wear, 1995, *The Western Medical Tradition: 800 BC to AD 1800*. Cambridge: Cambridge University Press.

Conroy, B. P., W. J. Kraemer, et al., 1993, "Bone Mineral Density in Elite Junior Olympic Weightlifters." *Medicine and Science in Sports and Exercise* 25(10): 1103.

Contopoulos-Ioannidis, D. G., E. E. Ntzani, et al., 2003, "Translation of Highly Promising Basic Science Research into Clinical Applications." *American Journal of Medicine* 114(6): 477–484.

Contopoulos-Ioannidis, D. G., G. A. Alexiou, et al., 2008, "Life Cycle of Translational Research for Medical Interventions." *Science* 321(5894): 1298–1299.

Convery, F. J., C. Di Maria, et al., 2010, "ESRI Discussion Paper Series No. 230."

Coulter, Harris L., 1994, *Divided Legacy: A History of the Schism in Medical Thought*, Vol. I. Center for Empirical Medicine.

Coulter, Harris L., 2000, *Divided Legacy: A History of Schism in Medical Thought*, Vol. II. North Atlantic Books.

Cowan, R., P. A. David, et al., 2000, "The Explicit Economics of Knowledge Codification and Tacitness." *Industrial and Corporate Change* 9(2): 211.

Coy, P., 2009, "What Good Are Economists Anyway?" *BusinessWeek* 27: 26–29.

Crafts, Nicholas F. R., 1985, *British Economic Growth During the Industrial Revolution*. New York: Oxford University Press.

Crafts, Nicholas F. R., and C. Knick Harley. "Output Growth and the British Industrial Revolution: A Restatement of the Crafts-Harley View." *Economic History Review* 45 (1992): 703–730.

Cretu, O., R. B. Stewart, et al., 2011, *Risk Management for Design and Construction*.

Crosby, Alfred W., 1997, *The Measure of Reality: Quantification and Western Society, 1250–1600*. Cambridge: Cambridge University Press.

Cuillerai, Marie, 2009, *Spéculation, éthique, confiance: Essai sur le capitalisme vertueux*. Éditions Payots-Rivages.

Cunningham, Solveig Argeseanu, Kristina Mitchell, K.M. Venkat Narayan, Salim Yusuf, 2008, "Doctors' Strikes and Mortality: A Review." *Social Science & Medicine* 67(11), 1784–1788.

Cypser, J. R., and T. E. Johnson, 2002, "Multiple Stressors in *Caenorhabditis Elegans* Induce Stress Hormesis and Extended Longevity." *Journals of Gerontology: Series A: Biological Sciences and Medical Sciences* 57(3): B109.

Czerlinski, J., G. Gigerenzer, et al., 1999, "How Good Are Simple Heuristics?"

Dahl, Robert A., and Edward R. Tufte, 1973, *Size and Democracy*. Stanford: Stanford University Press.

Danchin, A., P. M. Binder, et al., 2011, "Antifragility and Tinkering in Biology (and in Business) Flexibility Provides an Efficient Epigenetic Way to Manage Risk." *Genes* 2(4): 998–1016.

Darnton, Robert, 2010, *The Devil in the Holy Water, or The Art of Slander from Louis XIV to Napoleon*. University of Pennsylvania Press.

Daston, Lorraine, 1988, *Classical Probability in the Enlightenment*. Princeton, N.J.: Princeton University Press.

Davidson, P., 2010, "Black Swans and Knight's Epistemological Uncertainty: Are These Concepts Also Underlying Behavioral and Post-Walrasian Theory?" *Journal of Post Keynesian Economics* 32(4): 567–570.

Davis, Devra, 2007, *The Secret History of the War on Cancer*. Basic Books.

Dawes, Robyn M., 2001, *Everyday Irrationality: How Pseudo-Scientists, Lunatics, and the Rest of Us Systematically Fail to Think Rationally*. Westview.

De Finetti, B., 1937, *La prévision: ses lois logiques, ses sources subjectives*. Institut Henri Poincaré.

De Finetti, B., 1974, *Theory of Probability*, Vol. 1. London: John.

De Finetti, B., 1989, "Probabilism." *Erkenntnis* 31(2): 169–223.

De la Hunty, A., S. Gibson, and M. Ashwell, 2006, "A Review of the Effectiveness of Aspartame in Helping with Weight Control." *Nutrition Bulletin* 31(2):115–128.

De Long, J. Bradford, and Andrei Shleifer, 1993, "Princes and Merchants: European City Growth Before the Industrial Revolution." *Journal of Law and Economics* 36: 671–702.

De Soto, H., 2000, *The Mystery of Capital: Why Capitalism Triumphs in the West and Fails Everywhere Else*. Basic Books.

De Vany, A., 2011, *The New Evolution Diet*. Vermilion.

Delon, Michel, ed., 1997, *Dictionnaire européen des lumières*. Presses Universitaires de France.

Deneubourg, J. L., S. Goss, N. Franks, and J. M. Pasteels, 1989, "The Blind Leading the Blind: Modelling Chemically Mediated Army Ant Raid Patterns." *Journal of Insect Behavior* 2: 719–725.

Deneubourg, J. L., J. M. Pasteels, and J. C. Verhaeghe, 1983, "Probabilistic Behavior in Ants: A Strategy of Errors?" *Journal of Theoretical Biology* 105: 259–271.

Derman, E., and N. N. Taleb, 2005, "The Illusions of Dynamic Replication." *Quantitative Finance* 5: 4.

Dhabhar, F. S., 2009, "Enhancing Versus Suppressive Effects of Stress on Immune Function: Implications for Immunoprotection and Immunopathology." *Neuroimmunomodulation* 16(5): 300–317.

Dhabhar, F. S., A. N. Saul, C. Daugherty, T. H. Holmes, D. M. Bouley, T. M. Oberyszyn, 2010, "Short-term Stress Enhances Cellular Immunity and Increases Early Resistance to Squamous Cell carcinoma." *Brain, Behavior and Immunity* 24(1): 127–137.

Dhabhar, F. S., A. N. Saul, T. H. Holmes, C. Daugherty, E. Neri, J. M. Tillie, D. Kusewitt, T. M. Oberyszyn, 2012, "High-Anxious Individuals Show Increased Chronic Stress Burden, Decreased Protective Immunity, and Increased Cancer Progression in a Mouse Model of Squamous Cell Carcinoma." *PLOS ONE* 7(4): e33069.

Diamond, Jared, 1988, "Why Cats Have Nine Lives." *Nature,* Vol. 332, April 14.

Dixit, A. K. and R. S. Pindyck, 1994, *Investment Under Uncertainty.* Princeton, N.J.: Princeton University Press.

Djebbar, Ahmed, 2001, *Une histoire de la science arabe.* Éditions du Seuil.

Dook, J. E., C. James, N. K. Henderson, and R. I. Price, 1997, "Exercise and Bone Mineral Density in Mature Female Athletes." *Medicine and Science in Sports and Exercise* 29(3): 291–296.

Douady, R. and N. N. Taleb, 2011, "Statistical Undecidability," preprint.

Driver, P. M., and D. A. Humphries, 1988, *Protean Behaviour: The Biology of Unpredictability.* Oxford: Oxford University Press.

Duffin, Jacalyn, 1999, *History of Medicine: A Scandalously Short Introduction.* Toronto: University of Toronto Press.

Dunne, J. A., R. J. Williams, et al., 2002, "Network Topology and Biodiversity Loss in Food Webs: Robustness Increases with Connectance." *Ecology Letters* 5(4): 558–567.

Earle, J., 1975, "Thyroid Cancer. Delayed Effects of Head and Neck Irradiation in Children (Medical Information)." *Western Journal of Medicine* 123:340, October.

Easterly, W., 2001, *The Elusive Quest for Growth: Economists' Adventures and Misadventures in the Tropics.* Cambridge, Mass.: The MIT Press.

Easterly, W., and A. Kraay, 2000, "Small States, Small Problems? Income, Growth, and Volatility in Small States." *World Development* 28(11): 2013–2027.

Easterly, W., M. Kremer, L. Pritchett, and L. Summers, 1993, "Good Policy or Good Luck? Country Growth Performance and Temporary Shocks" *Journal of Monetary Economics* 32(3): 459–483.

Easterly, William, 2006, *The White Man's Burden: Why the West's Efforts to Aid the Rest Have Done So Much Ill and So Little Good.* Penguin Group.

Eberhard, Wolfram, 1950, 1977, *A History of China.* University of California Press.

Edelstein, Ludwig, 1987, *Ancient Medicine.* Johns Hopkins University Press.

Edgerton, David, 1996a, "The 'White Heat' Revisited: British Government and Technology in the 1960s." *Twentieth Century British History* 7(1): 53–82.

Edgerton, David, 1996b, *Science, Technology, and the British Industrial 'Decline,' 1870–1970.* Cambridge: Cambridge University Press.

Edgerton, David, 2004, "The 'Linear Model' Did Not Exist: Reflections on the History and Historiography of Science and Research in Industry in the Twentieth Century." In Karl Grandin and Nina Wormbs, eds., *The Science–Industry Nexus: History, Policy, Implications.* New York: Watson.

Edgerton, David, 2007, *The Shock of the Old: Technology and Global History Since 1900,* Oxford.

Ekern, S., 1980, "Increasing Nth Degree Risk." *Economics Letters* 6(4): 329–333.

Elkington, John, and Pamela Hartigan, 2008, *The Power of Unreasonable People: How Social Entrepreneurs Create Markets That Change the World.* Cambridge, Mass.: Harvard Business Press.

Emer, J., 2009, "An Evolution of General Purpose Processing: Reconfigurable Logic Computing." *Proceedings of the 7th Annual IEEE/ACM International Symposium.*

Esnault, Y., 2001, "Francois Jacob, l'éloge du bricolage." *Biofutur* (213).

Fabrizio, P., F. Pozza, S. Pletcher, C. Gendron, and V. Longo, 2001, "Regulation of Longevity and Stress Resistance by Sch9 in Yeast." *Science's STKE* 292(5515): 288.

Fejtö, François, 1989, *Requiem pour un Empire défunt. Histoire de la destruction de l'Autriche-Hongrie*. Paris: Lieu Commun.

Ferguson, Niall, 2011, *Civilization: The West and the Rest*. Penguin.

Fernandez, G., E. S. Spatz, C. Jablecki, P. S. Phillips, 2011, "Statin Myopathy: A Common Dilemma Not Reflected in Clinical Trials." *Cleveland Clinic Journal of Medicine* 78(6): 393–403.

Ferrante, Louis, 2011, *Mob Rules: What the Mafia Can Teach the Legitimate Businessman*. Penguin.

Finch, C., V. Longo, A. Miyao, T. Morgan, I. Rozovsky, Y. Soong, M. Wei, Z. Xie, and H. Zanjani, 2001, "Inflammation in Alzheimer's Disease." In M.-F. Chesselet, ed., *Molecular Mechanisms of Neurodegenerative Diseases*, pp. 87–110.

Fink, W., V. Lipatov, et al., 2009, "Diagnoses by General Practitioners: Accuracy and Reliability." *International Journal of Forecasting* 25(4): 784–793.

Finley, M. I., 1953, "Land, Debt, and the Man of Property in Classical Athens." *Political Science Quarterly* 68(2): 249–268.

Flyvbjerg, Bent, 2001, *Making Social Science Matter: Why Social Inquiry Fails and How It Can Succeed Again*. Cambridge: Cambridge University Press.

Flyvbjerg, Bent, and Alexander Budzier, 2011, "Are You Sitting on a Ticking Time Bomb?" *Harvard Business Review*, September.

Flyvbjerg, Bent, 2009, "Survival of the Unfittest: Why the Worst Infrastructure Gets Built—and What We Can Do About It." *Oxford Review of Economic Policy*, Vol. 25, No. 3, 344–367.

Fossedal, G. A., and A. R. Berkeley III, 2005, *Direct Democracy in Switzerland*. Transaction Pub.

Fourest, Caroline, and Fiametta Venner, 2010, *Les interdits religieux*. Éditions Dalloz.

Franklin, James, 2001, *The Science of Conjecture: Evidence and Probability Before Pascal*. Baltimore: Johns Hopkins University Press.

Freedman, D. A., and D. B. Petitti, 2001, "Salt and Blood Pressure: Conventional Wisdom Reconsidered." *Evaluation Review* 25(3): 267–287.

Freedman, D., D. Collier, et al., 2010, *Statistical Models and Causal Inference: A Dialogue with the Social Sciences*. Cambridge: Cambridge University Press.

Freeman, C., and L. Soete, 1997, *The Economics of Industrial Innovation*. London: Routledge.

Freidson, Eliot, 1970, *Profession of Medicine: A Study of the Sociology of Applied Knowledge*. Chicago: University of Chicago Press.

French, Roger, 2003, *Medicine Before Science: The Rational and Learned Doctor from the Middle Ages to the Enlightenment*. Cambridge: Cambridge University Press.

Froot, K. A., 2001, "The Market for Catastrophe Risk: A Clinical Examination," *Journal of Financial Economics* 60(2–3): 529–571.

Fujiwara, Y., 2004, "Zipf Law in Firms Bankruptcy." *Physica A: Statistical and Theoretical Physics* 337: 219–30.

Fukumoto, S., and T. J. Martin, 2009, "Bone as an Endocrine Organ." *Trends in Endocrinology and Metabolism* 20: 230–236.

Fuller, Steve, 2005, *The Intellectual*. Icon Books.

García-Ballester, Luis, 1995, "Health and Medical Care in Medieval Galenism." In Don Bates, ed., *Knowledge and the Scholarly Medical Traditions*. Cambridge: Cambridge University Press.

Garland, Robert, 1998, *Daily Life of the Ancient Greeks*. Indianapolis: Hackett.

Gauch, Ronald R., 2009, *It's Great! Oops, No It Isn't: Why Clinical Research Can't Guarantee the Right Medical Answers*. Springer.

Gawande, Atul, 2002, *Complications: A Surgeon's Note on an Imperfect Science.* Picador.

Geach, Peter, 1966, "Plato's Euthyphro," *The Monist* 50: 369–382.

Geison, Gerald L., 1995, *The Private Science of Louis Pasteur.* Princeton, N.J.: Princeton University Press.

Gems, D., and L. Partridge, 2008, "Stress-Response Hormesis and Aging: That Which Does Not Kill Us Makes Us Stronger." *Cell Metabolism* 7(3): 200–203.

Gibbert, M. and P. Scranton, 2009, "Constraints as Sources of Radical Innovation? Insights from Jet Propulsion Development." *Management & Organizational History* 4(4): 385.

Gigerenzer, Gerd, 2008, "Why Heuristics Work." *Perspectives on Psychological Science* 3(1): 20–29.

Gigerenzer, Gerd, and H. Brighton, 2009, "*Homo heuristicus:* Why Biased Minds Make Better Inferences." *Topics in Cognitive Science* 1(1): 107–143.

Gigerenzer, Gerd, and W. Gaissmaier, 2011, "Heuristic Decision Making." *Annual Review of Psychology* 62: 451–482.

Gladwell, Malcolm, 2009, *What the Dog Saw: And Other Adventures.* Hachette Group.

Glaeser, E., 2011, *Triumph of the City: How Our Greatest Invention Makes Us Richer, Smarter, Greener, Healthier, and Happier.* New York: Penguin

Glaser, Scott, and Rinoo Shah, 2010, "Root Cause Analysis of Paraplegia Following Transforaminal Epidural Steroid Injections." *Pain Physician* 13: 237–244.

Gold, Rich, 2007, *The Plenitude: Creativity, Innovation, and Making Stuff.* Cambridge, Mass.: The MIT Press.

Goldacre, B., 2007, "Benefits and Risks of Homoeopathy." *Lancet* 370(9600): 1672–1673.

Goldacre, B., 2009, *Bad Science: Quacks, Hacks, and Big Pharme Flacks.* London: Harper Perennial.

Goldstein, D. G., and G. Gigerenzer, 1999, "The Recognition Heuristic: How Ignorance Makes Us Smart."

Goldstein, D. G., and G. Gigerenzer, 2002, "Models of Ecological Rationality: The Recognition Heuristic." *Psychological Review* 109(1): 75.

Goldstein, D. G., and N. N. Taleb, 2007, "We Don't Quite Know What We Are Talking About When We Talk About Volatility," *Journal of Portfolio Management,* Summer.

Gott, J. Richard III, 1993, "Implications of the Copernican Principle for Our Future Prospects." *Nature* 363(6427): 315–319.

Gott, J. Richard III, 1994, "Future Prospects Discussed." *Nature* 368: 108.

Graeber, David, 2011, *Debt: The First 5000 Years.* Melville House Publishing.

Graham, M. R., C. J. Haberman, et al., 2005, "Mathematical Modelling to Centre Low Tidal Volumes Following Acute Lung Injury: A Study with Biologically Variable Ventilation." *Respiratory Research* 6(1): 64.

Granger, Clive W. J., 1999, *Empirical Modeling in Economics: Specification and Evaluation.* Cambridge: Cambridge University Press.

Grant, Ruth W., 2011, *Strings Attached: Untangling the Ethics of Incentives.* Princeton, N.J.: Princeton University Press.

Graver, M., 2007, *Stoicism and Emotion.* Chicago: University of Chicago Press.

Gray, John, 1998, *Hayek on Liberty.* Psychology Press.

Gray, John, 2002, *Straw Dogs: Thoughts on Humans and Other Animals.* London: Granta Books.

Gray, John, 2011, *The Immortalization Commission: Science and the Strange Quest to Cheat Death.* Allen Lane.

Greenwood, R., and R. Suddaby, 2006, "The Case of Disappearing Firms: Death or Deliverance?" *Journal of Organizational Behavior* 27(1): 101–108.

Grice, E. A., and J. A. Segre, 2011, "The Skin Microbiome." *Nature Reviews Microbiology* 9(4): 244–253.

Griffith, S. C., I.P.F. Owens, and K. A. Thuman, 2002, "Extrapair Paternity in Birds: A Review of Interspecific Variation and Adaptive Function." *Molecular Ecology* 11: 2195–212.

Grob, Gerald N., 2002, *The Deadly Truth: A History of Disease in America.* Cambridge, Mass.: Harvard University Press.

Gruber, Jonathan, and Samuel A. Kleiner, 2010, *Do Strikes Kill? Evidence from New York State* (NBER Working Paper No. 15855). National Bureau of Economic Research.

Guadalupe-Grau, A., T. Fuentes, B. Guerra, and J. Calbet, 2009, "Exercise and Bone Mass in Adults." *Sports Medicine* 39(6): 439–468.

Guarner, F., R. Bourdet-Sicard, et al., 2006, "Mechanisms of Disease: the Hygiene Hypothesis Revisited." *Nature Clinical Practice Gastroenterology & Hepatology* 3(5): 275–284.

Guidone, C., et al., 2006, "Mechanisms of Recovery from Type 2 Diabetes After Malabsorptive Bariatric Surgery." *Diabetes* 55: 2025–2031.

Hacking, Ian, 1984, *The Emergence of Probability: A Philosophical Study of Early Ideas About Probability, Induction and Statistical Inference.* Cambridge: Cambridge University Press.

Hacking, Ian, 1990, *The Taming of Chance.* Cambridge: Cambridge University Press.

Hacking, Ian, 2006, *The Emergence of Probability,* 2nd ed. New York: Cambridge University Press.

Hadler, Nortin M., M.D., 2008, *Worried Sick: A Prescription for Health in an Overtreated America.* Chapel Hill: University of North Carolina Press.

Hadler, Nortin M., M.D., 2009, *Stabbed in the Back.* Chapel Hill: University of North Carolina Press.

Haidt, J., 2012, *The Righteous Mind: Why Good People Are Divided by Politics and Religion.* New York: Pantheon.

Haigh, J., 2000, "The Kelly Criterion and Bet Comparisons in Spread Betting." *Journal of the Royal Statistical Society: Series D (The Statistician)* 49(4): 531–539.

Hajek, A., 2003, *Interpretations of Probability.* Citeseer.

Halagappa, V.K.M., Z. Guo, et al., 2007, "Intermittent Fasting and Caloric Restriction Ameliorate Age-Related Behavioral Deficits in the Triple-Transgenic Mouse Model of Alzheimer's Disease." *Neurobiology of Disease* 26(1):

Hald, Anders, 1998, *A History of Mathematical Statistics from 1750 to 1930.* New York: Wiley.

Hald, Anders, 2003, *A History of Probability and Statistics and Their Applications Before 1750.* Hoboken, N.J.: Wiley.

Haleblian, J., C. E. Devers, et al., 2009, "Taking Stock of What We Know About Mergers and Acquisitions: A Review and Research Agenda." *Journal of Management* 35(3): 469–502.

Hallström, H., H. Melhus, A. Glynn, L. Lind, A. Syvänen, and K. Michaëlsson, 2010, "Coffee Consumption and CYP1A2 Genotype in Relation to Bone Mineral Density of the Proximal Femur in Elderly Men and Women: A Cohort Study." *Nutrition and Metabolism* 7:12.

Hamazaki, T., et al, 2012, "Rethinking Cholesterol Issues," *Journal of Lipid Nutrition* 21.

Hammond, John S., Ralph L. Keeney, and Howard Raïffa, 1999, *Smart Choices: A Practical Guide to Making Better Life Decisions*. Cambridge, Mass.: Harvard Business Press.

Harrison, A.R.W., 1998, *The Law of Athens: The Family and Property*. Indianapolis: Hackett.

Harrison, D. E., J. R. Archer, and C. M. Astle, 1984, "Effects of Food Restriction on Aging: Separation of Food Intake and Adiposity." *Proceedings of the National Academy of Sciences USA* 81: 1835–1838.

Haug, E. G., 1998, *The Complete Guide to Option Pricing Formulas*. McGraw-Hill Companies.

Haug, E. G., and N. N. Taleb, 2010, "Option Traders Use Heuristics, Never the Formula Known as Black-Scholes-Merton Equation," *Journal of Economic Behavior and Organizations* 27.

Hayek, F. A., 1945, "The Use of Knowledge in Society." *American Economic Review* 35(4): 519–530.

Hayek, F. A., 1991, *The Fatal Conceit: The Errors of Socialism*. Chicago: University of Chicago Press.

Hayflick, L., 2001, "Hormesis, Aging and Longevity Determination." *Human & Experimental Toxicology* 20(6): 289.

Heyde, C. C., and E. Seneta, eds., 2001, *Statisticians of the Centuries*. New York: Springer.

Hilton-Jones, D., 2009, "I-7. Statins and Muscle Disease." *Acta Myologica* 28(1): 37.

Hind, K. and M. Burrows, 2007, "Weight-Bearing Exercise and Bone Mineral Accrual in Children and Adolescents: A Review of Controlled Trials." *Bone* 40: 14–27.

Holland, John H., 1995, *Hidden Order: How Adaptation Builds Complexity*. Basic Books.

Hollis, Martin, 1994, *The Philosophy of Social Science: An Introduction*. Cambridge: Cambridge University Press.

Horkheimer, Max, and Theodor W. Adorno, 2002, *Dialectic of Enlightenment*. Stanford: Stanford University Press.

Hu, M., B.M.Y. Cheung, et al., 2012, "Safety of Statins: An Update." *Therapeutic Advances in Drug Safety* 3(3): 133–144.

Huang, Chi-fu, and Robert H. Litzenberger, 1988, *Foundations of Financial Economics*. Prentice-Hall, Inc.

Hudson, M., M. Van de Mieroop, et al., 2002, *Debt and Economic Renewal in the Ancient Near East: A Colloquium Held at Columbia University*. Potomac: CDL Press.

Illich, Ivan, 1995, *Limits to Medicine: Medical Nemesis, the Expropriation of Health*. London: Marion Boyars.

Ioannidis, J.P.A., 2005, "Why Most Published Research Findings Are False." *PLoS Medicine* 2(8), 696–701, doi:10.1371/journal.pmed.0020124.

Ioannidis, J.P.A., and T. A. Trikalinos, 2007, "An Exploratory Test for an Excess of Significant Findings." *Clinical Trials* 4: 245–253, doi:10.1177/1740774507079944.

Issawi, Charles, 1988, *The Fertile Crescent, 1800–1914: A Documentary Economic History*. Oxford: Oxford University Press.

Issawi, Charles, 1966, in Charles Issawi, ed., *The Economic History of the Middle East, 1800–1914*. Chicago: University of Chicago Press.

Jacob, François, 1977a, "Evolution et bricolage." *Le Monde* 6(7): 8.

Jacob, François, 1977b, "Evolution and Tinkering," *Science* 196(4295): 1161–1166.

Janson, J., T. Laedtke, et al., 2004, "Increased Risk of Type 2 Diabetes in Alzheimer Disease." *Diabetes* 53(2): 474–481.

Jaynes, E. T., 2003, 2004, *Probability Theory: The Logic of Science.* Cambridge: Cambridge University Press.

Jensen, J.L.W.V., 1906, "Sur les fonctions convexes et les inégalités entre les valeurs moyennes." *Acta Mathematica* 30.

Johnsgard, P. A., 2010, "Ducks, Geese, and Swans of the World: Tribe Stictonettini (Freckled Duck)." In Paul A. Johnsgard, *Ducks, Geese, and Swans of the World.* University of Nebraska Press.

Johnson, P.D.R., 2011, "Extensively Resistant Tuberculosis in the Lands Down Under." *Medical Journal of Australia* 194(11): 565.

Johnson, Steven, 2010, *Where Good Ideas Come From: The Natural History of Innovation.* Riverhead Books.

Josipovici, Gabriel, 2010, *What Ever Happened to Modernism?* New Haven: Yale University Press.

Kahn, James, 2011, "Can We Determine the Optimal Size of Government?" *Cato Institute* No. 7, September.

Kahneman, D., 2011, *Thinking, Fast and Slow.* New York: Farrar, Straus and Giroux.

Kahneman, D., 1982, "On the Study of Statistical Intuitions." In D. Kahneman, P. Slovic, and A. Tversky, eds., *Judgment Under Uncertainty: Heuristics and Biases.* Cambridge: Cambridge University Press.

Kahneman, D., and Amos Tversky, 1979, "Prospect Theory: An Analysis of Decision Under Risk." *Econometrica* 46(2): 171–185.

Kaiser, Jocelyn, 2003, "Hormesis: Sipping from a Poisoned Chalice." *Science* 302 (5644): 376–379.

Kantorovich, Aharon, 1993, *Scientific Discovery: Logic and Tinkering.* State University of New York Press.

Kaplan, H., K. Hill, J. Lancaster, and A. M. Hurtado, 2000, "A Theory of Human Life History Evolution: Diet, Intelligence, and Longevity." *Evolutionary Anthropology* 9:156–185.

Karsenty, G., 2003, "The Complexities of Skeletal Biology." *Nature* 423 (6937): 316–318.

Karsenty, G., 2011, *Regulation of Male Fertility by Bone.* Cold Spring Harbor Laboratory Press.

Karsenty, G., 2012a, "Bone as an endocrine tissue." *Annual Review of Physiology* 74(1).

Karsenty, G., 2012b, "The Mutual Dependence Between Bone and Gonads." *Journal of Endocrinology* 213(2): 107–114.

Kauffman, Stuart, 1995, *At Home in the Universe: The Search for Laws of Self-Organization and Complexity.* Oxford: Oxford University Press.

Kay, John, 2010, *Obliquity.* Penguin.

Kealey, T., 1996, *The Economic Laws of Scientific Research.* London: Macmillan.

Kennedy, Michael T., 2004, *A Brief History of Disease, Science and Medicine: From the Ice Age to the Genome Project.* Mission Viejo, Calif.: Asklepiad Press.

Kerr, N. L., 1998, "HARKing: Hypothezising After the Results Are Known." *Personality and Social Psychology Review* 2: 196–217, doi:10.1207/s15327957 pspr0203_4.

Khanna, P., 2010, "Beyond City Limits." *Foreign Policy* 181: 120–128.

Khmaladze, E. V., R. Brownrigg, and J. Haywood, 2010, "Memoryless Reigns of the 'Sons of Heaven.'" *International Statistical Review* 78: 348–62.

Khmaladze, E., R. Brownrigg, and J. Haywood, 2007, "Brittle Power: On Roman Emperors and Exponential Lengths of Rule." *Statistics & Probability Letters* 77: 1248–1257.

Khosla, V., 2009, "Whose Rules? Terms of Discussions Around a Global Cap-and-Trade System." *Innovations: Technology, Governance, Globalization* 4(4): 23–40.

Kirikos, G., and D. Novak, 1997, "Convexity Conundrums." *Risk Magazine*, March: 60–61.

Kohr, Leopold, 1957, *The Breakdown of Nations*. Rinehart.

Kondo, Y., T. Kanzawa, and R. Sawaya, 2005, "The Role of Autophagy in Cancer Development and Response to Therapy." *Nature Reviews Cancer* 5: 726–734.

Krugman, P., 1998, "Why Intellectuals Don't Understand Comparative Advantage." *Freedom and Trade: The Economics and Politics of International Trade* 2: 22.

Kurzban, R., 2010, "Does the Brain Consume Additional Glucose During Self-Control Tasks?" *Evolutionary Psychology* 8: 244–259. Retrieved from http://www.epjournal.net/wp-content/uploads/ep08244259.pdf.

La Mattina, John L., 2009, *Drug Truths: Dispelling the Myths About Pharma R&D*. Wiley.

Latour, Bruno, and Steve Woolgar, 1996, *La vie de laboratoire: La production des faits scientifiques*. La Découverte.

Laumakis, M., C. Graham, et al., 2009, "The Sloan-C Pillars and Boundary Objects as a Framework for Evaluating Blended Learning." *Journal of Asynchronous Learning Networks* 13(1): 75–87.

Lavery, J. V., 2011, "How Can Institutional Review Boards Best Interpret Preclinical Data?" *PLoS Medicine* 8(3): e1001011.

Le Bourg, Eric, 2009, "Hormesis, Aging and Longevity." *Biochimica et Biophysica Acta (BBA): General Subjects* 1790(10): 1030–1039.

Le Breton–Miller, I., and D. Miller, 2006, "Why Do Some Family Businesses Out-Compete? Governance, Long-Term Orientations, and Sustainable Capability." *Entrepreneurship Theory and Practice* 30(6): 731–746.

Le Fanu, James, M.D., 2002, *The Rise and Fall of Modern Medicine*. Carroll and Graf.

Le Goff, Jacques, 1985, *Les intellectuals au moyen age*. Éditions du Seuil.

Le Goff, Jacques, 1999, *Un autre moyen age*. Gallimard.

Lebrun, François, 1995, *Se soigner: Médicins, saints et sorciers aux XVII et XVIII siècles*. Éditions du Seuil.

Leoni, B., 1957, "The Meaning of 'Political' in Political Decisions." *Political Studies* 5(3): 225–239.

Leoni, B., and A. Kemp, 1991, *Freedom and the Law*. Indianapolis: Liberty Fund.

Levi, Isaac, 1980, *The Enterprise of Knowledge*. Cambridge, Mass.: The MIT Press.

Lévi-Strauss, Claude, 1962, *La pensée sauvage*. Plon.

Lewis, Ben, 2008, *Hammer and Tickle*. London: Weidenfeld & Nicolson.

Lewontin, Richard, 1993, *Biology as Ideology: The Doctrine of DNA*, Harper Perennial.

Li, Jie Jack, 2006, *Laughing Gas, Viagra, and Lipitor: The Human Stories Behind the Drugs We Use*. Oxford: Oxford University Press.

Light, D. and J. Lexchin, 2012, "Pharmaceutical Research and Development: What Do We Get for All That Money?" *British Medical Journal*, 345.

Lim, E. L., et al., 2011, "Reversal of Type 2 Diabetes: Normalisation of Beta Cell Function in Association with Decreased Pancreas and Liver Triacylglycerol." *Diabetologia* 54: 2506–2514.

Lindsay, James E., 2005, *Daily Life in the Medieval Islamic World*. Indianapolis: Hackett.

Lloyd, R., K. Hind, et al., 2010, "A Pilot Investigation of Load-Carrying on the Head and Bone Mineral Density in Premenopausal, Black African Women." *Journal of Bone and Mineral Metabolism* 28(2): 185–190.

Longo, V., and B. Kennedy, 2006, "Sirtuins in Aging and Age-Related Disease." *Cell* 126(2): 257–268.

Longo, V., M. Lieber, and J. Vijg, 2008, "Turning Anti-Ageing Genes Against Cancer." *National Review of Molecular Cell Biology* 9(11): 903–910, 1471–1472.

Longrigg, James, 1998, *Greek Medicine from the Heroic to the Hellenistic Age: A Source Book*. London: Routledge.

Luchsinger, J. A., M. X. Tang, et al., 2004, "Hyperinsulinemia and Risk of Alzheimer Disease." *Neurology* 63(7): 1187–1192.

Luehrman, T. A., 1998, "Strategy as a Portfolio of Real Options." *Harvard Business Review* 76: 89–101.

Lustick, I., B. Alcorn, et al., 2010, "From Theory to Simulation: The Dynamic Political Hierarchy in Country Virtualization Models." *American Political Science Association*.

Machina, Mark, and Michael Rothschild, 2008, "Risk." In Steven N. Durlauf and Lawrence E. Blume, eds., *The New Palgrave Dictionary of Economics*, 2nd ed. London: Macmillan.

Mackie, R., 2001, "Family Ownership and Business Survival: Kirkcaldy, 1870–1970." *Business History* 43: 1–32.

Makridakis, S., and N. N. Taleb, 2009, "Decision Making and Planning Under Low Levels of Predictability," *International Journal of Forecasting* 25 (4): 716–733.

Makridakis, S., A. Andersen, R. Carbone, R. Fildes, M. Hibon, R. Lewandowski, J. Newton, R. Parzen, and R. Winkler, 1982, "The Accuracy of Extrapolation (Time Series) Methods: Results of a Forecasting Competition." *Journal of Forecasting* 1: 111–153.

Makridakis, S., and M. Hibon, 2000, "The M3–Competition: Results, Conclusions and Implications." *International Journal of Forecasting* 16: 451–476.

Makridakis, S., C. Chatfield, M. Hibon, M. Lawrence, T. Mills, K. Ord, and L. F. Simmons, 1993, "The M2–Competition: A Real-Time Judgmentally Based Forecasting Study" (with commentary). *International Journal of Forecasting* 5: 29.

Malhotra, Y., 2000, "Knowledge Assets in the Global Economy: Assessment of National Intellectual Capital." *Journal of Global Information Management* 8(3): 5.

Malmendier, U., and G. Tate, 2008, "Who Makes Acquisitions? CEO Overconfidence and the Market's Reaction." *Journal of Financial Economics* 89(1): 20–43.

Malmendier, U., and G. Tate, 2009, "Superstar CEOs." *Quarterly Journal of Economics* 124(4): 1593–1638.

Mandelbrot, Benoît B., 1983, *The Fractal Geometry of Nature*. W. H. Freeman.

Mandelbrot, Benoît B., 1997, *Fractals and Scaling in Finance: Discontinuity, Concentration, Risk*. New York: Springer-Verlag.

Mandelbrot, Benoît B., and N. N. Taleb, 2010, "Random Jump, Not Random Walk." In Richard Herring, ed., *The Known, the Unknown, and the Unknowable*. Princeton, N.J.: Princeton University Press.

Mansel, P., 2012, *Levant*. Hachette.

Marglin, S. A., 1996, "Farmers, Seedsmen, and Scientists: Systems of Agriculture and Systems of Knowledge." In Frédérique Apffel-Marglin and Stephen A. Marglin, *Decolonizing Knowledge: From Development to Dialogue*. Oxford University Press, 185–248.

Martin, B., M. P. Mattson, et al., 2006, "Caloric Restriction and Intermittent Fasting: Two Potential Diets for Successful Brain Aging." *Ageing Research Reviews* 5(3): 332–353.

Masoro, E. J., 1998, "Hormesis and the Antiaging Action of Dietary Restriction." *Experimental Gerontology* 33(1–2): 61–66.

Mattson, M. P., 2008, "Hormesis Defined." *Ageing Research Reviews* 7(1): 1–7.

Mattson, M. P., and R. Wan, 2005, "Beneficial Effects of Intermittent Fasting and Caloric Restriction on the Cardiovascular and Cerebrovascular Systems." *Journal of Nutritional Biochemistry* 16(3): 129–137.

Matz, David, 2002, *Daily Life of the Ancient Romans*. Indianapolis: Hackett.

McAleer, M., A. Pagan, and P. Volker, 1985, "What Will Take the Con Out of Econometrics?" *American Economic Review* 75(3): 293–307.

McCabe, D. P., and A. D. Castel, 2008, "Seeing Is Believing: The Effect of Brain Images on Judgments of Scientific Reasoning." *Cognition* 107: 343–352.

McCloskey, D., and S. Ziliak, 1996, "The Standard Error of Regressions." *Journal of Economic Literature* 34(1): 97–114.

McConaugby, D., C. Matthews, and A. Fialko, 2001, "Founding Family Controlled Firms: Performance, Risk and Value." *Journal of Small Business Management* 39: 31–49.

McCraw, Thomas 2007, *Prophet of Innovation: Joseph Schumpeter and Creative Destruction*. Cambridge, Mass.: The Belknap Press of Harvard University.

McGill, S., 2007, *Low Back Disorders: Evidence-Based Prevention and Rehabilitation*. Human Kinetics Publishers.

McGrath, R. G., 1999, "Falling Forward: Real Options Reasoning and Entrepreneurial Failure." *Academy of Management Review*: 13–30.

McKnight, Scot, 2009, *Fasting*. Thomas Nelson.

McMahon, Darrin M., 2001, *Enemies of the Enlightenment: The French Counter-Enlightenment and the Making of Modernity*. Oxford: Oxford University Press.

Mégraud, F., and H. Lamouliatte, 1992, "*Helicobacter pylori* and Duodenal Ulcer." *Digestive Diseases and Sciences* 37(5): 769–772.

Mehta, R., R. J. Zhu, et al., 2012, "Is Noise Always Bad? Exploring the Effects of Ambient Noise on Creative Cognition."

Meisenzahl, R., and J. Mokyr, 2011, *The Rate and Direction of Invention in the British Industrial Revolution: Incentives and Institutions*. National Bureau of Economic Research.

Menard, W., and G. Sharman, 1976, "Random Drilling." *Science* 192(4236): 206–208.

Meng, X., N. Qian, and P. Yared, 2010, *The Institutional Causes of China's Great Famine, 1959–61*. National Bureau of Economic Research.

Mercier, H., and D. Sperber, 2011, "Why Do Humans Reason? Arguments for an Argumentative Theory." *Behavioral and Brain Sciences* 34(2) 57–74.

Meslin, Michel, Alain Proust, and Ysé Tardan-Masquelier, eds., 2006, *La quête de guérison: Médecine et religions face à la souffrance*. Paris: Bayard.

Meyers, Morton A., M.D., 2007, *Happy Accidents: Serendipity in Modern Medical Breakthroughs*. New York: Arcade.

Michán, S., Y. Li, M. Chou, E. Parrella, H. Ge, J. Long, J. Allard, K. Lewis, M. Miller, and W. Xu, 2010, "SIRT1 Is Essential for Normal Cognitive Function and Synaptic Plasticity." *Journal of Neuroscience* 30(29): 9695–9707.

Micklesfield, L., L. Rosenberg, D. Cooper, M. Hoffman, A. Kalla, I. Stander, and E. Lambert, 2003, "Bone Mineral Density and Lifetime Physical Activity in South African Women." *Calcified Tissue International* 73(5): 463–469.

Miller, John H., and Scott E. Page, 2007, *Complex Adaptive Systems: An Introduc-*

tion to Computational Models of Social Life. Princeton, N.J.: Princeton University Press.

Mindell, D. A., 2002, *Between Human and Machine: Feedback, Control, and Computing Before Cybernetics.* Baltimore: Johns Hopkins University Press.

Mitchell, Mark T., 2006, *Michael Polanyi: The Art of Knowing.* ISI Books.

Mokyr, Joel, 1990, *The Lever of Riches: Technological Creativity and Economic Progress.* Oxford: Oxford University Press.

Mokyr, Joel, ed., 1999, *The British Industrial Revolution: An Economic Perspective.* Westview Press.

Mokyr, Joel, 2002, *The Gifts of Athena: Historical Origins of the Knowledge Economy.* Princeton, N.J.: Princeton University Press.

Mokyr, Joel, 2005, "Long-Term Economic Growth and the History of Technology." In Philippe Aghion and Steven N. Durlauf, eds., *Handbook of Economic Growth,* Vol. 1B. Elsevier.

Mokyr, Joel, 2009, *The Enlightened Economy: An Economic History of Britain, 1700–1850.* New Haven: Yale University Press.

Morens, David M., 1999, "Death of a President." *New England Journal of Medicine* 342: 1222.

Morris, Ivan I., 1975, *The Nobility of Failure: Tragic Heroes in the History of Japan.* Farrar, Strauss and Giroux.

Mudd, L., W. Fornetti, and J. Pivarnik, 2007, "Bone Mineral Density in Collegiate Female Athletes: Comparisons Among Sports." *Journal of Athletic Training,* Jul-Sep 42(3): 403–408.

Mudry, Philippe, 2006, *Medicina, soror philosophiae.* Éditions BHMS.

Muldrew, C., 1993, "Credit and the Courts: Debt Litigation in a Seventeenth-Century Urban Community." *Economic History Review* 46(1): 23–38.

Mutch, W.A.C., T. G. Buchman, et al., 2007, "Biologically Variable Ventilation Improves Gas Exchange and Respiratory Mechanics in a Model of Severe Bronchospasm." *Critical Care Medicine* 35(7): 1749.

Nasr, G., 2008, "Applying Environmental Performance Indices Towards an Objective Measure of Sustainability in the Levant." *International Journal of Sustainable Development* 11(1): 61–73.

Nasr, G., 2009, "Limitations of the Hydraulic Imperative: The Case of the Golan Heights." *Water Resources Development* 25(1): 107–122.

Nelson, R. R., 2005, *Technology, Institutions, and Economic Growth.* Cambridge, Mass.: Harvard University Press.

Neumaier, T., J. Swenson, et al., 2012, "Evidence for Formation of DNA Repair Centers and Dose-Response Nonlinearity in Human Cells." *Proceedings of the National Academy of Sciences* 109(2): 443–448.

Nicholas, Jean, 2008, *La rebellion française: Mouvements populaires et conscience sociale 1661–1789.* Gallimard.

Nichols, J. F., J. E. Palmer, et al., 2003, "Low Bone Mineral Density in Highly Trained Male Master Cyclists." *Osteoporosis International* 14(8): 644–649.

North, Douglass C., 1990, *Institutions, Institutional Change and Economic Performance.* Cambridge: Cambridge University Press.

Nowak, Martin A., 2006, *Evolutionary Dynamics: Exploring the Equations of Life.* Cambridge, Mass.: The Belknap Press of Harvard University.

Nutton, Vivian, 2004, *Ancient Medicine.* Psychology Press.

O'Hara, Kieron, 2004, *Trust: From Socrates to Spin.* Icon Books.

Oakeshott, Michael, 1975, *On Human Conduct.* Oxford: Clarendon Press.

Oakeshott, Michael, 1991, "The Rationalist." *Quadrant* 35(3): 87.

Oakeshott, Michael, 1962, 1991, *Rationalism in Politics and Other Essays*. Liberty Fund.

Ober, J., 2010, *Wealthy Hellas*, Vol. 140. Baltimore: Johns Hopkins University Press.

Ogilvie, Sheilagh, 2011, *Institutions and European Trade: Merchant Guilds 1000–1800*. Cambridge: Cambridge University Press.

Orlov, Dmitry, 2011, *Reinventing Collapse: The Soviet Experience and American Prospects*. New Society Publishers.

Palmieri, Nicoletta, ed., 2003, *Rationnel et irrationnel dans la médecine ancienne et médiévale*. Saint-Étienne: Université de Saint-Étienne.

Pamuk, Sevket, 2006, "Estimating Economic Growth in the Middle East Since 1820." *Journal of Economic History* 66(3).

Parsons, P. A., 2000, "Hormesis: An Adaptive Expectation with Emphasis on Ionizing Radiation." *Journal of Applied Toxicology* 20(2): 103–112.

Pat-Horenczyk, R., and D. Brom, 2007, "The Multiple Faces of Post-Traumatic Growth." *Applied Psychology* 56(3): 379–385.

Pautler, P. A., 2003, "Evidence on Mergers and Acquisitions." *Antitrust Bulletin* 48: 119.

Pavitt, K., 1998a, "The Inevitable Limits of EU R&D Funding." *Research Policy* 27(6): 559–568.

Pavitt, K., 1998b, "The Social Shaping of the National Science Base." *Research Policy* 27(8): 793–805.

Payer, Lynn, 1996, *Medicine and Culture*. New York: Henry Holt.

Pears, David, 2006, *Paradox and Platitude in Wittgenstein's Philosophy*. Oxford: Oxford University Press.

Pérez-Jean, Brigitte, 2005, *Dogmatisme et scepticisme*. Presses Universitaires du Septentrion.

Petchey, O. L., and J. A. Dunne, 2012, "Predator-Prey Relations and Food Webs." *Metabolic Ecology: A Scaling Approach*. Wiley, p. 86.

Petroski, Henry, 2006, *Success Through Failure: The Paradox of Design*. Princeton, N.J.: Princeton University Press.

Pigeaud, Jackie, 2006, *La maladie de l'âme*. Les Belles Lettres.

Pigolotti, S., A. Flammini, et al., 2005, "Species Lifetime Distribution for Simple Models of Ecologies." *Proceedings of the National Academy of Sciences of the United States of America* 102(44): 15747.

Pirenne, Henri, 2005, *Mahomet et Charlemagne*. Presses Universitaires de France.

Pisano, G. P., 2006a, "Can Science Be a Business?" *Harvard Business Review* 10: 1–12.

Pisano, G. P., 2006b, *Science Business: The Promise, The Reality, and the Future of Biotech*. Cambridge, Mass.: Harvard Business Press.

Pischon, T., et al., 2008, "General and Abdominal Adiposity and Risk of Death in Europe." *New England Journal of Medicine* 359: 2105–2120.

Pi-Sunyer, X., et al., 2007, "Reduction in Weight and Cardiovascular Disease Risk Factors in Individuals with Type 2 Diabetes: One-Year Results of the Look AHEAD Trial." *Diabetes Care* 30: 1374–1383.

Piterbarg, V. V., and M. A. Renedo, 2004, "Eurodollar Futures Convexity Adjustments in Stochastic Volatility Models." Working Paper.

Pluchino, A., C. Garofalo, et al., 2011, "Accidental Politicians: How Randomly Selected Legislators Can Improve Parliament Efficiency." *Physica A: Statistical Mechanics and Its Applications*.

Polanyi, M., 1958, *Personal Knowledge: Towards a Post-Critical Philosophy*. London: Routledge and Kegan Paul.

Pomata, Gianna, and Nancy G. Siraisi, eds., 2005, *Historia: Empiricism and Erudition in Early Modern Europe*. Cambridge, Mass.: The MIT Press.

Popkin, Richard, 2003, *The History of Scepticism: From Savonarola to Bayle*. Oxford: Oxford University Press.

Popper, Karl, 1961, *The Poverty of Historicism*. London: Routledge.

Pories, W. J., et al., 1995, "Who Would Have Thought It? An Operation Proves to Be the Most Effective Therapy for Adult-Onset Diabetes Mellitus." *Annals of Surgery* 222: 339–350; discussion 350–352.

Pormann, Peter E., and Emilie Savage-Smith, 2007, *Medieval Islamic Medicine*. Georgetown University Press.

Porter, Roy, 2002, *Blood and Guts: A Short History of Medicine*. Penguin.

Porter, Roy, 2003, *Flesh in the Age of Reason*. W. W. Norton.

Portet, P., 2002, *La mesure géométrique des champs au moyen âge*. Librairie Droz.

Posner, M. V., 1996, "Corrupted by Money?" *Nature* 382: 123–124.

Pratt, John W., 1964, "Risk Aversion in the Small and in the Large," *Econometrica* 32 (January–April), 122–136.

Pritchard, James B., ed., 2011, *The Ancient Near East: An Anthology of Texts and Pictures*. Princeton, N.J.: Princeton University Press.

Pritchett, L., 2001, "Where Has All the Education Gone?" *World Bank Economic Review* 15(3): 367.

Radak, Z., H. Y. Chung, et al., 2005, "Exercise and Hormesis: Oxidative Stress-Related Adaptation for Successful Aging." *Biogerontology* 6(1): 71–75.

Raffaghello, L., F. Safdie, G. Bianchi, T. Dorff, L. Fontana, and V. Longo, 2010, "Fasting and Differential Chemotherapy Protection in Patients." *Cell Cycle* 9(22): 4474.

Rashed, Marwan, 2007, *L'héritage aristotélien*. Les Belles Lettres.

Rattan, S.I.S., 2008, "Hormesis in aging." *Ageing Research Reviews* 7(1): 63–78.

Rautava, E., M. Lehtonen-Veromaa, H. Kautiainen, S. Kajander, and O. J. Heinonen, 2007, "The Reduction of Physical Activity Reflects on the Bone Mass Among Young Females: A Follow-Up Study of 143 Adolescent Girls." *Osteoporosis International* (18)7: 915–922.

Razay, G. and G. K. Wilcock, 1994, "Hyperinsulinaemia and Alzheimer's Disease." *Age and Ageing* 23(5): 396–399.

Read, D., S. Frederick, and M. Airoldi, 2012, "Four Days Later in Cincinnati: Longitudinal Tests of Hyperbolic Discounting." *Acta Psychologica* 140(2): 177–185, PMID: 22634266.

Redberg, R. F., and M. H. Katz, 2012, "Healthy Men Should Not Take Statins." JAMA 307(14): 1491–1492.

Rees, Martin, 2003, *Our Final Century: Will Civilisation Survive the Twenty-First Century?* Arrow Books.

Rein, R., K. Davids, et al., 2010, "Adaptive and Phase Transition Behavior in Performance of Discrete Multi-Articular Actions by Degenerate Neurobiological Systems." *Experimental Brain Research* 201(2): 307–322.

Ridley, Matt, 2010, *The Rational Optimist: How Prosperity Evolves*. 4th Estate.

Riffard, Pierre, 2004, *Les philosophes: Vie intime*. Presses Universitaires de France.

Robb, Graham, 2007, *The Discovery of France*. Picador.

Roberts, B. H., 2012, *The Truth About Statins: Risks and Alternatives to Cholesterol-Lowering Drugs*. New York: Simon and Schuster.

Roberts, Royston M., 1989, *Serendipity: Accidental Discoveries in Science*. Wiley.

Roll, R., 1986, "The Hubris Hypothesis of Corporate Takeovers." *Journal of Business* 59:197–216.

Rook, G.A.W., 2011, "Hygiene and Other Early Childhood Influences on the Subsequent Function of the Immune System." *Digestive Diseases* 29(2): 144–153.

Rose, K. A., I. G. Morgan, et al., 2008, "Outdoor Activity Reduces the Prevalence of Myopia in Children." *Ophthalmology* 115(8): 1279–1285.

Rothschild, M., and J. E. Stiglitz, 1970, "Increasing Risk: I. A Definition." *Journal of Economic Theory* 2(3): 225–243.

Rothschild, M., and J. E. Stiglitz, 1971, "Increasing Risk: II. Its Economic Consequences." *Journal of Economic Theory* 3(1): 66–84.

Rubino, F., et al., 2006, "The Mechanism of Diabetes Control After Gastrointestinal Bypass Surgery Reveals a Role of the Proximal Small Intestine in the Pathophysiology of Type 2 Diabetes." *Annals of Surgery* 244: 741–749.

Sackett, David L., W. Scott Richardson, William Rosenberg, and R. Brian Haynes, 1998, *Evidence-Based Medicine: How to Practice and Teach EBM*. Churchill Livingstone.

Safdie, F., T. Dorff, D. Quinn, L. Fontana, M. Wei, C. Lee, P. Cohen, and V. Longo, 2009, "Fasting and Cancer Treatment in Humans: A Case Series Report." *Aging* (Albany, N.Y.), 1(12): 988.

Salsburg, David, 2001, *The Lady Tasting Tea: How Statistics Revolutionized Science in the Twentieth Century*. Freemen.

Sandis, Constantine, 2012, *The Things We Do and Why We Do Them*. London: Palgrave Macmillan.

Scanu, A. M., and C. Edelstein, 2008, "HDL: Bridging Past and Present with a Look at the Future." *FASEB Journal* 22(12): 4044–4054.

Schlumberger, M. J., 1998, "Papillary and Follicular Thyroid Carcinoma," *New England Journal of Medicine* 338(5) 297–306.

Schnohr, P., J. L. Marott, et al., 2011, "Intensity Versus Duration of Cycling: Impact on All-Cause and Coronary Heart Disease Mortality: The Copenhagen City Heart Study." *European Journal of Cardiovascular Prevention & Rehabilitation*.

Schon, Donald, 1983, *The Reflective Practitioner: How Professionals Think in Action*. Basic Books.

Schumacher, E. F., 1973, *Small Is Beautiful: A Study of Economics as if People Mattered*. London: Blond & Briggs.

Schumpeter, Joseph A., 1942, *Capitalism, Socialism and Democracy*. New York: Harper and Brothers. 5th ed., London: George Allen and Unwin, 1976.

Schumpeter, Joseph A., 1994, *History of Economic Analysis*. Oxford: Oxford University Press.

Scott, A., K. M. Khan, V. Duronio, and D. A. Hart, 2008, "Mechanotransduction in Human Bone: In Vitro Cellular Physiology That Underpins Bone Changes with Exercise." *Sports Medicine* 38(2): 139–160.

Scott, James C., 1998, *Seeing like a State: How Certain Schemes to Improve the Human Condition Have Failed*. New Haven: Yale University Press.

Scranton, P., 2006, "Urgency, Uncertainty, and Innovation: Building Jet Engines in Postwar America." *Management & Organizational History* 1(2): 127.

Scranton, P., 2007, "Turbulence and Redesign: Dynamic Innovation and the Dilemmas of US Military Jet Propulsion Development." *European Management Journal* 25(3): 235–248.

Scranton, P., 2009, "The Challenge of Technological Uncertainty." *Technology and Culture* 50(2): 513–518.

Seery, M. D., 2011, "Resilience." *Current Directions in Psychological Science* 20(6): 390–394.

Sestini, P., and L. B. Irving, 2009. "The Need for Expertise and the Scientific Base of Evidence-Based Medicine." *Chest* 135(1): 245.

Shackle, G.L.S., 1992, *Epistemics and Economics: A Critique of Economic Doctrines*. Transaction Publishers.

Shah, A. K., and D. M. Oppenheimer, 2007, "Easy Does It: The Role of Fluency in Cue Weighting." *Judgment and Decision Making* 2(6): 371–379.

Sharpe, Virginia A., and Alan I. Faden, 1998, *Medical Harm: Historical, Conceptual, and Ethical Dimensions of Iatrogenic Illness*. Cambridge: Cambridge University Press.

Shelford, April G., 2007, *Transforming the Republic of Letters: Pierre-Daniel Huet and European Intellectual Life, 1650–1720*. Rochester, N.Y.: University of Rochester Press.

Shimabukuro, M., et al., 1998, "Lipoapoptosis in Beta-Cells of Obese Prediabetic Fa/Fa Rats. Role of Serine Palmitoyltransferase Overexpression." *Journal of Biological Chemistry* 273: 32487–32490.

Siegel-Itzkovich, Judy, 2000. "Doctors' Strike in Israel May Be Good for Health." *BMJ* 320(7249): 1561.

Silverman, William A., 1999, *Where's the Evidence: Debates in Modern Medicine*. Oxford: Oxford University Press.

Singer, S. Fred Charles A. S. Hall, Cutler J., 1981, Cleveland: Science, New Series, Vol. 213, No. 4515 (Sep. 25, 1981).

Singh, Simon, and Ernst Edzard, M.D., 2008, *Trick or Treatment: The Undeniable Facts About Alternative Medicine*. New York: W. W. Norton.

Skyler, J., R. Bergenstal, R. Bonow, J. Buse, P. Deedwania, E. Gale, B. Howard, M. Kirkman, M. Kosiborod, and P. Reaven (2009), "Intensive Glycemic Control and the Prevention of Cardiovascular Events: Implications of the ACCORD, ADVANCE, and VA Diabetes Trials." *Circulation* 119(2): 351–357.

Smith, V. L., 2008, *Rationality in Economics: Constructivist and Ecological Forms*. Cambridge: Cambridge University Press.

Sober, Elliott, 2008, *Evidence and Evolution: The Logic Behind Science*. Cambridge: Cambridge University Press.

Solomon, L., 1979, "Bone Density in Ageing Caucasian and African Populations." *Lancet* 2: 1326–1330.

Sorabji, Richard, 2000, *Emotion and Peace of Mind: From Stoic Agitation to Christian Temptation*. Oxford: Oxford University Press.

Sornette, Didier, and L. Knopoff, 1997, "The Paradox of the Expected Time Until the Next Earthquake." *Bulletin of the Seismological Society of America* 87(4): 789–798.

Sornette, Didier, and D. Zajdenweber, 1999, "Economic Returns of Research: The Pareto Law and Its Implications." *The European Physical Journal, B: Condensed Matter and Complex Systems* 8(4): 653–664.

Sornette, Didier, 2003, *Why Stock Markets Crash: Critical Events in Complex Financial Systems*. Princeton, N.J.: Princeton University Press.

Sornette, Didier, 2004, *Critical Phenomena in Natural Sciences: Chaos, Fractals, Self-organization and Disorder: Concepts and Tools*, 2nd ed. Berlin and Heidelberg: Springer.

Stanley, J., 2010, "Knowing (How)." *Noûs*.

Starbuck, W. H., 1992, "Strategizing in the Real World," in "Technological Foundations of Strategic Management." Special issue, *International Journal of Technology Management* 8, no. 1/2.

Starbuck, W. H., 2004, "Why I Stopped Trying to Understand the Real World." *Organizational Studies* 25(7).

Starbuck, W. H., M. L. Barnett, et al., 2008, "Payoffs and Pitfalls of Strategic Learning." *Journal of Economic Behavior & Organization* 66(1): 7–21.

Stasavage, D., 2012, "Was Weber Right? City Autonomy, Political Oligarchy, and the Rise of Europe." Preprint.

Steinmo, S., 2010, *The Evolution of Modern States: Sweden, Japan, and the United States (Cambridge Studies in Comparative Politics)*. Cambridge University Press

Steinmo, S., 2012, "Considering Swedish Exceptionalism," draft, European University Institute.

Sternberg, Robert J., 2003, *Wisdom, Intelligence and Creativity Synthesized*. Cambridge: Cambridge University Press.

Sternhell, Zeev, 2010, *The Anti-Enlightenment Tradition*. New Haven: Yale University Press.

Steven, S., et al., 2010, "Dietary Reversal of Type 2 Diabetes Motivated by Research Knowledge." *Diabetic Medicine* 27: 724–725.

Stigler, Stephen M., 1990, *The History of Statistics: The Measurement of Uncertainty Before 1900*. Cambridge, Mass.: The Belknap Press of Harvard University.

Stipp, David, 2010, *The Youth Pill*. Current.

Stokes, Donald E., 1997, *Pasteur's Quadrant: Basic Science and Techonological Innovation*. Brookings Institution Press.

Stranahan, A. M., and M. P. Mattson, 2012, "Recruiting Adaptive Cellular Stress Responses for Successful Brain Ageing." *Nature Reviews Neuroscience*.

Stroud, Barry, 1984, *The Significance of Philosophical Scepticism*. Oxford: Oxford University Press.

Stubbart, C. I., and M. B. Knight, 2006, "The Case of the Disappearing Firms: Empirical Evidence and Implications." *Journal of Organizational Behavior* 27(1): 79–100.

Sunstein, Cass, 2009, *On Rumors: How Falsehoods Spread, Why We Believe Them, What Can Be Done*. Allen Lane.

Taagepera, R., 1978, "Size and Duration of Empires: Growth-Decline Curves, 3000 to 600 B.C." *Social Science Research* 7: 180–196.

Tainter, J., 1988, *The Collapse of Complex Societies: New Studies in Archaeology*. Cambridge: Cambridge University Press.

Taleb, N. N., and M. Blyth, 2011, "The Black Swan of Cairo." *Foreign Affairs* 90(3).

Taleb, N. N., and A. Pilpel, 2007, "Epistemology and Risk Management." *Risk and Regulation* 13, Summer.

Taleb, N. N., and C. Tapiero, 2010, "The Risk Externalities of Too Big to Fail." *Physica A: Statistical Physics and Applications*.

Taleb, N. N., D. G. Goldstein, and M. Spitznagel, 2009, "The Six Mistakes Executives Make in Risk Management," *Harvard Business Review* (October).

Taleb, N. N., 2008, "Infinite Variance and the Problems of Practice." *Complexity* 14(2).

Taleb, N. N., 2009, "Errors, Robustness, and the Fourth Quadrant." *International Journal of Forecasting* 25.

Taleb, N. N., 2011, "The Future Has Thicker Tails than the Past: Model Error as Branching Counterfactuals." *Benoît Mandelbrot's Scientific Memorial*, Preprint (see Companion Volume).

Taleb, N. N., and R. Douady, 2012, "A Map and Simple Heuristic to Detect Fragility, Antifragility, and Model Error," arXiv Preprint.

Taleb, N. N., and G. Martin, 2012a, "How to Avoid Another Crisis," *SAIS Review of International Affairs*.

Taleb, N. N., and G. Martin, 2012b, "The Illusion of Thin Tails Under Aggregation (A Reply to Jack Treynor)." *Journal of Investment Management*.

Taleb, N. N., and D. Goldstein, 2012, "The Problem Is Beyond Psychology: The Real World Is More Random Than Regression Analyses," *International Journal of Forecasting* 28(3), 715–716.

Taleb, N. N., Elie Canetti, Elena Loukoianova, Tidiane Kinda, and Christian Schmieder, 2012, "A New Heuristic Measure of Fragility and Tail Risks: Application to Stress Testing," IMF Working Paper.

Tatonetti, Nicholas P., et al., 2012, "Data-Driven Prediction of Drug Effects and Interactions." *Science Translational Medicine* 4, 125ra31, doi: 10.1126/scitransl med.3003377.

Taubes, G., 2008, *Good Calories, Bad Calories: Fats, Carbs, and the Controversial Science of Diet and Health*. New York: Anchor Books.

Taubes, G., 2011, *Why We Get Fat: And What to Do About It*. New York: Anchor Books.

Taylor, R., 2008, "Pathogenesis of Type 2 Diabetes: Tracing the Reverse Route from Cure to Cause." *Diabetologia* 51: 1781–1789.

Tedeschi, R. G., and L. G. Calhoun, 1996, "The Posttraumatic Growth Inventory: Measuring the Positive Legacy of Trauma." *Journal of Traumatic Stress* 9(3): 455–471.

Tetlock, Philip E., Richard Ned Lebow, and Geoffrey Parker, eds., 2009, *Unmaking the West: "What-If?" Scenarios That Rewrite World History*. Ann Arbor: University of Michigan Press.

Thomas, Keith, 1997, *Religion and the Decline of Magic*. Oxford: Oxford University Press.

Thompson, M. R., 2010, "Reformism vs. Populism in the Philippines." *Journal of Democracy* 21(4): 154–168.

Thorp, E., 1971, "Portfolio Choice and the Kelly Criterion." *Stochastic Models in Finance*, 599–619.

Thorp, E., 1998, "The Kelly Criterion in Blackjack, Sports Betting, and the Stock Market." *Finding the Edge: Mathematical Analysis of Casino Games*.

Thorsrud, Harald, 2009, *Ancient Scepticism*. Acumen.

Todd, E., 2010, "The International Risk Governance Council Framework and Its Application to *Listeria monocytogenes* in Soft Cheese Made from Unpasteurised Milk." Food Control.

Townsend, A., A. Clark, and K. McGowan, 2010, "Direct Benefits and Genetic Costs of Extrapair Paternity for Female American Crows (*Corvus brachyrhynchos*)." *American Naturalist* 175 (1).

Trabelsi, K., K. El Abed, S. R. Stannard, K. Jammoussi, K. M. Zeghal, and A. Hakim, 2012, "Effects of Fed- Versus Fasted-State Aerobic Training During Ramadan on Body Composition and Some Metabolic Parameters in Physically Active Men." *International Journal of Sport Nutrition and Exercise*.

Triana, P., 2009, *Lecturing Birds on Flying: Can Mathematical Theories Destroy the Financial Markets?* Wiley.

Triana, P., 2011, *The Number That Killed Us: A Story of Modern Banking, Flawed Mathematics, and a Big Financial Crisis*. Wiley.

Trigeorgis, L., 1993, "Real Options and Interactions with Financial Flexibility." *Financial Management*, 202–224.

Trigeorgis, L., 1996, *Real Options: Managerial Flexibility and Strategy in Resource Allocation.* Cambridge, Mass.: The MIT Press.

Trivers, Robert, 2011, *The Folly of Fools: The Logic of Deceit and Self-Deception in Human Life.* Basic Books.

Turchin, P., 2003, *Historical Dynamics: Why States Rise and Fall.* Princeton, N.J.: Princeton University Press.

Turchin, P., 2009, "A Theory for Formation of Large Empires." *Journal of Global History* 4(02): 191–217.

Urvoy, Dominique, 1996, *Les penseurs libres dans l'Islam classique.* Champs Flammarion.

Valdovinos, F., R. Ramos-Jiliberto, et al., 2010, "Consequences of Adaptive Foraging for the Structure and Dynamics of Food Webs." *Ecology Letters* 13: 1546–1559.

Vanderbilt, T., 2008a, "The Traffic Guru." *Wilson Quarterly* (1976), 32(3): 26–32.

Vanderbilt, T., 2008b, *Traffic: Why We Drive the Way We Do (and What It Says About Us).* New York: Knopf.

Van Zwet, W. R., 1964, *Convex Transformations of Random Variables.* Mathematical Center Amsterdam, 7.

Velez, N., A. Zhang, B. Stone, S. Perera, M. Miller, and S. Greenspan, "The Effect of Moderate Impact Exercise on Skeletal Integrity in Master Athletes." *Osteoporosis International* (October 2008), 19(10): 1457–1464.

Vermeij, Geerat J., 2004, *Nature: An Economic History.* Princeton, N.J.: Princeton University Press.

Vernon, Mark, 2009, *Plato's Podcasts: The Ancient's Guide to Modern Living.* London: Oneworld.

Veyne, Paul, 1999, "Païens et chrétiens devant la gladiature." *Mélanges de l'École française de Rome. Antiquité,* vol. 111, issue 111–2, 883–917.

Veyne, Paul, 2001, *La société romaine.* Paris: Éditions du Seuil.

Vigarello, Georges, 1998, *Histoire des pratiques de santé.* Paris: Éditions du Seuil.

von Heyd, Wilhelm, 1886, *Histoire du commerce du Levant au moyen-âge* (French translation). Éd. fr., refondue et augmentée, Leipzig.

von Plato, Jan, 1994, *Creating Modern Probability: Its Mathematics, Physics and Philosophy in Historical Perspective.* New York: Cambridge University Press.

Wagner, Andreas, 2005, *Robustness and Evolvability in Living Systems.* Princeton, N.J.: Princeton University Press.

Wai-Hung, Wong, 2002, "The Problem of Insulation," *Philosophy,* vol. 77, no. 301 (July 2002), 349–373.

Wales, J. K., 1982, "Treatment of Type 2 (Non-Insulin-Dependent) Diabetic Patients with Diet Alone." *Diabetologia* 23: 240–245.

Wallenborn, White McKenzie, 1997, "George Washington's Terminal Illness: A Modern Medical Analysis of the Last Illness and Death of George Washington." The Papers of George Washington, University of Virginia.

Waller, John, 2002, *Fabulous Science: Fact and Fiction in the History of Scientific Discovery.* Oxford: Oxford University Press.

Waterfield, Robin, 2009, *Why Socrates Died: Dispelling the Myths.* London: Faber and Faber.

Wear, Andrew, 1995, "Anatomy." In Lawrence Conrad et al., eds., *The Western Medical Tradition,* Vol. 1, Cambridge: Cambridge University Press.

Weber, Max, 1905, 2000, *L'éthique protestante et l'esprit du capitalisme.* Flammarion.

Weindruch, R., 1996, "The Retardation of Aging by Caloric Restriction: Studies in Rodents and Primates." *Toxicologic Pathology* 24: 742–745.

Weisberg, D., F. Keil, J. Goodstein, E. Rawson, and J. R. Gray, 2008, "The Seductive Allure of Neuroscience Explanations." *Journal of Cognitive Neuroscience* 20: 470–477.

Welch, H. Gilbert, Lisa M. Schwartz, and Steven Woloshin, 2011, *Overdiagnosed: Making People Sick in the Pursuit of Health*. Boston: Beacon Press.

West, G. B., 2011, "Can There Be a Quantitative Theory for the History of Life and Society?" *Cliodynamics* 2(1).

Westman, E. and Vernon, M., 2008, "Has Carbohydrate Restriction Been Forgotten as a Treatment for Diabetes Mellitus? A Perspective on the ACCORD Study Design." *Nutrition and Metabolism* (Lond), 5:10.

Whitacre, J. M., 2010, "Degeneracy: A Link Between Evolvability, Robustness and Complexity in Biological Systems." *Theoretical Biology and Medical Modelling* 7(1): 6.

White, David A., and Thomas A. Fitzgerald, "On Menard and Sharman Random Drilling." *Science*, New Series, Vol. 192, No. 4236 (Apr. 16, 1976).

Whitehead, Alfred North, 1967, *Science and the Modern World*. The Free Press.

Wilcken, Patrick, 2010, *Claude Lévi-Strauss: The Poet in the Laboratory*. Penguin.

Wilson, E. A., et al., 1980, "Dietary Management of Maturity-Onset Diabetes." *BMJ* 280: 1367–1369.

Wilson, Emily, 2007, *The Death of Socrates: Hero, Villain, Chatterbox, Saint*. London: Profile Books.

Wilson, Stephen, 2003, *The Bloomsbury Book of the Mind*. London: Bloomsbury.

Winchester, Simon, 2008, *Bomb, Book and Compass: Joseph Needham and the Great Secrets of China*. New York: Viking.

Wolf, Alison, 2002, *Does Education Matter? Myths About Education and Economic Growth*. London: Penguin UK.

Wolff, J., 1892, *Das Gesetz der Transformation der Knochen*. Reprint: Pro Business, Berlin 2010.

Women, P., W. Speed, et al., 2012, "Statins and Musculoskeletal Pain."

Wootton, David, 2006, *Bad Medicine: Doctors Doing Harm Since Hippocrates*. Oxford: Oxford University Press.

Yaffe, K., T. Blackwell, et al., 2004. "Diabetes, Impaired Fasting Glucose, and Development of Cognitive Impairment in Older Women." *Neurology* 63(4): 658–663.

Yarkoni, T., 2009, "Big Correlations in Little Studies: Inflated Fmri Correlations Reflect Low Statistical Power," commentary on Vul et al., 2009, *Perspectives on Psychological Science* 4(3), 294–298, doi:10.1111/j.1745–6924.2009.01127.x.

Young, S. S., and A. Karr, 2011, "Deming, Data and Observational Studies." *Significance* 8(3): 116–120.

Yuan, K. H., and S. Maxwell, 2005, "On the Post Hoc Power in Testing Mean Differences." *Journal of Educational and Behavioral Statistics* 30(2), 141–167.

Zeller, Eduard, 1905 (reprint), *Outlines of History of Greek Philosophy*. Whitefish, Mont.: Kessinger Publishing.

Zerubavel, Eviatar, 2006, *The Elephant in the Room: Silence and Denial in Everyday Life*. Oxford: Oxford University Press.

Ziliak, S., and D. McCloskey, 2008, *The Cult of Statistical Significance: How the Standard Error Costs Us Jobs, Justice, and Lives*. Ann Arbor: University of Michigan Press.

Acknowledgments

Peter Bevelin, Jazi Zilber, and Peter Tanous read the entire manuscript several times in several different versions in great detail and provided generous comments or hints on relevant research. I had exceptional and enthusiastic contributions from Will Murphy, Evan Camfield, Alexis Kirshbaum, Cynthia Taleb, Will Goodlad, Stefan McGrath, and Asim Samiuddin, who witnessed the progress of the book and contributed to its development.

Generous comments and help: Peter Nielsen, Rory Sutherland, Saifedean Ammous, Michael Kraland, Ron Kennett (for, among other things, the prints concave/convex of the Metropolitan Museum), Max Brockman, John Brockman, Marcos Carreira, Nathan Myhrvold, Aaron Brown, Terry Burnham, Peter Boettke, Russ Roberts, Kevin Horgan, Farid Karkaby, Michael Schrague, Dan Goldstein, Marie-Christine Riachi, Ed Frankel, Mika Kasuga, Eric Weinstein, Emanuel Derman, Alberto Mingardi, Constantine Sandis, Guy Deutscher, Bruno Dupire, George Martin, Joelle Weiss, Rohan Silva, Janan Ganesh, Dan Ariely, Gur Huberman, Cameron Williams, Jacques Merab, Lorenzo Savorelli, Andres Velasco, Eleni Panagiotarakou, Conrad Young, Melik Keylan, Seth Roberts, John McDonald, Yaneer Bar-Yam, David Shaywitz, Nouriel Roubini, Philippe Asseily, Ghassan Bejjani, Alexis Grégoire Saint-Marie, Charles Tapiero, Barry Blecherman, Art De Vany, Guy Riviere, Bernard Oppetit, Brendon Yarkin, and Mark Spitznagel; and my online helpers Jean-Louis Reault, Ben Lambert, Marko Costa, Satiyaki Den, Kenneth Lamont, Vergil Den, Karen Brennan, Ban Kanj, Lea McKay, Ricardo Medina, Marco Alves, Pierre Madani, Greg Linster, Oliver Mayor, Satyaki Roy, Daniel Hogendoorn, Phillip Crenshaw, Walter Marsh, John Aziz, Graeme Blake, Greg Linster, Sujit Kapadia, Alvaro De La Paz, Apoorv Bajpai, Louis Shickle, Ben Brady, Alfonso Payno de las Cuevas, "Guru Anaerobic," Alexander Boland, David Boxenhorn, Dru Stevenson, and Michal Kolano. I am certain I have forgotten many more.

Index

ABOUT THE AUTHOR

NASSIM NICHOLAS TALEB spent twenty-one years as a risk taker before becoming a researcher in philosophical, mathematical, and mostly (very) practical problems with probability.